A DICTIONARY OF ECONOMETRICS

A Dictionary of Econometrics

Adrian C. Darnell

Edward Elgar

Published by
Edward Elgar Publishing Limited
Gower House
Croft Road
Aldershot
Hants GU11 3HR
England

Edward Elgar Publishing Limited
Old Post Road
Brookfield
Vermont 05036
USA

Reprinted 1995

British Library Cataloguing in Publication Data

Darnell, A. C.
Dictionary of Econometrics
I. Title
330.01

Library of Congress Cataloguing in Publication Data

Darnell, A.C.
A dictionary of econometrics/edited by Adrian C. Darnell.
480 p. 23 cm
Includes bibliographical references.
1. Econometrics — Dictionaries. I. Title.
HB139.D358 1994
330'.01'5195 — dc20 93–39138
CIP

ISBN 1 85278 389 3
ISBN 1 85898 328 2 (paperback)

Printed and bound in Great Britain by
Hartnolls Ltd, Bodmin, Cornwall

CONTENTS

PREFACE

This work began life as handouts I have provided to my students over recent years; that they have now grown in number and stature to become this volume is, in no small part, due to the unceasing encouragement of Edward Elgar (and I thank him for his patience). I must also thank my own undergraduate and postgraduate students whose criticisms have been invaluable. Several people have read this manuscript in draft form and I extend grateful thanks to my dear friend and colleague, Lynne Evans, not only for reading much of this work in draft form and offering many helpful comments but also for her untiring enthusiasm for the project. My thanks also go to Mark Blaug who read this manuscript in draft form and offered some very constructive comments, and to an anonymous reader whose suggestions led me to extend the coverage of the work. I must thank Thelma Ellison who typed the references with extraordinary speed and precision. Finally I extend my unlimited thanks to my wife Angela; she never once wavered in supporting me during the writing of this volume and I dedicate this work to her.

University of Durham ADRIAN C. DARNELL

INTRODUCTION

Students of econometrics are faced with a very great variety of literature; the purpose of this work is to provide yet more variety in that body of literature and, specifically, to provide students with a collection of 'bite-sized' reading on some of the most important topics of econometrics. It is intended to be used by students of econometrics to aid their understanding of key areas of the subject by presenting the material in a relatively non-technical fashion, but simultaneously providing sufficient technical material to enable the student to gain yet more from their reading of the standard texts and the primary material. Where formal presentations and proofs are provided it is done in the expectation that the expositions will offer a slightly different, and perhaps more accessible, account of the essential technical material than that found elsewhere.

This volume is certainly not intended for the professional econometrician, but is directly aimed at an undergraduate and an elementary postgraduate audience. It will also find use amongst the non-professional user of econometrics who finds the need to understand more about a computer print-out or who needs to know more about applied econometrics and the underlying econometric theory. The entries in this dictionary are, however, concerned with theoretical econometrics, and are not concerned, directly, with applied work. The topics are arranged in alphabetical order and are designed as short essays which will stand on their own; students will, of course, need to supplement their reading of this volume with other reading and with the more expansive and inevitably more detailed presentations to be found in the mainstream econometric theory texts and in the primary journal literature. Each entry will, nevertheless, provide a clear flavour of the topic under discussion and will also provide students with 'essential notes' on those topics. In using this dictionary not all topics are assigned their own entry; for example, material on Consistency, a large sample concept, is to be found in **Large sample theory**.

The choice of entries has been guided by my own view of the topics to which students, both undergraduate and elementary postgraduate, are typically exposed in the syllabi of econometric theory; the volume is intended to be used as a complement to the existing literature and is not a substitute. Each entry is designed to present the essential points of that particular concept or technique and to offer a concise guide to other relevant reading on that topic. Some entries are, inevitably, more elementary than others, and some are longer than others.

I have found, having given the entries to my own students, that they provide an effective learning resource when used in association with lecture material and directed reading of the primary and secondary literature. The literature of econometrics is, like that of most other disciplines of economics, expanding at a rapid rate and this volume will, hopefully, facilitate students to make reference to relatively concise material on strictly compartmentalized topics. Given the growing movement towards modularization in undergraduate and postgraduate courses, the present volume is within that spirit of providing easily digestible reading and should prove a most useful source of secondary reading for students.

An early issue faced in constructing this volume was the number of topics; it would, of course, have been possible to disaggregate the present entries into many more topics, but the inevitable fragmentation proved to be inefficient. The number of entries is now so constructed that cross-referencing within this volume has been minimized, and the entries may be read on their own with little need to enter a tour of the other entries. There are, of course, linkages across the entries, but they are intended as branch lines rather than main routes. The present arrangement is a compromise between the demands of academic coherence of the individual entries and the need to be sufficiently comprehensive over undergraduate and elementary postgraduate econometric theory syllabi. This is, I believe, a successful arrangement within the overall size constraint of the volume.

It is to be hoped the present arrangement will prove successful and students will make frequent reference to this volume to obtain concisely presented and accessible material on all the topics they seek.

This volume is intended to complement the standard texts such as Johnston (1984), Maddala (1977 and 1992), Wonnacott and Wonnacott (1979), Judge *et al.* (1982, 1985 and 1988) and Greene (1993); it also complements the *New Palgrave Dictionary* (Eatwell *et al.*, 1990a and b) and the excellent text by Kennedy (1992). It is not, however, an econometrics text, but rather a more compartmentalized encyclopaedic dictionary arrangement of material. For primary material the reader is referred to the many volumes in the series *The International Library of Critical Readings in Econometrics* (currently being published by Edward Elgar).

Analysis of variance in regression

Analysis of variance is a general technique by which the variance of a variable is broken down into a number of distinct components; in the regression model this has found particular application in disaggregating the variation of the dependent variable into those components due to the explanatory variables, and a remainder due to the inherent error term. That part of the total variation of the dependent variable which is due to the error term is the unexplained, or residual, variation, and that which may be attributable to the regressors is the explained variation which may, itself, then be broken down into explained variation attributable to specific regressors. Suppose the simple linear model with a constant and k other regressor is employed, under the usual assumptions, using n observations:

$$Y_i = \alpha + \beta_1 X_{i1} + \beta_2 X_{i2} + \ldots + \beta_k X_{ik} + \varepsilon_i;$$

where ε_i is a zero mean, homoscedastic, non-autocorrelated, normally distributed error term. A specific application of analysis of variance is in testing hypotheses: if the variation of Y_i which may be explained by the jth regressor is statistically significant then this provides evidence on which to reject the hypothesis that $\beta_j = 0$.

If this equation is estimated by ordinary least squares, the fitted equation may be written as:

$$\hat{Y}_i = \hat{\alpha} + \hat{\beta}_1 X_{i1} + \hat{\beta}_2 X_{i2} + \ldots + \hat{\beta}_k X_{ik};$$

or, equivalently:

$$Y_i = \hat{\alpha} + \hat{\beta}_1 X_{i1} + \hat{\beta}_2 X_{i2} + \ldots + \hat{\beta}_k X_{ik} + \hat{e}_i;$$

i.e. $$Y_i = \hat{Y}_i + \hat{e}_i.$$

The term $\hat{e}_i$ is the ith residual which measures the difference between the observed value of the dependent variable (Y_i) and fitted value ($\hat{Y}_i$). Let $y_i = Y_i - \overline{Y}$, the measure of y in deviation form, so that the total sum of squares (TSS) to be explained is given by:

$$TSS = \sum_{i=1}^{n} y_i^2 .$$

Because the regression model includes a constant term the average residual ($\overline{\hat{e}}$) is guaranteed to be zero; this follows from the normal equations from which the OLS estimates are derived. If the regression model is written in matrix notation as:

$$Y = Z\delta + \varepsilon$$

where Z is the $n \times (k+1)$ matrix given by $[\iota \;\; X]$, ι is a column vector every element of which is unity and $\delta = [\alpha \;\; \beta']'$, the normal equations may be written, as $Z'\hat{e}$ where $\hat{e}$ is the residual vector. Since the first row of Z' is [1 1

. . . 1], it follows that $\sum_{i=1}^{n}\hat{e}_i = 0$. Therefore $\hat{e}_i - \bar{\hat{e}} \equiv \hat{e}_i$, and so the unexplained sum of squares is given by the residual sum of squares (RSS) defined by:

$$RSS = \sum_{i=1}^{n} \hat{e}_i^2$$

Since $Y_i = \hat{Y}_i + \hat{e}_i$, and $\bar{\hat{e}} \equiv 0$ in this model, it follows that $\bar{Y} \equiv \bar{\hat{Y}}$, and so:

$$Y_i = \hat{Y}_i + \hat{e}_i \Rightarrow Y_i - \bar{Y} = \hat{Y}_i - \bar{\hat{Y}} + \hat{e}_i$$

hence: $\quad y_i = \hat{y}_i + \hat{e}_i$

where $\hat{y}_i$ measures the fitted value of Y from the sample mean. Hence:

$$\sum_{i=1}^{n} y_i^2 = \sum_{i=1}^{n} \hat{y}_i^2 + \sum_{i=1}^{n} \hat{e}_i^2 + 2\sum_{i=1}^{n} \hat{y}_i\hat{e}_i$$

but, defining the estimated parameter vector as $\hat{\delta}$ and $\hat{Y}$ as the vector of fitted values, given by $\hat{Y} = X\hat{\delta}$, $\sum_{i=1}^{n}\hat{y}_i\hat{e}_i = \hat{Y}'\hat{e} = \hat{\delta}'X'\hat{e}$. But $X'\hat{e} = 0$ by the normal equations and so the cross product term is identically zero. Hence:

$$\sum_{i=1}^{n} y_i^2 = \sum_{i=1}^{n} \hat{y}_i^2 + \sum_{i=1}^{n} \hat{e}_i^2 .$$

Defining $\sum_{i=1}^{n}\hat{y}_i^2$ as the 'explained sum of squares', ESS, this implies that:

$$TSS = ESS + RSS.$$

This decomposition may be used to test hypotheses within the regression model: if every β_i is, in fact, zero, then any apparent explanatory power of the regression is due only to chance variation in the particular sample, and the regressors contribute nothing to the explanation of Y in the population.

Under H_o: $\beta_i = 0$ for all i the implied model is $Y_i = \alpha + \varepsilon_i$; therefore, under H_o, $\sum_{i=1}^{n} y_i^2/(n-1)$ is an unbiased estimator of the variance of ε_i, σ^2. Whether or not H_o is true, the sum of squared residuals from the regression of Y on all the regressors is the basis for an unbiased estimator of σ^2, and $s^2 = \sum_{i=1}^{n}\hat{e}_i^2/(n-k-1)$ is always an unbiased estimator of σ^2. Now under H_o, $E(\sum_{i=1}^{n}y_i^2 - \sum_{i=1}^{n}\hat{e}_i^2) = (n-1)\sigma^2 - (n-k-1)\sigma^2 = k\sigma^2$; therefore, ESS/k = $(\sum_{i=1}^{n}y_i^2 - \sum_{i=1}^{n}\hat{e}_i^2)/k$ is an unbiased estimator of σ^2 under H_o.

Given the standard assumptions, it may be shown that RSS/σ^2 is always a χ^2 variate with $n-k-1$ degrees of freedom, and that ESS/σ^2 is a χ_k^2 only under H_o; it may further be shown that under H_o the two χ^2 variates are independent. Therefore, under H_o,

$$[ESS/k]/[RSS/(n-k-1)] \sim F_{k,n-k-1} \text{ on repeated sampling.}$$

Since the goodness of fit statistic, R^2, is given by the ratio of the explained to the total variation, ESS/TSS, this may be written as: under H_o:

$$[R^2/k]/[(1-R^2)/(n-k-1)] \sim F_{k,n-k-1} \text{ on repeated sampling.}$$

Now suppose that the regression is broken down into the first k – m regressors, and the last m regressors:

$$Y_i = \alpha + \beta_1 X_{i1} + \beta_2 X_{i2} \quad . \quad . \quad . \quad + \beta_{k-m} X_{i,k-m}$$
$$+ \beta_{k-m+1} X_{i,k-m+1} \quad . \quad . \quad . \quad + \beta_k X_{ik} + \varepsilon_i .$$

The total sum of squares may then be broken down into that due to the regressors X_1 to X_{k-m}, ESS_1, and that due to the regressors X_{k-m+1} to X_k, ESS_2. It may be easily shown that the variation explained by all k regressors, ESS, is simply the sum of ESS_1 and ESS_2, and hence that $TSS = ESS_1 + ESS_2 + RSS$.

ESS_1 is identical to the explained sum of squares that would be derived from a regression of Y on a constant and the first k – m regressors (that is, having deleted the last m regressors). Now consider the hypothesis:

$$H_o: \beta_i = 0, i = k - m + 1, \dots k.$$

In the full regression of Y on all k regressors, $s^2 = RSS/(n - k - 1)$ is always an unbiased estimator of σ^2 whether or not H_o is true. If H_o is true, ESS_2, the explanation due to the last k – m regressors, will only differ from zero by virtue of sampling variation. Under H_o,:

$$E(TSS - ESS_1 - RSS) = (n-1)\sigma^2 - (k-m)\sigma^2 - (n-k-1)\sigma^2 = m\sigma^2.$$

Thus, $E(ESS_2) = m\sigma^2$, i.e. ESS_2/m is an unbiased estimator of σ^2 under H_o. By using the standard assumptions, and proceeding to form an F-variable as before:

$$[ESS_2/m]/[RSS/(n - k - 1)] \sim F_{m,n-k-1} \text{ on repeated sampling;}$$

i.e. $$[(TSS - ESS_1 - RSS)/m]/[RSS/(n - k - 1)] \sim F_{m,n-k-1}.$$

The goodness of fit statistic from the regression of Y on the first k – m regressors is given by ESS_1/TSS, and may be denoted by R_r^2, the restricted R^2. Similarly, the R^2 from the regression Y on all the regressors is given by (TSS – RSS)/TSS, and this may be denoted by R_u^2, the unrestricted R^2. Hence, dividing the numerator and denominator of the F variate given above by TSS it follows that under H_o:

$$\frac{(R_u^2 - R_r^2)/m}{(1 - R_u^2)/(n-k-1)} \sim F_{m,n-k-1}.$$

This is a familiar result, and one which is derived in **Linear hypotheses**; however, this is an illuminating route which leads to the Analysis of Variance Table:

The analysis of variance table

Source of variation	Sum of squares	Degrees of freedom
$X_1, \ldots, X_k$	$ESS = ESS_1 + ESS_2 = TSS.R_u^2$	k
$X_1, \ldots, X_{k-m}$	$ESS_1 = TSS.R_r^2$	k – m
$X_{k-m+1}, \ldots, X_k$	$ESS_2 = TSS.(R_u^2 - R_r^2)$	m
Error	$RSS = TSS.(1 - R_u^2)$	n – k – 1
Total	$TSS = ESS_1 + ESS_2 + RSS$	n – 1

Note that rows 2 and 3 sum to row 1, and that rows 1 and 4 sum to row 5.

This analysis has disaggregated the variance of the dependent variable into its constituent components: that due to one set of regressors, that due to the other regressors, and that which remains as unexplained and due to the random error in the regression. This provides an alternative perspective on the traditional F-tests within regression. The F-test to examine the hypothesis that coefficients are zero is now seen as the ratio of two mean sums of squares; the numerator is the mean sum of squares of the variation in Y explained by the regressors in question and the denominator is the mean residual sum of squares. If the regressors in question make no contribution to the explanation of Y, the numerator of this statistic will be non-zero only because of sampling variation. If, however, the null hypothesis is false then the numerator will be significantly non-zero and the resulting F statistic will be larger than may be explained by random variation alone, leading to a rejection of the null hypothesis.

Further reading

Analysis of variance (ANOVAR) is described in all standard texts, the reader is referred to any of those standard texts for further details of this technique. See the related entry **Linear hypotheses**.

ARCH and GARCH

Heteroscedasticity is often a feature of models using cross-section data, and autocorrelation is often a feature of models using time-series data; however, in some time-series models (notably those using financial data) heteroscedasticity has been observed. The appearance of heteroscedasticity in time-series models may be rationalized in some cases as a reflection of the way in which the variability of the dependent variable changes systematically over time. The variance of the error term at time t represents the uncertainty at that point in time; a larger variance of ε_t indicates more noise and uncertainty at time t than does a smaller variance, and in some models it has been found useful to treat the variance of ε_t, conditional on the information available at time t, as a function of previous errors. Engle (1982, 1983) and Cragg (1982) have found evidence for such a phenomenon and Engle proposed the **A**uto**R**egressive **C**onditional **H**eteroscedastic (ARCH) model; the simplest version, an ARCH(1) process, may be written as:

$$Y = X\beta + \varepsilon$$

and $\varepsilon_t = u_t(\alpha_o + \alpha_1 \varepsilon_{t-1}^2)^{1/2}$ where u_t is an identically and independently distributed standard normal variate. It follows that:

$$E(\varepsilon_t | \varepsilon_{t-1}) = 0$$

and

$$V(\varepsilon_t | \varepsilon_{t-1}) = V(u_t)(\alpha_o + \alpha_1 \varepsilon_{t-1}^2) = (\alpha_o + \alpha_1 \varepsilon_{t-1}^2)$$

Thus, conditional on the previous error, ε_t is heteroscedastic. However, using the result of conditional expectation that E[E(w|z)] = E(w) for random variables w and z, the unconditional variance of ε_t is given by $E[V(\varepsilon_t | \varepsilon_{t-1})]$. Therefore, noting that ε_t has a zero (conditional and unconditional) mean:

$$E[V(\varepsilon_t | \varepsilon_{t-1})] = E(\alpha_o + \alpha_1 \varepsilon_{t-1}^2)$$

i.e. $$E[V(\varepsilon_t | \varepsilon_{t-1})] = V(\varepsilon_t) = \alpha_o + \alpha_1 V(\varepsilon_{t-1})$$

and assuming that the process is variance stationary (so that $V(\varepsilon_t)$ is constant for all t):

$$V(\varepsilon_t) = \alpha_o/(1 - \alpha_1)$$

Thus, even though ε_t is conditionally heteroscedastic, it is unconditionally homoscedastic; clearly there are constraints to be placed on the parameters of the ARCH process: in the ARCH(1) process it is sufficient that $\alpha_o > 0$ and $0 < \alpha_1 < 1$ to ensure that the variance is non-negative and that the error is stationary.

Since the error term in $Y = X\beta + \varepsilon$ is unconditionally homoscedastic the usual assumptions required to demonstrate that ordinary least squares yields best linear unbiased estimators (BLUE) are met. The OLS estimator of β, $\hat{\beta}$, may be shown to be BLUE. However, $\hat{\beta}$ is only the minimum variance estimator from amongst linear unbiased estimators, and it may be shown that there is an alternative non-linear estimator which is more efficient. If the conditional variance of ε_t is denoted by σ_t^2, then given normality of the errors and conditional upon initial values Y_o and X_o, the log-likelihood function for T observations may be written as:

$$\ell n L = -(n/2)\ell n(2\pi) - \tfrac{1}{2} \textstyle\sum_{t=1}^{T} (\varepsilon_t/\sigma_t)^2 - \tfrac{1}{2} \sum_{t=1}^{T} \ell n(\sigma_t^2)$$

The first two terms are the log-likelihood of the sample $u_t = \varepsilon_t/\sigma_t$, and the final term arises from the transformation from u_t to ε_t. Maximization of this log-likelihood may be achieved by the usual non-linear numerical routines, and many software packages have an ARCH option inbuilt. For an alternative estimation of the ARCH model, a staged feasible generalized least squares route is available (described in Greene, 1993). The staged procedure approximates the maximum likelihood solution, is asymptotically equivalent to it, and therefore generates a non-linear estimator which is more efficient than the best linear unbiased estimator (the OLS estimator).

A Lagrange multiplier (LM) test of the presence of an ARCH process is easily constructed and, if an ARCH process is suspected then the non-linear estimator is preferred on efficiency grounds to the OLS estimator. To test for ARCH effects, first estimate the model $Y = X\beta + \varepsilon$ by ordinary least squares to yield the vector of residuals given by $\hat{e}$. The artificial regression of $\hat{e}_t^2$ on a constant and $\hat{e}_{t-1}^2$ may then be used as the basis for an asymptotic test of an ARCH(1): R^2 denotes the goodness of fit statistic from this artificial regression and then TR^2 is distributed as a χ_1^2 variable under the null hypothesis of conditional homoscedasticity. This is rationalized by noting that $\hat{e}_t^2$ is a proxy for σ_t^2; hence in the absence of an ARCH effect $\hat{e}_{t-1}^2$ will not contribute any significant explanation of $\hat{e}_t^2$ and so the resulting R^2 statistic from this regression will be low. If the R^2 is so large that TR^2 exceeds the chosen critical value from the χ_1^2 distribution the null hypothesis is rejected. Also, this method may be expanded to accommodate higher orders of ARCH processes. Suppose the error follows an ARCH(p) process:

$$Y = X\beta + \varepsilon$$

and

$$\varepsilon_t = u_t(\alpha_o + \alpha_1 \varepsilon_{t-1}^2 + \alpha_2 \varepsilon_{t-2}^2 + \ldots . \alpha_q \varepsilon_{t-q}^2)^{1/2}$$

where u_t is a standard normal variate. Hence, in an ARCH(q) model, the conditional variance of ε_t, σ_t^2, is defined by:

$$\sigma_t^2 = \alpha_o + \alpha_1 \varepsilon_{t-1}^2 + \alpha_2 \varepsilon_{t-2}^2 + \ldots . \alpha_q \varepsilon_{t-q}^2.$$

To test for an ARCH(q) process, if the regression of Y on X is first performed by OLS to yield the residual vector $\hat{e}$ the R^2 statistic from the regression of $\hat{e}_t^2$ on a constant and the q lags $\hat{e}_{t-j}^2$ ($j = 1, \ldots, q$) provides the basis for a test of the model: TR^2 is then distributed, under the null of conditional homoscedasticity, as a χ_q^2 variate, and large values of TR^2 are evidence upon which to reject the null hypothesis and consider re-estimating the model as an ARCH error process.

In an ARCH process the error terms are not autocorrelated, but the fact that the conditional variance of ε_t depends on previous errors can give the misleading impression of autocorrelation (via, for example, a 'significant' Durbin–Watson statistic). The LM test suggested above is designed to distinguish between autocorrelation and ARCH. The general form of an ARCH process may be characterized as:

$$V(\varepsilon_t | \psi_t) = \sigma_t^2$$

where ψ_t is the information available at time t. In the ARCH process ψ_t consists only of previous realized errors, so that $\psi_t = \{\varepsilon_{t-j}; j = 1, 2, \ldots, q\}$. However, this may be generalized so that ψ_t also includes previous conditional variances: $\psi_t = \{\varepsilon_{t-j}, \sigma_{t-k}^2; j = 1, 2, \ldots, q; k = 1, 2, \ldots, p\}$. This is a Generalized ARCH (or GARCH) model in which:

$$\sigma_t^2 = \alpha_o + \alpha_1 \varepsilon_{t-1}^2 + \alpha_2 \varepsilon_{t-2}^2 + \ldots \alpha_q \varepsilon_{t-q}^2$$

$$+ \gamma_1 \sigma_{t-1}^2 + \gamma_2 \sigma_{t-2}^2 + \ldots + \gamma_p \sigma_{t-p}^2.$$

In this model the conditional variance is generated by an autoregressive moving average process with p autoregressive terms in $\{\sigma_{t-j}^2\}$ and q moving average terms in the innovations $\{\varepsilon_{t-j}^2\}$, and is described as an GARCH(p, q) process. It has been found that a GARCH process with few terms can perform at least as well, if not better, than an ARCH model with many more terms. The conditions required to ensure that a GARCH process is stationary become very complicated; if the model is written as:

$$\sigma_t^2 = \alpha_o + C(L)\sigma_t^2 + A(L)\varepsilon_t^2$$

where C(L) and A(L) are polynomials in the lag operator, of order p and q respectively, then if all the roots of $1 - C(z) = 0$ lie outside the unit circle and $A(1) + C(1) < 1$ then the process is covariance stationary. The GARCH model may be estimated by the ML method, and many software packages now incorporate GARCH options. The computational aspects of ARCH and GARCH, including constraints to ensure stationarity, are not explored here.

In testing for ARCH effects the LM test may be constructed from the OLS residuals: TR^2 from the auxiliary regression of $\hat{e}_t^2$ on a constant and the q lags $\hat{e}_{t-j}^2$, $j = 1, 2, \ldots, q$, is (asymptotically) distributed as χ_q^2 under the null of conditional homoscedasticity. If a significant value of TR^2 is found this rejects the null and may be an indication of ARCH, or GARCH, effects. Unfortunately, the LM test for ARCH(q) against ARCH(p+q) is identical to that for ARCH(q) against GARCH(p, q); this is because the candidate terms to proxy the autoregressive components are squared OLS residuals, and the candidate terms to proxy the moving average components of the GARCH are also the squared residuals. A more effective test of an ARCH against a GARCH model consists of estimating them both and making comparison of the finally estimated models.

The GARCH and ARCH models above are both linear, which implies that the conditional variance σ_t^2 depends on the size, but not the sign, of previous errors. The exponential GARCH(p, q) (known as the EGARCH(p, q) model) is asymmetric:

$$\varepsilon_t = u_t\sigma_t \quad \text{and}$$

$$\ell n\, \sigma_t^2 = \omega + \Sigma_{i=1}^{q}\alpha_i\left[\phi u_{t-i} + \gamma(|u_{t-i}| - E|u_{t-i}|)\right] + \Sigma_{k=1}^{q}\beta_k \ell n \sigma_{t-k}^2 .$$

The EGARCH model is an unrestricted ARMA(p, q) model, for it places no restrictions on the α_i or β_k parameters to ensure that σ_t^2 is non-negative; however, all the roots of the polynomial lag structure in $\ell n\sigma_{t-k}^2$ must lie outside the unit circle to ensure that ε_t is covariance stationary. If $\alpha_i\phi < 0$ then σ_t^2 tends to fall (rise) when $\varepsilon_{t-i} > 0$ (< 0), and this model has found application in financial economics. Other parametric representations of ARCH processes have also been suggested, including those which incorporate power transformations of ε_t^2.

ARCH models have also been extended to the ARCH-in-Mean (ARCH-M) model, in which the conditional mean of Y depends on the conditional variance:

$$Y_t = f(x_{t-1}, \sigma_t^2, \beta) + \varepsilon_t \quad \text{and } \varepsilon_t = u_t\sigma_t.$$

In such a model the conditional mean of Y_t varies systematically with the conditional variance of the error term and this model, too, has found application in financial economics.

Finally, in testing for ARCH and GARCH effects it has to be recognized, as in all tests utilizing OLS residuals, that a property of the residuals is not necessarily a reflection of that property amongst the true errors; hence, even if residuals exhibit ARCH effects this may be because the 'explanation' of $\hat{e}_t^2$ by the lags $\hat{e}_{t-j}^2$ is due to the latter acting as proxies for omitted variables in the original regression of Y on X. Specifically, if the original regression includes insufficient lagged values of regressand and regressors then a 'spurious' ARCH effect may be observed. The critical point is that if ARCH or GARCH processes are entertained only as a reaction to a test statistic, as opposed to being considered *a priori* as a potential way to model the underlying economic process, then the investigator needs to be assured that the interpretation of the test as an indication of GARCH effects (rather than an indication of some other form of misspecification) is appropriate. Such assurance may be sought by seeking to eliminate the alternative interpretations. However, in some areas (modelling asset prices, for example) it is becoming increasingly common to hypothesize GARCH effects *a priori* and to perform the estimation as a test of the hypothesis.

Further reading

See especially Engle (1982 and 1983), Engle and Kraft (1983) and Bollerslev (1986). Engle and Rothschild (1992) survey the use of ARCH models in the literature of finance.

ARMA and ARIMA models

An ARMA model is a univariate model which seeks to model a single variable as an **A**uto**R**egressive **M**oving **A**verage process; an ARMA process is fully described by two parameters, p and q, where p is the order of the autoregressive component, and q is the order of the moving average component. If y_t may be described by an ARMA(p, q) process then y_t is modelled as a stationary process which evolves according to the equation:

$$y_t = \mu + \alpha_1 y_{t-1} + \alpha_2 y_{t-2} + \ldots + \alpha_p y_{t-p}$$
$$+ \varepsilon_t + \beta_1 \varepsilon_{t-1} + \beta_2 \varepsilon_{t-2} + \ldots + \beta_q \varepsilon_{t-q}$$

where ε_t is a white-noise random variable (it is stationary with a zero mean, mutually uncorrelated and has a constant variance). The p terms in lagged y comprise the autoregressive component, and the q terms in the innovations ε_t comprise the moving average component. ARMA models have been found to provide parsimonious representations of a number of economic time series. Using the lag operator L, where $Lz_t = z_{t-1}$, this may be written as:

$$\alpha(L)y_t = \beta(L)\varepsilon_t$$

where $\alpha(L)$ and $\beta(L)$ are polynomials of order p and q respectively. Stationarity demands that all the roots of $\alpha(L)$ lie outside the unit circle. If the variable y is not stationary then an ARMA model could not be adequate, since it requires stationarity; however, if y_t is integrated of order d (see **Integration**), so that, using the difference operator, $\Delta = (1 - L)$, $z_t = \Delta^d y_t$ is stationary, z could then be modelled as an ARMA process, which constitutes an **A**uto**R**egressive **M**oving **I**ntegrated **A**verage (ARIMA) model of y, and is denoted by ARIMA(p, d, q), where p is the order of the autoregressive component, d is the order of integration and q is the order of the moving average component. If y_t is an ARIMA(p, d, q) process then:

$$\Delta^d y_t = \mu + \alpha_1 \Delta^d y_{t-1} + \alpha_2 \Delta^d y_{t-2} + \ldots + \alpha_p \Delta^d y_{t-p}$$
$$+ \varepsilon_t + \beta_1 \varepsilon_{t-1} + \beta_2 \varepsilon_{t-2} + \ldots + \beta_q \varepsilon_{t-q}$$

where the first p terms in $\Delta^d y_{t-i}$ comprise the autoregressive components of $\Delta^d y_t$, ε_t is a white-noise random variable, and the q terms in ε_{t-j} comprise the q moving average components.

One of the most influential expositions of ARIMA modelling is that of Box and Jenkins (1984), and one of the most common uses of ARIMA modelling is to provide a simple, somewhat mechanistic, process by which to forecast. It has been shown in many studies that macroeconomic variables can frequently be modelled as ARIMA(p, 1, q) models, that is, it has been shown in very many cases that macroeconomic variables may be modelled as integrated of order 1 with autoregressive and moving average components. It should be noted that to model a variable as an ARIMA(p, d, q) process is not to say that this is a complete and sufficient statement of the variable's determinants; it may be sufficient for some purposes, but 'y_t is an ARIMA(p, d, q) process' is not a statement of economic theory, but merely one way of describing the pure time series properties of $\{y_t\}$. In an ARIMA process, the current value of y is determined wholly by its own past values (its history) and the moving average error; there are no explanatory variables and an ARIMA model is atheoretical – it does not constitute a theoretical statement.

Tests which indicate the degree of differencing necessary to transform y_t into a stationary series are described in **Unit root tests**; once d has been found, estimation of the ARMA model of $z_t = \Delta^d y_t$ may be considered. If the moving average component is absent the model may be estimated by an ordinary least squares of the regression of current z_t on the p lagged values of z; the estimators of the parameters of $\alpha(L)$ are biased, but consistent. However, if both the autoregressive and the moving average component are present then OLS will yield biased and inconsistent estimators, since the lagged values of z used as regressors are always correlated with the moving average error term. To estimate an ARMA model requires the application of non-linear least squares (or, equivalently if the errors are normally distributed, maximum likelihood) which will yield consistent and asymptotically normal estimators of the parameters (conditional on the initial observations).

The Box–Jenkins approach to modelling consists of first identifying the appropriate order of differencing to ensure stationarity, and then examining the correlogram of the differenced data (see **Autocorrelation function**). For a low-order ARMA process the implied correlograms may be derived analytically and by examining the estimated (sample) correlogram it is possible to make a judgement regarding the appropriate orders of p and q. The principle of parsimony dictates that low values of both p and q should be chosen. Having chosen the order of integration, d, and having (tentatively) chosen the orders of the AR and MA processes as p and q, the model is then estimated (by non-linear least squares or maximum likelihood methods); the model is then subjected to diagnostic tests; if the model is deemed inadequate at this stage the entire process is repeated until an adequate model is identified.

A diagnostic test commonly used is the Box–Pierce Q statistic (described in **Autocorrelation function**), but this is strictly invalid in an autoregressive model (just as the Durbin–Watson statistic is invalid in a regression equation with a lagged dependent variable) and a Lagrange multiplier (LM) test should be used. The diagnostic LM test may be used to ensure not only that p and q are sufficiently large, but also that the model has not been over-fitted and may, then, be used to simplify a deliberately overparameterized ARIMA model.

ARIMA models may be extended to accommodate seasonalities in the data by using seasonal differences; if data are collected with frequency s then the seasonal difference defined by $\Delta_s y_t = y_t - y_{t-s}$ may be examined; with quarterly data s = 4 and with monthly data s = 12.

Once an ARIMA model has been estimated satisfactorily over the period 1, 2, . . , T it may be used as the basis for forecasting beyond the estimation period. The forecast of y_{T+1}, given the original observations and the estimated parameters, may be constructed by setting the error at T+1 to zero; the forecast of y_{T+2} may then be constructed given the original observations, the estimated parameters and the forecast of y_{T+1} and so on. If the data have been differenced then it is the differences of y_t which are forecast and which are then integrated back to obtain forecasts of y_t.

ARIMA modelling, at one time synonymous with time-series modelling and once thought of as distinct from econometrics, has had a profound influence upon econometrics in recent years. Econometricians working with time-series data now recognize that the concepts and tools of ARIMA modelling can offer a great deal in modelling economic time-series. The influence is most noticeable in analyses using distributed lag models, error correction mechanisms, vector autoregressions and is especially marked in analyses of stationarity and integration.

Further reading

Box and Jenkins (1984), Chatfield (1975) and Mills (1990) provide extensive additional material on time-series modelling and ARIMA processes. See also Granger (1990).

Autocorrelation

The assumption made within the standard regression model that the error terms are mutually independent is the assumption of no autocorrelation and when this assumption fails the error is described as autocorrelated. Within the standard model, $Y = X\beta + \varepsilon$, ε is assumed to be such that ε_t and ε_{t+s} are independent for all $s \neq 0$. This assumption may fail within time-series models (and may also fail if there is spatial autocorrelation in a cross-section model), and the interpretation of such a situation is that the error at time t influences not only the current value of the dependent variable but also, to some extent, other values of the dependent variable. Clearly, there are many possible specifications of dependence amongst the errors, each of which leads to a specific form of autocorrelation.

In general, if the errors are autocorrelated then some off-diagonal elements of the variance–covariance matrix of ε, which measure the covariance between different elements of the error term, are non-zero and the matrix is non-scalar so that $V(\varepsilon) = \sigma^2\Omega$, where Ω is a symmetric positive definite matrix having some non-zeros off the diagonal. If the errors are homoscedastic then the diagonal elements of Ω are identical.

The immediate consequence of autocorrelation for the ordinary least squares estimator of β is that while the estimator remains unbiased, it loses efficiency. This loss of efficiency follows directly from the Gauss–Markov theorem: that theorem shows that when the error term is wholly non-systematic (a white-noise random variable), then OLS produces Best Linear Unbiased (BLU) estimators. All the properties of a white-noise error are required in the proof of this theorem, and since in the case of autocorrelation the error does not have all the required properties, then OLS estimation cannot produce BLU estimators. Specifically, the consequences may be shown as follows. Let the estimator of β be denoted by $\hat{\beta}$ so that:

$$\hat{\beta} = (X'X)^{-1}X'Y = (X'X)^{-1}X'(X\beta + \varepsilon) = \beta + (X'X)^{-1}X'\varepsilon$$

i.e. $\hat{\beta}$ comprises two components, one the 'true' value of the parameter, β, and the other a linear combination of the random elements. Taking expectations, assuming that the X matrix is deterministic and that the errors are all drawn from a zero mean distribution:

$$E(\hat{\beta}) = \beta$$

Turning to the variance–covariance matrix of $\hat{\beta}$, by definition:

$$V(\hat{\beta}) = E\{[\hat{\beta} - E(\hat{\beta})][\hat{\beta} - E(\hat{\beta})]'\} = E\{[(X'X)^{-1}X'\varepsilon][(X'X)^{-1}X'\varepsilon]'\}$$

i.e. $$V(\hat{\beta}) = E\{(X'X)^{-1}X'\varepsilon\varepsilon'X(X'X)^{-1}\}.$$

Given that the X matrix is deterministic, this implies that:

$$V(\hat{\beta}) = (X'X)^{-1}X'E(\varepsilon\varepsilon')X(X'X)^{-1}.$$

Now $E(\varepsilon\varepsilon')$ is simply the variance–covariance matrix of ε, here equal to $\sigma^2\Omega$; hence:

$$V(\hat{\beta}) = \sigma^2(X'X)^{-1}X'\Omega X(X'X)^{-1}.$$

If and only if $\Omega = I$ does this condense to the familiar expression:

$$V(\hat{\beta}) = \sigma^2(X'X)^{-1}.$$

In the case of autocorrelation, this result is not attainable.

The familiar formula for the variance–covariance matrix is, then, not appropriate when the error term is autocorrelated; more importantly the estimation of $V(\hat{\beta})$ involves the estimation of σ^2, and the OLS method assumes that the error term is white-noise and the variance of the errors is estimated by $s^2 = RSS/(n - k)$ (where RSS is the residual sum of squares from the OLS regression, there are n observations and the β vector comprises k elements). s^2 is, however, only an unbiased estimator under the assumption of a scalar variance–covariance matrix and in the case of autocorrelation it is biased; this is easily shown. If the OLS residuals are denoted by $\hat{e}$, then $(n - k)s^2 = \hat{e}'\hat{e} = \varepsilon' M \varepsilon$, where M is the idempotent matrix $I - X(X'X)^{-1}X'$; now:

$$E(\hat{e}'\hat{e}) = E(\sum_{i=1}^{n} m_{ii}\varepsilon_i^2 + \sum_{i \neq j}^{n}\sum_{j=1}^{n} m_{ij}\varepsilon_i\varepsilon_j)$$
$$= \sigma^2 Tr(M) + \sum_{i \neq j}^{n}\sum_{j=1}^{n} m_{ij}\varepsilon_i\varepsilon_j.$$

This assumes that ε is homoscedastic with constant variance σ^2; since the trace of $M = n - k$:

$$E(s^2) = E(\hat{e}'\hat{e}/(n-k) = \sigma^2 + (1/(n-k))\sum_{i \neq j}^{n}\sum_{j=1}^{n} m_{ij}E(\varepsilon_i\varepsilon_j).$$

Hence $E(s^2) \neq \sigma^2$ since $E(\varepsilon_i \varepsilon_j) \neq 0$ in the case of autocorrelation. In general it is not possible to say whether s^2 will be an over- or an under-estimate of σ^2, but s^2 will certainly be a biased estimator in the presence of autocorrelation. The method of OLS reports the estimated variance–covariance matrix of $\hat{\beta}$ as:

$$\hat{V}(\hat{\beta}) = s^2(X'X)^{-1}$$

Clearly, two things 'go wrong' in the autocorrelated case:

1. the correct formula for the true variance of $\hat{\beta}$ is not given by the standard expression $\sigma^2(X'X)^{-1}$;
2. the standard formula for the estimator of the error variance, σ^2, is not applicable and s^2 is a biased estimator of σ^2.

Under autocorrelation, then, the OLS estimator of β is unbiased but is inefficient (and is asymptotically inefficient), the formula for the *true* variance of $\hat{\beta}$ is not given by $\sigma^2(X'X)^{-1}$ and the *estimator* of σ^2 is biased. Inefficiency of $\hat{\beta}$ is the least of the two problems, since inefficiency can be compensated by a large number of observations. The bias in $\hat{V}(\hat{\beta})$ is a serious problem: it means that conventionally computed test statistics do not have their assumed distribution and that conventionally constructed confidence regions are also invalid. Specifically, when $\Omega = I$ it may be shown that $(n - k)s^2/\sigma^2 \sim \chi^2_{n-k}$, but the distribution of $(n - k)s^2/\sigma^2$ when $\Omega \neq I$ is not χ^2 and so subsequent tests, using t- and F- distributions, which rely on the estimated variance–covariance matrix of $\hat{\beta}$, are no longer valid.

One must be careful to draw the distinction between the true variance of $\hat{\beta}$ and the estimated variance of $\hat{\beta}$. In the present case the former is given by $\sigma^2(X'X)^{-1}X'\Omega X(X'X)^{-1}$ and the latter is given by $s^2(X'X)^{-1}$.

If one knew Ω, it would then be possible to construct the best linear unbiased estimator of β using generalized least squares, but in most practical circumstances GLS cannot be applied since Ω is not known. The structure of the autocorrelation may be very complex, and depend on a large number of parameters; however, if Ω is to be estimated, so that feasible generalized least squares can be applied, it is necessary to restrict the structure of autocorrelation such as to ensure that it is determined by fewer than n – k parameters (the number of available degrees of freedom).

One of the simplest, and certainly one of the most popular, structures is that of first order autoregression whereby the current error depends linearly upon the immediate past error plus some white-noise:

$$\varepsilon_t = \rho\varepsilon_{t-1} + v_t$$

where v_t is a wholly non-systematic white-noise random variable. If ε_t is determined in this way it is described as autoregressive of order 1, written as AR(1). Using the lag operator, L, where $Lz_t = z_{t-1}$:

$$(1-\rho L)\varepsilon_t = v_t \Rightarrow \varepsilon_t = (1-\rho L)^{-1}v_t \Rightarrow \varepsilon_t = v_t + \rho v_{t-1} + \rho^2 v_{t-2} + \ldots$$

This expression, whereby ε_t is written as an infinite weighted sum of white-noise terms is only possible when $|\rho| < 1$ and given the assumption that the process has been in existence for the infinite past.

Hence, if ε_t is AR(1) and the autoregressive parameter is strictly less than one (absolutely) then ε_t is described as 'invertible' and may be written as an infinite weighted sum of white-noise random variables. The latter representation of ε_t is an infinite moving average process, and is written as MA(∞). If $\rho > 0$ then ε_t will tend to have the same sign as ε_{t-1}, and there will be few sign changes in the series of errors: the errors will exhibit 'sign persistence'. If $\rho < 0$ then ε_t will tend to have the opposite sign to ε_{t-1} and there will be many changes of sign amongst the errors. In econometric work $\rho > 0$ is far more common than is $\rho < 0$. This simple AR(1) case may be analysed as follows:

if $\quad Y_t = \Sigma_{j=1}^{k} X_{tj}\beta_j + \varepsilon_t \quad$ and $\quad \varepsilon_t = \rho\varepsilon_{t-1} + v_t$

then: $\quad Y_t - \rho Y_{t-1} = \Sigma_{j=1}^{k}(X_{tj} - \rho X_{t-1;j})\beta_j + \varepsilon_t - \rho\varepsilon_{t-1}$

i.e. $\quad Y_t^* = \Sigma_{j=1}^{k} X_{tj}^*\beta_j + v_t$

where $Y_t^* = (1-\rho L)Y_t$, $X_{tj}^* = (1-\rho L)X_{tj}$ and $v_t = (1-\rho L)\varepsilon_t$, for $t > 1$.

The transformed variables, Y_t^* and X_{tj}^*, are known as quasi-first differences, and the model in Y_t^* and X_{tj}^* has an error term (v_t) which is, by construction, white-noise; however, relative to the original model this model has less information since there are only T – 1 available observations (there are no observations on the variables at time zero from which to construct Y_1^* and X_{1j}^*). Denoting the (constant) variance of v_t by σ_v^2 :

$$\varepsilon_t = v_t + \rho v_{t-1} + \rho^2 v_{t-2} + \ldots \Rightarrow \qquad V(\varepsilon_t) = \sigma_v^2\,(1 + \rho^2 + \rho^4 + \ldots$$

$$\Rightarrow \sigma_\varepsilon^2 = \sigma_v^2 /(1-\rho^2)$$

The assumption that the autocorrelation process extends into the infinite past ensures that ε_t is stationary and specifically that it is homoscedastic. The assumption of an infinite past is a mathematical convenience; so long as the process has sufficient history to ensure that remote errors have very little influence on the present this assumption is innocuous. The term ε_t is, by definition, independent of all v_t terms, but the variance of ε_t is not that of v_t; however, the variance of $(1-\rho^2)^{1/2}\varepsilon_t$ is precisely σ_v^2. Hence, ε_1 is independent of all the v_t terms ($t \geq 2$), but has a different variance; to transform ε_1 into a new random variable having a variance of σ_v^2 is straightforward: $V[(1-\rho^2)^{1/2}\varepsilon_1] = \sigma_v^2$. To utilize all T observations, therefore, the following transformed model is constructed:

$$(1-\rho^2)^{1/2}Y_1 = \sum_{j=1}^{k}(1-\rho^2)^{1/2}X_{1j}\beta_j + (1-\rho^2)^{1/2}\varepsilon_1$$

$$Y_t - \rho Y_{t-1} = \sum_{j=1}^{k}(X_{tj} - \rho X_{t-1;j})\beta_j + v_t \qquad t \geq 2$$

This model is the basis for the Prais–Winsten feasible generalized least squares estimation and may be extended to higher order AR processes.

Moving average errors present more difficulties, and simple transformations of the original model are not available; however, for a given MA process the structure of the variance matrix of the error term is known, and this may be utilized. For example, if the error term is an MA(1) process:

$$\varepsilon_t = v_t + \theta v_{t-1}$$

where v_t is a white-noise random term. In this case: $E(\varepsilon_t) = 0$ for all t, $V(\varepsilon_t) = (1+\theta^2)\sigma_v^2$, $E(\varepsilon_t\,\varepsilon_{t+s}) = \theta\sigma_v^2$ if $s = 1$ and is zero for all $s > 1$. Assuming normality of the errors maximum likelihood may then be used to estimate the model's parameters, and this may extended to higher order moving average processes.

Test of autocorrelation are, since the true errors are not observable, based on the ordinary least squares residuals. If autocorrelation is indicated amongst the residuals, whether AR, MA or a mixture of the two, this may be interpreted in a variety of ways; the unambiguous interpretation is that the residuals contain a systematic component, and hence some unexplained variation of the regressand is systematic. In this sense the original regression is mis-specified, but it is not clear whether the mis-specification is due to autocorrelated true errors or to some other cause. If the former, then (ideally) the source of autocorrelation within the true errors demands an economic interpretation and an estimation technique such as maximum likelihood is required. If the latter then the form of mis-specification requires further investigation.

There are various forms of mis-specification which might lead to the appearance of autocorrelated residuals. The simplest is that of an omitted regressor which is itself autocorrelated, and its influence is therefore relegated to the residuals, giving rise to autocorrelated residuals. The omitted variables may reflect mis-specified dynamics, in which case the relationship should have been estimated as, for example:

$$Y_t = \alpha + \beta X_t + \gamma X_{t-1} + \rho Y_{t-1} + \varepsilon_t$$

but was estimated as the static regression $Y_t = \alpha + \beta X_t + \varepsilon_t$; for details of this example, see **Common factors**.

Equally, the regression may have been estimated as a linear from, when a non-linear form was appropriate; suppose the relationship between Y and X is actually a concave, not a linear function. If a straight line is fitted to observations from a concave function then the residuals will exhibit sign persistence, and this will manifest itself as the appearance of positive first-order autoregression. To examine this it is necessary to investigate the functional form of the relationship via, for example, the Ramsey RESET test (see **RESET tests**) or an application of the Box and Cox transformation (see the entry of that title). Further, if there is a structural break in the relationship, a similar picture of first-order positive autocorrelation may be apparent. This case may be examined by a Chow test or via the use of recursive residuals (see **Chow test** and **Recursive residuals**).

In the cases when the evidence of autocorrelation is a reflection of a mis-specification of the systematic component of the regression, as opposed to a reflection of a truly non-scalar variance–covariance matrix of the errors, estimation by some feasible generalized least squares or maximum likelihood method will yield most misleading results, as all estimators will then be biased due to the mis-specification. Evidence of autocorrelation should not, then, be interpreted simply as evidence that OLS is not applicable and that some other estimation technique should be used; the other interpretations of autocorrelation suggest that the specification of the model should be re-examined. Only when the evidence of residual autocorrelation is interpreted as a reflection of autocorrelated true errors should the model be re-estimated by feasible generalized least squares or maximum likelihood.

Further reading

The literature on autocorrelation has a long history, is extremely wide ranging and complex; the bibliography in Judge *et al.* (1982 and 1985) is very comprehensive, as is that of most modern texts (see, for example the references to the Chapter 15 of Greene, 1993). In addition to the references given above, the reader is best referred to such excellent texts and the references therein for further reading on this topic. See also **Autocorrelation – estimation methods** and **Autocorrelation Tests**.

Autocorrelation – estimation methods

If the error term in the model $Y = X\beta + \varepsilon$ is autocorrelated, whether in the form of an autoregressive or a moving average process then, if the regressors are fixed, ordinary least squares (OLS) leads to an unbiased but inefficient estimator of β. If, however, the regressors include the lagged dependent variable OLS will produce biased and inconsistent estimators (since the regressor Y_{t-1} and the error are then always correlated).

In the case of fixed regressors, the Cochrane–Orcutt procedure is a most popular alternative estimation technique of the model $Y = X\beta + \varepsilon$ when the error follows an AR(1) process: $\varepsilon_t = \rho\varepsilon_{t-1} + v_t$. Then:

$$Y_t - \rho Y_{t-1} = \Sigma_{j=1}^{k}(X_{tj} - \rho X_{t-1;j})\beta_j + \varepsilon_t - \rho\varepsilon_{t-1}$$

for $t \geq 2$. The Cochrane–Orcutt procedure is an iterative method and requires an initial estimate of ρ, say $\hat{\rho}$. The initial estimate may be derived from several sources. Since $\varepsilon_t = \rho\varepsilon_{t-1} + v_t$, and the true errors are not observable, the obvious possibility is to replace the true errors, ε_t, by the OLS residuals from the regression of Y on X, $\hat{e}_t$, and then run the regression of $\hat{e}_t$ on $\hat{e}_{t-1}$. The estimator of ρ, $\hat{\rho}$, is then the OLS estimator of ρ from the regression: $\hat{e}_t = \rho\hat{e}_{t-1} + \eta_t$.

i.e.

$$\hat{\rho} = \frac{\Sigma_{t=2}^{T}\hat{e}_{t-1}\hat{e}_t}{\Sigma_{t=2}^{T}\hat{e}_{t-1}^2}$$

Under appropriate assumptions about the limiting distribution of the regressors $\hat{\rho}$ is then a consistent estimator. An alternative approach to the estimation of ρ is to take the Durbin–Watson statistic, d, and note the following:

$$d = \frac{\Sigma_{t=2}^{T}(\hat{e}_t - \hat{e}_{t-1})^2}{\Sigma_{t=1}^{T}\hat{e}_t^2}$$

Expanding the numerator yields:

$$\Sigma_{t=2}^{T}(\hat{e}_t - \hat{e}_{t-1})^2 = \Sigma_{t=2}^{T}(\hat{e}_t^2 - 2\hat{e}_{t-1}\hat{e}_{t-1} + \hat{e}_t^2)$$

Hence, for large T: $d \cong 2(1 - \hat{\rho})$. Thus, $\hat{\rho}$ may be estimated by $1 - \frac{1}{2}d$, which provides a consistent estimator of ρ.

Given $\hat{\rho}^{(1)}$, an initial estimate of ρ, the estimated quasi-first differences, given by $Y_t - \hat{\rho}^{(1)}Y_{t-1}$ and $X_{tj} - \hat{\rho}^{(1)}X_{t-1,j}$, are constructed for $t > 1$ and the regression performed using these transformed variables. This yields estimates of the β_j parameters which, in turn, may be used to construct a revised estimate of ρ and this process may be iterated until the parameter estimates converge. This process may be summarized by the two-step procedure:

1. given the initial value of ρ, $\hat{\rho}^{(1)}$, construct the quasi-first differences $Y^*_t = Y_t - \hat{\rho}^{(1)}Y_{t-1}$ and $X^*_{tj} = X_{tj} - \hat{\rho}^{(1)}X_{t-1;j}$; for t > 1, run the OLS regression of Y^*_t on the variables X^*_{tj} to yield parameter estimates $\hat{\beta}^{(1)}$.
2. from the residuals, constructed as $\hat{e}^{(1)}_t = Y_i - \sum_{j=1}^{k} X_{tj}\hat{\beta}^{(1)}_j$, run the OLS regression of $\hat{e}^{(1)}_t$ on $\hat{e}^{(1)}_{t-1}$ to yield a new estimate of ρ, denoted by $\hat{\rho}^{(2)}$. Return to step one, replacing $\hat{\rho}^{(1)}$ by $\hat{\rho}^{(2)}$ and so on.

The iterations cease once the parameter estimates have converged (that is, change by less than some pre-specified amount from one iteration to another) or once the residuals from step 1 indicate no autocorrelation. The Cochrane–Orcutt procedure uses only T – 1 observations and one could use all T observations by incorporating the first observation as $(1 - \rho^2)^{½}Y_1$ and $(1 - \rho^2)^{½}X_{1j}$ (as explained in **Autocorrelation**); this is then known as the Prais–Winsten method. Since the Prais–Winsten method uses one more observation than the Cochrane–Orcutt it is expected to be more efficient.

If the regressors are not fixed, but include the lagged dependent variable, then the regression of Y on X does not produce consistent estimators, and so the residuals cannot be used to construct a consistent estimator for ρ. In this case an instrumental variable for the lagged dependent variable is employed to estimate the model $Y = X\beta + \varepsilon$, and from the resulting residuals an initial consistent estimate of ρ may be constructed which may then be improved upon in a two-step technique. This is the basis of Hatanaka's (1974) two-step efficient estimator which is equivalent to the maximum likelihood procedure.

Another method to obtain the initial estimate of ρ (in absence of a lagged dependent variable as a regressor) is to run the regression:

$$Y_t = \sum_{j=1}^{k} X_{tj}\beta_j + \sum_{j=1}^{k} X_{t-1;j}\phi_j + \rho Y_{t-1} + v_t \qquad t \geq 2$$

and taking the estimate of the coefficient on Y_{t-1} as the initial $\hat{\rho}$. The above method is due to Durbin (1960) and the regression suggested by Durbin represents the AR(1) model once the non-linear restrictions $\phi_j = -\rho\beta_j$ are imposed, but to obtain $\hat{\rho}$ this restriction is ignored. Monte Carlo evidence has suggested that the Durbin estimate of ρ followed by the Prais–Winsten method performs well. If the original model includes a constant, so that X_{i1} = 1 for all i, the Durbin equation, to avoid perfect multicollinearity, becomes:

$$Y_t = \alpha + \sum_{j=2}^{k} X_{tj}\beta_j + \sum_{j=2}^{k} X_{t-1;j}\phi_j + \rho Y_{t-1} + v_t \qquad t \geq 2$$

It is to be noted that, in the common case when the original model includes a constant term, the Durbin method demands that a regression involving a total of 2k parameters is run in order to obtain the estimate of $\hat{\rho}$, and this requires that there are sufficient degrees of freedom.

One problem which plagues all iterative approaches is that the final estimate may represent only a local, not a global, minimum of the sum of squares; to ensure that a global minimum has been achieved it is recommended that a search is performed over the relevant parameter space. In this case this would involve estimating step 1 of the Cochrane–Orcutt (or, better, the Prais–Winsten) method for values of ρ in the range $-1 < \rho < 1$ at, say 0.1 intervals, and computing the residual sum of squares for each value of ρ. The grid search could then be concentrated around that value of ρ which yields the least sum of squares in this grid.

The variance–covariance estimator of the parameters should be taken from the final regression, but tests which use it then have only asymptotic validity since the variance–covariance of the error terms has been estimated and the reported variance–covariance matrix is conditional on the final value of $\hat{\rho}$.

Yet another estimation method is that of maximum likelihood; in the case of a non-scalar error variance matrix term the concentrated log-likelihood function is given by:

$$\ell n\tilde{\mathrm{L}}(\tilde{\Omega}) = \text{constant} - (n/2)\ell n(\mathrm{RSS}(\tilde{\rho})) - \tfrac{1}{2}\ell n|\tilde{\Omega}(\tilde{\rho})|$$

where $\mathrm{RSS}(\tilde{\rho})$ is the residual sum of squares using a Prais–Winsten transformation and $\tilde{\Omega}(\tilde{\rho})$ is the estimated variance matrix of ε, for a given value of the autocorrelation parameter denoted by $\tilde{\rho}$. The general linear model $\mathrm{Y} = \mathrm{X}\beta + \varepsilon$ with $\mathrm{V}(\varepsilon) = \sigma^2\Omega$ may be transformed to a model with a scalar variance–covariance matrix, as is described in **Generalized least squares**: there exists a square non-singular matrix P such that $\mathrm{PP}' = \Omega$ from which it follows that:

$$\mathrm{P}^{-1}\mathrm{Y} = \mathrm{P}^{-1}\mathrm{X}\beta + \mathrm{P}^{-1}\varepsilon$$

and $\mathrm{V}(\mathrm{P}^{-1}\varepsilon) = \sigma^2\mathrm{I}$; P^{-1} disentangles the autocorrelation and since $\mathrm{PP}' = \Omega$ this fact may be used to compute $|\Omega|$. P^{-1} describes the transformation used in the Prais-Winsten method, and so the structure of P^{-1} is known:

$$\mathrm{P}^{-1} = \begin{bmatrix} (1-\rho^2)^{1/2} & 0 & \cdots & \cdots & 0 \\ -\rho & 1 & & & 0 \\ 0 & -\rho & 1 & & \vdots \\ \vdots & & \ddots & \ddots & \vdots \\ 0 & \cdots & \cdots & -\rho & 1 \end{bmatrix}$$

and it is easy to show that: $|\mathrm{P}^{-1}| = (1-\rho^2)^{1/2}$; hence $|\mathrm{P}| = (1-\rho^2)^{-1/2}$ and $|\Omega| = |\mathrm{PP}'| = |\mathrm{P}|^2 = (1-\rho^2)^{-1}$; hence:

$$\ell n\tilde{\mathrm{L}}(\tilde{\Omega}) = \text{constant} - (n/2)\ell n(\mathrm{RSS}(\tilde{\rho})) + \tfrac{1}{2}\ell n(1-\tilde{\rho}^2).$$

It is clear from this expression that the Prais–Winsten method, which minimizes $\mathrm{RSS}(\tilde{\rho})$, is not equivalent to the maximum likelihood (ML) method. Monte Carlo evidence suggests that the Prais–Winsten method is as efficient as the ML method; but the Prais–Winsten method reports the conditional estimated variance of the $\hat{\beta}$ estimates, not the unconditional estimated variances. Since the ML method, through estimation of the information matrix (see **Maximum likelihood**), yields unconditional estimates of the variances of $\hat{\beta}$, taking account of the fact that ρ has been estimated, the ML method offers a real advantage over other methods and is available as an option in most software packages for the general AR(p) model.

Since in all these methods an estimate of ρ is required, and this is derived from the same data set as that used to estimate β, the resulting estimator of β is not a linear estimator; the estimator is, in fact, neither linear nor is it unbiased, but all the above methods yield a consistent estimator of β.

If the error term in the model $Y = X\beta + \varepsilon$ is defined by a first-order moving average process then ordinary least squares leads to an unbiased, but inefficient estimator of β in the case of fixed regressors, but leads to inconsistent and inefficient estimators when the regressors include a lagged dependent variable. The simple transformations available in the case of AR errors are not available in the moving average case, and non-linear least squares or maximum likelihood estimation techniques are required. As an example, if the regressors are fixed and the error term follows an MA(1) process then:

$$Y = X\beta + \varepsilon \quad \text{and } \varepsilon_t = v_t + \theta v_{t-1}.$$

$E(\varepsilon_t) = 0$ for all t, $V(\varepsilon_t) = (1 + \theta^2)\sigma_v^2$, $E(\varepsilon_t \varepsilon_{t+s}) = \theta\sigma_v^2$ if $s = 1$ and is zero for all $s > 1$. Hence, writing $V(\varepsilon) = \sigma_v^2 \Omega$ and assuming normality of the errors, the log-likelihood function may be written as:

$$\ell nL(\beta, \theta, \sigma_v^2 \mid Y)$$
$$= -(n/2)\ell n(2\pi\sigma_v^2) - (1/2\sigma_v^2)(Y - X\beta)'\Omega^{-1}(Y - X\beta) - \tfrac{1}{2}\ell n|\Omega|$$

and this may be maximized by some appropriate non-linear routine or by a search over values of θ. This may, of course, be extended to higher order MA processes.

Most software packages include exact maximum likelihood estimation techniques for autoregressive and moving average errors.

Further reading

The literature on the estimation of models subject to autocorrelation has a long history, is extremely wide ranging and complex; the bibliography in Judge *et al.* (1982 and 1985) is very comprehensive, as is that of most modern texts (see, for example the references to the Chapter 15 of Greene, 1993). In addition to the references given above, the reader is best referred to such excellent texts and the references therein for further reading on this topic. See also **Autocorrelation** and **Autocorrelation tests**.

Autocorrelation function

It is typically impossible to characterize fully any time series (because only a finite and historical realization of that series may be observed); however, a very useful descriptor of a time series is its autocorrelation function. Simply, the autocorrelation function is a measure of the dependency between data points separated by time. For a time series $\{y_t\}$, denote the variance of y_t by σ_t^2 and the covariance between y_t and y_{t+s} by $\tau_{t,s}$. Since $\tau_{t,s}$ depends on the units of measurement, it is more common to measure the dependencies across time by the autocorrelation parameters of the series, denoted by $\rho_{t,s}$ where $\rho_{t,s}$ is the correlation between y_t and y_{t+s}:

$$\rho_{t,s} = \mathrm{Cov}(y_t, y_{t+s})/\sigma_t\sigma_s = \tau_{t,s}/\sigma_t\sigma_s$$

If $\{y_t\}$ is a stationary process then σ_t^2 is independent of t and may be written simply as σ^2; similarly, for a stationary series the covariance between any two values of the series, y_t and y_{t+s} depends only on the difference in time between those observations (the lag); hence $\tau_{t,s}$ may be written as τ_s.and so for a stationary series:

$$\rho_{t,s} = \rho_s = \tau_s/\sigma^2.$$

The terms ρ_s define the autocorrelation function of the series and a plot of ρ_s against the lag, s, is known as the correlogram of the series. The autocorrelation function may be used to test the properties of the time-series. As a special case, suppose $\{y_t\}$ is a white-noise process; then this may be described fully in terms of its autocorrelation function, for then $\rho_0 = 1$ and $\rho_s = 0$ for all $s \neq 0$.

The correlogram plays a critical role in identifying the order of an ARIMA model, since various standard patterns of the autocorrelation function are easy to recognize. If, for example, $\{y_t\}$ is a stationary AR(1) process then:

$$y_t = \rho y_{t-1} + \varepsilon_t, \quad |\rho| < 1 \text{ and } \varepsilon_t \text{ is a stationary white-noise random variable}$$

and it is easy to demonstrate that $\rho_s = \rho^s$, in which case the correlogram will constitute a geometrically declining series (if $\rho > 0$) or will alternate in sign and approach zero (if $\rho < 0$). If $\{y_t\}$ is an MA(1) process then:

$$y_t = \varepsilon_t + \lambda\varepsilon_{t-1},$$

where ε_t is a stationary white-noise random variable and $\rho_s \neq 0$ for $s = 1$ and $\rho_s = 0$ for all $s > 1$. Similarly, if $\{y_t\}$ is an MA(2) process then the only values of ρ_s which are non-zero refer to s = 0, 1 and 2. It is important to be able to infer the population autocorrelation function from the sample autocorrelation function, and a rough guide of the 95% confidence interval is provided by $\pm 2/\sqrt{T}$, where T is the sample size; if the estimated values of ρ_s are denoted by r_s, then the significance of the r_s terms may be judged by reference to this band, so that any r_s which lie within $2/\sqrt{T}$ of zero may be deemed statistically insignificant (with a Type I error of 5%).

The confidence band is due to a result of Bartlett (1946) who demonstrated that if $\{y_t\}$ is white-noise then its sample autocorrelation coefficients (that is the estimated values of ρ_s from a finite sample of T observations) are distributed approximately normally with zero mean and variance 1/T. This provides a simple test that a series is white-noise:

> The null hypothesis H_o: $\rho_s = 0$ may be tested by using the result that the estimated coefficient, r_s multiplied by $\sqrt{T}$ is, under the null hypothesis, approximately a standard normal variate; i.e. under the null, $\sqrt{T}r_s \sim N(0, 1)$.

Of more interest, perhaps, is the joint null hypothesis H_o: $\rho_s = 0$ for all s = 1, . . . , p. Under the null hypothesis, $\sqrt{T}r_s \sim N(0, 1)$ (approximately) and so $Q = T\Sigma_{s=1}^{p} r_s^2 \sim \chi_p^2$ (approximately). This is the Box–Pierce statistic, but the Ljung–Box statistic has better finite sample properties; the latter is defined by $[T(T+2)/(T-k)]\Sigma_{s=1}^{p} r_s^2$ and is a χ_p^2 variate under the null hypothesis of white-noise. The Box–Pierce and Ljung–Box tests are called portmanteau tests, but neither can be recommended with any confidence in identifying an ARMA model; the non-nested tests of McAleer *et al.* (1988) are superior.

The correlogram can also give a visual indication of seasonalities within data; if, for example, the data are quarterly and there is a marked cycle of significant r_s values for every fourth s then a quarterly seasonal effect is suggested.

Further reading

Box and Jenkins (1984) provide a thorough study of the autocorrelation function, with numerous examples. See also Box and Pierce (1970), Ljung and Box (1979), Godfrey (1979), McAleer *et al.*(1988) and **ARMA and ARIMA models**.

Autocorrelation tests

Many tests exist to detect autocorrelation. The most commonly reported statistic is the Durbin–Watson test, based on the statistic defined by:

$$d = \frac{\Sigma_{t=2}^{T}(\hat{e}_t - \hat{e}_{t-1})^2}{\Sigma_{t=1}^{T}\hat{e}_t^2}$$

where $\hat{e}_t$ is the tth ordinary least squares residual from the general model $Y = X\beta + \varepsilon$ based on T observations. The statistic is designed to test for first order autocorrelation, AR(1), when the regressors are non-stochastic. Under the null hypothesis of no autocorrelation the sampling distribution of the statistic can be derived, but it depends upon the actual values of the regressors, so that different X matrices lead to different distributions of d. However, the actual distribution of d, whatever the X matrix, is constrained within bounds which are defined only by the number of observations used in the regression and the number of regressors. Tables of the critical values for d offer two critical values, a lower critical value, d_l, and an upper value d_u, so that if the observed value of d is less than 2 and $d < d_l$ the null hypothesis of no autocorrelation is rejected in favour of positive first order autocorrelation, if $d > d_u$ the null hypothesis is not rejected; and if $d_l < d < d_u$ the test is inconclusive. If $d > 2$ then this procedure is followed using the test statistic $4 - d$ and the alternative hypothesis of negative autocorrelation. Most tables require there to be a constant in the regression, although Farebrother (1980) constructed critical values for use in the absence of a constant term. The Durbin–Watson test has drawbacks which include the fact that it is only applicable to regressions which have fixed regressors, it uses a specific alternative hypothesis of first order autocorrelation, and has a distribution, under the null hypothesis of no autocorrelation, which is dependent on the particular configuration of regressors. In consequence, even when applicable, for a given Type I error the Durbin–Watson statistic requires two critical values and so there is an 'indeterminate' range within which one can neither 'accept' nor 'reject' the null hypothesis; furthermore, the D–W statistic is only tabulated for a limited number of Type I errors.

When the regressors are stochastic the test is biased, and in the special case when the regression includes the lagged dependent variable as a regressor the statistic is biased towards the value of 2, leading to frequent erroneous non-rejection of the null hypothesis of no autocorrelation. The use of a lagged dependent variable as a regressor is common in time-series analysis, and in the presence of autocorrelation the regressor Y_{t-1} is then always correlated with the error ε_t; hence the presence of autocorrelation and a lagged dependent variable as a regressor leads to biased OLS estimators due to the non-independence of regressors and the error. For this special case Durbin (1970) derived an asymptotic test, known as Durbin's h-statistic:

$$h = r\sqrt{\frac{T}{1 - T\hat{V}(\hat{\gamma})}}$$

where there are T observation, $\hat{\gamma}$ is the estimate of the coefficient on the lagged dependent variable, $\hat{V}(\hat{\gamma})$ is its estimated variance and $r = 1 - \frac{1}{2}d$, where d is the usual Durbin–Watson statistic. Under the null hypothesis of no first-order autocorrelation, h is asymptotically distributed as a standard normal variate, and is used as a one-sided test.

Wallis (1972) extended the Durbin–Watson test for a special form of fourth-order autocorrelation, $\varepsilon_t = \rho\,\varepsilon_{t-4} + v_t$, in which case the test statistic becomes:

$$d = \frac{\sum_{t=5}^{T}(\hat{e}_t - \hat{e}_{t-4})^2}{\sum_{t=1}^{T}\hat{e}_t^2}$$

In order to test for the presence of more general forms of autocorrelation, the Breusch–Godfrey test is most commonly used and is reported by most software packages. This is a Lagrange multiplier (LM) test which is applicable in more general situations than any of the above tests; it is a test of general dependence amongst the errors and places no constraints on the regressors, so that it may be used with stochastic regressors; importantly, the test statistic has a known (asymptotic) distribution.

The LM statistic is designed to overcome the known weaknesses of the Durbin–Watson statistic and its immediate extensions; the LM statistic tests for general violations of the hypothesis independence amongst the errors (not simply autoregressive AR(p) structures of the form $\varepsilon_t = \sum_{j=1}^{p}\rho_j\varepsilon_{t-j} + v_t$ but also moving average MA(q) structures of the form $\varepsilon_t = \sum_{j=0}^{q}\rho_j v_{t-j}$), is applicable in the presence of non-fixed regressors, and because it has a known (asymptotic) distribution, for a given Type I error, there is a unique critical value.

The LM test is based upon an artificial regression and may be simply explained: within the general linear model, $Y = X\beta + \varepsilon$, suppose there are k regressors and T observations; the test proceeds by first computing the OLS estimate $\hat{\beta}$ and the residual vector, $\hat{e}$. The test is one of independence amongst the disturbances up to p^{th} order, namely that ε_t is independent of ε_{t-s} for all s = 1, 2 . . . , p and for all t (and it is irrelevant whether the dependence arises via AR, MA or ARMA structures). This test is carried out by forming an auxiliary regression of $\hat{e}_t$ on the p lagged residuals $\hat{e}_{t-1}, \hat{e}_{t-2}, \ldots, \hat{e}_{t-p}$ and the k original regressors; since this regression cannot immediately be carried out for t = 1, 2, . . p as there are no values available for $\hat{e}_{t-s}$ for $s \geq t$, the regression is performed using all T observations and setting $\hat{e}_{t-s} = 0$ for $s \geq t$. The auxiliary regression is, therefore:

$$\hat{e} = X\xi + W\delta + \text{error}$$

where W is the T×p matrix of additional regressors given by:

$$W = \begin{bmatrix} 0 & 0 & \cdots & \cdots & \cdots & 0 \\ \hat{e}_1 & 0 & \cdots & \cdots & \cdots & 0 \\ \hat{e}_2 & \hat{e}_1 & & & & \vdots \\ \vdots & & \ddots & & & \vdots \\ \vdots & & & \ddots & & \vdots \\ \vdots & & & & \ddots & \hat{e}_{T-p-1} \\ \hat{e}_{T-1} & \hat{e}_{T-2} & & & & \hat{e}_{T-p} \end{bmatrix}$$

If the hypothesis of independence amongst the errors is correct, then this auxiliary regression will have a very poor fit, for the following reasons: the true errors ε are independent of the full matrix of regressors X and, under the null hypothesis of independence, are also mutually independent; using the OLS residuals $\hat{e}$ as proxies for the true errors ε, when the null hypothesis is true neither X nor W contribute to the explanation of $\hat{e}$ and so the fit will be poor (that is, the R^2 statistic will be small). Clearly, a 'large' value of R^2 is evidence against the hypothesis of independence, and to decide 'how large is large' the distribution of R^2 must be investigated. It may be shown that, under the null hypothesis of independence:

$$TR^2 \sim \chi^2_p \text{ (asymptotically).}$$

Thus, if the observed value of TR^2 from the auxiliary regression is so large as to exceed the chosen critical value from the χ^2_p distribution, the null hypothesis of independence amongst the errors is rejected.

The asymptotic χ^2 distribution is derived from considering the F-test for the exclusion of W: under H_o: $\delta = 0$:

$$\frac{(R^2 - R^2_r)/p}{(1-R^2)/(T-k-p)} \sim F_{p,T-k-p}$$

where R^2_r is the R^2 statistic from the restricted regression of $\hat{e}$ on X alone (that is, having excluded W) and R^2 is the goodness-of-fit statistic from the unrestricted regression of $\hat{e}$ on both X and W. Since $\hat{e}$ and X are orthogonal, R^2_r is identically zero. Rearranging the test, noting that $R^2_r \equiv 0$:

$$TR^2 \sim [Tp/(T-k-p)](1-R^2)F_{p,T-k-p}$$

Now, as $T \to \infty$, $F_{p,T-k-p} \to \chi^2_p/p$ and $Tp/(T-k-p) \to p$; also, under the null hypothesis, $R^2 \to 0$. Hence the right hand side approaches χ^2_p. Thus:

$$TR^2 \xrightarrow{D} \chi^2_p.$$

The χ^2 form of this test is the asymptotic form, and the F-version, given above, is commonly employed as it has been shown that the asymptotic form rejects the null hypothesis too often (its actual Type I error exceeds the nominal level).

Further reading
Tests of autocorrelation are further described in all standard texts; see also Durbin and Watson (1950, 1951 and 1971), Durbin (1970), Breusch (1978) and Godfrey (1978a and 1978b) See also **Autocorrelation** and **Autocorrelation – estimation methods**

Bayesian estimation

The concepts of the prior and posterior distributions described in **Bayesian theory** provide the basis for Bayesian estimation; Bayesian estimation proceeds from the posterior distribution, but in order to obtain the posterior distribution it is necessary to specify a prior distribution of the parameters. Broadly speaking, two categories of prior distribution are used. The first is the non-informative prior which captures ignorance of the parameter in question, and the second is an informative prior.

Non-informative priors are often called Jeffrey's priors, and are also called improper or diffuse priors. If, for example, there is no prior information on mean of a distribution, μ, its prior distribution may be thought to take the form $f(\mu) = c$, where c is some constant, but this distribution does not integrate over the real line to unity. Notwithstanding this improper characteristic of the prior it is possible to combine improper priors with sample information to yield proper posterior distributions. A common example is that of a sample drawn from a normal population for which the priors of the mean and log of the variance are assumed to be independent and uniform distributions; in that case both marginal posterior functions are proper. If the posterior distribution is proper then it is legitimate to proceed to make inference, whatever the form of the prior.

Informative priors encapsulate prior information of the parameter(s) in question; it is common to use what are called conjugate priors. A conjugate prior distribution is from the same family of distributions as that which describes the distribution of the sample of observations, so that if the sample is assumed to be normally distributed a conjugate prior for the parameters would also be normal. The variance of the prior distribution is a measure of the prior information, and the inverse of the prior variance is known as the prior precision. The use of conjugate priors has analytic attractions and they may be used to capture the typical forms of prior information.

Bayesian estimation proceeds from the posterior distribution by use of a *loss function*; a loss function describes the losses which accrue given an action and a particular state of world. Suppose the posterior distribution for a parameter θ and given information (both sample and prior) D, is given by $f(\theta|D)$; estimation can be seen as the taking of an action, namely announcing $\hat{\theta}$ as the estimate, and the state of the world can be seen as the value of θ. If $\hat{\theta}$ is declared to be the estimate when the parameter's value is actually θ, then if $\hat{\theta} \neq \theta$ some loss will be incurred. Let $l(\theta, \hat{\theta})$ describe these losses. In general, $l(\theta, \hat{\theta}) = 0$ when $\theta = \hat{\theta}$. The Bayesian estimate is then given by that value $\hat{\theta}$ which minimises the expected loss:

$$\min_{\hat{\theta}} \int l(\theta, \hat{\theta}) f(\theta | D) d\theta$$

Denote the solution to this by $\hat{\theta}^*$, the Bayesian estimator. Clearly, $\hat{\theta}^*$ depends upon both the posterior distribution (and hence on the prior distribution) and on the loss function.

Various loss functions have been proposed, and the three most popular are the quadratic loss, $(\theta - \hat{\theta})^2$, the absolute loss, $|\theta - \hat{\theta}|$, and the zero-one loss, $l(\theta, \hat{\theta}) = 1$ if $\theta \neq \hat{\theta}$, and 0 otherwise. The Bayesian estimator is optimal with respect to a specific loss function, and for the three above it may be shown that:

$\hat{\theta}^*$ = the posterior mean, for a quadratic loss;

$\hat{\theta}^*$ = the posterior median, for an absolute loss;

$\hat{\theta}^*$ = the posterior mode, for a zero-one loss.

It should be noted that since all inference is based on the posterior distribution, which is conditional upon the sample data and the prior information, the Bayesian estimator is treated as a constant. Bayesian estimation thus reverses the more usual treatment in which the parameter is fixed and the estimator is random. In consequence, for example, a Bayesian interval estimate has non-random end-points and probability (in the sense of degrees of belief) is attached to the parameter.

To determine a $100(1 - \alpha)\%$ Bayesian confidence interval for the case when θ is a scalar quantity, what is sought is that interval (a, b) such that $\Pr\{a < \theta < b\} = (1 - \alpha)$; that is, a and b are required so that:

$$\int_a^b f(\theta|D)d\theta = (1-\alpha).$$

Since there is no unique solution to this equation, the condition that the interval be the shortest possible is added. The posterior density associated with this interval is higher than that attached to any other interval yielding $100(1 - \alpha)\%$ posterior probability and is thus referred to as a posterior highest density (PHD) interval.

In the case when θ is a vector of parameters, say $(\theta_1, \ldots, \theta_k)$, it is often the case that interest centres on a subset of these k parameters, say $(\theta_1, \ldots, \theta_r)$, $r < k$. In this case the parameters $\theta_{r+1}, \theta_{r+2}, \ldots \theta_k$ are called nuisance parameters, and the marginal posterior density function for the parameters of interest can be obtained by integrating out the nuisance parameters:

$$f(\theta_1, \ldots, \theta_r|D) = \int \ldots \int f(\theta_1, \ldots \theta_k | D) d\theta_{r+1} \ldots d\theta_k$$

$$= \int .. \int f(\theta_1, \ldots, \theta_r | \theta_{r+1}, \ldots, \theta_k, D) f(\theta_{r+1}, \ldots \theta_k | D) d\theta_{r+1} \ldots d\theta_k$$

Hence the marginal posterior distribution of $(\theta_1, \ldots, \theta_r)$ is simply a weighted average of the conditional pdfs of $(\theta_1, \ldots, \theta_r)$ given ($\theta_{r+1}, \ldots, \theta_k$ and D) where the weights are the marginal densities of $(\theta_{r+1}, \ldots, \theta_k)$ given the prior and sample data, D. Having integrated out the nuisance parameters, this marginal pdf can then be used, with a loss function, to compute Bayesian point and interval estimates of this subset of parameters. In this case the interval estimate is the region of highest posterior density in r-dimensional space.

In similar vein to point estimation, the Bayesian approach provides a conceptually simple approach to the comparison of hypotheses. In testing hypotheses in a Bayesian framework the investigator assigns prior probabilities to each hypothesis and then combines these with the sample information to obtain posterior probabilities which then determines the decision. Consider the following:

$$H_o: \theta_1 = 0$$

$$H_1: \theta_1 \neq 0$$

and the marginal posterior density function is given by $f(\theta_1|D)$. Suppose the prior probabilities of the hypotheses are given by $p(H_o) = p_o$ and $p(H_1) = 1 - p_o$; this yields the prior odds $p(H_o)/p(H_1) = p_o/(1 - p_o)$, and the sample information, denoted by Y, may be incorporated, via Bayes' Theorem, to yield the posterior odds, $p(H_o|Y)/p(H_1|Y)$. Now:

$$p(H_o, Y, \theta) = p(H_o)f(\theta|Y)f(Y|H_o, \theta) = p(H_o, \theta|Y)f(Y)$$

Hence:

$$p(H_o, \theta|Y) = p(H_o)f(\theta|Y)f(Y|H_o, \theta)/f(Y).$$

Integrating out the parameters, $\theta_1, \ldots, \theta_k$:

$$p(H_o|Y) = \frac{p(H_o)}{p(Y)}\int\ldots\int f(\theta_1,\ldots\theta_k|Y)f(Y|H_o,\theta_1,\ldots\theta_k)d\theta_1,\ldots d\theta_k.$$

The expression for $p(H_1|Y)$ is obtained similarly, and so:

$$\frac{p(H_o|Y)}{p(H_1|Y)} = \frac{p(H_o)\int\ldots\int f(\theta_1,\ldots\theta_k|Y)f(Y|H_o,\theta_1,\ldots\theta_k)d\theta_1,\ldots d\theta_k}{p(H_1)\int\ldots\int f(\theta_1,\ldots\theta_k|Y)f(Y|H_1,\theta_1,\ldots\theta_k)d\theta_1,\ldots d\theta_k}$$

Thus the posterior odds, $p(H_o|Y)/p(H_1|Y)$, are given by the prior odds, $p(H_o)/p(H_1)$, multiplied by the ratio of averaged likelihoods, where the likelihoods are averaged using the prior densities of parameters (given the respective hypotheses) as weighting functions. This ratio is known as the Bayes' factor. Bayesian analysis, as given above, thus provides a posterior comparison of hypotheses, rather than a test of hypotheses; moreover, the setting of prior odds may be seen to determine the critical Bayes factor which will be just sufficient to overturn the prior belief. Within a Bayesian analysis the approach to testing hypotheses is shown as in the table below:

	True state of the world	
Act	H_0 is true	H_0 is not true
H_0 is not rejected	0	L_{o1}
H_0 is rejected	L_{1o}	0
Probabilities	$p(H_o \vert Y)$	$p(H_1 \vert Y)$

L_{ij} denotes the loss incurred if hypothesis i is chosen when hypothesis j is the more appropriate; and the condition for choosing H_o is that the expected loss in choosing H_o, $L_{o1}p(H_1|Y)$, is less than that of choosing H_1, $L_{1o}p(H_o|Y)$. In this form it is clear that merely being the more likely hypothesis is insufficient to be chosen; the posterior odds may or may not favour the chosen hypothesis since choice depends not only upon the posterior odds, but also upon the losses incurred. Thus H_o is chosen relative to H_1 if:

$$\frac{L_{1o}p(H_o \mid Y)}{L_{o1}p(H_1 \mid Y)} > 1$$

i.e. if: (posterior odds)×(relative loss) < 1.

i.e. if: (prior odds)×(Bayes Factor)×(relative loss) < 1.

One should, perhaps, distinguish between the use of Bayesian analysis in estimation as opposed to hypothesis testing; in estimation the argument that all information should be utilized so as to maximize efficiency may be used to justify a Bayesian analysis, but in problems of hypothesis testing the Bayesian approach provides not so much a test but more a method of comparison. By incorporating prior beliefs in the posterior comparison, one might argue that 'objectivity' has been lost and that the prior odds imply the minimum weight of sample information which is sufficient to overturn the original ranking. The so-called loss of objectivity is an interesting perspective, but must be put in the light of classical hypothesis testing in which a test statistic is compared to a critical value and the decision to reject a null hypothesis is then based on a test statistic which is (absolutely) larger than the critical value. The question must be put: by what objective criteria was that critical value chosen, and does the critical value not simply identify the nature of sample information which would result in any given decision?

Bayesian analysis can be very expensive in terms of computing power for it requires the amalgamation of multi-dimensional information from the prior density function with that from the likelihood and then requires that any nuisance parameters are integrated out. When computing techniques were very costly these considerations were most important and Bayesian estimation found little favour on these grounds, but now that the costs of computing are less of a constraint, Bayesian analysis is more feasible and the debate over the use of Bayesian inferential techniques can move to the more proper grounds concerning the way in which prior information might be used and the nature of probability and inference. What is clear is that all inferential techniques involve the use of information other than that obtained from the sample at hand; indeed, given that theory precedes observation (all observation statements are made in the language of some theory) there is no such thing as 'pure sample information'. Inference, of whatever kind, proceeds by combining theoretical considerations with sample information and involves, of necessity, judgement. A judgement-free inferential process is not, nor will ever be, available, and what the Bayesian procedures offer is a conceptually simple method by which to combine information from various sources and within which the role of judgement is more explicit.

The flavour of the Bayesian approach may be applied in econometrics within the familiar regression model under the usual assumptions of that model and also under relaxations of those assumptions. One drawback of the approach, which becomes increasingly important as the number of parameters in the model increases, is that the Bayesian approach demands that the investigator can state a joint prior distribution of all the parameters and of all restrictions to be placed on the model. To the extent that not all prior information might be communicated concisely by a prior distribution, this can become extremely difficult. However, the great advantage claimed of Bayesian econometrics is that it makes explicit the 'mapping of the prior to the posterior', that is, the route by which inferences are constructed is made explicit by Bayesians. This is seen as an advantage over alternative methods which are open to the charge of using information in an implicit or, worse, an implicit and *ad hoc* manner. Adherents of non-Bayesian methods can, however, seek to defend themselves by improving the route by which they communicate their methods, methodologies and conclusions. Notwithstanding the claimed advantages of Bayesian methods the typical econometrics investigation is conducted by non-Bayesian methods.

Further reading

Most excellent sources of further reading on Bayesian econometrics are Zellner (1971 and 1985) and Box and Tiao (1973); see also Leamer (1978) and, for a survey of Bayesian theory in practice, Poirier (1991).

Bayesian theory

Bayesian inference has a long history, originating in the work of Thomas Bayes which was published two years after his death in 1763. The distinguishing characteristics of the Bayesian approach are the use made of prior information and the way in which probability is understood.

Specifically, Bayesian analysis formalizes the use of prior information in inference and utilizes a 'degrees of belief' concept of probability. Whereas the sampling approach takes the probability structure of an experiment as given and enquires of the probabilities of various stated outcomes of the experiment, the Bayesian approach seeks to infer the probability structure given an observed outcome. To illustrate this difference, in a coin-tossing experiment the sampling approach takes the probability of a head as given and determines the probability of r heads from n tosses; Bayesian analysis takes the observation of r heads in n tosses and seeks to infer the probability of a head. The heart of Bayesian analysis is Bayes' theorem. By the rule of conditional probability:

$$f(x|y) = f(x, y)/f(y)$$

where f(.) stands for a probability density function. Since $f(y|x) = f(x, y)/f(x)$, combining the two conditional expressions:

$$f(x|y) = f(y|x)f(x)/f(y).$$

This statement is commonly known as Bayes' theorem. If θ represents a vector of parameters, y represents sample information and I represents the set of prior information, then this may be written as:

$$f(y|\theta, I) = f(y, \theta, I)/f(\theta, I) = f(\theta, y|I)f(I)/f(\theta|I)f(I)$$

i.e. $$f(y|\theta, I) = f(\theta, y|I)/f(\theta|I)$$

and $$f(\theta|y, I) = f(\theta, y|I)/f(y|I)$$

hence: $$f(\theta, y|I) = f(\theta|y, I)f(y|I) = f(y|\theta, I)f(\theta|I)$$

i.e. $$f(\theta|y, I) = f(y|\theta, I)f(\theta|I)/f(y|I)$$

Denoting the set of both sample and prior data, (y, I), by D to represent all the available data, a more appropriate form of Bayes' theorem may be written:

$$f(\theta|D) \propto f(\theta|I)f(y|\theta, I).$$

$f(\theta|I)$ is the *prior* distribution of θ, given only prior information; $f(y|\theta, I)$ is the density function of the sample given the parameter vector and the prior information which, when viewed as a function of θ is the likelihood function, and $f(\theta|D)$ is the posterior distribution of θ given both the sample and prior information. This form of Bayes' theorem may be stated as: the posterior probability density function (pdf) is proportional to the product of the prior distribution and the likelihood; i.e. the posterior pdf $\propto$ (the prior pdf)$\times$(the likelihood function).

Since the prior distribution contains all available information on the probability of the possible values of θ *prior* to any observations, and the likelihood function contains the information contained in the observations, y, Bayes' theorem is a rule by which to incorporate all sources of information in order to form views on a parameter. The likelihood function is a complete summary of the information contained in the observations, the prior is a complete statement of the information known to the investigator prior to the experiment, and so the posterior distribution is a complete statement of that which is known after the experiment.

Several observations are in order:

1. Bayes' theorem is merely a statement of conditional probability, and as such is not contentious; contention, however, surrounds its interpretation and the implied interpretation of probability.
2. Of itself, Bayes' theorem does not provide an estimator; rather, the posterior pdf is a complete statement of knowledge regarding θ after the sample information has been combined with the prior information; an estimator is simply a single value drawn from the posterior pdf, and a Bayesian estimator can only be constructed once a rule has been invoked by which to choose a particular value of θ from the posterior pdf.
3. The likelihood function plays a crucial role, for it is the likelihood which dictates the nature of the mapping from the prior distribution to the posterior distribution.
4. The prior distribution is equally critical, for it represents a 'starting position'; if little is known about the parameter, then a 'diffuse' (or non-informative) prior is required, but if there is some prior knowledge of θ (available from previous studies, or economic theory for example), then an informative prior is required.

One very appealing property of Bayesian analysis is that given a posterior pdf, which is the product of a prior pdf and a likelihood, in a future investigation that posterior may now be used as the prior with the following result. If Y_1 is the first available set of observations, then:

$$f(\theta|D_1) \propto f(\theta|I)f(Y_1|\theta, I)$$

where $D_1 = (Y_1, I)$. Suppose a second independent set of observations, denoted by Y_2, becomes available; the prior information now comprises the original information I and the data set Y_1. The prior distribution which is now to be used incorporates all the information available and is given by the old posterior pdf: $f(\theta|D_1)$; then:

$$f(\theta|D_2) \propto f(\theta|D_1)f(Y_2|\theta, I)$$

where $D_2 = (Y_1, Y_2, I)$. But $f(\theta|D_1) = f(\theta|Y_1, I) = f(Y_1|\theta, I)f(\theta|I)/f(Y_1|I)$ and so:

$$f(\theta|D_2) \propto f(\theta|I)f(Y_1|\theta, I)f(Y_2|\theta, I).$$

Had the data set (Y_1, Y_2) been analysed, not sequentially as above, but as a complete whole, the posterior distribution would have been obtained as:

$$f(\theta|Y_1, Y_2, I) \propto f(\theta|I)f(Y_1, Y_2|\theta, I)$$

and since Y_1 and Y_2 are independent, the likelihood function may be split into the product of likelihoods:

$$f(\theta|Y_1, Y_2, I) \propto f(\theta|I)f(Y_1|\theta, I)f(Y_2|\theta, I)$$

which is identical to the result from sequential analysis. Thus, the same posterior distribution is obtained from sequential analysis, using the 'old' posterior as the 'new' prior, as if the whole set of observations were analysed as a complete whole.

The prior density function plays a crucial role in Bayesian analysis, and it is important to recognize the following:

1. A 'diffuse', non-informative, prior which is assumed to be uniform over an infinite range is improper in the sense that it will not integrate to unity; for example, if in analysing a population mean, μ, the prior $f(\mu|I) \propto$ constant for all μ on the real line is used, then $\int f(\mu|I)d\mu \to \infty$ and the prior is improper. Such priors are advocated by Jeffreys and are commonly known as Jeffreys' priors. For such diffuse priors the posterior distribution is simply proportional to the likelihood.
2. As the sample size grows the contribution of the likelihood dominates that of the prior in determining the posterior distribution. In the limit the posterior becomes, as in the case of diffuse priors, proportional to the likelihood.
3. In large samples the posterior distribution may be shown to adopt a normal distribution with a mean given by the maximum likelihood estimate and a covariance matrix given by the inverse of the information matrix. This result links Bayesian methods with maximum-likelihood methods. Moreover, the assumptions required to demonstrate asymptotic normality of the posterior distribution are identical to those required to show asymptotic normality of maximum likelihood estimators when the observations are identically and independently distributed; when the observations are not independent the assumptions needed to show asymptotic normality of the posterior distribution are weaker than those needed for the maximum likelihood case.
4. Importantly, the very use of a prior distribution encapsulates, in the form of a density function, an investigator's prior beliefs about a parameter. In that sense the parameter is treated as a random variable. Complications arise, however, for it is necessary that the prior information is capable of being communicated via the device of a density function, and some would argue that this is not always possible, especially when the parameters are many-dimensional. Moreover, non-Bayesians object to the fact that the

sensitivity of inference to the personally held prior denies the 'objectivity' of inferential procedures. This objection has little force, however, once it is recognized that there is no 'objective' inferential approach available.

The debate over Bayesian theory concerns the concept of probability and the proper use of prior information. What is clear is that all inferential techniques involve the use of information other than that obtained from the sample at hand; indeed, given that theory precedes observation (all observation statements are made in the language of some theory) there is no such thing as 'pure sample information'. Inference, of whatever kind, proceeds by combining theoretical considerations with sample information and involves, of necessity, judgement. A 'judgement-free' inferential process is not, nor will ever be, available, and what Bayesian procedures offer is a simple method by which to combine information from various sources and in which to make the role of judgement more explicit.

Further reading
Most excellent sources for further reading on Bayesian econometrics are Zellner (1971 and 1985) and Box and Tiao (1973); see also Jeffreys (1967 and 1973), Leamer (1978) and, for a survey of Bayesian theory in practice, Poirier (1991). See also **Bayesian estimation**.

Box and Cox transformations

Economic theory rarely specifies the precise functional form which relates dependent and independent variables; exceptions to this include some models of the demand for money in which square root and cube root relationships have been proposed. In the absence of any indications as to functional form, econometric models have typically used linear functions and such an assumption is testable. A common test is the Ramsey RESET test (described in **RESET tests**). If a linear form is used and this is incorrect then parameter estimators lose meaning, except in so far as linearity is an approximation to the 'true' non-linear form; also, the mis-specification leads to biased estimators of the variances of estimators which invalidate inferential procedures. However, since any non-linear relationship may be written as a Taylor series, the first term of which is linear, using a simple linear function may be analysed as an omitted variables issue – linearity omits higher order terms of the Taylor expansion and the Ramsey test utilizes this fact.

Some non-linearities may, of course, be transformed into linear form. If, for example, it is proposed that Y is a polynomial in X, then:

$$Y_t = \alpha + \beta_1 X_t + \beta_2 X_t^2 + \ldots + \beta_p X_t^p + \varepsilon_t.$$

This equation is, of course, linear in the variables X, X^2 . . X^p, and the standard application of ordinary least squares (OLS) will yield estimators with all the usual properties (given that this is a well-specified equation). The original equation in this case is linear in parameters but non-linear in variables and OLS may be applied. If the original equation is non-linear in both variables and parameters it may be possible to transform it into a linear form, and a common example of this is the multiplicative model:

$$Y_t = \alpha \prod_{j=1}^{k} X_{tj}^{\beta_j}.$$

By taking natural logarithms this becomes the linear model in logarithms:

$$\ell n Y_t = \ell n \alpha + \textstyle\sum_{j=1}^{k} \beta_j \, \ell n(X_{jt})$$

If the error term in the original model is multiplicative then it becomes additive in the logarithmic model, and OLS may be applied to the transformed model, subject to the normal caveat that the transformed model is well-specified.

A general class of models which admits, as special cases, the linear model and the common non-linear models, is given by the Box and Cox (1964) family of power transformations, defined by:

$$\begin{aligned} Z^{(\lambda)} &= (Z^{\lambda} - 1)/\lambda && \text{if } \lambda \neq 0 \\ &= \ell n(Z) && \text{if } \lambda = 0 \end{aligned}$$

The definition of $Z^{(\lambda)}$ at $\lambda = 0$ is the limit as $\lambda \rightarrow 0$ and ensures continuity. It should be noted that this transformation is only defined for all values of λ if Z is everywhere strictly positive. One may now consider the simple model with only one regressor:

$$Y_t^{(\lambda)} = \alpha + \beta X_t^{(\phi)} + \varepsilon_t.$$

For purposes of exposition this model utilizes only one regressor, but may be easily generalized to the k-variable case. It is, however, important to retain a constant term in this model so as to maintain the invariance of transformation parameter estimates to changes in the units of measurement. This simple model has, as special cases, most of the familiar models; for example:

- if $\lambda = 1 = \phi$ the model is linear in the variables;
- if $\lambda = 1$ and $\phi = 0$ the model is semi-logarithmic in the variables with a linear dependent variable and a logarithmic regressor;
- if $\lambda = 0$ and $\phi = 1$ the model is semi-logarithmic in the variables with a logarithmic dependent variable and a linear regressor;
- if $\lambda = 0 = \phi$ the model is linear in the logarithms of the variables (the log-linear model);
- if $\lambda = 1$ and $\phi = -1$ the model is the inverse or reciprocal model.

Using the method of maximum likelihood (ML) it is possible both to estimate the transformation parameters, λ and ϕ, and also to run hypothesis tests on λ and ϕ. In the transformed model $Y^{(\lambda)} = \alpha + \beta X^{(\phi)} + \varepsilon$, (where both $Y^{(\lambda)}$ and $X^{(\phi)}$ are vectors of observations) it is assumed that $\varepsilon \sim N(0, \sigma^2 I)$ and that a sample of size n is available; the log-likelihood is then given by:

$$\ell n L(\alpha, \beta, \sigma^2, \lambda, \phi | Y) = -(n/2)\ell n(2\pi\sigma^2)$$

$$-(1/2\sigma^2)(Y^{(\lambda)} - \alpha - \beta X^{(\phi)})'(Y^{(\lambda)} - \alpha - \beta X^{(\phi)}) + \ell n\, J$$

where $J = |\{dY_i^{(\lambda)}/dY_j\}|$; see the entry **Maximum likelihood**.

Given that there is no autocorrelation, the Jacobian of the transformation is diagonal, and the ith diagonal term is given by $Y_i^{\lambda-1}$ for all values of λ. Hence the determinant of J is the product of all the observations of Y, raised to the power $\lambda - 1$, i.e. $\ell n\, J = (\lambda - 1)\sum_{i=1}^{n} \ell n Y_i$.

The log-likelihood may be concentrated, using the ML estimator of σ^2; for given transformation parameters the OLS regression of $Y^{(\lambda)}$ on a constant and $X^{(\phi)}$ may be run to yield the residual sum of squares, $RSS(\lambda, \phi)$. The estimator of σ^2 is then given by $s^2(\lambda, \phi) = RSS(\lambda, \phi)/n$; hence the concentrated log-likelihood is given by:

$$-(n/2)\ell n[2\pi s^2(\lambda, \phi)] - [1/2s^2(\lambda, \phi)].RSS(\lambda, \phi) + (\lambda - 1)\sum_{i=1}^{n} \ell n Y_i$$

$$= \text{constant} - (n/2)\ell n[s^2(\lambda, \phi)] + (\lambda - 1)\sum_{i=1}^{n} \ell n Y_i$$

Choosing the transformation parameters so that the resultant residual sum of squares is a minimum will not maximize the likelihood, since the term from the Jacobian would then have been ignored. However, if $\sum_{i=1}^{n} \ell n Y_i$ were zero, choosing λ and ϕ to minimize the residual sum of squares would be equivalent to ML. This may be achieved by scaling the dependent variable by its geometric mean. The geometric mean of Y is given by:

$$GM(Y) = \left(\prod_{i=1}^{n} Y_i\right)^{1/n};$$

hence: $$\ell n[GM(Y)] = (1/n)\sum_{i=1}^{n} \ell n Y_i$$

Thus, defining Y_i^* by $Y_i^* = Y_i/GM(Y)$:

$$\ell n[GM(Y^*)] = (1/n)\sum_{i=1}^{n} \ell n(Y_i / GM(Y))$$

$$= (1/n)\sum_{i=1}^{n}[\ell n(Y_i) - \ell n GM(Y)] = 0.$$

Considering, then, the model given by

$$Y_t^{*(\lambda)} = \alpha_o + \beta_o X_t^{(\phi)} + \eta_t$$

the log-likelihood is given by:

$$\ell n L(\alpha_o, \beta_o, \sigma_0^2 | Y^*, \lambda, \phi) = \text{constant} - (n/2)\ell n[\hat{\sigma}_0^2(\lambda, \phi)]$$

where $\hat{\sigma}_0^2(\lambda, \phi)$ is the MLE of σ_0^2, the variance of η_t.

Thus if the original observations on Y are divided by their geometric mean (which acts only as a scale factor) to generate a variable Y*, the maximum likelihood estimates of the transformation parameters may be constructed by running $Y^{*(\lambda)}$ on a constant and $X^{(\phi)}$, using ordinary least squares; denote the residual sum of squares from such a regression by RSS(λ, ϕ). The ML estimators of λ and ϕ ($\tilde{\lambda}$, $\tilde{\phi}$) correspond to those for which the regression variance is minimized, and the ML estimates of α_0 and β_0 are then identical to the OLS estimates from the regression of Y*, transformed by $\tilde{\lambda}$, on a constant and X, transformed by $\tilde{\phi}$.

To compute $\tilde{\lambda}$ and $\tilde{\phi}$ a search method may be utilized: first scale the dependent variable by its geometric mean and then choose some start value for each parameter (λ_0, ϕ_0) and compute RSS(λ_0, ϕ_0); then increment the parameters in turn, computing the RSS for a whole set of pairs in some pre-specified region of parameter space. For some pair of transformation parameters, say (λ^*, ϕ^*), RSS(λ^*, ϕ^*) will achieve its least value, and the maximum likelihood solutions $\tilde{\lambda}$ and $\tilde{\phi}$ are then expected to lie in some neighbourhood of (λ^*, ϕ^*); the likelihood function may then be further explored around this point by a more detailed search (using smaller increments in the parameters than in the initial grid search) so as to achieve greater accuracy for the estimates $\tilde{\lambda}$ and $\tilde{\phi}$.

Once an acceptable degree of accuracy has been obtained it is then a simple matter of computing $\tilde{\alpha}_0$ and $\tilde{\beta}_0$ from the corresponding OLS regression. However, since those OLS estimators are constructed for given transformation parameter estimates, their unconditional standard errors are not as reported by the OLS regression (which takes the power transformations as given and fails to recognize that $\tilde{\lambda}$ and $\tilde{\phi}$ are both estimates). The conditional standard errors as reported by a simple OLS regression for given transformation parameters will underestimate the unconditional standard errors which should be obtained from the information matrix (see **Maximum likelihood**). To ensure that a global, not a local, maximum has been achieved, it is important that the original range of λ and ϕ is sufficiently large and that the increments are sufficiently small. Alternatively, a direct numerical maximization routine may be employed.

Tests of λ and ϕ may be constructed, as may a confidence region, from the distribution of the likelihood ratio:

$$2\ln[L(\tilde{\lambda}, \tilde{\phi})/L(\lambda, \phi)] \sim \chi_2^2$$

i.e.

$$n[\hat{\sigma}_0^2(\lambda, \phi) - \hat{\sigma}^2(\tilde{\lambda}, \tilde{\phi})] \sim \chi_2^2.$$

The χ^2 distribution has two degrees of freedom since, in this example, there are two transformation parameters. In testing H_0: $\lambda = \lambda_0$ and $\phi = \phi_0$, if $n[\hat{\sigma}^2(\lambda_0, \phi_0) - \hat{\sigma}^2(\tilde{\lambda}, \tilde{\phi})]$ exceeds the appropriate critical value from the right-hand tail of the χ_2^2 distribution, H_0 is rejected since, if the null hypothesis is true, $\hat{\sigma}^2(\lambda_o, \phi_o)$ will not be significantly larger than its maximum likelihood value at $(\tilde{\lambda}, \tilde{\phi})$.

The above analysis assumes that the error is normally distributed with a scalar variance–covariance matrix; this cannot, strictly, be the case, since $Y^{(\lambda)}$ is constrained to exceed $-1/\lambda$. The distribution of the errors must, therefore, strictly speaking be a truncated distribution but it may be shown that so long as the error term is sufficiently symmetric in its distribution, the ML method is robust. The model may be extended to the case when the original errors are autocorrelated, and may also be used in simultaneous models. It should be noted that when the original errors are heteroscedastic the estimator of λ is biased in the direction required to make the errors most nearly homoscedastic. In order to estimate the model with heteroscedasticity it is, of course, necessary to impose a specific form of the heteroscedasticity.

The main use of the Box–Cox transformation in applied work has been to generalize the linear functional form and to accommodate potential non-linearities, such as a liquidity trap. Also, it has been used to test specific functional forms; in this context it is to be noted that the ML estimates $(\tilde{\lambda}, \tilde{\phi})$ may not be capable of economic interpretation, and the investigator may only be interested in transformations which are capable of economic interpretation. In this case one may estimate the likelihoods associated with models of interest (which utilize only a limited set of transformation parameters), discriminate amongst them by identifying that functional form within this set which has the greatest likelihood, and then test, using the likelihood ratio, whether this functional form is significantly different from that freely estimated and given by $(\tilde{\lambda}, \tilde{\phi})$.

Further reading

In addition to Box and Cox (1964), see also Zarembka (1968) for an application of this technique, and Zarembka (1974) and Spitzer (1982).

Causality and Granger-causality

At first sight it appears that the simple question 'does X cause Y or does Y cause X?' should have a simple answer; in fact questions of causality are very difficult and no universally acceptable definition of causality has yet been developed. To illustrate an immediate difficulty, mere correlations between variables are insufficient to establish causation since correlation is a symmetric measure, and unidirectional causality is an asymmetric concept. The asymmetry is apparent from the following: the proposition 'if A then B' implies the logically true proposition 'if not B then not A', whereas the causal proposition 'A causes B' does not imply the proposition 'not B causes not A'. As a familiar example, 'rain causes wet pavements' does not imply 'dry pavements cause no rain'. Implication and causality are not synonymous. Also, causality may be unidirectional, so that for example X causes Y but Y does not cause X, or bidirectional so that Y and X cause each other. Further, a mere temporal ordering is not sufficient either to establish or dismiss causality: that A occurred before B is insufficient to establish that A caused B, and is insufficient to dismiss the possibility that B caused A. The latter possibility could be rationalized as follows: if B is predicted to occur, so that B is expected with a high probability, this may induce the event A now. As an example, if high inflation is predicted in the future this might induce consumers to bring forward purchases to the present. This example is, strictly, one in which expectations held in the present period of future events lead to specific events in the present, but given that event B occurs it would 'look like' the 'future' causing the past.

It may be argued that, concerning temporal causality, a cause cannot occur after the effect; indeed, it is frequently assumed that causes predate effects, but these views, as exemplified above, are not uncontentious. Moreover, causal variables are not synonymous with controlled variables: it might be argued that a controlled variable (such as the money supply) can only be a cause, not an effect, but in the case of policy instruments the policy makers may use feedback rules so that the instrument reacts both to the present economic environment and currently held expectations of the future environment. This is closely related to the concepts of exogeneity and endogeneity: a classical exogenous variable can only be a cause, and not an effect, whereas an endogenous variable may be both a cause and an effect. Causality questions are not confined to time-series data and also arise in cross-section analyses: if data are collected on a sample of agents' incomes and expenditures, the question of why some agents spend more than others is a cross-section causal question, but formal tests of causality in this context have received little attention.

Within a model of an economic phenomenon the notions of causality may be model-specific in the sense that the model is, inevitably, a sub-model of the larger economic system; hence an exogenous variable in one model (a potentially causal variable and not an effect) may be treated as an endogenous variable in a different model.

Notwithstanding any philosophical or other conceptual difficulties with the notion of causality, the so-called Granger causality test (1969) has become popular in applied work. Put in its simplest form, the Granger test utilizes F-statistic to examine whether lagged values of X contribute significantly (in the statistical sense) to the explanation of Y_t, once lagged values of Y have been incorporated; if they do not, then X is said not to 'Granger-cause' Y, and if they do, X 'Granger-causes' Y. Similarly, to examine whether Y 'causes' X, the contribution of lagged values of Y to the explanation of X is examined (having already accommodated the contribution of lagged X to its own explanation). The test, thus, consists of running regressions of Y on itself lagged and on a set of lagged X values; if the lagged values of X do not contribute a statistically significant explanation then X does not Granger-cause Y; similarly, to examine if Y causes X the regression of X on itself lagged and a set of lagged Y values is run and the contribution of the lagged Y values is examined by an F-test. Two regressions are run:

$$Y_t = \Sigma_{j=1}^{k}(\theta_j Y_{t-j} + \beta_j X_{t-j}) + \varepsilon_t$$

$$X_t = \Sigma_{j=1}^{k}(\lambda_j X_{t-j} + \alpha_j Y_{t-j}) + \upsilon_t$$

and the hypothesis H_{ox}: $\beta_j = 0$ for all j is tested in the first equation, and H_{oy}: $\alpha_j = 0$ for all j is tested in the second equation. If the former is not rejected then X does not Granger-cause Y and if the latter is not rejected then Y does not Granger-cause X. There are no obvious routes by which to determine the lag length, k. Clearly, several outcomes are possible: neither X nor Y Granger-cause each other (both H_{ox} and H_{oy} are not rejected), both X and Y Granger-cause each other, so that there is bidirectional causality (both H_{ox} and H_{oy} are rejected), X Granger-causes Y but Y does not Granger-cause X (H_{ox} is rejected but H_{oy} is not rejected) or Y Granger-causes X but X does not Granger-cause Y (H_{ox} is not rejected but H_{oy} is rejected). Note that in the regression the contemporaneous value of X plays no role in the first regression, and similarly the contemporaneous value of Y plays no role in the second regression.

Such a test of 'causality' does not allow any particular philosophical position to be adopted regarding the causal structure of the Y, X relationship excepting that 'Granger-causality' takes as its premiss that the past can cause the future, the future cannot cause the past and temporal ordering is insufficient evidence on which to assert causality. Thus, if event A occurs before event B it is possible that A causes B, impossible that B causes A and it is also possible that there is no causal relationship between the events. Granger-causality means that, having taken account of a variable's autocorrelation structure, the lags of some other variable are found to make a statistically significant contribution to its explanation. This may be formalized as follows: let Ω_{t-1} denote all the information available at time up to and including t−1, so that Ω_{t-1} includes all values of $X_{t-\tau}$ and $Y_{t-\tau}$, $\tau = 1, \ldots$ Given the definition of Granger-causality, X causes Y, given Ω_{t-1}, if Y_t can be better predicted using values $X_{t-\tau}$, $\tau > 0$, than without past X values, i.e. X Granger-causes Y if all the information of Ω_{t-1} is relevant in explaining Y_t. Similarly, Y causes X, given Ω_{t-1}, if X_t can be better predicted using values $Y_{t-\tau}$ $\tau > 0$, than without past Y values. It is, of course, possible for Granger-causality to run in one direction only (from X to Y or from Y to X) or in both directions simultaneously (that is, with feedback).

Sims (1972) provided an alternative test by which to examine causality; he proposed the following definition: X fails to cause Y (in the sense of Granger) if, in the regression of Y on past, present and future values of X, the future values of X are insignificant. This may be formalized in the regression:

$$Y_t = \sum_{j=-k_1}^{k_2} \beta_j X_{t-j} + \varepsilon_t .$$

If H_o: $\beta_j = 0$ for all $j = -1, \ldots, -k_1$ is not rejected then the prediction of Y from the present and past values of X is not improved by adding in future values of X. The Sims test and the Granger test, though exhibiting some slight differences, are actually testing exactly the same hypothesis.

Whether 'causality' is tested via the Granger or the Sims test, it is important to note that what is actually being tested is more a temporal ordering and a predictive ability rather than 'causality' as that word is commonly understood. In the Granger–Sims sense, X 'causes' Y if Y is better predicted using the history of X than ignoring that history (and *vice versa*). Because the test relies on a temporal ordering, Leamer (1985) has suggested replacing 'causality' by 'precedence', but the language of causality in the econometric literature is now too well-established for any change of nomenclature. Concepts of causality are intimately related to those of exogeneity and endogeneity; see **Exogeneity and endogeneity**.

Further reading

Many writers have addressed the issues of causality, but in addition to the references cited in the text above, see especially Wold (1954), Simon (1953 and 1970), Granger (1980) and Sims (1980).

Censored data

The linear probability model and the probit and logit model are appropriate vehicles by which to analyse models in which the dependent variable is a dummy variable (see **Limited dependent variables**); in many examples the dependent variable is not a dummy variable, but is censored by reference to the size of a latent variable, Y^*:

$$Y_i = Y_i^* \quad \text{if } Y_i^* > 0$$
$$= 0 \quad \text{if } Y_i^* < 0$$

It is assumed that the latent variable depends linearly on k explanatory variables, x_i', the $1 \times k$ vector of explanatory variables for observation i:

$$Y_i^* = x_i'\beta + \varepsilon_i \qquad \text{and } \varepsilon \sim N(0, \sigma^2 I)$$

The data to which such a model is applicable include data drawn from a population in which individuals make choices, and a positive choice results in observation Y_i^*, and a negative choice results in a zero observation on Y_i. The data on Y are censored by reference to the size of the latent variable, but observations on the explanatory variables are available for all individuals. As an example, consider a model which relates individuals' expenditures on a particular good (houses, cars, foreign holidays, etc.) to their income; in the sample of data some but not all individuals choose to purchase the good in question. If the model is written as:

$$Y_i = Y_i^* = x_i'\beta + \varepsilon_i > 0 \quad \text{for those with the positive characteristic}$$
$$= 0 \quad \text{for those with the zero characteristic,}$$

suppose the parameters are estimated using only the data on those n individuals for whom $Y_i = Y_i^*$ (that is, using only the subset of the data on those individuals with the positive characteristic). The implication is that those individuals for whom $x_i'\beta + \varepsilon_i < 0$ are simply ignored and only those for whom $x_i'\beta + \varepsilon_i > 0$ are included. A salient feature of this subset is that $\varepsilon_i > -x_i'\beta$ and so the usual assumption that the error has a zero mean is violated. It is also to be noted that the true response of the latent variable to x_i is given by $\partial E(Y_i^*)/\partial x_i = \beta$, but for the censored data $\partial E(Y_i)/\partial x_i = \beta \Pr\{x_i'\beta + \varepsilon_i > 0\} = \beta F(x_i'\beta/\sigma)$ where F is the cumulative distribution function of the standardized variable ε_i/σ. This is unambiguously less than β, and unless the focus of the investigation concerns only the censored data, as opposed to the latent variable, this difference must be acknowledged. The marginal effect of x_i on the observed value may be broken down into two components: x_i affects the mean of the latent variable and affects the probability that $Y_i > 0$.

In order to analyse censored data maximum likelihood may be used; assuming normality, the probability density function for a positive value of Y_i is given by:

$$(2\pi\sigma^2)^{-1/2}\exp[-(Y_i - x_i'\beta)^2/2\sigma^2] = \sigma^{-1}f(u)$$

where u is a standard normal variate, and $u = (Y_i - x_i'\beta)/\sigma$.

The probability of a zero value of Y_i depends on the value of $x_i'\beta$ and is given by:

$$\Pr\{\varepsilon_i < -x_i'\beta\} = \Pr\{\varepsilon_i/\sigma < -x_i'(\beta/\sigma)\} = F(-x_i'(\beta/\sigma))$$

The likelihood for the whole sample is then:

$$L = \left[\prod_1 \sigma^{-1} f(u)\right]\left[\prod_0 F(-x_i'(\beta/\sigma))\right]$$

where the first and second products refer to positive and zero values of Y respectively. This may be maximized with respect to β and σ using non-linear methods; the resulting maximum likelihood estimates are consistent and the information matrix provides the estimated variances from which the usual tests on the parameters may be constructed. This is the Tobit model (Tobin's probit model; see Tobin, 1958).

In cases when the observations on the dependent variable are missing it is appropriate to use the Tobit model if, when the latent variable is negative, the dependent variable is then censored to take the value zero. In some cases of missing observations such a model is not applicable, since the dependent variable is naturally constrained to lie within a specified range (such as the non-negative real line). When the variable is constrained, for example, to be non-negative (and one might argue that this is the case, for example, in analysing expenditures), the Tobit censored model is inapplicable, and if used will result in biased and inconsistent estimators. In the case of constrained dependent variables it is better to model the process as a truncated data set (see **Truncated variables**).

Further reading
See Tobin (1958), Amemiya (1984) and Maddala (1983) for details of applications of censored data analysis. See also Amemiya (1973), Blundell (1987) and Duncan (1986).

Central limit theorems

Limit theorems are concerned with the behaviour of sample statistics as the sample size gets large without limit; they are used extensively in the analysis of the asymptotic behaviour of estimators in those cases when small finite sample properties are not amenable to conclusive analysis. They are used in the regression context especially when normality is not assumed of the error term and, having obtained asymptotic results, these are then usually translated into finite sample properties as approximations.

In **Large sample theory**, a distinction is drawn between the concepts of convergence in probability and convergence almost surely. Limit theorems associated with the former concept are referred to as the 'weak law of large numbers' and those associated with the latter as the 'strong law of large numbers'. The laws given will not be proved here.

Kolmogorov's first Law of Large Numbers
Let $\{X_1, X_2, .. X_n\}$ be a sequence of independent random variables with finite variance $V(X_t) = \sigma_t^2$; if $\sum_{t=1}^{\infty} \sigma_t^2 / t^2$ is finite, then:

$$\overline{X}_n - E(\overline{X}_n) \xrightarrow{a.s.} 0$$

Kolmogorov's second Law of Large Numbers
Let $\{X_1, X_2, .. X_n\}$ be a sequence of independent and identically distributed random variables; then a necessary and sufficient condition that

$$\overline{X}_n \xrightarrow{a.s.} \mu$$

is that $E(\overline{X}_n)$ exists and $= \mu$.

The first law requires the X_t each to have a finite variance and be independent, whereas the second law relaxes the finite variance condition, replacing it by the requirement that the X_t be identically distributed. Kolmogorov's second law of large numbers implies

Khinchine's Weak Law of Large Numbers
Let $\{X_1, X_2, .. X_n\}$ be a sequence of independent and identically distributed random variables; then a necessary and sufficient condition that

$$\overline{X}_n \xrightarrow{p} \mu$$

is that $E(\overline{X}_n)$ exists and $= \mu$.

Chebyshev's Theorem
A further weak law of large numbers may be obtained from Chebyshev's inequality which states that:

$$\Pr\{X_n^2 > k^2\} \leq E(X_n^2)/k^2$$

for any real $k > 0$, from which Chebyshev's Theorem is obtained: if x_n = has mean μ_n and variance σ_n^2, and the limits of μ_n and σ_n^2 are μ and 0 respectively, then

$$E(x_n^2) \rightarrow 0 \quad \Rightarrow \quad x_n \xrightarrow{p} \mu.$$

Chebyshev's Theorem requires that the random variable have a finite mean and variance. A generalization of Chebyshev's Theorem, which does not require the condition of a finite variance, is given by Markov's weak law of large numbers.

Markov's Weak Law Of Large Numbers
Let $\{X_t\}$ be independent and suppose that $E(|X_t|^{1+\delta})$ is finite for some $\delta > 0$; then:

$$\overline{X}_n - E(\overline{X}_n) \xrightarrow{p} 0.$$

If interest centres on the distribution of $\overline{X}_n$ as n gets large, the above theorems imply that if a law of large numbers holds then

$$\overline{X}_n - E(\overline{X}_n) \xrightarrow{D} 0.$$

This follows because convergence almost surely implies convergence in probability which implies convergence in distribution; hence the difference between the (large sample) mean and its expectation is a degenerate distribution, concentrating all probability on the point zero. It is more meaningful, therefore, to examine the standardized variable given by:

$$Z_n = [\overline{X}_n - E(\overline{X}_n)]/\sqrt{V(\overline{X}_n)}.$$

If a limit distribution of Z_n exists this will then have a unit variance, and central limit theorems examine the conditions under which Z_n converges in distribution to the standard normal, N(0, 1).

The Lindeberg–Lévy Central Limit Theorem

This is the most familiar of the CLTs. Let $\{X_t\}$ be independently and identically distributed with finite mean and variance given by μ and σ^2 respectively; then

$$Z_n = [\overline{X}_n - E(\overline{X}_n)]/\sqrt{V(\overline{X}_n)} \xrightarrow{D} N(0, 1).$$

This may be generalized to a vector random variable, so that if the $\{X_t\}$ represent a random sample drawn from a multivariate distribution having a (vector) mean of μ and a finite non-singular variance–covariance matrix of V, then:

$$Z_n = \sqrt{n}[\overline{X}_n - \mu] \xrightarrow{D} N(0, V)$$

Other CLTs exist (notably the Liapounov and Lindeberg–Feller CLTs); these differ only in their assumptions of the $\{X_t\}$. The Lindeberg–Feller CLT is the most general, the other two being special cases of it.

The Lindeberg–Feller Central Limit Theorem

This theorem applies to a sample of random vectors, $\{X_t\}$, each of which has an identical mean, μ, but each vector X_t is assumed to have a variance–covariance matrix denoted by V_t. It is assumed that the multivariate distribution of X_t has finite third moments. Define:

$$\overline{V}_n = n^{-1}\Sigma_{t=1}^{n} V_t$$

and assume that $\overline{V}_n \rightarrow V$, where V is a non–singular positive definite matrix. Assume further that:

$$\lim_{n\to\infty} \left(\Sigma_{s=1}^{n} V_s\right)^{-1} V_t = 0$$

for all t. This assumption demands that the relative size of each V_t in the sum of the V_s tends to zero (it is also assumed that the average of the V_s matrices is a non-singular matrix).

Given these assumptions the Lindeberg–Feller CLT result is that:

$$Z_n = \sqrt{n}(\overline{X}_n - \mu) \xrightarrow{D} MVN(0, V)$$

Z_n comprises a sum of random variables, and the assumptions required in any CLT are to ensure that no one random variable is allowed to dominate the sequence of sums. Placing binding conditions on the behaviour of all the random variables (and in particular binding their higher moments) ensures that the distributional behaviour of a sum of an ever-increasing number of those random variables may be determined, since not one of the individual random variables is allowed to dominate the sum. The three CLTs noted differ only in the way these assumptions are phrased.

Use of CLTs in regression analysis utilize the following important result: in the familiar regression model, $Y = X\beta + \varepsilon$, suppose that the error terms are independently and identically distributed with a zero mean and finite variance σ^2. Now consider the random variable $X'\varepsilon$. This is a k×1 vector, every element of which is a weighted sum of T random variables (where there are T observations) and one may then consider the random sequence $X'\varepsilon$ as T gets large. The typical element of $X'\varepsilon$ is given by:

$$\Sigma_{t=1}^{T} X_{tj}\varepsilon_t$$

for j = 1, 2, . . k. Assuming that the regressors are uniformly bounded, in the sense that $|X_{tj}| \le c$ for all t and j, where c is some finite constant and that:

$$\lim_{T\to\infty} (T^{-1}X'X) = Q,$$

where Q is some finite non-singular positive definite matrix, then the conditions of the CLTs are satisfied and it may be shown that:

$$T^{-1/2}X'\varepsilon \xrightarrow{D} N(0, \sigma^2 Q).$$

The derivation of this result is not given here; it is, however, to be noted that it relies upon a most useful theorem:

> If $\{X_t\}$ is a sequence of m-dimensional vectors of random variables and $a'X_t$ converges to a normal random variable for every vector a ($a \neq 0$) then X_t converges to a multivariate normal random variable. (It is not sufficient merely to show that each element of X_t converges to a normal random variable.)

The importance of these theorems can be seen in the regression model in which the error term may be seen as the total contribution of many separate effects; those separate effects are due to omissions and approximations from the model $Y = X\beta + \varepsilon$, and so ε_i may be seen as the sum of a large number of distinct random variables. On the assumption that no one constituent of ε_i dominates, the requirements of the central limit theorems are met, and it may be assumed that in large samples proceeding with the assumption of normally distributed errors may be justified.

In applying large sample theory, and central limit theorems, to the standard regression model with non-stochastic regressors, it is sufficient to assume that the regressors are bounded (in some sense) and that the limit of $T^{-1}X'X$ exists and is non-singular to demonstrate the asymptotic normality and consistency of $\hat{\beta}$ and to show the consistency of s^2 (in standard notation). There are notable examples where these sufficient conditions fails, for example when regressors are trended; in such cases OLS may still yield estimators with acceptable asymptotically properties.

Of course, in applications one can only make assumptions about the large sample behaviour of regressors, and such assumptions are not amenable, typically, to testing. Particularly, without making some assumptions regarding the behaviour (and specifically, the boundedness) of regressors as the sample size gets large without limit, no central limit theorems may be applied. In **Ordinary least squares in large samples**, sufficient conditions for the application of CLTs, and hence the asymptotic normality of the estimators, are given.

Further reading

For proofs of these results, and discussion, see, for example, Chung (1974), Fomby *et al.* (1984) and Greenberg and Webster (1983).

Chow test

Tests of structural change are frequently carried out using an econometric model. There are at least two motivations for such tests: on the one hand, it might be thought *a priori* that there is a structural change in a relationship at some known point in time and the model may have been designed to examine and test that possibility formally; on the other hand, a test of structural change may be phrased as a test of predictive ability designed as a test of the model's specification. The former motivation might include, for example, an examination of the effectiveness of a policy which was designed to change behavioural parameters; the latter motivation is a diagnostic test designed to assess the worth of the model as an out-of-sample predictor.

The common form of testing structural change is due to Chow (1960) and examines the model's parameters for instability; this is a simple case of testing linear restrictions, and may be examined as below. Tests of parameter constancy based on the Chow test are predicated upon the presumption that there are two distinct regimes (it may easily be extended to more regimes). The whole sample may be split into two sub-samples, and while the parameter vector is assumed constant within each sub-sample, the test is of an abrupt shift in the parameter at the break between the sub-samples. The sample of T observations is split into the two sub-samples:

in period one $\quad Y_t = \sum_{j=1}^{k} X_{tj}\beta_{j1} + \varepsilon_t, \qquad (t = 1, 2, .. T_1)$

and in period two $\quad Y_t = \sum_{j=1}^{k} X_{tj}\beta_{j2} + \varepsilon_t, \qquad (t = T_1+1, T_1+2, .. T).$

In period two there are $T - T_1 = T_2$ observations. Denoting the $T_i \times 1$ vectors of observations on the dependent variable in period i by Y_i, the $T_i \times k$ data matrices in period i by X_i the $k \times 1$ vectors of parameters in period i by β_i and the $T_i \times 1$ vectors of errors in period i by ε_i $(i = 1, 2)$, this may be written as:

$$Y_1 = X_1\beta_1 + \varepsilon_1, \qquad \varepsilon_1 \sim N(0, \sigma_1^2 I),$$

and

$$Y_2 = X_2\beta_2 + \varepsilon_2, \qquad \varepsilon_2 \sim N(0, \sigma_2^2 I)$$

The errors, ε_1 and ε_2 are each assumed to be white-noise random variables and it assumed, in the first instance, that $\sigma_1^2 = \sigma_2^2 = \sigma^2$, namely that ε_1 and ε_2 have a common variance. The hypothesis of structural stability, translated into the simple null hypothesis that $\beta_1 = \beta_2$ may then be tested.

Running the regression only over the first T_1 observations yields a residual sum of squares, RSS_1; and running the regression over the second set of T_2 observations yields a residual sum of squares, RSS_2. Running the regression of Y on X for the whole sample of T observations yields a residual sum of squares, RRSS. This latter regression over the whole sample period effectively imposes the restriction that $\beta_1 = \beta_2$ and RRSS is, then, the restricted residual sum of squares. The individual regressions over the two sub-samples yield the unrestricted sum of squares, denoted by URSS, and this is computed as $URSS = RSS_1 + RSS_2$. If $\beta_1 = \beta_2$ then the difference between the restricted and unrestricted sum of squares is due to sampling variation only, and it may be shown (see **Restricted least squares**) that under the null hypothesis H_o: $\beta_1 = \beta_2$:

$$\frac{[RRSS - URSS]/k}{URSS/(T-2k)} \sim F_{k,T-2k}.$$

If the null hypothesis is true the numerator is expected to be small; rejection of the hypothesis of parameter constancy thus takes place in the right-hand tail of the relevant F distribution.

The test is sensitive to having correctly chosen the point at which the regimes shift, and choosing the switch point incorrectly will lead to a loss of power; also, the test is sensitive to violations of the assumption that the error term (comprising the T errors of both ε_1 and ε_2) is $MVN(0, \sigma^2 I)$: autocorrelation and heteroscedasticity will each affect the validity of the test statistic. Heteroscedasticity may be easily accommodated; the assumption of homoscedasticity is a testable proposition since the regressions over the sub-samples yield $s_i^2 = RSS_i/(T_i - k)$, i = 1, 2, which are unbiased estimators of σ_1^2 and σ_2^2 respectively. Given the assumptions of the error terms:

$$(T_1 - k)s_1^2/\sigma_1^2 \sim \chi_{T_1-k}^2 \quad \text{and} \quad (T_2 - k)s_2^2/\sigma_2^2 \sim \chi_{T_2-k}^2$$

and the random variables are independent given that each of ε_1 and ε_2 are not autocorrelated. Hence the F variable may be formed:

$$\frac{s_1^2/\sigma_1^2}{s_2^2/\sigma_2^2} \sim F_{T_1-k,\, T_2-k}.$$

Under H_o: $\sigma_1^2 = \sigma_2^2$, $s_1^2/s_2^2 \sim F_{T_1-k,\, T_2-k}$, and to test H_o the statistic $F = s_1^2/s_2^2$ is compared with critical values from the $F_{T_1-k,\, T_2-k}$ distribution. If the null hypothesis is not rejected the Chow test may be performed as above; if it is rejected then the test may proceed, but using a Wald statistic (see **Wald test**). If $\hat{\beta}_1$ is the estimator from the first sample then this has a mean of β_1 and an estimated variance given by $\hat{V}_1 = s_1^2(X_1'X_1)^{-1}$; $\hat{\beta}_2$ has a mean of β_2 and an estimated variance given by $\hat{V}_2 = s_2^2(X_2'X_2)^{-1}$. Given no autocorrelation, the estimators are independent and the hypothesis $\beta_1 = \beta_2$ may be examined by the Wald statistic:

$$W = (\hat{\beta}_1 - \hat{\beta}_2)'(\hat{V}_1 + \hat{V}_2)^{-1}(\hat{\beta}_1 - \hat{\beta}_2)$$

which, under the null hypothesis has a χ_k^2 distribution (asymptotically).

For the Chow test to be run it is essential that neither T_1 nor T_2 are less than k, for otherwise one or other of the RSS_i quantities cannot be computed (since it would then not be possible to run both regressions for the sub-samples). If, as is often the case, $T_2 < k$ the test of predictive failure (known also as the Chow 2 test or Chow's second test) may be run as follows:

$$Y_1 = X_1\beta_1 + \varepsilon_1, \qquad \varepsilon_1 \sim N(0, \sigma^2 I), \text{ for observations } t = 1, 2, \ldots T_1$$

$$Y_2 = X_2\beta_2 + \varepsilon_2, \qquad \varepsilon_2 \sim N(0, \sigma^2 I), \text{ for observations } t = T_1{+}1, T_1{+}2, \ldots T.$$

The second equation may be written as:

$$Y_2 = X_2\beta_1 + X_2(\beta_2 - \beta_1) + \varepsilon_2, \qquad t = T_1{+}1, T_1{+}2, \ldots T,$$

where $X_2(\beta_2 - \beta_1)$ is a $T_2 \times 1$ vector, and:

$$X_2(\beta_2 - \beta_1) = \begin{bmatrix} \sum_{j=1}^{k} X_{T_1+1j}(\beta_{j2} - \beta_{j1}) \\ \sum_{j=1}^{k} X_{T_1+2,j}(\beta_{j2} - \beta_{j1}) \\ \vdots \\ \vdots \\ \sum_{j=1}^{k} X_{T,j}(\beta_{j2} - \beta_{j1}) \end{bmatrix}$$

Setting $X_2(\beta_2 - \beta_1) = \gamma$, the second equation may be written as:

$$Y_2 = X_2\beta_1 + I\gamma + \varepsilon_2, \quad t = T_1+1, T_1+2, \ldots T$$

where I is an identity of order T_2 and represents a set of T_2 observation-specific dummy variables. Hence in the second period the typical observation may be written as:

$$Y_t = \sum_{j=1}^{k} X_{tj}\beta_{j1} + \gamma_t + \varepsilon_t, \quad \text{for } t = T_1+1, T_1+2, \ldots T)$$

where γ_t is the coefficient attached to an observation-specific shift dummy variable. Stacking the observations yields:

$$\begin{bmatrix} Y_1 \\ Y_2 \end{bmatrix} = \begin{bmatrix} X_1 & 0 \\ X_2 & I \end{bmatrix} \begin{bmatrix} \beta_1 \\ \gamma \end{bmatrix} + \begin{bmatrix} \varepsilon_1 \\ \varepsilon_2 \end{bmatrix}$$

The coefficient on the dummies, γ, equals $X_2(\beta_2 - \beta_1)$ and the null hypothesis H_o: $\beta_1 = \beta_2$ is thus equivalent to the hypothesis that $\gamma = 0$. If the stacked dependent variable is denoted by Y, the matrix of regressors is denoted by Z, the stacked coefficient vector by θ, and the error term by ε, this regression may be written as $Y = Z\theta + \varepsilon$. By OLS, the normal equations are given by $(Z'Z)\hat{\theta} = Z'Y$, which may be written out as:

$$\begin{bmatrix} X_1' & X_2' \\ 0 & I \end{bmatrix} \begin{bmatrix} X_1 & 0 \\ X_2 & I \end{bmatrix} \begin{bmatrix} \hat{\beta}_1 \\ \hat{\gamma} \end{bmatrix} = \begin{bmatrix} X_1' & X_2' \\ 0 & I \end{bmatrix} \begin{bmatrix} Y_1 \\ Y_2 \end{bmatrix}$$

$$\begin{bmatrix} X_1'X_1 + X_2'X_2 & X_2' \\ X_2 & I \end{bmatrix} \begin{bmatrix} \hat{\beta}_1 \\ \hat{\gamma} \end{bmatrix} = \begin{bmatrix} X_1'Y_1 + X_2'Y_2 \\ Y_2 \end{bmatrix}$$

which yield the two equations:

$$(X_1'X_1 + X_2'X_2)\hat{\beta}_1 + X_2'\hat{\gamma} = X_1'Y_1 + X_2'Y_2$$

$$X_2\hat{\beta}_1 + \hat{\gamma} = Y_2$$

Since the second equation yields the result that $\hat{\gamma} = Y_2 - X_2\hat{\beta}_1$, when inserted into the first equation it is apparent that $\hat{\beta}_1 = (X_1'X_1)^{-1}X_1'Y_1$, namely the OLS estimator of the coefficient from the regression of Y_1 on X_1, that is, using only the first T_1 observations. Further, the observation-specific dummies imply that $\hat{e}_2$, the vector of fitted residuals to the second set of T_2 observations, is given by $\hat{e}_2 = Y_2 - X_2\hat{\beta}_1 - \hat{\gamma} \equiv 0$; hence the effect of dummies is to guarantee that there is an exact fit to the second set of observations. Equivalently, since $\hat{\gamma} = Y_2 - X_2\hat{\beta}_1$, the terms γ_t are seen as the forecast errors, and the test of predictive failure is seen as a test that the forecast errors, taken together, are insignificantly different from zero. Since $\hat{e}_2 \equiv 0$, the unrestricted sum of squared residuals is obtained by running Y_1 on X_1; the restricted sum of squared residuals is computed by stacking the observations and running Y on X using all T observations:

$$\begin{bmatrix} Y_1 \\ Y_2 \end{bmatrix} = \begin{bmatrix} X_1 \\ X_2 \end{bmatrix} \beta_1 + \begin{bmatrix} \varepsilon_1 \\ \varepsilon_2 \end{bmatrix}$$

Thus, to test the hypothesis that $\gamma = 0$ in the case when $T_2 < k$, obtain the unrestricted sum of squared residuals by running Y_1 on X_1 for the first T_1 observations, and obtain the restricted sum of squared residuals by running Y on X using all T observations. Then, under H_o: $\gamma = 0$, one can use the familiar distributional expression:

$$\frac{[\mathrm{RRSS} - \mathrm{URSS}]/T_2}{\mathrm{URSS}/(T-k)} \sim F_{T_2,T-k}.$$

An alternative method of examining hypotheses of structural stability is based on the use of recursive residuals, and the CUMSUM and CUSUMSQ test statistics; this method is described in **Recursive residuals**, and is particularly useful in identifying points of change if they are not known *a priori*.

Finally, in using the test of stability as a test of predictive failure this is commonly seen as a method of mis-specification analysis: a model which fails a test of predictive ability is deemed inadequate on that ground. It is common, then, in applied work to split the available data into two samples, one of which is to be used for estimation and the other of which is to be used for a test of predictive ability. This is known as cross-validation. If the parameters are not stable then it is to be expected that the out-of-estimation-sample predictions will be poor, and this may be examined by the Chow test of predictive failure. As an extension of this idea of judging a model by reference to its predictive ability it has been suggested that the model be estimated n times, using all available samples of size n – 1 from the original data set which contains n observations; each regression uses exactly n – 1 sample points and each produces a prediction of the observation which has been omitted from the estimation. The sum of squared prediction errors is known as PRESS, but this takes no account of the fact that those residuals do not have a common variance, even under the assumption that the model is well specified. If a model's adequacy is to be judged by reference to its ability to predict, which is, in part, determined by the stability of the parameters, it is better to recognize the heteroscedasticity of the prediction residuals and use the sum of squared studentized residuals, known as the SSSR. Studentized residuals are defined in **Outliers**.

Tests of structural change have an important role to play in econometric analysis; in many investigations such tests are the focus of the exercise; in others they are used as a diagnostic test of model adequacy, and in this latter case may be carried out by using either the test of predictive failure or by some measure such as PRESS or SSSR. If the hypothesis of structural change is motivated by a desire to examine whether a known change in the economic environment resulted in a change in the parameters of a model, then a significant F-statistic is no surprise to the investigator and is a confirmation of the *a priori* hypothesis. If, however, an apparent structural change cannot be explained in terms of any known changes in the economic environment then this may be explained by reference to a rather more subtle change in the economy. Suppose that a model, $Y_1 = X_1\beta_1 + \varepsilon_1$, is estimated for observations t = 1, 2, . . T_1, and that in this period a potential explanatory variable, say Z, is deliberately omitted since it has a statistically insignificant role; if the values of Z in period 1 are such that Z has only a small, and statistically insignificant, effect on the dependent variable this may be due to a very small variance of Z in period 1 which implies that Z contains very little information in that period. Suppose further that in period 2 the influence of Z becomes quantitatively and statistically significant – in period 2 the values of Z exhibit a much greater variance and are such that predicting Y on the basis of the variables in X alone lead to significant prediction errors. In such a case the omission of Z leads to predictive failure, not because there has been any structural change, indeed the parameter values are assumed in this analysis to be unchanged, but rather the predictive failure is due to a change in the behaviour of a potential explanatory variable. Such an interpretation leads to a re-specification of the model, and an expansion of the set of regressors. Yet a further explanation of predictive failure is a mis-specification of the functional form, and in period 2 some form of nonlinearity becomes apparent. Of the three possible interpretations given here, the first is unexpected since a structural break was suspected (and that was the original motivation of the test); the second interpretation may be examined by respecifying the regressor set, and the last interpretation may be further examined by recursive residuals, for example, and by a more detailed examination of the functional form (see **Box and Cox transformations**).

Further reading
Chow (1960) is the original reference for stability tests. See Ohtani and Kobiyashi (1986) on the Wald test. Recursive residuals were introduced by Brown, Durbin and Evans (1975). On the use of SSSR in model choice, see, for example, Schmidt (1974).

Coherence principle

The coherence principle examines the condition under which betting odds may be interpreted as probabilities. Strictly speaking, betting odds refer to the amount of money which accrues to a successful wager of one unit. Odds, with regard to some uncertain event A (which need not necessarily be an event in the future), are written as 'r/1'; if $r > 1$ this is read as 'r to one against', and if $r < 1$ this would be typically written as '1/s', where $s = 1/r$, and is read as 's to one on'. For example, odds of 2/1 are read as '2 to 1 against' and mean that a wager of £1 will yield a return of £2 plus the original stake of £1 if event A occurs; if event A does not occur the stake is lost. Odds of 1/2 are read as '2 to 1 on' and mean that a wager of £1 will yield a return of £0.50 plus the original stake of £1 if event A occurs; again, if event A does not occur the stake is lost. In general one may write odds as 'x/y' (whether or not $x > y$) and this means that a stake of £1 yields a total return, including the original stake, of £$[(x/y) + 1]$ if event A occurs. The event A need not be a stochastic event, in the commonly understood sense; it is necessary only that event A be uncertain. Thus odds may be attached to events which are non-stochastic and to events which are non-repeatable, and also to uncertain historical events.

Now consider a universe in which there are n events, $\{A_i\}$, associated odds, written as $\{x_i/1\}$, and there are n stakes $\{S_i\}$; this forms a triple: $\{A_i, x_i, S_i; i = 1, 2, \ldots, n\}$. You are now asked to quote the odds $\{x_i/1\}$ such that you are willing to accept any stakes, positive or negative, and the purpose of this enquiry is to determine the properties of those odds and their relationship to 'probabilities'. The obvious property of the odds is that they will be set in such a way that no one can be guaranteed a sure thing – either a sure win or a sure loss. This proposition is known as the coherence principle.

If the events are disjoint and A_i occurs the total return to a gambler who placed a stake of S_i on the event A_i is denoted by R_i:

$$R_i = S_i x_i - \Sigma_{j \neq i}^{n} S_j$$

i.e.

$$R_i = S_i(x_i + 1) - \Sigma_{j=1}^{n} S_j .$$

If $R_i > 0$ for all i then $1/(x_i + 1) < S_i/\Sigma_{j=1}^{n} S_j$ for all i. Summing over i:

$$\Sigma_{i=1}^{n}[1/(x_i + 1)] < 1.$$

That is, gamblers are guaranteed a sure win if the odds are such that $\Sigma_{i=1}^{n}[1/(x_i + 1)] < 1$, and if the converse holds then gamblers are guaranteed a sure loss. If neither party to the gamble is to be guaranteed a sure thing it is necessary that:

$$\Sigma_{i=1}^{n}[1/(x_i + 1)] = 1.$$

Such odds may be described as 'actuarially fair', and the coherence principle implies that the odds obey this property.

Suppose that S_i is the only stake placed; then the return, if A_i occurs, is given by $S_i(x_i + 1) - S_i$, and if A_i does not occur the return is simply given by $-S_i$. Coherence demands that both returns not be of the same sign; hence:

$$-S_i^2(x_i + 1) + S_i^2 \leq 0 \quad \Rightarrow \quad x_i \geq 0.$$

Hence all x_i are not negative, and this implies:

$$x_i + 1 \geq 1 \quad \Rightarrow \quad 1/(x_i + 1) \leq 1$$

Denote $1/(x_i + 1)$ by $\tilde{p}_i$ and refer to this as a 'probability'; it has already been shown that, for disjoint events, $0 \leq \tilde{p}_i \leq 1$ which is the first axiom of a probability measure and that $\sum_{i=1}^{n} \tilde{p}_i = 1$ which is the second axiom.

The third axiom of probability is that if A_i and A_j are disjoint events then $P(A_i \cup A_j) = P(A_i) + P(A_j)$. To show this, let the stakes S_i, S_j and S_k be placed on events A_i, A_j and A_k where event A_k is given by $A_i \cup A_j$; all other stakes are zero. The possible outcomes are: A_i occurs, and hence A_k occurs; A_j occurs, and hence A_k occurs; neither A_i nor A_j occurs and hence A_k does not occur. If A_i occurs, A_k also occurs, and the gambler's net return is:

$$R_i = S_i(x_i + 1) + S_k(x_k + 1) - (S_i + S_j + S_k).$$

Similarly:

$$R_j = S_j(x_j + 1) + S_k(x_k + 1) - (S_i + S_j + S_k).$$

If neither A_i nor A_j occur then A_k does not occur, and the return is written as $R_{\neg k}$ where:

$$R_{\neg k} = -(S_i + S_j + S_k).$$

Coherence demands that, given the odds, there are no stakes such that R_i, R_j and $R_{\neg k}$ are not all of the same strict sign (and therefore that there are no stakes such that each return is strictly positive – a sure win – nor such that each return is strictly negative implying a sure loss); viewing the equations for the returns as three linear equations in the three stakes, they may be written as:

$$\begin{aligned} R_i &= S_i x_i - S_j + S_k x_k \\ R_j &= -S_i + S_j x_j + S_k x_k \\ R_{\neg k} &= -S_i - S_j - S_k \end{aligned}$$

If these equations can be solved to express the stakes in terms of the returns, it is then possible to set the stakes so the each return is strictly positive. To guarantee that the equations are not solvable, the determinant of the equations must be zero:

$$\begin{vmatrix} x_i & -1 & x_k \\ -1 & x_j & x_k \\ -1 & -1 & -1 \end{vmatrix} = 0$$

Subtracting the last row from both the first and the second:

$$\begin{vmatrix} x_i + 1 & 0 & x_k + 1 \\ 0 & x_j + 1 & x_k + 1 \\ -1 & -1 & -1 \end{vmatrix} = 0$$

i.e.

$$\begin{vmatrix} 1/\tilde{p}_i & 0 & 1/\tilde{p}_k \\ 0 & 1/\tilde{p}_j & 1/\tilde{p}_k \\ -1 & -1 & -1 \end{vmatrix} = 0$$

i.e. $\tilde{p}_i + \tilde{p}_j = \tilde{p}_k$ and thus coherence implies that all three axioms of a probability measure are satisfied.

Now consider a future state of the world in which A is either declared to have occurred or declared not to have occurred. Let the odds relating to the event 'not A' (which will be written as $\neg A$) be given by v/w and suppose that a gambler considers placing a stake of £S_1 on the event A occurring and also a stake of £S_2 on event A not occurring. The table below gives the net returns in the two future states of the world, where the odds on A occurring are x/y:

	State of the world declared to be	
Stake	A occurred	A did not occur
£S_1 on the event A	£S_1[x/y]	−£S_1
£S_2 on the event $\neg A$	−£S_2	£S_2[v/w]

Suppose now that the 'probability' of A occurring is p; therefore that of A not occurring is (1 − p). The expected net return of the stakes £S_1 and £S_2 is denoted by E(R) and may be written as:

$$E(R) = S_1\{p[(x/y) + 1] - 1\} + S_2\{(1 - p)[(v/w) + 1] - 1\}$$

Is it possible to choose the stakes S_1 and S_2 in such a way that a sure positive return can be made? That is, are there stakes S_i such that $E(R) > 0$ unambiguously? E(R) is a linear function of each S_i and if either of p[(x/y) + 1] − 1 or (1 − p)[(v/w) + 1] − 1 is positive then E(R) can be made arbitrarily large. Suppose (without loss of generality) that the former term is positive while the latter is negative; then set S_1 arbitrarily large and S_2 to zero and

E(R) is then large without limit. Since no bookmaker would offer odds such that the gambler could expect to secure a sure win from repeated plays of the game (and therefore the bookmaker make a sure loss) such odds will not be observed; i.e. $1/[(x/y) + 1] \geq p$ and $[1/(v/w) + 1] \geq 1 - p$. Also, since no stakes will be placed if the expected net return is strictly negative, this implies that $1/[(x/y) + 1] \leq p$ and $[1/(v/w) + 1] \leq 1 - p$; hence $x/y = w/v$ and $1/[(x/y) + 1] = p$. The expected net return is then zero and the game is fair.

Betting odds which satisfy the coherence principle, so that sure things are prohibited, may be interpreted as probabilities in the sense that they satisfy the axioms of a probability measure. In interpreting probabilities attached to non-repeatable events this means that the information may be conveyed by a statement of fair betting odds. This may be used, for example, in interpreting a 95% confidence interval which has been constructed from a single sample: the fair odds that the constructed interval includes the parameter of interest are 1/19, or 19 to 1 on, and the fair odds of exclusion are 19/1 or 19 to 1 against. The odds of inclusion are very short, reflecting the high degree of certainty attached to this outcome.

Further reading
DeFinetti (1937) provides an analysis of betting odds as probabilities.

Cointegration

Two time series $\{y_t\}$ and $\{x_t\}$ are said to be cointegrated if:

1. both x and y are individually integrated of the same order, say p; and:
2. there exists a linear combination of the variables which is integrated of an order lower than p; that is, α_1 and α_2 exist such that $\alpha_1 y_t + \alpha_2 x_t \sim I(q)$, $q < p$. The vector $[\alpha_1 \ \alpha_2]'$ is described as the cointegrating vector.

If y and x are cointegrated this is denoted by $y_t, x_t \sim CI(p, p - q)$.

In applications of cointegration one of the commonest forms is when both x and y are I(1) variables and the combination $y - \beta x$ is I(0), that is, when y and x are each integrated of order 1 and there is a linear combination of the variables which is stationary. In the case of more than two variables this definition may be generalized so that if z_{tj}, $j = 1, 2, \ldots, m$ represent m time-series variables, each of which is I(p) and there exists a vector α such that $\alpha' z_t \sim I(q)$, $q < p$ then the m variables z_j are cointegrated. (It is not strictly necessary that all m variables be I(p), some could be integrated of order lower than p, but this need not detain us here). In the case of $m = 2$ the cointegrating vector, if it exists, is unique up to a scalar multiple, but in the case of $m > 2$ there may be several linearly independent cointegrating vectors. This is easily shown: suppose $y_t \sim I(p)$ and $x_t \sim I(p)$ and that y_t, x_t

$\sim$ CI(p, p – q) with cointegrating vector $[\alpha_1 \ \alpha_2]'$. Now consider the linear combination:

$$\alpha_1 y_t + (\alpha_2 + \gamma)x_t = (\alpha_1 y_t + \alpha_2 x_t) + \gamma x_t$$

which is a linear combination of an I(q) variable, $(\alpha_1 y_t + \alpha_2 x_t)$, and an I(p) variable, γx_t; hence, since p > q, and in linear combination an I(p) variable dominates an I(q) variable, this linear combination is I(p), not I(q), and is I(q) only if $\gamma = 0$. Hence the cointegrating vector to construct the I(q) variable is unique. Now consider the more general case of m time-series variables, z_{tj}, and let A be an m×m matrix; suppose, for illustrative purposes, that each z_j variable is I(1) and now consider the m linear combinations Az. Let the matrix A comprise m linearly independent vectors and suppose that Az_t is stationary: $Az_t \sim I(0)$; but then one could write $Az_t = \varepsilon_t$ where ε_t is a stationary random variable and, since A is supposed to contain m linearly independent vectors, A is non-singular. Hence $A^{-1}\varepsilon_t$ is stationary but this implies that z_t is stationary ($Az_t = \varepsilon_t \Rightarrow z_t = A^{-1}\varepsilon_t$ when A is non-singular) and this contradicts the original supposition that z_t is I(1). Hence, given a set of m time series variables, there cannot be m linearly independent cointegrating vectors; if $z_t \sim I(1)$ and $Az_t \sim I(0)$ where A is some m×m matrix, A must be a singular matrix of rank r, where r < m. If A has rank r (denoted by $\rho(A) = r$) then there are precisely r linearly independent cointegrating vectors. If r = 0 then A is the null matrix and there are no cointegrating vectors. In the special case when m = 2, A has rank 0, 1 or 2; suppose that $Az_t \sim I(0)$. If $\rho(A) = 0$ then A is the null matrix and no cointegrating vector exists, if $\rho(A) = 1$ then there is exactly one cointegrating vector (unique up to a multiplicative constant) and if $\rho(A) = 2$ then the original variables are I(0), not I(1). See **Johansen method** where this analysis is examined further.

It is often remarked that if two variables are cointegrated then a time-series plot of them indicates that they do not drift apart; this is not strictly true but is a special case when the cointegrating vector is [1 –1]'. Suppose that $y_t, x_t \sim CI(1, 1)$ with cointegrating vector $[1 \ -\beta]'$; then $y_t - \beta x_t \sim I(0)$. The implication of cointegration is that the two series, each of which is I(1) (and hence exhibits a particular form of time trend), can be formed into a linear combination which is not integrated. If, as a special case, the variables do not drift apart over time then their simple difference, $y_t - x_t$, will appear to be stationary; this is, however, a special case when $\beta = 0$, and in the more general case the simple difference is itself non-stationary: $y_t - x_t = y_t - \beta x_t - (1 - \beta)x_t$ which is a combination of a stationary variable, $y_t - \beta x_t$, and an integrated variable, $(1 - \beta)x_t$ (unless $\beta = 1$). Hence in general two cointegrated variables will drift apart over time, and the difference is determined by the level of one of the variables (and equal to $(1 - \beta)x_t$).

In regression analysis it is important that the error term is stationary; one immediate reason for this is that a non-stationary error term necessarily contains some systematic components and a non-stationary error therefore denies the validity of the model (and denies the validity of subsequent test statistics). A second reason for this may be seen in terms of an economic interpretation of cointegration: suppose that theory proposes the existence of a 'long-run' relationship between y_t and x_t: $y_t = \beta x_t + \varepsilon_t$, where ε_t is stationary; then the combination $y_t - \beta x_t$ is stationary and if, as is not uncommon with economic time series, both y and x are I(1) variables, this implies that $y_t, x_t \sim CI(1, 1)$ with cointegrating vector $[1\ -\beta]'$. This simple example also illustrates the concept of a balanced equation: if, in a regression of y on x, y and x are integrated of different orders then the error term is necessarily non-stationary and the equation is described as unbalanced. It is very important to note that if y and x are integrated of the same order the regression is only amenable to interpretation if they may be cointegrated into a stationary variable. A most important result for the estimation of β when both variables are I(1) and cointegrated is that the simple regression of y_t on x_t will yield a super-consistent estimator of β; this is described in **Spurious regressions**. See also **Stationarity** and **Integration**.

Further reading
For further material on cointegration and the cointegrating regression, see, for example, Engle and Granger (1987); see also Charemza and Deadman (1992). For details of tests of integration and cointegration, see **Unit root tests**.

Common factors

Consider the very simple dynamic model which relates a variable Y to the current and one-period lagged explanatory variable, X, and also to its own lagged value:

$$Y_t = \alpha + \beta X_t + \gamma X_{t-1} + \theta Y_{t-1} + \varepsilon_t.$$

Suppose that the error term is a white-noise process. Using the lag operator, L, where $Lz_t = z_{t-1}$, this may be written as:

$$(1 - \theta L)Y_t = \alpha + \beta[1 + (\gamma/\beta)L]X_t + \varepsilon_t.$$

Now suppose that $\gamma/\beta = -\theta$; in this case the term $(1 - \theta L)$ is a 'common factor' of the lag polynomials attaching to the variables, and the relationship may be written as:

$$Y_t = a + \beta X_t + u_t$$

where $a = \alpha/(1 - \theta L)$ and $u_t = \varepsilon_t/(1 - \theta L)$.

From the former equation it is seen that $(1 - \theta L)a = \alpha$; i.e. $(1 - \theta)a = \alpha$ (since a is not time dependent) or, equivalently, $a = \alpha/(1 - \theta)$ and from the latter equation:

$$(1 - \theta L)u_t = \varepsilon_t \Rightarrow u_t - \theta u_{t-1} = \varepsilon_t \Rightarrow u_t = \theta u_{t-1} + \varepsilon_t.$$

Thus, when there is a common factor in the dynamic model, when $\theta = -\gamma/\beta$, the model may be written as the static model with an autocorrelated error:

$$Y_t = a + \beta X_t + u_t \quad \text{and} \quad u_t = \theta u_{t-1} + \varepsilon_t.$$

In this sense autocorrelation is a simplification, not a nuisance, for the original dynamic model with four parameters has been simplified, via the common factor restriction, to an autocorrelated static model with three parameters. As a corollary of this analysis, if one were to begin with the static model and then note the presence of first-order autocorrelation (by the Durbin–Watson statistic or the more general Lagrange multiplier statistic, for example; see **Autocorrelation tests**), this might be interpreted as an indication that the true model is actually a dynamic model with a common factor. This is a testable interpretation.

The test for the presence of a common factor involves testing a non-linear hypothesis; in this example the null hypothesis to be tested is that $\beta\theta + \gamma = 0$, which is clearly non-linear in the parameters. The alternative hypothesis is that $\beta\theta + \gamma \neq 0$ and the model under the alternative hypothesis is simply the more general unrestricted dynamic model. The Wald test is commonly used, since estimating the model under the alternative hypothesis is straightforward; the Wald statistic examines the computed value of $\hat{\beta}\hat{\theta} + \hat{\gamma}$ relative to its computed standard error and, under the null hypothesis, the Wald statistic is here distributed as a chi-squared variate with one degree of freedom (see **Non-linear hypothesis testing** and **Wald test**). If the null hypothesis is true, the statistic will be small and close to zero (since any difference between $\hat{\beta}\hat{\theta} + \hat{\gamma}$ and zero is due, then, to sampling variation); hence the null is rejected in the right-hand tail of the χ_1^2 distribution. The likelihood ratio test or the Lagrange Multiplier approach could be used, but the Wald approach is more usual due to its relative computational ease.

Suppose, in more general terms, the model is specified as:

$$\phi(L)Y_t = \beta(L)X_t + \varepsilon_t.$$

The error is a white-noise random variable and $\phi(L)$ and $\beta(L)$ are lag polynomials of order p and q respectively; these polynomials may be written as $\phi(L) = 1 - \phi_1 L - \phi_2 L^2 - \ldots - \phi_p L^p$ and $\beta(L) = \beta_o - \beta_1 L - \beta_2 L^2 - \ldots - \beta_q L^q$. The polynomial $\phi(L)$ is assumed to have roots which lie outside the unit circle, for otherwise Y_t would not be stationary. At most there could be r common factors where $r = \min(p, q)$. (In the particular example used above $p = q = 1$ and $\phi(L) = 1 - \theta L$, $\beta(L) = \beta + \gamma L$.) In general, to test for the presence of common factors one should first test the null hypothesis of one or more common factors, against the alternative hypothesis of no common factors; if the null is not rejected, the next test utilizes a null hypothesis of two or more common factors (with an alternative hypothesis of one common factor), and so on up to r common factors. A Wald statistic could be computed for each of the r hypotheses, but these statistics are not independent of each other.

It is not proper to examine the r Wald statistics *per se* but rather to examine the incremental Wald statistics as follows. First test whether $\phi(L)$ and $\beta(L)$ have one common factor; this involves a Wald statistic which is distributed (at least asymptotically) as χ_1^2 under the null hypothesis. If the computed statistic is denoted by W_1 and W_1 is not greater than the critical value chosen, then the null hypothesis of one or more common factors is not rejected and the investigation can proceed to test for the presence of two common factors. Let the computed Wald statistic for two or more common factors be denoted by W_2; W_2 is necessarily not smaller than W_1. Under the null hypothesis W_2 is drawn from the χ_2^2 distribution, but W_1 and W_2 are not independent, and the hypothesis of one common factor has already been tested (and not rejected) by reference to W_1. At this stage one is interested in testing the hypothesis of a second common factor, given that there is at least one such factor and the appropriate test is to use the incremental Wald statistic, $W_2 - W_1$; under the null hypothesis of a second common factor this is distributed as χ_1^2. If $W_2 - W_1$ is not significant (that is, $W_2 - W_1$ is less than the critical value), the investigation proceeds to examine the hypothesis of three common factors which utilizes the increment given by $W_3 - W_2$ and so on. All incremental Wald statistics are, under their respective null hypotheses, distributed as chi-squared variates with one degree of freedom.

In general, then, if W_1 is not significant one proceeds to test $W_2 - W_1$, and if this is not significant the investigation proceeds to examine $W_3 - W_2$ and so on; if $W_j - W_{j-1}$ is significant for some $j \leq r$, but $W_i - W_{i-1}$ is not significant for all $i < j$ and W_1 is not significant, then the hypothesis of j or more common factors can be rejected, but the hypothesis of $j - 1$ common factors cannot be rejected. In the yet more general model which involves a second explanatory variable:

$$\phi(L)Y_t = \beta(L)X_t + \gamma(L)Z_t + \varepsilon_t.$$

the first Wald statistic is distributed, under its null, as χ_2^2, and all subsequent incremental Wald statistics are similarly distributed (under their respective nulls) as χ_2^2; if there are k explanatory variables then the first Wald statistic and all subsequent incremental Wald statistics are distributed, under their nulls, as χ_k^2.

The simplification of a general autoregressive distributed lag model with a white-noise error by the extraction of common factors to a model involving fewer lags and an autocorrelated error term is known as COMFAC analysis. This has become a popular route of model specification and, when allied to the deletion of regressors via F-tests and extensive diagnostic tests, is critical to the process of general to specific modelling (see **General to specific modelling**).

Further reading
For further details, see, for example, Hendry and Mizon (1978), and for an exposition of some problems in the use of COMFAC analysis in the determination of model specification, see, for example, Harvey (1990).

Conditional omitted variable estimator

In selecting the regressors of a regression equation, and choosing a rule by which to delete some of the explanatory variables, one approach is to drop regressors which have insignificant t-statistics associated with them. Consider the model

$$Y_t = \alpha + \beta X_t + \gamma Z_t + \varepsilon_t$$

and the restricted version where Z has been deleted:

$$Y_t = \alpha_1 + \beta_1 X_t + u_t.$$

Denote the ordinary least squares estimators from the unrestricted equation by $\hat{\beta}$ and $\hat{\gamma}$, and from the restricted equation $\hat{\beta}_1$. Suppose the estimator of the coefficient on X is chosen by reference to the significance of Z in the unrestricted equation so that the estimator is given by:

$$\begin{aligned} \tilde{\beta} &= \hat{\beta} \quad \text{if } |\hat{t}_z| > t^* \\ &= \hat{\beta}_1 \quad \text{otherwise} \end{aligned}$$

where $\hat{t}_z$ is the computed t-statistic of γ in the first equation and t^* is the chosen critical value against which the significance of γ is tested. $\tilde{\beta}$ is known as the conditional omitted variable (COV) estimator, since it is the omitted variable estimator, $\hat{\beta}_1$, conditional upon $|\hat{t}_z| < t^*$ and is otherwise the unrestricted ordinary least squares estimator $\hat{\beta}$. This is a pre-test estimator, and as such its sampling properties are extremely difficult to analyse other than by Monte Carlo experiment (see **Pre-test estimators**).

An implication of the COV estimator for β is that the corresponding COV estimator for γ is given by $\hat{\gamma}$ if $|\hat{t}_z| > t^*$ and 0 otherwise. It is not clear quite why, in this circumstance, one should treat X and Z other than symmetrically; why should Z be the variable under consideration for omission rather than X? Unless the investigator holds a very strong prior view that X should always be included and that Z is a doubtful variable whose inclusion is merely being entertained, then a symmetric treatment would seem more appropriate. This would dictate that the COV estimator for γ be examined were X, rather than Z, be treated as the doubtful variable and that an informed decision be taken as to which variable should be dropped (if either). Of course, it is necessary that the diagnostic tests on the unrestricted equation and on the restricted equations be examined carefully before any decision to drop a variable is finally taken.

If the unrestricted equation is well-specified, then $\hat{\beta}_1$ will be biased, but more efficient than $\hat{\beta}$. To compare the two estimators the mean square error criterion may be used. The mean square error of an estimator is given by its variance plus the square of its bias, and it may be shown that:

$$\frac{\mathrm{MSE}(\hat{\beta})}{\mathrm{MSE}(\hat{\beta}_1)} = 1 + r_{12}^2\,(t_z^2 - 1)$$

where $t_z = \gamma/\sqrt{V(\hat{\gamma})}$ and r_{12}^2 is the squared correlation between X and Z. t_z is not observable, but it may be estimated by as $\hat{t}_z = \hat{\gamma}/\mathrm{se}(\hat{\gamma})$, where $\mathrm{se}(\hat{\gamma})$ is the square root of the estimated variance of $\hat{\gamma}$ from the regression of Y on X and Z; $\hat{t}_z$ is the computed t-ratio used to test the null hypothesis H_o: $\gamma = 0$. It is seen that the estimator $\hat{\beta}$ has a lower mean square error than the alternative $\hat{\beta}_1$ if and only if $|t_z| < 1$. If, then, the mean square error criterion is used to decide whether or not to drop Z this results in the COV estimator:

$$\begin{aligned} \tilde{\beta} &= \hat{\beta} \quad \text{if } |\hat{t}_z| > 1 \\ &= \hat{\beta}_1 \quad \text{otherwise} \end{aligned}$$

which is clearly a decision based on what is, implicitly, a very large significance level in testing the hypothesis $\gamma = 0$.

Instead of using either $\hat{\beta}$ or $\hat{\beta}_1$, a linear combination of the two might be considered:

$$\tilde{\beta}^* = \theta\hat{\beta} + (1 - \theta)\hat{\beta}_1.$$

This is the weighted estimator and its mean squared error is minimized by setting $\theta = t_z^2/(1 + t_z^2)$, which is estimated by replacing t_z by $\hat{t}_z$. It has been suggested that the weighted estimator is generally better than the COV estimator and that the weighted estimator is an improvement, in MSE terms, over the unrestricted ordinary least squares estimator for values of t_z (absolutely) less than 1.25. The unrestricted ordinary least squares estimator is superior to the COV estimator unless the investigator holds a very strong prior view that $|t_z| \leq 1$.

Further reading

The COV estimator is one proposed response to the presence of multicollinearity, and the properties of the conditional omitted variable estimator, and the weighted estimator are examined in Feldstein (1973).

Confidence intervals

Suppose $\hat{\theta}$ is an estimate of some parameter θ; the true value of θ is not known, nor is it knowable and, whatever estimation method is used, it is almost certain that $\hat{\theta}$ will not be identical to θ ($\Pr\{\hat{\theta} = \theta\} = 0$). Nevertheless, the estimate contains information on the true value of θ and $\hat{\theta}$ may be used to divide the parameter space into a 'plausible' and an 'implausible' set of values. One may then say that the plausible set is more likely to contain the unknown (and unknowable) parameter than is the implausible set, and the extent of 'likelihoodness' may be quantified. Estimation of a set of plausible parameter values is the focus of set estimation, otherwise known as the estimation of confidence intervals or confidence regions.

If θ is an m-dimensional vector the plausible set is known as a confidence region and is a set in m-dimensional space; in the special case when θ is a scalar quantity the region is a set on the one-dimensional real line and is then known as a confidence interval. A general form of a confidence region is:

$$R = \{\theta | g(\theta) < K\}$$

where g is some function of the unknown parameter, θ, and is determined by sample statistics; $g(\theta)$ is, therefore, a random variable. K is some constant. This statement defines the confidence region as that set of θ values such that $g(\theta) < K$, and since $g(\theta)$ is a random variable, the set R is also a random variable; a probability statement is associated with this region:

$$\Pr\{R \ni \theta\} = 1 - \alpha.$$

The probability that R contains θ is $1 - \alpha$, and $1 - \alpha$ is known as the confidence level. This statement attaches probability to the event that the random region R contains θ, and the confidence level determines the constant K in the general statement above. Having constructed a specific region from sample information, an estimate of R results and it may then be asserted that θ lies in the estimated region; one may have $100(1 - \alpha)\%$ confidence in the truth of such an assertion.

It is easiest to approach the construction and interpretation of a confidence region by using a familiar example. If a sample of size n, $\{x_1, x_2, .., x_n\}$, is taken at random from a population, then whatever the distribution of x in the population, central limit theorem considerations indicate that the sample mean is approximately normally distributed given only that the population distribution has a finite mean and variance and that n is sufficiently large:

$$\bar{x} \sim N(\mu, \sigma^2/n)$$

approximately, on repeated sampling. Since σ^2 is not known, the estimator, s^2, is used where:

$$s^2 = \frac{\sum_{i=1}^{n}(x_i - \overline{x})^2}{(n-1)}.$$

Then, using familiar distributional theory:

$$T(\mu) = \frac{(\overline{x} - \mu)}{s/\sqrt{n}} \sim t_{n-1}$$

approximately, on repeated sampling. From tables one can then find the 'critical value', $t_{n-1;\alpha/2}$, so that, even in ignorance of μ:

$$\Pr\{|T(\mu)| \geq t_{n-1;\alpha/2}\} = \alpha \quad \text{(approximately).}$$

Thus $\qquad \Pr\{T(\mu) \in (-t_{n-1;\alpha/2}, +t_{n-1;\alpha/2})\} = 1 - \alpha \quad \text{(approximately).}$

Now,

$$T(\mu) \in (-t_{n-1;\alpha/2}, +t_{n-1;\alpha/2}) \Leftrightarrow -t_{n-1;\alpha/2} < T(\mu) < t_{n-1;\alpha/2}$$

$$\Leftrightarrow -t_{n-1;\alpha/2} < \frac{(\overline{x} - \mu)}{s/\sqrt{n}} < t_{n-1;\alpha/2}$$

$$\Leftrightarrow \overline{x} - (s/\sqrt{n})t_{n-1;\alpha/2} < \mu < \overline{x} + (s/\sqrt{n})t_{n-1;\alpha/2}$$

Therefore,

$$\Pr\{-t_{n-1;\alpha/2} < \frac{(\overline{x} - \mu)}{s/\sqrt{n}} < t_{n-1;\alpha/2}\} = 1 - \alpha$$

$$\Leftrightarrow \Pr\{\overline{x} - (s/\sqrt{n})t_{n-1;\alpha/2} < \mu < \overline{x} + (s/\sqrt{n})t_{n-1;\alpha/2}\} = 1 - \alpha$$

i.e. $\qquad \Pr\{R \ni \mu\} = 1 - \alpha$

where R is the random interval given by $\overline{x} \pm (s/\sqrt{n})t_{n-1;\alpha/2}$. In the context of the general statement of a confidence region, this may be written as

$$R = \{\mu | n[(\overline{x} - \mu)/s]^2 < (t_{n-1;\alpha/2})^2\},$$

so that the general function, $g(\mu)$, is in this specific example $n[(\overline{x} - \mu)/s]^2$ which depends on the sample statistics $\overline{x}$ and s, and the constant, K, is here $(t_{n-1;\alpha/2})^2$.

R is defined as the $(1 - \alpha)$% confidence interval for μ. To interpret R note that the sample statistics $\overline{x}$ and s are random variables, and it is these which define the region R; μ is a fixed parameter, and $(t_{n-1;\alpha/2})$ is a fixed number; thus the interpretation of the probability statement associated with R is as follows:

> the probability that the random interval R contains the fixed (unknown) parameter μ is $1 - \alpha$ (approximately).

Since the classical interpretation of probability only allows probability to be attached to what are deemed to be random variables it is to be noted that this interpretation is careful to attach probability to the interval, and *not* to the fixed parameter.

In economic data analysis there is, typically, only one available sample from which inferences about the population are to be made, and it is natural to ask how one interprets the result of inserting the realized sample statistics into the formula for the interval. Suppose the sample size is 100, that a sample mean of 4 is observed and that s^2 is computed to be 2; the 95% confidence interval for μ is then given by $4 \pm (1.414/10)1.96 = (3.72, 4.28)$. This is a realization of the random interval $\overline{x} \pm (s/\sqrt{n})t_{n-1;\alpha/2}$, but since neither 3.72 nor 4.28 is a random variable, it is difficult to interpret this (or any other) specific realization in terms of the language of classical probability.

The language of classical probability is strictly reserved for random variables; hence one can legitimately state that the probability of the interval $\overline{x} \pm (s/\sqrt{n})t_{n-1;\alpha/2}$ containing μ is $1 - \alpha$, given the following interpretation:

> If, on taking random samples of size n repeatedly from the population, one were to construct, for each sample, the interval $\overline{x} \pm (s/\sqrt{n})t_{n-1;\alpha/2}$ then, in the long run, $100(1 - \alpha)\%$ of all such intervals will contain the parameter μ, while $100\alpha\%$ of such intervals will not.

It is, however, not immediately obvious that one could legitimately say that the probability that the interval (3.72, 4.28) contains μ is 0.95, nor is it immediately obvious that one could say the probability that μ lies between 3.72 and 4.28 is 0.95, even though there is great temptation to say this. Somewhat simplistically one can state the obvious, namely, either μ lies between 3.72 and 4.28 or it does not. But this was known before the sample was drawn; so in what way has knowledge of μ been improved by the construction of the confidence interval?

The sample information provides real information, encapsulated in the expression 'the 95% confidence interval for μ is (3.72, 4.28)'; the parameter space, here the real line, has been divided into two mutually exclusive and exhaustive sets, (3.72, 4.28) and its complement, such that (3.72, 4.28) is the plausible set for μ (with confidence level 95%). This means that one would now be very surprised to be told that the true value of μ is actually outside this specific interval. How surprised would one be? The degree of surprise is indicated by the degree of confidence used to construct the interval, here 95%; one interpretation, familiar to those who gamble, is to say that the fair odds of μ lying within (3.72, 4.28) are 1/19 (that is, 19 to 1 on); these odds are derived from the construction which attaches 95% probability to inclusion and 5% to exclusion and so their ratio yields the odds of 19 to 1 on inclusion. Equally, one can say that the fair odds that μ lies outside (3.72, 4.28) are 19/1 (read as '19 to 1 against'). This represents a pair of fair odds: the odds of inclusion are *very* short, while those of exclusion are *very* long. The odds are constructed by reference to the degree of confidence, and the interval is constructed by reference to the conceptualized act of repeatedly sampling from the (possibly conceptual) population. In general, having constructed an interval with confidence level $1 - \alpha$ the fair odds of any specific estimated interval including the unknown parameter may be written as $\alpha{:}1 - \alpha$, or as $1{:}[(1/\alpha) - 1]$.

Clearly, if more certainty is required, then shorter odds of inclusion are required; this requires a larger value of $(1/\alpha) - 1$ and hence a smaller value of α. If odds of 99 to 1 on that μ lies in an interval (A, B) are required, then this requires an α value of 0.01, or a 99% confidence level. The smaller is α the greater is the critical value used to construct the interval, and so greater confidence implies, necessarily, a wider interval. It follows that the greater the level of confidence, the more certain is inclusion, the shorter are the odds of inclusion and hence the larger is the interval (and *vice versa*).

The concept of betting odds may be used in order to formalize the pursuit of knowledge: information leads investigators to change their assessment of the fair odds on an event of interest. An 'event of interest' may be the 'truth status' of a theory or the value of a parameter and sample information may lead the investigator to be able to quote new fair odds on the event. In this example the 'event of interest' is the value of μ, and it may be said that the very short odds of 19 to 1 on are a fair reflection of the event 'μ lies between 3.72 and 4.28': it is very likely that μ lies within this interval and most unlikely that it lies outside. Those who adhere strictly to the rules of classical probability would not attach probability to the event 'μ lies within the interval (A, B)' if neither A nor B were random variables, but this does not deny the use of fair odds to communicate the result of an analysis of a single data set. (See **Coherence principle**.)

It should be noted that, for a given level of confidence, there is no unique confidence interval. In the above example one could construct the interval for a $1 - \alpha$ confidence level by noting that, since $T(\mu) \sim t_{n-1}$:

$$\Pr\{-t_{n-1;\gamma} < T(\mu) < t_{n-1;\alpha-\gamma}\} = 1 - \alpha$$

for any γ, $0 < \gamma < \alpha$. There are, then, an infinity of confidence intervals for a given level of confidence. Which is to be chosen in any given situation depends upon the purpose, and one might want to choose that which is, in some sense, smallest, and this may be achieved by uniformly minimizing the probability of covering false values of the parameter. The question of which interval to choose is related to optimal hypothesis tests. The symmetric interval for μ constructed above is that which is smallest in length and is optimal with respect to a two-sided hypothesis test of μ.

The allocation of $\frac{1}{2}\alpha$ probability in each tail of the t-distribution results in the shortest length interval as the distribution in question is unimodal and symmetric. If, however, one were constructing an interval for a variance then consider the following:

$$(n - 1)s^2/\sigma^2 \sim \chi^2_{n-1}$$

and so:

$$\Pr\{\chi^2_{n-1;1-\alpha/2} < (n - 1)s^2/\sigma^2 < \chi^2_{n-1;\alpha/2}\} = 1 - \alpha$$

where $\Pr\{v^2 > \chi^2_{n-1;\alpha/2} \mid v^2 \sim \chi^2_{n-1}\} = \alpha/2$. Manipulation of this expression yields a confidence interval for σ^2 given by $([(n - 1)s^2]/\chi^2_{n-1;\alpha/2}, (n - 1)s^2/\chi^2_{n-1;1-\alpha/2})$; this is not symmetric about the observed value of s^2, and nor is it of shortest length as the χ^2 distribution is not symmetric. By allocating more probability to the left-hand tail, and removing the same amount from the right-hand tail, a shorter confidence interval may be constructed. Nevertheless, the non-symmetric interval quoted above is that commonly derived.

In the context of economic data analysis, it is often the case that one is interested in not only constructing a confidence interval for a single coefficient, but also in constructing the analogue – a confidence region – for more than one parameter. For details see **Confidence regions**.

Further reading

The construction and interpretation of confidence intervals and confidence regions, and their relationship with hypothesis tests are discussed in every econometrics text, and the texts cited in the Introduction are appropriate further reading, but see Geary and Leser (1968) for a most interesting discussion on the relationship between hypothesis tests and confidence regions.

Confidence regions

Suppose $\hat{\theta}$ is an estimate of a multi-dimensional parameter θ; the true value of θ is not known, nor is it knowable and, whatever estimation method is used, it is almost certain that $\hat{\theta}$ will not be identical to θ ($\Pr\{\hat{\theta} = \theta\} = 0$). Nevertheless, the estimate obtained contains information on the true value of θ and one can use $\hat{\theta}$ to divide the parameter space into a 'plausible' and an 'implausible' set of values. One may then say that the plausible set is more likely to contain the unknown (and unknowable) parameter than is the implausible set, and the extent of 'likelihoodness' may be quantified. Estimation of a set of plausible parameter values is the focus of set estimation, otherwise known as the estimation of confidence regions.

If θ is an r-dimensional vector the plausible set is known as a confidence region and is a set in m-dimensional space (the special case when $r = 1$ concerns the construction of confidence intervals). A general form of a confidence region is:

$$R = \{\theta | g(\theta) < K\}$$

where g is some function of the unknown parameter, θ, and is determined by sample statistics; $g(\theta)$ is, therefore, a random variable. K is some constant. This statement defines the region as that set of θ values such that $g(\theta) < K$, and since $g(\theta)$ is a random variable, the set R is also a random variable; a probability statement is associated with this region:

$$\Pr\{R \ni \theta\} = 1 - \alpha$$

The probability that R contains θ is $1 - \alpha$, and $1 - \alpha$ is known as the confidence level. This probability statement attaches probability to the (random) region R containing θ, and the confidence level determines the constant K in the general statement above. Having constructed a specific region from sample information, an estimate of R results and it may then be asserted that θ lies in the estimated region; one may have $100(1 - \alpha)\%$ confidence in the truth of such an assertion.

Within the familiar regression model $Y = X\beta + \varepsilon$, one can (under standard assumptions) construct the sampling distribution of the $r \times 1$ vector $C\hat{\beta}$ (where C is a known $r \times k$ matrix of constants and $\hat{\beta}$ is the OLS estimator of β) and derive:

$$\frac{(C\hat{\beta} - C\beta)'[C(X'X)^{-1}C']^{-1}(C\hat{\beta} - C\beta)}{rs^2} \sim F_{r,n-k}.$$

To construct the $100(1 - \alpha)\%$ confidence region for two of the elements of β, say β_i and β_j, the C matrix would take the form:

$$C = \begin{bmatrix} 0 & \cdots & 0 & \overset{\text{the } i^{\text{th}} \text{ position}}{\overset{\downarrow}{1}} & 0 & \cdots & & \cdots & 0 \\ 0 & \cdots & & & 0 & \underset{\underset{\text{the } j^{\text{th}} \text{ position}}{\uparrow}}{1} & 0 & \cdots & 0 \end{bmatrix}$$

Then $C\beta = [\beta_i \;\; \beta_j]'$ and, denoting the $(i, j)^{\text{th}}$ element of $(X'X)^{-1}$ by v_{ij},

$$C(X'X)^{-1}C' = \begin{bmatrix} v_{ii} & v_{ij} \\ v_{ji} & v_{jj} \end{bmatrix}$$

and substituting these expressions into the distributional statement above, and noting that $v_{ij} \equiv v_{ji}$, yields:

$$\frac{(\hat{\beta}_i - \beta_i)^2 v_{jj} - 2(\hat{\beta}_i - \beta_i)(\hat{\beta}_j - \beta_j) v_{ij} - (\hat{\beta}_j - \beta_j)^2 v_{ii}}{2s^2(v_{ii} v_{jj} - v_{ij}^2)} \sim F_{2,n-k}$$

which may be simplified markedly, and the left hand side expression may be shown to be equivalent to:

$$\left[\frac{(\hat{\beta}_i - \beta_i)^2}{s^2 v_{ii}} - \frac{2(\hat{\beta}_i - \beta_i)(\hat{\beta}_j - \beta_j) r_{ij}}{\sqrt{s^2 v_{ii} s^2 v_{jj}}} + \frac{(\hat{\beta}_j - \beta_j)^2}{s^2 v_{jj}}\right]\left[\frac{1}{2(1 - r_{ij}^2)}\right]$$

where r_{ij} is given by $v_{ij}/\surd(v_{ii} v_{jj})$, which is the correlation coefficient between the estimators $\hat{\beta}_i$ and $\hat{\beta}_j$. Denoting this expression by F, the 100(1 – α)% confidence region is given by:

$$\{(\beta_j, \beta_j) | F < F_{2,n-k;\alpha}\}$$

where $F_{2,n-k;\alpha}$ is defined by $\Pr\{F < F_{2,n-k;\alpha} | F \sim F_{2,n-k}\} = 1 - \alpha$. F is a quadratic form in (β_i, β_j) and the boundary of the inequality can be shown to define, in general, an ellipse in (β_i, β_j) space. A special case occurs when r_{ij} is zero; in this case the correlation between $\hat{\beta}_i$ and $\hat{\beta}_j$ is zero and the ellipse has its major and minor axes parallel to the β_i and β_j axes. When $r_{ij} \neq 0$ the ellipse is tilted in (β_i, β_j) space.

In general, the region can be most easily drawn if, instead of using (β_i, β_j) space, β_i is standardized by the estimate $\hat{\beta}_i$ and its estimated standard error, $s\surd v_{ii}$; defining t_i by $(\beta_i - \hat{\beta}_i)/s\surd v_{ii}$, and t_j similarly, the ellipse then has the equation:

$$t_i^2 - 2t_i t_j r_{ij} + t_j^2 - 2(1 - r_{ij}^2) F_{2,n-k;\alpha} = 0.$$

The importance of the transformation from $(\beta_i . \beta_j)$ to (t_i, t_j) is that if the ellipse is drawn in the new space of (t_i, t_j) it is always centred on the origin, always has its major axis at a 45° angle (+45° if $r_{ij} > 0$ and –45° if $r_{ij} < 0$), and is always circumscribed exactly by a square whose side is $2\surd(2F_{2,n-k;\alpha})$ long. In the special case of $r_{ij} = 0$ the 'ellipse' is a circle of radius $\surd(2F_{2,n-k;\alpha})$ and this case is drawn below in the upper half of Figure 1. The outer square has sides of length $2\surd(2F^*)$ where F^* denotes the critical value $F_{2,n-k;\alpha}$, and the inner square ABCD has sides of length $2t^*$ where t^* denotes the critical value $t_{n-1;\alpha/2}$. It is important to note that t_i and t_j are now considered as functions of their respective parameters, β_i and β_j, given the sample information on $\hat{\beta}_i$, $\hat{\beta}_j$, s, v_{ii} and v_{jj}; the ellipse can then be drawn given only the additional sample information of v_{ij}, and the chosen critical value $F_{2,n-k;\alpha}$. The resulting ellipse may be thought of as a 'confidence region' for (t_i, t_j).
The 100(1 – α)% confidence interval for β_i is $(\hat{\beta}_i - t^* s\surd v_{ii}, \hat{\beta}_i + t^* s\surd v_{ii})$ (see **Confidence intervals**); this may be written as 'all values of β_i which satisfy $-t^* < (\hat{\beta}_i - \beta_i)/s\surd v_{ii} < +t^*$' or, equivalently, as 'all values of β_i which satisfy $-t^* < t_i < +t^*$'. The interval for β_i is thus given by those β_i values

Figure 1

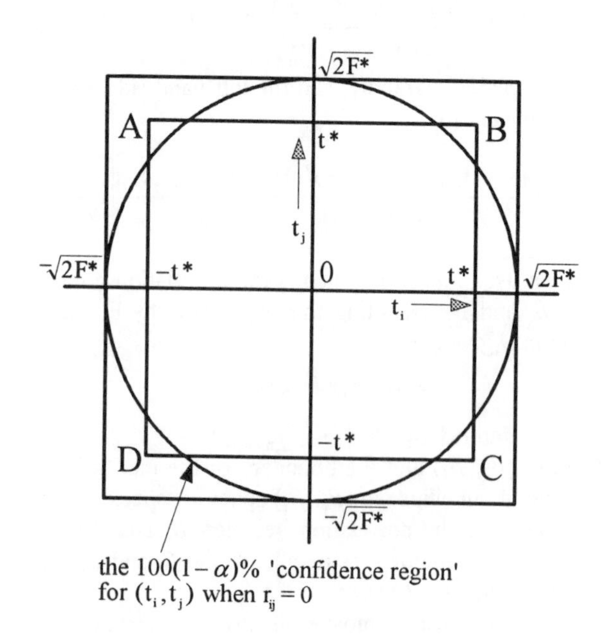
√2F*
A
B
t*
t_j
−√2F*
−t*
0
t*
√2F*
t_i
−t*
D
C
−√2F*
the 100(1 − α)% 'confidence region' for (t_i, t_j) when r_{ij} = 0

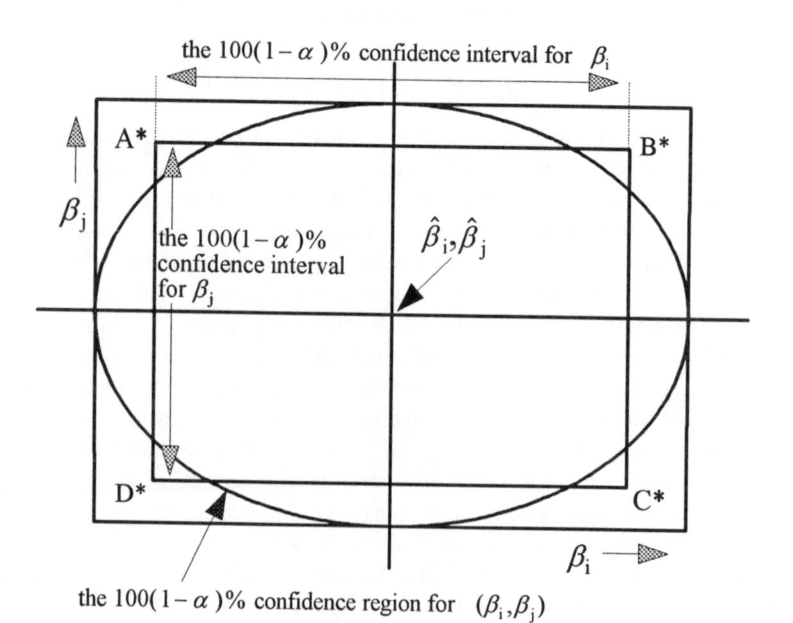
the 100(1 − α)% confidence interval for β_i
A*
B*
β_j
the 100(1 − α)% confidence interval for β_j
$\hat{\beta}_i, \hat{\beta}_j$
D*
C*
β_i
the 100(1 − α)% confidence region for (β_i, β_j)

defined by the length AB (or DC) on the diagram, and that for β_j is given by those β_j values defined by the length BC (or AD). Note that since the upper half of the figure is drawn in (t_i, t_j) space the sides of the square ABCD are not confidence intervals for β_i and β_j; for those intervals it is necessary to transform the upper half of the diagram into (β_i, β_j) space, and this is shown in the lower half of Figure 1. In transforming from (t_i, t_j) space, the length AB is transformed into the length A*B*; now AB is of length 2t* and A*B*, which is the confidence interval for β_i, has length $2t^*s\sqrt{v_{ii}}$. Similarly, BC has length 2t* but is transformed into B*C* which is the confidence interval for β_j and is therefore of length $2t^*s\sqrt{v_{jj}}$. Equally, the square which circumscribes the circle in (t_i, t_j), whose sides are each $2\sqrt{(2F^*)}$ long, is transformed into a rectangle which has sides of length $2s\sqrt{(2F^*v_{ii})}$ in the β_i direction and $2s\sqrt{(2F^*v_{jj})}$ in the β_j direction. The circle of (t_i, t_j) space thus becomes, in general when $v_{ii} \neq v_{jj}$, an ellipse in (β_i, β_j) space. In the special case when $r_{ij} \neq 0$ the ellipse has its major and minor axes parallel to the axes in that space. This technical argument which leads to an ellipse in (β_i, β_j) space may be offered in a more intuitively appealing fashion by reference to the joint confidence region for the two parameters.

The $100(1 - \alpha)\%$ region for the two parameters taken together is that region which covers the 'true' value (β_i, β_j) in $100(1 - \alpha)\%$ of all samples (on repeated sampling). The most efficient such region is that which covers least area, and it is natural, in (t_i, t_j) space, to consider the square ABCD as defining such a region; however, in the case when $r_{ij} = 0$, the two estimators are independent, and the square represents a confidence level of $(1 - \alpha)^2$ which is strictly less than $(1 - \alpha)$. ABCD is thus smaller than a $100(1 - \alpha)\%$ confidence region and must be enlarged; in order to ensure that the enlargement is only in those directions most likely to cover the true point, consider the corners of the square. At each corner the 'true' value of the parameters are distant from the unbiased estimators and there is little likelihood of the true (t_i, t_j) lying in the neighbourhood of the corners. The likelihood of β_i is concentrated around $\hat{\beta}_i$, that is, in a vertical slice around $t_i = 0$ and that for β_j is similarly concentrated in a horizontal slice around $t_j = 0$; indeed, the concentration is so great in these two slices that the regions just *outside* the square ABCD in these slices are more likely to contain the true (t_i, t_j) values than the areas just *inside* the corners of ABCD. The most efficient $100(1 - \alpha)\%$ confidence region is thus constructed by taking away some of the area near the extremities and extending the square at each side's mid-point, so as to create a circle in (t_i, t_j) space.

This argument may be put in a slightly different form, by considering the shape of the likelihood function over (t_i, t_j) space. This function is a symmetric bell-shape, and to cover a part of that space with $(1 - \alpha)$ probability creates a perfectly symmetric region, and hence a circle.

Figure 2

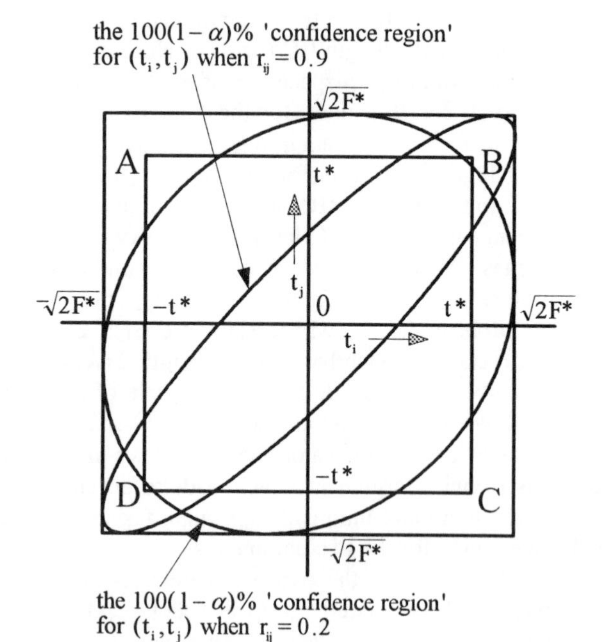
the 100(1 − α)% 'confidence region'
for (t_i, t_j) when r_ij = 0.9
√2F*
A
B
t*
t_j
0
−t*
t*
−√2F*
√2F*
t_i
−t*
D
C
−√2F*
the 100(1 − α)% 'confidence region'
for (t_i, t_j) when r_ij = 0.2

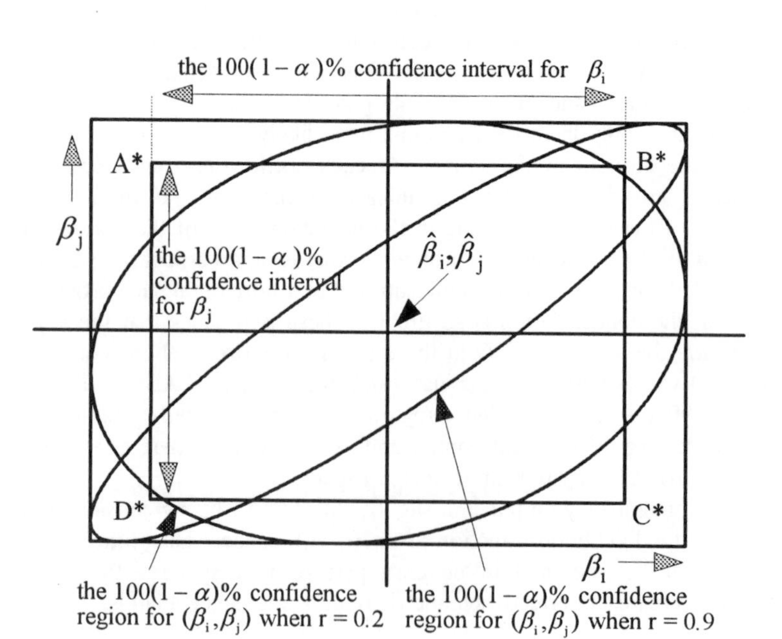
the 100(1 − α)% confidence interval for β_i
A*
B*
β_j
the 100(1 − α)%
confidence interval
for β_j
β̂_i, β̂_j
D*
C*
β_i
the 100(1 − α)% confidence
region for (β_i, β_j) when r = 0.2
the 100(1 − α)% confidence
region for (β_i, β_j) when r = 0.9

When that circle of $(1 - \alpha)$ probability is transformed into (β_i, β_j) space the resultant region is, in general, an ellipse due to differences between the sampling variances of the two estimators (if those sampling variances are identical then the region is also a circle in (β_i, β_j) space). In the upper diagram of Figure 1 the line AB, which only *represents* the confidence interval for β_i is transformed into the line A*B* on the lower diagram which is the confidence interval for β_i; similarly for BC and B*C* which is the confidence interval for β_j. The circle of the upper diagram, when mapped into (β_i, β_j) space, is an ellipse; this reflects the differing sampling variances of the two estimators and, as drawn, $\hat{\beta}_i$ has a larger sampling variance than $\hat{\beta}_j$ so that A*B* > B*C*.

Considering now the case when r_{ij} is not zero, suppose that r_{ij} is positive. Referring to the upper diagram of Figure 1, the argument that ABCD is insufficiently large is no longer valid, nor is the region in (t_i, t_j) space a circle. Consider the vertices of ABCD as before: in the case when $r_{ij} > 0$, if $\hat{\beta}_i$ overestimates β_i (the actual estimate obtained exceeds the true parameter, $\hat{\beta}_i > \beta_i$), then $\hat{\beta}_j$ is also likely to be an overestimate and it is more likely that $\hat{\beta}_j > \beta_j$ than $\hat{\beta}_j < \beta_j$ Thus, the regions in the neighbourhoods of the two vertices B and D are very much more likely to cover the true values of t_i and t_j than the regions in the neighbourhoods of A and C: it is unlikely, with a positive correlation between the estimators, that one be an overestimate while the other be an underestimate. Thus, in this case, the $100(1 - \alpha)\%$ confidence region should be constructed from the square ABCD by taking away some of the area around A and C and expanding the area around B and D. The likelihood of the pair (t_i, t_j) is concentrated around the diagonal BD, and an ellipse is formed having BD as an axis; the ellipse *may or may not* enclose the vertices B and D – this depends critically upon the confidence level used and the extent of the correlation. The greater the correlation between the two estimators, the more elongated is the ellipse; if the correlation is weak then B and D will remain outside the ellipse, but if the correlation is strong then B and D will be enclosed by the ellipse. Two ellipses in (t_i, t_j) space are shown in Figure 2 for the case when r_{ij} is not zero – the more elongated ellipse corresponds to $r_{ij} = 0.9$, and the larger ellipse corresponds to $r_{ij} = 0.2$. Were $r_{ij} < 0$ the ellipse in (t_i, t_j) space the ellipse would have its major axis along AC rather than BD. It is to be noted that the greater is r_{ij} (absolutely) the more elongated is the ellipse and the less area it covers as the more is the joint probability concentrated along the relevant diagonal.

The ellipse in (t_i, t_j) space is always centred on the origin and has its major axis along BD if r_{ij} is positive, and along AC otherwise; its area depends critically upon the correlation coefficient between the estimators and it is necessary, then, to enquire what determines r_{ij}. It may be shown that $v_{ij} = -\hat{b}_{ij}v_{jj}$ where $\hat{b}_{ij}$ is the estimated coefficient of X_j in the auxiliary regression of X_i on all the other regressors (see **Variance inflation factor**). Since $r_{ij} = v_{ij}/\sqrt{(v_{ii}v_{jj})}$, $r_{ij}^2 = v_{ij}^2/(v_{ii}v_{jj}) = v_{ij}v_{ji}/(v_{ii}v_{jj})$ (since $v_{ij} = v_{ji}$). It follows, then, that:

$$r_{ij} = \text{sgn}(-\hat{b}_{ij})\sqrt{\hat{b}_{ij}\hat{b}_{ji}}$$

and thus the correlation between the estimators $\hat{\beta}_i$ and $\hat{\beta}_j$ is simply given by the geometric mean of the estimates of coefficients from two auxiliary regressions, and the sign of this correlation is the sign of $(-\hat{b}_{ij})$. This result may be interpreted as follows:

> If X_i cannot explain X_j in the auxiliary regression of X_i on X_j and all other independent variables from the original regression, then $\hat{b}_{ij}$ is zero (and *vice versa* for $\hat{b}_{ji}$); thus, in the special case of orthogonal regressors, the correlation between the estimators $\hat{\beta}_i$ and $\hat{\beta}_j$ (from the regression of Y on all the regressors) is precisely zero. If, however, X_i and X_j are positively related in the artificial regression, then the estimate $\hat{b}_{ij}$ is positive and so the correlation between $\hat{\beta}_i$ and $\hat{\beta}_j$ is negative; moreover, the more closely are X_i and X_j linearly related, the more $\hat{b}_{ij}\hat{b}_{ji}$ approaches unity, and the more $|r_{ij}|$ approaches one. Thus the term r_{ij} is a simple measure of the degree of collinearity between the regressors.

From this it is readily seen that, in (t_i, t_j) space, the ellipse is actually a circle in the special case of orthogonal regressors, and in the case of collinear regressors (though not perfectly collinear) it is an ellipse whose precise shape is determined uniquely by the degree of collinearity. In the case of $r_{ij} > 0$ the upper diagram of Figure 2 is the 'confidence region' drawn in (t_i, t_j) space and the lower half transforms that into (β_i, β_j) space. Just as the degree of collinearity determines whether the vertices B and D are enclosed by the region in (t_i, t_j) space, the vertices B* and D* lie within the confidence region for (β_i, β_j) when the collinearity is sufficiently strong. Whatever the degree of collinearity, the upper diagram is always an ellipse (having either BD or AC as its major axis) circumscribed by a square whose sides are $2\sqrt{(2F^*)}$ long and the lower diagram is always an ellipse circumscribed by a rectangle whose sides are $2s\sqrt{(2F^*v_{ii})}$ and $2s\sqrt{(2F^*v_{jj})}$ long. When drawing the confidence region in (β_i, β_j) space it is, then, clearly a mistake to project the extremities of the $1 - \alpha$ ellipse to the axes and describe the resulting intervals as 'approximate $100(1 - \alpha)\%$ confidence intervals'; such intervals are always too long. The true interval for β_i has length $2t^*s\sqrt{v_{ii}}$ whereas the projection of the ellipse onto the β_i axis has length $2s\sqrt{(2F^*v_{ii})}$; the ratio is, therefore, $\sqrt{(2F^*)}/t^*$. This may be written as $\sqrt{(2F_{2,n-k;\alpha}/F_{1,n-k;\alpha})}$ (since $F_{1,n-k;\alpha} = (t_{n-1;\alpha/2})^2$ and the extent of overstatement by the projection to the axis relative to the true interval, when $\alpha = 5\%$, ranges from 58% (when there is 1 degree of freedom) to a limit of 25% when there are unlimited degrees of freedom.

Further reading

The construction and interpretation of confidence intervals and confidence regions, and their relationship with hypothesis tests are discussed in every econometrics text, and the texts cited in the Introduction are appropriate further reading, but see Geary and Leser (1968) for a most interesting discussion on the relationship between hypothesis tests and confidence regions. For further interpretations, see also **Linear hypotheses**, **Multicollinearity**, **t- and F-tests** and **Venn diagrams**.

Constant term

It is common in regression analysis to include a 'constant term'. This may have several justifications, and it has many implications. Among the justifications of a constant term are that this represents part of the approximation which any functional form necessarily represents. If, for example, a linear form is used then the constant term is part of the approximation and may be justified by the implications of its absence, namely that in the absence of a constant the regression line is necessarily forced to pass through the origin. This would be an unnecessary, and possibly damaging, constraint on the estimated parameters; moreover, by including a constant term the constraint encapsulated by its omission becomes a testable proposition. When viewed merely as a part of the approximate functional form the interpretation of the constant term as the intercept, the expected value of the dependent variable when all regressors are zero, is not necessarily tenable (and may be meaningless). Further justifications follow from a consideration of the statistical model.

Consider a most general model in which a vector of variables $Z_t = [Y_t \; X_t']'$ is to be explained; X_t' is a $1 \times k$ vector of observations on k variables. It is assumed that Z_t is normally identically and independently distributed, so that:

$$E\begin{bmatrix} Y_t \\ X_t \end{bmatrix} = \begin{bmatrix} m_Y \\ m_X \end{bmatrix}$$

and:

$$V\begin{bmatrix} Y_t \\ X_t \end{bmatrix} = \begin{bmatrix} \sigma_{11} & \sigma_{12} \\ \sigma_{21} & \Sigma_{22} \end{bmatrix}$$

where σ_{11} is the variance of Y, Σ_{22} is the $k \times k$ variance matrix of the variables of X and σ_{12} is the $1 \times k$ vector of covariances between Y and the variables of X. The general linear model proposes that:

$$Y_t = \mu_t + \varepsilon_t$$

where $\mu_t = E(Y_t|X_t)$, the systematic component of Y_t, and ε_t is the non-systematic component. In view of the normality, it may easily be demonstrated that this implies that:

$$\mu_t = \beta_o + X_t'\beta$$

i.e. μ_t is linear in the variables of X, and the parameters β_o and β are given by:

$$\beta_o = m_y - \sigma_{12}\Sigma_{22}^{-1}m_x \qquad \text{and} \qquad \beta = \Sigma_{22}^{-1}\sigma_{21}.$$

The natural candidate estimate for β is, therefore, given by the inverse of the sample variance matrix of X post-multiplied by the sample covariance vector between Y and X (this is an example of estimation by the method of moments). Suppose the sample mean of the ith variable is subtracted from all observations on the ith variable, so that x is the matrix of observations on X written in terms of deviations from the respective sample means; similarly, let y be vector of observations on Y in deviations from the sample mean of Y. Then the estimate of β is given by:

$$[x'x/n]^{-1}[x'y/n] = (x'x)^{-1}x'y.$$

Clearly, then, an appropriate estimate of β is given, in the simple case of $Y_i = \alpha + \beta X_i + \varepsilon_i$, by:

$$\hat{\beta} = \Sigma_{i=1}^{n} x_i y_i / \Sigma_{i=1}^{n} x_i^2 \quad \text{and} \quad \hat{\alpha} = \overline{Y} - \overline{X}\hat{\beta}.$$

These are seen as the ordinary least squares estimates. Without a constant term, β would be estimated as:

$$\hat{\beta}_c = \Sigma_{i=1}^{n} X_i Y_i / \Sigma_{i=1}^{n} X_i^2$$

which is different from $\hat{\beta}$ unless the data were originally in deviation form.

In general, the constant term may be seen as the coefficient on a dummy variable, every value of which is unity. Let ι denote a vector, every element of which is unity; then denoting the other k regressors by X a linear regression with a constant term may be written as:

$$Y = \iota\alpha + X\beta + \varepsilon \quad \text{or} \quad Y = W\delta + \varepsilon$$

where $W = [\iota \;\; X]$ and $\delta = \begin{bmatrix} \alpha \\ \beta \end{bmatrix}$.

The normal equations may then be written as $W'W\hat{\delta} = W'Y$; expanding these equations yields:

$$\iota'\iota\hat{\alpha} + \iota'X\hat{\beta} = \iota'Y \qquad \text{and} \qquad X'\iota\hat{\alpha} + X'X\hat{\beta} = X'Y$$

But $\iota'\iota = n$, the number of observations, $\iota'Y = n\overline{Y}$ ($\overline{Y}$ is the sample mean of the dependent variable) and $\iota'X = n\overline{X}'$ where $\overline{X}'$ is a $1 \times k$ row vector of the sample means of the k regressors in X. Hence:

$$\hat{\alpha} + \overline{X}'\hat{\beta} = \overline{Y} \qquad \text{and} \qquad n\overline{X}\hat{\alpha} + X'X\hat{\beta} = X'Y.$$

Solving: $$\hat{\alpha} = \overline{Y} - \overline{X}'\hat{\beta} \qquad \text{and} \qquad n\overline{X}(\overline{Y} - \overline{X}'\hat{\beta}) + X'X\hat{\beta} = X'Y.$$

The equation for $\hat{\beta}$, noting the definitions of $\overline{X}$ and $\overline{Y}$, may be written as:

$$X'\iota(\iota'Y/n - \iota'(X/n)\hat{\beta}) + X'X\hat{\beta} = X'Y$$

i.e. $X'(I - \iota\iota'/n)X\hat{\beta} = X'(I - \iota\iota'/n)Y$. Denoting the matrix $(I - \iota\iota'/n)$ by A this may be written as:

$$\hat{\beta} = (X'AX)^{-1}X'AY.$$

The matrix A is square, symmetric, idempotent, and its operation on a vector, say Y, is as follows:

$$AY = Y - (\iota\iota'/n)Y = Y - \iota\overline{Y}.$$

Hence the ith element of AY is given by $Y_i - \overline{Y}$ (where Y_i is the ith element of Y).

The effect of pre-multiplying a matrix by A is to generate a new matrix whose elements are those of the original matrix less the mean value of the corresponding column of the original matrix; i.e. AX generates the matrix of X expressed in deviation form. It is easily demonstrated that A is idempotent; indeed, given the effect of A, A(AX) must equal AX as the columns of AX necessarily have a zero mean and so AA = A.

Clearly, then, $(1/n)(X'AX)^{-1}$ is the sample estimate of the variance matrix of the variables of X, and $(1/n)X'AY$ is the sample estimate of the covariance between Y and X. Hence $\hat{\beta}$ as reported by the OLS regression including a constant term provides the sample analogues of the population parameters; without a constant term this is not the case.

Since A is idempotent $\hat{\beta}$ may be written as:

$$\hat{\beta} = [(AX)'(AX)]^{-1}(AX)'(AY)$$

which is clearly the OLS estimator of β in the regression of AY on AX; hence the estimates of the coefficients of X in a regression of Y on a constant and X are identical to those obtained from a regression of Y in deviation form on X in deviation form. It is to be noted that when all the regressors are at their sample means, the predicted value of Y is given by $\hat{\alpha} + \overline{X}'\hat{\beta}$ and by the formula for $\hat{\alpha}$ this is equal to $\overline{Y}$; hence the regression line with a constant term necessarily passes through the centre of gravity of the data ($\overline{Y}$, $\overline{X}'$).

A regression without a constant term means that the estimates of the regression parameters are not their population analogues; the constant term should, therefore, never be dropped for otherwise the regression does not report estimates of the true regression parameters. Moreover, it is not only the regression estimates which lose meaning if the constant term is dropped; as a consequence other statistics, such as the R^2, also lose meaning. It is important to note that the regression normal equations may be written as:

$$W'\hat{e} = 0$$

where $\hat{e}$ is the vector of regression residuals; with a constant term the first row of W' is given by ι' and so the first normal equation is $\iota'\hat{e} = 0$ which implies that the average regression residual, when a constant is included, is zero. (The average residual will also be zero if a constant is implicitly, rather then explicitly, included.) Given that the average residual is zero, this implies that the average predicted value of Y, $(1/n)\iota'\hat{Y}$, is identical to the sample average of Y. This follows because:

$$Y = \hat{Y} + \hat{e} \Rightarrow (1/n)\iota'Y = (1/n)\iota'\hat{Y} + (1/n)\iota'\hat{e} \Rightarrow \overline{Y} = \overline{\hat{Y}}.$$

It is usual to define the multiple correlation coefficient, R^2, as:

$$R^2 = 1 - \hat{e}'\hat{e}/y'y$$

Defining the deviations of the fitted values from their sample average (which is identical to the sample average of the observations on Y) by $\hat{y}$, then: $y = \hat{y} + \hat{e}$ and this implies that $y'y = \hat{y}'\hat{y} + \hat{e}'\hat{e}$ (since $\hat{y}'\hat{e} = 0$); i.e. the total variation of Y about its sample mean is the sum of the variation of the fitted values around their sample mean plus the variation of the fitted residuals. This is usually written as:

$$TSS = ESS + RSS$$

where ESS is the explained sum of squares and RSS is the residual sum of squares. This decomposition is not valid without a constant term, for without a constant term there is a difference between the average fitted and average observed values (due to the non-zero average of the residuals). Hence, with a constant term one may write:

$$R^2 = 1 - RSS/TSS = ESS/TSS$$

R^2 may then be interpreted as 1 minus the ratio of the unexplained variation to the total variation, which is equal to the ratio of the explained variation to the total variation. When a constant term is included, this formula (and interpretation) is implied by the definition of R^2 as the correlation between the fitted and observed values of the dependent variable, and $0 \leq R^2 \leq 1$. A value of 0 indicates no degree of fit whatsoever, and the inclusion of the regressors over and above the constant term offers no explanation of Y, whereas a value of unity implies a perfect linear fit. Without a constant term this formula no longer represents the correlation between the fitted and observed values of Y, and were R^2 to be computed according to this formula there is no guarantee that it will be positive.

The use of regression without a constant term is not generally recommended. It destroys the relationship between the estimated coefficients and their population counterparts, and has very damaging implications for the usual statistics reported by the regression output, with consequential implications for hypothesis testing.

Further reading

See Theil (1971) for further details; see also Spanos (1986). It should also be added that most software packages provide the user with a health warning if an attempt is made to run a regression without a constant term.

Data generating processes

Much recent work in econometrics seeks to identify and estimate the so-called 'data generating process' (DGP). If a data set consists of n observations on a total of g variables, let the g-dimensional vector y_t denote the observations on all the variables at time t, and let Ω_{t-1} denote the observations on all g variables up to period t−1. If the probability function of the data is parameterized by θ, where θ is a vector, some of whose elements are the focus of interest, then the joint probability of the entire sample of T observations may be written as:

$$\prod_{t=1}^{T} f(Y_t \mid \Omega_{t-1}; \theta).$$

This joint probability is the data generating process, and the process of econometric modelling is seen as providing a route by which the DGP may be simplified, estimated and interpreted. As written, the DGP is a wholly general statement: the joint density function of the current data depends upon the history of the process and the parameters which govern that process, combined via the function f. The process of simplification consists of at least four different sub-processes:

1. Not all the variables in Y will be of concern to the problem at hand; the 'true' DGP is, therefore, marginalized with respect to those variables so as to concentrate interest on those variables germane to the study.
2. Some of the variables in the reduced vector of interest y_t will be endogenous, and others will be (weakly) exogenous (see **Exogeneity and endogeneity**); the variables are categorized appropriately and the endogenous variables are modelled conditionally on the exogenous variables.
3. The reduced and conditioned DGP, written in terms of a smaller set of variables than originally, and written whereby the distinction between endogenous and exogenous variables is explicit, is examined with the objective of finding some simple and interpretable form of the DGP.
4. The reduced, conditioned and simplified DGP is estimated.

This description applies, for example, to 'general to specific' modelling (see **General to specific modelling**). The independent existence of the DGP is not an uncontroversial position to adopt, and this approach to econometrics sets out with the objective of discovering an acceptable model of the true DGP. However, since economic theory informs the act of marginalization the ensuing steps in this process are, in part, determined by the choice of which variables are the focus of interest and which are to be ignored by marginalization. Whatever the purity of the true DGP, the reduced, conditioned and simplified DGP is a model and must, therefore, be subjected to appropriate tests of its adequacy. If the finally chosen model satisfies criteria of model adequacy it is described as congruent with the evidence, but there is no guarantee that by starting with an agreed and common concept of the DGP that any two investigators, using exactly the same data set, will derive identical congruent models; indeed, both might derive congruent (i.e. acceptable) models, but those models need not be identical. This concerns the very important issue of model discovery, and the concept of the DGP has little to offer with regard to this question.

On the other hand, one might view an acceptable model as representing the estimated form of a reduced, conditioned and simplified DGP and view the concept of the DGP as important to the process of testing a model's adequacy. Of course, a vital stage in the process of moving from the DGP to an estimated model is stage 3, which in Leamer's terminology is a simplification (and, possibly, an interpretative) search (see **Specification searches**); all resulting estimates are, therefore 'testimates' since they depend on the outcome of previous tests. In this respect the final model is subject to all the usual criticisms of pretest estimation, but the proposal by which the general DGP is the starting point is claimed to have advantages over the alternative, of starting with a simple model and expanding upwards towards the DGP. It is argued that by starting with the concept of the DGP and modelling downwards the resulting model is far more likely to be an acceptable, congruent, model than if one were to model upwards towards the DGP. One of the most persuasive arguments leading to this position is that in modelling upwards the investigator responds at each stage of the process to test statistics which are not capable of an unambiguous interpretation – for example, in responding to autocorrelated residuals, should the next stage consider omitted variables, common factors, mis-specified dynamics, etc? If one starts with a very general equation which is the closest approximation to the true DGP it will be intentionally over-parameterized and include some variables which are of little relevance to the issues at hand; by reducing, conditioning and simplifying this over-parameterized DGP the outcome is more likely to be an acceptable model. A counter view is that although modelling upwards does not guarantee a properly specified model, nor does modelling downwards; moreover, it may be argued that starting with the simplest model and, having estimated that model, responding to its imperfections and respecifying it by reference to economic theory, is a strategy having some merit.

Further Reading

Gilbert (1986) provides a clear description of the concept of the DGP and its role in econometric modelling; see also Hendry and Richard (1982 and 1983) and Spanos (1988).

Data transformation tests

If the regression model is specified as $Y = X\beta + \varepsilon$ where Y is an n×1 vector of observations on the dependent variable, X is an n×k matrix of observations on the regressors and $\varepsilon \sim N(0, \sigma^2 I)$, then this specification may be tested by considering a data transformation. Suppose this model is transformed by the non-stochastic m×n matrix P, where $k < m \le n$, to yield the transformed model $PY = PX\beta + P\varepsilon \Rightarrow Y^* = X^*\beta + u$, where $u \sim N(0, \sigma^2 PP')$; it is assumed that P is of full rank. A test of the specification of the model may then be performed by estimating both the original and the transformed models and comparing the estimators. If the original specification is correct then the ordinary least squares estimator of β from the original model is the best linear unbiased estimator, while that from the transformed model is linear unbiased, consistent but inefficient. Denoting the estimators from the original and transformed model by $\hat{\beta}$ and $\tilde{\beta}$ respectively then, under the null hypothesis that $Y = X\beta + \varepsilon$ is well-specified, $\hat{\beta} - \tilde{\beta}$ will be zero, in probability.

The simplest case arises when P is a square matrix of order n, so that the original and transformed models both use the same number of observations.

$$\hat{\beta} = (X'X)^{-1}X'Y \quad \text{and} \quad \tilde{\beta} = (X'P'PX)^{-1}X'P'PY$$

If the original model is well specified then $\text{plim}(\hat{\beta} - \tilde{\beta}) = 0$. The ordinary least squares residuals from the original model are given by $\hat{e} = Y - X\hat{\beta}$. Hence $Y = X\hat{\beta} + \hat{e}$, $\tilde{\beta} = \hat{\beta} + (X'P'PX)^{-1}X'P'P\hat{e}$, and so $(X'P'PX)(\tilde{\beta} - \hat{\beta}) = (X'P'PX)^{-1}X'P'P\hat{e}$. Now consider the auxiliary regression:

$$Y = X\beta + (P'PX)\alpha + \eta.$$

The OLS estimator of α, $\hat{\alpha}$, is given by:

$$\hat{\alpha} = [X'P'PM_xP'PX]^{-1}X'P'PM_xY$$

where M_x is the idempotent matrix $I - X(X'X)^{-1}X'$; but $M_xY = \hat{e}$, and so $\hat{\alpha}$ may be written as $\hat{\alpha} = [X'P'PM_xP'PX]^{-1}(X'P'PX)(\tilde{\beta} - \hat{\beta})$; hence a test of the difference $\tilde{\beta} - \hat{\beta}$ is equivalent to a test of the hypothesis $\alpha = 0$. A test of the original specification may, therefore, be carried out by a simple F-test of the hypothesis $\alpha = 0$ in the auxiliary regression equation

$$Y = X\beta + (P'PX)\alpha + \eta.$$

If the computed F statistic is larger than the chosen critical value then the null hypothesis of a correct specification is rejected. The F-test will, in general, have k and n – 2k degrees of freedom. Two complications arise: it is possible that the additional set of variables, P'PX, is not of full rank in which case some columns of P'PX should be deleted to remove all the linear dependencies, and the degrees of freedom in the F-test should then be correspondingly adjusted. The other problem which may arise occurs if either X or P is stochastic and $\text{plim}(n^{-1}X'P'P\eta) \neq 0$ in which case the auxiliary regression yields inconsistent estimators. This case can occur particularly in the differencing test (see **Differencing test**).

If the transformation matrix is of order m×n and m < n then the transformed model has fewer observations than the original. In this case the above auxiliary regression and the test of $\alpha = 0$ remain appropriate, and is equivalent to a test of $\alpha = 0$ in the auxiliary model

$$Y = X\beta + (\hat{X})\alpha + \eta$$

where $\hat{X}$ is the matrix of predicted values of X from a regression of X on P', given by $P'(PP')^{-1}PX$. Again, if the additional regressors in the auxiliary regression are not of full rank then the redundant columns are deleted.

This test of specification is not at all unlike the Hausman test (see **Exogeneity tests**). It provides a general test of specification and is used particularly in the Plosser–Schwert–White differencing test (see **Differencing test**).

Further reading

Data transformation tests are analysed fully in Breusch and Godfrey (1986).

Datamining

The word 'datamining' is used as a pejorative term to describe an unstructured search for a 'good' regression equation; datamining exercises are characterized by reporting the finally chosen equation with little (if any) indication of the search process which led to it, and interpreting the one reported equation as if it were the first regression examined. In this context a 'good' equation is one whose parameter estimates are all of the 'right' sign (i.e. all estimates have their *a priori* sign as indicated by theoretical considerations), all of whose estimates are deemed 'significant' by reference to standard t- and F-tests using conventional levels of statistical significance, with a 'high' R^2 statistic and a 'good' Durbin–Watson statistic (i.e. one which is close to 2). Such an equation, therefore, is one which at least superficially conforms to the underlying economic theory. The investigator who has performed the exercise might wish to present the outcome of the empirical analysis as a demonstration that the economic theory it supports is robust and interpret the equation as if the economic theory had withstood an attempted falsification.

Unfortunately such a presentation and interpretation is invalid. The standard application of regression theory to the testing of hypotheses refers to an equation which is properly specified and which is not the result of pre-tests; interpreting an equation in 'textbook' fashion disallows the investigator from using the same data set for both a specification search and the testing of meaningful economic hypotheses. Datamining need not be overt and may be a hidden activity, not apparent to the final user of the model; if it is overt then its implications are that although the reported equation is incapable of providing a basis for standard inferential statistical analysis the equation will, nevertheless, be interpreted in standard fashion (and this can constitute a serious misinterpretation). The classic examples of datamining involve the running of many regressions and reporting just one which, in some sense, is best suited to the investigator's purpose. Since economic theory may dictate a large number of potential regressors to explain a chosen dependent variable and is largely silent on both the functional form and, in time-series work, the lag structure, it has not been uncommon for investigators to run the most general form of the equation and discard variables on the basis of the t- and F-statistics to arrive at one equation which performs well on some pre-chosen, and implicit, criteria. The use of goodness-of-fit statistics and t-statistics as criteria for model selection is fraught with dangers and can, very easily, lead to poor models.

Simply adding new regressors to an equation cannot cause the R^2 statistic to fall. This is most easily demonstrated by recognizing that a model which regresses a variable, Y, on k variables $X_1, \ldots, X_k$ is equivalent to a regression of Y on the k + 1 variables $X_1, \ldots, X_{k+1}$ subject to the restriction that the coefficient on X_{k+1} is zero; in comparing the residual sum of squares from the regression of Y on the k regressors with that from the unconstrained regression of Y on the k + 1 regressors the latter may be seen as an unrestricted sum of squares and the former a restricted sum of squares. Imposing a restriction can only cause the residual sum of squares to rise, and so the R^2 from the unrestricted model is either equal to, or greater than, that from the restricted model. (The R^2 is unchanged if and only if the estimated coefficient on X_{k+1} is identically zero, that is if the restriction is exactly true in the sample.) The R^2 criterion for model choice is, then, inadequate since larger models (those with more regressors) will exhibit larger R^2 statistics whatever the underlying relationship in the population. To overcome this deficiency of R^2 the $\bar{R}^2$ statistic, defined by:

$$\bar{R}^2 = 1 - [RSS/(n - k)]/[TSS/(n - 1)]$$

has been suggested. RSS is the residual sum of squares, TSS is the total sum of squares of the dependent variable and the regression includes a total of k regressors. This is the R^2 'adjusted for degrees of freedom' and, since $R^2 = 1 - RSS/TSS$, the two are related by:

$$\bar{R}^2 = 1 - [(n - 1)/(n - k)](1 - R^2).$$

On the argument that, on average, a 'true' regression equation will have a larger R^2 and a larger $\bar{R}^2$ than a 'false' model it was not uncommon to use either statistic as a criterion of model choice; however, this argument is only true on average and there is nothing to prohibit a false model from having a larger $\overline{R}^2$ than the 'true' model in a given sample. Hence this criterion can lead to incorrect model choice. Moreover, it may be shown as a result of adding one new regressor to an equation that the $\overline{R}^2$ will increase if the added regressor has a t-statistic which (absolutely) exceeds unity; hence accepting the enlarged model because the $\overline{R}^2$ has risen is equivalent to accepting the additional variable on the basis of what may be a very small t-statistic; this criterion of model choice implicitly uses very low critical t-values and significance levels which are very much larger than those in conventional use (an additional candidate regressor will be admitted on the effective basis of a small t-statistic and a correspondingly large Type I error).

A further consideration relates to the sample size used in conventional testing. Suppose one were to use a standard F-test of the inclusion of an additional regressor, using the statistic:

$$F = (T - k - 1)(R_u^2 - R_r^2)/(1 - R_u^2) \sim F_{1,T-k-1}$$

as a test of the inclusion of X_{k+1}. R_u^2 is the R^2 statistic from the regression on all k+1 regressors, and R_r^2 is that from the regression having deleted X_{k+1}. Rejection of the null hypothesis leads to the retention of the variable X_{k+1}, and this will occur when the computed value of F lies in the right-hand tail of the $F_{1,T-k-1}$ distribution. However, the F-statistic is clearly an increasing function of the sample size and so the use of a fixed Type I error on this test can lead to a 'rejection' of the null hypothesis that $\beta_{k+1} = 0$ which is more a reflection of the large sample size than of the underlying 'truth'. Such considerations lead to the proposition that Type I errors should diminish with sample size for those test statistics which are increasing functions of sample size. Such a practice would allow the additional information in a larger sample to be reflected in both a smaller Type I error and smaller Type II errors and would avoid the above problem. The use of a fixed Type I error leads to the rejection of all null hypotheses for a sufficiently large sample size: 'significant' test statistics are only to be expected with large samples and in this sense such tests reflect the large sample size, not necessarily the underlying relationship in the population. The answer is to allow the significance level to be a decreasing function of sample size.

Finally, goodness-of-fit statistics cannot be used to compare models with different dependent variables; R^2 measures the proportion of the variation in the dependent variable which is explained by the regressors, and R^2 statistics can only be compared directly if the dependent variable is the same in the models being compared. This is to be noted especially in attempting to choose between linear and log-linear models; methods other than a simple comparison of R^2 are to be used (see **Box and Cox transformations** for a further discussion of this particular issue).

The issue of sample size is also pertinent in considering the use of a coefficient's t-statistic as a simple criterion of model selection. If a fixed Type I error is used in all instances, independently of sample size, then a 'significant' t-statistic may merely reflect the sample size and not the underlying relationship. Hence 'significant' t-statistics, using conventional significance levels, from models estimated with large data sets should be treated with caution. The converse of this should also be noted: the 'significance' of variables at conventional levels from models using small sample sizes may be interpreted as a more meaningful result than from models with larger sample sizes and, more importantly, 'non-significant' t-statistics from models with large sample sizes is a *prima facie* strong indication of the irrelevance of those variables.

Some of the most important issues in datamining derive from processes of search which result in a given equation which is then interpreted in 'standard' fashion. If a variable, Y, is thought, for example, to be determined by at most k_1 of k potential regressors $\{X_j; j = 1, 2, \ldots, k\}$, the investigator might run all the regressions of Y on the possible combinations of k_1 regressors from the list of k potential regressors and choose the 'best' regression. The best regression might be chosen on fairly standard criteria of having 'significant' t- and F-statistics, and a large R^2, together with a Durbin–Watson statistic close to 2. If the typical parameter in a regression is denoted by β_j, then in examining the null hypothesis H_o: $\beta_j = 0$ at a Type I error of, say 5%, the null hypothesis will be rejected, when true, on 5% of all occasions. If this hypothesis test is examined once within each of 20 different regression equations then it is expected that on one occasion H_o will be rejected, even though it is true. In a datamining exercise, the null hypotheses of no-effect (tests involving null hypotheses such as $\beta_j = 0$) are examined a large number of times, using the same data set on each occasion, and it is only to be expected that some true null hypotheses will be rejected. A rejection of a null hypothesis which posits no effect leads to the acceptance of that regressor and a claim that the dependent variable is affected by the regressor in question. The more regressions that are run in the search for a 'good' result the greater is the chance of 'finding' that good result; however, the result may be nothing but a Type I error, and the process of unstructured search invalidates the use of traditional inferential procedures.

In a datamining search it has been argued above that the 'significant' test statistics may reflect Type I errors, and that the probability of committing such errors rises as the number of regressions increases; specifically, the true Type I error of a hypothesis test, run using a critical value commensurate with a Type I error of α, is α only if a single regression is run and the test in question does not depend on the outcome of any previous regressions using that data set, nor does it depend on the outcome of any other tests on that one regression equation. The distinction must be drawn between the true significance level of a test and the nominal significance level; the nominal significance level is the claimed Type I error. An immediate, and critical, consequence of datamining is that nominal significance levels are smaller than the true levels.

This issue has been investigated in simple experiments by Lovell (1983) who examined the performance of ten orthogonal candidate regressors as explanatory variables for a variable Y. In choosing just two regressors the two candidates most highly correlated with Y were chosen and it was demonstrated that even when not one of the candidates is related to the dependent variable, the probability of observing the result of no dependence when all possible regressions are run is only 0.6, using conventional significance levels of 5%. The probability of not rejecting a null hypothesis when it is true is $(1 - \alpha)$, and in a sequence of p independent tests the probability of not rejecting all p null hypotheses if they are true is then given by $(1 - \alpha)^p$. If the overall Type I error of the p tests is denoted by α^*:

$$(1 - \alpha^*) = (1 - \alpha)^p$$

Hence if the overall Type I error is to be controlled and is set to equal α^*, this implies that the individual tests should be performed at Type I errors given by:

$$1 - (1 - \alpha^*)^{1/p}.$$

The relationship between nominal and true significance levels may be easily computed if the tests are independent, but cannot, typically, be derived analytically in the case of non-independent tests.

Datamining also opens the investigation to the charge of pre-test-bias: the common form of pre-test bias results when a regressor is dropped on the basis of a low t-statistic and the regression re-run with the reduced set of regressors. Since the decision to drop the regressor may have been in error (a Type II error – not rejecting the null hypothesis when it is false) all subsequent regressions are susceptible to mis-specification. This is further examined in **Pre-test estimators**.

Datamining leads to exaggerated claims of significance; nevertheless it is inconceivable that the finally reported regression equation from any investigation is the first equation which was run. Some form of specification search is almost always undertaken, and this may be seen as the intelligent use of data information to inform the model's specification. The important message from considerations of datamining is that the confidence placed in the final equation should be tempered by the knowledge that previous equations were run, and that the reported equation reflects the results of those previous regressions. The issue is not whether or not to engage in datamining, but how to perform specification searches which mitigate the most damaging consequences of mining. Particularly, a battery of specification tests and evaluation procedures (provided, for example, by the extensive use of diagnostic tests; see **Diagnostic tests**) are required in order to establish the worth of the model and to generate confidence in it.

Further reading

The original paper by Lovell (1983) sets out the essentials of datamining; see also Karni and Shapiro (1980), Denton (1985) and Caudill (1988).

Deductive fallacies

There are, inevitably, a number of fallacies which may be committed within deductive reasoning. Fallacies may take many forms, but the following are particularly worth noting.

Affirming the consequent

One of the most common fallacies is that of 'affirming the consequent'. This is a formal, or logical, fallacy since it involves a breach of the formal rules of logic. Consider the following hypothetical syllogism:

1. If $A_1, A_2, \ldots, A_n$ are all true then B is true;
2. B is true;
3. therefore $A_1, A_2, \ldots, A_n$ are all true.

In this form, the minor premiss is an affirmation of the consequent (not the antecedent), and while the conclusion may be true, it is not necessarily true. The rules of formal logic only allow a weak conclusion, which reads:

3 Therefore each of $A_1, A_2, \ldots$ and A_n is not-necessarily-not-true.

This fallacy is the basis of the problems associated with the attempt to verify theories.

Post hoc ergo propter hoc

The fallacy of *post hoc ergo propter hoc* (literally translated as 'after this because of this') lies in the assumption that simply because one event, E_1, occurred after event E_2, then E_2 was necessarily the cause of E_1. In an evaluation of economic policy, for example, it is always tempting to conclude that a policy designed to achieve a specific objective was effective if it is observed that the objective has been met. Specifically, consider a policy of tight monetary control designed to reduce the rate of inflation. After the imposition of the policy, suppose that the rate of inflation is observed to have fallen and the policy-maker then concludes 'the policy was effective'. This commits the fallacy of *post hoc ergo propter hoc*. Equally importantly, suppose that in this example the inflation rate is observed *not* to have changed at all after the imposition of a tight money policy; is it then legitimate, logically, to conclude that the policy has been a failure? The answer is no, for this too would commit the *post hoc ergo propter hoc* fallacy: there is no way of knowing what would have happened in the absence of the policy (the inflation rate may have accelerated in the absence of the policy and then the judgement would have been that the policy had been effective!).

Fallacies of composition

The fallacy of composition occurs when it assumed that what is true for a part of a whole is also true of the whole. As an example, suppose an individual finds that they currently hold an excess of real money balances and, therefore, seek to spend the excess; in so doing they reduce their real balances (by reducing their nominal balances) towards their own optimum level and have no effect on the price level. Now if everyone were in this position, then the aggregate effect of the spending would, in part at least, be to increase prices, and individuals' real balances would be reduced as the price level rose. The effect here is akin to that of the spectator who rises from his or her seat in order to gain a better view; if everyone were to stand the individual's gain would be nullified. One message from this fallacy is that what is true for individuals is not always true for the aggregation of those individuals, and in this sense the fallacy alerts economists to some potential dangers of aggregation. It also applies in forecasting where it is assumed (implicitly) that what is true of the data set used for estimation is also true of the entire population and may, therefore, be extrapolated to form a forecast. This is also related to the problem of induction (see **Induction**).

Appeals to authority

Arguments which seek their justification from an appeal to the known practice of certain individuals or schools of thought are fallacious, for they require the minor premiss that the individuals or schools in question are correct. Amongst such fallacious arguments are those that appeal to conventionalism such as, for example, the attempt to justify the (almost universal) use of a 5% Type I error in statistical testing 'because that is the Type I error most commonly utilized'; on those grounds this is not an acceptable argument.

Begging the question

Strictly, this fallacy occurs when a conclusion is based upon a proposition which has not been agreed to be materially true. It is particularly common when syllogistic reasoning is employed and one of the premisses is left unstated, but is merely implied.

Circular reasoning
This fallacy occurs when that which was to be demonstrated is assumed as true within the argument:

High R^2 are a good thing.
Why?
Because the best econometricians obtain high R^2.
What makes them the best?
They get high R^2.

Within econometrics, the most common fallacies concern logical fallacies of affirming the consequent in the attempt to 'prove' theories 'true' and within statistical testing much practice seeks its justification by appeals to schools of thought. Also, attempts to examine issues of causality must beware the *post ergo propter hoc* fallacy.

Further reading
Stewart (1979) provides an excellent source of further material on fallacies in reasoning, especially within economics and econometrics.

Diagnostic tests

Diagnostic tests, or mis-specification tests, are designed to test the adequacy of the specification of a regression equation. The possible ways in which an equation might have been mis-specified are large; they include:

1. the set of regressors may be incomplete – some important variables may have been omitted;
2. the parameter vector may not be constant;
3. the functional form may be incorrect;
4. one or more of the regressors may not be exogenous;
5. the error term may be autocorrelated;
6. the error term may be heteroscedastic;
7. the error term may be non-normally distributed.

If a specification error has been committed under any one (or more) of the above headings, then the standard interpretation of the estimated equation is invalid in some way. To take a familiar example, if one presumes the regression equation to be well-specified, but the error term is in fact autocorrelated, then the application of ordinary least squares results in estimators of the parameters which are linear and unbiased but which are no longer efficient and, more importantly, the standard formula for the estimators of the parameters' variances will yield biased estimators and so all inferences based on standard t- and F- tests are invalidated.

In general, in order to utilize the textbook results the investigator must be assured that the assumptions upon which those results depend are themselves satisfied; it is vitally important to confirm that those assumptions are valid and the purpose of diagnostic tests is to provide tests of the underlying assumptions of a model. The tests are described in separate entries, detailed in the further reading.

Before any regression model is deemed acceptable it is subjected to a battery of diagnostic tests, and any reported regression will be the outcome of some iterative process in which an initial model has first been estimated and has been modified in some regard as a result of the outcome of diagnostic tests. The tests are conducted with a null hypothesis which states that the regression is well-specified but do not have well-defined alternative hypotheses; hence if any diagnostic test results in a significant statistic the unambiguous conclusion is that the regression model is, in some way, mis-specified, but the direction of the mis-specification is not indicated. Therefore, any significant diagnostic test may be capable of several interpretations, and the investigator should explore those interpretations. For example, if autocorrelation is present in the residuals this may be due to any one of several causes: a salient regressor may have been omitted (and its influence is felt via the residuals); the functional form may be incorrect; there may be a structural break in the relationship; the true error term may itself be autocorrelated or it may follow some more complex ARCH or GARCH process. If the model is to be modified in consequence of a significant diagnostic test is it advisable that any modification is made in the light of relevant economic theory, rather than as a mechanical reaction. Hence any modification is best made as a result of a re-examination of the assumptions which underpin the original model. Notably, the regression equation $Y = X\beta + \varepsilon$ assumes that all approximations and omissions are captured in the non-systematic error term, ε, and a failure of that assumption, as indicated by a diagnostic test, is evidence upon which the model must be re-specified.

If, as is common, many diagnostic tests are performed on a series of regression equations in the search for a well-specified model, the finally chosen equation is subject to the objection of pre-test bias, that is, the final equation represents a modification of (at least one) previous equation, and the decision to change the equation's specification, based on a significant test statistic, could have been a Type I error.

Suppose the ith diagnostic test has a null hypothesis denoted $H_o^{(i)}$ and is run using a nominal significance level of α; then the overall significance level of p diagnostic tests taken together is the probability of rejecting the joint null hypothesis ($H_o^{(1)}$ and $H_o^{(2)}$ . . . and $H_o^{(p)}$) when all the individual null hypotheses are true. The tests are not independent, and the overall significance level, denoted by α^*, can only be described as lying between the limits given by α and $p\alpha$; in order to control the overall size of the joint diagnostic tests, given that the upper limit increases as the number of tests increases, it is necessary to run such tests with small Type I errors (and ½% is not uncommon). However, one might argue that, since the consequences of failing to reject the null hypothesis of a diagnostic test when it is false are large (since the regression is then interpreted as if it were correctly specified, but in fact the underlying assumptions are false) it is important to keep the Type II errors small and use, in consequence, a relatively large overall Type I error. Given the bounds on α^*, even a relatively large overall Type I error (and a correspondingly small overall Type II error) leads to small Type I errors on individual tests, since to be sure that $\alpha^* < \alpha_o$, each test should be run using a Type I error of α, where $\alpha < \alpha_o/p$, and this is a declining function of the number of tests.

Further reading
Tests of omitted variables may be carried out as a linear hypothesis test – additional variables are included in the model and their exclusion is tested as an F-test (see **Linear hypotheses**); constancy of the parameter vector may be examined using a Chow test or a test of predictive failure or may be examined using recursive residuals (see **Chow test** and **Recursive residuals**); the functional form may be examined using a Box and Cox test or by Ramsey's RESET test (see **Box and Cox transformations** and **RESET tests**); exogeneity may be examined by Hausman's test (see **Exogeneity tests**); autocorrelation and heteroscedasticity may be examined by various tests (see **Autocorrelation tests** and also **Heteroscedasticity tests**); normality may be examined by the Jarque–Bera statistic and by testing for outliers (see **Normality tests** and **Outliers**). See also the excellent comprehensive monograph by Godfrey (1988).

Differencing test

If the regression model $Y = X\beta + \varepsilon$, $\varepsilon \sim N(0, \sigma^2 I)$ is properly specified, the regressors are all exogenous or pre-determined, then the ordinary least squares estimator of β will be consistent. In the particular case of time-series data, if the data were analysed in first difference form, where ΔY is the vector of observations on the differenced dependent variable, whose typical element is $\{Y_t - Y_{t-1}\}$, ΔX is the matrix of differenced regressors, whose typical element is $\{X_{tj} - X_{t-1,j}\}$, and $\Delta\varepsilon$ is the differenced error term, with typical element $\{\varepsilon_t - \varepsilon_{t-1}\}$, then the differenced model could be constructed:

$$\Delta Y = \Delta X\beta + \Delta\varepsilon$$

If the original regressors do not include any lags of the dependent variable then, notwithstanding the fact that the error term in the differenced specification is a moving average, the ordinary least squares estimator of β from the differenced model will also be consistent (but inefficient). A test of the original model's specification may, therefore, be performed by estimating the model in both levels and in first differences and comparing the two estimates; this is a special case of the more general tests described in **Data transformation tests**. If the estimator from the levels equation is given by $\hat{\beta}$ and that from the differenced data is $\tilde{\beta}$, then $\hat{\beta} - \tilde{\beta}$ has a probability limit of zero under the hypothesis that the levels equations is well-specified. This test may be carried out easily by using an auxiliary regression of the form:

$$Y = X\beta + Z\alpha + \eta$$

where, as is shown in **Data transformation tests**, $Z = P'PX$, and P is the transforming matrix. A test of $\alpha = 0$ is then a test of the adequacy of the model specified in levels. If the original model is estimated using T observations then, in this specific case, the transforming matrix produces first differences and may, therefore, be written as:

$$P = \begin{bmatrix} -1 & 1 & 0 & \cdots & \cdots & \cdots & 0 \\ 0 & -1 & 1 & 0 & \cdots & \cdots & 0 \\ \vdots & \ddots & \ddots & & & & \vdots \\ \vdots & & \ddots & \ddots & & & \vdots \\ \vdots & & & 0 & -1 & 1 & 0 \\ 0 & 0 & \cdots & \cdots & 0 & -1 & 1 \end{bmatrix}$$

P is of order $T-1 \times T$, and it is easy to show that P'P is given by:

$$P'P = \begin{bmatrix} 1 & -1 & 0 & \cdots & \cdots & 0 \\ -1 & 2 & -1 & \cdots & \cdots & \vdots \\ \vdots & \ddots & \ddots & \ddots & & \\ \vdots & & \ddots & \ddots & \ddots & \\ \vdots & & & -1 & 2 & -1 \\ 0 & 0 & \cdots & \cdots & -1 & 1 \end{bmatrix}$$

Hence, given an appropriate treatment of $X_{-1,j}$ and $X_{T+1,j}$, P'PX has a typical element given by $-X_{t-1,j} + 2X_{t,j} - X_{t+1,j}$, which may be written as $-\Delta^2 X_{t+1,j}$. If the matrix of additional variables, Z, is defined by $Z = -\Delta^2 X$ using only the observations from $t = 2$ to $T - 1$, a test of the specification in levels may, therefore, be carried out by running the model:

$$Y = X\beta + Z\alpha + \eta$$

where this is defined for only T − 2 observations. An F-test of the hypothesis $\alpha = 0$ then yields the necessary test statistic. The F-statistic to test $\alpha = 0$ is, under the null hypothesis of a correct specification, distributed as $F_{k,T-2-2k}$. If the hypothesis is not rejected then the specification of the model in levels is deemed adequate. If, however, the F-test is so large as to result in a rejection of the hypothesis $\alpha = 0$ then the model specified as $Y = X\beta + \varepsilon$ is rejected. The additional regressors may be simply defined as $(X_{t-1,j} + X_{t+1,j})$, since the influence of the current regressors is already accommodated in the matrix X.

If the original model includes, as is most likely, a constant term then the first column of Z is zero and this is then discarded; equally, if X contains any variables so that $\Delta^2 X$ is not of full rank then they are simply discarded in the construction of Z, the number of parameters in α is reduced, and the degrees of freedom of the F-test are adjusted accordingly.

A more serious problem arises with this test if the original regressors, X, include lags of the dependent variable; then the additional regressors in the auxiliary regression will include terms like $(Y_{t-2} + Y_t)$, and the appearance of Y_t in this additional regressor will result in biased and inconsistent ordinary least squares estimators from the auxiliary regression. In this case the test is, therefore, performed by running the auxiliary regression of Y on X and all additional variables of the form $(X_{t-1,j} + X_{t+1,j})$ as required plus the additional regressor Y_{t-2}.

The differencing test is a most useful test of the specification of a time-series model, and is due to Plosser, Schwert and White (1982).

Further reading

See, especially, Plosser, Schwert and White (1982) and also Davidson and MacKinnon (1985).

Distributed lag models

Economic theory is phrased, typically, in terms of static equilibrium; however, in many situations it is not reasonable to assume that the observed data have been generated from an equilibrium state. Moreover, economic theory is usually silent on adjustment processes and out-of-equilibrium behaviour, although many *ad hoc* adjustment processes have been proposed in the literature. It is, therefore, incumbent upon econometricians to recognize the possibility of disequilibrium and to construct models in this light. Particularly, this means that while economic theory tends to concentrate upon equilibrium behaviour, the time-series data available to econometricians reflects short-run disequilibria positions. One way to model short-run deviations from 'long-run' equilibria is to incorporate lags into the process: suppose economic theory predicts that a variable, Y, is determined by a single explanatory variable, X, then one way to model data generated by out-of-equilibrium states is to examine an equation which recognizes that the influence of X on Y may be other than just instantaneous. The equilibrium relationship might be modelled, in the simplest of deterministic linear forms, by:

$$Y_t = \alpha + \beta X_t.$$

However, this equilibrium relationship assumes that all the adjustment of Y to the current value of X occurs within the period of the data (which might be monthly, quarterly, annual, etc.). Whether or not such an assumption is *a priori* reasonable demands that the nature and frequency of the data collection exercise be carefully considered, but the assumption is testable. Data from the material world may have been generated from out-of-equilibrium states and to accommodate this one approach is to allow the effect of X_t to be spread over several periods, so that the effect of current X is felt not only by current Y but also by future values of Y. This may reflect adjustment costs, so that, for example, agents choose not to react instantaneously and fully to the current value of X but to allow the effect of X to be felt in part in the current value of Y and in part in future values of Y. This may be modelled as the following deterministic equation:

$$Y_t = \alpha + \beta_o X_t + \beta_1 X_{t-1} + \beta_2 X_{t-2} + \ldots + \beta_m X_{t-m}.$$

Such a model allows current X to affect current Y with coefficient β_o, to affect next period's Y with coefficient β_1 and to affect the value of Y j periods in the future with coefficient β_j (where $j \leq m$). The history of X more than m periods in the past is not directly relevant to the determination of current Y. In such a simple deterministic distributed lag model Y is, in one sense, in equilibrium only when X has been unchanged for at least m+1 consecutive periods: if $X_{t-s} = X^*$ for all s then:

$$Y^* = \alpha + (\Sigma_{j=0}^{m} \beta_j) X^* = \alpha + \beta X^*.$$

m may be finite or infinite; if m is infinite it is necessary, for this equilibrium to exist, that $\beta = \Sigma_{j=0}^{m} \beta_j$ is finite. β is called the equilibrium multiplier, and β_o is called the short-run, or impact, multiplier. It is useful to define the lag weights:

$$w_j = \beta_j / \beta$$

and then:

$$Y_t = \alpha + \beta(\Sigma_{j=0}^{m} w_j X_{t-j}).$$

In order to examine the period of adjustment it is common to report the median lag, j^*, defined as the period within which half the total adjustment occurs: j^* is such that

$$\Sigma_{j=0}^{j^*} w_j = 0.5.$$

The mean lag is also a useful summary figure, defined as $\sum_{j=0}^{m} jw_j$. If the lag weights are not all the same sign then neither the median nor the mean lag are easily interpreted; indeed, a change of sign in the lag weights is commonly interpreted as a sign of mis-specification.

To estimate a distributed lag model several issues emerge; one is that economic theory may not have informed the model's specification and the distributed lag is merely used as some form of proxy for disequilibrium processes. The important implication of this is that since theory may have nothing to say about the sign or size of any individual β_j, there is no value of any one β_j which is in conflict with the underlying theory (although there may be theory which constrains the signs of the lag weights); the theoretical prediction concerns the equilibrium relationship between Y^* and X^*, and a test of this proposition is a test of $\sum_{j=0}^{m}\beta_j$. Also, the value of m will have to be determined empirically, according to some criterion (such as goodness-of-fit, subject to degrees-of-freedom constraints dictated by the size of the data set). Another issue concerns the degree of multicollinearity between the regressors (in economic time series it is common for X_{t-s} and X_{t-s-1} to be collinear), and the associated loss of precision in the estimated coefficients.

In seeking to fit a general unrestricted distributed lag model the choice of m may be taken by reference to the adjusted R^2 statistic, or Akaike's Information Criterion (see **Selection of regressors**); alternatively, m could be chosen by simplifying down an over-parameterized model by the use of sequential F-tests, stopping when the last test rejects the null hypothesis of zero parameters.

In the development of the distributed lag model there is, of course, nothing which guarantees that m is finite; that is, it may be the case that the relevant history of X is its entire history, and not just the last m periods. In this case the model cannot be estimated unless some restricting structure is placed upon the β_j parameters. In the case of a non-finite m, the earliest proposal was that of Koyck (1954) who suggested the geometric lag whereby $\beta_j = \beta\lambda^j$ for all values of j and where $0 < \lambda < 1$. This may be written as the following stochastic equation:

$$Y_t = \alpha + \sum_{j=0}^{\infty}\beta\lambda^j X_{t-j} + \varepsilon_t$$

where it is assumed that the error is a white-noise random variable. This may be solved to yield:

$$Y_t = \alpha(1-\lambda) + \beta X_t + \lambda Y_{t-1} + v_t$$

where $v_t = \varepsilon_t - \lambda\varepsilon_{t-1}$.

Given the assumptions made of ε_t, v_t is a moving average random variable of order 1; that is, v_t is MA(1). This may be estimated, but by methods other than OLS since OLS will not yield best linear estimators in the presence of a lagged dependent variable and an MA(1) error (since the regressor Y_{t-1} and the error v_t are correlated). This model has been examined extensively, and the assumption made above regarding ε, namely that it is white-noise, has been relaxed in many ways to accommodate autocorrelation and moving average components. Much research energy had been devoted to devising the appropriate estimation techniques under such alternative error specifications.

The Koyck lag structure is relatively simple, it depends on only two parameters, but the weights are monotonically declining; thus this structure imposes the restriction that X_t has its greatest impact upon current Y and its influence on future values of Y diminishes geometrically. More flexible schemes are required for lag structures which allow the impact of current X to be greatest on some future value of Y.

If m is large, but finite, the immediate issues concern the loss of degrees of freedom and multicollinearity; one of the earliest, and once very popular, approaches to imposing structure on the β_j parameters (due to Almon, 1965) is to require that the β_j all lie on a polynomial of small order. That is:

$$\beta_j = \gamma_o + \gamma_1 j + \gamma_2 j^2 + \ldots + \gamma_p j^p \qquad j = 0, 1, \ldots m.$$

In matrix notation: $\beta = A\gamma$, where A is an $(m+1)\times(p+1)$ matrix whose $(j+1)^{th}$ row ($j = 0, 1, 2, \ldots, m$) is given by $[1\ j\ j^2 \ldots j^p]$. Hence:

$$Y = \alpha + X\beta + \varepsilon$$

where X is the $T\times(m+1)$ matrix of lagged independent variables. Hence:

$$Y = \alpha + XA\gamma + \varepsilon$$

and so α and γ may be estimated by running the regression of Y on a constant and the regressors constructed according to XA. This device has reduced the number of response parameters to be estimated from m+1 β terms to p+1 γ terms; the reduction is thus $m - p$ and an efficiency gain will be realized (whether or not imposing the polynomial constraint is correct). Given the estimate of γ the estimate of β is obtained directly from $\hat{\beta} = A\hat{\gamma}$. Some work using Almon lags also constrains either or both of the end values of β to be zero; this amounts to setting $\beta_{-1} = 0$ and/or $\beta_{m+1} = 0$. Such a proposal has little merit: the model's parameters would all be affected by imposing either constraint, but the model itself does not utilize coefficients outside the (0, m) interval. Clearly, in order to estimate an Almon lag structure both the order of the polynomial, p, and the lag length, m, must be chosen.

The objective of both the Koyck and polynomial lag model is to impose some structure on the parameters to facilitate estimation. Other particular schemes exist for finite structures, notably the arithmetic lag and the inverted V. However, the advantages of the infinite lag are not inconsiderable, and to remove the restriction of the Koyck lag that the weights are monotonically declining, the rational lag model has been proposed; defining the lag operator L by $Lz_t = z_{t-1}$, the rational lag is defined by:

$$Y_t = \mu + [B(L)/A(L)]X_t + \varepsilon_t$$

where A(L) and B(L) are polynomials in L, and this equation has been written in terms of one regressor variable only. This model may, of course, be extended to accommodate any number of regressors, each of which might then have its own dynamic structure attached to it. This scheme allows great flexibility of the lag structure using relatively small order polynomials. The autoregressive distributed lag (ADL) form of the model is simply:

$$A(L)Y_t = \alpha + B(L)X_t + A(L)\varepsilon_t.$$

If A(L) is of order p and B(L) is of order q and attention is, for purposes of exposition only, confined to a single regressor variable, this may be written as:

$$Y_t = \alpha + \Sigma_{j=0}^{q}\beta_j X_{t-j} + \Sigma_{i=1}^{p}\alpha_j Y_{t-i} + \Sigma_{i=0}^{p}\alpha_j \varepsilon_{t-i}.$$

In this form of the model the current value of Y_t is determined by lagged values of Y_t (via the operation of A(L)), the current and lagged values of X_t (via the operation of B(L)) and has a moving average error term in $A(L)\varepsilon_t$. This form has been restricted so that the same lag structure applies to the dependent variable as to the error term, and a yet more flexible structure is to let the error term have a unique dynamic structure; the resulting equation is:

$$A(L)Y_t = \alpha + B(L)X_t + C(L)\varepsilon_t.$$

This is an ARMAX (**A**uto**R**egressive **M**oving **A**verage **X**) model ; this label distinguishes it from the ARMA model (see **ARMA and ARIMA models**) in which there is no regressor, X. The ARMAX model combines an econometric model (which includes regressors chosen by reference to *a priori* propositions from economic theory) with a time-series approach, and is sometimes referred to as SEMTSA – the **S**tructural **E**conometric **M**odel **T**ime **S**eries **A**pproach.

If, as a special case, there is no autocorrelation (whether of an autoregressive or moving average from) in the error $v_t = C(L)\varepsilon_t$, then the ARMAX model may be estimated consistently by OLS; this is effectively a regression of Y_t on itself lagged p times (where A is of order p) and on current and lagged X_t where the lag length of X_t reflects the order of the polynomial B. If the error term is autocorrelated, however, the lagged dependent variables will be correlated with it, even in the limit, and OLS will be inconsistent; consistent and efficient estimation methods do, of course, exist.

A final consideration of distributed lag models is their stability; if X_t is fixed at some value, X^*, and the disturbances are fixed at their expected values of zero, then:

$$A(L)Y_t = \alpha + B(L)X^*.$$

This may be written as:

$$Y_t = \alpha + B(1)X^* + \alpha_1 Y_{t-1} + \alpha_2 Y_{t-2} \ldots + \alpha_p Y_{t-p}.$$

B(L) has been replaced by B(1) since X^* is unchanged through time and so $LX_t^* = X^*$ for all t. The stability of the system is ensured if, in such a case, Y_t converges to a constant value. If it does, then the value, Y^*, is defined by:

$$Y^* = [\alpha + B(1)X^*]/A(1)$$

and this clearly demands that $A(1) \neq 0$. This stability condition may be shown to be that all the roots of $A(z) = 0$ are absolutely greater than 1.

The use of distributed lag models is now most commonly seen in the form of the ADL or ARMAX models, and such models are at the heart of vector autoregressive (VAR) models. They provide very flexible ways of modelling short-run deviations from long-run equilibrium relationships, but they are not commonly grounded in economic theory; a distributed lag model provides a means of modelling short-run behaviour, but is not a device for testing short-run behaviour since rarely, if ever, does theory offer meaningful predictions about the short-run responses (and there are, then, no hypotheses to test). Economic theory is concerned with the specification of the regressors and with their associated long-run multipliers and has little to say about adjustment processes. Notwithstanding that, many economic models posit adjustment processes (such as the partial adjustment mechanism or adaptive expectations) which give rise to distributed lag models, and in the absence of imposing any such structure on the adjustment the ARMAX model allows a very flexible route by which the data are allowed to indicate the adjustment processes at work. However, in a many-regressor equation, unless the regressors specified in the variables of X are complete, then the flexibility offered by the ARMAX model may mean that the lagged variables behave as proxies for omitted regressors and care must be exercised in the specification of the regressors so that the adjustment derived from the model may, indeed, be interpreted as the short-run responses. When allied to extensive diagnostic tests and simplifications tests (via F-tests of zero parameters and Wald tests of common factors, for example) ARMAX models have become the basis for much of the modern approach to time-series modelling. A general model such as the ADL or ARMAX may also be re-parameterized as an error correction model and when expressed in differences of the variables in question has found great application with integrated data series; see

Common factors, Error correction models, Integration and **Cointegration**.

Further reading

Important references to the literature on distributed lags include the surveys by Griliches (1967), Dhrymes (1971) and Nerlove (1972). See also Koyck (1954), Almon (1965), Jorgenson (1966), Hendry *et al.* (1984) and Harvey (1990); Trivedi and Pagan (1979) discuss the use of optimal significance levels in sequential testing; Godfrey and Poskitt (1975) discuss the choice of polynomial in the Almon lag. See Mills (1990) for a discussion of forecasting with the ARMAX model.

Distribution theory: the relationships between normal, chi-squared, t- and F- distributions

The normal distribution is the commonest starting point of analysis, and tables of the standardized normal distribution are widely available. The shape of the density function of z is the familiar symmetric bell-shape; any value of z on the real line is possible, but the probability is concentrated around the mean of zero and there is little probability in the extreme tails. Just over 68% of the probability lies within one standard deviation of the mean, and a little over 95% lies within two standard deviations.

If y is a single normally distributed random variable written as $y \sim N(\mu, \sigma^2)$ then the standardized form of y is given by $z = (y - \mu)/\sigma$ (see **Standardized random variables**). This is written as:

$$(y - \mu)/\sigma = z \sim N(0, 1).$$

The probability density function of z is then given by $(2\pi)^{-\frac{1}{2}}\exp\{-z^2/2\}$.

If y is a standardized vector of normal variates then y has a zero mean and its variance–covariance matrix is the identity, written as $y \sim MVN(0, I)$. Consider the linear transformation of y given by $q = By$:

$$\text{If} \qquad y \sim MVN(0, I) \qquad \text{then} \qquad q = By \sim MVN(0, BB').$$

Strictly speaking, this is only true for matrices B such that BB' is non-singular; when BB' is singular By is described as multivariate normal only as a matter of *convention*. This results from the following: if $y \sim MVN(0, I)$ then the density function of a typical element, y_i, is given by:

$$f(y_i) = (2\pi)^{-\frac{1}{2}}\exp\{-y_i^2/2\}$$

and since the elements of y are mutually independent, the joint density function of $(y_1, y_2, \ldots, y_n)$ is the product of the individual density functions:

$$f(y_1, y_2, \ldots, y_n) = (2\pi)^{-n/2}\exp\{-\tfrac{1}{2}\sum_{i=1}^{n} y_i^2\}$$

To derive the distribution function of $q = By$ suppose that B is a square matrix and use the following general result:

$$f(q_1, q_2, \ldots, q_n) = f(y_1, y_2, \ldots, y_n).|J|.$$

where J is an n×n matrix known as the Jacobian of the transformation and $|J|$ is the determinant of J; this equation relates the distribution of the original variable, y, and the transformed variable, q. The typical element of J, j_{ik}, is given by:

$$j_{ik} = \frac{\partial y_i}{\partial q_k}$$

and so long as B is not singular, $y = B^{-1}q$ and so j_{ik} is simply given by the (i, k)th element of the matrix B^{-1}. Thus, the determinant of the Jacobian is the determinant of B^{-1}. By the rules of determinants, $\det(B^{-1}) = [\det(B)]^{-1}$. Hence:

$$f(q_1, q_2, \ldots, q_n) = f(y_1, y_2, \ldots, y_n).|B|^{-1}.$$

If B is singular, $|B| = 0$ and so q (= By) does not have a well-defined density function. It is for this reason that By is *by convention only* described as multivariate normal. If B is not a square matrix, but of order r×n, then the above reasoning may be used to show that in this case By has a multivariate normal distribution with a well-defined density function if and only if BB' is of full rank. Since BB' is a square matrix of order r, it is required that $\rho(BB') = r$; but $\rho(BB') = \rho(B)$, and $\rho(B) \leq \min(r, n)$, and so it is necessary that $\rho(B) = r$ (which in turn demands that $r \leq n$).

The standardized normal variable is the commonest starting point of distributional analysis in econometrics; from it many other common distributions are derived.

The chi-squared distribution

The first distribution to be defined is the square of a standard normal: if z is a single standardized normal random variable, then z^2 has a central chi-squared distribution with one degree of freedom: if $z \sim N(0,1)$ then $z^2 \sim \chi^2_1$, read as 'chi-squared with one degree of freedom'. The central chi-squared distribution is uniquely defined by its degrees of freedom (the word 'central' is frequently dropped from its title). Since $z^2 \geq 0$, a chi-squared variable can take all values on the non-negative real line. An important property of this distribution is that if two independent chi-squared distributions, each having 1 degree of freedom, are added, then the resulting random variable is also distributed as chi-squared but has 2 degrees of freedom. In general, therefore, if $w^2 \sim \chi^2_n$ and $v^2 \sim \chi^2_p$ and w^2 and v^2 are independent, then:

$$w^2 + v^2 \sim \chi^2_{n+p}\,.$$

The mean and variance of a χ^2_n variate are given by n and 2n respectively; the actual shape of the chi-squared distribution depends on the degrees of freedom, is skewed and has a long right hand tail.

From this definition of the central chi-squared distribution the following result may be derived: if z is an n×1 vector, and each element z_i is a standard normal variate and each z_i is independent of all other z_j then z is described as having a standardized multivariate normal distribution:

$$z \sim MVN(0, I); \qquad \text{also,} \quad z_i^2 \sim \chi^2_1 \quad \text{for all } i = 1, 2, \ldots, n$$

and since the z_i variables are mutually independent:

$$\sum_{i=1}^{n} z_i^2 \sim \chi^2_n \qquad \text{i.e.} \quad z'z \sim \chi^2_n.$$

Hence, if the n×1 random vector y has a multivariate normal distribution with a mean of μ and a variance matrix of Ω, then:

$$y \sim MVN(\mu, \Omega) \Rightarrow Q^{-1}(y - \mu) \sim MVN(0, I) \text{ where } QQ' = \Omega;$$

$$\Rightarrow (y - \mu)'(Q^{-1})'Q^{-1}(y - \mu) \sim \chi^2_n$$

$$\Rightarrow (y - \mu)'\Omega^{-1}(y - \mu) \sim \chi^2_n.$$

The above analysis shows that a (central) chi-squared distribution may be created by taking the sums of squared mutually independent standard normal variates. However, this is not the only form in which the chi-squared distribution appears in econometric work; a very important special case arises as follows: if y is an n×1 vector and has a standard normal multivariate distribution, then by forming the quadratic form y'By, where B is a square idempotent matrix of order n and rank p ($p < n$), also yields a chi-squared variable:

$$y'By \sim \chi^2_p$$

The case when $p = n$ is already shown; the proof of this result when $p < n$ requires the use of eigenvalues and is demonstrated in most advanced texts on statistics. The result is most important and is much used in econometric work.

From the normal and chi-squared distributions, several other common and important distributions may be defined.

The augmented chi-squared distribution

If $w^2 \sim \chi^2_n$ then $w^2/n \sim C^2_n$; that is, a (central) chi-squared variate with n degrees of freedom, when divided by n, is an augmented (or modified) chi-squared variate with n degrees of freedom. From the mean and variance of the chi-squared distribution, it is seen that:

$$E(w^2/n) = 1 \quad \text{and} \quad V(w^2/n) = 2/n.$$

Hence, as $n \to \infty$, $V(w^2/n) \to 0$; that is, as n gets large without limit, the augmented chi-squared distribution tends, in probability, to unity.

The t-distribution

If $z \sim N(0, 1)$, $w^2/n \sim C_n^2$ and z and w^2 are independent, then $z/\sqrt{(w^2/n)} \sim t_n$; that is, a standard normal variate, divided by the square root of an independent augmented (central) chi-squared variate with n degrees of freedom is a '(central) t-variate with n degrees of freedom'. Clearly, as $n \to \infty$ the denominator tends, in probability, to unity, and so $t_n \xrightarrow{D} N(0, 1)$. In fact, as is evident from tables of the standard normal and t-distributions, for $n > 30$ there is very little error in approximating the t distribution by the standard normal. For any finite degrees of freedom, the t-distribution has a similar shape to the standard normal: it is symmetric about its zero mean and has a bell-shape; however, in comparison to the normal, all t-distributions have more probability in the tails (put equivalently, all t-distributions with finite degrees of freedom have a variance which exceeds unity).

The F-distribution

If $w^2 \sim \chi_n^2$ and $v^2 \sim \chi_m^2$ and w^2 and v^2 are independent, then:

$$\frac{w^2/n}{v^2/m} \sim F_{n,m}$$

that is, an augmented (central) chi-squared variate with n degrees of freedom, divided by an independent augmented (central) chi-squared variate with m degrees of freedom, is a '(central) F-variate with n and m degrees of freedom'.

From this definition several properties are evident; firstly, if F is a random variable distributed as $F_{n,m}$, then this has the same distribution as the random variable $(1/F_{m,n})$. Secondly, there is a direct relationship between a t-variate and an F-variate: since $z/\sqrt{(w^2/n)} \sim t_n$, then the square of a t_n random variable is given by $z^2/(w^2/n)$; the numerator, z^2, is by definition distributed as χ_1^2 (identical to an augmented chi-squared with one degree of freedom) and the denominator is an independent augmented chi-squared variable with n degrees of freedom; hence this new random variable is, by definition, an F variable with 1 and n degrees of freedom. Thus, the square of a t_n variate is an $F_{1,n}$ variate Finally, since the denominator of a random variable distributed as $F_{n,m}$ approaches unity (in probability) as $m \to \infty$, then the $F_{n,m}$ distribution approaches C_n^2 as $m \to \infty$. Moreover, as both n and m approach infinity, the $F_{n,m}$ variable approaches unity in probability.

Independence of random variables

In order to determine whether random variables are, or are not, independent, the following result is critical and widely used in econometrics: if z is an n-dimensional random variable and $z \sim MVN(0, I)$ and A and B are two $n \times n$

symmetric matrices then, if AB = 0, the two quadratic forms z'Az and z'Bz are mutually independent. This result is used in constructing independent χ^2 variables, and hence F- and t- random variables, and is used frequently in econometrics, as are all the above results which relate the normal, chi-squared, t- and F-distributions.

All the results given above facilitate the application of inferential statistics – the construction of confidence regions and hypothesis testing – in econometrics, and most of the standard texts provide sets of tables of each of these common distributions in order that such regions and tests may be constructed.

Non-central distributions

Strictly speaking, the chi-squared, augmented chi-squared, t- and F-distributions defined above are all 'central' distributions. The 'non-central' forms of each distribution are also important in hypothesis testing work, especially in evaluating the power of a test (see, for example, **Hypothesis testing** and **Power function**). The 'non-central' forms are defined as below.

The non-central chi-squared distribution

If y is an n-dimensional vector, and y ~ MVN(η, I) then y'y ~ $\chi^2_n(\lambda)$ where λ is the non-centrality parameter, and is given by $\lambda = \eta'\eta$; i.e. the sum of squares of n independent normal variables, each of which has a non-zero mean but a unit variance, is a non-central chi-squared variable. If $\lambda = 0$ (which implies that $\eta = 0$), this result defines the central chi-squared distribution.

The non-central t-distribution

If z ~ N(λ, 1) and $w^2 \sim \chi^2_n(0)$ (i.e. w^2 is a central χ^2_n variable) and z and w^2 are independent, then $z/\sqrt{(w^2/n)} \sim t_n(\lambda)$ where λ is the non-centrality parameter; i.e. a non-central, unit variance, normal variable divided by the square root of a central augmented chi-squared variable is a non-central t-variable. This distribution is of particular importance in evaluating the power of t-tests.

The non-central F-distribution

If $w^2 \sim \chi^2_n(\lambda_1)$ and $v^2 \sim \chi^2_m(\lambda_2)$ and w^2 and v^2 are independent, then:

$$\frac{w^2/n}{v^2/m} \sim F_{n,m}(\lambda_1, \lambda_2)$$

that is, a non-central augmented chi-squared variate with n degrees of freedom and non-centrality parameter λ_1, divided by an independent non-central augmented chi-squared variate with m degrees of freedom and non-centrality parameter λ_2, is a non-central F-variate with n and m degrees of freedom and non-centrality parameters λ_1 and λ_2.

The above distributions form the basis of the techniques of hypothesis testing and inferential statistics within econometrics; each has a common parent, namely the normal distribution. It is important, therefore, to be able to examine and to test for normality; the Jarque–Bera test is a common test for normality (see **Diagnostic Tests** and **Normality tests**), but, in large samples, central limit theorems may be used. Those theorems identify the conditions under which random variables may, in large samples, be assumed to have approximate normal distributions. They, and their implications, are explained in **Central limit theorems**.

Further reading
The essential distribution theory for econometrics is discussed further in all econometrics texts. See, for example, Greene (1993).

Dummy variables

Economic models often incorporate qualitative, rather than quantitative, explanatory variables; examples include male/female, north/south, policy on/off, quarter I/quarter II/quarter III/quarter IV. In such cases a quantitative proxy is constructed to represent qualitative variables in the corresponding econometric model, and such proxy variables are known as dummy variables. The simplest form of dummy variable is one which takes the value of one when the qualitative effect is in place, and zero otherwise. In the above examples a dummy, D, is constructed which takes the value one if the observation relates to male and zero if female, one if north and zero if south, one if policy is on and zero otherwise; the last example requires more than one dummy and one might use three dummies, Q_i, i = 1, 2 and 3 so that $Q_i = 1$ if the observation relates to quarter i and is zero otherwise (the reason for three, not four, dummies is explained below). Once constructed these dummies are used in the standard regression model just like any other regressor, but care must be taken both in their incorporation and their interpretation.

Consider a very simple model in which the regressand is hours of labour supplied (Y) and the regressor is the wage rate (X); data are available at the level of individuals and it is decided that the individual's sex is potentially an important determinant of labour supply. Let D_i be a dummy which takes the value one if the individual is male and zero otherwise. The simple linear regression model, excluding the dummy variable, may be written as $Y_i = \alpha + \beta X_i + \varepsilon_i$; if the dummy for the individual's sex is now included, where $D_i = 1$ if individual i is male and $D_i = 0$ if female:

$$Y_i = \alpha + \beta X_i + \gamma D_i + \varepsilon_i$$

which implies that the expected hours of labour supplied by a male, facing a wage rate of X_o, is given by $\alpha + \beta X_o + \gamma$; that for a female facing the same wage rate is given by $\alpha + \beta X_o$. The parameter γ thus represents the difference between the expected labour supplies of men and women who face the same wage rate. It is to be noted immediately that in this case there are two categories to be distinguished, namely male and female, but only one dummy is used. Suppose two dummies were used: D_i^m takes the value one if the individual is male and zero otherwise while D_i^f takes the value one if the individual is female and zero otherwise; then:

$$Y_i = \alpha + \beta X_i + \gamma D_i^m + \xi D_i^f + \varepsilon_i.$$

This model cannot be estimated, for it suffers perfect multicollinearity. This may be noted from the fact that the parameter α may be seen as the coefficient on a dummy variable, ι, every one of whose elements is unity; hence, in the model with the two dummies there is an exact linear relationship between the regressors ι, D_m and D_f: $\iota = D^m + D^f$. This situation is referred to as the 'dummy variable trap' and occurs when, with p dichotomous qualitative categories, the regression equation is specified to include p linearly independent 0-1 dummies and also a constant term. With p categories, if a constant term is to be included, one category should be set as the 'base' and only p – 1 dummies are included so that their associated parameters are then interpreted as differences with respect to the base. Hence in the model with only one dummy for the individual's sex, female labour supply is the base and γ represents the difference between men and women. One could, of course, use two dummies in such a situation but one would then omit the constant term:

$$Y_i = \beta X_i + \gamma_m D_i^m + \gamma_f D_i^f + \varepsilon_i.$$

This model, without a constant term, may be estimated and here $\gamma_m + \beta X_o$ is the expected labour supply of a male facing a wage rate of X_o, while a female is expected to supply $\gamma_f + \beta X_o$. In the model with only one dummy, the corresponding supplies are $\alpha + \beta X_o + \gamma$ and $\alpha + \beta X_o$; hence $\alpha + \gamma = \gamma_m$ and $\alpha = \gamma_f$ demonstrating that the use of the one dummy sets the female as the base. Including a constant term, then, in a model which incorporates dichotomous dummy variables demands that with p categories only p – 1 dummies are used, and their associated parameters represent differences with respect to a chosen base; the choice of base is without loss of generality. The alternative is to exclude the constant explicitly and use all p dummies; however, one use of dummies is to test for differences, and so the former approach allows a direct examination of hypotheses of differences, via simple t-tests of the coefficients on the dummy variables.

A given regression equation may contain dummies for more than one qualitative variable; suppose that the above model is extended to incorporate education as a dummy variable where D_i^e is defined as 1 if the individual has enjoyed education only to the age of 16 and is zero otherwise:

$$Y_i = \alpha + \beta X_i + \gamma D_i + \theta D_i^e + \varepsilon_i.$$

In this model the following expectations may be constructed:

E(Y|wage rate X_o, male and educated to 16 only) = $\alpha + \beta X_o + \gamma + \theta$;
E(Y|wage rate X_o, male and educated beyond 16) = $\alpha + \beta X_o + \gamma$;
E(Y|wage rate X_o, female and educated to 16 only) = $\alpha + \beta X_o + \theta$;
E(Y|wage rate X_o, female and educated beyond 16) = $\alpha + \beta X_o$.

This model does not include 'interaction' effects, for γ measures the expected difference between men and women, independently of their education level and θ measures the difference attributable to education level, independent of sex. Interaction may be accommodated by introducing a third dummy: D^{mo} = 1 if the individual is both male and educated to 16 only and = 0 otherwise; D^{ml} = 1 if the individual is both male and educated beyond 16 and = 0 otherwise; D^{fo} = 1 if the individual is both female and educated to 16 only and = 0 otherwise; the category of being both female and educated beyond 16 now becomes the reference category (the base). The model is then estimated as:

$$Y_i = \alpha + \beta X_i + \lambda_1 D_i^{mo} + \lambda_2 D_i^{ml} + \lambda_3 D_i^{fo} + \varepsilon_i.$$

The following expectations may be constructed:

E(Y|wage rate X_o, male and educated to 16 only) = $\alpha + \beta X_o + \lambda_1$;
E(Y|wage rate X_o, male and educated beyond 16) = $\alpha + \beta X_o + \lambda_2$;
E(Y|wage rate X_o, female and educated to 16 only) = $\alpha + \beta X_o + \lambda_3$;
E(Y|wage rate X_o, female and educated beyond 16) = $\alpha + \beta X_o$.

Now, the difference between men and women is $\lambda_1 - \lambda_3$ if educated to 16 only and is λ_2 if education was pursued beyond 16; the difference ascribed to education is now $\lambda_1 - \lambda_2$ if male and λ_3 if female. If $\lambda_1 - \lambda_3 = \lambda_2$ (and so $\lambda_1 - \lambda_2 = \lambda_3$) the model with interaction simplifies to that without; these restrictions are testable by an F-test.

Further, dummy variables may interact with quantitative variables; in the above example the dummy variables are used to model differences in average labour supply according to sex and education, but as modelled all individuals react to a change in the wage rate identically. To allow individuals to react differently, one may construct the new variables: $X_i D_i^{mo}$, $X_i D_i^{ml}$ and $X_i D_i^{fo}$ and run the model:

$$Y_i = \alpha + \beta X_i + \lambda_1 D_i^{mo} + \lambda_2 D_i^{ml} + \lambda_3 D_i^{fo} + \beta_1 X_i D_i^{mo} + \beta_2 X_i D_i^{ml} + \beta_3 X_i D_i^{fo} + \varepsilon_i.$$

Now:

$E(Y|\text{wage rate } X_o, \text{ male and educated to 16 only}) = \alpha + (\beta + \beta_1)X_o + \lambda_1;$
$E(Y|\text{wage rate } X_o, \text{ male and educated beyond 16}) = \alpha + (\beta + \beta_2)X_o + \lambda_2;$
$E(Y|\text{wage rate } X_o, \text{ female and educated to 16 only}) = \alpha + (\beta + \beta_3)X_o + \lambda_3;$
$E(Y|\text{wage rate } X_o, \text{ female and educated beyond 16}) = \alpha + (\beta + \beta_1)X_o.$

In this model, each of the four categories is parameterized differently, and it is to be noted that for each case the constant term and coefficient on the wage rate are unique to the specific category. This is, then, equivalent to running a separate regression for each category and demands, therefore, that there are sufficient observations in each category to allow such a regression. The advantage of running the regression over all available observations and using dummies is that the detail of difference may be tested via standard t- and F-tests (given that the model is deemed satisfactory and passes the diagnostic tests). It is very important to recognize that in running one regression with dummies makes the assumption that the error variance is constant across all observations (a testable assumption). Dummy variables accommodate abrupt shifts; in some cases (such as modelling a reaction to a policy shift) a more smooth adjustment to the two regimes is called for, and dummy variables may be used to model smooth transitions between states (see **Spline functions** and also **Varying parameter models**). Dummy variables may also be used to quantify polytomous qualitative variables.

The interpretation of intercept dummies must be carried out with care; suppose that an intercept shift dummy is included in a simple linear function:

$$Y_i = \alpha + \gamma D_i + \beta X_i + \varepsilon_i$$

where $D_i = 0$ for some observations (regime 0) and unity for the remainder (regime 1). The parameter γ measures the change in expected Y due to moving from regime 0 to regime 1. Now suppose, for example, that the relationship is log-linear:

$$\ell n Y_i = \alpha + \gamma D_i + \beta \ell n X_i + \varepsilon_i.$$

The parameter β is immediately recognized as the (point) elasticity of Y with respect to X; γ cannot be interpreted as an elasticity because the dummy takes on values of zero and one only, and the shift between the two values is not a marginal change. The interpretation of dummies in such a regression is related to the difference between point and arc elasticities. Consider the following deterministic relationship: let

$$\ell n Y_i = \alpha + \beta \ell n X_i$$

and suppose X_i grows by 100g% to become X_{i+1}: $X_{i+1} = (1 + g)X_i$; then:

$$\ell n Y_{i+1} = \alpha + \beta \ell n X_i + \beta \ell n(1 + g) = \ell n Y_i + \beta \ell n(1 + g)$$

that is, $$Y_{i+1}/Y_i = (1+g)^\beta$$

i.e. Y_i has grown by $100[(1 + g)^\beta - 1]\%$; if and only if g is small does this approximate to $100\beta g\%$.

Since ℓn and exp are inverse functions, the log-linear model with a shift dummy may be written as:

$$\ell n Y_i = \alpha + \gamma\, \ell n(\exp(D_i)) + \beta\, \ell n X_i + \varepsilon_i$$

and between regimes 0 and 1 the variable $\exp(D_i)$ changes from 1 to e; hence the percentage change in this variable, $\exp(D_i)$, from regime 0 to regime 1 is $100(e - 1)$ and so the percentage change in Y is given by $100(e^\gamma - 1)\%$.

Dummy variables allow the investigator to examine hypotheses of parameter shifts due to qualitative variables; it is not the only means by which such hypotheses may be examined, and variance component models (considered in **Panel data and variance component models**) and random coefficient models (see the entry of that title) may be better suited to particular applications. Other uses of dummy variables allow the investigator to examine issues of forecasting (see **Forecasting**).

This entry has only considered the use of dummies when they appear as regressors. For the important case of dummies as independent variables in regression analysis, see **Limited dependent variables**.

Further reading

Suits (1984) examines the use of dummies to test hypotheses of differences; see also Greene and Seaks (1991). The interpretation of dummies in logarithmic models is considered in Halvorsen and Palmquist (1980) and also in Kennedy (1981a).

Encompassing tests

Encompassing tests are used increasingly as a test of a model's acceptability. A model is said to encompass another if the former can explain the results of the latter, and a good model should not only explain the data at hand but also be capable of explaining a rival model's success or failure in explaining the same data set. Encompassing may be defined at a high level of generality, and can be used when competing models differ, for example, by reference to their choice of endogenous variables, their functional form or their choice of explanatory (conditioning) variables. Encompassing tests are similar to, but different from, non-nested hypothesis tests (see **Non-nested hypotheses**).

There are three forms of encompassing: mean encompassing, variance encompassing and forecast encompassing. Model H_1 mean encompasses model H_2 if the residuals of model H_2 can be explained by model H_1; model H_1 variance encompasses model H_2 if the variance of errors from model H_2 can be explained by model H_1; model H_1 forecast encompasses model H_2 if the latter's forecasts can be explained by those of the former. If the models are:

$$\text{Model } H_1\text{: } Y = X\beta + \varepsilon \quad \text{and} \quad \text{Model } H_2\text{: } Y = Z\gamma + \nu$$

Model 1 defines the conditional distribution of Y given X and model 2 defines the conditional distribution of Y given Z and the principle of encompassing tests is that they examine the conditional distributions of Y given X and Z under both H_1 and H_2. If the parameter estimates are $\hat{\beta}$ and $\hat{\gamma}$ and the model's error variances are estimated as $\hat{\sigma}_1^2$ and $\hat{\sigma}_2^2$ respectively, then the mean encompassing test, when H_2 is viewed as the rival model, is performed by comparing $\hat{\gamma}$ with $\text{plim}(\hat{\gamma}|H_1)$ and the variance encompassing test is performed by comparing $\hat{\sigma}_2^2$ with $\text{plim}(\hat{\sigma}_2^2|H_1)$. It is also possible to perform the complete encompassing test (CET) which examines jointly $\hat{\gamma}$ and $\hat{\sigma}_2^2$ with their plims under H_1.

In a linear framework the more general encompassing tests link the J- and F-tests of non-nested hypotheses. In comparison to the more traditional non-nested tests, the F-test of this model comparison involves running model 1 with, as additional regressors, those variables of Z which are not already accommodated within X and testing their inclusion by an F-statistic (and then the roles of the models is reversed so that model 2 is examined with the inclusion of those variables of X not accommodated within Z). It may be shown that the F-test is a mean encompassing test.

The non-nested J-test of these models requires that the predicted values from model 2, given by $Z\hat{\gamma}$, are included as an additional regressor in model 1 and the significance of this regressor is examined by a t-statistic. This is equivalent, here, to a variance encompassing test.

The forecast encompassing test is carried out as follows. Let the two models be estimated recursively to obtain the one-step-ahead forecasts.

Denoting by $\hat{\beta}_{(t-1)}$ the estimate of β using only the data up to and including period t−1, the one-step-ahead forecast of Y is given by $\hat{Y}_{(t)} = X\hat{\beta}_{(t-1)}$; define $\hat{\gamma}_{(t-1)}$ similarly and denote the one-step-ahead forecasts from model 2 by $\tilde{Y}_{(t)}$. If model 2 is the rival model then the forecast errors are given by $\tilde{\varepsilon}_t = Y_t - \tilde{Y}_{(t)}$; consider now the artificial regression:

$$\tilde{\varepsilon}_t = \delta(\tilde{Y}_{(t)} - \hat{Y}_{(t)}) + \eta_t$$

and test, by a t-statistic, the significance of δ. If $\delta = 0$ is rejected then the difference in the forecasts is significant in explaining the one-step-ahead forecast errors from model 2 and model 1 then forecast encompasses model 2. This test has at least two important features: it is easy to implement, and to run the test it is not in fact necessary to know the specification of the rival model. In the example used here the forecasts from model 2 have been constructed as one-step-ahead forecasts, but if only the *ex ante* forecasts of the rival model were known (and not its full specification) this test could still be performed by the artificial regression.

Notwithstanding any results from encompassing tests, it is very important to examine the diagnostic tests associated with the competing models, for these are good indicators of false models.

Further reading
See Mizon and Richard (1986) and Chong and Hendry (1986).

Engle–Granger representation theorem

The general autoregressive distributed lag model of order m (ADL(m)), which is written in terms of zero-mean variables and with one regressor only for ease of exposition, is:

$$Y_t = \Sigma_{j=0}^{m}\beta_j X_{t-j} + \Sigma_{j=1}^{m-1}\gamma_j Y_{t-j-1} + \varepsilon_t$$

and this may be re-parameterized as the error correction model (ECM):

$$\Delta Y_t = \Sigma_{i=1}^{m-1}(\lambda_i \Delta X_{t-i} + \theta_i \Delta Y_{t-i}) + \beta_o \Delta X_t + (\theta - 1)(Y_{t-1} - \phi X_{t-1}) + \varepsilon_t$$

where $\beta = \Sigma_{i=0}^{m}\beta_i$, $\lambda_i = -\Sigma_{j=i+1}^{m}\beta_j$, $\theta = \Sigma_{i=0}^{m-1}\gamma_i$, $\theta_i = -\Sigma_{j=i}^{m-1}\gamma_j$ and $\phi = \beta/(1-\theta)$ (assuming that $\theta \neq 1$) (this transformation is described in **Error correction models**).

If the variables under consideration are integrated, then the ECM representation has significant advantages over the ADL form; one of the important messages from the work on integration and cointegration is that one cannot freely mix variables of differing orders of integration in a regression equation. Suppose that both Y and X are I(1) variables; then the original ADL form of the model involves a regression of an I(1) variable on I(1) regressors and standard regression theory is not applicable to such a regression. However, if Y and X are not only I(1) variables but are also cointegrated, with a cointegrating coefficient ϕ, then ΔX_t and ΔY_t are both I(0) variables and, by the cointegrating relationship, $(Y_{t-1} - \phi X_{t-1})$ is also an I(0) variable. Hence a regression taking the form of the ECM is a regression equation involving only stationary (that is, I(0)) variables, and standard regression theory applies. The Engle–Granger representation theorem demonstrates that if two variables are each I(1) but cointegrated then the short-run dynamics may be written as an error correction model (that is, there is a mechanism which constrains the errors between the two series to be bounded); it also shows the converse, that for an error correction model to hold over I(1) variables they must also be cointegrated. This result facilitates estimation of the cointegrating relationship between two variables.

Knowledge of the 'error', $Y_{t-1} - \phi X_{t-1}$, and hence knowledge of the cointegrating coefficient ϕ, is required in order to pursue estimation of the ECM equation. One could run the regression:

$$\Delta Y_t = \sum_{i=1}^{m-1}(\lambda_i \Delta X_{t-i} + \theta_i \Delta Y_{t-i}) + \beta_o \Delta X_t + \xi Y_{t-1} + \eta X_{t-1} + \varepsilon_t$$

by OLS without restriction and then recover the cointegrating coefficient as $-\eta/\xi$, but this involves a regression utilizing variables of differing orders of integration and then standard regression theory is not applicable. The common estimation route is known as the Engle–Granger two-step procedure. First test that both Y and X are I(1), then run the simple regression of Y on X by OLS and test the residuals for stationarity; let the estimated coefficient be $\hat{\phi}$ so that the residuals are given by $\hat{e}_t = Y_t - \hat{\phi} X_t$. If Y and X are cointegrated then these residuals will exhibit stationarity, and suppose that the Dickey–Fuller (or Augmented Dickey–Fuller) test confirms that the residuals from the regression of Y on X are stationary and hence that variables are cointegrated. The second step is to run the ECM form of the model replacing the true error, $(Y_{t-1} - \phi X_{t-1})$, with the 'estimated error', $\hat{e}_{t-1} = (Y_{t-1} - \hat{\phi} X_{t-1})$; in this form all the variables are stationary and estimation of the ECM equation may proceed. An alternative approach to the estimation of the error correction is to run the unrestricted ADL(m) model and estimate $\hat{\phi}$ by $\sum_{i=1}^{m} \hat{\beta}_i / (1 - \sum_{i=1}^{m-1} \hat{\gamma}_i)$, and use this estimate in the ECM representation.

Using the ADL model, or the Engle–Granger procedure, to estimate the ECM model is appropriate when the coefficient of the long-run relation is not known *a priori*. In some circumstances economic theory may indicate the long-run coefficient; for example, in examining consumption expenditures, economic theory may indicate that the long-run consumption elasticity with respect to income is unity. This may be translated into the restriction that the cointegrating coefficient is unity, which is a testable proposition. If, in this example, $\hat{e}_t$ is defined by $(\ell n\,\text{consumption} - \ell n\,\text{income})_t$, and a Dickey–Fuller (or Augmented DF) test does not deny the hypothesis of a unit cointegrating parameter (that is both ℓn(consumption) and ℓn(income) are

I(1) variables, and $\hat{e}_t \sim I(0)$), then the ECM model may be estimated by OLS using $\hat{e}_{t-1}$ as the errors. The errors in this example have been constructed from considerations of economic theory, rather than having been constructed from a regression of ℓn(consumption) on ℓn(income). The hypothesis that the cointegrating coefficient is one is testable: if the variable $Y_t - X_t$ is stationary, but both Y and X are I(1) variables then the hypothesis that the cointegrating coefficient is unity may be accepted.

With more than one regressor, say k regressors, the ADL model becomes:

$$Y_t = \sum_{i=0}^{m} \sum_{j=1}^{k} \beta_{ij} X_{t-i,j} + \sum_{j=1}^{m-1} \gamma_j Y_{t-j-1} + \varepsilon_t$$

which may be written as

$$\Delta Y_t = \sum_{i=1}^{m-1} \left[\sum_{j=1}^{k} \lambda_{ij} \Delta X_{t-i,j} + \theta_i \Delta Y_{t-i} \right] + \sum_{j=1}^{k} \beta_{oj} \Delta X_{tj}$$

$$+ (\theta - 1)(Y_{t-1} - \sum_{j=1}^{k} \phi_j X_{t-1,j}) + \varepsilon_t .$$

When the variables are integrated of order one, this model seeks to impose a cointegrating vector given by $(1\ -\phi_1\ -\phi_2 \ldots -\phi_k)'$ and to estimate this model one may, having confirmed that Y_t and X_{tj} (j = 1, 2, . . , k) are all I(1) variables, run the regression of Y on the k regressors and test that the residuals are stationary; if their stationarity is confirmed then they may be inserted into this ECM and OLS will yield estimates of the short-run parameters and of the speed of adjustment. However, this assumes that there is just one cointegrating vector which relates Y_t to the k regressors, X_{tj}. If there is more than one cointegrating vector (and amongst any k I(1) variables they may be up to k – 1 cointegrating vectors) then the regression of Y_t on the k regressors X_{tj} will not yield the appropriate 'error', as more than one 'error' exists. For more details of this, see **Integration**, **Cointegration** and also **Johansen method** and **Vector autoregressions**.

If the X variables are not all exogenous then this equation is better examined as one of a set of simultaneous equations; a VAR approach, utilizing a Johansen test is an appropriate test of the single-equation specification. If the Johansen test indicates the existence of just one cointegrating vector then the above method is legitimized, since the 'error' is then unique and the regression of Y on the k regressors will be a super-consistent estimating approach. Because the single-equation approach is justified only when there is exactly one cointegrating vector an initial examination of the model as a VAR representation in which the existence and number of cointegrating vectors is examined using the Johansen method is favoured. If only one such vector exists, the single equation ECM model is justified, and if more than one such vector exists the single equation approach is deficient.

Further reading
Further details may be found in Engle and Granger (1987); see also Stock (1987) and Banerjee *et al.* (1986) for discussion of the estimation of cointegrating vectors. Cointegrated variables and error correction models are further discussed in **Johansen method**.

Error correction models

Error correction mechanisms were introduced into the economics literature by Phillips (1954) and by Sargan (1964). Consider the general autoregressive distributed lag model of order m (ADL(m)), which is written in terms of zero-mean variables and with one regressor only for ease of exposition:

$$Y_t = \Sigma_{j=0}^{m} \beta_j X_{t-j} + \Sigma_{j=1}^{m-1} \gamma_j Y_{t-j-1} + \varepsilon_t .$$

The m + 1 terms in current and lagged X may be re-written as:

$$- \beta_m (X_{t-m+1} - X_{t-m}) - (\beta_m + \beta_{m-1})(X_{t-m+2} - X_{t-m+1})$$
$$- (\beta_m + \beta_{m-1} + \beta_{m-2})(X_{t-m+3} - X_{t-m+2})$$
$$- \ldots\ldots$$
$$- (\beta_m + \beta_{m-1} + \ldots \beta_2)(X_{t-1} - X_{t-2})$$
$$+ (\beta_m + \beta_{m-1} + \ldots + \beta_2 + \beta_1) X_{t-1} + \beta_o X_t$$

which may be written as:

$$-\beta_m \Delta X_{t-m+1} - (\beta_m + \beta_{m-1}) \Delta X_{t-m+2} - \ldots - (\beta_m + \beta_{m-1} + \ldots + \beta_2) \Delta X_{t-1}$$
$$+ \beta_o \Delta X_t + (\beta_m + \beta_{m-1} + \ldots + \beta_o) X_{t-1}$$

which is equal to:

$$\Sigma_{i=1}^{m-1} \lambda_i \Delta X_{t-i} + \beta_o \Delta X_t + \beta X_{t-1}$$

where $\beta = \Sigma_{i=0}^{m} \beta_i$ and $\lambda_i = -\Sigma_{j=i+1}^{m} \beta_j$.

The m terms in lagged Y may be written, similarly, as:

$$- \gamma_{m-1}(Y_{t-m+1} - Y_{t-m}) - (\gamma_{m-1} + \gamma_{m-2})(Y_{t-m+2} - Y_{t-m+1})$$
$$- (\gamma_{m-1} + \gamma_{m-2} + \gamma_{m-3})(Y_{t-m+3} - Y_{t-m+2})$$
$$- \ldots\ldots$$
$$- (\gamma_{m-1} + \gamma_{m-2} + \ldots \gamma_2 + \gamma_1)(Y_{t-1} - Y_{t-2})$$
$$+ (\gamma_{m-1} + \gamma_{m-2} + \ldots \gamma_1 + \gamma_o) Y_{t-1}$$

which may be written as:

$$-\gamma_{m-1}\Delta Y_{t-m+1} - (\gamma_{m-1} + \gamma_{m-2})\Delta Y_{t-m+2} - \ldots - (\gamma_{m-1} + \gamma_{m-2} + \ldots \gamma_1)\Delta Y_{t-1}$$

$$+ (\gamma_{m-1} + \gamma_{m-2} + \ldots \gamma_o)Y_{t-1}$$

which is equal to:

$$\Sigma_{i=1}^{m-1} \theta_i \Delta Y_{t-i} + \theta Y_{t-1}$$

where $\theta = \Sigma_{i=0}^{m-1} \gamma_i$ and $\theta_i = -\Sigma_{j=i}^{m-1} \gamma_j$.

Hence the ADL(m) model may be written as:

$$Y_t = \Sigma_{i=1}^{m-1} \lambda_i \Delta X_{t-i} + \beta_o \Delta X_t + \beta X_{t-1} + \Sigma_{i=1}^{m-1} \theta_i \Delta Y_{t-i} + \theta Y_{t-1} + \varepsilon_t$$

that is:

$$\Delta Y_t = \Sigma_{i=1}^{m-1}(\lambda_i \Delta X_{t-i} + \theta_i \Delta Y_{t-i}) + \beta_o \Delta X_t + (\theta - 1)(Y_{t-1} - \phi X_{t-1}) + \varepsilon_t$$

where $\phi = \beta/(1 - \theta)$ (assuming that $\theta \neq 1$).

Re-parameterized in this way the ADL(m) model is now in the form of an error correction model (ECM) in which the current change in Y (ΔY_t) is a linear function of changes in X (ΔX_{t-i} for i = 0, 1, . . m−1), previous changes in Y (ΔY_{t-i} for i = 1, . . m−1) and the error correction term ($Y_{t-1} - \phi X_{t-1}$). This last term may be interpreted as follows: in the steady state, when X_t = X* and Y_t = Y* for all t, the static long-run equilibrium solution of the ADL(m) model is $Y^* = \phi X^*$. This may also be seen from the ECM representation, for when $\Delta Y_t = \Delta X_t = 0$ (all t) it is clear that $Y_t = \phi X_t$; this defines the long-run relationship between the variables, and so if $Y_t \neq \phi X_t$ the difference can be described as the 'error' between Y and its long-run value.

Now suppose that Y is not presently on its long-run path, and suppose that $Y_{t-1} > \phi X_{t-1}$; from the ECM representation this ensures that there is pressure, from the error correction term, for $\Delta Y_t < 0$, so long as $(\theta - 1) < 0$; i.e. $(\theta - 1) < 0$ ensures that when Y_{t-1} lies above its long-run value Y_t will be less than Y_{t-1} due to this correction term. Similarly, $(\theta - 1) < 0$ ensures that when Y_{t-1} lies below its long-run value $Y_t > Y_{t-1}$. Thus, if $\theta < 1$, in 'disequilibrium' Y_t will move towards its long-run path, both from above and below, and the movement will be in proportion to the last period's 'error' given by $(Y_{t-1} - \phi X_{t-1})$. Clearly, however, if $\theta < 0$ the 'correction' is explosive and the process of adjustment will not be stable. A stability condition of the original ADL(m) model is, therefore, $0 < \theta < 1$ and this condition ensures that the adjustment process exhibits stable negative feedback. The coefficient $\theta - 1$ measures the speed of adjustment of Y_t to disequilibrium.

Error correction models are used widely in econometrics; when economic theory proposes an equilibrium relationship between two variables this may be viewed as the 'long-run' steady-state solution to an unrestricted ADL(m) model which may be written equivalently as an ECM. The ECM form of the model may be seen as comprising the short-run transitory effects and the long-run relationship and describes how the long-run solution is achieved via negative feedback and error correction.

If the variables under consideration are integrated, then the ECM representation has significant advantages over the ADL form; one of the important messages from the work on integration and cointegration is that one cannot freely mix variables of differing orders of integration in a regression equation. Suppose that both Y and X are I(1) variables; then the original ADL form of the model involves a regression of an I(1) variable on I(1) regressors and standard regression theory is not applicable to such a regression. However, if Y and X are not only I(1) variables but are also cointegrated, with a cointegrating coefficient ϕ, then ΔX_t and ΔY_t are both I(0) variables and, by the cointegrating relationship, $(Y_{t-1} - \phi X_{t-1})$ is also an I(0) variable. Hence a regression taking the form of the ECM is a regression equation involving only stationary (that is, I(0)) variables, and standard regression theory applies. The Engle and Granger Representation Theorem demonstrates that if two variables are each I(1) but cointegrated then the short-run dynamics may be written as an ECM and this facilitates estimation of such a model (this is discussed further in **Engle–Granger representation theorem**).

Further reading

Davidson *et al.* (1978) is a very good example of the error correction model in practice.

Error term

The error term in a regression equation arises for a variety of reasons. Suppose it is proposed that some economic variable, Y, is determined by some other economic variable, X: Y = f(X) where f is some function. Here, Y and X refer to the theoretical constructs of the variables and not to their measured counterparts; thus Y = f(X) is a theoretical model, not a data model.

Because Y = f(X) is a theoretical proposition it necessarily resides in the c-domain (the domain of theoretical constructs). The theoretical proposition is a simplification of reality, the partial nature of the analysis ensures that it is made subject to a *ceteris paribus* clause, and it is expressed in terms of theoretical variables. In an important sense the act of simplification, an essential component of theorizing, may be seen to define the elements of the *ceteris paribus* clause: all variables whose influence is excluded from the theory are effectively placed in the *ceteris paribus* clause. The conceptual world of *ceteris paribus* will, almost certainly, be violated within the material world, and the violation may be of any magnitude and may be in any particular dimension (that is, those other variables which influence the dependent variable but which have been excluded from the analysis may vary from one observation to another and may be of any number). Moreover, it is unusual for any theoretical proposition to state fully the contents of the *ceteris paribus* clause; thus any deviation of an observed value of Y from the predicted value, given by f(X), may be attributed, rather generally, to the violation of *ceteris paribus* (or it may be attributed to the falsity of the theoretical proposition).

To be able to attribute deviations between Y and f(X) in this simple dichotomous fashion (either the theory is 'true' but the *ceteris paribus* clause is violated in the data set or the theory is 'false') presumes that there are precise observations on the theoretical variables, and that the functional form f is known. In any particular situation, however, it is typically the case that theoretical variables are not themselves measured but, rather, proxies are used and, moreover, the measures of those proxies are typically subject to measurement error; equally, theory typically does not indicate the precise nature of the functional form, and a particular investigation assumes a (simple) functional dependence, denoted by f*. Let the measured proxy for Y be denoted by Y^m, and that for X be denoted by X^m; at any point in time, then, Y^m differs from the predicted value given by $f^*(X^m)$ because:

either **A**: The theory is 'true' but:
1. the *ceteris paribus* clause is violated;
2. the measured proxies are not identical to the values of the theoretical variables;
3. the function used, f*, does not correspond exactly with the theoretical function, f;

or **B:** The theory is 'false'.

Typically, the (tentatively) assumed function, f*, is a simple linear form written as $Y^m = \alpha + \beta X^m$; this particular form may be called a 'model' (though not a fully specified model) of the theoretical process: the 'theory' *per se* is the statement that Y is determined by X *ceteris paribus*, and to encapsulate this in the equation $Y^m = \alpha + \beta X^m$ is a specific (and not unique) way of writing this statement. In fact, for any given theoretical proposition there are many (actually an infinity) of potential corresponding models.

The theory states that Y is determined by X *ceteris paribus*, and observations denoted by Y^m and X^m are available; they are examined using an imposed functional form, typically linear: $Y^m = \alpha + \beta X^m$. Because the theory is inevitably expressed in the language of theoretical constructs and within a world of *ceteris paribus*, the data are not all expected to lie exactly on a straight line. Let these anticipated differences be denoted by ε so that the model is written as $Y^m_i = \alpha + \beta X^m_i + \varepsilon_i$ where there are n observations: i = 1, . . , n. ε_i is the error term and may be described as an 'anticipated difference' since the data are not expected to lie exactly on a straight line; for any given observation the realized value of ε_i may take on any value.

In this form the parameters α and β are unknown and ε_i is also unknown; but then the equation $Y^m_i = \alpha + \beta X^m_i + \varepsilon_i$ simply defines ε_i in terms of unknowns. This is a position of some circularity, and to proceed it is necessary to impose some particular structure on the error. It is helpful to note that one goal of econometric modelling is to specify the relationship between the variables in such a way as to minimize the contribution of the factors encapsulated by ε_i. If the relationship is represented by the simple linear dependence of measured Y on measured X, then the dependence on X^m is the systematic component of measured Y and the term ε_i may be called the non-systematic component: the former component represents what is thought to be known about the determination of Y^m while the latter represents the element of ignorance.

Although the error term may be seen as encapsulating ignorance, it is important to understand precisely what is meant by ignorance; specifically, ε is a non-systematic error. That ε is non-systematic is equivalent to saying that there is no available information which could be used to predict any particular realized value of the error. ε is, thus, an indicator of ignorance of the process which relates the measured proxies, and the concept of a random variable can be utilized to capture this notion of ignorance. Treating ε_i as if it were a random variable with a probability density function given by $g_i(\varepsilon_i)$, the concept of 'non-systematic' may be made operational by imposing the following characteristics on ε_i and g_i:

1. each g_i is a zero mean, symmetric distribution;
2. $g_i = g_j$ (= g) for all $i \neq j$;
3. ε_i is independently distributed of ε_j for all $i \neq j$;
4. ε_i is independently distributed of all X^m, for all i;
5. g is such that 'small' values of ε_i are more likely than 'large' values: g is a distribution which places little probability in the tails, and concentrates the probability symmetrically around the value of zero.

Of course, to utilize the concept of a random variable as an indicator of ignorance requires that there is some conceptual population from which the actual value of each ε_i (i = 1, . . , n) may be viewed as a random drawing. In the case of regression analysis the population, typically, does not exist – it is a theoretical construct and is the route by which a theory of inference based upon statistical theory may be constructed.

The theory states Y = f(X) *ceteris paribus*; this could be written as Y = f(X) + F(X, Z); Z is the complete set of other theoretical variables which contribute to the determination of Y. The term F(X, Z) thus encapsulates both the role of the interactions between X and other variables, Z, and the direct contributions of the variables in Z to the determination of Y. In a world of *ceteris paribus* the analysis abstracts from the role of the variables in Z (which may, or may not, be a finite set) and treats them as 'held constant'; the theorizing has chosen to concentrate on X as the salient variable and in this theoretical world the role F(X, Z) is, then, *deemed* constant. Definitionally, one could then write the following:

$$Y_i^m = \alpha + \beta X_i^m + [F(X, Z) + (Y^m - Y) + \{f(X) - (\alpha + \beta X^m)\}]_i;$$

and thus $$Y_i^m = \alpha + \beta X_i^m + \varepsilon_i$$

where $$\varepsilon_i = [F(X, Z) + (Y^m - Y) + \{f(X) - (\alpha + \beta X^m)\}]_i.$$

The first term of ε indicates the error due to the potential failure of the *ceteris paribus* assumption in the material world; the second term is due to the difference between the theoretical construct, Y, and its material counterpart Y^m, the measured proxy; and the third term reflects the difference between the theoretical determination of Y attributable to the direct influence of X with Z fixed, f(X), and the linear way in which this is encapsulated in the model.

This model focuses only upon the role of the variable X and is, therefore, a less than complete statement of the way the world was; also, the available data are not, typically, drawn from anything which remotely resembles a repeatable experiment. Nevertheless, there is nothing in this statement which prevents the errors, ε, from being treated *as if* they were random variables. The 'population' from which they are drawn is a theoretical construct, and it arises from consideration of the counter-factual situation: if those myriad factors which determined the nature of the *ceteris paribus* failure had been different and if those myriad factors which determined the difference between the theoretical constructs and their measured counterparts had been different, then the realized error would have been different. That any realized value of the error *could* take on any value is the justification for treating it as if it were a random variable, and the nature of various factors which determine the value of the error, in part a consequence of the level of abstraction, is the source of the population concept.

The level of abstraction is a choice to be exercised by the investigator, and the above argument of a conceptual population not only puts limits on that abstraction (the error must be non-systematic and more likely to be 'small' than 'large') but also, by treating the net result of a model's omissions, approximations and errors *as if it were* a realization of a random variable, allows statistical inference of the underlying behavioural relationship. Model-building, certainly, seeks to reduce the error term as far as is required by the purpose at hand, but model-building does not seek to eliminate the error completely: if there is no error term the model does not represent a theory since there is no abstraction.

The population from which the error term in a regression analysis is drawn is commonly, if not always, a conceptual population; it typically has no material counterpart but is, rather, a device, a mechanism, by which it is recognized that the actual error could have taken on any value. The error at any point could have taken on any value, but the investigator deems just one value to have been realized; the one realized value is, further, deemed to be like a random drawing from a probability distribution. The implications of this view of the world are at least two-fold: first, although only one value of the measured dependent variable actually occurred, the full model allows any number of possible values to have theoretically occurred; second, by the use of a theoretical population from which the observations are deemed to be a random drawing, one can then utilize the technology of statistical inference in order to further understanding of the underlying economic behaviour. That only one 'sample' from the conceptualized population is available is no handicap in the use of statistical theory; indeed, even when repeated sampling is *actually* possible, inference may proceed legitimately from just one sample.

This approach largely follows that of Haavelmo (1944) who, in a classic paper, sought to justify the use of a stochastic model in the analysis of economic data on the grounds that one can only interpret such concepts as 'mean', correlation', 'estimator', 'variance', etc., if there is an underlying model of the process which is stochastic in nature. He argued that it is proper to

> assume that the *whole* set of, say n, observations may be considered as *one* observation of n variables (or a 'sample point') following an n-dimensional *joint* probability law, the 'existence' of which may be purely hypothetical. Then, one can test hypotheses regarding this joint probability law, and draw inference as to its possible form, by means of *one* sample point (in n dimensions). (p. iii)

Haavelmo's use of joint probability is, therefore, not designed to be a perfect portrayal but rather a reflection of, a way of modelling, the real world: it is not necessary that this probability distribution exists in the material world, what is important is that the probability model is a convenient and powerful tool of abstraction. Here, the word 'powerful' is used in the sense that such a model is capable of facilitating an understanding of the material world. The purpose of the stochastic model is to enable data analysis to contribute to an understanding of economic phenomena via the use of statistical inference, and to this end the stochastic model has proved to be successful. Whether the probabilities 'exists' or not is irrelevant; if analysis proceeds *as if* they existed it is possible to make statements about real phenomena that are sufficient for practical purposes.

Much of econometrics is concerned with establishing whether the general model $Y_i = f(X_{i1}, \ldots, X_{ik}) + \varepsilon_i$ is adequate; this model posits that the variable Y is determined systematically by the k explanatory variables specified by $\{X_j, j = 1, , , k\}$ via the function specified as f, and all non-systematic components are relegated to the error term ε_i. If the measured proxies are inadequate, if the set of explanatory variables is improperly specified, if the chosen function f is inadequate, if Y is not only determined by the explanatory variables but they are, in turn, dependent on Y, then the error term will lose its desirable non-systematic characteristics. In such circumstances the model will be inadequate and require some modifications. Tests of the model's specifications via test of the error term, therefore, critically important to econometric analysis.

Further reading

See Haavelmo (1944) especially, and for a historical perspective on the use of stochastic models in economics, see Morgan (1990).

Errors in variables

Economic theory is expressed in terms of theoretical variables, but empirical analysis demands the availability of measured counterparts. Measured variables are proxies of their theoretical counterparts and are often measured with error. As an example, consider a model of money demand: economic theory is expressed in terms of a theoretical measure of the money supply and the officially available statistics are only proxies for this concept; moreover, the available data are almost certainly measured with error. As evidence of the latter point, consider the frequent 'revisions' to official statistics. The simplest analysis of errors in variables supposes that the available measure comprises the 'true' measure plus a non-systematic error, and this model will first be explained for the simple case of regression with one regressor. If the 'true' model is $Y_i = \alpha + \beta X_i + \varepsilon_i$ but both regressand and regressor are measured with error, suppose that:

$$\tilde{Y}_i = Y_i + u_i \quad \text{and} \quad \tilde{X}_i = X_i + v_i$$

where the variables with a tilde indicate the available measure. Substitution yields:

$$\tilde{Y}_i - u_i = \alpha + \beta(\tilde{X}_i - v_i) + \varepsilon_i$$

i.e.

$$\tilde{Y}_i = \alpha + \beta\tilde{X}_i + (\varepsilon_i - \beta v_i + u_i).$$

Suppose that all three random terms, ε_i, u_i and v_i, are from zero mean distributions, are independently distributed, are mutually independent and are independent of all the X_i; their variances are denoted by σ_ε^2 , σ_u^2 and σ_v^2 respectively. Under these assumptions, it is clear that:

$$\text{Cov}(\tilde{X}_i, \varepsilon_i - \beta v_i + u_i) = \text{Cov}(X_i + v_i, \varepsilon_i - \beta v_i + u_i) = -\beta\sigma_v^2 .$$

Thus, when measured Y is regressed on measured X, the regressor is correlated with the error term and one of the assumptions necessary for ordinary least squares estimators to be unbiased is violated. The source of the problem is the error in measuring X; if the only source of measurement error were in measuring Y then this problem would not arise. If OLS is applied, to yield the estimator $\hat{\beta}$, then:

$$\text{plim}(\hat{\beta}) = \beta + \text{plim}\frac{\sum_{i=1}^{n}\tilde{x}_i(\varepsilon_i - \beta v_i + u_i)}{\sum_{i=1}^{n}\tilde{x}_i^2}$$

$$= \beta - \beta\sigma_v^2/(\sigma_x^2 + \sigma^2{}_v)$$

where σ_x^2 is the variance in X. Since all the variances are positive, $\hat{\beta}$ is necessarily biased and inconsistent: $\hat{\beta}$ underestimates β. The traditional model without errors in the regressor is a special case of this model; setting $\sigma_v^2 = 0$ the familiar model reappears and then it is seen that OLS produces an unbiased estimator. The probability limit of $\hat{\beta}$ may also be written as $\beta/[1 + (\sigma_v^2/\sigma_x^2)]$ from which it is clear that the smaller is the ratio of the variance of the error in measurement to the variance of the true regressor the smaller is the bias. It is also clear that the larger is σ_v^2 the smaller is plim($\hat{\beta}$), and the effect of biasing the estimate towards zero is known as attenuation.

In the more general case of several regressors, all of which are measured with error, the only unambiguous conclusion is that OLS produces biased and inconsistent estimators; however, the direction of bias cannot be stated in general and both over- and under-estimation can occur.

The errors in variables 'problem' arises because the regressor is stochastic and not independent of the error; hence bias results if OLS is applied. The standard response is to use an instrumental variable estimation technique; for example, with time-series data, assuming that the (composite) error is not autocorrelated it is possible to use the lagged value of $\tilde{X}$ as an instrument for, given no autocorrelation in the error term, this is independent of the current error but is (most likely to be) highly correlated with the current value of $\tilde{X}$. Alternative instruments are derived from so-called 'grouping' methods. Consider splitting the data into two groups by reference to the size of $\tilde{X}$: group 1 consists of those observations on $\tilde{X}$ below the median and group 2 consists of those observation above the median. Then consider the estimator:

$$\tilde{\beta}_{IV} = (\bar{\tilde{Y}}_2 - \bar{\tilde{Y}}_1)/(\bar{\tilde{X}}_2 - \bar{\tilde{X}}_1)$$

where $\bar{\tilde{Y}}_i$ and $\bar{\tilde{X}}_i$ represent the mean values of $\tilde{Y}$ and $\tilde{X}$ in group i, i = 1, 2. This estimator is the instrumental variable estimator when the instrument, Z_i, is defined by:

$$\begin{aligned} Z_i &= 1 \text{ if } \tilde{X}_i > \text{median of } \tilde{X} \\ &= -1 \text{ if } \tilde{X}_i < \text{median of } \tilde{X}. \end{aligned}$$

This method, necessarily, splits the data by reference to the values of $\tilde{X}$ as a proxy for a division based upon the unobservable values of X. However, if the measurement error variance is large the actual division will not correspond closely to a division based upon X and by using more groups the efficiency of the instrumental variable estimator may be improved.

A more efficient IV estimator may be constructed by splitting $\tilde{X}$ into three groups, retaining the top and bottom thirds and constructing the respective means. Then:

$$\tilde{\beta}_{IV} = (\bar{\tilde{Y}}_3 - \bar{\tilde{Y}}_1)/(\bar{\tilde{X}}_3 - \bar{\tilde{X}}_1)$$

which is the instrumental variable estimator when the instrument, Z_i, is defined by:

$$\begin{aligned} Z_i &= 1 \text{ if } \tilde{X}_i \text{ lies in the top 1/3 of observations} \\ &= -1 \text{ if } \tilde{X}_i \text{ lies in the bottom 1/3 of observations.} \end{aligned}$$

The object of these grouping methods is to reduce the influence of the measurement error by averaging the data; a yet more efficient approach is to use the rank of $\tilde{X}$ as an instrument: $Z_i = i$ where the $\tilde{X}_i$ have been ranked by size. Each method, under fairly general conditions, generates consistent estimators, but there is a loss of efficiency relative to OLS.

One approach to this issue is to combine the (inconsistent) OLS estimator with a consistent IV estimator in order to improve efficiency but accept some bias. It is possible to arrange the weights so that the weighted average of the OLS and IV estimators is consistent and, by the mean square error criterion, is an improvement.

In the absence of any prior information maximum likelihood estimation breaks down in the case of errors in variables because each observation is associated with an unknown parameter, X_i, notwithstanding the other parameters (intercept and slope parameters and the variances). If the error variances are known or, less restrictively, their ratio is known, maximum likelihood may be used, but such knowledge may not be available. Such information might, however, be available in the case of official statistics: it is not unusual for official statistics to be published with a given range of error attached to them, and in the familiar case of data revisions it may be possible to estimate the error variances by examining the relationship between the first announcement of the data and the latest revised figures.

It may be argued that all data available to economists are flawed by measurement error and that, therefore, OLS always produces inconsistent estimators. This source of potential inconsistency may, or may not, be large relative to any specification error and other sources of bias and inconsistency. If the measurement error variance is small relative to the variance of the underlying variable then the inconsistency due to this source will not be large. This represents an argument that the data are not so bad as to cause serious concern. A different response argues that if the data available to the economist are those to which the economic agents themselves are reacting then the model should, properly, be expressed in terms of observable data and in this case there is no errors-in-variables problem at all. This argument does not, however, address the 'proxy variable' issue when it is known that the observable variables are merely (imperfect) proxies for those which determine behaviour (see **Proxy variables**), nor does it address the extreme errors in variables problem of missing observations (when some observations on variables are simply not available – see **Missing observations**). Of course, economists can only utilize the data which are available, and to concentrate upon the errors in variables issue can become nihilistic towards empirical research: the data, dirty as they are (or may be) are all that there is to go on, and the econometrician must enquire of the extent of the impact upon bias and inconsistency by investigating the source of the data (in an attempt to understand better the construction of the data set and seek improvements to the data), the nature of the behavioural relationship (to determine those variables to which agents actually react) and the potential size of any problems which arise from using the imperfect data, and temper any conclusions accordingly.

Further reading

The earliest work on errors-in-variables is due to Wald (1940), Bartlett (1949) and Durbin (1954). See also Theil (1961), Levi (1973), Garber and Klepper (1980), Klepper and Leamer (1983) and Griliches (1986). See also Hansen (1982) and White (1984) on the use of optimal instruments.

Exogeneity and endogeneity

Exogeneity is a property of a variable in an economic model; it is to be contrasted with endogeneity. The concepts of exogeneity and endogeneity are most important in model-building, model specification and model estimation, but there is some ambiguity over their precise meaning; the ambiguity arises particularly as they are used differently in deterministic and stochastic models, and within stochastic models the term exogeneity has at least three meanings, which are distinguished by the terms weakly exogenous, strongly exogenous and super exogenous.

In a deterministic economic model a variable is said to be exogenous when its value is not determined within the model; an exogenous variable is to be contrasted with an endogenous variable, namely one whose value is determined within the model in question. A deterministic model specifies certain relationships which a vector of variables, Y, must satisfy; these relationships may be seen as a set of constraints on the values which Y may adopt and the relationships typically include other variables, denoted here by the vector X. Further, the relationships may hold only for values of X within some specified range. A deterministic model, then, may be characterized by taking the form:

$$\text{for all } X \in R,\ f_j(Y, X) = 0 \ \text{ for } j = 1, 2, \ldots g.$$

R is the range of X for which the model is constructed, and there are g equations in the model which constrain the possible values of Y. The variables in X are exogenous and those in Y are endogenous; the distinction cannot be gleaned from the model's relationships alone. Although $f_j(Y, X) = 0$ indicates no distinction between Y and X, the distinction arises from the specification which dictates that the values of Y are constrained by those of X, *but not vice versa*. If there are g variables in Y, and the g equations $f_j(Y, X)$ are independent, then in principle these equations can be 'solved' to yield a further g equations:

$$Y_k = h_k(X) \ \text{ for all } X \in R \text{ and } k = 1, 2, \ldots, g.$$

In this way the restrictions (the g equations $f_j(Y, X) = 0$) *determine* Y, but the existence of such a solution (unique or otherwise) is not a characteristic of exogeneity or endogeneity. The distinguishing feature is that an endogenous variable is constrained by the values of (at least some of) the exogenous variables, *but not vice versa*. This is the most familiar variant of the distinction, but it is within stochastic models that the distinction is most important.

In their work on simultaneous equation models, the Cowles Commission were concerned with general models of the form:

$$B(L)Y_t + \Gamma(L)X_t = u_t$$

$$A(L)u_t = \varepsilon_t$$

where L is the lag operator, defined by $Lz_t = z_{t-1}$, and B, Γ and A are polynomials; u_t and ε_t are unobservable disturbances and Y_t and X_t are observable economic variables. B and A are assumed to have roots which guarantee stability of this system. It is further assumed that:

$$\text{cov}(\varepsilon_t, Y_{t-s}) = 0 \quad \text{for all } s > 0 \text{ and all } t;$$

$$\text{cov}(\varepsilon_t, X_{t-s}) = 0 \quad \text{for all } s \text{ and all } t; \text{ and}$$

$$\varepsilon_t \sim MVN(0, \Sigma) \quad \text{for all } t \ \text{ and}$$

$$\varepsilon_t \text{ and } \varepsilon_s \text{ are independently distributed for all } t \neq s.$$

These conditions on the vector of disturbances ε_t ensure that each ε_t is identically and independently distributed and that:

1. ε_t is independent of all Y_{t-s}, $s > 0$; that is, the current error vector is independent of all previous Y vectors;
2. ε_t is independent of all X_{t-s}, all s; that is, the current error vector is independent of all previous, present and future values of X.

In such a model exogeneity is defined by the following:

> In a stochastic model a variable is exogenous if its value at each and every observation point is statistically independent of the values of all the disturbance terms in the model at all observation points.

Endogeneity is defined by:

> In a stochastic model all variables which are not exogenous are endogenous.

These definitions arise in a special class of models, namely linear models with normally distributed disturbances. To further the analysis, note that the model may be 'solved':

$$Y_t = -B(L)^{-1}\Gamma(L)X_t + B(L)^{-1}A(L)^{-1}u_t.$$

X is then a set of exogenous variables and the above equations which constitute the 'solution' of the model may be seen as the equations which determine the value of the endogenous variables, for given exogenous variables and for given realizations of the disturbances. In this solution each equation expresses one endogenous variable as a linear function of the exogenous variables and the error terms. In estimation it is then possible to treat the exogenous variables as fixed, but exogeneity is not a necessary condition for this treatment (though it is sufficient).

To expand upon this, suppose that the data are time-series and that the polynomial A(L) is the identity matrix; then the disturbances u_t are not autocorrelated, and so in the specification:

$$B(L)Y_t + \Gamma(L)X_t = u_t$$

the typical equation expresses all endogenous variables as linear functions of their own lagged values, all exogenous variables and their lagged values, and the current error term. Given the assumption of no autocorrelation amongst the errors all lagged values of Y are independent of the current disturbance, u_t. Hence, in the special case of no autocorrelation the lagged values of Y may also be treated as fixed for the purposes of estimation; this leads to the definition of a pre-determined variable:

> A pre-determined variable in a stochastic model utilizing time-series data is one whose current and all previous values are statistically independent of the current disturbance terms in the model, and these disturbances are not autocorrelated.

These definitions arise in the simplest of models (linear models with normally distributed disturbances), and in recent work which utilizes non-linearities, rational expectations for example, the definitions have proved inadequate. In general terms, following Sims (1977) and Geweke (1982), one may define X_t as model exogenous as follows:

> X_t is model exogenous if, given $\{X_t, t \leq T\} \in R(T)$, the model may restrict $\{Y_t, t \leq T\}$, but given $\{X_t, t \leq T + s\} \in R(T + s)$, there are no further restrictions on $\{Y_t, t \leq T\}$ for any $s > 0$.

Hence X_t is model exogenous if, given the history of this vector of variables up to and including time T, the model may restrict the values realized by the variables in Y up to and including time T, *but* values of X_t beyond time T provide no additional restrictions on Y_t, $t \leq T$. Model exogeneity/endogeneity is a most useful definition, but it is not sufficient that a variable be model exogenous to be treated as fixed for the purposes of estimation.

In the considering a simple single-equation model (using time-series data) of the form $Y = X\beta + \varepsilon$, the analysis concentrates on the conditional distribution of the $\{Y_t: t = 1, 2, \ldots, T\}$ given the value of the regressors at time t, X_t, and the parameters. Let ψ represent the parameters of the joint distribution of Y_t and X_t: $f(Y_t, X_t; \psi)$. Suppose further that ψ may be split into (ψ_1, ψ_2) where ψ_1 is related directly to the parameters of interest and ψ_2 is a vector of nuisance parameters so that f(.) may be written in terms of the conditional distribution of Y_t given X_t and ψ_1:

$$f(Y_t, X_t; \psi) = f(Y_t|X_t; \psi_1)\times f(X_t; \psi_2)$$

then X_t is weakly exogenous and inference of the parameters of interest may be constructed by reference to the conditional distribution only. To concentrate upon the conditional distribution is to ignore the marginal distribution $f(X_t; \psi_2)$, and this is valid only if that distribution contains no information relevant to the estimation (and hence the testing) of the parameters of interest. Denoting the parameters of interest by θ (where θ typically comprises the response vector, β, and the error variance, σ^2), this approach implies that the stochastic nature of X_t is irrelevant with regard to inference of θ. The definition of weak exogeneity may be expressed as: X_t is weakly exogenous over the period $t = 1, 2, \ldots, T$ if there exists a re-parameterization of the model with $\psi = (\psi_1, \psi_2)$ so that θ is some function of ψ_1 only and ψ_1 and ψ_2 are variation free (which means that for any specific value of ψ_1 in its parameter space ψ_2 is free to take any value from its parameter space). If these conditions are *not* met then the marginal distribution of X_t contains relevant information for the estimation of θ. Weak exogeneity of X_t implies, then, that the parameters in the marginal distribution of X_t are nuisance parameters and that nothing is lost in the estimation and testing of the parameters of interest by proceeding to examine the model conditional upon X_t. If the question of exogeneity is examined in order to determine an appropriate estimation method for the parameters of interest, then weak exogeneity is sufficient.

The definition of super exogeneity is related to the Lucas Critique (Lucas, 1976); the Lucas Critique concerns the potential for economic agents to modify their behaviour according to the economic environment and addresses, in particular, the possibility that in response to a change in the economic environment agents change their behaviour; viewed in this way the coefficients in a regression equation are seen as conditional upon the economic environment. If the events to which agents react concern policy variables which are viewed as 'exogenous' then the Lucas Critique proposes that a model's parameters are dependent on exogenous variables. One response to this is to model such a dependence explicitly, and this leads to a varying parameter model. The definition of super exogeneity is that a variable is exogenous if the Lucas Critique does not apply to it:

$$f(Y_t, X_t; \psi) = f(Y_t | X_t; \psi_1) \times f(X_t; \psi_2).$$

If X_t is weakly exogenous and the parameters ψ_1 are invariant to any changes in the marginal distribution of X_t then X_t is super exogenous.

Strong exogeneity is defined in terms of Granger causality (See **Causality and Granger causality**). The variable X_t is strongly exogenous if it is both weakly exogenous and not Granger-caused by any of the endogenous variables in the system. Granger-non-causality is neither necessary nor sufficient for exogeneity, however defined; it is, though, necessary (but not sufficient) for strong exogeneity. Hence a test of Granger causality by itself provides only negative information regarding exogeneity: if X_t is Granger-caused by any of the endogenous variables in the system then it cannot be strongly exogenous.

In early econometric work exogeneity was not treated as a testable proposition, but was rather treated as a matter of *a priori* specification. The commonest tests of exogeneity are based on Hausman's (1978) test, described in **Exogeneity tests**.

Considerations of exogeneity, and tests of exogeneity, are important in order to determine an appropriate estimating technique, and especially in an examination of the appropriateness of using single equation methods and ordinary least squares, as opposed to other techniques such as two stage least squares (TSLS) or instrumental variables (IV). If all the potential regressors in an equation are found to be exogenous then a single equation estimation method is appropriate; if some are found to be endogenous this implies that a larger, simultaneous, model is more appropriate and indicates that, for the purpose of estimation, ordinary least squares is not appropriate.

Further reading
The Cowles Commission approach is exemplified by Christ (1966). In addition to the references in the text above, see also Engle, Hendry and Richard (1983) and Geweke (1984).

Exogeneity tests

In the standard linear model $Y = X\beta + \varepsilon$ it is important to be able to test for the exogeneity of a regressor (or set of regressors) since, in the presence of endogenous regressors the ordinary least squares estimator $\hat{\beta}$ is inconsistent, and so standard inferential techniques will lead to misleading interpretations. A common means of testing for the exogeneity of regressors is to compare two alternative estimators of the model's parameters, one of which is consistent under certain conditions, and the other only consistent under more particular, more restrictive, conditions. In such tests it is common to compare an instrumental variable estimator of β with the ordinary least squares estimator; the former is consistent (but inefficient) always, while the latter is only consistent under the hypothesis of exogeneity. Hence a significant difference between the two estimators is evidence of the presence of at least one endogenous regressor. This construction is the basis of tests suggested by Hausman (1978) (and may be found in Durbin, 1954, and Wu, 1973). Such tests are sometimes referred to as Durbin-Wu-Hausman (DWH) tests.

Such a test may be set in a general framework, so that two estimators are to be compared, one of which is always consistent, the other of which is consistent only when a set of restrictions is true. If the restrictions hold true in the sample, then the difference between the two estimators will have a probability limit of zero and if the restrictions are false the difference between the estimators will have a non-zero probability limit. Hence a test of the difference between the estimates provides a test of those conditions. In the context of a simple examination of specification, where the alternative models under consideration are:

$$Y = X\beta + \varepsilon \quad \text{and} \quad Y = X\beta + Z\gamma + \nu$$

then a test of the difference between $\hat{\beta}$ and $\tilde{\beta}$, where $\hat{\beta}$ is the OLS estimator from the regression of Y on X alone and $\tilde{\beta}$ is the estimator from the regression of Y on both X and Z, provides a suitable test. Under the assumption that the model of Y on X alone is well-specified, the estimator $\hat{\beta}$ is consistent and efficient; if this model suffers mis-specification then $\hat{\beta}$ is efficient, but inconsistent. If the extended model of Y regressed on both X and Z is correct then $\tilde{\beta}$ is consistent always and, even if $\gamma = 0$, $\tilde{\beta}$ retains its consistency but is then inefficient. $\hat{\beta}$ is consistent only under the particular restriction that $\gamma = 0$. If $\gamma = 0$ the difference between $\hat{\beta}$ and $\tilde{\beta}$ will, asymptotically, have a zero mean and it has been proposed that the test:

$$(\hat{\beta} - \tilde{\beta})'[\hat{V} - \tilde{V}]^{-1}(\hat{\beta} - \tilde{\beta})$$

be used, where $\hat{V}$ and $\tilde{V}$ are the estimated variances of $\hat{\beta}$ and $\tilde{\beta}$ respectively; under the null hypothesis that $\gamma = 0$ this statistic is not expected, in large samples, to differ significantly from zero. The immediate problem with this statistic arises since there is no guarantee that the difference between the variance estimates, $\hat{V} - \tilde{V}$, will be non-singular and positive definite. To overcome this the test may be carried out using an auxiliary regression, as described below.

In general the test consists of comparing one estimator of β, namely $\hat{\beta} = (X'X)^{-1}X'Y$, with another, namely $\tilde{\beta} = (X'AX)^{-1}X'AY$ where A is some square non-singular matrix chosen so that $\tilde{\beta}$ is consistent if $Y = X\beta + \varepsilon$. It is easy to demonstrate, assuming the model $Y = X\beta + \varepsilon$ to be true, that $Y = X\hat{\beta} + \hat{e}$, and so:

$$\tilde{\beta} = \hat{\beta} + (X'AX)^{-1}X'A\hat{e}.$$

Hence the test is effectively examining whether $X'A\hat{e}$ has a zero expectation. The case of potentially omitted variables considered above is equivalent to setting $A = M_z = I - Z(Z'Z)^{-1}Z'$ and the test is then identical to the traditional F-test of $\gamma = 0$ so long as $k \geq r$, where k is the number of regressors in X and r is the number of regressors in Z. Interpreting the test as a test of zero parameters in an auxiliary regression facilitates its use and computation.

As a specific example, suppose that $A = W(W'W)^{-1}W'$ then $\tilde{\beta}$ is given by $\tilde{\beta} = (X'W(W'W)^{-1}W'X)^{-1}X'W(W'W)^{-1}W'Y$, and if W is a matrix of order $n \times k$ and has full rank, where there are n observations in the original model, then the matrix X'W is of order $k \times k$ and is non-singular; hence $\tilde{\beta}$ may be written as $(W'X)^{-1}W'Y$ which is seen as the instrumental variable estimator of β given the instruments W.

The essence of the specific test, as described above, is especially useful in testing for the possible inconsistency of $\hat{\beta}$ due to the potential endogeneity of the regressors. Consider the regression model $Y = X\beta + \varepsilon$ and suppose a test of the exogeneity of the regressors is required. The hypotheses are:

H_o: X and ε are independent

H_1: X and ε are not independent.

If there are instruments W which satisfy the requirements:

$$\text{plim}(n^{-1}W'\varepsilon) = 0$$

and
$$\text{plim}(n^{-1}W'X) = Q,$$

where Q is some finite non-singular matrix, then the instrumental variable estimator, $\tilde{\beta} = (W'X)^{-1}W'Y$, is consistent always.

The OLS estimator, $\hat{\beta} = (X'X)^{-1}X'Y$, is consistent only under the assumption that $\text{plim}(T^{-1}X'\varepsilon) = 0$; hence the difference between $\tilde{\beta}$ and $\hat{\beta}$ has a probability limit of zero under the hypothesis that X is exogenous, and a test of the difference $\tilde{\beta} - \hat{\beta}$ provides the test of exogeneity. Strictly speaking this test examines whether the possible endogeneity of X is causing the inconsistency of $\hat{\beta}$. If the variances of $\hat{\beta}$ and $\tilde{\beta}$, computed under H_o, are denoted by V_1 and V_2 respectively, then Hausman's test relies on the fact that the variance of the difference $\hat{\beta} - \tilde{\beta}$ is given by $V_1 - V_2 = V$, so that if $\hat{V}$ is a consistent estimator of V:

$$(\hat{\beta} - \tilde{\beta})'\hat{V}^{-1}(\hat{\beta} - \tilde{\beta}) \sim \chi^2_k$$

Clearly, if H_o is true then $\hat{\beta}$ and $\tilde{\beta}$ are both consistent in which case their difference approaches zero in probability; hence, when H_o is true the test statistic will be small. A large value of the test statistic leads to a rejection of H_o in favour of H_1.

This special case may be tested easily by an auxiliary regression; consider regressing the variables of X on the instruments, W; the corresponding matrix of fitted values is given by $W(W'W)^{-1}W'X$ and if these are used as additional regressors in the regression of Y on X then, if $Y = X\beta + \varepsilon$ is a properly specified model, their addition is the addition of redundant regressors. Hence the test statistic may be computed by regressing the original regressors on the available instruments, of which there must be at least k, running the auxiliary regression:

$$Y = X\beta + Z\gamma + \varepsilon$$

where $Z = W(W'W)^{-1}W'X$ and testing, via an F-test, the hypothesis $\gamma = 0$. If the test statistic exceeds the chosen critical value then $\hat{\beta}$ and $\tilde{\beta}$ are significantly different and the original model yields inconsistent estimators; consequently its specification as a single equation with exogenous regressors is rejected. Clearly, this test could equally be carried out with the additional regressors equal to the residuals from the regression of X on W:

$$Y = X\beta + \hat{v}\gamma + \varepsilon$$

where $\hat{v} = X - W(W'W)^{-1}W'X = M_wX$. Again, the F-test on γ yields the desired test statistic.

Such specification tests offer a general method of specification testing, and the particular form is commonly employed as a test of the inconsistency of ordinary least squares estimators due to the endogeneity of the regressors.

When written in their general form, these tests are very similar to data transformation tests (see **Data transformation tests**).

Further reading
The test was introduced by Durbin (1954), Wu (1973) and its application to a test of endogeneity is due to Hausman (1978). See the discussion in MacKinnon (1992).

Extreme bounds analysis

Extreme bounds analysis (EBA) is designed to improve the information content of an econometric investigation, is introduced within a Bayesian framework and is an examination of the sensitivity of inferences to a range of prior distributions. Critical to the discussion of EBA is the fact that the explanatory variables in a regression equation are categorized as 'doubtful' or 'focus' and while these terms are not unambiguously defined, it suffices to define them as follows: for any investigation, different individuals will hold different priors regarding the role of potential explanatory variables and, with respect to a given prior, those variables whose role is zero are termed doubtful, and the remaining variables are focus, or free, variables. The former variables are those which the investigator is prepared to entertain, while the latter variables are certainties for inclusion.

By considering a very general family of models attention may then be concentrated upon inferences of parameters of interest (those parameters attached to focus, or free, variables) and by examining the sensitivity of those inferences to particular prior distributions, an extreme bounds analysis is constructed. Formally, if the general model is of the form:

$$Y_t = \Sigma_{k=1}^{K} \beta_k X_{tk} + \Sigma_{j=1}^{J} \gamma_j Z_{tj} + \varepsilon_t$$

where the K variables of X are focus variables, and the J variables of Z are doubtful variables, then EBA examines the minimum and maximum values of each $\hat{\beta}_k$ from the regressions which always include all focus variables and include all possible linear combinations of the doubtful variables. This is equivalent to a Bayesian analysis utilizing diffuse priors on β (hence the term 'free') and a host of arbitrary and specific priors on γ. It may be shown that:

$$[\hat{V}(\hat{\beta}_k)]^{-1/2} |\hat{\beta}_k^{max} - \hat{\beta}_k^{min}| = \phi \chi_\gamma^2$$

where $\hat{V}(\hat{\beta}_k)$ is the estimated variance of $\hat{\beta}_k$ from the unconstrained OLS regression of Y on all free and doubtful variables, χ_γ^2 is the chi-squared test statistic for the hypotheses $\gamma = 0$ in that regression (the large-sample Wald test statistic) and $0 \leq \phi \leq 1$. ϕ is a function specific to the general regression equation, and is determined, in part, by the collinearity of the regressors.

The quantity $[\hat{V}(\hat{\beta}_k)]^{-½}|\hat{\beta}_k^{max} - \hat{\beta}_k^{min}|$ is called the specification uncertainty. Suppose that χ^2_γ is small; in the traditional approach to modelling, this would indicate that the simplified model, excluding the variables of Z, is an appropriate model from which to make inferences of β. In the EBA analysis much the same message is conveyed: the range on $\hat{\beta}_k$ is small, indicating a low degree of specification uncertainty. (The problem of choosing an appropriate size of the test of $\gamma = 0$ is not removed in this analysis, and that choice dictates the measure of the importance, or otherwise, of the specification uncertainty.) It is also to be noted that if $\gamma \neq 0$, then as the sample size increases so the test statistic, χ^2_γ, increases without bound; hence the range of $\hat{\beta}_k$ also increases without bound.

As the number of doubtful variables increases, the critical value applied to χ^2_γ increases (for a fixed Type I error); in classical hypothesis testing it is not the size *per se* of χ^2_γ which is of importance, but its size relative to a chosen critical value. In an extreme bounds analysis the larger is the dimension of the set of doubtful variables, the larger is the potential range in any $\hat{\beta}_k$ and the estimate of the parameter attached to a focus variable, β_k, may become very sensitive to the way in which doubtful variables are combined. The construction of the extreme bounds on the coefficients on focus variables might appear, then, to be more important the larger is the number of doubtful variables deleted in a simplification exercise.

In the non-Bayesian tradition, a large value of χ^2_γ relative to the chosen critical value will lead to retention of the general model; in EBA a large value of χ^2_γ leads to a wide range on the possible estimates of β_k. The former approach, then, retains the general model as the basis for inference, while advocates of EBA conclude that the data are uninformative about β_k since there are many different, and conflicting, inferences which might be drawn, depending on the model's specification. A large range of $(\hat{\beta}_k^{max}, \hat{\beta}_k^{min})$ would lead an advocate of EBA to describe any subsequent inference of β_k as 'fragile'.

EBA concentrates upon the possible inferences one might make regarding a number of particular parameters; it does not address the wider issues of the model's specification, and in this respect it differs markedly from other approaches to econometric modelling. In many instances the investigator is interested in the model as a whole, and not just in any specific parameter; if, however, a particular investigation is so tightly focused that the inference on one parameter is the objective, then EBA may be seen to have a role; equally, in a simplification of a general equation in which a large number of variables are deleted, performing an EBA may convey useful information.

Further reading

Leamer (1983) introduces EBA, and is extended in Leamer and Leonard (1983); for an appraisal see, for example, Pagan (1987).

Falsification

Falsification is the attempt to demonstrate, by empirical testing, that a theory is materially false, and falsificationism is associated with the methodological perspective which regards theories and hypotheses as 'scientific' if and only if their material predictions are, in principle, empirically falsifiable. There is a logical force to the process of falsification or refutation: if a theory's predictions are refuted by material observations then it is logically valid to conclude that the antecedent of the major premiss is therefore false (see **Syllogistic reasoning**). This process is known as 'denying the consequent'. If H represents a main hypothesis and A_1, A_2, , and A_n are auxiliary hypotheses which, when taken together, logically imply a prediction, P, then the syllogism runs thus:

1. If H and A_1, A_2, , and A_n are all true then P is true;
2. P is false;
3. therefore at least one of the n + 1 propositions H, A_1, A_2, . . , and A_n is false (and therefore the theory encapsulated by these propositions is false).

To many, science comprises a body of synthetic propositions regarding the real world which, at least in principle, is capable of refutation through the use of empirical observations, and the syllogism which illustrates the act of denying the consequent is critical to science. In this syllogism the theory is encapsulated in the major premiss: the main hypothesis, H, with the assumptions, or tentative hypotheses, $\{A_i; i = 1, . . , n\}$, combine together to yield the prediction, P, and for this theory to be viewed as a part of 'science' the proposition P must be capable, at least in principle, of being refuted by material observations.

Naïve falsificationism holds that a theory may be decisively refuted on the basis of a single refutation. If decisive falsification of the proposition P were feasible then this syllogism does indeed indicate that the entire theory, as described by the main hypothesis with its tentative hypotheses, is also decisively refutable in principle. However, the technology of falsification does not allow decisive refutation, as is described below, and so naïve falsificationism is not tenable.

Nevertheless, suppose it were possible, after gathering and analysing data, to deny, decisively, the proposition P; what, then, could be said of the theory? If a theory's predictions (P) do not conform to what is observed, the conclusion is to reject the theory as encapsulated in the propositions H and $A_1, . . , A_n$. It may be the case that some of those propositions are materially true while others are materially false, but the empirical evidence does not identify which particular propositions have been refuted – the precise reason for the refutation of a composite hypothesis cannot be immediately located. In the absence of further information it is, therefore, possible for an investigator to declare that the case is 'not proven' against any one of the hypotheses under test {H and A_i; i = 1, . . , n}. This illustrates Duhem's irrefutability thesis, namely that there are no crucial experiments by which a single hypothesis can be conclusively refuted.

It might be inferred from this that, since no single hypothesis can be refuted decisively once it is embedded with auxiliary hypotheses, single hypotheses are not falsifiable in practice and that any hypothesis, however ridiculous it might appear, can hold the status of a maintained hypothesis. Were this the case then scientists would be criticized for holding on to hypotheses even in the face of contrary evidence, and there are certain types of stratagems, called immunizing stratagems, which have been adopted solely to protect theories from refutation. Popper, amongst others, has condemned the use of such stratagems and, in testing, it is vitally important that the investigator states, prior to the test, precisely what conditions in the material world would constitute a refutation of the theory. It is precisely because, following Duhem's irrefutability thesis, no critical experiments exist that, in order to demarcate science from non-science, it is necessary to set methodological limits on the stratagems which are admissible in the attempt to avoid falsifying any single hypothesis.

In the context of economic theories the testing apparatus involves statistical analysis; statistical inference involves the examination of data in order to infer something about the material world and in order to utilize statistical theory econometricians typically choose to view a data set as if it were a sample drawn randomly from a 'population'. In testing a hypothesis it is always the case that a single hypothesis is never examined in isolation; rather, a main hypothesis, with its associated auxiliary hypotheses, is tested against an alternative hypothesis (which, too, has associated auxiliary hypotheses). In the formal framework of statistical testing the main hypothesis may be either the null or the alternative hypothesis, and the presence and role of the necessary auxiliary hypothesis are not always fully recognized.

The main hypothesis, H, cannot be tested individually since the prediction, P, is the result of the conjunction of H with the associated auxiliary hypotheses. Thus the practicality of naïve falsificationism is denied: if the result of testing is a 'rejection' of the prediction then, because at least one of the auxiliary hypotheses could be false and therefore responsible for the falsity of the prediction, whatever the status of the main hypothesis, the conclusion can only be that the composite hypothesis of the main and auxiliary hypotheses is rejected.

Some of the auxiliary hypotheses are required to justify the statistical testing procedure (such as the hypothesis that the errors in a regression are independently distributed), and if a main hypothesis is tested and a 'rejection' results this does not allow anything else, logically, but a rejection of the composite hypothesis; moreover, the sophisticated falsificationist recognizes that, since it is possible for an investigator to be unaware of the full set of auxiliary hypotheses, even the most exhaustive examination of $A_1, \ldots A_n$ which still leads to a 'refutation' cannot necessarily be viewed as a conclusive refutation of the main hypothesis H: there could be other auxiliary hypotheses in play of which the investigator is ignorant and which are false. Thus, repeated tests (perhaps with different data sets) which generate the same 'rejection' result, do not allow a *certain* rejection of the main hypothesis; however, in order to avoid the use of immunizing stratagems, it is necessary to adopt methodological norms which allow the investigator to declare that the main hypothesis is 'false'. It is to be noted that a declaration of a theory's falsity within stated methodological norms is not the same as the definitive statement that a theory is materially false.

Since some of the auxiliary hypotheses are required in order to justify the use of a particular test statistic in the testing of the main hypothesis, the statistic used has validity only when those auxiliary hypotheses are materially true. This appears to require investigators to 'verify' at least some of the auxiliary hypotheses simply in order to use a particular test statistic; however, syllogistic reasoning demonstrates that there is no logic of verification. Typically, auxiliary hypotheses are capable at least in principle of refutation; having tested some of the auxiliary hypotheses, and having not rejected any of them, their 'non-refutation' cannot be taken, logically, as a verification but one can set methodological norms of confirmation so that one can declare the conditions under which one might deem 'non-refuted' hypotheses to be 'true'. Indeed, the effort devoted in regression analysis to an examination of diagnostic tests utilizes, albeit implicitly, norms of confirmation.

Additionally, it must be recognized that any statistical test which leads to a rejection at a given level of significance is, of course, subject to a potential error and thus, as Popper observed, probability statements are inherently non-falsifiable because they:

> **do not rule out anything observable**; . . 'practical falsification' can only be obtained through a methodological decision to regard highly improbable events as ruled out – as prohibited. . . Where does this high improbability begin? (Popper, 1968, pp. 190 and 191, original emphasis)

This demands that in any testing framework the investigator explicitly recognizes the limits of any conclusions; specifically, no single hypothesis can ever be declared, demonstrably, to be materially false. It is equally important to recognise that a non-rejection of a hypothesis, at a given significance level, is also subject to potential error and non-rejection is not equivalent to verification. Hence no single hypothesis can ever be declared, demonstrably, to be materially true or materially false.

Since there is no logic of verification and no demonstrative logic of practical falsification, no attempts to test theories can ever be conclusive, one way or the other: there is no certain empirical knowledge. This, then, sets the limits and the challenges to econometrics. The limits are enshrined in the knowledge that our beliefs constitute only tentatively held hypotheses; those hypotheses are the currently maintained hypotheses because, given our methodological norms regarding falsification, confirmation and immunizing stratagems, they have successfully withstood attempts to refute them. The challenge to econometrics lies in recognizing that we cannot be at all sure that those maintained hypotheses are the best which are available, and one of the most important roles which econometricians can fulfil is, therefore, the search for and identification of better scientific theories of economic phenomena. However, what we cannot do is 'to pretend that there is on deposit somewhere a perfectly objective method, that is, an intersubjectively demonstrative method, that will positively compel agreement on what are or are not acceptable scientific theories' (Blaug, 1992, p. 26).

In practice, then, neither demonstrative falsification nor demonstrative verification is feasible; there is, however, practical falsification and practical confirmation. Specifically, the only way to arrive at a position of practical falsification is to view those events which are 'highly improbable' given the truth of the main and auxiliary hypotheses as evidence upon which to assert the falsity of that hypothesis. Clearly, therefore, practical falsification is probabilistic falsification, for rejection of the main hypothesis under these conditions is liable to a potential error. Nevertheless, the adoption of such a norm is the only way forward: this explains Popper's statement that 'practical falsification can be obtained only through a methodological decision to *regard* highly improbable events as ruled out – as prohibited'.

Thus the position of the 'naïve falsificationist' is wholly improper for a falsifying instance can never be decisive. The sophisticated falsificationist recognizes this. However, although neither verification nor falsification can ever be decisive, with regard to the testing of a main hypothesis the informational content of confirmation and falsification are quite different: a further confirmation of an often confirmed hypothesis has little information content (although it may be suggested that the hypothesis is either insufficiently well defined to allow falsification or that there are but few states of the world which are inconsistent with that theory and if this latter is the case then the information content of the hypothesis itself is low). In contrast, falsification of a main economic hypothesis does provide information – it indicates the presence of a problem and provides the challenge to address that problem.

Further reading

On falsification in economics, see especially Popper (1968), Stewart (1979) and Blaug (1992). See also Chalmers (1976).

Forecast accuracy

Suppose the general linear model $Y = X\beta + \varepsilon$ with $E(\varepsilon) = 0$, $V(\varepsilon) = \sigma^2 I$ and fixed regressors is estimated by ordinary least squares using T observations. This yields $\hat{\beta}$ and the associated estimated variance–covariance matrix of the estimators $s^2(X'X)^{-1}$. Now suppose that observations for period s (where s > T) become available and it is intended to forecast the value of Y_s given the observations on the regressors for period s (denoted by the 1×k row vector x_s'). The purpose of forecasting might be to assess the worth of the chosen model (better forecasts will be generated by better models) or it might be to forecast the phenomenon under consideration to feed into policy-making or it might be to predict the likely outcome of a particular policy. The best predictor of Y_s is given by:

$$\hat{Y}_s = x_s'\hat{\beta}$$

Since $\hat{\beta} = \beta + (X'X)^{-1}X'\varepsilon$:

$$\hat{Y}_s = x_s'\beta + x_s'(X'X)^{-1}X'\varepsilon$$

and so $E(\hat{Y}_s) = x_s'\beta = E(Y_s)$; that is, $\hat{Y}_s$ is an unbiased predictor of the expected value of Y_s; the variance of the prediction is given by $V(x_s'(X'X)^{-1}\varepsilon) = \sigma^2 x_s'(X'X)^{-1}x_s$ which may be estimated by $s^2 x_s'(X'X)^{-1}x_s$. The variance of the prediction increases the more distant is x_s from the sample used for estimation; this is easily demonstrated in the simple model $Y_i = \alpha + \beta X_i + \varepsilon_i$ with n observations: in this case it is easily shown that:

$$x_s'(X'X)^{-1}x_s = \left(\frac{1}{n\sum_{i=1}^{n} x_i^2}\right)\left(1 + (X_s - \overline{X})^2\right)$$

where $x_i = X_i - \overline{X}$. The further is X_s from the mean of the sample used for estimation ($\overline{X}$), the greater is the variance of the forecast.

The above provides a prediction for the expected value of Y_s given x_s and this is to be contrasted with the prediction of a particular value of Y_s given x_s. Now $Y_s = x_s'\beta + \varepsilon_s$, and using the same prediction, namely $x_s'\hat{\beta}$, the prediction error is given by $\tilde{e}_s = Y_s - x_s'\hat{\beta}$; both components of the prediction error are stochastic, but since $\hat{\beta}$ utilizes information other than that for observation s, given independence of the error terms the two components are independent of each other. Hence the variance of $\tilde{e}_s$ is given by $V(Y_s) + V(x_s'\hat{\beta}) = \sigma^2 + \sigma^2 x_s'(X'X)^{-1}x_s$ and the first term, σ^2, provides an additional source of variance in the prediction error due to the stochastic nature of Y_s. The prediction error is particularly important in the construction of recursive residuals (see **Recursive residuals**), which use the 'one-step ahead prediction error', namely the error in predicting Y_{T+1} when $\hat{\beta}$ has been estimated using the observations up to and including T.

If the forecast is generated *ex post*, that is with full knowledge of both Y_s and x_s, then it is possible to construct confidence intervals and form hypothesis tests. For example:

$$x_s'\hat{\beta} \pm t_{\alpha/2;n-k}\, s[x_s'(X'X)^{-1}x_s]^{½}$$

is the $(1 - \alpha)$% confidence interval for the expected value of Y given x_s and under the null hypothesis that the particular observation Y_s comes from the same underlying structure as that which generated the data used for estimation purposes. If the observed value of Y_s lies outside this interval then the hypothesis of structural stability is rejected (using a Type I error of α). This test could, equally, have been carried out directly with a t-statistic, and if the test were carried out with several forecast periods then a test such as the Chow test could be used (see **Forecasting** and **Chow test**).

A forecast may be in error because the specification of the model from which it is derived is in error; it will also be in error because it utilizes estimated parameters ($\hat{\beta}$ is an estimate and will, with probability one, differ from β) and, in forecasting a particular value of Y_s there will be error due to the associated error term ε_s. The interval $x_s'\hat{\beta} \pm t_{\alpha/2;n-k}\, s[1 + x_s'(X'X)^{-1}x_s]^{½}$ provides a confidence interval for a forecast of a particular value of Y_s and this demonstrates that the error due to the estimate of β is incorporated via the forecast itself and also in the term $(X'X)^{-1}$; the error due to the error term associated with an individual Y_s is incorporated via the additional term in s. Effective use of tests of specification and mis-specification can reduce the potential impact of the first source of error; a well-fitting equation will reduce the impact of the second term; neither potential error can be eliminated. Only if the specification is correct does $x_s'\hat{\beta}$ provide a best unbiased forecast; if x_s is itself a forecast then unbiasedness is only retained if, in conjunction with a well-specified model, the estimated value of x_s is also unbiased. This fact leads some forecasters to utilize 'judgement' in modifying the point prediction in the light of 'relevant' circumstances not incorporated into the estimated model. *Ex post* forecasts may be assessed for their accuracy, but forecasting unknown values, typically using forecast values of x_s, cannot easily be assessed at the time they are made. Forecasting unknown values is known as *ex ante* forecasting and is subject to the three sources of error noted above; the potential error which arises from the use of a forecast value of x_s is known as the conditioning error. The use of best practice in forecasting x_s can reduce the impact of this error but it cannot be eliminated.

Ex post forecasts may be used to evaluate the estimated model, but *ex ante* forecasts are made without knowledge of Y_s and typically with forecasts of x_s. The forecasts of Y_s may be constructed as a means of forecasting the effect of a policy or simply as a means of foretelling the future (typically in the form of a confidence interval) on the basis of prior data analysis. The accuracy of an *ex ante* forecast cannot be assessed directly, but *ex post* forecasts may be constructed and evaluated by reserving some of available data set for this purpose, so that a sub-set of the data are used for estimation, and the remaining sub-set for *ex post* forecasting. This is a common form of diagnostic testing, known as cross-validation: models which perform well in *ex post* forecasting may be expected, given stability of the economic system, to generate 'good' *ex ante* forecasts.

There are many measures of *ex post* forecast accuracy; for any given measure one may, given two or more forecast methods, choose that which provides the 'best' forecasts. Simply choosing the 'best' forecast (best in the sense of generating the best measure of accuracy) requires only a relative judgement and does not require an absolute judgement of 'how good was this forecast method by reference to this measure?' Indeed, absolute measures of accuracy are only available by the use of an explicit loss function. *Ex post* assessment of accuracy is, then, of more use in comparing alternative forecasts (derived from alternative models or alternative methodologies) than in assessing the absolute accuracy of any one approach to forecasting.

Having estimated the model the forecast error is given by $\tilde{e}_s = Y_s - x_s'\hat{\beta}$; we suppose that x_s constitutes an extra-sample observation, of which there may be many. A good forecast method is one for which the $\tilde{e}_s$ are, in some sense, small; this in turn demands that the forecasts, $x_s'\hat{\beta}$, are 'close' to the outcomes, Y_s, and various measures of 'smallness' and 'closeness' are available.

Suppose that Y is forecast for a total of p periods. The mean absolute deviation (MAD), also known as the mean absolute error (MAE), is given by $(1/p)\ \Sigma_{s=1}^{p}|\tilde{e}_s|$; it is appropriate when the cost of forecast error is proportional to the absolute error. If the cost of error increases more than proportionately with the absolute size the MAD is not appropriate and, given the widespread use of the quadratic loss function, the alternative is to use the root mean square error (RMSE), given by $\sqrt{[(1/p)\Sigma_{s=1}^{p}\tilde{e}_s^2]}$; clearly this attaches greater weight to large errors than to small errors. The mean squared error may be decomposed to yield:

$$\text{MSE} = (1/p)\Sigma_{s=1}^{p}\tilde{e}_s^2 = (\overline{\hat{Y}} - \overline{Y})^2 + (\hat{s} - rs)^2 + (1 - r^2)s^2$$

where $\overline{\hat{Y}}$ and $\overline{Y}$ are the mean of the forecast and actual values respectively, $\hat{s}^2$ and s^2 are the estimated variances of the forecasts and actual values, and r is the correlation between the forecasts and the actual values. Dividing through by MSE, and denoting the resulting ratios by UM, UR and UD:

$$1 = \text{UM} + \text{UR} + \text{UD}.$$

UM is the proportion of the MSE due to bias in the forecasts (the mean error); UR and UD are best interpreted by considering the artificial regression relationship between the actual values and the forecasts:

$$Y_s = \alpha + \beta\hat{Y}_s + \text{error}.$$

A perfect set of forecasts would yield $\alpha = 0$ and $\beta = 1$. The OLS estimate of β may be written as $\hat{\beta} = rs/\hat{s}$, and so $\hat{s} - rs = \hat{s}(1 - \hat{\beta})$, and the R^2 statistic from this auxiliary regression is, of course, identical to the r^2, the simple correlation coefficient between the actual and fitted values. Hence UR, the regression error, is the proportion of the MSE due to the estimate $\hat{\beta}$ differing from unity and UD, the disturbance error, is due to unexplained error (if the fit of the auxiliary regression were exact then UD = 0). UD may be interpreted as the proportion of error in the MSE which is unexplained. A good forecast, therefore, has a low UM, a low UR and a high UD.

Both MAD and RMSE focus on the size of $\tilde{e}_s$ and both are dependent on the units of measurement. In some circumstances the relative error, $\tilde{e}_s/Y_s$, is more important. The relative error is dimensionless, and the mean absolute percentage error (MAPE) is often used, defined by $(100/p)\Sigma_{s=1}^{p}|\tilde{e}_s/Y_s|$. These measures concern the errors directly. Other measures are concerned with the 'closeness' of the forecasts and the outcomes: the correlation of the forecasts and the outcomes may be used, as may the correlation between the actual changes $(Y_s - Y_{s-1})$ with the forecast changes $(x_s - x_{s-1})'\hat{\beta}$ or one might utilise the extent to which the forecasts accurately predict turning points in the outcomes (this may be measured by computing the percentage of turning points which were actually forecast: let $\delta_s = 1$ if $(Y_s - Y_{s-1})$ and $(x_s - x_{s-1})'\hat{\beta}$ are of the same sign and zero otherwise so then the required percentage is $(100/p)\Sigma_{s=1}^{p}\delta_s$. These latter measures are dimensionless.

Other measures are based on Theil's inequality coefficients, the U statistics:

$$U_1 = \frac{\sqrt{(1/p)\Sigma_{s=1}^{p}\tilde{e}_s^2}}{\left(\sqrt{(1/p)\Sigma_{s=1}^{p}\hat{Y}_s^2} + \sqrt{(1/p)\Sigma_{s=1}^{p}Y_s^2}\right)}.$$

The numerator may be written the root squared error, but the denominator is difficult to interpret; nevertheless, if all the forecasts were correct, then $U_1 = 0$, and if all forecasts were exactly zero, then $U_1 = 1$. A large U_1 statistic is an indicator of poor performance, while a low statistic is an indicator of a better forecasting performance. The interpretative difficulties with the denominator led Theil to propose the U_2 statistic:

$$U_2 = \frac{\sqrt{(1/p)\Sigma_{s=1}^{p}\tilde{e}_s^2}}{\sqrt{(1/p)\Sigma_{s=1}^{p}Y_s^2}}.$$

U_2 may thus be written as the root mean square error scaled by the mean square of the actual values. U_2 has a minimum of zero, but is not bounded. This measure has also been proposed in terms of changes, so that it becomes the ratio of the root mean error of the forecast changes to the mean squared actual change, in which case it measures the ability of the forecasts to track turning points.

Further reading
Theil (1961) and Fair (1984) are excellent sources on the measuring the accuracy of forecasts; see also Holden, Peel and Thompson (1990).

Forecasting

One of the objectives of econometric models is to produce good forecasts; the accuracy of a forecast depends on several factors which include:

1. the specification of the model which generates the forecasts;
2. the accuracy of the estimates of that model;
3. the goodness of fit of that model;
4. the accuracy of any forecasts which are necessary to construct forecasts of the variable(s) in question.

A well-specified model is more likely to generate good forecasts than a poorly specified model. If the model on which the forecast is based is subject to some serious form of specification error, such as an omitted variable, or an incorrect functional form, then the estimation of that model is flawed and the estimators derived from it will be biased; to the extent that all models omit some variables (whether deliberately or by design) and all models impose a functional form, such specification errors are not all avoidable. However, if the error term in a forecasting equation does not exhibit any systematic components, as revealed by the use of diagnostic tests, the investigator may be content that the specification is fit for the purpose.

The variance of the residual error is a measure of the goodness of fit of the model within the sample of estimation, and it is tempting to argue that the better a model fits the data used for estimation, the better will it forecast; unfortunately this cannot be demonstrated. Indeed, if the equation fits the data used for estimation extremely well, and has been designed to account for certain idiosyncrasies of that data set, it need not necessarily be a good forecasting equation if the future is not like the past. If there are characteristics of the data set unique to the estimation period then it is possible that the fitted model may account for so many of the data's peculiarities that it 'over-fits' that data set and becomes, in consequence, a poor forecasting equation outside the sample of estimation. Forecasting is an exercise in generalizing from a specific data set; success in forecasting is, then, to a significant extent dependent on the extent to which the estimation sample is representative of the phenomenon under consideration.

Since forecasting is a generalization of a specific data set it is always subject to the inductivist critique, and it is necessary to assume that the future will be sufficiently like the past; however acceptable such an assumption may be for the immediate future, the further is the forecast period from the present the less tenable does this implicit assumption become. In constructing a confidence interval for a forecast constructed from a regression model this is accommodated, in part, by the fact that the further is the forecast from the data set used for estimation the larger is the confidence interval, and the lower is the precision in the forecast (see **Forecast accuracy**). Dummy variables may be used both to construct forecasts from the regression model and to examine their precision by using observation-specific dummies. Suppose the model $Y = X\beta + \varepsilon$ is estimated using T observations, and it is intended to forecast the dependent variable for the next p periods and the future values of the regressors are available. Denote the first T observations on the regressand and the regressors by Y_1 and X_1 respectively, and the regressors in the next p periods are denoted by X_2. Construct the artificial regression model:

$$\begin{bmatrix} Y_1 \\ 0 \end{bmatrix} = \begin{bmatrix} X_1 & 0 \\ X_2 & -I \end{bmatrix} \begin{bmatrix} \beta \\ \gamma \end{bmatrix} + \begin{bmatrix} \varepsilon_1 \\ \varepsilon_2 \end{bmatrix}$$

where the identity matrix, I, is of order p and represents a set of p dummy variables. The jth dummy variable takes the value zero for all observations, except T+j for which it takes the value $-1(j = 1, 2, \ldots, p)$.

If the stacked dependent variable is denoted by Y, the matrix of regressors is denoted by Z, the stacked coefficient vector by θ, and the error term by ε, this regression may be written as $Y = Z\theta + \varepsilon$. By ordinary least squares, the normal equations are given by $(Z'Z)\hat{\theta} = Z'Y$, which may be written out in full:

$$\begin{bmatrix} X_1' & X_2' \\ 0 & -I \end{bmatrix} \begin{bmatrix} X_1 & 0 \\ X_2 & -I \end{bmatrix} \begin{bmatrix} \hat{\beta}_1 \\ \hat{\gamma} \end{bmatrix} = \begin{bmatrix} X_1' & X_2' \\ 0 & -I \end{bmatrix} \begin{bmatrix} Y_1 \\ 0 \end{bmatrix}$$

$$\begin{bmatrix} X_1'X_1 + X_2'X_2 & -X_2' \\ -X_2 & I \end{bmatrix} \begin{bmatrix} \hat{\beta}_1 \\ \hat{\gamma} \end{bmatrix} = \begin{bmatrix} X_1'Y_1 \\ 0 \end{bmatrix}$$

which yield the two equations:

$$[X_1'X_1 + X_2'X_2]\hat{\beta} - X_2'\hat{\gamma} = X_1'Y_1 \quad \text{and} \quad -X_2\hat{\beta} + \hat{\gamma} = 0$$

Hence: $\hat{\gamma} = X_2\hat{\beta}$ and $\hat{\beta} = (X_1'X_1)^{-1}X_1'Y_1$.

Thus, $\hat{\beta}$ is given by OLS estimator of the coefficient from the regression of Y_1 on X_1, that is, using only the first T observations and the coefficients on the dummies are seen as precisely equal to the forecast values of Y for the later period using $\hat{\beta}$ estimated from the first. Moreover, the reported standard errors on the individual coefficients on the dummies are the standard errors of the forecasts, and this then represents a very simple way of computing what are, otherwise, burdensome calculations.

If the observations on Y for the later period were available the method of dummy variables may be used to compute the forecast errors, and their associated standard errors. This is described in detail in **Chow test**.

In the case when the future values of the regressors are not available X_2 must be replaced by a set of forecast values. In this case the forecast values of Y will be subject to an additional source of error, namely that arising from the fact that X_2 is not known but is itself forecast. This is known as a conditioning error.

In time-series analysis, one of the simplest forms of forecasting uses a same as before model: $Y_t = Y_{t-1}$, rather than an econometric regression equation. The same-as-before model is extremely naïve, and is based on the random walk model:

$$Y_t = Y_{t-1} + \varepsilon_t$$

where ε_t is a stationary random variable. This model, and extensions of it, form the literature of time-series forecasting; many time-series forecasts are based on univariate models in which the variable Y_t is examined as an ARIMA(p, d, q) process (see **ARMA and ARIMA models**). In many contexts ARIMA models have enjoyed great success. Such a model may be written as:

$$\alpha(L)\Delta^d Y_t = \beta(L)\varepsilon_t$$

where $\alpha(L)$ and $\beta(L)$ are polynomials of order p and q respectively, L is the lag operator and Δ is the difference operator. Such models are not econometric models since they do not take into account anything other than the history of the series itself – there are no explanatory variables as such, only the previous values of the variable under consideration. Vector autoregressions also provide an atheoretical method of forecasting. To accommodate genuine explanatory variables the ARMAX model (see **Distributed lag models**) may be used.

An ARMAX model is an econometric model in which a variable is modelled as a function both of its own past history and the current and past values of other economic explanatory variables. To the extent that such an econometric model is based within a theoretical model which seeks to explain the variable in question, an ARMAX may be expected to be a better forecaster. However, in forecasting from an ARMAX model it is necessary to have forecasts of the explanatory variables, whereas an ARIMA model can generate dynamic forecasts since the only data requirements of a forecast from an ARIMA model are the estimated lag polynomials, $\alpha(L)$ and $\beta(L)$, and the history of Y_t; if the model is estimated over the period 1, 2, . . , T, then to forecast Y_{T+1} the relevant history of Y_t constitutes the original data. To forecast Y_{T+2} the relevant history of Y_t includes the original data set plus the forecast value of Y_{T+1} from the first step. In this way successive forecasts depend on previous forecasts. Obviously, if any of those forecasts are in serious error then such errors will accumulate the further one forecasts into the future.

An alternative forecasting method, which may have no dependence upon theoretical considerations, is to model Y_t as if its path were wholly time dependent: one could model Y_t as a linear function of time (and dummy variables may be included to accommodate any seasonalities) so that:

$$Y_t = \alpha + \beta t + \sum_{i=1}^{3} \gamma_i D_{ti} + \varepsilon_t$$

where $D_{ti} = 1$ if observation Y_t is in quarter i and is zero otherwise (i = 1, 2, 3). The fitted equation then provides a simple method of forecasting Y, and assumes that Y has a deterministic trend and seasonal component. This constitutes trend extrapolation.

The variable could, alternatively, be modelled as if it had a constant growth rate which, in its simplest form, is the model:

$$\ell n Y_t = \alpha + \beta t + \varepsilon_t .$$

The simplest time-series models, using deterministic trends, are not favoured in comparison to the more complex ARIMA models and econometric models, such as ARMAX.

All forecasting techniques require judgement, whether that concerns a judgement of the underlying model, a judgement of the future values of explanatory variables which are required to construct the forecast, or of the model's applicability to the particular period of the forecast. One way to reduce the variance of a forecast is to use several different, unbiased, forecasts and combine them optimally so as to reduce the variance of their weighted average. This has been the subject of an extensive literature. One commonly observed method of combining forecasts is to take various 'expert' opinions and average them – the so-called Delphic method of forecasting.

Further reading

See Holden, Peel and Thompson (1990) who survey the various methods of forecasting; see also Granger and Newbold (1977), and see Winkler and Makridakis (1983) especially on combining forecasts. Salkever (1976) and Kennedy (1990) examine the use of observation-specific dummies in the context of prediction.

Fragility

The concept of fragility is closely associated with the construction and use of extreme bounds analysis (EBA) (see **Extreme bounds analysis**). From an EBA, inference of a parameter, say β_1, is described as fragile if the estimates of β_1 from a variety of regression equations (which differ in the way in which explanatory variables are included) cover a wide range which cannot be reduced by imposing plausible restrictions. Hence, having constructed the extreme bounds for the parameter and found a wide range, the analysis of fragility concerns the form of restrictions necessary to reduce that range; if the restrictions are deemed implausible then inference is described as fragile.

A Bayesian analysis combines prior information with sample information to produce the posterior distribution; the posterior distribution, defined on the parameters, is the product the prior distributions and the likelihood function. The examination of fragility is concerned with the way in which the mean of the posterior distribution changes as the prior variance is changed. Specifically, starting with a prior variance–covariance matrix V, fragility analysis examines the effect of using a different matrix, Ω, where Ω is defined by:

$$(1-\lambda)V \leq \Omega \leq [1/(1-\lambda)]V \quad \text{where } 0 \leq \lambda \leq 1.$$

When $\lambda = 0$ Ω is equal to the prior variance–covariance matrix and as λ increases from 0 to 1 the prior precision, as measured by the diagonal elements of Ω^{-1}, falls; fragility analysis considers, for each value of λ, the posterior means which result from using each side of the inequality on Ω. This is a sensitivity analysis, and is in one sense an examination of the shape of the likelihood function: if the likelihood is very peaked around the maximum likelihood estimate then increasing λ will cause the posterior mean to shift away from the prior mean to the maximum likelihood estimate; however, if the likelihood function is very flat the posterior and prior means will always be very close. Changing λ will have an effect on the posterior mean which reflects the role of the likelihood function: changing λ reflects the relative roles of prior and sample information. When the dimension of the likelihood function is high this approach provides a simple method of examining the curvature of the likelihood since the high dimensionality of the problem is captured by a single parameter, λ. As an example of a sensitivity analysis it is, however, a very limited approach, concentrating as it does on the relationship between the posterior means and the prior variances.

Nevertheless, fragility analysis does address one of the criticisms of Bayesian econometrics, namely the potential sensitivity of inferences to the particular prior distribution; by reporting the posterior means which result from a variety of priors (which vary according to the precision they embody) the relationship of the posterior to the prior is made more clear. If the posterior means are relatively insensitive to the precision of the prior then greater confidence may be attached to the information contained in the posterior distribution (but this is, then, only a reflection of the high degree of curvature of the likelihood function); also, if the posterior mean is very sensitive to the prior precision the inferences are then claimed to be 'too fragile' to be the basis of inference. Extreme Bounds Analysis examines the sensitivity of the posterior distribution to the prior means on the doubtful variables and taken together with fragility analysis it is argued that the two approaches provide a useful reporting device.

Further reading

Leamer (1986) provides the original source of this analysis; the software package SEARCH (**S**eeking **E**xtreme and **A**verage **R**egression **C**oefficient **H**ypotheses) facilitates fragility analysis. See also Ziemer (1984) for a discussion of potential applications of the approach and, for a critique, see Pagan (1987).

Frisch–Waugh theorem

The Frisch–Waugh theorem is a very powerful and useful theorem. It was developed in the context of regression models involving variables each of which is subject to a time trend and it shows that by regressing Y on the k variables $X_1, X_2, \ldots, X_k$ and a time trend as an additional regressor results in estimates of the relationship between Y and the k regressors $\{X_j\}$ which are identical to those which result from regressing Y purged of its time trend on the k regressors $\{X_j\}$, each of which has been purged of its time trend. In this context, 'purging' means regressing each variable on the time trend and treating the ordinary least squares residuals from such auxiliary regressions as the 'purged' variable. Since the residuals from the auxiliary regressions on a time trend are necessarily orthogonal to the trend the residuals contain information on Y and X *except* that which is linearly related to the trend.

In general the theorem shows that if variables are subject to prior adjustment by ordinary least squares and the residuals subsequently used in a regression equation then the resulting estimates are identical to those from a regression which uses unadjusted data but includes the adjustment variables explicitly.

Suppose, in the general linear model, the regressors are split into two disjoint sets, X and Z, containing k_1 and k_2 linearly independent regressors respectively, so that:

$$Y = X\beta + Z\gamma + \varepsilon$$

which may be written as $Y = W\delta + \varepsilon$, where $W = [X \;\; Z]$ and $\delta = \begin{bmatrix} \beta \\ \gamma \end{bmatrix}$.

The OLS estimator, $\hat{\delta}$, is given by $(W'W)^{-1}W'Y$ and the normal equations are given by $W'W\hat{\delta} = W'Y$ which may be expanded as:

$$X'X\hat{\beta} + X'Z\hat{\gamma} = X'Y \quad \text{and} \quad Z'X\hat{\beta} + Z'Z\hat{\gamma} = Z'Y.$$

From the second equation:

$$\hat{\gamma} = (Z'Z)^{-1}(Z'Y - Z'X\hat{\beta})$$

and substituting into the first equation yields:

$$X'X\hat{\beta} + X'Z(Z'Z)^{-1}(Z'Y - Z'X\hat{\beta}) = X'Y$$

hence:
$$X'[I - Z(Z'Z)^{-1}Z']X\hat{\beta} = X'[I - Z(Z'Z)^{-1}Z']Y$$

Denoting $I - Z(Z'Z)^{-1}Z'$ by M_z, this may be written as:

$$\hat{\beta} = (X'M_zX)^{-1}X'M_zY$$

and by symmetry:

$$\hat{\gamma} = (Z'M_xZ)^{-1}Z'M_xY$$

Now suppose Y and X are purged of Z by regressing each on Z and retaining the residuals; denote the residuals of Y on Z by Y* and those of X on Z by X*:

$$Y^* = Y - Z(Z'Z)^{-1}Z'Y = M_zY \quad \text{and} \quad X^* = X - Z(Z'Z)^{-1}Z'X = M_zX.$$

Note that both Y* and X* are orthogonal to Z since $Z'M_z \equiv 0$. If Y* is now regressed on X* in the auxiliary regression: $Y^* = X^*b + v$, the OLS estimate is given by:

$$\hat{b} = (X^{*\prime}X^*)^{-1}X^{*\prime}Y^* = (X'M_zX)^{-1}X'M_zY$$

(noting that M_z is idempotent); i.e. $\hat{b} = \hat{\beta}$.

Hence using the 'purged', adjusted, variables in a regression yields exactly the same estimate for the response of Y to X as using the unadjusted variables but including Z in the multiple regression.

Not only is $\hat{b}$ identical to $\hat{\beta}$, but so is the estimated variance–covariance matrix; in regressing Y on X and Z the estimated variance of $\hat{\delta}$ is given by:

$$\hat{V}(\hat{\delta}) = s^2(W'W)^{-1}$$

where $s^2 = (Y - X\hat{\beta} - Z\hat{\gamma})'(Y - X\hat{\beta} - Z\hat{\gamma})(n - k_1 - k_2)$. Now:

$$(W'W)^{-1} = \begin{bmatrix} X'X & X'Z \\ Z'X & Z'Z \end{bmatrix}^{-1}$$

And by application of the rules of inverting a partitioned matrix (see **Matrix algebra**), the upper left sub-matrix of $(W'W)^{-1}$ is given by $(X'M_zX)^{-1}$. Hence:

$$\hat{V}(\hat{\beta}) = s^2(X'M_zX)^{-1}$$

but from the regression of Y* on X*, the estimated variance of $\hat{b}$ is given by $\hat{V}(\hat{b}) = \hat{\sigma}^2(X'M_zX)^{-1}$ where $\hat{\sigma}^2$ is the estimated variance of this regression. $\hat{V}(\hat{\beta})$ and $\hat{V}(\hat{b})$ are identical if s^2 and $\hat{\sigma}^2$ are identical. $\hat{\sigma}^2$ is equal to the residual sum of squares from the regression of T* on X*, divided by the degrees of freedom; the degrees of freedom are given by the degrees of freedom in Y* minus k_1, the number of variables in X. Y* only has $n - k_2$ degrees of freedom (since k_2 degrees have been consumed in the regression of Y on Z to yield Y*) and so the degrees of freedom in $\hat{\sigma}^2$ is $n - k_1 - k_2$, which is identical to the degrees of freedom in s^2. Hence $s^2 = \hat{\sigma}^2$ if the residual sums of squares from the multiple regression of Y on X and Z and from the purged regression of Y* and X* are identical. The latter is given by $(Y^* - X^*\hat{b})'(Y^* - X^*\hat{b})$ and to compute the former, note that:

$$\hat{e} = Y - X\hat{\beta} - Z\hat{\gamma};$$

but it was shown above that:

$$\hat{\gamma} = (Z'Z)^{-1}(Z'Y - Z'X\hat{\beta})$$

and so:

$$\hat{e} = Y - X\hat{\beta} - Z[(Z'Z)^{-1}(Z'Y - Z'X\hat{\beta})] = M_zY - M_zX\hat{\beta} = M_z(Y - X\hat{\beta})$$

Hence, noting that M_z is symmetric and idempotent:

$$s^2 = \hat{e}'\hat{e}/(n - k_1 - k_2) = (Y - X\hat{\beta})'M_z(Y - X\hat{\beta})/(n - k_1 - k_2)$$

But:

$$\begin{aligned}\hat{\sigma}^2 &= (Y^* - X^*\hat{b})'(Y^* - X^*\hat{b})/(n - k_1 - k_2)\\ &= (Y^* - X^*\hat{\beta})'(Y^* - X^*\hat{\beta})/(n - k_1 - k_2) \qquad \text{since } \hat{b} = \hat{\beta}\\ &= [M_z(Y - X\hat{\beta})]'[M_z(Y - X\hat{\beta}]/(n - k_1 - k_2)\\ &= (Y - X\hat{\beta})'M_z(Y - X\hat{\beta})/(n - k_1 - k_2) = s^2\end{aligned}$$

Hence, in a multiple regression of Y on X and Z exactly the same inferences are made regarding the relationship between Y and X from this multiple regression as from the 'adjusted' regression of Y purged of Z on X purged of Z, given that the 'purging' consists of utilizing the residuals from regressing each of Y and X on Z. This result may be illustrated by the Venn diagram approach (detailed in **Venn diagrams**).

One immediate implication of this result may be seen in terms of deseasonalization and detrending: if deseasonalization and detrending consist of regressing variables on seasonal dummies and a time trend and labelling the residuals as the deseasonalized (or detrended) variables, then using the 'raw' data in a multiple regression which includes seasonal dummies and a time trend results in exactly the same inferences as those which result from using the deseasonalized and detrended data in a regression model (see **Seasonality**).

Further reading
See Frisch and Waugh (1933) in which this theorem was first introduced.

Full information maximum likelihood

In estimating the structural parameters of a system of simultaneous equations it is common for a limited information method, such as two-stage least squares, to be used or, if a full information method is used, three stage least squares is the commonest approach; the staged least squares methods owe their popularity to their relative ease of computation. The full information maximum likelihood (FIML) estimation method is a method which estimates the system as a whole and, with normally distributed errors, is efficient amongst all estimators. Unlike staged least squares methods, the estimates obtained are invariant to normalization.

Suppose that there are T observations available; denote by Y_t the $G\times 1$ vector of observations on the G endogenous variables at time t, by X_t the $K\times 1$ vector of observations on the K exogenous and pre-determined variables at time t and by ε_t the $G\times 1$ vector of disturbances. Let B be the $G\times G$ matrix of parameters $\{\beta_{pi}\}$ and let Γ be the $G\times K$ matrix of parameters $\{\gamma_{pj}\}$; the tth observations of this system of G equations may then be written as:

$$BY_t + \Gamma X_t = \varepsilon_t$$

B contains G^2 parameters and Γ contains GK parameters; this equation, therefore, contains the $G^2 + GK$ structural parameters of the system, and the G equations $BY_t + \Gamma X_t = \varepsilon_t$ are called the structural equations. If the G equations are linearly independent, that is, no equation can be obtained as a linear combination of any of the other equations, the structure can be 'solved' so as to express each of the G endogenous variables in terms of the other variables:

$$Y_t = -B^{-1}\Gamma X_t + B^{-1}\varepsilon_t, \qquad t = 1, 2, \ldots, T$$

i.e.

$$Y_t = \Pi X_t + v_t.$$

where $\Pi = -B^{-1}\Gamma$ and $v_t = B^{-1}\varepsilon_t$

The FIML method assumes that the errors in the reduced-form equations are multivariate normally distributed, with a zero mean and unknown covariance matrix. The log-likelihood of the reduced form may be expressed in terms of the unknown parameters, which may then be maximized subject to all the zero restrictions on the structure. To compute the FIML estimates it is necessary to maximize a log-likelihood function in many parameters subject to the restrictions imposed by the exclusion restrictions on the structural form (which must, of course, be sufficient to satisfy the identification of each equation by the rank condition, see **Identification**). This constrained maximization procedure can be very cumbersome and very expensive in terms of computing time. The question to be answered is: what is to be gained from FIML?

It has been shown (Hausman, 1975 and 1983) that the FIML estimator is actually an instrumental variable estimator and its asymptotic covariance matrix is identical to that of the three-stage least squares estimator. It may be concluded, therefore, that the three-stage least squares estimator and the FIML estimator have identical asymptotic distributions in the case of normally distributed errors. This result means that the more costly estimator (FIML) provides no asymptotic efficiency gains over the less costly approach of three-stage least squares. This result has certainly meant that FIML is the less popular estimation technique. Moreover, if the equations are exactly identified, then the FIML estimates are identical to those from indirect least squares, again obviating any need to use FIML in the exactly identified case.

One further important analytic result from analysis of FIML is that if the structural equations are not related via error covariances then the FIML estimates of the parameters are ordinary least squares estimators applied equation by equation to the structural equations. These estimators are, by virtue of being maximum likelihood estimators, consistent and asymptotically efficient. The special case in which OLS applied to the structural equations of a simultaneous system yields optimal estimators is considered further in **Recursive systems**.

Further reading

See Hausman (1975 and 1983), and Chow (1968) who presents two methods by which the FIML estimates may be computed. See also Maddala (1977).

Gauss–Markov theorem

The Gauss–Markov theorem shows that, in a well-specified general linear model, the ordinary least square estimators are linear, unbiased and, within the class of linear unbiased estimators, have least variance. In the sense of having least variance, such estimators are known as 'best' and hence OLS estimators are described as the BLUE (**B**est **L**inear **U**nbiased **E**stimators).

To prove this theorem is straightforward. Within the model $Y = X\beta + \varepsilon$ (in standard notation) suppose that β is estimated by $\tilde{\beta}$ where:

$$\tilde{\beta} = [A + (X'X)^{-1}X']Y$$

where A is some non-stochastic k×n matrix. The ordinary least squares estimator of β is given by $\hat{\beta} = (X'X)^{-1}X'Y$, and so $\tilde{\beta}$ is a linear estimator (a linear combination of the observations on the regressand), and is the sum of some linear combination, AY, of the observations Y and the ordinary least squares estimator, $\hat{\beta}$:

$$\tilde{\beta} = AY + \hat{\beta}$$

then: $E(\tilde{\beta}) = [A + (X'X)^{-1}X']E(Y) = [A + (X'X)^{-1}X']X\beta = (AX + I)\beta$
Thus $E(\tilde{\beta}) = \beta$ if and only if $AX = 0$; i.e. $\tilde{\beta}$ is unbiased if and only if $AX = 0$; thus, if $\tilde{\beta}$ is unbiased:

$$\tilde{\beta} = [A + (X'X)^{-1}X'](X\beta + \varepsilon) = \beta + [A + (X'X)^{-1}X']\varepsilon \quad \text{(since } AX = 0\text{)}.$$

Given that ε has a zero mean and a scalar variance matrix, the variance of $\tilde{\beta}$ may now be evaluated:

$$V(\hat{\beta}) = [A + (X'X)^{-1}X']\, \sigma^2 I\, [A + (X'X)^{-1}X']' = \sigma^2[AA' + (X'X)^{-1}].$$

The diagonal terms of AA' are sums of squares, which may be denoted by λ_i^2, $i = 1, 2, \ldots, k$; denoting the typical term of $(X'X)^{-1}$ by v_{ij}:

$$V(\tilde{\beta}_i) = \sigma^2(\lambda_i^2 + v_{ii});$$

but by ordinary least squares, $V(\hat{\beta}) = \sigma^2(X'X)^{-1}$, and so $V(\hat{\beta}_i) = \sigma^2 v_{ii}$; hence:

$$V(\tilde{\beta}_i) = \sigma^2\lambda_i^2 + V(\hat{\beta}_i) \geq V(\hat{\beta}_i)$$

The unbiased linear estimator $\tilde{\beta}_i$ thus has a variance which is always at least as great as that of the ordinary least squares estimator and the two have equal variances if and only if $\lambda_i^2 = 0$ for all i. Therefore,

$$V(\tilde{\beta}_i) = V(\hat{\beta}_i)$$

for all i if and only if $\lambda_i^2 = 0$ for all i. But $\lambda_i^2 = 0$ for all i if and only if $A = 0$. Therefore, the ordinary least squares estimator is, within the class of linear unbiased estimators, that with least variance.

This theorem establishes that within a well-specified model the OLS estimators have very desirable properties, and it should be noted that this proof has required only that ε have a zero mean and a scalar variance matrix and that the regressors are non-stochastic (that is, no assumption of normality has been required). In fact, under the assumption of normally distributed errors, the OLS estimator has the minimum variance of any unbiased estimator.

The attractiveness of best linear unbiased estimators is that:

1. by their linearity are they easy to compute and are analytically tractable;
2. by their unbiasedness they are 'right' 'on average';
3. by their 'bestness' they are, within the class of linear unbiased estimators, those with least variance.

Ease of computation is far less important now than was once the case; the advent of high-speed electronic computers, obviating the need for investigators to grind through the necessary arithmetic to obtain estimates, means that estimators which are numerically cumbersome can be computed with relative ease. This was once the preserve of linear estimators. Nevertheless, in order to examine the properties of an estimator, analytical tractability remains an important aspect of desirability (though this does not establish an argument for linear estimators – nonlinear estimators may also be analytically tractable). However, if the finite sample properties of estimators are not easily analysed then there are two approaches available: on the one hand one may consider the results of Monte Carlo experiments and on the other one may consider the large sample (asymptotic) properties of estimators; neither approach provides unambiguous evidence of the small finite sample properties of such estimators.

The second and third properties are to be considered together; unbiasedness is not, of itself, a decisive criterion by which to choose one estimator over another, and nor is efficiency. Were efficiency a decisive criterion one might take, as an extreme example, $\hat{\theta} = \theta_0$ as an estimator of some parameter θ, where θ_0 is some fixed number; clearly this estimator has no variance in repeated sampling and so is most efficient. But it is only 'right' if the true parameter is given by θ_0 and is otherwise always 'wrong'. This estimator is, in general, biased but its efficiency cannot be improved upon. In general if one is confronted with two estimators, say $\hat{\theta}_1$ and $\hat{\theta}_2$, and the former is unbiased but the latter is biased then, if $V(\hat{\theta}_1) < V(\hat{\theta}_2)$ the choice is simple: not only is $\hat{\theta}_1$ 'right' on average (while $\hat{\theta}_2$ is not) but the probability of an estimate being within some distance δ of θ using the $\hat{\theta}_1$ rule will be greater than that of an estimate using the $\hat{\theta}_2$ rule. This is a simple case and it is this kind of comparison which is made in the Gauss–Markov theorem: of all linear and unbiased estimators none has a variance smaller than that of the OLS estimator. However, if the comparison is between a biased estimator and an unbiased estimator, and the biased is the more efficient, the choice is not necessarily so clear. If the bias is small and the difference in variance large, then one might prefer the biased estimator to the unbiased. To construct a formal trade-off between bias and efficiency the mean square error (MSE) criterion is often used.

The converse of the Gauss–Markov theorem is that if any one of the assumptions necessary in its derivation fails, then OLS will not necessarily yield BLU estimators: to demonstrate unbiasedness it is required that the error term has a zero mean and is independent of the regressors (an extreme case of which is the familiar assumption that the regressors are fixed in repeated samples), and to show minimum variance it is necessary that the error term has a scalar variance–covariance matrix. Hence, for example, if the error term has a zero mean and is independent of the regressors but $\varepsilon \sim (0, \sigma^2\Omega)$, where $\Omega \neq I$, then $\hat{\beta}$ will be linear, unbiased but inefficient and if $\varepsilon \sim (0, \sigma^2 I)$ but ε and X are correlated then $\hat{\beta}$ will be biased (and possibly inconsistent).

It is not uncommon to compare two estimators, one of which is linear and the other of which is nonlinear; the Gauss–Markov theorem is only concerned with linear estimators and there are circumstances (such as feasible generalized least squares and, as a particular example, the estimation of ARCH or GARCH models) in which a nonlinear estimator is more efficient than the best available linear estimator.

Many of the early concerns of econometric theory, especially during the period up to the 1970s, were focused on the generation of BLU estimators. In this period, were any of the critical assumptions of OLS found wanting, the concern was to overcome the deficiencies of the OLS estimator and construct an alternative estimator which was the BLUE, or at least the nonlinear approximation to the BLUE (consider, especially, the feasible generalized least squares estimation of models characterized by heteroscedasticity and autocorrelation). Modern econometrics is far more concerned with wider matters of model specification and testing, rather than with merely constructing 'good' estimators of the parameters of a model whose specification is deemed correct with respect to its regressors and functional form.

Further reading

The Gauss–Markov theorem is presented and discussed in all econometrics texts, and the reader is referred to those and the references therein.

General linear model

Suppose there are n observations Y_i (i = 1, 2, . . , n) on some variable and it is proposed to regress this variable on a set of k regressors. Denote the ith observation on the jth regressor by X_{ij} and denote the coefficient attached to the jth regressor by β_j. Denoting the error term by ε_i the regression equation may then be written as:

$$Y_i = \beta_1 X_{i1} + \beta_2 X_{i2} + \; . \; . \; . \; . \; . + \beta_k X_{ik} + \varepsilon_i \quad \text{for } i = 1, 2, \ldots n.$$

It is common to include a constant term in regression equations, in which case set the first variable to be a dummy variable so that $X_{i1} = 1$ for all i; then β_1 is the 'constant' in the regression. Analysis of this general equation using only the tools of scalar algebra is extremely tedious and complicated, but the methods of matrix algebra provide a most compact and efficient form in which to analyse the model. Writing out all the n equations:

$$\begin{array}{lllllll} Y_1 & = & \beta_1 X_{11} & + \beta_2 X_{12} & + \; \ldots \ldots & + \beta_k X_{1k} & + \varepsilon_1 \\ Y_2 & = & \beta_1 X_{21} & + \beta_2 X_{22} & + \; \ldots \ldots & + \beta_k X_{2k} & + \varepsilon_2 \\ \vdots & = & \vdots & \vdots & & \vdots & \vdots \\ \vdots & = & \vdots & \vdots & & \vdots & \vdots \\ Y_n & = & \beta_1 X_{n1} & + \beta_2 X_{n2} & + \; \ldots \ldots & + \beta_k X_{nk} & + \varepsilon_n \end{array}$$

'Stacking' the equations, matrix notation may be used; defining the following terms:

$$Y = \begin{bmatrix} Y_1 \\ Y_2 \\ \vdots \\ \vdots \\ Y_n \end{bmatrix} \qquad X = \begin{bmatrix} X_{11} & X_{12} & \cdots & \cdots & X_{1k} \\ X_{21} & X_{22} & & & X_{2k} \\ \vdots & & \ddots & & \vdots \\ \vdots & & & \ddots & \vdots \\ X_{n1} & \cdots & \cdots & \cdots & X_{nk} \end{bmatrix}$$

$$\beta = \begin{bmatrix} \beta_1 \\ \beta_2 \\ \vdots \\ \beta_k \end{bmatrix} \qquad \varepsilon = \begin{bmatrix} \varepsilon_1 \\ \varepsilon_2 \\ \vdots \\ \vdots \\ \varepsilon_n \end{bmatrix}$$

Y represents the n observations on the regressand, X represents all n observations on all k regressors, β represents the k parameters and ε represents the n disturbances. Y and ε are both vectors of order n, β is a vector of order k and X is the data matrix of order n×k. The definitions and rules of matrix algebra allow the general linear model to be written as:

$$Y = X\beta + \varepsilon$$

The usual assumptions are as follows:

1. $E(\varepsilon_i) = 0$ for all i;
2. $Var(\varepsilon_i) = \sigma^2$ for all i;
3. ε_i and ε_j are independent for $i \neq j$;
4. all errors are independent of the regressors;
5. the regressors are 'fixed on repeated sampling';
6. each error, ε_i, is normally distributed.

It is to be noted that assumption (5) actually implies (4) since a random term is necessarily independent of X if X is non-stochastic. The distributional assumption (6) is required for the purpose of making inferences. These assumptions can be translated into matrix notation as follows: let $E(\varepsilon)$ be the n-dimensional vector comprising the terms $E(\varepsilon_i)$; then $E(\varepsilon) = 0$. Since ε is an n-dimensional random variable, not only must the variance of each ε_i be considered, but the covariances between all ε_i and ε_j $(i \neq j)$ must also be analysed. The variance–covariance matrix of ε is defined as:

$$V(\varepsilon) = \begin{bmatrix} V(\varepsilon_1) & Cov(\varepsilon_1\varepsilon_2) & \dots & \dots & Cov(\varepsilon_1\varepsilon_n) \\ Cov(\varepsilon_2\varepsilon_1) & V(\varepsilon_2) & & & Cov(\varepsilon_2\varepsilon_n) \\ \vdots & & \ddots & & \vdots \\ \vdots & & & \ddots & \vdots \\ Cov(\varepsilon_n\varepsilon_1) & \dots & \dots & \dots & V(\varepsilon_n) \end{bmatrix}$$

Since it has already been established that $E(\varepsilon) = 0$, $V(\varepsilon_i) = E(\varepsilon_i^2)$ and $Cov(\varepsilon_i, \varepsilon_j) = E(\varepsilon_i \varepsilon_j)$; hence:

$$V(\varepsilon) = E\begin{bmatrix} \varepsilon_1^2 & \varepsilon_1\varepsilon_2 & \dots & \dots & \varepsilon_1\varepsilon_n \\ \varepsilon_2\varepsilon_1 & \varepsilon_2^2 & & & \varepsilon_2\varepsilon_n \\ \vdots & & \ddots & & \vdots \\ \vdots & & & \ddots & \vdots \\ \varepsilon_n\varepsilon_1 & \dots & \dots & \dots & \varepsilon_n^2 \end{bmatrix}$$

Now consider the n×n matrix given by $\varepsilon \varepsilon'$:

$$\varepsilon\varepsilon' = \begin{bmatrix} \varepsilon_1 \\ \varepsilon_2 \\ \vdots \\ \vdots \\ \varepsilon_n \end{bmatrix} \begin{bmatrix} \varepsilon_1 & \varepsilon_2 & \dots & \dots & \varepsilon_n \end{bmatrix}$$

The typical element of this matrix is $\varepsilon_i \varepsilon_j$, and so:

$$V(\varepsilon) = E(\varepsilon \varepsilon').$$

The assumptions made regarding ε can now be used: $E(\varepsilon_i^2) = \sigma^2$ for all i, and $E(\varepsilon_i \varepsilon_j) = 0$ for $i \neq j$. Hence, under these standard assumptions $V(\varepsilon) = \sigma^2 I$, that is, the variance–covariance matrix of ε is a scalar matrix.

The general linear model, with its assumptions, may then be written compactly as:

$$Y = X\beta + \varepsilon$$

$\varepsilon \sim MVN(0, \sigma^2 I)$, and X is fixed on repeated sampling.

The statement regarding ε is to be read as 'ε is distributed multivariately normally with a zero mean and a scalar variance–covariance matrix'; this is the vector generalization of the distribution of a single random variable; it is often written simply as $\varepsilon \sim N(0, \sigma^2 I)$. The assumption that $\varepsilon \sim N(0, \sigma^2 I)$ may be relaxed to allow a more general form of $\varepsilon \sim N(0, \sigma^2 \Omega)$

Estimation of the parameters, β and σ^2 is considered in **Ordinary least squares**, **Generalized least squares**, **Maximum likelihood** and **Instrumental variables**.

Further reading

Chapter 4 of Johnston (1984) is an excellent presentation of the matrix algebra necessary for econometric work, illustrated with many examples, as is Chapter 2 of Greene (1993).

General to specific modelling

General to specific modelling is particularly designed to address issues of model specification using time-series data; it may be seen as comprising four stages:

1. Economic theory is used to specify the economic variables which enter a relationship; economic theory is seen as specifying an equilibrium relationship and it is assumed that the available data are a reflection of the short-run disequilibria around the long-run equilibrium. To accommodate the disequilibrium, the general equation which is first estimated includes lags of all the variables (exogenous variables and the dependent variable) as regressors. The dynamics inherent in this equation are unrestricted, except for their assumed linearity and the lag length. The starting position is, therefore, to specify an equation of the form (here written without an explicit constant term):

$$Y_t = \sum_{i=0}^{m} \sum_{j=1}^{k} \beta_{ij} X_{t-i,j} + \sum_{s=0}^{m-1} \gamma_s Y_{t-s-1} + \varepsilon_t .$$

The k variables, X_j, are chosen by reference to economic theory and the lag length, m, is chosen to be as large as possible, given the available data; ε_t is an error term having all the usual desirable properties of a zero mean, no autocorrelation, homoscedastic and uncorrelated with the X_j variables.

2. The above equation is in the form of a general autoregressive distributed lag (ADL) equation, and it may be re-parameterized in many ways; one immediate issue which arises in an ADL model is the potential multicollinearity among the lagged variables, and at stage two the equation is rewritten with the twin objectives of making the explanatory variables as nearly orthogonal as is possible and of constructing an easily interpretable equation. The common form of re-parameterization is the error correction mechanism (see **Error correction models**):

$$\Delta Y_t = \sum_{i=1}^{m-1}\left[\sum_{j=1}^{k}\lambda_{ij}\Delta X_{t-i,j} + \theta_i \Delta Y_{t-i-1}\right] + \sum_{j=1}^{k}\beta_{oj}\Delta X_{tj}$$
$$+ (\theta - 1)(Y_{t-1} - \sum_{j=1}^{k}\phi_j X_{t-i,j}) + \varepsilon_t.$$

The parameters λ_{ij}, θ_i and ϕ_j are all functions of the parameters of the original formulation in levels. The changes in the variables, the first differences, are closer to being orthogonal than are the levels of the variables. In the long run all such first differences are zero in which case the relationship between Y and the k variables, X, is given by $Y = \sum_{j=1}^{k}\phi_j X_j$; hence the term $Y_{t-1} - \sum_{j=1}^{k}\phi_j X_{t-1,j}$ may be interpreted as the difference, the 'error', between the actual value of Y and its long-run equilibrium value.

3. The third stage of the process seeks to simplify the general model to a more parsimonious equation; simplifying the model takes at least two quite different forms: variables may be deleted individually, or in sets, as a result of 'insignificant' F-statistics, and variables may be deleted as a result of testing for common factors (see **Common factors**). The former simplification is a straightforward application of testing a linear hypothesis; the latter simplification reduces the number of parameters to be estimated by, for example, deleting the longest lags on the variables and accommodating them by introducing autocorrelation into the error term. One objection to the process of simplification is that this is an obvious form of search, and unless the investigator reports exactly the particular route by which the general model is cut down to become the finally reported more parsimonious model, it is difficult for other users of the model to make informed assessments of its worth. One advantage claimed of this search is that when the process forms a sequence of nested

models (all later models are special cases of previous models) then the overall Type I error of the simplifications may be computed (unlike the case of modelling from a specific equation to a more general equation).

4. The final stage of general to specific modelling involves extensive testing of the specification via diagnostic tests; this comprises the so-called 'test, test and test' methodology, whereby the simplified equations at each stage are subjected to a battery of tests designed to test their adequacy. Adequacy is here defined in terms of the equation's residuals, both within the sample of estimation and outside the sample as a test of predictive performance. The simplified equation should possess certain characteristics: it should be data admissible, consistent with economic theory, have weakly exogenous regressors, have constant parameters, be data coherent and encompass rival models.

The criteria imply that the finally chosen equation is properly specified as a single equation (if the regressors are not weakly exogenous then single equation estimation would lead to biases), its parameters are constant (and so the equation may be used for policy analysis and forecasting), has an acceptable error structure (the error contains no systematic components which are deserving of further attention) and the equation is capable of explaining the results of other, rival, models; also, the equation may be interpreted with the context of some economic theory. The economic interpretation of the equation is conducted via an examination of the implied long-run steady-state relationship, $Y = \sum_{j=1}^{k} \phi_j X_j$; this has to be the case since economic theory typically provides no testable predictions on the short-run equation which incorporates the dynamic adjustment. This does not necessarily mean that the estimated equation may be used as a test of economic theory or that such an equation provides particular support for any particular economic theory. That the long-run form of the equation is consistent with one theory does not mean that it is inconsistent with any other theory, and this approach to model specification is not obviously capable of making a contribution to the formal testing of economic theory (since the investigator does not specify, prior to estimation, what observations would constitute a refutation of the main economic hypothesis). The general model which began the sequence of testing down involves what some would see as an *ad hoc* inclusion of lags and is, in that sense, not driven by theory; the general model may be consistent with a number of theories, and in consequence the finally chosen model may also be consistent with many theories and inconsistent with none. Moreover, if one were to treat the simplified equation as an adequate description of the way in which the data were generated in the real world (i.e. it represents the data-generating process), even then it is not immediately apparent that one could proceed to testing economic hypotheses using the equation. This follows from recognizing the fact that the simplification path is not unique, the parsimonious equation is not, then, unique, and if economic theory provides a yet simpler form of the equation (by imposing constraints which are not rejected by the data) then this would already have been accomplished in stage 3.

Notwithstanding criticisms of this approach it is extremely popular; it may be described as an intended over-parameterization followed by data-based simplifications. As a method of model specification it has advantages in its claimed ability to control the overall size of simplification tests, but it can resemble an uneasy interface between economic theory and applied econometrics.

Further reading

The general to specific approach may be traced back to Sargan (1964); see especially the papers by Mizon (1977) and Hendry and Mizon (1978), Hendry (1980) and Hendry and Richard (1983). For an overview of this modelling strategy, see Gilbert (1986).

Generalized least squares

Suppose the general linear model, $Y = X\beta + \varepsilon$, is specified; there are T observations available, and β contains k parameters. Suppose further that the usual assumption that the error term is white-noise is replaced by a more general assumption which allows ε to be both autocorrelated and heteroscedastic:

$$V(\varepsilon) = \sigma^2\Omega$$

where Ω is some positive definite non-stochastic matrix with (possibly) non-zeros off the diagonal and (possibly) non-constant diagonal elements; the former relaxation allows for the possibility of autocorrelation, and the latter for heteroscedasticity.

Since Ω is positive definite there exists a non-singular matrix P such that $PP' = \Omega$; P plays a role in matrix algebra similar to that of the square root operation in scalar algebra. Given the definition of P, pre-multiplying by P^{-1} and post-multiplying by P'^{-1}:

$$P^{-1}PP'P'^{-1} = P^{-1}\Omega P'^{-1}$$

i.e.
$$P^{-1}\Omega P'^{-1} = I$$

It is also to be noted that $(PP')^{-1} = \Omega^{-1}$, that is, $P'^{-1}P^{-1} = \Omega^{-1}$. Now consider the random variable given by $v = P^{-1}\varepsilon$ if the typical element of P^{-1} is p^{ij} then the typical element of v is given by:

$$v_t = \sum_{s=1}^{T} p^{ts}\varepsilon_s$$

that is, v_t is simply a linear combination of the elements of ε. Hence:

$$E(v) = E(P^{-1}\varepsilon) = P^{-1}E(\varepsilon) = 0 \qquad \text{since } E(\varepsilon) = 0.$$

and so $\quad V(P^{-1}\varepsilon) = E[P^{-1}\varepsilon][P^{-1}\varepsilon]' = E[P^{-1}\varepsilon\varepsilon'P^{-1\prime}]$

since P is a non-stochastic matrix, this simplifies to:

$$V(P^{-1}\varepsilon) = P^{-1}E(\varepsilon\varepsilon')P^{-1\prime}$$

But $E(\varepsilon\varepsilon') = V(\varepsilon)$, and the operations of inversion and transposition can be interchanged:

$$V(v) = V(P^{-1}\varepsilon) = \sigma^2 P^{-1}\Omega P'^{-1} = \sigma^2 I.$$

Thus, the transformed variable $P^{-1}\varepsilon$ has a scalar variance–covariance matrix; the effect of transforming the original random error by P^{-1} is to 'unscramble' the mutual dependencies and the heteroscedasticity to create a new random variable, $P^{-1}\varepsilon$, which has all the 'desirable' properties of a homoscedastic and non-autocorrelated term. If the entire model is then transformed by P^{-1} the result is a model which conforms to the usual OLS assumptions:

$$P^{-1}Y = P^{-1}X\beta + P^{-1}\varepsilon \qquad \text{which may be written as:} \qquad Y^* = X^*\beta + v$$

where $Y^* = P^{-1}Y$, $X^* = P^{-1}X$ and $v = P^{-1}\varepsilon$. The new dependent variable, Y^*, is simply a linear transformation of the original variable Y, and the same remark holds for X^*:

$$Y_t^* = \Sigma_{s=1}^{T} p^{ts} Y_s \text{ for all t} \quad \text{and} \quad X_{tj}^* = \Sigma_{s=1}^{T} p^{ts} X_{sj} \text{ for all t and j.}$$

Since the assumptions of the Gauss–Markov Theorem are satisfied in the transformed model, ordinary least squares may be applied to yield the best linear unbiased estimator of β:

$$\hat{\beta} = (X^{*\prime}X^*)^{-1}X^{*\prime}Y^* = (X'P^{-1\prime}P^{-1}X)^{-1}X'P^{-1\prime}P^{-1}Y = (X'\Omega^{-1}X)^{-1}X'\Omega^{-1}Y$$

and $\qquad V(\hat{\beta}) = \sigma^2(X^{*\prime}X^*)^{-1} = \sigma^2(X'\Omega^{-1}X)^{-1}$

$\hat{\beta}$ is known as the generalized least squares (GLS) estimator (or sometimes as the Aitken estimator).

Were Ω, the variance matrix of ε, known, then $\hat{\beta}$ could be computed; however, Ω is typically not known and must, then, be estimated. The estimator of Ω is, typically, constructed from the very same sample of observations which is then subsequently used to estimate β by generalized least squares; in that case the linearity and other finite sample properties of the estimator are lost. If Ω is not known but is estimated as $\hat{\Omega}$ then the estimated generalized least squares estimator is given by:

$$\tilde{\beta} = (X'\hat{\Omega}^{-1}X)^{-1}X'\hat{\Omega}^{-1}Y$$

It is clear, from the Gauss–Markov theorem, that when Ω is not an identity matrix the ordinary least squares estimator of β is linear and unbiased, but inefficient; it should also be noted that in such a circumstance the standard OLS formulae for the estimators of variances are no longer valid (the OLS formula is $s^2(X'X)^{-1}$, but this is constructed on the assumption that $V(\varepsilon) = \sigma^2 I$). Hence the application of OLS leads to improper inferences: even though $\hat{\beta}$ is not biased the standard formula for the estimators of the variances results in biased variance estimators and standard test statistics no longer have their assumed distributions.

If, as is usual, Ω is not known but is estimated, then using an estimated value, $\hat{\Omega}$, in the generalized least squares formula as written above leads to a feasible generalized least squares estimator of β, commonly denoted by FGLS (or EGLS, the estimated GLS estimator). However, Ω contains $T(T + 1)/2$ different elements (T diagonal elements plus only the lower diagonal elements since Ω is symmetric), and so it is essential that some restrictions are placed on Ω in order that it may be estimated. In general, suppose Ω is determined by j parameters which are independent of the k elements in β; then the model as a whole contains $k + j$ parameters (k elements in β and j parameters to determine Ω) and so given T observations it is essential that $k + j < T$, for otherwise all degrees of freedom would be consumed. Hence the restrictions on Ω must be such as to enable it to be determined by fewer than $T - k$ parameters. Most importantly, the estimate of Ω which is used must satisfy the requirements that $\hat{\Omega}^{-1}$ exists (that is, $\hat{\Omega}$ must be of full rank). One most important consequence of the requirement that $\hat{\Omega}^{-1}$ exists is that an obvious candidate is ruled out: having estimated the regression of Y on X by ordinary least squares and having obtained the OLS residuals, $\hat{e}$, it is tempting to construct the estimate:

$$\hat{\Omega} = \hat{e}\hat{e}'$$

However, the elements of the residual vector are not linearly independent (since they are defined by $X'\hat{e} = 0$) and so it is immediately obvious that this proposed estimator of Ω is not of full rank. This is not, then, an operational route. For approaches to estimation in the case of a non-scalar variance matrix see, for example, **Autocorrelation – estimation methods**, **Heteroscedasticity – estimation methods** and **Maximum likelihood**.

When Ω is known the GLS estimator is the best linear unbiased estimator; but the relevant practical consideration is not a comparison of the efficiency of the OLS and GLS estimators, but rather a comparison of the OLS and FGLS estimators (since Ω is, typically, not known). As is noted above, the FGLS estimator is not, in general, a linear estimator, and this makes analysis of finite sample results difficult. In finite samples there is not a unique definitive conclusion to the relevant efficiency comparison. However, Monte Carlo analysis indicates that, at least in moderately sized samples, the efficiency gain from FGLS is usually significant, although this will not always be the case and is specific to the particular model. Asymptotic results may be derived, however. The consistency of the GLS estimator is assured if:

$$\text{plim } T^{-1}(X'\Omega^{-1}X) = Q$$

where Q is finite and non-singular. If $\hat{\Omega}$ is such that:

$$\text{plim } T^{-1}(X'\hat{\Omega}^{-1}X) = \text{plim } T^{-1}(X'\Omega^{-1}X) = Q$$

and

$$\text{plim } T^{-1/2}X'\hat{\Omega}^{-1}\varepsilon = \text{plim } T^{-1/2}X'\Omega^{-1}\varepsilon$$

then both the GLS and FGLS estimators are consistent, both being asymptotically normal with mean β and variance matrix given by $T^{-1}\sigma^2Q^{-1}$. Moreover, if

$$\text{plim } T^{-1}\varepsilon'(\hat{\Omega}^{-1} - \Omega^{-1})\varepsilon = 0$$

then σ^2 may be consistently estimated.

Hence, when these conditions hold the FGLS estimator may be computed according to:

$$\tilde{\beta} = (X'\hat{\Omega}^{-1}X)^{-1}X'\hat{\Omega}^{-1}Y$$

and $\tilde{\beta}$ has a covariance estimator which may be estimated consistently by:

$$\tilde{\sigma}^2(X'\hat{\Omega}^{-1}X)^{-1}$$

where $\tilde{\sigma}^2 = \tilde{e}'\hat{\Omega}^{-1}\tilde{e}/(T-k)$ and $\tilde{e} = Y - X\tilde{\beta}$.

The FGLS estimator is, under these conditions, asymptotically more efficient than the OLS estimator. However, it should be noted that the requirement that $\hat{\Omega}$ represents a consistent estimator of Ω is not sufficient for this result. For a method by which to estimate Ω consistently when Ω depends in an assumed fashion on a limited number of parameters, see **Maximum likelihood**. Given the above conditions, the FGLS estimator has identical large sample properties to its GLS counterpart; thus in large samples all conventional test statistics (t- and F-tests for example) are valid. However in small samples the FGLS estimator is, in general, neither unbiased nor normally distributed, and conventional statistics may be seen as only approximations and are, then, to be used with caution.

Most importantly, even if the diagnostic tests from a regression indicate residuals which are inconsistent with white-noise errors this does not constitute sufficient evidence upon which to discard the OLS technique and proceed to an FGLS estimation. Autocorrelated or heteroscedastic residuals may be a symptom of some form of mis-specification of the regression equation, such as mis-specified dynamics, omitted variables, incorrect functional form, random coefficients, etc., as opposed to the interpretation that the properties of residuals are merely a reflection of the very same properties of the true errors. The investigator should therefore explore the possible interpretation of the autocorrelated or heteroscedastic residuals and only if satisfied that this reflects a non-scalar variance–covariance matrix of the true errors should an EGLS estimation technique be adopted.

Further reading
The derivation of the generalized least squares estimator uses the result of the theorem due to Aitken (1935). For an examination of the small sample properties of the estimated, feasible, generalized least squares estimator, see, for example, Griliches and Rao (1969) and Taylor (1977). Estimation of the GLS model is further examined in Schmidt (1976) and Magnus (1978).

Grouped data

Grouped data is a particular case of censored data; grouped data refers to data for which the actual observations are not reported but either a range, or the mean value within a class, are reported. For example, in order to preserve the anonymity of respondents, it is common practice for survey data to be reported as a set of mean values for given groupings of respondents – for respondents within a given income range their average income and the average expenditure on various categories of goods are reported, rather than the actual incomes and expenditures of each respondent. For large data sets compiled by survey methods considerations of pragmatism may lead to an analysis of the grouped data, even if the original data are available (this can facilitate computation and lower the costs of analysis, for example). Suppose at the micro level a relationship is posited:

$$Y = X\beta + \varepsilon;$$

but that data are available only on group means; a group mean is simply an average of certain rows of the Y and X matrices, and since the regression relationship is assumed to hold for all individuals, it will also hold across the group means. However, by using group means some information is inevitably lost, and this may be expected to lead to some loss of efficiency in estimation. Suppose that of the original n observations, data are only available on G groups, where G is very much smaller than n. The ith group is an aggregation of n_i observations (so that $\sum_{i=1}^{G} n_i = n$), and observations are available of the group averages of both the dependent variable y and the k regressors. Let the G group averages of Y be denoted by the vector $\overline{y}$, the G group averages of the k regressors be denoted by the matrix $\overline{x}$, and the corresponding G group averages of the true errors be denoted by the vector $\overline{\varepsilon}$, then:

$$\overline{y} = \overline{x}\beta + \overline{\varepsilon}.$$

Clearly, given that $E(\varepsilon) = 0$, $E(\overline{\varepsilon}) = 0$; ordinary least squares applied to the G observations will, given non-stochastic regressors, yield an unbiased estimator of β; however, this will not be efficient, since the error term $\overline{\varepsilon}$ is no longer homoscedastic (in general). Denoting by $\overline{\varepsilon}_i$ the average true error of the ith group, $V(\overline{\varepsilon}_i) = \sigma^2/n_i$, and so the error term $\overline{\varepsilon}$ is heteroscedastic unless the groups are all of an identical size. This is a particularly straightforward example in which the heteroscedasticity is of a known form; weighting the means of the ith group by $\sqrt{n_i}$, so that $y_i^* = \overline{y}_i \sqrt{n_i}$, and $x_{ij}^* = \overline{x}_{ij} \sqrt{n_i}$ allows a regression of y* on x* which yields the best linear unbiased estimator of β. This is, however, only the BLUE of β given the data on group means, and a yet more efficient estimator would result if all n original data observations could be used.

There is a loss of efficiency due to the loss of information and, not surprisingly, the loss in efficiency is greater the greater is the variability of the data within the groups. If the variation within the groups is large a great deal of information is lost once that variability is collapsed into one reported data point. However, a consequence of this is that having averaged the true disturbance terms the variation to be explained by the regression may be much smaller, leading to a larger R^2 statistic for the grouped mean regression than could be obtained from the original raw data. This is an important issue, for the aggregation of the raw data into group averages may actually be beneficial if the original data suffer measurement errors, for example; in that case the aggregation may lead to a cancelling out of such errors and lead to more precise estimators (as suggested by an improved goodness-of-fit from the grouped regression).

Further reading

The potential benefits from aggregation are discussed in Grunfeld and Griliches (1960) and developed in Ringwald (1980). See **Pooling data**.

Heteroscedasticity

The assumption that the error term in a regression model has a constant variance for all observations is the assumption of homoscedasticity; when this assumption fails the error is described as heteroscedastic. Within the standard model, $Y = X\beta + \varepsilon$, ε is assumed to be such that $V(\varepsilon_i) = \sigma^2$ for all i = 1, 2, . . . n. This assumption may fail within time-series or cross-section data; in time-series data the failure may be complex and of the form of an ARCH or GARCH process (see **ARCH and GARCH**) and in cross-section models the failure may be much more simple, in which the error variance may be related to the size of the cross-section units under consideration.

If this assumption fails (but the errors are not autocorrelated) then the variance–covariance matrix of ε is a diagonal matrix so that $V(\varepsilon) = \sigma^2 \text{diag}\{\lambda_1^2, \lambda_2^2, \quad \lambda_n^2\} = \sigma^2\Omega$; the variance of ε_i is given by $\sigma^2\lambda_i^2$, and the covariance between ε_i and ε_j, $i \neq j$, is zero.

The immediate consequence of heteroscedasticity for the ordinary least squares estimator of β is that while the estimator remains unbiased, it loses efficiency. This loss of efficiency follows directly from the Gauss–Markov theorem: that theorem shows that when the error term is wholly non-systematic (a white-noise random variable), then ordinary least squares estimation produces best linear unbiased estimators. All the properties of a white-noise error are required in the proof of this theorem, and in the case of heteroscedasticity the error does not have all the required properties; therefore, OLS estimation cannot produce BLU estimators. Specifically, the consequences may be shown as follows. Let the estimator of β be denoted by $\hat{\beta}$ so that:

$$\hat{\beta} = (X'X)^{-1}X'Y = (X'X)^{-1}X'(X\beta + \varepsilon) = \beta + (X'X)^{-1}X'\varepsilon$$

i.e. $\hat{\beta}$ comprises two components, one the 'true' value of the parameter, β, and the other a linear combination of the random elements. Taking expectations, assuming that the X matrix is deterministic and that the errors are all drawn from a zero mean distribution:

$$E(\hat{\beta}) = \beta.$$

Turning to the variance–covariance matrix of $\hat{\beta}$, by definition:

$$V(\hat{\beta}) = E\{[\hat{\beta} - E(\hat{\beta})][\hat{\beta} - E(\hat{\beta})]'\} = E\{[(X'X)^{-1}X'\varepsilon][(X'X)^{-1}X'\varepsilon]'\}$$

i.e. $$V(\hat{\beta}) = E\{(X'X)^{-1}X'\varepsilon\varepsilon'X(X'X)^{-1}\}.$$

Given that the X matrix is deterministic, this simplifies to:

$$V(\hat{\beta}) = (X'X)^{-1}X'E(\varepsilon\varepsilon')X(X'X)^{-1}$$

Now $E(\varepsilon\varepsilon')$ is simply the variance–covariance matrix of ε, here equal to $\sigma^2\Omega$; hence:

$$V(\hat{\beta}) = \sigma^2(X'X)^{-1}X'\Omega X(X'X)^{-1}$$

If $\Omega = I$, then this condenses to the familiar expression:

$$V(\hat{\beta}) = \sigma^2(X'X)^{-1}$$

However, in the heteroscedastic case, this result is not attainable. The familiar formula for the variance–covariance matrix is, then, not appropriate in this case; more importantly the estimation of $V(\hat{\beta})$ involves the estimation of σ^2, and the OLS method assumes that the error term is white noise and estimates the variance of the errors by $s^2 = RSS/(n - k)$ (where RSS is the residual sum of squares from the OLS regression, there are n observations and β comprises k elements). s^2 is, however, only unbiased under the assumption of a scalar variance–covariance matrix and in the case of heteroscedasticity it is biased; this is easily shown. If the OLS residuals are denoted by $\hat{e}$, then $(n - k)s^2 = \hat{e}'\hat{e} = \varepsilon'M\varepsilon$, where M is the idempotent matrix $I - X(X'X)^{-1}X'$; now:

$$E(\hat{e}'\hat{e}) = E(\Sigma_{i=1}^{n} m_{ii}\varepsilon_i^2 + \Sigma_{i\neq j}^{n}\Sigma_{j=1}^{n} m_{ij}\varepsilon_i\varepsilon_j)$$

$$= \sigma^2\Sigma_{i=1}^{n} m_{ii}\lambda_i^2 \qquad (\text{since } E(\varepsilon_i\varepsilon_j) = 0,\ i \neq j)$$

and $$E(s^2) = \left(\sigma^2\sum_{i=1}^{n} m_{ii}\lambda_i^2\right)\Big/(n-k) \text{ which implies that } E(s^2) \neq \sigma^2.$$

The estimated variance–covariance matrix of $\hat{\beta}$ reported by the method of OLS is:

$$\hat{V}(\hat{\beta}) = s^2(X'X)^{-1}$$

Clearly, two things 'go wrong' in the heteroscedastic case:

1. the correct formula for the true variance of $\hat{\beta}$ is not given by the standard expression $\sigma^2(X'X)^{-1}$;
2. the standard formula for the estimator of the error variance, σ^2, is not applicable since the concept of *the* error variance assumes homoscedasticity and s^2 is a biased estimator of σ^2.

When the errors are heteroscedastic the OLS estimator of the coefficient β is unbiased but is inefficient (and is asymptotically inefficient), the formula for the *true* variance of $\hat{\beta}$ is not given by $\sigma^2(X'X)^{-1}$ and the estimator of the variance, $\hat{V}(\hat{\beta})$, is biased. Inefficiency of $\hat{\beta}$ is the least of the two problems, since inefficiency can be compensated by a large number of observations. The bias in $\hat{V}(\hat{\beta})$ (produced by an invalid formula for $V(\hat{\beta})$ and a biased estimator of σ^2) is a serious problem: it means that conventionally computed test statistics do not have their assumed distribution and that conventionally constructed confidence regions are also invalid. Specifically, when $\Omega = I$ it may be shown that $(n-k)s^2/\sigma^2 \sim \chi^2_{n-k}$, but the distribution of $(n-k)s^2/\sigma^2$

when $\Omega \neq I$ is not χ^2 and so subsequent tests, using t- and F-distributions, which rely on the estimated variance–covariance matrix of $\hat{\beta}$ are no longer valid.

One must be careful to draw the distinction between the true variance of $\hat{\beta}$ and the estimated variance of $\hat{\beta}$. In the present case the former is given by $\sigma^2(X'X)^{-1}X'\Omega X(X'X)^{-1}$ and the latter is given by $s^2(X'X)^{-1}$.

If Ω were known the then it would be possible to construct the best linear unbiased estimator of β by using generalized least squares. In most practical circumstances, however, GLS cannot, typically, be applied since Ω is not known (an exception is described in **Grouped data**). If Ω is to be estimated, so that feasible generalized least squares can be applied, it is then necessary to restrict the structure of heteroscedasticity such as to ensure that it is determined by fewer than $n - k$ parameters (the number of available degrees of freedom).

Tests of heteroscedasticity are based on an examination of the ordinary least squares residuals. If evidence of heteroscedasticity is found, the unambiguous conclusion is that the original model, together with the assumption that $V(\varepsilon) = \sigma^2 I$, is mis-specified. This may be due to heteroscedasticity in the true errors of the model $Y = X\beta + \varepsilon$; in that case it would be appropriate to try to identify the precise form of the heteroscedasticity and then estimate the model's parameters by, for example, feasible generalized least squares or, better, maximum likelihood methods. It is important that any form of heteroscedasticity has an economic justification in the context of the model. In some cases the form of the heteroscedasticity might be relatively easy to identify and justify in terms of economic theory. For example, in cases of cross-section data with units of differing sizes (such as households in an income-expenditure analysis) it might be possible to identify an appropriate scale factor (such as household size) and if it is possible then to argue that the variance of the error might be expected to vary systematically with the scale variable the model may be re-estimated taking explicit account of the heteroscedasticity. Where a number of potential weight functions are available they may be tested by comparison of the resulting estimated models.

However, the residuals from the regression of Y on X may exhibit heteroscedasticity because the systematic component of the model is mis-specified and when the presence of heteroscedasticity is interpreted as evidence of a mis-specification the direction of that mis-specification must be further investigated. It could be due, for example, to the use of an incorrect functional form and a regressor, such as x_j^2, has been omitted; in this case the influence of the quadratic term may have been translated into the residuals to give the appearance of heteroscedasticity. This is a testable source of heteroscedasticity via tests such as the RESET test (see the entry of that title). Another interpretation of heteroscedasticity arises if the parameter β is not constant but is a random variable; for analysis of this case see **Random coefficient model**. Only if the heteroscedastic residuals are interpreted as a reflection of heteroscedastic true errors should an estimation method such as feasible generalized least squares or maximum likelihood be employed. In the event of residual heteroscedasticity being observed in the model $Y = X\beta + \varepsilon$, and having explored and discarded the mis-specification alternatives and having tried various (economically) justifiable weighting schemes and having discarded all such interpretations, inferences based on the OLS results will be misleading since the OLS reported variances will be biased. In that case, as a 'last resort', it is possible to construct estimators of the variances which are robust to heteroscedasticity (see **White's test**).

Further reading
The literature on heteroscedasticity is extremely wide ranging and complex; the bibliography in Judge *et al.* (1982 and 1985) is very comprehensive, as is that of most modern texts (see, for example, the references to chapter 14 of Greene (1993)). The reader is best referred to such texts and the references therein for further reading on this topic. See also **Heteroscedasticity – estimation methods** and **Heteroscedasticity tests**.

Heteroscedasticity – estimation methods

If, in the general linear model $Y = X\beta + \varepsilon$ the error term ε is heteroscedastic then $V(\varepsilon_i) = \sigma^2\lambda_i^2$ and the λ_i^2 terms are not constant over the observations ($i = 1, 2, \ldots, n$). In this case the variance matrix of ε may be written as $V(\varepsilon) = \sigma^2\Omega$ where $\Omega = \text{diag}\{\lambda_i^2\}$; it is assumed that the error terms are mutually independent so that the off-diagonal elements of Ω are all zero. Although ε_i is heteroscedastic it is easy to transform ε_i into a homoscedastic variable: $V(\varepsilon_i/\lambda_i) = (1/\lambda_i^2)V(\varepsilon_i) = \sigma^2$. Hence the new variable, ε_i/λ_i, is homoscedastic; this transformation gives rise to the estimation method known as weighted least squares (WLS).

Define the n×n matrix P by $P = \text{diag}\{\lambda_i\}$; hence $P^{-1} = \text{diag}\{\lambda_i^{-1}\}$. Thus:

$$P^{-1}\varepsilon = \begin{bmatrix} \varepsilon_1/\lambda_1 \\ \varepsilon_2/\lambda_2 \\ \vdots \\ \vdots \\ \varepsilon_n/\lambda_n \end{bmatrix}$$

Hence, if Ω were known, P would then be known, and the best linear unbiased estimator of β could then be produced by running the regression:

$$P^{-1}Y = P^{-1}X\beta + P^{-1}\varepsilon$$

In this special case this amounts to running the ordinary least squares regression:

$$Y_i/\lambda_i = \sum_{j=1}^{k}(X_{ij}/\lambda_i)\beta_j + \varepsilon_i/\lambda_i;$$

that is, dividing each observation of the regressand and regressors by λ_i (which is proportional to the standard deviation of the error for that observation) and then using standard ordinary least squares. This technique takes its name from the fact that observation i is weighted by λ_i. The rationale for this technique is seen immediately from the fact that observations associated with a relatively large error variance (a large value of λ_i) are less reliable and so are given relatively less weight; those observations associated with a smaller error variance are, definitionally, more reliable and are therefore given more weight.

In most practical circumstances, however, WLS cannot be applied since Ω, and hence P, is not known. In the more usual case when only the *structure* of Ω is known as diag$\{\lambda_i^2\}$ it is not possible to proceed without imposing some structure on the λ_i terms. This is immediately clear once the unknowns in the general heteroscedastic model have been counted: if $Y = X\beta + \varepsilon$ and $V(\varepsilon) = \sigma^2\text{diag}\{\lambda_i^2\}$ then the model contains k unknown parameters in β and n unknown parameters in Ω. With only n observations available, it is not possible to estimate k + n parameters. To proceed it is therefore necessary to impose a structure on the n λ_i terms so that they depend upon fewer than n – k parameters. If the weights are estimated as $\hat{\lambda}_i$, and WLS then applied, the reported estimated variances of $\hat{\beta}$ will be conditional on the estimates of the weights, and will be underestimates of the unconditional variances which take into account the fact that the weights have been estimated. Using the maximum likelihood method to estimate both the weights and the parameters produces, via the information matrix, estimates of the unconditional variances.

From the entry **Maximum likelihood** it is known that the concentrated likelihood may be written as:

$$-(n/2)\ell n(\text{RSS}(\tilde{\Omega})) - \tfrac{1}{2}\ell n|\tilde{\Omega}|$$

where RSS($\tilde{\Omega}$) is the residual sum of squares from the weighted least squares regression using weights given by $\tilde{\lambda}_i$ and $\tilde{\Omega} = \text{diag}\{\tilde{\lambda}_i^2, \tilde{\lambda}_2^2, \ldots, \tilde{\lambda}_n^2\}$. In the case of heteroscedasticity, therefore,

$$|\tilde{\Omega}| = \prod_{i=1}^{n}\tilde{\lambda}_i^2 \qquad \text{and hence}$$

$$\ell n|\tilde{\Omega}| = \sum_{i=1}^{n}\ell n\tilde{\lambda}_i^2 = 2\sum_{i=1}^{n}\ell n\tilde{\lambda}_i.$$

The method of maximum likelihood produces, then, a method by which to estimate all the model's parameters and this is achieved by choosing the weights to minimize the expression:

$$(n/2)\ell n(RSS(\tilde{\Omega})) + \Sigma_{i=1}^{n} \ell n\tilde{\lambda}_i .$$

The solution to this minimization produces consistent estimators of all the parameters (given that the model is correctly specified), and the information matrix produces unconditional estimates of the variances. Clearly, with only n observations no more than n parameters can be estimated, and so the structure of Ω must be constrained to depend on fewer than n – k parameters. It is also to be noted that simply choosing the weights to minimize the residual sum of squares of the weighted regression is not equivalent to maximum likelihood, since such a procedure effectively ignores the term $\Sigma_{i=1}^{n} \ell n\tilde{\lambda}_i$.

As an example, suppose λ_i^2 depends linearly on one of the regressors, say X_j:

$$\lambda_i^2 = \alpha_o + \alpha_1 X_{ij}$$

It is essential that the parameters α_o and α_1 are such as to ensure that for all values of X_{ij}, $\alpha_o + \alpha_1 X_{ij} > 0$. Ω now depends on only two parameters, α_o and α_1 and the method of maximum likelihood may be used; analytic solutions are not available to solve this problem, and numerical routines are required.

A number of special cases of heteroscedasticity have been proposed. The general case of heteroscedasticity which depends linearly on a known set of variables is given by $\sigma_i^2 = \sigma^2 \alpha' z_i$ where α is a vector of parameters (of dimension less than n – k) and z_i represents a vector of observations of (less then n – k) variables thought to determine σ_i^2. α may be estimated consistently be running the regression of $\hat{e}_i^2$ (the best available estimate of σ_i^2) on the variables of z_i, using OLS, and the original regression may then be re-run as a weighted regression, using $\sqrt{\tilde{\alpha}' z_i}$ as the weights. Alternatively, α and β may be estimated together using maximum likelihood. A popular variant of this model occurs when it is assumed that $\sigma_i^2 = \sigma^2[E(Y_i)]^2$ and the weighted least squares regression may then be run using $\hat{Y}_i$, the fitted value of Y_i from the simple OLS regression, as the ith weight.

The simple case of heteroscedasticity which depends multiplicatively on a known variable is given by $\sigma_i^2 = \sigma^2 z_i^{\alpha}$ where α is a scalar parameter and z_i represents the ith observation on the one variable z thought to determine σ_i^2; α may be estimated consistently by running the regression of $\ell n\, \hat{e}_i^2$ on a constant and $\ell n(z_i)$ and then WLS may be used. Maximum likelihood may be used in this case very easily, since the concentrated likelihood function is given by:

$$-(n/2)\ell n(RSS(\tilde{\alpha})) - (\tilde{\alpha}/2)\, \Sigma_{i=1}^{n} \ell n(z_i) .$$

$RSS(\tilde{\alpha})$ is the residual sum of squares from the weighted regression. A simple search over positive values of α will yield the required estimates.

Another popular form of multiplicative heteroscedasticity is given by $\sigma_i^2 = \sigma^2\exp(\alpha' z_i)$ which may also be estimated by maximum likelihood.

Having adopted a given structure of heteroscedasticity it is a relatively easy task to estimate the resulting model, using either weighted least squares or, better, maximum likelihood; the latter is preferable for not only does it allow simultaneous estimation of all the model's parameters (including those which determine the heteroscedasticity) but the reported variance matrix of parameter estimates, derived from the information matrix, is the unconditional variance estimator, taking account of the fact that the heteroscedastic structure has been estimated.

Further reading

The literature on estimating heteroscedastic models is extremely wide-ranging and complex; the bibliography in Judge *et al.* (1982 and 1985) is very comprehensive, as is that of most modern texts (see, for example, the references to chapter 14 of Greene (1993)). The reader is best referred to such texts and the references therein for further reading on this topic. See also **Heteroscedasticity**, **Heteroscedasticity tests** and **Grouped data**.

Heteroscedasticity tests

If, in the general linear model $Y = X\beta + \varepsilon$, the error term has a non-constant variance it is described as heteroscedastic and in such circumstances ordinary least squares will not yield the best linear unbiased estimator of the parameters. It is important, therefore, to test for heteroscedastic errors and, if found, respond to their presence. The starting point of heteroscedasticity tests are the ordinary least squares residuals from the regression of Y on X; denoting the vector of residuals by $\hat{e}$, most tests then proceed to use $\hat{e}$ as the best proxy for the unknown and unobservable errors, ε, and the nature of the residuals is examined.

A common test of heteroscedasticity, due to Goldfeld and Quandt (1965), is applicable if the error variance is believed to be a monotonic function of one of the regressors. The test proceeds by ordering the observations according to the regressor in question, omitting c central observations, and running the ordinary least squares regressions for the first and last ½(n–c) observations; denote the two residual sums of squares by RSS_1 and RSS_2. Then, under the null hypothesis of homoscedasticity, $RSS_i/[\frac{1}{2}(n-c)-k]$ is an unbiased estimator of the common and constant error variance (i = 1, 2); hence RSS_1/RSS_2 may be used to test this hypothesis since RSS_1/RSS_2 is distributed as $F_{\frac{1}{2}(n-c)-k,\frac{1}{2}(n-c)-k}$ under the null hypothesis of homoscedasticity. It is usual to arrange this statistic so that the larger residual sum of squares is the numerator, and then large values of the test statistic lead to rejection of the null. The power of this test depends critically upon the number of omitted observations, c. For further details, see, for example, Harvey and Philips (1973).

Most other tests require that some more specific form be imposed on the heteroscedasticity. In the general case of heteroscedasticity, $V(\varepsilon_i^2) = \sigma_i^2 = \sigma^2\lambda_i^2$, and the λ_i^2 terms are not constant; however, it is common to examine a number of special cases (see **Heteroscedasticity – estimation methods**). Two special cases assume that σ_i^2 takes a simple form: $\sigma_i^2 = \sigma^2\alpha z_i$ and $\sigma_i^2 = \sigma^2\exp(\alpha' z_i)$, where α is a vector of parameters which determine the heteroscedastic process and z_i is a vector of variables thought to determine σ_i^2. In the first example a test is easily constructed by running the implied auxiliary regression of $\hat{e}_i^2$ (the proxies for σ_i^2) on the variables of z_i and, so long as z_i contains a constant term, an F-test that the slope parameters of α are zero constitutes a test of the heteroscedastic model. In the second case a regression of $\ell n(\hat{e}_i^2)$ on a constant and the variables of z_i also provides an F-test of heteroscedasticity. A third special case arises when it is assumed that $\sigma_i^2 = \sigma^2 z_i^\alpha$ where z_i represents the one variable thought to determine the error variance; in this case a regression of $\ell n(\hat{e}_i^2)$ on a constant and $\ell n(z_i)$ provides a test of heteroscedasticity since, if the coefficient on $\ell n(z_i)$ is insignificantly different from zero the error may be treated as homoscedastic.

In general, following the work of Glesjer (1969), a specific form of heteroscedasticity may be examined as a special case of the general model $\sigma_i^2 = \sigma^2 f(\alpha' z_i)$ where f is a known function and the z_i represents either a single variable or a vector of variables; the appropriate artificial regression, replacing σ_i^2 by $\hat{e}_i^2$, may then be run and a Wald statistic (or some other appropriate method) may be used to test the slope parameters of the heteroscedastic model and if all slope parameters are insignificantly different from zero the homoscedastic model may be adopted.

The Glesjer tests are often carried out by taking the ordinary least squares residuals $\hat{e}$ and then performing the regression of the absolute residuals, $|\hat{e}_i|$, or their squares $\hat{e}_i^2$, on a constant and variables of Z_i (the variables of Z may, or may not, include any or all of the original regressors). Under the hypothesis of homoscedasticity, the coefficients on Z variables are all zero, and so a test of the significance of the coefficients is carried out. If some, or all, of the coefficients are significantly different from zero this constitutes not only a rejection of homoscedasticity, but also provides some indication of the nature of the heteroscedasticity which may then be utilized in a weighted least squares regression (see **Heteroscedasticity – estimation methods**. Such tests are constrained by the proposed form of the heteroscedasticity, and a much more general test is available via the Lagrange multiplier approach.

The Breusch–Pagan (1979) test is a general Lagrange multiplier test which requires only that the investigator can correctly specify the variables which potentially determine the heteroscedasticity; it uses a general model which may be written as $\sigma_i^2 = \sigma^2 f(\alpha' z_i)$, where the first variable in the vector z_i is a constant term. It is not necessary to specify the function f, and a test that the slope parameters in this model are all zero provides the test (the relevant test statistic is commonly reported by software packages where z_i is assumed to constitute a constant term and the squares of the fitted Y_i values from the original OLS regression).

Suppose that z_i represents a constant term and p other variables; ε_i is thus assumed to have a variance given by $f(\alpha_o + \sum_{j=1}^{p} z_{ij}\alpha_j)$. f is assumed to be continuous and have at least first and second derivatives. If the error is homoscedastic with respect to the variables in z, then $\sigma_i^2 = \sigma^2$ for all i; hence, in this case, $\alpha_i = 0$, $j = 1, \ldots, p$. Thus the hypothesis of homoscedasticity may then be tested as a test of the joint hypothesis: H_o: $\alpha_i = 0, j = 1, \ldots, p$.

The test statistic is calculated as follows: from the original OLS regression given by $Y = X\beta + \varepsilon$, take the residuals, $\hat{e}$, and compute the mean squared residual, s^2, where $s^2 = \hat{e}'\hat{e}/T$; and also compute the series $v_i = \hat{e}_i^2/s^2$. The p variables in z must then be specified; these variables are not necessarily either the original regressors or a sub-set of them, but may be and should be chosen by reference to economic theory. An auxiliary regression of v_i on a constant and the p variables z_{ij} is then run, and the explained sum of squares (ESS) from this regression is calculated. If the null hypothesis is true, then there will be no 'explanation' due to the z_j variables.

Asymptotically, under H_o, ½ESS ~ χ^2_p. The rationale is as follows: if the errors are homoscedastic, then their proxies, the squared residuals, are, in large samples, explained only by the constant term in the auxiliary regression; on the other hand, if there is heteroscedasticity then the v_i terms will be explained not only by the constant term but also by the variables in z_i (so long as those variables are appropriately specified). Thus, under H_o, the explained sum of squares will be small, and the question of 'how small is small' is measured by reference to the distribution of ½ESS; an observed value of ½ESS which exceeds the chosen critical value from the χ^2_p results in a rejection of H_o. The use of ½ESS as the test statistic may be derived from considerations of the R^2 from the auxiliary regression. A test of the significance of the R^2 from the artificial regression may be carried out by the familiar F-statistic:

$$\frac{R^2/p}{(1-R^2)/(n-p)} \sim F_{p,n-p}.$$

Rearranging this:

$$nR^2 \sim n[p/(n-p)](1-R^2)F_{p,n-p}$$

But under H_o: $\sigma_i^2 = \sigma^2$ for all i, $(1 - R^2) \rightarrow 1$; also, as $n \rightarrow \infty$, $np/(n-p) \rightarrow p$ and $F_{p,n-p} \rightarrow \chi_p^2/p$ and so the right-hand side of the expression $\rightarrow \chi_p^2$. Thus, under H_o:

$$nR^2 \xrightarrow{D} \chi_p^2.$$

However, the R^2 statistic may be written as:

$$R^2 = ESS/TSS$$

where $TSS = \sum_{i=1}^n v_i^2$. TSS measures the variation of v_i, the dependent variable. Under the null hypothesis each $v_i \sim \chi_1^2$ and so each v_i has a variance of 2; hence, as $n \rightarrow \infty$, $TSS \rightarrow V(\sum_{i=1}^n v_i^2) \rightarrow 2n$. Thus:

$$nR^2 \rightarrow n(ESS)/2n = ½ESS;$$

hence $½ESS \xrightarrow{D} \chi_p^2$, as given above. It is, however, common to use the F-version of this test in finite samples as the asymptotic χ^2 version has been found to reject the null hypothesis too often (its actual Type I error exceeds the nominal level used). An extension of this test is the so-called ARCH test: this is a test of **A**uto**R**egressive **C**onditional **H**eteroscedasticity (see **ARCH and GARCH**).

A general test to examine the most general hypothesis that $\sigma^2 = \sigma_i^2$ for all i would be most useful, and White (1980) provided such a test. If the model is of the form $Y = X\beta + \varepsilon$ and $V(\varepsilon) = \sigma^2 \text{diag}\{\lambda_1^2, \lambda_2^2, \lambda_n^2\} = \sigma^2\Omega$ then the true variance of $\hat{\beta}$ is given by $\sigma^2(X'X)^{-1}X'\Omega X(X'X)^{-1}$ and this may be consistently estimated by replacing $\sigma^2\Omega$ by the diagonal matrix whose typical term is given by $\hat{e}_i^2$, the square of the ith residual from the OLS regression of Y on X. It should be noted that this does not provide the basis for a consistent estimator of Ω, but it may be used to yield a consistent estimator of $V(\hat{\beta})$:

$$\hat{V}(\hat{\beta}) = (X'X)^{-1}[\sum_{i=1}^n \hat{e}_i^2 x_i x_i'](X'X)^{-1}$$

where x_i' is the $1 \times k$ i^{th} row of X, the ith observations on all k regressors.

However, by the usual ordinary least squares formula, the variance of $\hat{\beta}$ is given by:

$$s^2(X'X)^{-1}$$

where $s^2 = \hat{e}'\hat{e}/(n-k)$. A test of heteroscedasticity may then be formed by computing the difference:

$$(X'X)^{-1}[\sum_{i=1}^n \hat{e}_i^2 x_i x_i'](X'X)^{-1} - s^2(X'X)^{-1}$$

A large difference is indicative of a general form of heteroscedasticity. White's test may be carried out by running the regression of $\hat{e}_i^2$ on all the unique variables in $x \otimes x$, where these comprise all the original regressors (X_j, $j = 1, \ldots, k$), and all the distinct products $X_i X_j$, $i > j$, $j = 1, 2, \ldots k-1$; the test is then based on the R^2 from this auxiliary regression, and nR^2 is distributed (asymptotically) as χ^2_{p-1} where p is the number of regressors in the auxiliary regression (including the constant term). A significant White test statistic is indicative of mis-specification, which may be due to heteroscedasticity; if it is interpreted as indicating heteroscedasticity the very generality of the White test then means that no particular model of heteroscedasticity is suggested. While a significant test statistic is indicative of a mis-specification, the test does not indicate in which direction the mis-specification has occurred.

Further reading

The literature on testing for the presence of heteroscedasticity is extremely wide-ranging and complex; the bibliography in Judge *et al.* (1982 and 1985) is very comprehensive, as is that of most modern texts (see, for example, the references to chapter 14 of Greene (1993)). In addition to the references given above, see Godfrey (1988) and see also **Heteroscedasticity** and **Heteroscedasticity – estimation methods**.

Hypothesis testing

Hypothesis testing is critically important both within the methodology of econometrics and within the method of econometrics; indeed, since one of the main functions of econometrics is to utilize data in order to assess the validity or otherwise of economic theory, the techniques of econometrics are intimately concerned with the testing of economic hypotheses. The typical classical hypothesis test consists of several distinct stages:

1. a 'null' hypothesis is stated, and this is tested against an 'alternative' hypothesis; the null hypothesis is usually a simple hypothesis;
2. given a data set, a 'test statistic' is computed;
3. the model within which the null hypothesis is tested is stochastic in nature and, from considerations of statistical distribution theory, the 'sampling properties' of the test statistic, under the truth of the null, are analysed;
4. a rule is invoked by which a 'rejection region' of the null hypothesis is constructed;
5. if the observed test statistic lies within the rejection region the null hypothesis in question is rejected, otherwise it is not rejected; it is to be noted that 'non-rejection' of a null hypothesis is *not* equivalent to 'accepting' that null hypothesis.

If the test statistic is denoted by T and the rejection region by R, the null hypothesis is rejected if $T \in R$. From considerations of the model from which the test statistic is constructed, T has either a known exact sampling distribution under the truth of H_0 or its distribution is known approximately (from analysing its asymptotic distribution); whatever the distribution of T, no value of the test statistic (within its feasible range) is ruled out, but some values are markedly less likely than others. It is this feature which allows practical falsification of the null hypothesis, and R is chosen in such a way that the test statistic is unlikely to fall in that region when H_0 is true. The probability of T lying in R when the null hypothesis is true is known as the significance level, or size, of the test and is denoted by α.

In the framework of classical testing (as opposed to Bayesian testing) the null hypothesis is either true or it is false and hence either decision (to reject or not reject the null hypothesis) may be at variance with the (inherently unknown and unknowable) 'true' state of the world. A hypothesis is described as simple if it uniquely defines the sampling distribution of the test statistic, and is otherwise described as composite. In most examples in econometrics, hypothesis testing concerns the testing of a simple null hypothesis against a composite alternative hypothesis.

The test statistic may, given the truth of the null hypothesis take on any value within the feasible range, and so no observed value of T is incompatible with the null hypothesis, and equally, no value of T is incompatible with the alternative hypothesis either. Herein lies the difficulty with hypothesis testing: the null hypothesis cannot be ruled out by any observable test statistic. In order to make hypothesis testing operational, what is required is a methodological norm which dictates that some observed values of T are so extreme that they are *deemed* to be incompatible with the null hypothesis. This is done by defining the statistical test, Γ, as follows:

> If $T \in R$ then H_0 is rejected; R is the rejection region of the test and is chosen to be such that $\Pr\{T \in R|H_0 \text{ is true}\} = \alpha$, where α is chosen, prior to the test, as some small number, typically 0.05.

The argument which leads to the rejection of H_0, given that the observed value of T lies in R, runs as follows:

> Given the truth of the auxiliary hypotheses (notably the assumptions of the model), the null hypothesis could be true, but then the observed sample would have to be interpreted as atypical. This is because the computed value of the test statistic could only have been generated, if the null hypothesis were true, on $100\alpha\%$ of all occasions (that is, the observed result could only be generated from $100\alpha\%$ of all possible samples in a repeated sampling world). By setting α as a small number, this is deemed to be so unlikely (i.e. the particular sample is deemed not to be atypical) that the decision is to reject the null hypothesis.

The role of α is crucial for it encompasses the investigator's concept of atypicality. There is no obvious reason for any two investigators to hold the same view on atypicality, but in statistical testing values of 0.05 and 0.01 are most common. Clearly, the null hypothesis may, if true, be incorrectly rejected (the Type I error or, equivalently, the size of the test), and, if false, it may be not rejected (a Type II error). Hence practical falsification, through its use of a methodological norm, provides a rule by which a null hypothesis may be rejected, but only at the cost of occasionally rejecting a true null hypothesis and of occasionally failing to reject a false null hypothesis.

The probability of false rejection of a null hypothesis is given by α, the size of the test, but it is also of importance to know, for a given α, how occasional is non-rejection of the null hypothesis when it is false, and this is determined by the power function of the test, denoted by π (see **Power function**). The power function yields the probability of rejecting the null hypothesis for all values of the parameter under test, and to examine the power it is necessary to examine the distribution of T whatever the status of the null and alternative hypotheses. If the test concerns some parameter denoted by λ, then:

$$\pi(\lambda) = \Pr\{T \in R|\lambda\}.$$

The significance level is the supremum of π when H_0 true; if the null hypothesis is the simple hypothesis that $\lambda = \lambda_0$ then $\alpha = \pi(\lambda_0)$. When H_0 is false π yields the probability of rejecting the false null hypothesis. The test statistic and the size of the test are choices to be made. In order to choose amongst different tests of the same hypothesis it is useful to recognize certain desirable properties of a test.

A test is described as *most powerful* if it has greater power than any other test of the same size; a test is described as *unbiased* if its power is at least as great as its size for all values of the parameter; and a test is described as *consistent* if its power approaches one as the sample size grows without limit. A *uniformly most powerful* (UMP) test is one which has greater power than any other test of the same size for all admissible values of the parameter, though there are few circumstances in which an UMP test exists. The comparison of tests is typically based upon their power functions.

Considering H_0: $\lambda = \lambda_0$ and comparing two possible tests, Γ_1 and Γ_2, with test statistics and power functions denoted by (T_1, π_1) and (T_2, π_2) respectively, the first characteristic dictates that if:

$$\pi_1(\lambda_0) = \alpha = \pi_2(\lambda_0),$$

then Γ_1 is preferred to Γ_2 if $\pi_1(\lambda) \geq \pi_2(\lambda)$ for all $\lambda \neq \lambda_0$. Clearly, both tests have identical size, but the probability of rejecting a given false null hypothesis is greater using Γ_1 than using Γ_2.

The unbiasedness of a test is most important; this dictates that

$$\pi(\lambda) \geq \pi(\lambda_0) \quad \text{for all } \lambda.$$

If the test is biased then $\pi(\lambda) < \pi(\lambda_o)$ for some λ. Suppose this last inequality is true for λ_1; then $\pi(\lambda_1) < \pi(\lambda_o)$ implying that $1 - \pi(\lambda_1) > 1 - \pi(\lambda_o)$, which states that the probability of accepting the null when it is false (when $\lambda = \lambda_1$) is more likely than accepting the null when it is true (when $\lambda = \lambda_o$); this is clearly a most undesirable possibility.

Consistent tests, as a general rule, are constructed from consistent estimators (see **Large sample theory**). Consistency requires that:

$$\pi(\lambda) \rightarrow 1 \text{ as } n \rightarrow \infty \text{ for all } \lambda \neq \lambda_o.$$

A consistent test thus has the desirable property that as n, the sample size, grows without limit the probability of rejecting any false hypothesis approaches unity.

Economists have adopted the Neyman–Pearson methodology of hypothesis testing. This consists of choosing that test which, for a given size, is most powerful. However, it is to be noted that even a uniformly most powerful unbiased and consistent test may have a large probability of not-rejecting a false null hypothesis. The errors which may be committed in testing can be expressed as in the table below.

	State of the world	
Decision	H_0 is true	H_0 is not true
H_0 is not rejected	A 'correct' decision	A Type II error
H_0 is rejected	A Type I error	A 'correct' decision

The Neyman–Pearson route, as adopted by economists, entails setting the Type I error as a small number, and effectively leaves the Type II error to the vagaries of the sample.

The typical framework of hypothesis testing in economics consists of a substantive theory statement which takes the form of 'some variable is determined (is affected) by some other variable'. In the context of the regression model, this is represented by the hypothesis that some parameter, β_i, is non-zero. Observations are used to test this hypothesis, and the most common form of a test is as follows:

1. the precise negation of the substantive hypothesis is stated as the null hypothesis, H_o, so that H_o is $\beta_i = 0$ and the substantive hypothesis of interest becomes the alternative hypothesis, H_1: $\beta_i \neq 0$;
2. a test of this null is constructed, and if the observed phenomenon is not markedly different from the null, the substantive theory is rejected (i.e. the null hypothesis is 'accepted');

3. because one would only be willing to 'accept' a substantive theory if the evidence were strong, the observed phenomenon must be very different from the null before the substantive theory is deemed to have 'passed' the test.

The principle in 3 may be called the *Principle of Academic Conservatism*.

Of course, in inferring the 'truth status' of theories from observations, mistakes can be made as set out in the table above and in order to determine the methodological norms of acceptance and rejection appropriate to any particular investigation, a 'hurdle' (or a series of hurdles) are set over which the theory, to be 'accepted', must jump. The real question to be addressed is how high should that hurdle be set?

The process of setting the methodological norm of rejecting H_0 fixes the probability of the Type I error and the principle of academic conservatism dictates that substantive theories should only be 'accepted' when the evidence is strong; since, in this framework, the substantive theory is encapsulated in the alternative hypothesis (*not* the null), this is equivalent to saying that the costs of 'accepting' H_1 when it is false are very much greater than those of rejecting H_1 when it is true (which is the same as saying that the costs of rejecting H_0 when it is true are very much greater than those of 'accepting' H_0 when it is false).

This leads to setting the probability of a Type I error as some very small number. Unfortunately, the Type II error probability may, in fact, be absolutely large for some degrees of falsity, and the above description of a testing procedure has actually left its determination to the vagaries of the particular experiment.

One issue which this approach fails to address explicitly is the costs of the two sorts of error; however, by fixing the probability of a Type I error at 5%, and effectively allowing the Type II error probability to be arbitrarily close to 95% (when the null hypothesis is 'only just' false) suggests that the cost of a Type I error is 19 times that of the maximum Type II error.

Within econometrics there are many forms of hypothesis testing. Whatever the example, in testing a function of a single parameter, or functions of several parameters, and whatever the distribution of the test statistic (normal, t, χ^2, F etc.) the same principles apply whenever the null hypothesis is simple:

> Testing involves the computation of a test statistic whose sampling properties (under the null hypothesis) are derived (exactly or asymptotically) from a consideration of the particular model; a rejection region is determined by the setting of a Type I error (by the use of a methodological norm and, ideally, by a consideration of the costs of the two sorts of error); if the observed test statistic lies within the rejection region the null

hypothesis is rejected, and if it lies outside the rejection region the null is not rejected.

Econometricians are concerned with tests of 'main' hypotheses – those which address parameters of primary economic interest – but are equally concerned with tests of model specification and mis-specification. See also **Diagnostic tests**, **Linear hypotheses** and **Non-linear hypothesis testing**. Also, there is an equivalence between testing by the use of test statistics and by the construction of confidence intervals and regions (see **Confidence intervals** and **Confidence regions**).

Further reading
Material on hypothesis testing is available in all econometrics texts but see, for example, Neyman and Pearson (1933), Lehman (1959) and Mood, Graybill and Boes (1974). For material which considers the choice of the significance level and the power function, see, for example, Arrow (1960), Morrison and Henkel (1970), McCloskey (1985), and Denton (1988). See also De Long and Lang (1992).

Hypothetico-deductive method

There is no logic of verification, but there is a logic of falsification (see **Falsification**). From this asymmetry one can distinguish between science and non-science, and define science as that body of synthetic propositions regarding the real world which, at least in principle, are capable of refutation through the use of observations. A synthetic proposition is one based upon premisses which make assertions about the material world (in contrast to an 'analytic' proposition which is based wholly within a deductive argument and which relies only on the concept of logical truth). Science, as a label, is independent of its subject matter, but is characterized, rather, by its method of formulating and testing propositions; moreover, science is independent of the degree of certainty which is attached to its propositions. The line between science and non-science is, inevitably, thin and falsifiability is itself more a matter of degree than an absolute criterion.

Science concerns the generation and testing of hypotheses in which falsified hypotheses are replaced by hypotheses which, though capable in principle of refutation, successfully withstand attempts to falsify them. A science bases its conclusions on the outcome of attempts to establish 'facts' about the material world; it is not based on mere opinions or superstitions or prejudices. Simple though this statement might appear, one can debate what constitutes a 'fact', and much statistical testing is directed at determining what evidence provides confirmation, and what provides disconfirmation, of hypotheses. A science may characterized by its appeal to empirical observations, and hence to measurement and instrumentation.

The hypothetico-deductive model of science argues that all scientific explanations of phenomena have a common logical structure: they involve at least one universal law plus a statement of relevant initial (or boundary) conditions which, in combination, form the *explanans* (or premisses) from which the *explanandum* is derived using only the rules of logic; the *explanandum* is a statement about the phenomenon of interest. The universal law(s) and the relevant conditions form the antecedent clause of the hypothetical syllogism used to test the explanation (or theory):

1. If the main hypothesis, H, and auxiliary hypotheses, $A_1, \ldots, A_n$, are all true then P (a logically derived prediction) is true;

EITHER
2. P is not true;
3. therefore H and $A_1, \ldots, A_n$ are not true as a composite hypothesis;

OR
2. P is not true;
3. therefore H and $A_1, \ldots, A_n$ are corroborated as a composite hypothesis.

The prediction, P, is a claim about the material world which is, in principle, capable of refutation. The syllogism of testing highlights the appeal to 'fact' (and hence to measurement and instrumentation): the minor premiss, in which P is declared 'not true' or 'true', where truth is here material truth, is based on a confrontation between P and the material world.

In science the origin of the universal law is not relevant to an assessment of the scientific explanation: the source of such hypotheses is not a matter for concern, though one can insist that induction is not a true source (see **Induction**). All 'facts', all 'observations', are theory laden and thus induction cannot constitute unprejudiced generalization since all observations are made in the language of some theory (if only implicitly). This view undermines the position of the extreme inductivists, the logical positivists, who argued that theories only have meaning in so far as they can be verified by direct observation; since there is no sharp distinction between theory and observation (or rather between theory and the statements which result from observations), logical positivism is not tenable. It follows that theories provide only a window through which the real world may be viewed and the real world cannot be viewed unless a theoretical window is available. Unprejudiced windows are not attainable, and what science provides is a route by which to determine which windows to use, and which not to use.

The argument which denies induction as a basis for the source of universal laws is based upon an argument of 'begging the question' (see **Deductive fallacies**): since the world is viewed through a window provided by theory, all observations are tainted by some theory. Moreover, induction cannot provide verification of the theory since this would involve the fallacy of affirming the consequent. This is actually a denial of induction as a source of demonstrative argument; however, what induction offers is a non-demonstrative argument which attempts to suggest that a particular theory is supported by the observations. Such presentations of inductive evidence and their associated conclusions are non-demonstrative since the conclusion, while in some sense supported by the premisses, is not a logical *sequitur*: even if the major and minor premisses are materially true, a non-demonstrative inductively based conclusion cannot logically exclude the possibility that the conclusion is false. Indeed, induction can and does provide useful non-demonstrative conclusions (sometimes described as the 'logic of confirmation') but the important point to be made is that the real contrast is not between deduction, on the one hand, and induction on the other, but between demonstrative and non-demonstrative arguments.

The testing of a main hypothesis is actually carried out in conjunction with 'relevant conditions', otherwise known as auxiliary hypotheses or assumptions or tentative hypotheses; what is actually tested is a composite hypothesis 'H and A_1, A_2, . . ,A_n'. Suppose the prediction P is declared to be false. What is refuted by this experiment is not H, but the composite hypothesis H and the auxiliary hypotheses. This is the essence of the Duhem–Quine thesis, from which it follows that there are no crucial experiments with respect to any main hypothesis: if P is not true this may be due to a failure of H itself or of any one (or more) of the auxiliary hypotheses, but the evidence does not allow the investigator to identify the cause of that failure. Clearly, it is possible, then, to declare that falsification of a main hypothesis is, in principle, impractical, but to 'blame' the false prediction on the failure of auxiliary hypotheses while maintaining the truth of the main hypothesis in the face of such evidence is an 'immunizing stratagem' – belief in H is immunized from any contradictory evidence by this device. Therefore, in scientific endeavour it is essential that the investigator identify, prior to a test, what evidence would be deemed sufficient to declare H false, and it is necessary, then, to set limits on the stratagems which are admissible in the attempts to avoid falsifying a main hypothesis.

There are obvious differences between sciences, notably between the experimental and non-experimental sciences. Economic data are, typically, non-experimental, and economics cannot boast of such universal laws as those found in physics or chemistry, for example. Although, in principle, economics might choose to adopt the same methodology and methodological norms as the hard sciences, the differences in practical terms are great; claims about economic phenomena do not have the same forecasting accuracy, nor are they characterized by 'great numerical constants', nor are they characterized by such universal laws as is common in hard science.

Further reading

See especially Blaug (1992) and Hausman (1992). See also **Falsification**.

Identification

Identification is an issue which arises in the analysis of simultaneous equations models (such as the determination of price in a supply and demand model). Suppose an economic system is modelled as a set of G equations in G endogenous variables and K exogenous or pre-determined variables. The pth equation may be written as:

$$\sum_{i=1}^{G} \beta_{pi} Y_{it} + \sum_{j=1}^{K} \gamma_{pj} X_{jt} = \varepsilon_{pt}.$$

Not all the β_{pi} and γ_{pj} parameters are necessarily non-zero; the G variables denoted as Y_i are the endogenous variables, and the K variables denoted X_j are the exogenous or pre-determined variables. Suppose that there are T observations available; denote by Y_t the $G \times 1$ vector of observations on the G endogenous variables at time t, by X_t the $K \times 1$ vector of observations on the K exogenous and pre-determined variables at time t and by ε_t the $G \times 1$ vector of disturbances. Let B be the $G \times G$ matrix of parameters $\{\beta_{pi}\}$ and let Γ be the $G \times K$ matrix of parameters $\{\gamma_{pj}\}$; then the tth observations of this system of G equations may then be written as:

$$BY_t + \Gamma X_t = \varepsilon_t.$$

B contains G^2 parameters and Γ contains GK parameters; this equation, therefore, contains the $G^2 + GK$ structural parameters of the system, and the G equations $BY_t + \Gamma X_t = \varepsilon_t$ are called the structural equations. Some authors write the structural form equivalently as $Y_t'B' + X_t'\Gamma' = \varepsilon_t'$; there is no particular advantage gained from either representation. If the G equations are linearly independent, that is, no equation can be obtained as a linear combination of any of the other equations, the structure can be 'solved' so as to express each of the G endogenous variables in terms of the other variables:

$$Y_t = -B^{-1}\Gamma X_t + B^{-1}\varepsilon_t, \qquad t = 1, 2, \ldots, T$$

i.e.

$$Y_t = \Pi X_t + v_t.$$

The G equations in this 'solution' each express one endogenous variable in terms of the exogenous and pre-determined variables only; these equations are known as the 'reduced form' of the simultaneous system. The matrix Π, which is of order $G \times K$ is the matrix of reduced form parameters, and the identification issue may be phrased as follows: 'if Π were known, could one then derive the structural form parameters? That is, given Π can B and Γ be derived?'

The identification problem condenses to the question: 'Are the structural equations sufficiently well defined that the true structure can be distinguished from a bogus structure?' If there are two possible structures which are consistent with the data, and they are not distinguishable, then those structures are said to be observationally equivalent and the structure is then unidentified. Consider again the structural form:

$$BY_t + \Gamma X_t = \varepsilon_t, \qquad t = 1, 2, \ldots, T$$

and suppose that $V(\varepsilon_t) = \Omega$. Ω is the variance–covariance matrix of all the errors and contains information on the error term as it relates to individual structural equations and also contains information on the contemporaneous cross-equation covariances. The errors are here assumed to have the same covariance structure at all points in time. Now consider the reduced form:

$$Y_t = -B^{-1}\Gamma X_t + B^{-1}\varepsilon_t, \qquad t = 1, 2, \ldots, T.$$

i.e. $$Y_t = \Pi X_t + v_t \quad \text{and} \quad V(v_t) = B^{-1}\Omega B^{-1\prime} = \Sigma$$

If Ω were known, and Π were known, then knowledge of B would allow identification of the structure, for then Γ and Σ are derivable. Now consider a bogus (false) structure:

$$B_o Y_t + \Gamma_o X_t = \eta_t, \qquad t = 1, 2, \ldots, T$$

where this is obtained from the true structure by pre-multiplying by the square non-singular matrix F:

$$B_o = FB; \quad \Gamma_o = F\Gamma; \quad \eta_t = F\varepsilon_t \qquad \text{and so } V(\eta_t) = F\Omega F'.$$

The reduced form corresponding to this bogus structure is:

$$Y_t = -B_o^{-1}\Gamma_o X_t + B_o^{-1}\eta_t, \qquad t = 1, 2, \ldots, T.$$

i.e. $$Y_t = \Pi X_t + v_t \quad \text{and} \quad V(v_t) = B^{-1}\Omega B^{-1\prime} = \Sigma$$

which is identical to the reduced form of the true structure for any arbitrary non-singular matrix F. The bogus structure is observationally equivalent to the true structure, and the identification problem concerns the form of prior information which enables the true structure to be distinguished from such bogus structures.

The identification issue is not one which concerns estimation techniques, but is a pre-estimation issue. Clearly, since Π contains only GK parameters, and there are G^2 + GK structural parameters, unless there are sufficient restrictions on the structure of the simultaneous system, the answer to the identification must be in the negative. In fact there are fewer than G^2 unknowns in B by virtue of normalization: each structural equation may be normalized so that one endogenous variable in each structural equation has its parameter set to unity. Normalization is logically equivalent to placing one endogenous variable on the left-hand side of a regression equation, but since this is a simultaneous system there is no such thing as 'the' dependent variable of a structural equation, and so normalization does not equate to setting any variable as the dependent variable. For the purposes of identification, normalization is without loss of generality, and may be carried out arbitrarily; for the purposes of estimation there may be some natural candidate endogenous variable whose coefficient is set to unity, but many methods of estimation (including the popular two stage least squares approach) are not invariant to normalization. In order to count the number of unknowns in the structural form, normalization implies that there are G(G – 1) unknowns in B, and GK unknowns in Γ.

The restrictions which will allow identification represent additional information, and this may arise from various sources. Some of the structural equations may be identities (equations to which no error is attached); these may take the form of market clearing equations, for example, and can be easily dealt with by substituting them into the rest of the equations, so as to produce a structural form consisting only of stochastic equations. The other two common forms of restrictions consist of non-sample information which provides restrictions on some of the structural parameters, B and Γ, or provide restrictions on the covariance matrix, Ω.

The commonest form of restrictions on the structure are simple linear restrictions on the parameters in B and Γ, and the very simplest form of linear restrictions which are in evidence are so-called 'exclusion restrictions'. First note that if all elements of B and Γ are non-zero then each structural equation has exactly the same form: each equation relates all G endogenous variables to all K exogenous and pre-determined variables. In such a circumstance, all structural equations are observationally equivalent and are not distinguishable. If, on the other hand, β_{pi} is zero then in the pth structural equation the endogenous variable Y_i is omitted and, similarly, if γ_{pj} is zero then in the pth structural equation the exogenous (or predetermined) variable X_j is omitted. Suppose that, in the first structural equation the endogenous and exogenous variables are so ordered that only the first G_1 endogenous variables are included while only the first K_1 exogenous variables are included. The first structural equation then relates G_1 endogenous variables to K_1 exogenous variables. If such exclusion restrictions are imposed on the structure then the matrices B and Γ may be partitioned:

$$B = \left[\begin{array}{c|c} \beta_1' & 0 \\ \hline B_{21} & B_{22} \end{array}\right] \qquad \Gamma = \left[\begin{array}{c|c} \gamma_1' & 0 \\ \hline \Gamma_{21} & \Gamma_{22} \end{array}\right]$$

where:

β_1' is a row vector of order $1 \times G_1$
0 is a row vector of order $1 \times G_2$
B_{21} is a $(G-1) \times G_1$ matrix
B_{22} is a $(G-1) \times G_2$ matrix

γ_1' is a row vector of order $1 \times K_1$
0 is a row vector of order $1 \times K_2$
Γ_{21} is a $(G-1) \times K_1$ matrix
Γ_{22} is a $(G-1) \times K_2$ matrix

and let Π be partitioned as:

$$\Pi = \left[\begin{array}{c|c} \Pi_{11} & \Pi_{12} \\ \hline \Pi_{21} & \Pi_{22} \end{array}\right]$$

where:

Π_{11} is of order $G_1 \times K_1$
Π_{12} is of order $G_1 \times K_2$ where $K_2 = K - K_1$
Π_{21} is of order $G_2 \times K_1$ where $G_2 = G - G_1$
Π_{22} is of order $G_2 \times K_2$

Now $-B^{-1}\Gamma = \Pi$, and so: $B\Pi = -\Gamma$.

Hence: $\beta_1' \Pi_{11} = -\gamma_1'$ and $\beta_1' \Pi_{12} = 0$.

The latter set of equations represent K_2 linear homogeneous equations in the G_1 unknowns (the elements of β_1). To be able to solve these equations it must be recognized that they can only be solved up to a scalar multiple and so, by fixing, say, the first element of β_1 to unity there are $G_1 - 1$ remaining unknowns. It is necessary and sufficient, then, that these equations constitute exactly $G_1 - 1$ linearly independent equations; hence the necessary and sufficient condition is that the rank of Π_{12} is exactly $G_1 - 1$ (i.e. Π_{12} contains exactly $G_1 - 1$ pieces of linearly independent information). If this is the case then given Π, Π_{12} is known and the linear homogeneous equations may be solved for β_1; having solved for β_1 then γ_1 is given by $\gamma_1' = -\beta_1' \Pi_{11}$.

The necessary and sufficient condition for identification, in the special case of exclusion restrictions, is that:

$$\rho(\Pi_{12}) = G_1 - 1.$$

This is the so-called 'rank condition'.

Since Π_{12} is of order G_1 by K_2 it follows that $\rho(\Pi_{12}) \leq \min(G_1, K_2)$ and it is necessary, though not sufficient, that $G_1 - 1 \leq K_2$. This condition requires that the number of exogenous variables omitted from the first equation (K_2) is at least as great as the number of endogenous variables in the first equation (G_1) less one. This is the so-called 'order condition'.

The order condition may be easily rationalized as follows: since each equation of the structural form includes endogenous variables which are, by definition, not independent of the error term, the structural parameters cannot be estimated consistently by the use of ordinary least squares (an exception to this general remark is described in **Recursive Systems**). Suppose the first equation of the structure were written as below:

$$Y_{1t} = -\sum_{i=2}^{G_1} \beta_{1i} Y_{it} - \sum_{j=1}^{K_1} \gamma_{1j} X_{jt} + \varepsilon_{1t}$$

The coefficient on Y_1 has been set to unity (without loss of generality). This equation cannot be estimated consistently by ordinary least squares but, if $G_1 - 1$ instruments were available to apply to the $G_1 - 1$ endogenous variables on the right-hand side of this equation then instrumental variable estimation could be used to construct consistent estimators of the parameters. In such an equation the exogenous variables of the simultaneous system are obvious candidates as instruments; however, the first K_1 exogenous variables are required as instruments for themselves, and so there are only $K - K_1$ candidate instruments. It is necessary, therefore, that $K - K_1$ is at least as large as $G_1 - 1$, for otherwise instrumental variable estimation cannot be used with the exogenous variables as instruments. Therefore, a necessary though not sufficient condition is that:

$$K - K_1 \geq G_1 - 1$$

i.e. $K_2 \geq G_1 - 1$, which is exactly the form of the order condition.

If, for the first equation, the order condition is not satisfied, then the rank condition cannot hold, and such an equation is said to be not-identified (or, equivalently, under-identified). If the order condition is satisfied it does not follow that the rank condition is satisfied, and the rank of Π_{12} must be investigated. Unfortunately, Π_{12} is a matrix of reduced-form parameters, and it would be much simpler if the rank condition were phrased in terms of the structural form. It may be shown that:

$$\rho(\Pi_{12}) = G_1 - 1 \Leftrightarrow \rho(A) = G - 1$$

where the matrix A is defined by:

$$A = \left[B_{22} \mid \Gamma_{22}\right]$$

That is, A consists of that $(G-1)\times(G_2 + K_2)$ matrix of structural form parameters which relate to the other $G - 1$ equations and are attached to those endogenous and exogenous variables omitted from the first equation.

This form of the rank condition is easy to apply, since it demands only an investigation of the structural form. If the rank condition were to fail for a given structural equation, this is a reflection of the fact that a linear combination of other equations is observationally equivalent to the equation in question; observational equivalence means that a linear combination of other equations includes exactly the same variables (exogenous and endogenous) as the equation whose identification status is being examined. The extreme form of observational equivalence occurs when two structural equations are identical with respect to the included variables (and this is, of course, independent of the satisfaction or otherwise of the order condition).

Identification is not an estimation issue *per se*, but a structural equation's parameters cannot be estimated if that equation is not identified.

Consideration of exclusion restrictions allows identification to be considered as above. Other forms of prior information can also facilitate identification: information may be available on linear combinations of parameters (a more general case than exclusion restrictions) and information on the covariance structure can also facilitate identification. The structure may be written as:

$$BY_t + \Gamma X_t = \varepsilon_t, \qquad V(\varepsilon_t) = \Omega$$

and any linear transformation of this structure yields the bogus structure:

$$FBY_t + F\Gamma X_t = F\varepsilon_t, \qquad V(F\varepsilon_t) = F\Omega F' = \Psi$$

If there are known restrictions on Ω then any admissible transformation must ensure that those restrictions are also satisfied by the new covariance matrix Ψ. A particularly important case of such restrictions arises when Ω is known to be diagonal, and this forms the basis of the so-called recursive system .

Further reading
Fisher (1976) is a classic in the field of identification; see also Hsiao (1983) for a survey of this issue. For estimation of simultaneous systems see **Two-stage least squares, Instrumental variables, Three-stage least squares** and **Recursive systems**.

Indirect least squares

Indirect least squares (ILS) is an estimation technique applied to exactly identified equations of a simultaneous system and yields consistent estimators of the structural parameters. Suppose that the first structural equation of a simultaneous system of G equations is given by:

$$Y_{1t} = \sum_{q=2}^{g_1} \beta_{1q} Y_{qt} + \sum_{r=1}^{k_1} \gamma_{1r} X_{rt} + \varepsilon_{1t}$$

where Y_{it} represents the endogenous variables of the system, and Y_{it}, $i = 1, 2, \ldots, g_1$ are included in the first equation; X_{rt} represents the exogenous or pre-determined variables of the system and X_{rt}, $r = 1, 2, \ldots, k_1$ are included in the first equation. The equation has been normalized so that variable Y_1 has been given a unit coefficient. The T observations may be written as:

$$Y_1 = Z\beta_1 + X_1\gamma_1 + \varepsilon_1$$

Z represents the endogenous variables placed on the right-hand side of this equation and is a matrix of order $T \times (g_1 - 1)$; X_1 represents all the included exogenous variables and is of order $T \times k_1$. Since the regressors include endogenous variables, the application of ordinary least squares will, in general, result in biased and inconsistent estimators of the parameters. This may easily be seen as the equation in question is one of the G structural equations, described by the equations:

$$BY_t + \Gamma X_t = \varepsilon_t, \qquad t = 1, 2, \ldots, T$$

where B and Γ are matrices of structural coefficients, of order G×G and G×K respectively; Y_t is a G×1 vector of observations on all the endogenous variables at time t and X_t is a K×1 vector of observations on all the exogenous (and pre-determined) variables at time t. The reduced form may be derived, assuming that the G equations of the structural form are linearly independent:

$$Y_t = -B^{-1}\Gamma X_t + B^{-1}\varepsilon_t, \qquad t = 1, 2, \ldots, T.$$

i.e.

$$Y_t = \Pi X_t + v_t.$$

where $\Pi = B^{-1}\Gamma$ and $v_t = B^{-1}\varepsilon_t$. Hence the covariance between each variable of Y_t and the error v_t is, in general, non-zero. (The exception to this is described in **Recursive systems**.) The reduced form expresses each endogenous variable as a function of exogenous and pre-determined variables only; the matrix Π is of order G×K and its elements are the reduced form parameters.

The typical equation of the structural form, when written as a regression, involves the regression of one endogenous variable on other endogenous variables and a set of exogenous variables; however, the reduced form equations indicate that, in general, the endogenous variables employed as regressors will be correlated with the error term and so such a regression violates a requirement of OLS that the regressors, if they are stochastic, be independent of the error. Using ordinary least squares on a structural equation will result in biased and inconsistent estimators, in general.

Considering the regressions implied by the reduced form, since each equation expresses just one endogenous variable in terms of the exogenous variables only, the requirements of ordinary least squares are met.

The first structural equation, written above, excludes $K - k_1$ exogenous variables and, if the only restrictions on the structure take the form of exclusions, the order condition for identification requires that $K - k_1 \geq g_1 - 1$. Suppose this is satisfied and that the rank condition for this equation is also satisfied (see **Identification**). Indirect least squares proceeds by estimating the reduced form parameters by ordinary least squares and then solves for the structural parameters.

The ith reduced form equation may be written as:

$$Y_{it} = \sum_{j=1}^{K} \pi_{ij} X_{tj} + v_{it}.$$

Definitionally, all the regressors are exogenous, or pre-determined variables of the system and running the regression of Y_i on all the K variables of X yields estimates $\hat{\pi}_{ij}$, j = 1, 2, . . . , K. Given that the regressors are, at least in the limit, uncorrelated with the error, the estimators, $\hat{\pi}_{ij}$, are consistent, and if the regressors may be treated as fixed in repeated sampling, then the estimators are also unbiased. By the ordinary least squares formula:

$$\hat{\pi}_i = (X'X)^{-1}X'Y_i$$

where $\hat{\pi}_i$ is the K×1 vector of reduced form estimates relating to i^{th} endogenous variable, Y_i represents the T×1 vector of observation on the ith endogenous variable and X is the T×K matrix of observations on all the exogenous variables; in terms of the definition of X_t above, X_t' is the tth row of X. $\hat{\pi}_i'$ is the estimate corresponding to the ith row of Π. Define $\hat{\Pi}$ by:

$$\hat{\Pi} = \begin{bmatrix} \hat{\pi}_1' \\ \hat{\pi}_2' \\ \vdots \\ \hat{\pi}_G' \end{bmatrix}.$$

Denoting the G×T matrix of observations on all the endogenous variables by Y (so that the ith row of Y is given by Y_i'):

$$\hat{\Pi} = YX(X'X)^{-1}$$

The reduced form and structural form parameters are related, linearly, by the G equations $\Pi = B^{-1}\Gamma$ which may be written equivalently as $\Pi'B' = \Gamma'$. The first equation of the structural form only includes the first g_1 endogenous variables, so the first row of B is given by $[1\ -\beta_1'\ 0]$, where β_1' is a row vector of order $1\times(g_1-1)$ and the first element of the row has been set to unity to reflect the normalization in effect (the parameter on Y_1 in the first structural equation has been normalized to one); similarly the first row of Γ is given by $[\gamma_1'\ 0]$, where γ_1' is a row vector of order $1\times k_1$. Writing the equations $\Pi'B' = \Gamma'$ in terms of the corresponding estimates: $\hat{\Pi}'\hat{B}' = \hat{\Gamma}'$, and the first equation then yields:

$$\hat{\Pi}'\begin{bmatrix} 1 \\ -\hat{\beta}_1 \\ 0 \end{bmatrix} = \begin{bmatrix} \hat{\gamma}_1 \\ 0 \end{bmatrix}$$

This expression constitutes exactly K equations in $g_1 - 1 + k_1$ unknowns. If the first structural equation is identified, then $K - k_1 \geq g_1 - 1$, i.e. $K \geq g_1 - 1 + k_1$. Therefore, when the first equation of the structural form is *exactly* identified there are precisely the same number of equations as unknowns, and the equations may be solved for unique solutions, $\hat{\beta}_1$ and $\hat{\gamma}_1$. Hence indirect least squares, by estimating the reduced form parameters consistently by ordinary least squares and then solving back for the structural parameters, works when the equation in question is exactly identified by exclusion restrictions (and, more generally, when it is exactly identified by linear restrictions across its parameters). It is to be noted that the structural estimators obtained by this route are non-linear transformations of the reduced form estimators, and so $\hat{\beta}_1$ and $\hat{\gamma}_1$ are consistent, but they will exhibit small sample bias. Furthermore, in the case of an exactly identified equation, it may be shown that the ILS estimators are identical to the two-stage least estimators.

If the structural equation in question is under-identified, so that $K - k_1 < g_1 - 1$, the number of equations, K, now is strictly less than the number of unknowns, in which case no solution is possible. This provides a good illustration of the identification issue; the prior information, in the form of exclusion restrictions, is insufficient and there are too many unknowns in this set of equations. It now becomes apparent that the order condition for identification, $K - k_1 \geq g_1 - 1$, guarantees that the structural parameters can be recovered from knowledge of the reduced form parameters.

If the structural equation is strictly over-identified, then $K - k_1 > g_1 - 1$, and the number of equations, K, exceeds the number of unknowns; the equations now yield multiple solutions for $\hat{\beta}_1$ and $\hat{\gamma}_1$. The amount of available information is, in this case, more than sufficient. Given the non-uniqueness of the solution to these equations the issue to be addressed is how best to combine the multiple solutions. For over-identified equations the method of ILS offers no immediate answers, and for such a situation other methods are required. Indeed, because the ILS estimator only yields a unique solution in the exactly identified case it is rarely used; however, it is a most useful device by which to illustrate the nature of the identification issue.

Further reading

Indirect least squares is a little-used technique, but illustrates the identification issue; it may be found in all the standard texts. For other material on simultaneous systems, see **Identification**, **Instrumental variables**, **Full information maximum likelihood**, **Limited information maximum likelihood** and **Two-stage least squares**.

Induction

Economists (of whom econometricians are a sub-group) use data in a variety of ways but particularly in the derivation of general results and of general predictions. Such use of data implicitly (or explicitly) utilizes the method of induction.

Consider why it is believed that the sun will rise tomorrow: the belief is based upon inductive reasoning which takes the following form:

> All observations of past mornings reveal that the sun has risen on such occasions; therefore the sun will continue to rise each morning.

The characteristic of inductive reasoning is that a generalization is derived from consideration of a number of particular observations. To illustrate the nature of induction it is helpful to state the above inductive argument in the form of deductive syllogistic reasoning:

1. The sun has always risen on mornings in the past.
2. What has happened in the past will continue to happen in the future.
3. Therefore the sun will rise tomorrow.

This syllogism highlights the nature (and therefore the fallacy) of inductive reasoning. The observations which form the basis of induction (the major premiss) are particular to a historic period and a specific location. However, the conclusion of inductive reasoning is a generalization which seeks to make some statement (a prediction) beyond the range of the observations (the data) upon which it is based: induction seeks to predict what will happen in circumstances similar to its premisses but at different points in time or at different locations. In order to form the logical link between the major premiss and the conclusion it is necessary to invoke (either explicitly, as in the syllogism, or, more commonly, implicitly) a minor premiss of regularity.

In inductive reasoning, the essential problem concerns the minor premiss, for this requires an appeal to a 'Principle of Regularity' (that is, a principle which states that what has been will continue to be). If the regularity principle is accepted for the purpose of the argument, that is, it has logical truth, the conclusion is also logically true; moreover, were one to be convinced of the material truth of such a principle, one would have no objection to the material truth of inductively based predictions. Unfortunately, any attempt to establish the material truth of the Principle of Regularity itself requires an appeal to an inductively based conclusion (which would require an appeal to the very principle whose truth is to be demonstrated). This circularity cannot be broken which is why the principle is often described as a statement of faith.

From the perspective of a scientist, it is important to ask to what extent can inductive reasoning provide proof? Unfortunately, because of the nature of the minor premiss, conclusive material proof cannot be derived from inductive reasoning, and the simple familiar example given earlier makes this clear. This logical problem of induction has concerned philosophers, and others, ever since Hume who, in 1748, wrote

> If a body of like colour and consistency with that bread which we have formerly eaten be presented to us, we make no scruple of repeating the experiment and foresee with certainty like nourishment and support. Now this is a process of mind or thought of which I would willingly know the foundation. (Quoted from Hume, 1955, p. 47)

An inductively based conclusion cannot be said to be materially true since there is no way of establishing the material truth of the minor premiss (that of regularity); the question to be answered is simply how, logically, one may infer anything regarding future experience when the evidence is nothing but historical experience. It is not possible to construct inductive inferences with certainty, but induction does provide evidence of a non-demonstrative kind (but it would never convince a committed sceptic). Nevertheless. a large number of confirming instances that a hypothesis is true is seen as a weighty accumulation of evidence that the hypothesis is true.

The inductivist critique is particularly relevant to the issue of forecasting where the implicit minor premiss is that the future will be like the past. Lucas provided a specific form of the inductivist critique when he argued that the parameters of a relationship are sensitive to the economic environment and are likely to change when, for example, the policy environment changes.

It follows from the above that there is a fundamental asymmetry between induction and deduction. The problem of induction is that no universal statement may be logically derived, or established with certainty, from a finite number of singular statements; in contrast, a universal statement may be logically refuted with the aid of deductive reasoning from one single contrary event. This observation is critical to an understanding of the methodology of testing; see **Falsification** and **Hypothesis testing**.

Further reading

On the use of induction in economics see, especially, Stewart (1979) and Blaug (1992). See also Lucas (1976).

Instrumental variables

In the general linear model, $Y = X\beta + \varepsilon$, the unbiasedness of the ordinary least squares estimator, $\hat{\beta}$, depends upon the two assumptions: first, that the data matrix, X, is either not stochastic or, if stochastic, is independent of the error term, and second, that the error term is drawn from a zero mean distribution. Suppose that the data matrix is stochastic; then:

$$\hat{\beta} = \beta + (X'X)^{-1}X'\varepsilon$$

and taking expectations:

$$E(\hat{\beta}) = \beta + E[(X'X)^{-1}X'\varepsilon].$$

If X and ε are independently distributed, then the expectation of the product is the product of expectations and:

$$\begin{aligned} E(\hat{\beta}) &= \beta + E[(X'X)^{-1}X']E[\varepsilon] \\ &= \beta \end{aligned}$$

given that ε is drawn from a zero mean distribution.

However, if X and ε are not independent then the ordinary least squares estimator is characterized by bias, which may or may not persist in samples of all sizes; in such circumstances $\hat{\beta}$ is biased and may or may not be consistent.

Suppose the general linear model is specified in the usual fashion as $Y = X\beta + \varepsilon$, there are T observations and suppose that the regressors are stochastic variables with the following properties (the definition of plim and the properties of this operator are found in **Large sample theory**):

$$\text{plim}(T^{-1}X'X) = Q, \quad \text{where Q is some positive definite non-singular matrix}$$

and

$$\text{plim}(T^{-1}X'\varepsilon) \neq 0. \quad \text{(i.e. in the limit, the errors are correlated with at least one regressor).}$$

The application of ordinary least squares to this equation yields the estimator $\hat{\beta}$ which has the following properties:

$$\text{plim}(\hat{\beta}) = \beta + \text{plim}(T^{-1}X'X)^{-1}(T^{-1}X'\varepsilon).$$

But the plim of a product is the product of plims; hence:

$$= \beta + \text{plim}(T^{-1}X'X)^{-1}.\text{plim}(T^{-1}X'\varepsilon)$$

$$= \beta + Q^{-1}.\text{plim}(T^{-1}X'\varepsilon)$$

$$\neq \beta.$$

Hence ordinary least squares leads to an inconsistent estimator in this case. However, if the moments of X have a finite probability limit (Q) and if ε is uncorrelated, in the limit, with all the regressors, then $\hat{\beta}$ is a consistent estimator:

if $\text{plim}(T^{-1}X'X) = Q$, where Q is some positive definite non-singular matrix

and $\text{plim}(T^{-1}X'\varepsilon) = 0$

then: $\text{plim}\hat{\beta} = \beta$, that is, $\hat{\beta}$ is then a consistent estimator.

An inconsistent estimator results when there is dependence between the regressors and the error term, whatever the sample size. It is then necessary to consider an alternative estimation technique by which to derive a consistent estimator. Suppose there exists a $T \times k$ matrix W such that:

$$\text{plim}\,(T^{-1}W'X) = \Sigma \quad \text{where } \Sigma \text{ is a finite and non-singular } k \times k \text{ matrix}$$

and $\text{plim}\,(T^{-1}W\varepsilon) = 0.$

Thus the k variables in W are such that there are uncorrelated (in the limit) with the error term, but are related to the k variables in X. Now consider the estimator:

$$\tilde{\beta} = (W'X)^{-1}W'Y$$

and substituting for Y:

$$\tilde{\beta} = (W'X)^{-1}W'(X\beta + \varepsilon) = \beta + (W'X)^{-1}W'\varepsilon$$

Taking probability limits:

$$\begin{aligned} \text{plim}\tilde{\beta} &= \beta + \text{plim}[(T^{-1}W'X)^{-1}].\text{plim}[T^{-1}W'\varepsilon] \\ &= \beta + [\text{plim}(T^{-1}W'X)]^{-1}.\text{plim}[T^{-1}W'\varepsilon] \\ &= \beta + \Sigma^{-1}.0 \\ &= \beta. \end{aligned}$$

Hence this estimator is consistent; $\tilde{\beta}$ is known as the instrumental variables (IV) estimator, and the k variables in W are known as the instruments. It is to be noted that ordinary least squares can be seen as a special case of IV estimation: if the original regressors, X, are uncorrelated with the errors in the limit, then the k variables in X may be used as instruments for themselves, in which case the instrumental variable estimator becomes $(X'X)^{-1}X'Y$ which is the standard formula for the OLS estimator. The asymptotic variance of the IV estimator may be examined as follows.

Defining asymptotic variance as the variance of the limiting distribution:

$$\begin{aligned} \sqrt{T}.(\tilde{\beta} - \beta) &= \sqrt{T}.(W'X)^{-1}W'\varepsilon \\ &= (T^{-1}W'X)^{-1}(T^{-1/2}W'\varepsilon) \end{aligned}$$

Assuming that $T^{-1/2}W'\varepsilon$ converges in distribution to a multivariate normal random variable (see **Central limit theorems**):

$$T^{-1/2}W'\varepsilon \xrightarrow{D} N(0, \sigma^2\Sigma_W)$$

where $\text{plim}(T^{-1}W'W) = \Sigma_W$ and $V(\varepsilon) = \sigma^2 I$, using Cramer's Theorem, it follows that $\sqrt{T}.(\tilde{\beta} - \beta)$ has the limiting distribution given by:

$$MVN(0, \sigma^2\Sigma^{-1}\Sigma_W\Sigma^{-1}).$$

One may write, then:

$$\tilde{\beta} \sim AN(\beta, T^{-1}\sigma^2\Sigma^{-1}\Sigma_W\Sigma^{-1})$$

where AN is read as 'asymptotically normal'.

In practical applications neither Σ nor Σ_W are known, and so they are estimated by the following:

$$\tilde{\Sigma} = (1/T)W'X \quad \text{and} \quad \tilde{\Sigma}_W = (1/T)W'W$$

Further, σ^2 is not known and this is estimated by:

$$s^2 = \tilde{e}'\tilde{e}/(T-k)$$

where $\tilde{e} = Y - X\tilde{\beta}$. Thus the asymptotic variance of $\tilde{\beta}$ is estimated by:

$$\widetilde{\text{asyvar}}(\tilde{\beta}) = s^2(W'X)^{-1}W'W(W'X)^{-1}.$$

The importance of the role of the dependence between the instruments, W, and the original regressors, X, should be noted; the lower is the correlation between regressors and instruments the smaller are the sample moments as reflected in the matrix $T^{-1}W'X$ and hence the greater is the estimated variance of $\tilde{\beta}$ (since this depends on $(W'X)^{-1}$). In this sense there is a trade-off between consistency and efficiency. Indeed, the asymptotic variance of $\tilde{\beta}$ depends critically on the term $\Sigma^{-1}\Sigma_W\Sigma^{-1}$, and it may be shown formally that the more highly correlated are the regressors and the instruments the more efficient are the instrumental estimators.

The choice of instruments is critically important to the properties of the instrumental variable estimator, and there may be more than one set of available instruments. An admissible set of instruments must satisfy the requirements that, in the limit, the instruments are correlated with the regressors but uncorrelated with the errors; if more than one set of admissible instruments is considered then that set which is most highly correlated with the regressors will result in the most (asymptotically) efficient consistent estimator, but it may also be possible to construct a linear combination of admissible instruments which is yet more efficient than any individual set. The case of two-stage least squares applied to an over-identified equation of a simultaneous system provides a simple example in which an optimal linear combination of instruments can be constructed in order to maximize asymptotic efficiency.

In some examples, such as the estimation of the parameters of a simultaneous equation system, the choice of available instruments is relatively straightforward; however, in other cases, such as estimating an errors in variables equation, the choice is not so readily made.

Further reading

White (1984) and Hansen (1982) discuss the use of 'optimal instruments'. See also **Exogeneity tests** for a test of independence between regressors and the error.

Integration

An integrated variable is a special case of a non-stationary random variable: if x_t is an integrated variable it may be transformed into a stationary variable simply by taking sufficient numbers of first differences. Formally, if the time-series $\{x_t\}$ is non-stationary, but $\Delta^d x_t$ is stationary for some $d > 0$ (where Δ is the difference operator) and $\Delta^q x_t$ is not stationary for all $0 \leq q < d$, then x_t is said to be integrated of order d and is denoted by $x_t \sim I(d)$. Equivalently, if x_t must be differenced at least d times in order to construct a stationary variable then x_t is integrated of order d. Using the lag operator L, where $Lz_t = z_{t-1}$, a series is then integrated of order d if $(1 - L)^q x_t$ is non-stationary for all $0 \leq q < d$ but is stationary for $q = d$. The order of integration of a series which is characterized by seasonality is more complex, and then the integration is typically captured by two parameters: if a series x_t is measured s times per year and has a seasonal component, then the seasonal difference $\Delta_s = x_t - x_{t-s}$ $[= (1 - L^s)x_t]$ may be required to remove the seasonality, and a non-stationary time-series which is transformed into a stationary series by D seasonal differences (that is, by the operation of $(1 - L^s)^D$) and d first differences is said to be seasonally integrated of order (d, D), denoted by $SI_s(d, D)$. If quarterly data are used then $s = 4$, and if monthly data are used $s = 12$ and so on.

An integrated variable presents challenges to the regression model; in particular, one of the familiar assumptions of the regression model is that all regressors and the error term are stationary and so the use of an integrated variable denies this assumption. Most importantly, a characteristic of an integrated variable is that it has some form of stochastic trend – the simplest I(1) variable evolves according the equation $x_t = x_{t-1} + \varepsilon_t$ which implies that the current value of x is given by the previous value plus some white-noise error. The time dependence of an integrated variable can give rise to what are called spurious regressions; if one integrated variable is regressed on another then the fact that both have some form of trend can give the appearance of there being some relationship between the two variables, even though the variables are independent of each other. This is examined in **Spurious regressions**.

A series which is integrated of order one is generated according to the general equation:

$$x_t = \mu + x_{t-1} + \varepsilon_t$$

where ε_t is a stationary random error (ε_t is, therefore, homoscedastic but not necessarily white-noise as an autocorrelated error may be stationary). If ε_t is white-noise, so that the errors are mutually uncorrelated, then x_t is a random walk; hence a random walk is a special case of an integrated process. Taking x_{t-1} from both sides of the equation:

$$\Delta x_t = \mu + \varepsilon_t$$

If $\mu = 0$ then x_t is integrated of order 1 without drift and if $\mu \neq 0$ then x_t is described as integrated of order 1 with drift. If x_t is I(1) without drift then its expected value, given x_{t-1}, is x_{t-1} and a feature of such a series is that its variance is an increasing function of time: suppose that x_t is a random walk without drift; then:

$$x_t = x_{t-1} + \varepsilon_t$$

where ε_t is a white-noise error. By repeated substitution:

$$x_t = \sum_{s=0}^{\infty} \varepsilon_{t-s}$$

and so $\text{Var}(x_t) \to \infty$; i.e. the variance of an integrated series is not bounded. This has important implications for the analysis of integrated series within the regression model.

If $\mu \neq 0$ then x_t will tend to drift, since the expected value of x_t, given x_{t-1}, is $\mu + x_{t-1}$; i.e. the change in x_t is expected to be μ and the series will tend to drift according to this equation and such a variable has a time-dependent mean and variance.

Any series may drift simply as a consequence of random shocks; however, an integrated series has the property that consecutive values of the series are correlated positively with each other and in consequence an integrated series may, for long periods, be very distant from its unconditional mean.

An integrated variable is a random variable and is a special case of a non-stationary variable. The results from the standard regression model assume that the error term is stationary and that the regressors, if random, are also stationary. Clearly, then, if the regressand or any one of the regressors in the standard model is integrated the usual results regarding the properties of the estimators are no longer valid. The implications of integrated variables for the regression model are further examined in **Stationarity**, **Spurious regressions** and **Cointegration**; see also **Engle–Granger representation theorem** and **Johansen method**. Tests of the degree of integration are examined in **Unit root tests**.

Further reading

See the important papers by Dickey and Fuller (1979 and 1981), and also the earlier work of Mann and Wald (1943) and Rubin (1950). See also Nelson and Plosser (1982), Evans and Savin (1981 and 1984), Nerlove and Diebold (1990) and Charemza and Deadman (1992).

Johansen method

The Johansen method is concerned with identifying the number of cointegrating vectors within a general n variable vector autoregression. Consider the unrestricted n-equation vector autoregression (VAR) model in n variables and m lags:

$$Z_t = \sum_{i=1}^{m} A_i Z_{t-i} + \varepsilon_t .$$

Z_t is a vector of n variables, the A_i matrices are all of order n×n, and ε_t is an n×1 vector of stationary and non-autocorrelated random variables. The m terms in lagged Z may be re-written as:

$$Z_{t-1} + (A_1 - I)(Z_{t-1} - Z_{t-2}) + (A_2 + A_1 - I)(Z_{t-2} - Z_{t-3}) + \ldots$$

$$+ (A_{m-1} + \ldots + A_1 - I)(Z_{t-m+1} - Z_{t-m}) + (A_m + A_{m-1} + \ldots + A_1 - I)Z_{t-m}$$

which may be written as:

$$Z_{t-1} + \sum_{i=1}^{m-1} \lambda_i \Delta Z_{t-i} + \lambda_m Z_{t-m} \qquad \text{where } \lambda_i = \sum_{j=1}^{i} A_j - I,\ i = 1, \ldots, m$$

hence: $$\Delta Z_t = \sum_{i=1}^{m-1} \lambda_i \Delta Z_{t-i} + \lambda_m Z_{t-m} + \varepsilon_t .$$

The unrestricted VAR has now been rewritten by what the literature refers to as a 'cointegrating transformation'. All the λ_j are n×n matrices. Since the error term is stationary these equations must be balanced, that is the orders of integration of ΔZ_t and $\sum_{i=1}^{m-1} \lambda_i \Delta Z_{t-1} + \lambda_m Z_{t-m}$ must be the same. If all n elements of Z_t are stationary this is denoted by $Z_t \sim I(0)$ and if all n elements of Z_t are integrated of order 1 this is denoted by $Z_t \sim I(1)$; if $Z_t \sim I(1)$ and the linear combination $\gamma' Z_t \sim I(0)$ this is denoted by $Z_t \sim CI(1, 1)$ with cointegrating vector γ. Z_t is here restricted to be either I(0) or I(1).

Suppose that $\lambda_m = 0$; this may be interpreted as meaning that in the steady state, when $\Delta Z_t = 0$ for all t, there is no equilibrium relationship defined between the levels of Z_t. This denies the existence of a vector γ such that $\gamma' Z_t$ is stationary, for $\gamma' Z_t \sim I(0)$ represents an equilibrium relationship between the variables in levels; hence there can be no cointegrating vectors. Moreover, since there is no γ such that $\gamma' Z_t$ is stationary, Z_t cannot itself be stationary; but the requirement that the equation be balanced implies that ΔZ_t is stationary for all t which then implies that $Z_t \sim I(1)$. To consider this from the other perspective, suppose that $Z_t \sim I(1)$ and there are no cointegrating relationships amongst the Z_t; then $\Delta Z_t \sim I(0)$ and $\lambda_m Z_t \sim I(1)$ (for $\lambda_m \neq 0$) which implies that $\varepsilon_t \sim I(1)$. However, this denies the proposition that $\varepsilon_t \sim I(0)$ and hence λ_m must be the null matrix. The condition $\lambda_m = 0$ and $\varepsilon_t \sim I(0)$ may thus be interpreted as implying that Z_t is I(1) and that there are no cointegrating relationships amongst the n variables of Z_t. If the square n×n matrix λ_m is not the null matrix attention then focuses on its rank; clearly $\rho(\lambda_m) \leq n$.

Suppose that λ_m is of full rank; consider the consequences of $Z_t \sim I(1)$; $Z_t \sim I(1)$ implies $\Delta Z_t \sim I(0)$, and so all the terms in ΔZ_t are stationary (in fact if Z is not stationary and ΔZ_t is stationary this only requires that some, not all, elements of Z are I(1) – those elements of Z which are not I(1) are then I(0)). If λ_m is of full rank, then $\lambda_m Z_t$ is simply a vector of n linearly independent combinations of the n elements of Z_t. In that case, suppose $\lambda_m Z_t \sim I(0)$, so that $\lambda_m Z_t = \eta_t \sim I(0)$; but λ_m is of full rank, is non-singular, and hence $Z_t = \lambda_m^{-1}\eta_t$. However, $\lambda_m^{-1}\eta_t$ is simply a vector of n linearly independent combinations of the random vector η_t, and η_t is stationary; hence $\lambda_m^{-1}\eta_t$ is stationary and therefore $Z_t \sim I(0)$ – which is a contradiction. Hence if λ_m is of full rank, Z_t cannot be an I(1) variable; this demonstrates the fact that of n independent linear combinations of n I(1) variables, at least one must be integrated. The conclusion is that if $\rho(\lambda_m) = n$ and $Z_t \sim I(1)$ then $\lambda_m Z_t$ is not stationary, and at least one element of $\lambda_m Z_t$ will be I(1). But as at least one element of $\lambda_m Z_t \sim I(1)$ the equation involving the first differences and levels of Z_t is then unbalanced (denying $\varepsilon_t \sim I(0)$); hence $\rho(\lambda_m) = n$, $Z_t \sim I(1)$ and $\varepsilon_t \sim I(0)$ is a contradiction. If, however, Z_t is stationary, then $\lambda_m Z_t$ is stationary, ΔZ_t is also stationary, and the equation is balanced as required; therefore, if $\varepsilon_t \sim I(0)$ and $\rho(\lambda_m) = n$ it must be the case that $Z_t \sim I(0)$.

Now suppose that $\rho(\lambda_m) = r < n$; in the steady state $-\lambda_m Z_t = \varepsilon_t$ which is stationary. Since λ_m is singular, $-\lambda_m Z_t = \varepsilon_t \sim I(0)$ implies that there are only r (< n) independent linear combinations of Z_t which are stationary (and the remaining n – r linear combinations may be derived from the first r such combinations). If Z_t were stationary there would then be n independent linear combinations each of which is stationary; however, $\rho(\lambda_m) = r < n$ denies the existence of n such combinations and denies, then, that Z_t is stationary. Therefore, when $\rho(\lambda_m) = r < n$ this implies that $Z_t \sim I(1)$ and there are exactly r (< n) cointegrating vectors of Z_t. Three possibilities therefore exist:

1. λ_m is the null matrix: therefore $Z_t \sim I(1)$ and there are no cointegrating relationships;
2. λ_m is non-singular, $\rho(\lambda_m) = n$: therefore $Z_t \sim I(0)$;
3. λ_m is singular, $\rho(\lambda_m) = r$, $0 < r < n$: therefore $Z_t \sim I(1)$ and there are r cointegrating relationships.

Tests of the rank of λ_m are, therefore, tests of the degree of integration and of the extent of cointegration of the Z_t vector. If $\rho(\lambda_m) = r$ then λ_m may be written as $\alpha\beta'$ where α and β are both n×r matrices, each of full rank. When $0 < r < n$, β is known as the cointegrating matrix, since this defines the r cointegrating relationships: $\beta' Z_{t-m} \sim I(0)$. The VAR model, written in differences and levels, may then be interpreted as a generalization of the error correction model:

$$\Delta Z_t = \Sigma_{i=1}^{m-1} \lambda_i \Delta Z_{t-1} + \alpha\beta' Z_{t-m} + \varepsilon_t$$

where the term $\beta' Z_{t-m}$ is a set of r stationary terms, and may be interpreted as r errors (differences between the observations and the long-run equilibrium position as defined by the cointegrating relationships) at time t − m. The above equation re-parameterizes the VAR as an error correction model and the matrix α reflects the speed of adjustment of Z_t from disequilibrium positions towards equilibrium. The interpretation of α as an adjustment, or feedback, matrix, would appear to have implications for the lag length, m; m must be chosen to be sufficiently large to ensure that ε_t is not autocorrelated, but must be sufficiently short to allow the interpretation of this form of the VAR as an error correction model. This apparent conflict in the choice of m is, however, only superficial, and the only criteria for the choice of m are economic criteria (how long the influence of any variable is likely to last) allied to the statistical criterion of ensuring that ε_t is free from autocorrelation. There is no issue in the choice of m relating to the interpretation of $\beta' Z_{t-m}$ as a set of r errors from the long-run equilibrium. To demonstrate this, consider an alternative re-parameterization of the original VAR:

$$Z_t = \sum_{i=1}^{m} A_i Z_{t-i} + \varepsilon_t$$

The terms in Z_{t-i} may be written as:

$$-A_m(Z_{t-m+1} - Z_{t-m}) - (A_m + A_{m-1})(Z_{t-m+2} - Z_{t-m+1}) - \dots$$
$$- (A_m + A_{m-1} \dots + A_2)(Z_{t-1} - Z_{t-2}) + (A_m + A_{m-1} \dots + A_1)Z_{t-1}$$

Therefore:

$$Z_t = -\Sigma_{i=1}^{m-1} \theta_i \Delta Z_{t-1} + \theta_o Z_{t-1} + \varepsilon_t \quad \text{where } \theta_i = \Sigma_{j=i+1}^{m} A_j,\ i = 1, ., m-1.$$

i.e. $$\Delta Z_t = -\Sigma_{i=1}^{m-1} \theta_i \Delta Z_{t-i} + (\theta_o - I) Z_{t-1} + \varepsilon_t .$$

This form of the VAR is to be compared with that arrived at above:

$$\Delta Z_t = \Sigma_{i=1}^{m-1} \lambda_i \Delta Z_{t-i} + \lambda_m Z_{t-m} + \varepsilon_t .$$

The critical difference is that although both representations express ΔZ_t in terms of lagged first differences (ΔZ_{t-i}, i = 1, 2, . . , m−1), the term in the level of Z is, in the original form, the most historic lagged level (Z_{t-m}), whereas that in the new form is the most recent lagged level (Z_{t-1}). The two forms are equivalent, and $\theta_o - I = \lambda_m$. Hence the argument used above regarding the interpretations of the rank of λ_m applies equally to the new equation, translated into $\theta_o - I$. If $\theta_o - I$ is singular, $\rho(\theta_o - I) = r$, $0 < r < n$, then $Z_t \sim I(1)$ and there are r cointegrating relationships and $\theta_o - I$ may be written as $\alpha\beta'$ (where α and β are precisely as defined above), in which case the error correction form of the VAR becomes:

$$\Delta Z_t = -\Sigma_{i=1}^{m-1} \theta_i \Delta Z_{t-i} + \alpha\beta' Z_{t-1} + \varepsilon_t$$

where, in this representation, $\beta'Z_{t-1}$ is stationary just as $\beta'Z_{t-m}$ is stationary in the original exposition. To interpret $\beta'Z_{t-1}$ as r stationary errors from the long-run equilibrium path, and α as the adjustment matrix, has more appeal than to consider $\beta'Z_{t-m}$ as the errors (with exactly the same adjustment matrix, α) since here the correction is to the most recent, as opposed to the most historic, error. The adjustment matrix only depends on m via the number of lags which are incorporated into the short-run dynamics (i.e. on the original specification of the VAR), and not on the long-run relationships. Indeed, the interpretation of α as the adjustment matrix is independent of whether the error ($\beta'Z$) is dated at t – 1 (the most recent error) or t – m (the most historic error), and the economic interpretation of the $(i, j)^{th}$ element of α as yielding that multiple of the jth error as it affects the adjustment of the ith variable of Z to its long run position is independent of the dating of the error, and depends on the lag length m only in so far as m encapsulates the short-run dynamics admitted by the model. If a model of n I(1) variables interlinked by r cointegrating relationships may be properly specified as a VAR then m should be (just) large enough to yield an error ε_t which is free from autocorrelation and which is such as to model effectively the short-run dynamics (as captured by the variables ΔZ_{t-i}; i = 1, . . m – 1) in association with the error correction mechanism (the adjustment matrix α applied to the r long run relationships given by either $\beta'Z_{t-m}$ or $\beta'Z_{t-1}$).

There is, however, a problem in interpreting β' as a set of r cointegrating vectors and α as the adjustment matrix. These two matrices are defined by $\lambda_m = \alpha\beta'$, but α and β are not unique. Suppose Q is any non-singular r×r matrix; define α_o and β_o by $\alpha_o = \alpha Q'$ and $\beta_o = \beta Q^{-1}$; it is then apparent that $\alpha_o\beta_o' = \alpha Q'Q^{-1'}\beta' = \alpha\beta' = \lambda_m$. One might then describe β_o as the set of r cointegrating vectors and α_o as the adjustment matrix. This is a form of a 'normalization' issue; in the simple two variable world, if $Y_t - \gamma X_t$ is I(0) while both Y and X are I(1) the cointegrating vector is given by $[1 \; -\gamma]$, but this is unique only up to a scalar multiple, and has been normalized so that Y_t has a unit coefficient. The r cointegrating vectors of Z_t in the VAR may be written as $Q^{-1'}\beta'$, where $\beta'Z_t$ is stationary and Q is an arbitrary non-singular matrix; one might choose Q such that the $(p, p)^{th}$ elements of $Q^{-1'}\beta'$ are all unity so that the pth equation of $Q^{-1'}\beta'Z_t = 0$ yields an equation which states that Z_{pt} is linear in the other n – 1 variables of Z , but this is entirely arbitrary. Hence, there is an infinity of 'cointegrating vectors'; each is, however, associated with a unique 'adjustment matrix' but interpretation of any one 'cointegrating relationship' is not aided by this observation. To interpret $\beta'Z_t$ it is necessary to consider all r relationships taken together.

The Johansen method involves estimating the rank of the λ_m matrix by an examination of its characteristic roots. The rank of a matrix is equal to the number of its non-zero characteristic roots, or eigenvalues. The test proceeds by estimating the VAR model and then estimating the eigenvalues of the matrix λ_m. Let the estimates of the n roots of λ_m be denoted by $\hat{\omega}_j$, j = 1, 2, . . n, and be ordered such that $\hat{\omega}_j > \hat{\omega}_{j+1}$; all the roots satisfy $0 \leq \hat{\omega}_j < 1$. The likelihood ratio statistic is used:

$$LR = -T \sum_{j=r+1}^{n} \ell n(1-\hat{\omega}_j).$$

The LR statistic has a non-standard distribution, but critical values to test the null hypothesis that there are at most r cointegrating vectors are tabulated in Johansen (1988) and some software packages also report the critical values. Clearly, if $\hat{\omega}_1$ is close to zero then $-\ell n(1 - \hat{\omega}_1)$ is small and positive, and if all roots are close to zero then a small test statistic results. Starting with r = 0, a small value of the test statistic indicates that all the roots are close to zero, and is an indication that $\rho(\lambda_m) = 0$; equally, a large value of the test statistic indicates that at least the largest root is very different from zero, and that $\rho(\lambda_m) \geq 1$.

When r = 0, the null hypothesis is that there are no cointegrating vectors; if there are no cointegrating vectors all the roots of λ_m are zero. If this null is not rejected one may conclude that λ_m has zero rank and is the null matrix. Hence non-rejection of the hypothesis when r = 0 implies that $Z_t \sim I(1)$ and no cointegrating vectors exist.

However, if this hypothesis is rejected one cannot conclude that all the roots of λ_m are non-zero, and setting r = 1 allows examination of the hypothesis that the largest root of λ_m is different from zero, but that all remaining roots are zero. If the test statistic computed with r = 1 is not rejected the conclusion is that the largest root of λ_m is not zero, but that all subsequent roots are zero. Thus rejection of the hypothesis with r = 0 followed by non-rejection with r = 1 implies that the rank of λ_m is one, that $Z_t \sim I(1)$ and $Z_t \sim CI(1, 1)$ with one cointegrating vector. If the hypothesis r = 1 is rejected then the test is conducted with r = 2, and so on. If the hypotheses when $r \leq r_o - 1$ are rejected then λ_m has at least r_o non-zero roots; if the hypothesis when $r = r_o$ is not rejected then the conclusion is that $\rho(\lambda_m) = r_o$ and the testing stops. If all n hypotheses are rejected (for r = 0, . . . n – 1) then the conclusion is that λ_m is of full rank and hence that $Z_t \sim I(0)$.

The Johansen method estimates, by maximum likelihood, all the distinct cointegrating vectors which may exist, provides a test of their statistical significance and also provides a likelihood ratio test by which to examine linear restrictions on the vectors.

Suppose more than one cointegrating vector is found. An immediate, but unappealing, conclusion is that there is more than one long-run equilibrium relationship between the n variables of Z_t. But the long run is uniquely defined, even when there are several cointegrating vectors, and the interpretation demands that cointegrating relationships amongst sub-sets of the n variables are recognized. More than one cointegrating vector is to be seen as implying that there are long-run relationships amongst sub-sets of the n variables, and not just amongst the complete set of n variables. Of course, the number of cointegrating vectors must be less than, or equal to, n – 1. Suppose n = 3 and there are two cointegrating relationships:

$$Z_1 - \beta_{12}Z_2 - \beta_{13}Z_3 \sim I(0) \quad \text{and} \quad Z_1 - \beta_{22}Z_2 - \beta_{23}Z_3 \sim I(0).$$

These equations are of the form $\beta'Z = 0$; the 'normalization' used here sets the coefficients on Z_1 to unity in both relationships. Any linear transformation of these cointegrating relationships, as represented by $Q^{-1'}\beta'Z \sim I(0)$, simply yields two linearly independent combinations of I(0) variables both of which are, necessarily, also I(0) variables. One may, therefore, take the following linear combinations:

$$(\beta_{22} - \beta_{12})Z_2 + (\beta_{23} - \beta_{13})Z_3 \sim I(0)$$

and $$(\beta_{23} - \beta_{13})Z_1 + (\beta_{13}\beta_{22} - \beta_{23}\beta_{12})Z_2 \sim I(0)$$

and $$(\beta_{22} - \beta_{12})Z_1 + (\beta_{12}\beta_{23} - \beta_{22}\beta_{13})Z_3 \sim I(0)$$

Therefore, with two cointegrating vectors and three variables, each possible pairing of variables is also cointegrated. Thus, in the long run, there is a unique equilibrium relationship between the three pairings of variables which implies that, taking all three variables together, there are two cointegrating vectors. Thus, no two variables are independent in the long run, in the sense that there is a unique (up to a multiplicative factor) cointegrating relationship between each pair, and it is not just that Z_1, Z_2 and Z_3 are jointly cointegrated, but so are Z_1 and Z_2, Z_1 and Z_3, and Z_2 and Z_3. The operation of a linear transformation leaves the underlying cointegrated relationships unaltered, but the long-run position can be seen as the conjunction of three separate I(0) relationships each of which is defined on two variables.

This may be thought of as follows: a linear relationship between three variables defines a three-dimensional plane, and the existence of two distinct cointegrating vectors defines two distinct, but intersecting, planes. The intersection of two planes defines a line in three-dimensional space which defines *the* unique long-run equilibrium path. It is not that there are two equilibria in the long run, but rather that there is a unique path defined by the conjunction of three cointegrated relationships between the three pairs of variables. Equivalently, one can think of either cointegrating vector defining a plane in (Z_1, Z_2, Z_3) space, and then, say, take the cointegrating line in (Z_1, Z_2) space which is projected onto the plane; the resulting line on the plane is the unique long-run equilibrium relationship between the three variables. In the long run, the three variables lie in two intersecting planes, and the intersection is invariant to any linear transformation. Neither plane is, itself, invariant to such a transformation, but since it is the two planes *taken together* which defines the long run this does not generate any ambiguity. If the cointegrating vector is unique then there are no cointegrated relationships between any of the three possible pairs, and the long-run relationship is a unique plane in (Z_1, Z_2, Z_3) space, but in the absence of any information on the long-run path which relates any two of these variables no *line* can be identified as the long-run path.

In general, with n variables, if the cointegrating vector is unique then there are no cointegrated relationships amongst any subset of the n variables, and the long-run relationship then lies within a unique hyper-plane in n-dimensional space. If there are r_o ($0 < r_o < n$) cointegrating vectors then there are cointegrated relationships between sub-sets of the variables, and the long-run path may be more sharply defined as having fewer dimensions. If $r_o = n - 1$ there is a unique (up to a scalar multiple) linear combination of every possible pair of variables Z_i and Z_j which is stationary (and hence there are stationary combinations of any two or more variables), in which case the long-run equilibrium relating all n variables is a unique one-dimensional line in n-space; if $r_o = n - 2$ no pairs are cointegrated, but all possible triples of variables Z_i, Z_j and Z_k are cointegrated (as are all sets of three or more variables), and so the long run lies on a two-dimensional plane in n-space; and so on. The number of cointegrating vectors indicates the number of cointegrated relationships amongst the n variables of Z_t, so that with r_o cointegrating vectors every set of $n - r_o + 1$ variables is cointegrated, but no linear combination of $n - r_o$ (or fewer) variables is cointegrated.

Since the VAR approach makes no endo-exogenous variable distinction this is a quite different approach from the Engle–Granger single equation approach (which imposes a distinction; see **Engle–Granger representation theorem** and **Error correction models**); however, if the Johansen method indicates just one cointegrating vector this may be seen as some justification for using a single-equation error correction model (ECM). If more than one cointegrating vector is indicated by the Johansen method then any model utilizing a single equation defined on those same variables will be deficient and will incorrectly utilize a unique error in its ECM form when there are at least two errors to take into consideration. Hence when $r_o > 1$ the model is better examined as a set of equations, rather than as a single equation. Moreover, as a test of cointegration, the Johansen method has better statistical properties than the Engle–Granger approach, as the power of the cointegration test is higher.

Further reading

The most important papers in this field are Johansen (1988) and also Engle and Granger (1987). For applications of this approach, see, for example, Johansen and Juselius (1990). See also **Cointegration**, **Engle–Granger representation theorem**, **Error correction models**, **Integration**, **Stationarity** and **Vector autoregressions**.

Kalman filter models

The Kalman Filter was introduced by Kalman (1960) and is a powerful technique which may be used to model time-varying parameters. The principle of the Kalman filter is that the investigator first specifies a time path for the varying parameter of the form $\beta_t = \Gamma\beta_{t-1} + \eta_t$, where β_t is the value of the k-dimensional parameter at time t, Γ is some known (or imposed) k×k transition matrix and η_t is a random term. At time t = 0 the investigator holds an initial guess of β, say $\hat{\beta}_o$, and forms a prediction of β_1, denoted by $\hat{\beta}_{1/0;}$; when information becomes available at time t = 1 this prediction is updated optimally to form a new prediction, $\hat{\beta}_{2/1}$, which incorporates both the new information and the known transition path of the βs. The Kalman filter has many special cases, which include the pure random coefficient model and recursive least squares.

To formalize the ideas of the Kalman filter, suppose that in general an economic agent has both sample and prior information; the sample information is contained in the linear model $Y = X\beta + \varepsilon$, $\varepsilon \sim N(0, V)$, data are available on X and Y, and there is also prior information of the form $\beta = \beta_o + \eta$, $\eta \sim N(0, \Omega)$, where both β_o and Ω are known. It is common to assume that Ω is diagonal. The information may be combined by the Theil–Goldberger estimation technique (see **Mixed estimation**):

$$\begin{bmatrix} Y \\ r \end{bmatrix} = \begin{bmatrix} X \\ R \end{bmatrix} \beta + \begin{bmatrix} \varepsilon \\ \eta \end{bmatrix}$$

i.e. $Y^* = Z\beta + u$ where u has a variance–covariance matrix given by:

$$V(u) = \begin{bmatrix} V & 0 \\ 0 & \Omega \end{bmatrix}$$

Applying generalized least squares to this set of equations yields:

$$\hat{\beta} = \beta_o + K(Y - X\beta_o)$$

and

$$V(\hat{\beta}) = (I - KX)\Omega$$

where $K = [X'V^{-1}X + \Omega^{-1}]^{-1}X'V^{-1}$ which may be written equivalently as $\Omega X'(V + X\Omega X')^{-1}$; denoting the term $(Y - X\beta_o)$ by $\tilde{e}$, the prediction error using only the prior information, β_o, then $\hat{\beta} = \beta_o + K\tilde{e}$. Since $\tilde{e} = (Y - X\beta_o)$, $V(\tilde{e}) = V + X\Omega X' = \Phi$, and so $K = \Omega X'\Phi^{-1}$; K is known as the Kalman gain and clearly depends on both the sampling variance and the prior variance and when written as $\Omega X'\Phi^{-1}$, K is seen to depend on the prior variance, Ω, and the forecast variance, Φ.

The Kalman filter uses the above results in a recursive formula, whereby the estimate of a parameter is updated sequentially as new information becomes available. Consider the following simple structure:

$$y_t = x_t'\beta_t + \varepsilon_t, \quad \varepsilon_t \sim N(0, \sigma^2)$$

$$\beta_t = \Gamma\beta_{t-1} + \eta_t, \quad \eta_t \sim N(0, Q)$$

$$\hat{\beta}_o = \beta_o + \phi_o, \quad \phi_o \sim N(0, \Phi_o)$$

x_t' is a $1\times k$ vector, β_t is a $k\times 1$ vector, Γ, Q and Φ_o are known $k\times k$ matrices. The random error terms, ε_t, η_t and ϕ_o are assumed to be independent of each other.

The first equation is the measurement equation, the second is the transition equation, and the third provides the prior estimate. This system is known as the state-space model. At $t = 0$ the structure of the model, in terms of the fixed values of x, and the fixed matrices Γ, Q and Φ_o are all known, as is σ^2. Starting with an initial fixed guess of β, $\hat{\beta}_o$, the problem is how to use the sequential information y_t in order to form an optimal sequence of updated predictions of β_t and their associated variance matrices. Given $\hat{\beta}_o$ the optimal prediction of β_1 is denoted by $\hat{\beta}_{1/0} = \Gamma\hat{\beta}_o$; $\hat{\beta}_{1/0}$ is the prediction of β_1 using only information available at time 0. The error between $\hat{\beta}_{1/0}$ and its true value β_1 is given by $\beta_1 - \hat{\beta}_{1/0} = \Gamma\beta_o + \eta_1 - \Gamma(\beta_o + \phi_0) = -\Gamma\phi_0 + \eta_1 = \delta_1$, and so the variance of $\hat{\beta}_{1/0}$ is $V(\delta_1) = \Gamma\Phi_o\Gamma' + Q = P_{1/0}$. The state vector β_1 and its variance matrix are thus predicted, one-step-ahead, without any reference to y_1, which is of course not known at this time. At $t = 1$ the new information in the form of y_1 becomes available, and it, together with the prediction of β_1, may be used in a mixed estimation so as to combine the sample information with the prediction:

$$\begin{bmatrix} y_1 \\ \hat{\beta}_{1/0} \end{bmatrix} = \begin{bmatrix} x_1' \\ I \end{bmatrix}\beta_1 + \begin{bmatrix} \varepsilon_1 \\ \delta_1 \end{bmatrix}$$

This is precisely the form of the Theil–Goldberger model, and so using the expressions above, the optimal updating equations are:

$$\hat{\beta}_1 = \beta_{1/0} + K_1(y_1 - x_1'\beta_{1/0})$$

$$V(\hat{\beta}_1) = (I - K_1 x_1')P_{1/0},$$

where $K_1 = P_{1/0}x_1/f_1$ and $f_1 = (\sigma^2 + x_1 P_{1/0} x_1')$. These values may then be used to form predictions $\beta_{2/1}$ and $P_{2/1}$, which are then updated once y_2 becomes available, and so on. In general:

$$\hat{\beta}_t = \hat{\beta}_{t/t-1} + K_t(y_t - x_t'\hat{\beta}_{t/t-1})$$

$$V(\hat{\beta}_t) = (I - K_t x_t')P_{t/t-1},$$

where $K_t = P_{t/t-1}x_t/f_t$ and $f_t = (\sigma^2 + x_t P_{t/t-1} x'_t)$. The forecasts of $\hat{\beta}_t$, $\hat{\beta}_{t/t-1}$, are optimal in the sense of minimum mean square error and if normality of the errors is assumed they are also the maximum likelihood estimators of $\hat{\beta}_t$.

The one-step-ahead prediction errors, $\tilde{\varepsilon}_t$, are given by $(y_t - x'_t\hat{\beta}_{t/t-1})$, and so the updating formula may be written as:

$$\hat{\beta}_t = \beta_{t/t-1} + K_t\tilde{\varepsilon}_t.$$

Since $K_t = P_{t/t-1}x_t/f_t$, K_t is smaller the larger is f_t, and since $f_t = V(\tilde{\varepsilon}_t)$, the adjustment made to $\beta_{t/t-1}$ is smaller the larger is the variance of the prediction error. This model may also be used to make multi-period forecasts of the β values, rather than one-step-ahead forecasts:

$$\hat{\beta}_{t+n} = \Gamma^n\hat{\beta}_t \quad \text{and} \quad \tilde{y}_{t+n/t} = x'_{t+n}\hat{\beta}_{t+n}.$$

The filter can be employed in reverse: by using all available data to time T a smoothed estimate may be obtained, and the updating equations may be used to obtain backward-looking predictions.

This model has found application in many areas. As a special case, the simple unobservable components model may be written as:

$$y_t = \beta_t + \varepsilon_t, \quad \varepsilon_t \sim N(0, \sigma^2)$$

and
$$\beta_t = \beta_{t-1} + \eta_t, \quad \eta_t \sim N(0, \sigma^2_\eta)$$

and
$$\hat{\beta}_o = \beta_o + \phi_o, \quad \phi_o \sim N(0, \sigma^2_o).$$

This scheme could be used, for example, to model unobservable permanent income, β_t, whereby observable income, y_t, is assumed to comprise permanent income and a white-noise component, ε_t; permanent income, β_t, is assumed to follow a random walk. The updating equations are given by

$$\hat{\beta}_t = \hat{\beta}_{t/t-1} + K_t(y_t - \hat{\beta}_{t/t-1})$$

and may then be interpreted as modelling the way in which permanent income evolves through the gradual incorporation of some proportion of unexpected income, $y_t - \hat{\beta}_{t/t-1}$ (the prediction error given information available prior to time t), and may also be interpreted as providing a set of expectations about permanent income. The Kalman gain is simply a function of the variances of this model.

As another special case, the standard ordinary least squares recursions (see **Recursive residuals**) may be written as a Kalman filter:

$$y_t = x'_t\beta_t + \varepsilon_t, \quad \varepsilon_t \sim N(0, \sigma^2)$$

and
$$\beta_t = \beta_{t-1}$$

and
$$\hat{\beta}_o = \hat{\beta}_{t-1} \sim N(\beta_{t-1}, P_{t-1}).$$

In this model the true β is assumed to be constant, and is further analysed in **Recursive residuals**, where the updating equations may be seen as an application of the Kalman filter formulae.

As another special case, the autoregressive model, $y_t = \alpha y_{t-1} + \varepsilon_t$ may be written as:

$$y_t = \beta_t + \varepsilon_t$$

and

$$\beta_t = \alpha \beta_{t-1} + \eta_t.$$

As a final pair of special cases, the pure random coefficient model may be written as a Kalman filter by setting Γ as the null matrix, and systematic behaviour of the parameters over time may be established by, for example, setting $\Gamma = I$ in which case the parameters vary through time systematically and follow a random walk.

The Kalman filter is both a general and powerful model for analysing time-varying parameter models and many software packages incorporate estimation routines which allow the specification of the measurement, transition and prior estimate equations.

Further reading

See Kalman (1960), Harvey (1981) and Cuthbertson, Hall and Taylor (1992).

Lagrange multiplier tests

In testing a hypothesis one approach is to view that hypothesis as imposing a set of constraints on a more general model. Estimation of the model subject to the constraints may then be seen as a case of constrained optimization, and is often achieved by maximizing the likelihood of the model, subject to the constraints. Using the methods of traditional calculus, this can be effected by introducing a set of Lagrange multipliers, one for each constraint. If the constraints are satisfied exactly in the sample, then the resulting Lagrange multipliers will be exactly zero; however, even if a constraint is exactly true in the population, it is not likely to be exactly true in any one sample and so even a true constraint is likely to result in non-zero Lagrange multipliers. Of course, the multipliers are shadow prices of the constraints, and the smaller is the multiplier the less binding is the associated restriction and *vice versa*. One approach to testing restrictions is, therefore, to test that the Lagrange multipliers are zero.

An advantage of using the Lagrange multiplier (LM) approach to testing hypotheses is that the multipliers are evaluated from the constrained model, and this form of testing requires, therefore, that only the constrained model be estimated. The Lagrange multiplier approach may be seen as an examination of the curvature of the log-likelihood function: the slope of the log-likelihood function, evaluated at the maximum likelihood estimate, is zero, and if the restrictions are true then the slope of the log-likelihood function will be insignificantly different from zero when evaluated at the constrained estimate. In general, if the estimated multipliers are given by the vector $\hat{\lambda}$, then the test statistic is computed as:

$$LM = \hat{\lambda}'[\hat{V}(\hat{\lambda})]^{-1}\hat{\lambda}$$

where $\hat{V}(\hat{\lambda})$ is the variance matrix of the multipliers; it may be shown that LM has an asymptotic distribution given by χ^2_m where m is the number of constraints imposed by the hypothesis under test.

In the simple example of testing the linear restriction $R\beta = r$ in the general linear model $Y = X\beta + \varepsilon$, the Lagrange multipliers are given by:

$$\hat{\lambda} = -[R(X'X)^{-1}R']^{-1}R(\hat{\beta} - \tilde{\beta})$$

where $\hat{\beta}$ and $\tilde{\beta}$ are the unconstrained and constrained estimators respectively (see **Restricted least squares**). Noting that $R\tilde{\beta} = r$, the variance of $\hat{\lambda}$ is then given by:

$$\begin{aligned} V(\hat{\lambda}) &= \sigma^2[R(X'X)^{-1}R']^{-1}R(X'X)^{-1}R'[R(X'X)^{-1}R']^{-1} \\ &= \sigma^2[R(X'X)^{-1}R']^{-1} \end{aligned}$$

assuming that $V(\varepsilon) = \sigma^2 I$, and so the test statistic is computed as:

$$LM = \hat{\lambda}'[R(X'X)^{-1}R']\hat{\lambda}/s^2$$

where s^2 is the estimator of σ^2. In this example $(\tilde{\beta} - \hat{\beta}) = (X'X)^{-1}R'\hat{\lambda}$, and so:

$$(\tilde{\beta} - \hat{\beta})'X'X(\tilde{\beta} - \hat{\beta}) = \hat{\lambda}'R(X'X)^{-1}R'\hat{\lambda}$$

i.e.
$$LM = (\tilde{\beta} - \hat{\beta})'X'X(\tilde{\beta} - \hat{\beta})/s^2$$

but $(\tilde{\beta} - \hat{\beta})'X'X(\tilde{\beta} - \hat{\beta})$ may be shown to be the difference between the restricted residual sum of squared residuals (RRSS), obtained from running the regression of Y on X subject to the restriction $R\beta = r$, and the unrestricted residual sums of squares, URSS, obtained from running the regression of Y on X without any constraints. Also, $s^2 = URSS/(n - k)$, so the LM statistic is simply given by:

$$LM = (n - k)[(RRSS/URSS) - 1].$$

As a special case, if the restrictions express the hypothesis that all the slope parameters in the model are zero, then the RRSS is simply the sum of squared observations of the dependent variable, and the R^2 statistic from the restricted model will be exactly zero. Denoting the uncentred R^2 statistic from the unrestricted model by R_u^2 (= 1 − RRSS/URSS), the LM statistic may be written as:

$$LM = (n - k)[R_u^2/(1 - R_u^2)]$$

The exact test is given by the standard F statistic:

$$\frac{R_u^2\ /k}{(1-R_u^2)/(n-k)} \sim F_{k,n-k}$$

so the distribution of LM may be written as:

$$LM \sim kF_{k,n-k}$$

As $n \to \infty$, $F_{k,n-k} \xrightarrow{D} \chi_k^2/k$ and so in large samples:

$$LM \xrightarrow{D} \chi_m^2.$$

Also, in large samples under the truth of the restrictions, $R_u^2 \to 0$, and so $R_u^2/(1 - R_u^2) \to R_u^2$; hence in large samples $LM \to (n - k)R_u^2 \to nR_u^2$ which leads to the common form of the statistic:

$$LM = nR_u^2 \sim \chi_m^2.$$

This form of the Lagrange multiplier statistic, as the sample size multiplied by the uncentred goodness of fit statistic from the unrestricted regression, is most uncommon; it is to be noted that the R^2 in question is the uncentred R^2 (that is, expressed as the sum of squared fitted values divided by the sum of squares of the dependent variable, rather than as sums of squares of deviations from their sample means). This form of the statistic is used, for example, in the large sample LM test of autocorrelation amongst the errors of a regression equation.

The Lagrange multiplier test is commonly used in econometrics; it has intuitive appeal as a measure of the shadow price of constraints, and has the advantage of requiring the model to be estimated only subject to the constraints. It is used particularly for large sample tests of linear constraints when there are no small sample exact results available, and may also be used in testing non-linear hypotheses. Since it requires only that the model be estimated subject to the constraints, there may be computational gains to be enjoyed from this aspect of the test. In finite samples it is quite common to use the F-version of the test, rather than the large sample χ^2-version, since the χ^2-version has been found to reject the null hypothesis too frequently; use of the F-version is particularly common in small samples when using the LM test of autocorrelation or of heteroscedasticity.

Further reading

The derivation and use of the Lagrange multiplier test is examined in comprehensive detail in Godfrey (1988). and also Breusch and Pagan (1980). See also **Nonlinear hypothesis testing**, **Autocorrelation tests** and **Heteroscedasticity tests**.

Large sample theory

In many circumstances, for example when, in a regression equation, the investigator is not prepared to assert that the regressors are all non-stochastic, the small sample properties of estimators cannot be derived analytically. However, it is typically the case that the large sample properties of the estimators (that is, the properties of the estimators as the sample size gets large without limit) can be derived. It is then possible to choose from amongst alternative estimators by reference to their asymptotic properties (on the argument that if the estimator does not have desirable properties in large samples, then it is even less worthy as an estimator in small, finite samples and *vice versa*). Some definitions are required to pursue this discussion.

A random sequence is a set of random variables, each element of which depends critically upon the sample size from which the random variable is constructed. Let $\{\hat{\theta}_1, \hat{\theta}_2, \ ,\hat{\theta}_n\}$ be a random sequence, where $\hat{\theta}_i$ is a scalar random variable constructed from a sample of size i. As examples of a random sequence, $\hat{\theta}_i$ could be the mean value of a sample of size i or it could be the ordinary least squares estimator of one parameter of a model based on a sample of size i.

Convergence in probability can now be defined: $\hat{\theta}_n$ converges in probability to η (either a constant or a random variable) as $n \rightarrow \infty$ if:

$$\lim_{n\to\infty} \Pr(|\hat{\theta}_n - \eta| > \delta) = 0, \quad \text{for any } \delta > 0.$$

If this is the case, it may be written as:

$$\hat{\theta}_n \xrightarrow{p} \eta \qquad \text{or as} \qquad \text{plim}(\hat{\theta}_n) = \eta.$$

The first statement is read as '$\hat{\theta}$ converges in probability to η', and the second is read as 'the probability limit of $\hat{\theta}$ is η'; the two statements are equivalent. Following common practice, the sample size subscript on $\hat{\theta}$ may be dropped. The formal statement says that the probability that $\hat{\theta}_n$ is different from η tends to zero as the sample size increases; this implies that the distribution of $\hat{\theta}_n$, in the limit, becomes that of η.

Convergence in probability is not the same as convergence in quadratic mean, sometimes called convergence in mean square: if $\hat{\theta}$ converges to η in mean square then:

$$\lim_{n\to\infty} E(\hat{\theta}_n - \eta)^2 = 0;$$

which may be written as $\hat{\theta} \xrightarrow{m} \eta$.

A third concept of convergence is that of convergence in distribution: if $\{\hat{\theta}_1, \hat{\theta}_2, \ ,\hat{\theta}_n\}$ is a sequence of random variables with cumulative distribution functions $\{F_1, F_2, \ldots\}$ then $\hat{\theta}$ converges in distribution to the random variable η which has the cumulative distribution function F if:

$$\lim_{n\to\infty} F_n = F \text{ at every continuity point of F;}$$

which may be written as $\hat{\theta}_n \xrightarrow{D} \eta$.

A final concept of convergence is convergence almost surely: the sequence of random variables $\{\hat{\theta}_1, \hat{\theta}_2, \ ,\hat{\theta}_n\}$ converges almost surely to η if

$$\Pr\{\lim_{n\to\infty} \hat{\theta}_n = \eta\} = 1;$$

which may be written as $\hat{\theta}_n \xrightarrow{a.s.} \eta$.

The four concepts of convergence are related by:

$$\begin{array}{c} \hat{\theta} \xrightarrow{a.s.} \eta \\ \Downarrow \\ \hat{\theta} \xrightarrow{m} \eta \Rightarrow \hat{\theta} \xrightarrow{p} \eta \Rightarrow \hat{\theta} \xrightarrow{D} \eta \end{array}$$

that is, convergence in mean square and convergence almost surely each imply convergence in probability which implies convergence in distribution. Demonstration of this relationship may be found in most advanced texts; sufficient for the present purpose is to note that Chebyshev's inequality plays an important role in such demonstrations. This inequality states that for a scalar random variable, x, having a finite mean of μ and a finite variance σ^2:

$$\Pr\{x^2 > k^2\} \leq E(x^2)/k^2 \quad \text{for any real } k > 0.$$

Applying this inequality:

$$\Pr\{|x - \mu| > k\} \leq \sigma^2/k^2 \qquad \text{for any real } k > 0;$$

this inequality holds, whatever the distribution of x.

If $\hat{\theta}_n$ converges in mean square to η then $E(\hat{\theta}_n - \eta)^2$ has a limit of zero; Chebyshev's inequality then implies:

$$\lim_{n\to\infty} \Pr\{|\hat{\theta}_n - \eta| > k\} = 0, \qquad \text{that is, } \operatorname{plim}(\hat{\theta}_n) = \eta.$$

It is also clear from using Chebyshev's inequality that convergence of $\hat{\theta}_n$ to η in mean square implies convergence in probability of $\hat{\theta}_n$ to η where η may be regarded as a random variable or as a constant.

In general, convergence in distribution does not imply convergence in probability (although the converse is always true); however, in the special case when η is a constant, convergence of $\hat{\theta}_n$ to η in distribution implies that $\operatorname{plim}(\hat{\theta}_n) = \eta$.

If $\hat{\theta}_n$ is an estimator of the parameter θ then it is described as a consistent estimator if $\operatorname{plim}(\hat{\theta}_n) = \theta$ (some authors refer to this definition as that of weak consistency and convergence of $\hat{\theta}_n$ to θ almost surely as strong consistency). Given the above relationships between the concepts of convergence, this is equivalent to defining $\hat{\theta}_n$ as consistent if the limiting distribution of $\hat{\theta}$ collapses upon θ (since, in this case, θ is a constant). To make clear the role of convergence in mean square in the definition of consistency, consider the following:

$$\begin{aligned} E(\hat{\theta}_n - \theta)^2 &= E[(\hat{\theta}_n - E(\hat{\theta}_n)) + (E(\hat{\theta}_n) - \theta)]^2 \\ &= E(\hat{\theta}_n - E(\hat{\theta}_n))^2 + (E(\hat{\theta}_n) - \theta)^2 \\ &\qquad + E[(\hat{\theta}_n - E(\hat{\theta}_n))\times(E(\hat{\theta}_n) - \theta)]. \end{aligned}$$

The cross-product term is zero since $[E(\hat{\theta}_n) - \theta]$ is not a random variable and $E(\hat{\theta}_n - E(\hat{\theta}_n)) \equiv 0$, and so:

$$E(\hat{\theta}_n - \theta)^2 = V_n^2 + B_n^2$$

where V_n^2 is the variance of $\hat{\theta}_n$ and B_n^2 is the squared bias of $\hat{\theta}_n$. Thus the mean squared error of $\hat{\theta}_n$ comprises the sum of its variance and the square of its bias. Hence a sufficient (though not necessary) condition for consistency is that the variance and bias of the estimator both approach zero as the sample size increases.

In defining asymptotic unbiasedness, there are three different limit operators to consider; plim is defined above, and the other two limit operators are Lim E and AE which are read as 'the limit of the expectation' and the 'asymptotic expectation' respectively.

$$\lim_{n\to\infty} E(\hat{\theta}_n) = \lim_{n\to\infty} \int \hat{\theta}_n \, f(\hat{\theta}_n) \, d(\hat{\theta}_n)$$

$$AE(\hat{\theta}_n) = \int \hat{\theta} \, f(\hat{\theta}) \, d\hat{\theta}$$

where $f(\hat{\theta}_n)$ is the probability density function of $\hat{\theta}_n$ and $f(\hat{\theta})$ is the limiting probability density function of $\hat{\theta}_n$.

Hence, Lim E is the limit of the expectation of $\hat{\theta}_n$ as $n \to \infty$ and AE is the mean of the limiting distribution. The three limit operators may yield different results; in particular it should be noted that of the three only plim can be a non-degenerate random variable and so if $\text{plim}(\hat{\theta}_n)$ is a non-degenerate random variable it must differ from both Lim $E(\hat{\theta}_n)$ and $AE(\hat{\theta}_n)$. It should also be noted that since convergence in probability implies convergence in distribution, then if $\text{plim}(\hat{\theta}_n) = \theta$ where θ is a constant, $AE(\hat{\theta}_n) = \theta$.

$\hat{\theta}$ is described as an asymptotically unbiased estimator of θ if $AE(\hat{\theta}_n) = \theta$; the asymptotic bias of the estimator, which may or may not be zero, is defined as $AE(\hat{\theta}_n) - \theta$. The definition of asymptotic unbiasedness given is not, in general, equivalent to the statement that Lim $E(\hat{\theta}_n) = \theta$ since $AE(\hat{\theta}_n) = \theta$ does not, in general, imply that Lim $E(\hat{\theta}_n) = \theta$.

It is important to note the condition under which Lim E and AE are equivalent; it may be shown that (see Rao, 1973):

$$\text{if } E|\hat{\theta}_n|^r < K \quad \text{for all n, then} \quad \text{Lim } E(\hat{\theta}_n^i) = AE(\hat{\theta}_n^i) \quad \text{for all } i < r.$$

In particular, suppose that $E(\hat{\theta}_n^2) < K$ for all n; then the limiting expectation and the expectation of the limit distribution are identical.

As a consequence of the above, since $\text{plim}(\hat{\theta}_n) = \theta$ implies $AE(\hat{\theta}_n) = \theta$ when θ is a constant, if $\hat{\theta}_n$ is a consistent estimator is it asymptotically unbiased (but not necessarily *vice versa*).

If $\hat{\theta}$ is a consistent estimator then its probability density function collapses on the true parameter θ as the sample size tends to ∞. Since two consistent estimators ultimately concentrate all probability on the unknown parameter value, their limiting density functions have zero variance; this makes comparison of consistent estimators by reference to their efficiency difficult. In order that comparisons can be made the usual approach is to consider the behaviour of the scaled random variable $\sqrt{n}(\hat{\theta}_n - \theta)$. If $\hat{\theta}$ is a consistent estimator and $\sqrt{n}(\hat{\theta}_n - \theta)$ converges in distribution to $N(0, \Sigma)$ then $\hat{\theta}_n$ is said to have the asymptotic distribution given by $N(\theta, \Sigma/n)$. Suppose that $\hat{\theta}$ and $\tilde{\theta}$ are each consistent and asymptotically normal estimators with asymptotic variances given by Σ/n and Ω/n respectively, then $\hat{\theta}$ is said to be asymptotically efficient relative to $\tilde{\theta}$ if the matrix $\Omega - \Sigma$ is positive definite.

The plim operator has the following properties:

1. if $\text{plim}(\hat{\theta}) = \theta$ and g(.) is any continuous function not involving n, then $\text{plim}[g(\hat{\theta})] = g(\theta)$;
2. if $\hat{\theta}$ and $\hat{\lambda}$ are both random sequences and $\text{plim}(\hat{\theta})$ and $\text{plim}(\hat{\lambda})$ both exist then:
   a. $\text{plim}(\hat{\theta} + \hat{\lambda}) = \text{plim}(\hat{\theta}) + \text{plim}(\hat{\lambda})$;
   b. $\text{plim}(\hat{\theta} - \hat{\lambda}) = \text{plim}(\hat{\theta}) - \text{plim}(\hat{\lambda})$;
   c. $\text{plim}(\hat{\theta}\hat{\lambda}) = \text{plim}(\hat{\theta})\text{plim}(\hat{\lambda})$;
   d. $\text{plim}(\hat{\theta}/\hat{\lambda}) = \text{plim}(\hat{\theta})/\text{plim}(\hat{\lambda})$ for $\text{plim}(\hat{\lambda}) \neq 0$.

The following rules hold with regard to convergence in distribution:

1. if $\text{plim}(\hat{\theta} - \hat{\lambda}) = 0$ and $\hat{\theta} \xrightarrow{D} \eta$ where η is a random variable then $\hat{\lambda} \xrightarrow{D} \eta$;
2. if $\text{plim}(\hat{\lambda}) = 0$ and $\hat{\theta} \xrightarrow{D} \eta$ where η is a random variable then $\text{plim}(\hat{\lambda}\hat{\theta}) = 0$;
3. if $\text{plim}(\hat{\lambda}) = \lambda$ where λ is some constant and $\hat{\theta} \xrightarrow{D} \eta$ where η is a random variable then:
   a. $\hat{\lambda} + \hat{\theta} \xrightarrow{D}$ to the random variable $\lambda + \eta$;
   b. $\hat{\lambda}\hat{\theta} \xrightarrow{D}$ to the random variable $\lambda\eta$;
   c. $\hat{\theta}/\hat{\lambda} \xrightarrow{D}$ to the random variable η/λ for $\lambda \neq 0$;
4. if $\hat{\theta} \xrightarrow{D} \theta$, g is any continuous function not involving n, then $g(\hat{\theta}) \xrightarrow{D} g(\theta)$;
5. if $\hat{\theta} \xrightarrow{D} \theta$ and $\text{plim}(\hat{\theta} - \hat{\lambda}) = 0$, g is any continuous function not involving n, then $\text{plim}(g(\hat{\theta}) - g(\hat{\lambda})) = 0$.

In examining the large sample properties of estimators a most useful application of 3 is Cramer's Theorem:

> If A_n is a random sequence and $\text{plim}(A_n) = A$, where each A_n is a matrix and $\hat{\theta}_n$ is a vector random sequence such that $\hat{\theta}_n \xrightarrow{D} \theta \sim MVN(0, \Sigma)$, then $A_n\hat{\theta}_n \xrightarrow{D} A\theta \sim MVN(0, A\Sigma A')$.

The above concepts and definitions may be used to analyse the large sample properties of estimators within regression theory; however, any such analysis requires some form of central limit theorem to establish convergence in distribution. To demonstrate asymptotic normality of the ordinary least squares estimators requires the use of central limit theorems and demands that certain regularity conditions are satisfied. These are detailed in **Central limit theorems** and **Ordinary least squares in large samples**.

In examining the efficiency of estimators, the Cramer–Rao lower bound is an important concept; this states that, given certain regularity conditions, the variance matrix of an unbiased estimator of some parameter θ has a lower bound. The lower bound is defined in terms of the likelihood function (see **Maximum likelihood**) and is given by the inverse of the information matrix, $[I(\theta)]^{-1}$, where $I(\theta)$ is defined in terms of the likelihood function, L, by:

$$I(\theta) = E\left[-\frac{\partial^2 \ell n L}{\partial\theta\partial\theta'}\right]$$

The variance of $\hat{\theta}$ (where $\hat{\theta}$ is an unbiased or consistent estimator of θ) cannot be less than $[I(\theta)]^{-1}$; hence, denoting the variance–covariance matrix of $\hat{\theta}$ by V, this theorem states that $V - [I(\theta)]^{-1}$ is always a positive semi-definite matrix. Since the maximum likelihood estimator (MLE) is consistent and may be shown to achieve the Cramer–Rao lower bound this provides strong justification for using maximum likelihood estimation techniques.

Further reading

A clear summary of large sample theory may be found in White (1984); see also Greenberg and Webster (1983) and Rao (1973).

Likelihood ratio tests

Likelihood ratio tests are common ways of testing hypotheses; a hypothesis places restrictions on a more general model, and the essence of the likelihood ratio test is to estimate the model by maximum likelihood freely, that is without any constraints, and then estimate the model subject to the constraint. If the model is parameterized by θ, let $\hat{\theta}$ denote the maximum likelihood estimator of θ, and let the associated likelihood function be estimated by $L(\hat{\theta})$. If the model is then re-estimated subject to the constraints imposed by the hypothesis, the resulting estimator may be denoted by $\tilde{\theta}$ and the associated likelihood is computed as $L(\tilde{\theta})$. Definitionally, $L(\hat{\theta}) \geq L(\tilde{\theta})$ and a test of the difference between the two likelihoods constitutes a test of the hypothesis. This is usually performed by constructing the likelihood ratio, $\lambda = L(\tilde{\theta})/L(\hat{\theta})$, and it may be shown that, asymptotically $-2\ell n\lambda$ has a χ^2 distribution and the degrees of freedom are given by the number of constraints which the hypothesis imposes.

In the simple regression model $Y = X\beta + \varepsilon$ this could be used to test the m linear restrictions embodied in the m equations $R\beta = r$; the log-likelihood function of the model when estimated freely is given by

$$-(n/2)\ell n(2\pi\sigma^2) - (1/2\sigma^2)(Y - X\beta)'(Y - X\beta)$$

which may be concentrated, using the fact that $n\tilde{\sigma}^2 = (Y - X\hat{\beta})'(Y - X\hat{\beta})$, to $-(n/2)\ell n(2\pi\tilde{\sigma}^2) - (1/2\tilde{\sigma}^2)n\tilde{\sigma}^2 = -(n/2)(1 + \ell n2\pi) -(n/2)\ell n(\tilde{\sigma}^2)$; since the unrestricted sum of squares is given by $URSS = (Y - X\hat{\beta})'(Y - X\hat{\beta})$ the concentrated likelihood is proportional to $(URSS)^{-n/2}$. Similarly, the concentrated likelihood function of the model subject to the constraint is proportional to $(\text{RRSS})^{-n/2}$, where RRSS is the restricted sum of squares from the constrained regression. Hence the likelihood ratio test of the restrictions is conducted according to the test statistic:

$$\text{LR} = n[\ell n\text{RRSS} - \ell n\text{URSS}]$$

and this is distributed, in large samples, as χ^2_m under the truth of the hypothesis $R\beta = r$. Of course, for such a simple hypothesis an exact small sample F-statistic is available, and the LR test is not typically used in such situations. However, to demostrate this result, in the general LR test of m linear hypotheses H_o $R\theta = \theta_o$, the statistic is given by:

$$\text{LR} = 2\ell n\text{L}(\hat{\theta}) - 2\ell n\text{L}(\tilde{\theta})$$

where $\hat{\theta}$ and $\tilde{\theta}$ are the unconstrained and constrained maximum likelihood estimators respectively. Expanding $\ell n\text{L}(\tilde{\theta})$ in a Taylor series about $\hat{\theta}$, ignoring higher order terms:

$$\ell n\text{L}(\tilde{\theta}) \cong \ell n\text{L}(\hat{\theta}) + [\partial\ell n\text{L}(\hat{\theta})/\partial\theta]'(\tilde{\theta} - \hat{\theta}) - \tfrac{1}{2}(\tilde{\theta} - \hat{\theta})'\text{I}(\hat{\theta})(\tilde{\theta} - \hat{\theta})$$

where $\text{I}(\theta)$ is the information matrix. But $[\partial\ell n\text{L}(\hat{\theta})/\partial\theta] = 0$, hence:

$$\text{LR} \cong (\tilde{\theta} - \hat{\theta})'\text{I}(\hat{\theta})(\tilde{\theta} - \hat{\theta})$$

It may be shown that under regularity conditions and under H_o:

$$\sqrt{n}.(\tilde{\theta} - \theta) \xrightarrow{D} P\eta$$

where $P = Q^{-1} - Q^{-1}R'[RQ^{-1}R]^{-1}RQ^{-1}$, Q is defined by $n^{-1}\text{I}(\theta) \rightarrow Q$ and $\eta \sim N(0, Q)$. It is show in **Maximum likelihood** that $\sqrt{n}.(\hat{\theta} - \theta) \xrightarrow{D} Q^{-1}\eta$; therefore under H_o:

$$\sqrt{n}.(\hat{\theta} - \tilde{\theta}) \xrightarrow{D} (Q^{-1} - P)\eta$$

from which (using the concept of a generalized inverse since $(Q^{-1} - P)$ is generally singular) it may be concluded that asymptotically:

$$n(\hat{\theta} - \tilde{\theta})'Q(\hat{\theta} - \tilde{\theta}) \xrightarrow{D} \chi^2_m$$

i.e.

$$(\hat{\theta} - \tilde{\theta})'[\text{I}(\hat{\theta})](\hat{\theta} - \tilde{\theta}) \sim \chi^2_m$$

where nQ has been replaced by $\text{I}(\hat{\theta})$. This demonstrates that $\text{LR} \sim \chi^2_m$ in large samples.

The principles of the LR test, and its asymptotic distribution as a χ^2, may be extended to the case of non-linear hypotheses. The main applications of the LR test are in testing non-linear hypotheses where finite sample tests are not available or in testing other hypotheses for which exact finite sample tests are not available. The likelihood ratio test is based on the ratio of the restricted to the unrestricted likelihood. It is important to note that in performing an LR test it is required that the model be estimated both freely, to obtain $\hat{\theta}$, and subject to the constraints embodied in the hypothesis, to obtain $\tilde{\theta}$. This is not the case with alternative large sample tests of hypotheses, such as the Lagrange multiplier test or the Wald test. (See **Lagrange multiplier test**, **Wald test** and **Non-linear hypothesis testing**.

Further reading
See particularly Godfrey (1988). The use of the LR test is discussed further in **Non-linear hypothesis testing**, where it is compared with the alternative large sample tests of hypotheses, the Lagrange multiplier and the Wald tests.

Limited dependent variables

Limited dependent variables are limited in the values they can adopt; for example, in an examination of car ownership the dependent variable may be dichotomous – effectively a dummy variable which takes the value of zero if a car is not owned and unity otherwise. As another example the dependent variable may be constrained to be non-negative (such as in a production function for which output cannot be negative) or, in an examination of wage-rates, observations are only available for those individuals for whom the actual wage exceeds their reservation rate and all other individuals represent missing observations. Broadly there are two forms of limited dependent variables:

1. dichotomous and polytomous variables: dichotomous variables take one of only two values, such as the zero/one case of car ownership, and apply to variables which are binary; polytomous variables take one of more than two values, such as a response to a questionnaire involving one answer chosen from Yes, No or Don't Know or a qualitative response from n categories which is then coded numerically (such as 'was your car manufactured in Britain, Germany, Japan, France, Italy, Spain or elsewhere?' which might be coded as a dependent variable taking the value of 0, 1, 2, 3, 4, 5 and 6);
2. censored or truncated variables: if the data on the dependent variable are systematically missing for some observations, but data on the relevant explanatory variables are available, the data are said to be censored; if the data are drawn from a truncated distribution, so that observations on both the dependent and explanatory variables are systematically missing the data are said to be truncated. (See **Censored data** and **Truncated variables**).

Dichotomous dependent variables are not at all uncommon in economics. Suppose, for simplicity, Y_i is a dichotomous dependent variable which takes the value zero if individual i does not own a car and is one otherwise and suppose that car ownership is thought to be determined by some variable X and an error term:

$$Y_i = \alpha + \beta X_i + \varepsilon_i.$$

This is the linear probability model. Clearly, given the nature of the observations on Y_i, the error ε_i may only take one of two values for a given X_i, namely $-(\alpha + \beta X_i)$ or $1 - (\alpha + \beta X_i)$. Suppose these two values are taken with probabilities given by p_i and $1 - p_i$; then, defining θ_i by $\alpha + \beta X_i$, $E(\varepsilon_i) = -p_i\theta_i + (1 - p_i)(1 - \theta_i)$; therefore $E(\varepsilon_i) = 1 - p_i - \theta_i$ and for this to be zero demands that $p_i = 1 - \theta_i$. It is necessary that $0 \leq p_i \leq 1$, but there is no guarantee that θ_i lies in the closed interval [0, 1] and this creates an immediate difficulty. Moreover, the binary nature of Y_i implies that the variance of ε_i is given by $p_i(1 - p_i)$ and, since $p_i = 1 - (\alpha_i + \beta X_i)$, this depends critically on the value of X_i. The errors, therefore, are non-normal, have Bernouilli distribution characteristics and are heteroscedastic. Even if the estimation process constrained the parameters so that $\alpha + \beta X_i$ lies in the [0, 1] interval for all observed X_i, this does not guarantee that all predictions, $\hat{\alpha} + \hat{\beta} X_i$, also lie in the [0, 1] interval; clearly, then, the standard application of ordinary least squares to such a model is fraught with problems in estimation, inference and prediction. It is possible to proceed with a constrained estimation technique which takes account of the need to constrain $\alpha_i + \beta_i X_i$ to the [0, 1] interval and also recognizes the heteroscedastic nature of the error, but such a technique is not widely used. The so-called Probit and Logit approaches are much more popular.

In such models a latent, unobservable, variable, Y_i^*, is introduced; in general Y_i^* is specified as a linear combination of k variables, denoted for the ith individual by $1 \times k$ vector x_i', so that:

$$Y_i^* = x_i'\beta + \varepsilon_i;$$

Y_i^* is the latent variable specific to individual i, and is determined by the characteristics as measured by x_i and the random term, ε_i. The underlying behavioural theory then proposes that the observed dichotomous variable, Y_i, is determined by reference to the relative size of the latent variable with respect to a 'threshold' value. For ease of exposition, the threshold may be taken to be zero, so that:

$$\begin{aligned} Y_i &= 1 \qquad \text{if } Y_i^* > 0 \\ &= 0 \qquad \text{if } Y_i^* < 0. \end{aligned}$$

The latent variable is not constrained in any way, and the probability that $Y_i = 1$ is equal to the probability that $Y_i^* > 0$; hence:

$$\Pr\{Y_i = 1\} = \Pr\{Y_i^* > 0\} = \Pr\{x_i'\beta + \varepsilon_i > 0\} = \Pr\{\varepsilon_i > -x_i'\beta\}.$$

If F(.) is the cumulative probability function of ε_i, then:

$$P_i = \Pr\{Y_i = 1\} = 1 - \Pr\{\varepsilon_i < -x_i'\beta\} = 1 - F(-x_i'\beta)$$

and if the distribution of ε is symmetric about zero, $1 - F(-x_i'\beta) = F(x_i'\beta)$, so that:

$$P_i = \Pr\{Y_i = 1\} = F(x_i'\beta).$$

In this model the cumulative probability function maps the individual's characteristics $(x_i'\beta)$ into probabilities, and since Y_i is invariant to the scaling of the latent variable the model may be standardized so that $\sigma_\varepsilon^2 = 1$ (or any other convenient value). It remains to choose an appropriate cumulative probability function F, and then estimate the model's parameters, β.

Two common forms of the probability function are in use; the standard normal function produces the probit model, and the standard logistic function generates the logit model. The logit model is easier to analyse, since its probability function may be expressed in a relatively simple analytic form, whereas that for the standard normal may only be expressed as an integral. If the probit model is used, then:

$$F(x_i'\beta) = \int_{-\infty}^{x_i'\beta} (2\pi)^{-1/2} \exp(-w^2/2)dw.$$

And if the logistic function is used then:

$$F(x_i'\beta) = \exp(x_i'\beta)/(1 + \exp(x_i'\beta)).$$

It is to be noted that in the logit model the probabilities, P_i, are given by:

$$P_i = F(x_i'\beta) = \exp(x_i'\beta)/(1 + \exp(x_i'\beta))$$

$$\Rightarrow \quad 1 - P_i = 1 - F(x_i'\beta) = 1/(1 + \exp(x_i'\beta))$$

$$\Rightarrow \quad P_i/(1 - P_i) = \exp(x_i'\beta) \quad \Rightarrow \quad \ell n[P_i/(1 - P_i)] = x_i'\beta.$$

That is, in the logit model the log-odds ratio is a linear function of the explanatory variables, in contrast with the linear probability model in which the probabilities are specified as linear in the explanatory variables.

The interpretation of the β parameters is not standard in a these models; the expected value of Y_i is given by $\Pr\{Y_i^*|x_i' > 0\} = F(x_i'\beta)$, and so $\partial E(Y_i)/\partial x_i = \beta f(x_i'\beta)$, where f is the probability density function corresponding to the cumulative function F. The response of the expected value to a change in the explanatory variables is non-linear, and having estimated the model it is usual to report the response terms at the mean value of the x_i vectors and at other relevant values.

To estimate the parameters, let the sample be ordered so that the first n_1 observations relate to realizations $Y = 1$, and the remaining $n_2 = n - n_1$ observations relate to realizations $Y = 0$. Given independence, the observed

Y_i values may be viewed as the realizations of a binomial process, and the likelihood may be written as:

$$L = \left(\prod_1 P_i\right)\left(\prod_0 (1 - P_i)\right)$$

where the first product is taken over observations for which Y = 1, and the second over observations for which Y = 0. For a given form of the probability function, this model may estimated by maximum likelihood; the solutions, whether for the probit or logit model, require non-linear optimization, and the details are not given here. Most software packages contain a routine for solving such models, and there are many iterative methods which will suffice; the maximum likelihood estimates are consistent, and the information matrix provides a consistent estimator of the variances. Restrictions on the parameters may be tested using the usual methods. Test of the specification may also be carried out, and tests of omitted variables and of heteroscedasticity are commonly performed using Lagrange multiplier test statistics.

Although the two probability functions in common use are very similar in shape, except at the tails, the estimates of the parameters tend to be similar; they are not, however, directly comparable since the probit model has an error variance normalized to unity and the logit model has an error whose variance is $\pi^2/3$. It is necessary, then, to multiply the estimates from the logit model by $\sqrt{3}/\pi$ in order to make comparison. The models may be extended to polytomous (multiple choice) dependent variables.

Further reading

See Fomby *et al.* (1984) for discussion of modifications to the linear probability model and Caudill (1988) and Heckman and Macurdy (1985) for its application. See especially Tobin (1958), Amemiya (1981) and Maddala (1983). On specification tests in probit and logit models see, especially, Davidson and MacKinnon (1984) and Blundell (1987).

Limited information maximum likelihood

The limited information maximum likelihood (LIML) estimation method is a technique used to estimate the parameters of a structural equation of a simultaneous system. It is a limited information method because it seeks to construct estimates of a structural equation's parameters by examining that particular equation in isolation; it does not take into account any information concerning the other structural equations nor does it take into account anything about the relationship between the particular equation of interest and the other structural equations. By ignoring such information as might be contained in the system as a whole, it is to be expected that LIML estimators will be inefficient relative to alternative estimation methods that utilize such information. When the errors in question are assumed to be multivariate normally distributed, the LIML estimator is identical to the least variance ratio (LVR) estimator and the least generalized residual variance (LGRV) estimator. With normality, LIML is efficient amongst all the single equation estimation methods.

The method proceeds by considering a single structural equation, which may be written as:

$$Y_1 = Y\beta_1 + X_1\gamma_1 + \varepsilon_1$$

where Y_1 is the endogenous variable whose parameter has been normalized to unity, Y contains the other $g_1 - 1$ endogenous variables included in this equation and X_1 contains the k_1 exogenous or pre-determined variables included in the equation; β_1 and γ_1 are vectors of structural parameters. The LIML approach then considers the likelihood function of the reduced form equations for the endogenous variables $[Y_1 \ \ Y]$ and maximizes this subject to the constraints imposed by the exclusion restrictions on the structural equation in question. If the equation is exactly identified, then LIML estimates are identical to two-stage least squares estimates and no gain in efficiency is obtained; however, if the equations are over-identified there is some gain. Of course, if the structural equation is not identified the structural parameters cannot all be estimated. The over-identified case is difficult to analyse as a maximum likelihood method, but can easily be explained as a least variance ratio estimator.

The structural equation of interest may be written as:

$$Y_1 - Y\beta_1 = X_1\gamma_1 + \varepsilon_1 \qquad \text{i.e.} \quad y = X_1\gamma_1 + \varepsilon_1$$

where y is the linear combination of endogenous variables $Y_1 - Y\beta_1$; in this equation the structural restrictions of exclusion dictate the construction of y in terms of the endogenous variables Y_1 and Y only, and also dictate that in explaining y only the exogenous variables of X_1 are relevant. In consequence, additional exogenous variables should make insignificant contributions to the explanation of y. If β_1 were known then the regression of y on X_1 could be performed, and the residual sum of squares would then be given by:

$$RSS_1 = y'M_1y \qquad \text{where } M_1 = I - X_1(X_1'X_1)^{-1}X_1'$$

and if the regression of y on all the exogenous variables in the system, denoted by X, were run, the residual sum of squares would be given by:

$$RSS = y'My \qquad \text{where } M = I - X(X'X)^{-1}X'.$$

The set of all exogenous variables is given by $X = [X_1 \ X_2]$, where X_2 represents the exogenous variables excluded from the equation in question. Hence, in adding the regressors X_2 to the regression of y, their contribution should, given the exclusion restrictions, be due to sampling variation only.

The least variance ratio method proposes that β_1 is chosen so that the incremental contribution of X_2 is minimized; hence, β_1 is chosen so that:

$$(RSS_1 - RSS)/RSS_1$$

is minimized. By definition $y = [Y_1 \ \ Z]\beta^*$, where $\beta^* = [1 \ -\beta_1']'$; this may be written as $y = Y^*\beta^*$, and so the residual sums of squares may be written as:

$$RSS_1 = \beta^{*\prime}Y^{*\prime}M_1Y^*\beta^* \quad \text{and} \quad RSS = \beta^{*\prime}Y^{*\prime}MY^*\beta^*.$$

Hence β^* is chosen to minimize:

$$RSS_1/RSS = (\beta^{*\prime}Y^{*\prime}M_1Y^*\beta^*)/(\beta^{*\prime}Y^{*\prime}MY^*\beta^*).$$

Application of the differential calculus yields the solution as:

$$(W_1 - \lambda W)\beta^* = 0 \quad \text{where } W_1 = Y^{*\prime}M_1Y^* \quad \text{and } W = Y^{*\prime}MY^*.$$

This requires that the matrix $(W_1 - \lambda W)$ is singular and that the solution for λ solves the determinantal equation:

$$|W_1 - \lambda W| = 0;$$

if $\hat{\lambda}$ is the minimum value which solves this equation, then $\hat{\beta}^*$ is found by solving the equations:

$$(W_1 - \hat{\lambda}W)\hat{\beta}^* = 0.$$

Given the estimate $\hat{\beta}^*$, $\hat{\gamma}$ is easily found from the ordinary least squares regression of the estimated $\hat{y} = [Y_1 \ \ Z]\hat{\beta}^*$ on X_1.

The LIML estimator, in this form, uses exactly the same information as two stage least squares (TSLS) with the added assumption of normally distributed errors. It has the advantage over TSLS in that the estimates are invariant to the normalization of the equation, but it may be shown that the asymptotic variance matrix of the LIML estimators is identical to that of the TSLS estimators, and so TSLS is just as efficient asymptotically.

Further reading

The LIML estimation technique was first suggested by Anderson and Rubin (1949 and 1950). See also Theil (1971) Johnston (1984) and Schmidt (1976) and see **Full information maximum likelihood**, **Identification**, **Indirect least squares**, **Two stage-least squares** and **Three-stage least squares**.

Linear and log-linear models

In examining the functional form of a regression model one approach is to use the general class of models defined by the Box and Cox transformations and to consider the linear and log-linear models as special cases (see **Box and Cox transformations**). A more direct test exists, however. Suppose, for the purposes of exposition only, that the model involves one regressor and the choice is between the linear and log-linear model:

$$H_o: \; Y_t = \alpha_o + \beta_o X_t + \varepsilon_t$$

$$H_1: \; \ell n(Y_t) = \alpha_1 + \beta_1 \ell n(X_t) + \eta_t$$

Neither model is a special case of the other, and a comparison of the two models is therefore a non-nested hypothesis test. Suppose both models are estimated by ordinary least squares to yield:

$$\hat{Y}_t = \hat{\alpha}_o + \hat{\beta}_o X_t \qquad \text{and} \qquad \widehat{\ell n}(Y_t) = \hat{\alpha}_1 + \hat{\beta}_1 \ell n(X_t) = \hat{Z}_t.$$

The predicted values of Y from the log-linear model are given by $\exp(\hat{Z}_t)$, and the predicted values of $\ell n(Y_t)$ from the linear model are given by $\ell n(\hat{Y}_t)$. Hence $\hat{Z}_t - \ell n(\hat{Y}_t)$ is the difference between the prediction of $\ell n Y$ obtained directly from the log-linear model and from the log of the prediction from the linear model; if the linear model is correct then the addition of this regressor to the linear model will be a redundant regressor and, similarly, if the log-linear model is correct, then the addition of the regressor $\hat{Y}_t - \exp(\hat{Z}_t)$ to the log-linear model will be a redundant regressor. Hence the models are compared by running the auxiliary regressions:

$$Y_t = \alpha_o + \beta_o X_t + \gamma_o [\hat{Z}_t - \ell n(\hat{Y}_t)] + \varepsilon_t$$

$$\ell n(Y_t) = \alpha_1 + \beta_1 \ell n(X_t) + \gamma_1 [\hat{Y}_t - \exp(\hat{Z}_t)] + \eta_t$$

The hypotheses $\gamma_o = 0$ and $\gamma_1 = 0$ are each examined by a t-test; if $\gamma_o = 0$ is not rejected but $\gamma_1 = 0$ is rejected then the log-linear model is preferred; if $\gamma_o = 0$ is rejected but $\gamma_1 = 0$ is not rejected then the linear model is preferred. If both are rejected then neither model is properly specified and some more complex functional form is called for; if neither hypothesis is rejected then the models cannot be distinguished from the available data set, but neither model is rejected in favour of the other. This test is clearly a form of the J-test, described in **Non-nested hypotheses**, and is known as the P_E test.

The P_E test is particularly simple to compute and though not as powerful as, for example, the likelihood ratio test which may be derived from the Box and Cox transformations, has sufficiently high power to be a popular tool in applied work. As in all tests of non-nested models it is important to examine the associated diagnostic tests with each model, for these can give significant indications of the appropriate choice between the models.

Further reading

The J-test was extended to applications with non-linear models in Davidson and MacKinnon (1983); the P_E test described here is a special case of the extension given in that paper.

Linear hypotheses

Consider the general linear model: $Y = X\beta + \varepsilon$ where Y represents the n observations on the regressand, X represents the n observations on the k regressors, β represents the k parameters and ε represents the n disturbances. It is assumed that $\varepsilon \sim MVN(0, \sigma^2 I)$, X is non-stochastic and of full rank. Suppose it is proposed to test a main economic hypothesis via the simple null linear hypothesis:

$$H_o: R\beta = r$$

where R is an m×k ($m \leq k$) matrix of full rank of known constants and r is an m×1 vector, also of known constants.

The simplest form of this test occurs when the investigation concentrates upon only one element of the β vector, in the form of H_o: $\beta_i = 0$. This hypothesis states that the ith regressor has no effect upon the dependent variable. Most commonly economic theory actually predicts the precise negation of this hypothesis, namely that $\beta_i \neq 0$, but the standard framework of hypothesis testing uses the 'no effect' hypothesis as the null hypothesis (see **Hypothesis testing**). This simple example is a special case of the general linear hypothesis: R is here a row vector with zeros everywhere except the ith position which is unity and r is zero.

Given the ordinary least squares estimator, $\hat{\beta}$, under the truth of the null hypothesis, $R\hat{\beta}$ is expected to be zero. Now $\hat{\beta} = \beta + (X'X)^{-1}X'\varepsilon$ and so:

$$R\hat{\beta} = R\beta + R(X'X)^{-1}X'\varepsilon;$$

hence

$$R\hat{\beta} - R\beta = R(X'X)^{-1}X'\varepsilon.$$

Also $\hat{\beta} \sim MVN(\beta, \sigma^2(X'X)^{-1})$, and therefore:

$$R\hat{\beta} \sim MVN(R\beta, \sigma^2 R(X'X)^{-1}R')$$

Hence:

$$(R\hat{\beta} - R\beta)'[\sigma^2 R(X'X)^{-1}R']^{-1}(R\hat{\beta} - R\beta) \sim \chi^2_m.$$

Now the OLS residuals are given by $\hat{e} = (I - X(X'X)^{-1}X')\varepsilon = M\varepsilon$, and so $\hat{e}'\hat{e} = \varepsilon' M\varepsilon$; but M is a square idempotent matrix of rank k, and therefore using a result from **Distribution theory**, $\varepsilon' M\varepsilon/\sigma^2 \sim \chi^2_{n-k}$:

$$\varepsilon' M\varepsilon/\sigma^2 = \hat{e}'\hat{e}/\sigma^2 \sim \chi^2_{n-k}.$$

Given the relationship between $R\hat{\beta}$ and ε, and that between $\hat{e}$ and ε, the χ^2_m distribution may be written as:

$$\varepsilon' X(X'X)^{-1}R'[\sigma^2 R(X'X)^{-1}R']^{-1}R(X'X)^{-1}X'\varepsilon \sim \chi^2_m$$

and the χ^2_{n-k} distribution may be written as:

$$\varepsilon'[I - X(X'X)^{-1}X']\varepsilon/\sigma^2 \sim \chi^2_{n-k}.$$

Using the important result from **Distribution theory**: if z ~ MVN(0, I) then the quadratic forms z'Az and z'Bz are independent χ^2 distributions if A and B are both idempotent *and* their product is zero. The two chi-squared distributions above may be seen to be quadratic forms of the variable $\sigma^{-1}\varepsilon$, which is, indeed, MVN(0, I); moreover, the matrices in question may easily be verified as both idempotent and having a zero product. Therefore the F distribution may be formed:

$$\frac{(R\hat{\beta}-R\beta)'[\sigma^2 R(X'X)^{-1}R']^{-1}(R\hat{\beta}-R\beta)/m}{[\hat{e}'\hat{e}/\sigma^2]/(n-k)} \sim F_{m,n-k}.$$

From this expression it is seen that the nuisance parameter, σ^2, disappears; noting that $\hat{e}'\hat{e}/(n-k) = s^2$, in standard notation:

$$\frac{(R\hat{\beta}-R\beta)'[R(X'X)^{-1}R']^{-1}(R\hat{\beta}-R\beta)/m}{s^2} \sim F_{m,n-k}.$$

From this distributional expression, any linear hypothesis concerning the parameters of the general linear model may be examined. When the null hypothesis is true, $R\beta = r$, and therefore the test statistic, F, is constructed simply by replacing $R\beta$ by r in the above to yield:

$$F = \frac{(R\hat{\beta}-r)'[R(X'X)^{-1}R']^{-1}(R\hat{\beta}-r)/m}{s^2} \sim F_{m,n-k}.$$

Under the truth of the null hypothesis the estimate $R\hat{\beta}$ will be close to r; thus, if null hypothesis is true F will be small, and if the null is false the test statistic will be large. Hence rejection takes place in the right-hand tail of the appropriate F-distribution and, having set a Type I error of α, and finding that critical value $F_{m,n-k;\alpha}$ from tables such that an F-variate with m and n–k degrees of freedom only exceeds $F_{m,n-k;\alpha}$ with probability α, a test statistic larger than this critical value is deemed evidence upon which to reject the null hypothesis; any value of the test statistic less than this critical value leads to the non-rejection of the null. The choice of α, the Type I error, is critically important to the decision rule.

Testing this simple linear hypothesis may be seen to have an intimate relationship with the construction of confidence regions (see **Confidence regions**); defining the $(1-\alpha)\%$ confidence region for $R\beta$ by:

$$\left\{ R\beta \,\middle|\, \frac{(R\hat{\beta}-R\beta)'[R(X'X)^{-1}R']^{-1}(R\hat{\beta}-R\beta)/m}{s^2} < F_{m,n-k;\alpha} \right\}$$

then, clearly, if the hypothesized value of $R\beta$, r, lies outside the region, this is equivalent to the decision to reject the null hypothesis.

To illustrate the above in the very simplest of cases, suppose the hypothesis of exclusion $\beta_k = 0$ is to be tested. In this case R is a $1 \times k$ matrix and $r = 0$. Specifically, R is given by:

$$R[0 \quad 0 \quad \dots \quad \dots \quad 1]$$

Then it is easy to show that $R(X'X)^{-1}R' = v_{kk}$, where $(X'X)^{-1} = \{v_{ij}\}$; also, $R\beta = \beta_k$ and so:

$$(\hat{\beta}_k - \beta_k)' v_{kk}^{-1} (\hat{\beta}_k - \beta_k) / s^2 \sim F_{1,n-k}.$$

But all the terms in this expression are scalar quantities, and so:

$$(\hat{\beta}_k - \beta_k)^2 / s^2 v_{kk} \sim F_{1,n-k}.$$

Now $s^2 v_{kk}$ is simply the estimator of the sampling variance of $\hat{\beta}_k$, and $s\sqrt{v_{kk}}$ is the estimated standard error of $\hat{\beta}_k$, denoted by $se(\hat{\beta}_k)$. Further, the square root of the $F_{1,n-k}$ distribution is simply the t_{n-k} distribution, so the familiar distributional statement is derived:

$$t = (\hat{\beta}_k - \beta_k)/s\sqrt{v_{kk}} \sim t_{n-k}.$$

Under H_o: $\beta_k = 0$, the test statistic, t, is simply the ratio of the estimate, $\hat{\beta}_k$, to its estimated standard error, $se(\hat{\beta}_k)$. H_o is rejected with respect to the two-sided alternative, H_1: $\beta_k \neq 0$, if t exceeds, absolutely, $t_{n-k;\alpha/2}$, the $(\alpha/2)$% critical value from the t_{n-k} distribution. Equally, the $(1 - \alpha)$% confidence region for β_k is given by:

$$\hat{\beta}_k \pm t_{n-k;\alpha/2}\, se(\hat{\beta}_k);$$

thus, if H_o is not rejected:

$$|\hat{\beta}_k / se(\hat{\beta}_k)| < t_{n-k;\alpha/2}; \text{ i.e. } \quad -t_{n-k;\alpha/2} < \hat{\beta}_k / se(\hat{\beta}_k) < t_{n-k;\alpha/2};$$

but this implies that:

$$\hat{\beta}_k - t_{n-k;\alpha/2} se(\hat{\beta}_k) < 0 < \hat{\beta}_k + t_{n-k;\alpha/2} se(\hat{\beta}_k)$$

i.e. when H_o: $\beta_k = 0$ is not rejected at a significance level of α this is equivalent to the $(1 - \alpha)$% confidence interval for β_k including zero.

The relationship between hypothesis testing and confidence regions may be generalized, so that the hypothesis $R\beta = r$ is rejected (not rejected) in favour of the two-sided alternative $R\beta \neq r$, using a Type I error of α, if r lies outside (inside) the $(1 - \alpha)$% confidence region for $R\beta$ of least area.

For tests of linear hypotheses which involve more than one parameter there is an alternative approach which is often easier to put into practice than the F-test described above. Suppose the general linear hypothesis $R\beta = r$ is to be tested within the model $Y = X\beta + \varepsilon$; consider running the restricted, or constrained, regression (see **Restricted least squares**) and computing the restricted (constrained) estimator $\tilde{\beta}$ which minimizes the residual sum of squares $(Y - X\tilde{\beta})'(Y - X\tilde{\beta})$ subject to the constraint $R\tilde{\beta} = r$.

Defining the unrestricted residual sum of squares, $(Y - X\hat{\beta})'(Y - X\hat{\beta})$, as URSS and the restricted residual sum of squares, $(Y - X\tilde{\beta})'(Y - X\tilde{\beta})$, as RRSS, it may be shown that under the truth of the null hypothesis:

$$(\text{RRSS} - \text{URSS})/\sigma^2 = [(R\hat{\beta} - r)'[R(X'X)^{-1}R']^{-1}(R\hat{\beta} - r)]/\sigma^2.$$

But this expression is precisely that which has been shown above to be distributed as χ^2_m and forms the numerator in the F-test of the restriction. Hence there are two equivalent forms of the F-test; it has already been shown that:

$$\frac{(R\hat{\beta} - r)'[R(X'X)^{-1}R]^{-1}(R\hat{\beta} - r)/m}{s^2} \sim F_{m,n-k}$$

but the numerator is identical to (RRSS – URSS)/m and the denominator is, of course, equal to URSS/(n – k). Hence:

$$\frac{[\text{RRSS} - \text{URSS}]/m}{\text{URSS}/(n-k)} \sim F_{m,n-k}.$$

This is a particularly useful result. To test a set of linear restrictions two regressions are run: one unconstrained (to yield URSS) and the other constrained by the linear hypothesis (to yield RRSS); except in the very rare case when the hypothesis is exactly satisfied in the data, the restricted residual sum of squares exceeds the unrestricted. If the hypothesis is true, though not exactly satisfied in the data, any difference between RRSS and URSS will be the result of sampling variation only; however, if the hypothesis is false, then imposing it will effect a very large RRSS relative to URSS. Hence the same result as before is derived, but via a slightly different route. The F-test, when expressed in terms of residual sums of squares, can easily be translated into a difference of R^2: denote by R^2_r and R^2_u the goodness of fit statistics from the restricted and unrestricted regressions respectively; then it is easy to show that:

$$\frac{(R^2_u - R^2_r)/m}{(1 - R^2_u)/(n-k)} \sim F_{m,n-k}.$$

When these tests are carried out as tests of exclusion (perhaps the commonest case), they can be readily interpreted as a test of an area within a Venn diagram.

Further reading

Material on linear hypotheses is covered in all econometrics texts, and the reader is referred to the standard texts for further discussion. See also **Venn**

diagrams, **Hypothesis testing**, **Confidence intervals**, **Confidence regions**, **Non-linear hypothesis testing**, **Restricted least squares** and **Multicollinearity**.

Matrix algebra

Formal econometric theory is frequently presented using matrix algebra; this algebra allows very general models to be analysed with an economy of notation and is a very powerful tool.

Some useful definitions

1. A matrix is a rectangular array of elements; a general matrix, denoted by A, has n rows and m columns; it thus has n×m elements, and the typical element is a_{ij} ($i = 1, 2, \ldots, n$; $j = 1, 2, \ldots, m$); a_{ij} is the element in the ith row and j^{th} column. The matrix A is said to be of order n×m (to be read as 'n by m'). In describing the order of a matrix the number of rows is always given first. The matrix may be written compactly as $A = \{a_{ij}\}$ and written in full as.

$$A = \begin{bmatrix} a_{11} & a_{12} & \ldots & \ldots & a_{1m} \\ a_{21} & a_{22} & & & a_{2m} \\ \vdots & & \ddots & & \vdots \\ \vdots & & & \ddots & \vdots \\ a_{n1} & \ldots & \ldots & \ldots & a_{nm} \end{bmatrix}$$

2. If A is of order n×n it is called a square matrix of order n.
3. If A is a square matrix of order n and all off-diagonal elements are zero ($a_{ij} = 0$ for all $i \neq j$ then A is called a diagonal matrix and is often written as $A = \text{diag}\{a_{11}, a_{22}, \ldots, a_{nn}\}$.
4. If A is an n×n diagonal matrix, and $a_{ii} = 1$, for all i, then A is called the identity matrix of order n, written as I_n; the order subscript, n, is frequently dropped since it may always be inferred from the context. If A is an n×n diagonal matrix, and $a_{ii} = \lambda$, for all i, where λ is some real number, then A is called a scalar matrix and may be written as $A = \lambda I_n$ or simply as $A = \lambda I$. The identity matrix plays a similar role in matrix multiplication to unity in scalar algebra.
5. If A is such that $a_{ij} = 0$ for all i and j, A is called a zero, or null, matrix.
6. The transpose of the n×m matrix A is written A' (which is read as 'A trans'); A' is a matrix of order m×n and is obtained from A by transposing the rows of A into columns; thus if B = A', then B is of order m×n and $b_{ij} = a_{ji}$ for $i = 1, \ldots, m$ and $j = 1, \ldots, n$. Clearly, $(A')' = A$, that is, the act of transposing a matrix twice results in the original matrix. If $A' = A$ then A is symmetric and implies, and is implied by, $a_{ij} = a_{ji}$ for all i and j.
7. If A is a square matrix of order n, then its trace, written as Tr(A), is defined as the sum of the diagonal elements of A: $\text{Tr}(A) = \sum_{i=1}^{n} a_{ii}$.
8. If A is of order n×1, it has only one column and is usually referred to as an n-dimensional column vector, or simply a vector of order n; if A is of

order $1 \times n$ it has only one row and is usually referred to as an n-dimensional row vector, or simply a vector of order n.

Some rules of matrix algebra

1. Addition: two matrices A and B may be added if and only if they are of identical order; if A and B are both of order $n \times m$, then denoting the typical elements of A and B by a_{ij} and b_{ij} respectively, the $n \times m$ matrix C, which is given by (A + B), has a typical element c_{ij} where $c_{ij} = a_{ij} + b_{ij}$. Clearly the associative law then holds: $(A + B) + D = A + (B + D)$.
2. Multiplication of a matrix by a scalar: if λ is any scalar number then the matrix λA has typical element given by λa_{ij}. From this rule and rule 1 subtraction is defined: if A and B are matrices of the same order, $A - B = A + (-1 \times B)$ and so the typical element of A – B is $a_{ij} - b_{ij}$. Two matrices A and B are said to be equal if and only if $a_{ij} = b_{ij}$ for all i and j; in this case, then, $A - B = 0$, where 0 is a zero matrix.
3. Multiplication of two matrices: the two matrices, A and B, may be multiplied together (in the order of A postmultiplied by B) if and only if the number of columns in A is identical to the number of rows in B. Thus, if A is of order $n \times m$ and B is of order $p \times q$ then the product AB exists if and only if $m = p$; AB is described as A postmultiplied by B and is of order $n \times q$; typically AB is different from BA which is B postmultiplied by A. It is to be noted that BA exists if and only if $q = n$ and is then a matrix of order $p \times m$; the existence of AB (which requires $m = p$) does not imply the existence of BA (which requires $q = n$). Denote the product AB by C; c_{ij} is defined by:

   $$c_{ij} = \sum_{k=1}^{m} a_{ik} b_{kj} \qquad \text{for } i = 1, \ldots n \text{ and } j = 1, \ldots, q.$$

   That is, the $(i, j)^{th}$ element of AB is given by multiplying the elements of the ith row of A by the corresponding elements of the jth column of B and summing. If the product AB exists, A and B are described as conformable. This rule may be shown to imply the associative law of multiplication: (AB)D = A(BD), and the distributive law of multiplication: A(B + D) = AB + AD, where A, B and D are, in each case, of the appropriate orders for the multiplications to exist. Given the definition of the identity matrix, this rule also implies that, for any matrix A (of order $n \times m$), $I_n A = A I_m = A$; and, given the definition of a zero matrix, multiplying any matrix by a zero matrix results in a zero matrix. Using the definition of transpose, it may be shown that $(AB)' = B'A'$. Also, from the definition of the trace of a matrix, it can be shown easily that if both AB and BA exist, then Tr(AB) = Tr(BA).
4. If A and B are both square matrices of order n and AB = I, then B is called the inverse of A, and is written as $B = A^{-1}$. Only a square matrix can have such an inverse, but it is not sufficient that A be square for its

inverse to exist; if A does not have an inverse it is described as a singular matrix. It is easy to show that, if A is a square non-singular matrix, then $(A^{-1})^{-1} = A$; it may also be shown that if A and B are each square non-singular matrices of the same order then $(AB)^{-1} = B^{-1}A^{-1}$. Further, it may be shown that $(A')^{-1} = (A^{-1})'$. Particular formulae for inverting matrices which are extremely useful in econometrics are:
for any non-singular matrix A:

$$(I + A)^{-1} = I - (I + A^{-1})^{-1};$$

if A and B are m×n matrices, then:

$$[I_m + AB']^{-1} = I_m - A(I_n + B'A)^{-1}B'$$

and if A and D are any non-singular square matrices of order m and n respectively, and B is any m×n matrix, then:

$$[A + BDB']^{-1} = A^{-1} - A^{-1}B(B'A^{-1}B + D^{-1})^{-1}B'A^{-1}$$

5. Differentiation: if a and x are both column vectors of order n then $a'x = \sum_{i=1}^{n} a_i x_i$ consider the partial differentiation of a'x with respect to one of the elements of x, say x_j:

$$\frac{\partial(a'x)}{\partial x_j} = \frac{\partial(\sum_{i=1}^{n} a_i x_i)}{\partial x_j}$$

Define $\partial(a'x)/\partial x$ as the n×1 vector with typical element $\partial(a'x)/\partial x_j$, then:

$$\frac{\partial(a'x)}{\partial x} = \begin{bmatrix} a_1 \\ a_2 \\ \vdots \\ \vdots \\ a_n \end{bmatrix}$$

i.e. $$\partial(a'x)/\partial x = a.$$

If A is a symmetric matrix of order n, then x'Ax is called a quadratic form, and may be written out in full as:

$$x'Ax = \sum_{i=1}^{n} a_{ii} x_i^2 + 2\sum_{i=1}^{n-1}\sum_{j=i+1}^{n} a_{ij} x_i x_j$$

That is, x'Ax comprises the sum of all the squared terms plus twice all the cross-product terms; note that the symmetry of A ensures that $a_{ij}x_i x_j = a_{ji}x_i x_j$.

then: $$\frac{\partial x'Ax}{\partial x_k} = 2a_{kk}x_k + 2\sum_{j=k+1}^{n} a_{kj}x_j + 2\sum_{i=1}^{k-1} a_{ik}x_i$$

but $a_{ik} = a_{ki}$, for all i and k; therefore:

$$\frac{\partial x'Ax}{\partial x_k} = 2a_{kk}x_k + 2\sum_{j\neq k}^{n} a_{kj}x_j$$

$$= 2\sum_{j=1}^{n} a_{kj}x_j = 2a_k x$$

where a_k is the $1\times n$ vector which is the kth row of A. Thus:

$$\frac{\partial(x'Ax)}{\partial x} = 2\begin{bmatrix} a_1x \\ a_2x \\ \vdots \\ \vdots \\ a_nx \end{bmatrix}$$

i.e.
$$\frac{\partial(x'Ax)}{\partial x} = 2Ax$$

Given these rules of matrix algebra, it is now possible to offer some more definitions:

9. If A is a square symmetric matrix such that AA = A, then A is said to be idempotent. The only idempotent matrix which is non-singular is the identity matrix.
10. If x and y are both non-zero vectors of order n, then x and y are said to be linearly dependent if a real number λ exists such that $x + \lambda y = 0$. Conversely, if there is no such number λ which solves the equation $x + \lambda y = 0$ then x and y are said to be linearly independent.
11. If A is a matrix of order $n\times m$, let the maximum number of linearly independent rows be denoted by r; clearly $r \leq n$, and if $r < n$ then this implies that $n - r$ rows can be expressed as a linear combination of the other r rows. Denoting the maximum number of linearly independent columns by c then $c \leq m$. It may be shown that $r = c$, and the maximum number of linearly independent rows (or columns) of A is known as the rank of A, written as $\rho(A)$. It follows that $\rho(A) \leq \min(n, m)$ and if $\rho(A) = \min(n, m)$ then A is said to be of full rank. It also follows that $\rho(A) = \rho(A')$. If A is a square matrix of order n and of full rank, $\rho(A) = n$, then A^{-1} exists; it is a necessary and sufficient condition for A to be non-singular that A is of full rank. It may be shown that $\rho(A'A) = \rho(A)$.
12. Let A be a square, symmetric, matrix of order n and x be some n-dimensional vector; then if $x'Ax > 0$ for *all* vectors x ($x \neq 0$), A is said to a positive definite matrix; if $x'Ax \geq 0$ for all x ($x \neq 0$), and $x'Ax = 0$ for some vector x, $x \neq 0$, then A is a positive semi-definite matrix. If the inequalities are reversed, A is then a negative definite, or negative semi-definite, matrix.

13. For a square symmetric non-singular positive definite matrix A of order n, there exists a square, non-singular matrix P of order n such that A = PP'. P plays a role in matrix algebra not dissimilar from that of the square root in scalar algebra.
14. The determinant of a square matrix A is written as |A| or as det(A); det(A) is a scalar quantity and is a function of each and every element of A. If A is a 2×2 matrix, det(A) can be evaluated easily:

if $A = \begin{bmatrix} a_{11} & a_{12} \\ a_{21} & a_{22} \end{bmatrix}$ then $|A| = a_{11}a_{22} - a_{12}a_{21}$

If A is a 3×3 matrix then |A| is more complex:

if $A = \begin{bmatrix} a_{11} & a_{12} & a_{13} \\ a_{21} & a_{22} & a_{23} \\ a_{31} & a_{32} & a_{33} \end{bmatrix}$ then

$$|A| = a_{11}\begin{vmatrix} a_{22} & a_{23} \\ a_{32} & a_{33} \end{vmatrix} - a_{12}\begin{vmatrix} a_{21} & a_{23} \\ a_{31} & a_{33} \end{vmatrix} + a_{13}\begin{vmatrix} a_{21} & a_{22} \\ a_{31} & a_{32} \end{vmatrix}$$

i.e. $$|A| = a_{11}a_{22}a_{33} - a_{11}a_{23}a_{32} - a_{12}a_{21}a_{33} + a_{12}a_{23}a_{31} + a_{13}a_{21}a_{32} - a_{13}a_{22}a_{31}.$$

If A is of higher order the expressions become most unwieldy. In general, |A| involves all possible products of elements of A. The determinant of A in the 3×3 case has here been evaluated by taking the elements of the first row, and multiplying each by a 2×2 determinant; those 2×2 determinants are seen as the determinants of the matrices which result when the relevant row and column of A have been deleted; they are known as *cofactors* and, in general, if C_{ij} is the cofactor of the element a_{ij} it is obtained by deleting both the ith row and the jth column from A, and evaluating the determinant of the resulting (n–1)×(n–1) matrix; the sign of the cofactor is given by $(-1)^{i+j}$. The determinant of A can then be expressed as:

$$|A| = \Sigma_{i=1}^{n} a_{1i}C_{1i}.$$

This expresses |A| according to its first row, but any row (or column) could have been used:

$$|A| = \Sigma_{i=1}^{n} a_{ij}C_{ij} \qquad \text{for any given } j = 1, \ldots, n.$$

and $$|A| = \Sigma_{j=1}^{n} a_{ij}C_{ij} \qquad \text{for any given } i = 1, \ldots, n.$$

Via the definition of a cofactor, the inverse of A may be written out in full as:

$$A^{-1} = |A|^{-1} \begin{bmatrix} C_{11} & C_{21} & \cdots & \cdots & C_{n1} \\ C_{12} & \ddots & & & \vdots \\ \vdots & & \ddots & & \vdots \\ \vdots & & & \ddots & \vdots \\ C_{1n} & \cdots & \cdots & \cdots & C_{nn} \end{bmatrix}$$

That is, the inverse of A is given by the transpose of the matrix of cofactors, each of which is divided by the determinant of A. For A to be non-singular it is clear from this that a necessary and sufficient condition is that det(A) is not zero.

If A is any matrix of order n×m, the generalized inverse, denoted by A^+, may be computed; A^+ satisfies the requirements that $AA^+A = A$, $A^+AA^+ = A^+$ and both A^+A and AA^+ are symmetric. Such a matrix is known as the Moore-Penrose inverse, or pseudo-inverse of A. If A is a square matrix and A^{-1} exists then $A^{-1} = A^+$.

Some properties of determinants

For any square matrix, A, of order n:

1. $|A| = |A'|$;
2. if B is obtained from A by interchanging any two rows (or columns) then $|B| = -|A|$;
3. if A has any two rows (or columns) which are identical, then $|A| = 0$;
4. if A has any row (column) which may be expressed as a linear combination of other rows (columns) then $|A| = 0$; indeed, $|A| \neq 0$ if and only if $\rho(A) = n$;
5. if B is also a square matrix of order n, then $|AB| = |A|.|B|$.

Partitioned matrices

There is one other form of a matrix which is common in econometrics; this is the partitioned matrix: a partitioned matrix contains submatrices, rather than scalar quantities, as elements. For example, if A is written as:

$$A = \left[\begin{array}{c|c} A_{11} & A_{12} \\ \hline A_{21} & A_{22} \end{array}\right]$$

where A_{ij} is each a matrix then A is a partitioned matrix. It is clearly necessary that the A_{ij} are of appropriate order. Thus, for example A_{11} and A_{21} must have the same number of columns and, for example, A_{11} and A_{12} must have the same number of rows. The rules of matrix operations carry over to partitioned matrices, but one must be careful of the order of the submatrices. For example, in multiplying two partitioned matrices, each of which is partitioned into four submatrices:

$$AB = \left[\begin{array}{c|c} A_{11} & A_{12} \\ \hline A_{21} & A_{22} \end{array}\right]\left[\begin{array}{c|c} B_{11} & B_{12} \\ \hline B_{21} & B_{22} \end{array}\right]$$

$$= \left[\begin{array}{c|c} A_{11}B_{11} + A_{12}B_{21} & A_{11}B_{12} + A_{12}B_{22} \\ \hline A_{21}B_{11} + A_{22}B_{21} & A_{21}B_{12} + A_{22}B_{22} \end{array}\right]$$

Thus, for AB to exist, and to be written in this form, not only must A and B be conformable, but each product $A_{ij}B_{ji}$ must also exist.

Two further operations on partitioned matrices are deserving of attention. First is a consideration of the inverse of a partitioned matrix: the derivation is tedious, but the result is of primary importance.

If $$A = \left[\begin{array}{c|c} A_{11} & A_{12} \\ \hline A_{21} & A_{22} \end{array}\right] \quad \text{let} \quad A^{-1} = \left[\begin{array}{c|c} B_{11} & B_{12} \\ \hline B_{21} & B_{22} \end{array}\right]$$

Assuming that both A_{11} and A_{22} are square non-singular matrices; the terms B_{ij} are given by:

$$B_{11} = (A_{11} - A_{12}A_{22}^{-1}A_{21})^{-1}$$
$$B_{22} = (A_{22} - A_{21}A_{11}^{-1}A_{12})^{-1}$$
$$B_{21} = -A_{22}^{-1}A_{21}B_{11}$$
$$B_{12} = -A_{11}^{-1}A_{12}B_{22}$$

This is not the only way of writing the B_{ij} terms and the following form is equivalent:

$$B_{11} = A_{11}^{-1}(I + A_{12}B_{22}A_{21}A_{11}^{-1})^{-1}$$
$$B_{22} = (A_{22} - A_{21}A_{11}^{-1}A_{12})^{-1}$$
$$B_{21} = -B_{22}A_{21}A_{11}^{-1}$$
$$B_{12} = -A_{11}^{-1}A_{12}B_{22}$$

The final operation involving partitioned matrices which is in use in econometrics is the special form of multiplication, known as Kronecker multiplication. If A is some n×m matrix, and B is some p×q matrix, then the Kronecker product of A and B is defined as:

$$A \otimes B = \begin{bmatrix} a_{11}B & a_{12}B & \cdots & \cdots & a_{1m}B \\ a_{21}B & \ddots & & & \vdots \\ \vdots & & \ddots & & \vdots \\ \vdots & & & \ddots & \vdots \\ a_{n1}B & \cdots & \cdots & \cdots & a_{nm}B \end{bmatrix}$$

By this definition, $A \otimes B$, is of order $np \times mq$. If both A and B are square, non-singular matrices, then it may be shown that:

1. $(A \otimes B)' = (A' \otimes B')$;
2. $(A \otimes B)(C \otimes D) = (AC \otimes BD)$ where A and C, and B and D are conformable;
3. the above implies that: $(A \otimes B)^{-1} = A^{-1} \otimes B^{-1}$.

Systems of linear equations

Matrix algebra allows a concise route by which to analyse a deterministic system of linear equations. The typical problem may be written as a set of linear equations such as $Ax = b$, where A is some known $m \times n$ matrix, b is a known $n \times 1$ vector and x is an unknown $n \times 1$ vector. If $m < n$ the equations cannot be solved for there are fewer equations than unknowns; if $m > n$ and $\rho(A) = n$ then there are some redundant equations and the system may be solved by extracting a square non-singular matrix from A and proceeding as below; if $m > n$ and $\rho(A) > n$ no unique solution exists. If A is square and non-singular the solution may be written, compactly, as $x = A^{-1}b$. If A is square and singular a unique solution does not exist since then not all n equations are linearly independent and there is insufficient information in the equations to solve for the n unknowns of x. Sometimes, as in the analysis of principal components and some VAR models (see **Principal components** and **Johansen method**), the system of equations take the particular form:

$$Ax = \lambda x$$

where λ is an unknown scalar quantity. This is known as the eigenvalue problem, and the solutions are pairs such as (x^*, λ^*); if x^*, λ^* is a solution then x^* is known as the eigenvector corresponding to the eigenvalue λ^*. To solve the equations in question they may be written as:

$$(A - \lambda I)x = 0$$

and this is the characteristic equation. Clearly, if the matrix $A - \lambda I$ is non-singular there are no non-trivial solutions and $x^* = 0$. Cases of interest, therefore, occur when $A - \lambda I$ is singular. The equations $\det(A - \lambda I) = 0$ provide a polynomial equation in λ of order n which yields n solutions $\{\lambda_i^*; i = 1, 2, \ldots, n\}$, although not all solutions need be distinct. Eigenvalues and eigenvectors have many important properties.

Properties of eigenvalues and eigenvectors
For any square matrix A:

1. The sum of eigenvalues is equal to the trace.
2. The product of eigenvalues is equal to the determinant.
3. The rank of A is equal to the number of non-zero eigenvalues.
4. The eigenvalues of A^2 are the squares of the eigenvalues of A, but the eigenvectors are the same.
5. The eigenvalues of A^{-1} are the reciprocals of the eigenvalues of A, but the eigenvectors are the same.
6. If A is idempotent the eigenvalues are all either zero or one.
7. The rank of an idempotent matrix is equal to its trace.

and if A is symmetric:

8. The eigenvalues are real.
9. The eigenvectors which correspond to distinct eigenvalues are pairwise orthogonal.
10. If an eigenvalue is repeated r times then there are r orthogonal eigenvectors corresponding to this one root.
11. If A is of order n there are n orthogonal eigenvectors.
12. If X denotes the matrix of eigenvectors of the symmetric matrix A, and all eigenvectors are normalized to have unit length so that $X'X = I$, $X' = X^{-1}$. Also, X diagonalizes A:

$$X'AX = \Lambda, \quad \text{where} \quad \Lambda = \text{diag}(\lambda_1, \ldots, \lambda_n).$$

Matrix algebra is the most powerful of languages with which to analyse econometric models; it provides a compact tool which reduces the (otherwise tedious) algebraic manipulations. The above definitions and rules are used most extensively in the study of econometrics.

Further reading
See **General linear model**. Chapter 4 of Johnston (1984) is an excellent presentation of the matrix algebra necessary for econometric work, illustrated with many examples, as is Chapter 2 of Greene (1993).

Maximum likelihood

Maximum likelihood (ML) estimation provides a conceptually appealing method of estimating a model's unknown parameters. It is first necessary to define likelihood. Suppose a sample $\{Y_1, Y_2, .. Y_n\}$ is available, and each Y_i is drawn from some particular distribution which has the probability density function $f(Y_i|\theta)$, where θ is a set of parameters. Assuming that the Y_i are independent, the joint distribution of the sample is then given by the product of individual density functions:

$$g(Y_1, Y_2, \ldots Y_n) = f(Y_1|\theta).f(Y_2|\theta)\ldots f(Y_n|\theta) = \prod_{i=1}^{n} f(Y_i|\theta).$$

$\prod f(Y_i|\theta)$ is the joint density function of the observations and it involves the unknown parameters θ; once a sample of data has been drawn $\prod f(Y_i|\theta)$ may be viewed as a function of the unknown parameters and may then be written as:

$$L(\theta|Y) = \prod_{i=1}^{n} f(Y_i|\theta).$$

$L(\theta|Y)$ is the likelihood function which is a function of the parameters for a given set of observations; clearly, the value of the likelihood will be higher for some values of θ than for others, and the method of maximum likelihood answers the simple question: what value of the parameters maximizes the likelihood? Denoting the parameter value which maximizes the likelihood by $\tilde{\theta}$, the joint density function of the observations is then maximized at $\tilde{\theta}$, and so $\tilde{\theta}$ is that parameter value which maximizes the probability of observing the sample at hand; it must be stressed that this does not allow the interpretation that $\tilde{\theta}$ is the most probable value of θ.

In practice, maximum likelihood estimation typically does not use the likelihood function itself, but uses the log-likelihood function:

$$\ell n L(\theta|Y) = \Sigma_{i=1}^{n} \ell n f(Y_i|\theta).$$

The advantage of working with the log-likelihood is that this is an additive, rather than a multiplicative, function and maximizing this function is analytically easier than maximizing the likelihood directly. Of course, the value $\tilde{\theta}$ which maximizes $\ell n L$ also maximizes L. It is assumed in the following that L has first and second derivatives with respect to θ and that they are continuous functions of the sample data $(Y_1, \ldots, Y_n)$; this allows the derivatives to treated as random variables.

$\tilde{\theta}$ is chosen so that $L(\theta|Y)$ is at its maximum value. The rationale for this approach has conceptual appeal: a sample of observations, Y, is more likely to have been generated by a particular θ parameter for which the likelihood is large than a θ parameter for which the likelihood is small. The likelihood principle takes as relevant information only that which is encapsulated within the likelihood function itself, based upon a particular assumption about the joint density function of the sample.

Maximum likelihood estimation not only has this intuitively appealing property, but also has many desirable large sample properties: asymptotically, $\tilde{\theta}$ is unbiased, consistent, efficient and distributed normally. The only major conceptual disadvantage of the approach is that the investigator must specify a precise form of the density function $f(.|\theta)$, but f is most commonly assumed to be the normal density function.

The only other disadvantage of maximum likelihood estimation is not conceptual, but pragmatic; in many situations when θ is a of high dimension (that is, the parameter θ is a vector of many elements), the maximization of L (or, equivalently ℓnL) has no analytic solution, but must be approached as a problem of numerical optimization. The consequence of this is that maximum likelihood estimation can have a high computational cost, but most software packages now include appropriate numerical methods and this disadvantage is diminishing rapidly.

From the log-likelihood function two important functions may be derived; the first of these is the efficient score and the second is the information matrix. From the general statement of the log-likelihood, $\ell n \mathrm{L}(\theta|\mathrm{Y}) = \sum_{i=1}^{n} \ell n \mathrm{f}(\mathrm{Y}_i|\theta)$, the efficient score, $\mathrm{S}(\theta)$, is defined by:

$$\mathrm{S}(\theta) = \frac{\partial \ell n \mathrm{L}(\theta|Y)}{\partial \theta}$$

and so at the maximum likelihood estimate (MLE), $\mathrm{S}(\tilde{\theta}) = 0$.

The information matrix, $\mathrm{I}(\theta)$, is formally defined as:

$$\mathrm{I}(\theta) = \mathrm{E}\left[-\frac{\partial^2 \ell n \mathrm{L}(\theta|\mathrm{Y})}{\partial \theta \partial \theta'}\right].$$

In these expressions it is to be remembered that the likelihood function, when viewed as a function of the sample, is a random variable: hence $\mathrm{S}(\theta)$ is a random variable and in $\mathrm{I}(\theta)$ the expectation is with respect to the random variables $\{\mathrm{Y}_i\}$.

$\mathrm{I}(\theta)$ is a measure of the curvature of the log-likelihood function. Under a set of general regularity conditions the inverse of the information matrix evaluated at $\tilde{\theta}$ provides an estimate of the variance–covariance matrix of $\tilde{\theta}$.

The efficient score and the information matrix are most useful in solving for $\tilde{\theta}$, as is described in **Method of scoring**, where it is shown that:

$$\mathrm{S}(\theta) = \frac{\partial \ell n \mathrm{L}}{\partial \theta} \sim [0, \mathrm{I}(\theta)];$$

i.e., the efficient score is distributed with a zero mean and variance matrix $\mathrm{I}(\theta)$. Since $\mathrm{S}(\tilde{\theta}) = 0$, expanding the efficient score around the true value θ in a Taylor series, and ignoring all terms other than the linear term:

$$\mathrm{S}(\tilde{\theta}) = 0 \cong \frac{\partial \ell n \mathrm{L}}{\partial \theta} + \frac{\partial^2 \ell n \mathrm{L}}{\partial \theta \partial \theta'}(\tilde{\theta} - \theta).$$

Assuming $\partial^2 \ell n \mathrm{L}/\partial \theta \partial \theta'$ is non-singular:

$$(\tilde{\theta} - \theta) \cong -\left[\frac{\partial^2 \ell n \mathrm{L}}{\partial \theta \partial \theta'}\right]^{-1} \mathrm{S}(\theta).$$

If it is assumed that $n^{-1}I(\theta) \to Q$, where Q is some non-singular matrix, then under standard conditions it may be asserted that:

$$\text{plim}\left[-n^{-1}\frac{\partial^2 \ell n L(\theta|Y)}{\partial\theta\partial\theta'}\right] = Q$$

and since

$$(\tilde{\theta}-\theta) \cong -\left[n^{-1}\frac{\partial^2 \ell n L}{\partial\theta\partial\theta'}\right]^{-1} n^{-1}\frac{\partial \ell n L}{\partial\theta},$$

it follows that: $(\tilde{\theta}-\theta) \xrightarrow{p} Q^{-1}.0 = 0$. Hence $\tilde{\theta} \xrightarrow{p} \theta$ which shows that the maximum likelihood estimator $\tilde{\theta}$ is consistent, and so $\text{plim}(\tilde{\theta}) = \theta$. To examine the asymptotic distribution of $\tilde{\theta}$, note that:

$$n^{1/2}(\tilde{\theta}-\theta) \cong -\left[n^{-1}\frac{\partial^2 \ell n L}{\partial\theta\partial\theta'}\right]^{-1} n^{-1/2}S(\theta).$$

But it is assumed that $n^{-1}I(\theta) \to Q$ and so $n^{-1/2}S(\theta) \xrightarrow{D} \eta \sim N(0, Q)$. Using Cramer's Theorem (see **Large sample theory**) this implies that:

$$n^{1/2}(\tilde{\theta}-\theta) \xrightarrow{D} Q^{-1}\eta \sim N(0, Q^{-1}QQ^{-1})$$

i.e.:

$$n^{1/2}(\tilde{\theta}-\theta) \xrightarrow{D} Q^{-1}\eta \sim N(0, Q^{-1}).$$

Hence $\tilde{\theta}$ is approximately distributed as $N(\theta, n^{-1}Q^{-1})$ in large samples; although $n^{-1}Q^{-1}$ is not known, $n^{-1}I(\tilde{\theta})$ is a consistent estimator of Q under the regularity conditions used here and so $I(\tilde{\theta})$ is a consistent estimator of nQ and $[I(\tilde{\theta})]^{-1}$ is a consistent estimator of $n^{-1}Q^{-1}$. Thus $\tilde{\theta} \sim N(\theta, [I(\tilde{\theta})]^{-1})$ in large samples (approximately).

In efficient estimation the Cramer–Rao lower bound is an important concept: given certain regularity conditions, the variance matrix of an unbiased estimator is bounded below by $[I(\theta)]^{-1}$; the above shows that the $\tilde{\theta}$ achieves the Cramer–Rao lower bound, i.e. $\tilde{\theta}$ has the minimum variance achievable by a consistent estimator. This result, together with the result that the MLE is consistent and asymptotically normal, ensures the popularity of maximum likelihood estimation. A further most useful result is the invariance property of maximum likelihood estimators: if $\tilde{\theta}$ is the MLE of θ then $g(\tilde{\theta})$ is the MLE of $g(\theta)$, where g is any continuous function.

The method of maximum likelihood provides a basis for both estimation and hypothesis testing. For applications of ML to the latter, see especially **Non-linear hypothesis testing**.

In the context of the familiar general linear model, $Y = X\beta + \varepsilon$, where it is assumed that $\varepsilon \sim MVN(0, \sigma^2 I)$ and there is a sample of n observations $(Y_1, \ldots, Y_n)$, the density function of each Y_i is:

$$f(Y_i|\beta,\sigma^2) = (2\pi\sigma^2)^{-1/2}\exp\{-(1/2\sigma^2)(Y_i - X_i'\beta)^2\}$$

where X_i' is the $1 \times k$ i^{th} row of the data matrix X (i = 1, 2, . . . , n). Given independence of the Y_i observations, the joint density is then given by the product of each of the n terms, $f(Y_i|\beta, \sigma^2)$:

$$L(\beta, \sigma^2|Y_1, \ldots Y_n) = (2\pi\sigma^2)^{-n/2}\exp\left\{-(1/2\sigma^2)\Sigma_{i=1}^{n}(Y_i - X_i'\beta)^2\right\}$$

and the log-likelihood is given by:

$$\ell nL(\beta, \sigma^2|Y_1, \ldots Y_n) = -(n/2)\ell n(2\pi\sigma^2) - (1/2\sigma^2)\Sigma_{i=1}^{n}(Y_i - X_i'\beta)^2 .$$

Of course, $\Sigma_{i=1}^{n}(Y_i - X_i'\beta)^2 = (Y - X\beta)'(Y - X\beta)$ is matrix notation. To maximize the likelihood with respect to the k parameters of β note that ℓnL depends only on β via the term $-(\frac{1}{2}\sigma^2)(Y - X\beta)'(Y - X\beta)$ and maximizing the likelihood with respect to β is achieved by minimizing $(Y - X\beta)'(Y - X\beta)$. Thus, in the special case when the errors are distributed normally with a scalar variance–covariance matrix, the MLE, $\tilde{\beta}$, is identical to the OLS solution. Since the estimator of β is identical to the OLS solution, it follows that the fitted residuals are, in this case, identical to those obtained by OLS.

The MLE for σ^2 is obtained by taking the first derivative of ℓnL with respect to σ^2 and setting this to zero (the second-order conditions ensures that this provides a maximum position). Denoting the fitted residuals by $\hat{e}$, where $\hat{e} = Y - X\tilde{\beta}$ (and $\hat{e}$ is, of course, identical to the ordinary least squares residual vector), the MLE for σ^2 is then given by:

$$\tilde{\sigma}^2 = \hat{e}'\hat{e}/n.$$

The OLS estimator for the error variance is given by $s^2 = \hat{e}'\hat{e}/(n-k)$, and this is known to be an unbiased estimator. The two estimators are related, then, by the simple expression:

$$\tilde{\sigma}^2 = [(n-k)/n]s^2$$

and as n gets large $\tilde{\sigma}^2$ approaches s^2; since s^2 is unbiased, $\tilde{\sigma}^2$ is, therefore, asymptotically unbiased but is subject to small sample bias.

Within the general linear model, the example provided above is cast within the context of a simple error term which is distributed MVN(0, σ^2I); this can be extended to the case of an error which is MVN(0, $\sigma^2\Omega$). Since Ω is a positive definite matrix, there exists a matrix P such that $PP' = \Omega$. The random variable $P^{-1}\varepsilon$ has a zero mean and a variance–covariance matrix given by $\sigma^2P^{-1}\Omega P^{-1\prime}$; but since $PP' = \Omega$, pre-multiplying by P^{-1} and post-multiplying by $P^{-1\prime}$, yields $P^{-1}(PP')P^{-1\prime} = P^{-1}\Omega P^{-1\prime} = I$. Hence the transformed model $P^{-1}Y = P^{-1}X\beta + P^{-1}\varepsilon$ has an error term with a scalar variance–covariance matrix, and the log-likelihood of this model is:

$$\begin{aligned}\ell nL(\beta, \sigma^2|P^{-1}Y) \\ &= -(n/2)\ell n(2\pi\sigma^2) - (1/2\sigma^2)(P^{-1}Y - P^{-1}X\beta)'(P^{-1}Y - P^{-1}X\beta) \\ &= -(n/2)\ell n(2\pi\sigma^2) - (1/2\sigma^2)(Y - X\beta)'\Omega^{-1}(Y - X\beta).\end{aligned}$$

However, this is the log-likelihood given a sample of $P^{-1}Y$, whereas the focus of interest is the log-likelihood given the data Y. In order to translate from $L(\beta, \sigma^2|P^{-1}Y)$ to $L(\beta, \sigma^2|Y)$ one further analytic device is required, namely that if Y^* is some function of Y, then:

$$L(\theta|Y) = L(\theta|Y^*).J$$

where J is the Jacobian of the transformation, defined by:

$$J = |\{dY_i^*/dY_j\}|$$

i.e. J is the determinant of the matrix whose typical term is the derivative of Y_i^* with respect to Y_j. In this case, $Y^* = P^{-1}Y$ and so, denoting the (i, j)th element of P^{-1} by p_{ij}, $dY_i^*/dY_j = p_{ij}$. Hence, here, $J = |P^{-1}|$. Using the rules of determinants, $|P^{-1}| = |P|^{-1}$; also $|PP'| = |P||P'| = |P|^2$; but $|PP'| = |\Omega|$ and so $|P| = |\Omega|^{½}$. Therefore, $J = |P^{-1}| = |\Omega|^{-½}$. Hence, $L(\theta|Y) = L(\theta|Y^*).|\Omega|^{-½}$ and so, in this case,

$$\ell nL(\beta, \sigma^2, \Omega|Y) =$$

$$-(n/2)\ell n(2\pi\sigma^2) - (1/2\sigma^2)(Y - X\beta)'\Omega^{-1}(Y - X\beta) - ½\ell n|\Omega|.$$

This is a most useful statement of the log-likelihood, especially when dealing with a model which has an unknown but non-scalar variance–covariance matrix (for example, a model which is characterized by either autocorrelation or heteroscedasticity) since one can now estimate all the model's parameters, β, σ^2 and Ω, by the method of maximum likelihood simply by maximizing the above expression. This is, of course, only possible when Ω is defined by a sufficiently small number of parameters, j, where $j < n - k$, the number of available degrees of freedom. (For further details of this, see **Autocorrelation – estimation methods** and **Heteroscedasticity – estimation methods**.)

To utilize this expression, it is to be noted that given an estimate of the variance–covariance matrix, say $\tilde{\Omega}$, the maximum likelihood estimate of β is given by:

$$\tilde{\beta} = (X'\tilde{\Omega}^{-1}X)^{-1}X'\tilde{\Omega}^{-1}Y$$

and the maximum likelihood estimate of σ^2 is given by:

$$\tilde{\sigma}^2 = (Y - X\tilde{\beta})'\tilde{\Omega}^{-1}(Y - X\tilde{\beta})/n$$

The likelihood function may then be concentrated to yield:

$$\begin{aligned}\ell n\tilde{L}(\tilde{\Omega}|Y) &= -(n/2)\ell n(2\pi\tilde{\sigma}^2) - (1/2\tilde{\sigma}^2)n\tilde{\sigma}^2 - ½\ell n|\tilde{\Omega}| \\ &= -(n/2)\ell n(2\pi) - (n/2)\ell n\tilde{\sigma}^2 - (n/2) - ½\ell n|\tilde{\Omega}|\end{aligned}$$

which may be written as:

$$\ell n \tilde{L}(\tilde{\Omega}) = \text{constant} - (n/2)\ell n(\text{RSS}) - \tfrac{1}{2}\ell n|\tilde{\Omega}|$$

where RSS denotes the residual sum of squares from the least squares regression using transformed data, namely that of $\tilde{P}^{-1}Y$ on $\tilde{P}^{-1}X$ given an estimated variance–covariance matrix, $\tilde{\Omega}$ (and $\tilde{P}\tilde{P}' = \tilde{\Omega}$). (Equivalently RSS denotes the residual sum of squares from the feasible generalized least squares regression of Y on X given an estimated variance–covariance matrix, $\tilde{\Omega}$.) It should now be noted that the likelihood is not maximized simply by minimizing this residual sum of squares since the term in $-\tfrac{1}{2}\ell n|\tilde{\Omega}|$ would be effectively ignored in such an estimation process. The likelihood, as given above, is maximized by choosing that value of the variance–covariance matrix, $\tilde{\Omega}$, which minimizes the expression:

$$(n/2)\ell n(\text{RSS}(\tilde{\Omega})) + \tfrac{1}{2}\ell n|\tilde{\Omega}|.$$

Hence the technique of maximum likelihood may be carried out by a numerical procedure of computing the residual sum of squares for a chosen variance–covariance matrix, computing the log-likelihood function, and then carrying out exactly the same computations for a different variance matrix and so on. The maximum likelihood estimate of Ω, $\tilde{\Omega}$, is chosen as that which maximizes the likelihood; the maximum likelihood estimates of β and σ^2 are then given directly as functions of $\tilde{\Omega}$.

Further reading

Maximum likelihood is discussed in almost all econometrics texts; for discussion of the likelihood principle, see, for example, Edwards (1972), and for discussion of the method in the context of mathematical statistics, see, for example, Mood, Graybill and Boes (1974).

Method of moments

In cases when a consistent estimator is required, and efficiency is a secondary concern, the method of moments may be used to great effect. Suppose a random sample of size n, $x_1, x_2, \ldots, x_n$, is taken from a population described by the probability density function $f(x|\theta_1, \ldots, \theta_k)$; it is supposed that the population has finite moments. The uncentred moments of the distribution are defined by the equations:

$$\mu'_j = E[x_i]^j \quad j = 1, 2, \ldots, k.$$

The uncentred j^{th} population moment is the expectation of the jth power of the raw data. The population moments have sample analogues:

$$m'_j = (1/n)\Sigma_{i=1}^{n}[x_i]^j.$$

The fundamental idea in the method of moments is that the sample moments converge in probability to constants which are defined in terms of the parameters of the distribution, and so by computing the sample moments and equating them to their population counterparts, sufficient equations will be available from which estimates of the underlying parameters may be constructed. It is to be noted that:

$$E(m'_j) = \mu'_j = E(x^j_i)$$

and $V(m'_j) = (1/n^2)\Sigma^n_{i=1} V[x_i]^j = (1/n^2)\Sigma^n_{i=1}\{E[x^{2j}_i] - [E(x^j_i)]^2\}$

i.e. $$V(m'_j) = (1/n)[\mu'_{2j} - (\mu'_j)^2].$$

Also, $\text{plim}(m'_j) = \mu'_j$ and $\sqrt{n}(m'_j - \mu'_j) \xrightarrow{D} N(0, (\mu'_{2j} - (\mu'_j)^2))$.

By constructing k raw moments, m'_j, and equating them to their population counterparts, μ'_j, the k equations may be solved to yield the moment estimators of the k parameters $\{\theta_j, j = 1, 2, \ldots, k\}$. Since $\text{plim}(m'_j) = \mu'_j$ these estimators will be consistent and are derived as (possibly non-linear) functions of sample data. Although the simple moments may be used, other functions of the data could equally be used; if g_j is any continuous function whose parameters do not depend on the sample size, then:

$$\tilde{g}_j = (1/n)\Sigma^k_{i=1} g_j(x_i) \qquad j = 1, 2, \ldots, k$$

are also sample moments, and $E(\tilde{g}_j) = \phi_j(\theta_1, \ldots, \theta_k)$. These equations may, given that the equations are independent, be solved to yield consistent estimators of the population parameters. Since the resulting estimators are, in general, complicated non-linear functions of the sample moments $\tilde{g}_j$, it may be difficult to compute their variances. The methods of ordinary and generalized least squares are moment estimation techniques (OLS solves $E(X'\varepsilon) = 0$ and GLS solves $E(X'\Omega^{-1}\varepsilon) = 0$), and in those cases there are exactly as many moment equations as parameters (known as the exactly identified case).

In some cases, however, there are more moment equations than parameters (the over-identified case) and then the system of equations to be solved becomes over-determined. In such cases the method of moments seeks to reconcile all the available information in order to produce a unique estimate for each parameter. This is the subject of the generalized method of moments (GMM) which leads to an analysis of optimal instruments as a method of combining sample information in the best possible way.

Suppose a model is defined on the variables y_t and x'_t and is parameterized by k parameters, θ_i i =1 ,2, . . , K; suppose there are p moment equations:

$$E[m_j(y_t, x'_t, \theta_1, \ldots, \theta_k)] = 0 \qquad i = 1, 2, \ldots, p$$

Denoting the whole sample of T observations on y and x by Y and X, and the parameter vector by θ, the sample sums are:

$$\overline{m}_j = \frac{1}{T}\sum_{t=1}^{T} m_j(y_t, x_t', \theta)$$

and if the p equations $m_j' = 0$ are independent no unique solution exists for the k unknown parameters. To solve this over-identified system of equations, one approach is to minimize the sums of squares of sample sums: minimize $\overline{m}(\theta)'\overline{m}(\theta)$; this is a least squares method. Another approach is to minimize a weighted sum of squares; since the $\overline{m}_j$ are sums of random variables their sampling variances may be computed, and if W is defined as the diagonal matrix whose j^{th} diagonal term is the asymptotic variance of $\overline{m}_j$, minimizing $\overline{m}(\theta)'W^{-1}\overline{m}(\theta)$ is a weighted squares method. This method ignores the fact that the $\overline{m}_j$ terms will be correlated with each other, and if W is defined as the symmetric matrix whose typical element is the asymptotic covariance between $\overline{m}_i$ and $\overline{m}_j$, minimizing $\overline{m}(\theta)'W^{-1}\overline{m}(\theta)$ yields the minimum distance estimators. If W is a positive definite matrix and $\text{plim}(\overline{m}) = 0$ the resulting estimator $\hat{\theta}$ is consistent.

If W is chosen as the asymptotic variance matrix of the $\overline{m}$ this is the generalized method of moments, and defining Σ by:

$$\Sigma = [G'W^{-1}G]^{-1}$$

where G is the k×m matrix whose j^{th} row is the partial derivatives of $\overline{m}_j$ with respect to the k parameters θ_i, then it may be shown that the resulting estimate, $\hat{\theta}$, has an asymptotic normal distribution, $N(\theta, \Sigma)$.

The GMM estimators are consistent, and the familiar Wald test for examining restrictions may be used in the case of GMM estimation. Although most of the common estimators are special cases of the GMM approach, the method of moments provides a useful addition to the econometricians' stock of tools, and is especially useful when the moment equations are over-identified

Further reading

GMM estimation is described in detail in Pagan and Wickens (1989); for applications see, for example, Pagan and Vella (1989). For technical presentations of the GMM estimator, see Hansen (1982), Newey (1984, 1985a and 1985b) and Davidson and MacKinnon (1993).

Method of scoring

If the log-likelihood function of a sample of observations $\{Y_i\}$, parameterized by a vector θ is given by

$$\ell n L(\theta|Y) = \sum_{i=1}^{n} \ell n f(Y_i|\theta)$$

then two important functions may be derived; the first of these is the efficient score and the second is the information matrix. From the general statement of the log-likelihood the efficient score, $S(\theta)$, is defined by:

$$S(\theta) = \frac{\partial \ell n L(\theta|Y)}{\partial \theta}$$

and the information matrix, $I(\theta)$, is formally defined as:

$$I(\theta) = E\left[-\frac{\partial^2 \ell n L(\theta|Y)}{\partial \theta \partial \theta'}\right].$$

In these expressions the likelihood function, when viewed as a function of the sample, is a random variable: $S(\theta)$ is a random variable and in the expression for $I(\theta)$ the expectation is with respect to the random variables $\{Y_i\}$.

The efficient score and the information matrix are most useful in solving for the maximum likelihood estimator (MLE), $\tilde{\theta}$. $\tilde{\theta}$ clearly solves the equations $S(\theta) = 0$, and when these cannot be solved analytically, consider the following: suppose $\partial \ell n L/\partial \theta$ is expanded around a trial value of θ, say θ_o, retaining only the first power of $\delta\theta = \theta - \theta_o$:

$$\frac{\partial \ell n L}{\partial \theta} \cong S(\theta_o) + \left.\frac{\partial^2 \ell n L}{\partial \theta \partial \theta'}\right|_{\theta_o} \delta\theta.$$

In large samples $\partial^2 \ell n L/\partial \theta \partial \theta'$, evaluated at θ_o, may be replaced by $-I(\theta_o)$:

$$\frac{\partial \ell n L}{\partial \theta} \cong S(\theta_o) - I(\theta_o)\delta\theta.$$

Since $S(\tilde{\theta}) = 0$, the correction, $\delta\theta$, from the initial value of θ_o is given by $S(\theta_o)/I(\theta_o)$. This method of correction can then be repeated until the process converges sufficiently: this technique of obtaining the MLE is known as the method of scoring. Although this appears to require the second-order derivatives of the log-likelihood function (to evaluate the information matrix), this is not the case since it can be shown, relatively easily, that:

$$E\left[-\frac{\partial^2 \ell n L}{\partial \theta \partial \theta'}\right] = E\left[\frac{\partial \ell n L}{\partial \theta}\right]\left[\frac{\partial \ell n L}{\partial \theta}\right]' = I(\theta).$$

To demonstrate this result note that the likelihood function, when viewed as a function of the observations, is a joint density function. Hence:

$$\int\int \ldots \int L \, dY_1 \, dY_2 \ldots dY_n = 1$$

for any admissible value of θ. Differentiating with respect to θ_i, given that the limits of integration are independent of the parameters:

$$\iint \dots \int \left[\frac{\partial L}{\partial \theta_i} \right] dY_1 \, dY_2 \dots dY_n = 0 \quad \text{for all i}$$

which may be written as:

$$\iint \dots \int \left[\frac{1}{L} \frac{\partial L}{\partial \theta_i} \right] L \, dY_1 \, dY_2 \dots dY_n = 0 \quad \text{for all i.}$$

Since L is formally equivalent to the probability density function of Y, this implies that $E(\partial \ell n L / \partial \theta_i) = 0$ for all i; this is, of course, equivalent to:

$$E(S(\theta_i)) = 0 \Rightarrow E(S(\theta)) = 0.$$

Differentiating again with respect to $\hat{\theta}_j$:

$$\iint \dots \int \left\{ \left[\frac{1}{L} \frac{\partial L}{\partial \theta_i} \right] \left[\frac{1}{L} \frac{\partial L}{\partial \theta_j} \right] + \frac{\partial}{\partial \theta_j} \left[\frac{1}{L} \frac{\partial L}{\partial \theta_i} \right] \right\} L \, dY_1 \, dY_2 \dots dY_n = 0$$

which implies:

$$E[(\partial \ell n L / \partial \theta_i)(\partial \ell n L / \partial \theta_j)] + E(\partial^2 \ell n L / \partial \theta_j \partial \theta_i) = 0 \qquad \text{for all i and j.}$$

Hence, in matrix notation:

$$E[\partial \ell n L / \partial \theta][\partial \ell n L / \partial \theta]' + E[\partial^2 \ell n L / \partial \theta \partial \theta') = 0$$

i.e.

$$I(\theta) = E\left[-\frac{\partial^2 \ell n L}{\partial \theta \partial \theta'} \right] = E\left[\frac{\partial \ell n L}{\partial \theta} \right] \left[\frac{\partial \ell n L}{\partial \theta} \right]'$$

and so, to evaluate the information matrix, only the first partial derivatives of the log-likelihood function are required. Now $E[\partial \ell n L / \partial \theta][\partial \ell n L / \partial \theta]'$ is the matrix of second moments of $S(\theta)$, and since $E(S(\theta)) = 0$ this is the variance –covariance of $S(\theta)$. Hence:

$$S(\theta) = \frac{\partial \ell n L}{\partial \theta} \sim [0, I(\theta)];$$

that is, the efficient score is distributed with mean zero and variance $I(\theta)$.

If it is not difficult to estimate the information matrix the method of scoring provides a most effective method of deriving the maximum likelihood estimates, and is often easier to use that other numerical optimization methods.

Further reading

The method of maximum likelihood is discussed in almost all econometrics texts; for discussion of the likelihood principle, see, for example, Edwards (1972), and for discussion of the method of scoring in relation to other numerical optimization routines see, for example, Cuthbertson, Hall and Taylor (1992) or Fomby *et al.* (1984). See also **Maximum likelihood**.

Missing observations

It is not uncommon for economic data to be incomplete; gaps in data occur most commonly in survey data when not all respondents have answered all the questions. Gaps also occur in time-series data when, for example, some of the required data are available only at quarterly intervals, while other data series are available monthly. These two cases are examples of quite different possibilities. In both examples the data set could, in principle, have been complete but is not, and what distinguishes them is the reason why the data are incomplete. The first example is one in which it is quite reasonable to assume that the reasons for the missing data are independent of the available observations, known as the 'ignorable case'; the second case is one in which the available data is incomplete and the missing observations may be systematically related to the available data. In the former case one might ask how, if at all, the known data might cast light on the missing data, and in the final analysis one might simply ignore the missing observations and use only the available data. However, in the latter case the missing data may be a consequence of 'self-selection bias' – the data collection process has not captured a sample from the entire population (a form of this problem is examined in **Truncated variables**).

The case of using the regression model when there are missing observations in the ignorable case may be subdivided into three possibilities: for some observations (say n_1) there will be complete data on the regressand, denoted by Y_1, and all the k regressors, denoted by X_1; for some observations (say n_2) there will be complete data on Y, denoted by Y_2, but incomplete observations on X, denoted by X_2; and for some observations (say n_3) there will be no data on Y, but complete data for X, denoted by X_3. In the second case it is assumed that there is incomplete data on only some, not all, of the regressors.

Clearly, the regression of Y_1 on X_1 will produce an estimator, $\hat{\beta}$, which has all the usual properties (given that this is a properly specified regression equation), but this effectively ignores the incomplete data on $n_2 + n_3$ observations, and the issue is whether the incomplete data might be used so as to increase the efficiency of the estimator.

In the second case, the regressor matrix is incomplete; if the regression involves only a constant term and one regressor then there is insufficient information on which one may act. However, in the many-regressor case, suppose that there is complete data for at least one of the regressors but incomplete for the others. In order to fill the gaps it is possible to use the information from the first n_1 observations if the missing regressors are not orthogonal to the non-missing regressors. Consider, for illustrative purposes only, the case of a regression model:

$$Y_t = \alpha + \beta X_t + \gamma Z_t + \varepsilon_t .$$

Complete data are available for the first n_1 observations; running this regression yields estimates $\hat{\alpha}$, $\hat{\beta}$ and $\hat{\gamma}$. If data on X is missing for n_2 observations but is available on Z then the missing observations could be replaced by the prediction of X given Z; this involves running the auxiliary regression of X on a constant and Z for the first n_1 observations to yield estimates $\hat{\theta}$ and $\hat{\delta}$ and predicting X for the missing n_2 observations:

$$\hat{X}_t = \hat{\theta} + \hat{\delta} Z_t \qquad \text{for } n_2 \text{ observations}$$

One may then run the regression using $n_1 + n_2$ observations:

$$Y_t - \hat{\beta} D_t X_t - \hat{\beta}(1 - D_t)\hat{X}_t = \alpha + \gamma Z_t + v_t$$

where D_t is a dummy variable taking the value 1 for the first n_1 observations and zero for the next n_2 observations so that the dependent variable is Y 'purged' of the influence of X. For the first n_1 observations Y has been exactly purged, as $Y_t - \hat{\beta} X_t$, and for the next n_2 observations Y has been purged using the unbiased estimator of β, and the best predictor of X, given the auxiliary relationship between X and Z, so that $Y_t - \hat{\beta}\hat{X}_t$.

One cannot improve upon the efficiency of $\hat{\beta}$ (indeed, the estimate of β is that from the complete data set) but this route uses the available yet incomplete data on a further n_2 observations and should, therefore, yield a gain in efficiency in the estimation of γ. The estimator of γ obtained may, then, be more efficient than that obtained from using the first n_1 observations only.

Returning to the general model, if the regressor matrix is complete for $n_1 + n_3$ observations, but the data on Y is missing for the n_3 observations, one could use a similar technique to that above: regress Y_1 on X_1 to yield $\hat{\beta}$ using the complete n_1 observations and predict Y_3 for the missing observations using $\hat{\beta}$ and X_3 as $X_3\hat{\beta}$ one could then run the regression:

$$\begin{bmatrix} Y_1 \\ \hat{Y}_3 \end{bmatrix} = \begin{bmatrix} X_1 \\ X_3 \end{bmatrix} \beta + \text{error}$$

Ordinary least squares yields:

$$\tilde{\beta} = [X_1'X_1 + X_3'X_3]^{-1}[X_1'Y_1 + X_3'\hat{Y}_3]$$

But

$$\hat{Y}_3 = X_3\hat{\beta} \quad \text{and} \quad X_1'X_1\hat{\beta} = X_1'Y_1$$

and so:

$$\tilde{\beta} = [X_1'X_1 + X_3'X_3]^{-1}[X_1'X_1\hat{\beta} + X_3'X_3\hat{\beta}]$$

i.e.

$$\tilde{\beta} = \hat{\beta}.$$

Thus the 'mixed estimator' from using the OLS predicted values of Y_3 is identical to the unbiased estimator from the first n_1 observations; the residuals sum of squares from this regression is equal to:

$$(Y_1 - X_1\hat{\beta})'(Y_1 - X_1\hat{\beta}) + (\hat{Y}_3 - X_3\hat{\beta})'(\hat{Y}_3 - X_3\hat{\beta}) = (Y_1 - X_1\hat{\beta})'(Y_1 - X_1\hat{\beta})$$

and so the estimated variance of the regression appears to be smaller by virtue of the additional degrees of freedom. There is an apparent gain in efficiency, but this may be a misleading impression, since the OLS computation ignores the additional variation in $\hat{Y}_3$ due to the fact this has been estimated.

The method of predicting the missing values from the ordinary least squares regressions is known as the 'first-order regression method'. If the first-order method is used to predict the regressors, and observations for which the regressand is missing are discarded, the method is known as the 'modified first-order regression'.

The 'zero-order regression method' is achieved by replacing missing values by their average value over the observations for which the variable is available, and the 'modified zero-order regression method' assumes that the missing values are, for each variable, constant and uses a regression to estimate them, along with the parameters. Zero-order methods do not produce unbiased estimators of the parameters.

It is difficult to analyse the sampling properties of parameter estimators based on methods which have filled in the gaps in the dependent variable, but Monte Carlo evidence leads to the conclusion that, at least for single equation models, it is better not to fill in missing Y values. This conclusion is in contrast to that for filling in the gaps in a regressor, where the evidence suggests that there is an efficiency gain in the estimation of the parameters attached to non-missing regressors.

Further reading

Afifi and Elashoff (1966 and 1967) are amongst the early important papers on this subject; see also Kosobud (1963), Kelejian (1969) and Griliches (1986).

Mixed estimation

Consider the general linear model $Y = X\beta + \varepsilon$ for which there is prior stochastic information on the parameters of the form $r = R\beta + \eta$ where r is a known m×1 vector, R is a known m×k matrix of full rank, $m < k$, and η is an m×1 stochastic term with a zero mean and a known variance–covariance matrix, $\sigma^2\Omega$. The information may arise from previous empirical studies which provide unbiased estimators of some components (or linear combinations) of the β vector (with their associated variances and covariances), or the information may arise in the form of inequalities which stipulate upper and lower bounds on particular coefficients (in which case the variance of η will be set so that $R\beta - r$ is most unlikely to fall outside those bounds). Theil and Goldberger (1961) combined the model $Y = X\beta + \varepsilon$ with the stochastic information in the form of:

$$\begin{bmatrix} Y \\ r \end{bmatrix} = \begin{bmatrix} X \\ R \end{bmatrix} \beta + \begin{bmatrix} \varepsilon \\ \eta \end{bmatrix}$$

i.e. $Y^* = Z\beta + u$ where u has a variance–covariance matrix given by:

$$V(u) = \sigma^2 \begin{bmatrix} V & 0 \\ 0 & \Omega \end{bmatrix} = \sigma^2 U$$

(this formulation assumes that $V(\varepsilon) = \sigma^2 V$ and that ε and η and independent random variables). If U is known then β may be estimated using generalized least squares and, given that the stochastic restrictions are correct on average (i.e. $E(\eta) = 0$), this is the best linear unbiased estimator which utilizes both the sample and the prior information. In this case the estimator of β, $\hat{\beta}$, is given by:

$$\hat{\beta} = [X'V^{-1}X + R'\Omega^{-1}R]^{-1}[X'V^{-1}Y + R'\Omega^{-1}r]$$

and the variance–covariance matrix is given by:

$$V(\hat{\beta}) = \sigma^2[X'V^{-1}X + R'\Omega^{-1}R]^{-1}.$$

The estimate and its variance are weighted sums of the sample and prior information; it is, of course, possible to use the prior information in an alternative fashion and determine whether the prior information is consistent with the sample information. To this end Theil (1963) proposed the compatibility test statistic:

$$(r - R\tilde{\beta})'[\tilde{\sigma}^2 R(X'V^{-1}X)^{-1}R' + \sigma^2\Omega]^{-1}(r - R\tilde{\beta})$$

which utilizes the sample information to examine the stochastic hypothesis that $E(r) - R\beta = 0$; $\tilde{\beta}$ is the generalized least squares estimator of β, and $\tilde{\sigma}^2$ is the corresponding estimator of σ^2. Under the null hypothesis that the prior information is correct, this statistic is asymptotically distributed as χ^2_K. A large value of the compatibility statistic is evidence upon which to reject the hypothesis of correspondence between the prior and sample information. If this test is used to determine whether or not to utilize the prior information, then the resulting pre-test estimator is inferior to the least squares solution for large areas of the mis-specification parameter space under both risk matrix and squared error loss criteria. If the stochastic restrictions are correct on average, so that $E(r) = R\beta$, then the mixed estimator is superior to the unrestricted least squares estimator on both criteria. This case could also be examined in a Bayesian framework using an informative prior distribution. However, the mixed estimator is conceptually different from a Bayesian estimator; mixed estimation treats parameters as fixed, and the prior estimator is random; moreover, this present approach does not demand that the investigator hold priors on all parameters, but offers a simple route by which to combine some prior information with sample information.

The mixed estimator has a special case when R = I. In this case r represents a prior estimate of β, with a prior covariance of Ω. $\hat{\beta}$ may then be written as:

$$\begin{aligned}\hat{\beta} &= [X'V^{-1}X + \Omega^{-1}]^{-1}X'V^{-1}Y + [X'V^{-1}X + \Omega^{-1}]^{-1}\Omega^{-1}r \\ &= KY + P_1\Omega^{-1}r\end{aligned}$$

where $K = [X'V^{-1}X + \Omega^{-1}]^{-1}X'V^{-1}$ and $P_1 = [X'V^{-1}X + \Omega^{-1}]^{-1}$. Hence:

$$P_1\Omega^{-1} = [\Omega X'V^{-1}X + I]^{-1}$$

and $$KX = [X'V^{-1}X + \Omega^{-1}]^{-1}X'V^{-1}X = [I + (X'V^{-1}X)^{-1}\Omega^{-1}]^{-1}.$$

It is may easily be demonstrated that, for any non-singular matrix A, $(I + A)^{-1} = I - (I + A^{-1})^{-1}$. Hence $P_1\Omega^{-1} = I - KX$. Therefore:

$$\hat{\beta} = KY + (I - KX)r = r + K(Y - Xr).$$

This provides an updating equation, for $\hat{\beta}$ is seen as the prior vector, r, plus the term K(Y – Xr) which updates the first value in the light of sample information. Equally, the variance matrix of $\hat{\beta}$ is given by σ^2P_1, and $P_1 = (I - KX)\Omega$, where $\sigma^2\Omega$ is the prior variance matrix; hence $V(\hat{\beta}) = \sigma^2\Omega - \sigma^2KX\Omega$ which demonstrates how sample information leads to greater precision in the mixed estimator. These results are critical to the Kalman filter approach.

Further reading

Theil and Goldberger (1961) is the original presentation of the mixed estimator; see also Theil (1963) and **Kalman filter**.

Monte Carlo methods

In circumstances when the finite sample properties of a particular estimation technique are not known, and cannot be derived analytically, Monte Carlo methods may be used. Data, Y, are assumed to be generated according to some function parameterized by θ: $Y = f(\varepsilon|X, \theta)$, where ε is a random variable having an assumed density function and X represents other determining variables. An estimator of θ, say $\hat{\theta}$, is to be investigated, and the Monte Carlo method generates artificial data on Y, having fixed the variables X, having fixed the value of θ and having repeatedly sampled from the distribution of ε. Each drawing of ε generates a vector of observations, Y, and any number of drawings may be made. Suppose each vector of Y is n-dimensional and that m samples of ε are drawn. The data generated by the ith drawing allows the estimate $\hat{\theta}_i$ to be computed, and the immediate outcome of the repeated drawing experiment is a set of estimates $\{\hat{\theta}_1, \ldots, \hat{\theta}_n\}$. For a sufficiently large value of m the distribution of these estimates provides an estimate of the sampling distribution of $\hat{\theta}$. Given the empirically derived distribution of $\hat{\theta}$, its finite sample properties may be examined (its bias and efficiency particularly); Monte Carlo methods allow comparison of alternative estimators in finite samples.

In the absence of analytic information on the properties of $\hat{\theta}$ the Monte Carlo method provides a substitute. One of the major difficulties in a Monte Carlo study is to be able to sample, repeatedly and independently, from the distribution of ε, and computer technology only allows what are called pseudo-random variables. The outcome of such a study is dependent, in part, on the particular random number generator. Also, the outcome is dependent on the particular specification of the model $f(\varepsilon|X, \theta)$, on the chosen values of X, and on the chosen value of the parameter, θ, but these dependencies may be overcome by examining the estimator for various models, various values of X and various values of θ. If the specification of the model is varied it is then possible to construct the response surface which describes how the estimator's properties vary with respect to the parameter's true value and with respect to other conditions of the model.

The method is dependent upon the chosen distribution of the errors. One technique designed to address this issue is that of bootstrapping; the bootstrap technique is a special case of a Monte Carlo study. If real data are available for n observations, the model's parameters are first estimated by the chosen method; let the estimate be $\hat{\theta}$ and the fitted residuals be denoted by $\hat{e}$. If the estimator's properties are not amenable to analysis then a Monte Carlo experiment is constructed by taking the given parameter estimate as the 'true' value for the purpose of constructing artificial data. The distribution of the errors is not assumed, but is taken from that of the fitted residuals from the actual model. Artificial data are then constructed using the fixed parameter given by the one available estimate, $\hat{\theta}$, and by choosing, randomly and with replacement, a set of n_1 residuals from the vector $\hat{e}$. If a subset of residuals of size n_1 is chosen m times, and the estimator rule is applied to the resulting m sets of data, m estimates $\{\hat{\theta}_1, \ldots, \hat{\theta}_n\}$ are obtained and the distribution of these estimates from this Monte Carlo experiment may be compared with the fixed parameter value which generated them. Bootstrapping may be used for two distinct purposes: it may be used to produce an estimate of the bias in $\hat{\theta}$, and it may be used to construct an estimate of the variance of $\hat{\theta}$. If the bootstrap indicates a bias in $\hat{\theta}$, say B, this may then be subtracted from $\hat{\theta}$ to yield $\hat{\theta} - B$, which is then the bootstrap estimator.

Monte Carlo methods may also be used to examine the behaviour of test statistics, and are particularly useful in constructing empirical estimates of a test statistic's power function.

Further reading

Hendry (1984) provides a survey of Monte Carlo methods; Hsu *et al.* (1986) and Peters and Freedman (1984) discuss bootstrapping.

Multicollinearity

Multicollinearity arises in the general linear model $Y = X\beta + \varepsilon$ when the regressors are linearly related. Perfect multicollinearity is extremely rare, but can occur accidentally in a regression involving dummy variables, for example, when the investigator falls victim to the 'dummy variable trap' (see **Dummy variables**) and inadvertently specifies perfectly collinear variables.

In practice it is common for regressors to exhibit multicollinearity; this a data phenomenon and does not depend on any theoretical relationship between regressors. Since economic data are not, typically, collected from a controlled experiment, multicollinearity cannot, generally, be avoided by experimental design (in the experimental sciences it may be possible to design an experiment so that the regressors are orthogonal and exhibit no linear relationship at all – the precise opposite of multicollinearity).

In a well-specified regression equation multicollinearity implies that, while the estimators exhibit their usual desired properties, their precision is small. It is to be stressed that the ordinary least squares estimator of β remains the best linear unbiased estimator, given that the equation is well-specified. However, multicollinearity means that there is some common variation in at least two regressors and this common variation reduces the extent of the variation in Y uniquely explained by each regressor. Since the variance of an individual estimator is partly determined (inversely) by the variation uniquely explained by that regressor, the less is the unique variation, the higher is the variance of the respective estimator. See **Venn diagrams**.

In the model $Y = X\beta + \varepsilon$, $\varepsilon \sim N(0, \sigma^2 I)$, the true variance of $\hat{\beta}_i$ is given by $\sigma^2 v_{ii}$, where v_{ii} is the ith diagonal term of $(X'X)^{-1}$; v_{ii} may be written as $1/RSS_i$, where RSS_i is the sum of squared residuals from the auxiliary regression of X_i on all the other $k - 1$ regressors, $X_1, \ldots X_{i-1}, X_{i+1}, \ldots, X_k$ and so $V(\hat{\beta}_i) = \sigma^2/RSS_i$. The more is X_i collinear with any one or more of the other regressors the smaller is the residual sum of squares from this auxiliary regression and so the greater is the variance of $\hat{\beta}_i$. Hence multicollinearity yields imprecise estimators. The ratio of the actual variance in $\hat{\beta}_i$ to that which would obtain in the absence of any intercorrelations is referred to as the variance–inflation factor (VIF). The larger the VIF the lower is the precision of $\hat{\beta}_i$ (see **Variance inflation factor**).

The implications of a large VIF for hypothesis testing are serious: hypothesis tests lose power the greater is the variance in the estimator. Put equivalently, the standard $100(1 - \alpha)\%$ confidence interval is $2t^*s\sqrt{v_{ii}}$ long (where t^* is the appropriate critical value) and so the greater is the extent of multicollinearity, the wider is the confidence interval, and wide confidence intervals rule out fewer hypotheses than shorter intervals. There are also implications for joint hypothesis tests; collinearity between the regressors X_i and X_j means that the confidence region for (β_i, β_j) is very elongated and covers little area. In such circumstances, then, the imprecision which affects the individual parameters (measured by wide confidence intervals) is countered by the precision of the joint confidence region (as measured by its small area); a classic consequence of multicollinearity is that neither of the hypotheses $\beta_i = 0$ and $\beta_j = 0$ are rejected when tested as individual hypotheses, but the joint hypothesis $\beta_i = 0 = \beta_j$ is rejected.

Of course, although this is a classic consequence of multicollinearity it is a situation which could have other causes. Moreover, in applied research when a coefficient is found to have a low t-statistic it may be tempting, believing that variable to be important, to adopt an immunizing stratagem and claim multicollinearity to be at work. A low t-statistic is a potential indicator of many situations, including the irrelevance of that variable, and further investigation is required before more definitive conclusions may be reached.

There are other consequences of multicollinearity. These include the sensitivity of estimates both to the inclusion of particular observations and to the inclusion of particular variables; in the presence of multicollinearity merely dropping one observation can have large effects upon both parameter estimates and their variances, and dropping a collinear regressor will have similar consequences. If, in the regression $Y_i = \alpha + \beta X_i + \gamma Z_i + \varepsilon_i$, Z were be dropped and Y regressed on X alone, then, since OLS seeks to minimize the sum of squared errors and some of the variation of Z is explicable by the variation of X, when Z is dropped all variation in Z common to that in X is then ascribed to X; only that variation in Y which is uniquely due to Z is pushed into the now unexplained residual. As such the estimate of the coefficient on X changes markedly (and similarly if X were dropped and the regression of Y on Z alone were run).

Detecting multicollinearity is not easy: observing its consequences does not allow the assertion that multicollinearity is the cause (for this would commit the logical fallacy of affirming the consequent). One consequence of severe multicollinearity is that the matrix of moments, X'X, is near singular, but one cannot simply compute the determinant of X'X and describe a small value as an indicator of multicollinearity because the value of |X'X| is critically affected by the units of the regressors and may be changed by using different units. To overcome this it is more common to examine the correlation matrix, R, where $R = \{r_{ij}\}$ and $r_{ij} = \text{Cor}(X_i, X_j)$. In the presence of multicollinearity this matrix, whose elements are dimensionless, has a determinant close to zero. Another suggested measure is to normalize each regressor by its sample variation, and then compute the eigenvalues of the resulting moment matrix; the condition number of a matrix is the square root of the ratio of the maximum to the minimum eigenvalue, and the greater is the intercorrelation amongst the regressors the smaller is the minimum eigenvalue, implying a large condition number. If the regressors are orthogonal the condition number is unity.

A further symptom of multicollinearity is that the regression equation has an R^2 statistic which is large relative to the partial r^2 (see **Partial correlation**.). In regressing Y on two regressors, X and Z, R^2 is the usual coefficient of determination and is the proportion of the variation Y explained by the variables X and Z; if the two partial r^2 are both low then the addition of the variable X or Z adds little to the explanation and, in conjunction with a relatively high R^2, is a symptom of multicollinearity. However, multicollinearity does not necessarily result in this consequence.

Other rules of thumb have been developed, including whether the overall R^2 is smaller than that of any auxiliary regression of a regressor on the other regressors. Such tests are of limited value since multicollinearity is an issue which concerns the sample to hand, not the population from which the regressors are drawn. Whether multicollinearity is, or is not, a problem is a matter of judgement; if it is decided that the particular data to hand do suffer multicollinearity the question then is whether or do anything.

If one does nothing, then all inference from the regression model is based upon estimators of parameters which have high variances. If the model is well-specified those estimators are, however, still BLUE and the precision cannot be improved upon if the estimators are to remain linear and unbiased. Moreover, in the presence of multicollinearity confidence regions for sets of parameters attached to collinear regressors have small area and so a linear combination of the parameters is precisely estimated; if that linear combination is a focus of the investigator's interest then multicollinearity is no real concern. Also, if the purpose of the investigation were to predict out-of-sample and the multicollinearity were expected to be maintained then, again, it is of no real concern. If the investigator were to respond to the presence of multicollinearity, there are several possible courses of action:

1. Collect more data. Since multicollinearity is a problem associated with the data set to hand, more data would help. The problem would be most effectively alleviated by new data which do not exhibit multicollinearity, but even if the additional data exhibit the same extent of multicollinearity this would reduce variances as the degrees of freedom have increased.
2. Formalize a relationship between regressors. If the multicollinearity is believed not merely to be a sample but also a population phenomenon, then this implies that the relationship between regressors is a reflection of

behaviour which may be formalized. By formalizing the relationship, and modelling the entire process, the presence of multicollinearity may be seen as having provided information which has facilitated an improved specification.

3. Formalize a relationship between parameters. Since multicollinearity makes single parameter estimators imprecise, but generates much more precise estimators of certain linear combination of those parameters, it may be possible to formalize combinations. However, any such formalization should not merely be an *ad hoc* response to multicollinearity but should be grounded in economic theory and subjected to appropriate tests. As an example, suppose one were estimating a production function and the inputs are collinear, then the precision of the estimators could be improved if constant returns to scale were to prevail and be imposed. This will result in improved precision since there is a gain in degrees of freedom (there is one less parameter to estimate).
4. Drop one (or more) of the multicollinear regressors. This is a very common approach but should be adopted only with very great care. If the original specification was correct, and all originally included regressors are associated with non-zero parameters, then dropping any one of them will lead to bias in the OLS estimators of the restricted model. By dropping one variable what is gained in precision in estimating the remaining parameters is paid for in bias; the question is whether the gain in precision is sufficient, or otherwise, to compensate for the resulting bias. (See **Conditional omitted variable estimator**.)
5. Use an extraneous estimate. If the value of a parameter has been estimated satisfactorily from other studies then it may be incorporated into the regression quite easily. This has the effect of an efficiency gain immediately as it removes a parameter to be estimated, thus increasing the degrees of freedom. There are two issues to note in this procedure. First, the fact that a parameter has been replaced by an estimate should be taken into account in computing the estimated variances of the estimators of the remaining parameters. More importantly, the extraneous estimate may be 'too' extraneous and be a measure of a quite different concept. For example, a cross-section estimate used in a time-series analysis may be too extraneous since the latter takes no account of any dynamic structure to the model. Care should be taken to ensure as far as possible that the extraneous estimates are relevant to the purpose at hand.
6. Use principal components (linear amalgamations of variables into composite orthogonal indexes). One of the most serious challenges facing their use is the economic interpretation of a principal component. (See **Principal components**.)
7. Shrink the estimators towards zero. This approach has the objective of reducing the overall risk, the sum of the mean squared errors of all the

estimators in a model, and this may be accomplished by shrinking the estimates towards zero. (See **Ridge regression** and **Stein estimators**.)

8. Use ratio or first-differenced data. In time-series data when individual series are collinear by virtue of time trends, for example, it is tempting to re-specify the equation into first differences or ratios. If the well-specified equation is of the form: $Y_t = \beta_o + \beta_1 X_t + \beta_2 Z_t + \varepsilon_t$ then taking first differences results in:

$$\Delta Y_t = \beta_1 \Delta X_t + \beta_2 \Delta Z_t + u_t$$

where $u_t = \Delta\varepsilon_t = \varepsilon_t - \varepsilon_{t-1}$. If X_t and Z_t are collinear, each with a trend, then their first differences are less likely to be collinear; however, if ε_t were white-noise, then u_t is not white-noise but a moving average process, u_t and u_{t-1} are correlated (since both depend on ε_{t-1}) and OLS will yield unbiased, but inefficient estimators; moreover, in dealing with trended time-series data it is better to utilize the concepts and constructs of integration and cointegration (see **Integration**, **Cointegration** and also **Spurious regressions**).

If ratios with respect to X_t, for example, were taken:

$$Y_t/X_t = \beta_o(1/X_t) + \beta_1 + \beta_2(Z_t/X_t) + (\varepsilon_t/X_t)$$

and again, even if the collinearity between $(1/X_t)$ and (Z_t/X_t) is less than that between X_t and Z_t, OLS will yield unbiased, but inefficient estimators for, if ε_t were white-noise then the error in the transformed equation, given by ε_t/X_t, is heteroscedastic (and using the obvious weights so as to employ weighted least squares leads straight back to the original equation in levels). Such transformed equations are an *ad hoc* response to multicollinearity, and are not an appropriate solution.

There is no real answer to the 'problem' of multicollinearity; if the multicollinearity is severe then the problem is that the data contain insufficient information to serve the purpose at hand. In that case the only genuine response is to gather more information or, if this is not possible, to identify what questions may be addressed given the available data. If the former route cannot be adopted the investigator must be content to offer less precise answers to the questions posed of the data.

Further reading

The literature on multicollinearity is immense; an important early paper is Farrar and Glauber (1967); see also Feldstein (1973), Leamer (1973), Chatterjee and Price (1977) and Belsley *et al.* (1980).

Non-linear hypothesis testing

In testing a general hypothesis about some parameter, such as $f(\beta) = 0$ (where β may be a vector), there are three commonly used test procedures: the likelihood ratio (LR), the Wald (W) and the Lagrange multiplier (LM) tests (described in **Likelihood ratio tests**, **Wald tests** and **Lagrange multiplier tests**). Their particular usefulness lies in the fact that they are applicable to general hypotheses, which may be non-linear; asymptotically all three are equivalent, but they have quite different computational requirements.

In testing $f(\beta) = 0$, suppose data, Y, are available, that the likelihood function is given by $L(\beta; Y)$, and that the maximum likelihood estimator of β is given by $\hat{\beta}$ so that the maximized likelihood is given by $L(\hat{\beta}) = \hat{L}$.

The LR test has its rationale in the following: suppose that $\tilde{\beta}$ maximizes the likelihood subject to the constraint, so that $f(\tilde{\beta}) = 0$ and the corresponding likelihood is denoted by $\tilde{L}$. The likelihood ratio is then given by:

$$LR = \tilde{L}/\hat{L} \quad \text{and so} \quad \ell n(LR) = \ell n(\tilde{L}) - \ell n(\hat{L}).$$

$\hat{\beta}$ is a consistent estimator, and so if the hypothesis $f(\beta) = 0$ is true, then the unconstrained and the constrained estimates will be 'close', as will the corresponding likelihoods. Since $0 < \tilde{L} \leq \hat{L}$, $0 < LR \leq 1$, values of LR 'distant' from unity (equivalently values of $\ell n(LR)$ which are very negative) are evidence on which one would reject the null hypothesis. It may be shown that the large sample distribution of $-2\ell n(LR)$ is χ^2_m where there are m restrictions within the null hypothesis (i.e. there are m independent equations in the null hypothesis $f(\beta) = 0$), and a significant value of $-2\ell n(LR)$ leads to rejection of the null hypothesis. The LR test is not applicable in testing a simple null hypothesis against a simple alternative: the degrees of freedom is equal to the reduction in the parameter space which the hypothesis imposes and in testing for example $\beta = \beta_o$ against $\beta = \beta_1$ there is no reduction in the parameter space; moreover, in such a case there is no necessity that $LR \leq 1$.

Clearly, for any given difference between $\hat{\beta}$ and $\tilde{\beta}$, the value of the likelihood ratio will depend upon the curvature of the likelihood function. To accommodate the degree of curvature, both of the likelihood function and of the constraint function, two other tests of the hypothesis have been developed.

The Wald test is a more direct test of the hypothesis $f(\beta) = 0$ in the sense that it is a direct comparison of $f(\hat{\beta})$ and its hypothesized value. Clearly, if the null hypothesis is true, then $f(\hat{\beta})$ will be close to zero. The Wald test is a traditional test in that it measures the 'closeness' of $f(\hat{\beta})$ to zero by reference to the estimated covariance of $f(\hat{\beta})$. It may be shown that:

$$V(f(\hat{\beta})) = [\partial f(\hat{\beta})/\partial\hat{\beta}]' V(\hat{\beta}) [\partial f(\hat{\beta})/\partial\hat{\beta}]$$

where $[\partial f(\hat{\beta})/\partial\hat{\beta}']$ is the m×k matrix whose (i, j)th term is the derivative of ith equation of $f(\beta)$ with respect to β_j, evaluated at the maximum likelihood estimator of β; let this matrix of derivatives be denoted by $D(\hat{\beta})'$. To evaluate $V(\hat{\beta})$ the information matrix, defined in **Maximum likelihood**, may be used; the information matrix, I, is formally defined as:

$$I(\beta) = E\left[\frac{\partial^2 \ell n L(\beta)}{\partial\beta\partial\beta'}\right]$$

$I(\beta)$ is a measure of the curvature of the log-likelihood function. Under a set of general regularity conditions, $[I(\hat{\beta})]^{-1}$ provides the estimator of variance–covariance matrix for $\hat{\beta}$ (see **Maximum likelihood**), and so the Wald statistic takes the form:

$$W = f(\hat{\beta})'[D(\hat{\beta})'[I(\hat{\beta})]^{-1}D(\hat{\beta})]^{-1}f(\hat{\beta}).$$

It is to be noted that the Wald test utilizes the curvature of the log-likelihood function evaluated at the maximum likelihood value of the parameter, namely $I(\hat{\beta})$. It may be shown that, under very general conditions, the large sample distribution of the W statistic is χ^2_m. A large value of W leads to rejection of the null hypothesis, as this would constitute evidence that the difference between $f(\hat{\beta})$ and zero is too large to be explained by sampling variation.

The Lagrange multiplier (LM) test, also known as the efficient score test, derives from an application of constrained optimization in the case of maximizing the log-likelihood subject to the constraint. Denote the m×1 vector of Lagrange multipliers by λ, and define the Lagrangian:

$$\ell n L(\beta) + \lambda' f(\beta)$$

The first-order conditions are:

$$\frac{\partial \ell n L(\beta)}{\partial\beta} + D(\beta)\lambda = 0$$

and $$f(\beta) = 0$$

where the matrix $D(\beta)'$ is as defined above, the m×k matrix of derivatives of $f(\beta)$ with respect to β.

$\partial \ell n L(\beta)/\partial\beta$ represents the first derivatives of the log-likelihood function and, if the restrictions are valid, this will be close to zero when evaluated at $\tilde{\beta}$, the estimator which satisfies the constraints: $f(\tilde{\beta}) = 0$. The derivatives of the log-likelihood function form the vector of efficient scores, and its variance matrix is simply the information matrix, evaluated at $\tilde{\beta}$; hence the appropriate test is that the vector of efficient scores is zero at the constrained estimator, and may be written as:

$$\text{LM} = \left[\frac{\partial \ell n \text{L}(\beta)}{\partial \beta}\right]_{\tilde{\beta}}' \left[\text{I}(\tilde{\beta})\right]^{-1} \left[\frac{\partial \ell n \text{L}(\beta)}{\partial \beta}\right]_{\tilde{\beta}}$$

It may be shown, under general conditions, that the large sample distribution of LM is χ^2_m.

The figure below illustrates the rationale for these tests, in the simple case when β is one-dimensional.

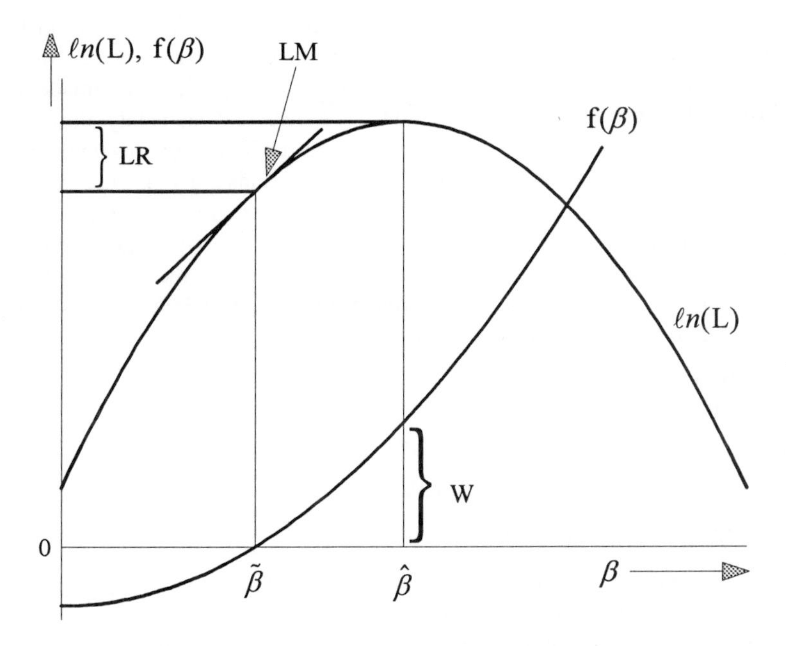

All three tests have the same asymptotic distribution, and:

$$\text{plim(LR)} = \text{plim(W)} = \text{plim(LM)}.$$

Thus the three statistics are asymptotically equivalent; in finite samples, however, the three approaches will, in general, yield different test statistics. If, however, the model has a known covariance matrix and the restrictions are linear, then the three tests will yield identical results; further, even if the covariance structure is to be estimated along with other parameters then, if the unrestricted maximum likelihood estimators of these two sets of parameters are asymptotically uncorrelated, the statistics will satisfy the inequality:

$$\text{W} \geq \text{LR} \geq \text{LM}.$$

Hence it is possible to reject a hypothesis by the Wald test, but not reject it by the other two tests. It should be noted that this inequality does not, of itself, indicate anything about the relative power of the tests. This inequality does not necessarily hold if the errors are non-normal, nor if the restrictions are non-linear; however, in the latter case LR ≥ LM. If the errors in the regression model are assumed to be identically distributed independent normal variates and the regressors are fixed then there is no need to use these asymptotic tests; in this case the three likelihood-based tests are each monotonic functions of the usual F statistic, and there is no conflict amongst the exact forms of the W, LR and LM tests.

The small finite sample properties of these tests are not known except for a limited number of special cases; given their different computational requirements, the particular choice in any context is typically made by reference to their ease of calculation. The LR test demands both the constrained and unconstrained estimates, while the Wald test demands only the unconstrained estimate and the LM test demands only the constrained estimate. Since both the LM and the LR test require the model to be estimated subject to the restrictions embodied in the hypothesis, and the Wald statistic demands only the unconstrained estimate, the Wald test has proved to be a particularly useful approach when the problems of estimating the restricted model are formidable.

Further reading

These three tests are further discussed in Buse (1982), and their use in the regression model is discussed in Berndt and Savin (1977) and Engle (1984).

Non-linear least squares

If variables enter an economic model in non-linear fashion the model can still be handled within the linear framework by a simple redefinition of variables (so that, for example, a model involving the variable X^2 may be seen as linear in the variable Z where $Z = X^2$). Some models which are non-linear in variables or parameters may be linearized by a simple transformation (for example, the Cobb–Douglas production function is non-linear, but may be linearized by taking the simple logarithmic transformation so long as the error term in the original equation enters multiplicatively). Other, more complex, models may be examined by use of the Box–Cox transformation which may then be analysed using linear models. However, models which cannot be made linear by a suitable transformation (either because of the non-linearity in variables and/or parameters or because of the way in which the error term is introduced) are called intrinsically non-linear, and the methods and analysis developed for linear models is not applicable. Two basic approaches exist for the estimation of the parameters of intrinsically non-linear models: minimizing the residual sum of squares and maximizing the likelihood. The distinguishing feature of a non-linear regression model is that its first-order conditions which define the solution are non-linear functions of the parameters.

A non-linear model may, however, always be approximately linearized by expanding the non-linear function as a Taylor series; consider a non-linear model:

$$Y_t = f(X_t, \beta) + \varepsilon_t$$

where f is a non-linear function, X_t is a vector of k explanatory variables and β is a k-dimensional vector of unknown parameters. If the function $f(X_t, \beta)$ is expanded around a given value of β, say β^o, the linear Taylor approximation is:

$$f(X_t, \beta) \cong f(X_t, \beta^o) + \sum_{j=1}^{k} \left[\frac{\partial f(X_t, \beta)}{\partial \beta_j} \right]_{\beta^o} (\beta_j - \beta^o).$$

Denoting $f(X_t, \beta^o)$ by f_t^o, and the partial derivative of $f(X_t, \beta)$ with respect to β_j evaluated at β^o by z_{tj}^o, this may be written as:

$$f(X_t, \beta) - f_t^o \cong \sum_{j=1}^{k} z_{tj}^o \beta_j - \sum_{j=1}^{k} z_{tj}^o \beta_j^o$$

i.e.

$$f(X_t, \beta) - f_t^o + \sum_{j=1}^{k} z_{tj}^o \beta_j^o = \sum_{j=1}^{k} z_{tj}^o \beta_j + \varepsilon_t$$

For a given value of β^o the left-hand side variable could be computed, as could the variables z_{tj}^o; the parameters β could then be computed from this linearized regression by ordinary least squares.

This solution to the non-linear regression, has properties which, although not amenable to exact finite sample results, may be shown to include consistency and asymptotic normality. The non-linear least squares solution may, however, be shown to be the most efficient estimator only when the errors are normally distributed. The usual asymptotic assumption made regarding the regressors for such a demonstration is that the sample moment matrix of regressors in the linearized model, when evaluated at the true value of β, has a finite, non-singular limit:

$$\text{plim} \left[T^{-1} \sum_{t=1}^{T} \frac{\partial f(X_t, \beta^o)}{\partial \beta} \cdot \frac{\partial f(X_t, \beta^o)}{\partial \beta'} \right] = Q$$

where β^o is the true value, and Q is a positive definite k×k matrix. A necessary condition for this assumption is that the T×k matrix $\partial f(X, \beta^o)/\partial \beta'$ is of full rank. In the case of the non-linear model the sum of squares to be minimized is given by:

$$RSS(\beta) = \sum_{t=1}^{T}[Y_t - f(X_t,\beta)]^2 = [Y - f(X,\beta)]'[Y - f(X,\beta)]$$

The first-order conditions (the k normal equations) are given by:

$$\frac{\partial RSS(\beta)}{\partial \beta} = -2\sum_{t=1}^{T}\frac{\partial f(X_t,\beta)}{\partial \beta_j}[Y_t - f(X_t,\beta)].$$

Defining the T×k matrix $Z(\beta)$ whose typical term is $\partial f(X_t, \beta)/\partial \beta_j$, that is, $Z(\beta) = \partial f(X, \beta)/\partial \beta'$: the first order conditions may then be written compactly as:

$$Z(\beta)'[Y - f(X, \beta)] = 0$$

These are the normal equations for the non-linear model and comprise a set of k non-linear equations. They may be solved by a variety of methods; a commonly used numerical routine is the Gauss–Newton algorithm which makes use of the first-order Taylor expansion of a non-linear function. In the linearized regression, for a given value of the parameter vector β^o the regression may be run; this yields an estimate of the parameters which becomes the β^o at the next iteration; iterations continue until convergence is satisfactory, and the sample value of Q^{-1} obtained at the final iteration is, excepting a scalar factor (s^2/T), the estimated variance matrix of the parameters. An alternative is the Newton–Raphson algorithm which uses a second-order Taylor expansion. Such numerical approaches demand a starting value of β and may not 'work' in the sense that they may not converge to a solution, or may converge to a local minimum, as opposed to a global minimum. The way to guard against such possibilities is to use different starting values of the unknown parameter.

If the errors are independently distributed with a zero mean and constant variance, σ^2, if the non-linear function $f(X, \beta)$ is continuous in both arguments and at least twice continuously differentiable in β, if $\text{plim}(1/T)Z(\hat{\beta})'Z(\hat{\beta})$ is a positive definite matrix, and if the sequence X_t is bounded and well behaved then $\hat{\beta}$ is approximately normally distributed with mean β and has a variance matrix which may be consistently estimated by $\hat{\sigma}^2[Z(\hat{\beta})'Z(\hat{\beta})]^{-1}$ where $\hat{\sigma}^2 = RSS(\hat{\beta})/(T - k)$ (or $\hat{\sigma}^2 = RSS(\hat{\beta})/T$, since the correction for the degrees of freedom is irrelevant to this asymptotic result). The goodness-of-fit statistic, R^2, defined as 1 minus the ratio of the sum of squared residuals to the variation of Y around its sample mean is, in this case, not constrained to the [0, 1] interval, but it does offer some description of the fit.

Maximum likelihood estimation may proceed from assuming a particular distribution of the errors. Taking ε to be distributed as $N(0, \sigma^2 I)$ the likelihood function of the non-linear model is given by:

$$L(\beta, \sigma^2|Y) = (2\pi\sigma^2)^{-T/2}\exp(-RSS(\beta)/2\sigma^2)$$

The ML estimator of σ^2 is given by RSS(β)/T, denoted by $\tilde{\sigma}^2$, and writing the likelihood function in terms of β alone concentrates the likelihood to:

$$L^*(\beta|Y) = (2\pi\tilde{\sigma}^2)^{-T/2}\exp(-T\tilde{\sigma}^2/2\tilde{\sigma}^2)$$

i.e.

$$L^*(\beta|Y) = (2\pi\tilde{\sigma}^2)^{-T/2}\exp(-T/2)$$

so that the concentrated log-likelihood may be written as:

$$\ell n L^*(\beta|Y) = -(T/2)(1 + \ell n(2\pi)) - (T/2)\ell n(RSS(\beta)/T)$$
$$= \text{constant} - (T/2)\ell n(RSS(\beta)).$$

Hence if $\tilde{\beta}$ minimizes the residual sum of squares it maximizes the likelihood also, and the non-linear least squares estimator, $\hat{\beta}$, is identical to the non-linear maximum likelihood estimator. This result is true of non-linear models for which the error is both additive and has a multivariate standard normal distribution. Under appropriate regularity conditions the large sample properties of the ML estimator may be derived. Defining the $1\times(k+1)$ vector θ by:

$$\theta = \begin{bmatrix} \tilde{\beta} \\ \tilde{\sigma}^2 \end{bmatrix},$$

$$\sqrt{T}(\tilde{\theta} - \theta) \xrightarrow{D} N(0, \lim[I(\theta)/T]^{-1})$$

where $I(\theta)$ is the information matrix given by $-E[\partial^2 \ell n L/\partial\theta\partial\theta']$; here:

$$I(\theta) = \begin{bmatrix} \sigma^{-2}[Z(\beta)'Z(\beta)] & 0 \\ 0 & T/2\sigma^4 \end{bmatrix}$$

so that $\tilde{\beta}$ has an asymptotic variance matrix given by $\sigma^2[Z(\beta)'Z(\beta)]^{-1}$ which is precisely the result demonstrated for the non-linear least squares estimator.

An extension of the likelihood approach allows estimation of non-linear models such as:

$$h(Y_t, \gamma) = f(X_t, \beta) + \varepsilon_t.$$

Defining the sum of squares as $RSS(\gamma, \beta) = \sum_{t=1}^{T}[h(Y_t,\gamma) - f(X_t,\beta)]^2$, and given normality, the likelihood function is given by:

$$L(\gamma, \beta, \sigma^2|Y) = (2\pi\sigma^2)^{-T/2}[\exp(-RSS(\gamma, \beta)/2\sigma^2)].J$$

where J is the determinant of the Jacobian matrix of the transformation from $h(Y_t, \gamma)$ to Y_t, whose typical element is $\partial h(Y_t, \gamma)/\partial Y_s = j_{ts}$; j_{ts} is a function of γ. However, if Y_t and Y_s are independently distributed, then $\partial h(Y_t, \gamma)/\partial Y_s = 0$ for all $t \neq s$ and then the Jacobian matrix is diagonal . Hence the log-likelihood function is given by:

$$\ell n L(\gamma, \beta, \sigma^2|Y) = -(T/2)\ell n(2\pi\sigma^2) - (1/2\sigma^2)RSS(\gamma, \beta) + \sum_{t=1}^{T}\ell n(j_{tt})$$

Since σ^2 is estimated as RSS(γ, β)/T, the log-likelihood may be concentrated to yield:

$$\hat{\ell n}L(\gamma,\beta|Y) = -(T/2)(1+\ell n(2\pi)) + \sum_{t=1}^{T}\ell n(j_{tt}) - (T/2)\ell n(RSS(\gamma,\beta)/T)$$

and this may be maximized by numerical routines to obtain the estimates of γ and β, from which the estimate of σ^2 may then be computed.

The simple non-linear model, with a scalar variance matrix, may be extended to more general models with autocorrelation and heteroscedasticity, and to models involving sets of non-linear equations which are contemporaneously correlated. Naturally, given the asymptotic properties of the non-linear estimator, standard tests and inferential statistics may be employed within this class of model, and they have asymptotic validity. The increasing availability of software capable of computing estimators of non-linear models facilitates the use of these models; due to the lack of such software, or computational cost, simpler estimators were utilized as a second best some years ago but they are now being displaced by the computationally more demanding maximum likelihood (ML) non-linear estimators. The ML non-linear estimators have desirable large-sample properties and research has shown that they have better finite sample properties than the computationally simpler 'second best' alternatives.

In practical terms there are various algorithms available for deriving the estimators in non-linear models; some use first-order Taylor expansions, some use second-order expansions, some use numerically constructed first derivatives of the non-linear function whereas others require the investigator to provide those derivatives in analytic form. It is important, also, to note that the 'solutions' obtained by numerical methods may only be local, not global, solutions, and so it is important that various starting values are employed to ensure that the true global solutions may be obtained.

Further reading
A comprehensive discussion of non-linear least squares may be found in Amemiya (1985).

Non-nested hypotheses

A nested hypothesis is a hypothesis which, when true, generates a special case of a more general family of models. Nested hypothesis tests include, for example, all tests of the exclusion of explanatory variables in the regression model. However, some hypothesis tests of great interest cannot be so described. Suppose one were to test the model $Y = X\beta + \varepsilon$ against the model $Y = Z\gamma + \nu$ where neither X nor Z is a subset of the other; it is assumed that $\varepsilon \sim N(0, \sigma_1^2 I)$ and $\nu \sim N(0, \sigma_2^2 I)$. Label the former model as

H_1 and the latter as H_2; note that here the models are the hypotheses, and the hypotheses do not relate to the parameters *per se*.

One of the simplest approaches to testing one model against another, when neither model is a special case of the other and in particular when X and Z have no variables in common, takes the following form: construct the artificial model $Y = X\delta + Z\xi + \nu$ and then test, separately, the hypotheses $\delta = 0$ and $\xi = 0$, using appropriate F-statistics. If the latter hypothesis is not rejected while the former hypothesis is rejected, then the model H_2 is rejected in favour of H_1; if $\delta = 0$ is not rejected while $\xi = 0$ is rejected, then the model H_1 is rejected in favour of H_2. Of course, it is also possible that the hypotheses, $\delta = 0$ and $\xi = 0$, are both either rejected or not rejected; if both are rejected then the data are incapable of discriminating between the two models to the extent of rejecting one in favour of the other (or neither model is adequate), and if both hypotheses are not rejected then both models described by H_1 and H_2 are rejected. In the case when neither model is rejected, the data can still be used to discriminate between the models in the sense that one of the models will, on some criteria, perform better than the other. In this context it is tempting to measure the 'better' model by reference to the R^2 statistics of the two models; even though in this example the two models utilize exactly the same dependent variable it would be incorrect simply to choose that model with the higher R^2 since this does not take into account the possibility that the regressors X and Z contain a different number of explanatory variables.

Since the goodness of fit statistic, R^2, cannot fall as the number of regressors in a model increases one might 'improve' the R^2 of either model simply by adding regressors, and in comparing two models it is important to take into account not only the goodness of fit, but also the degree of parsimony (as indicated by the number of regressors). Various measures exist which formalize the trade-off between goodness of fit and parsimony (see **Selection of regressors**), most notably the $\bar{R}^2$, Amemiya's prediction criterion PC, Akaike's information criterion AIC, Sawa's BIC criterion, Mallows' C_p statistic and the posterior odds criterion. Each criterion depends on specific assumptions, and by using different loss functions the investigator may be led to use any one of them; this arbitrariness of choice has led to their relative non-use in favour of other approaches: the F-test, J-test, Cox test and encompassing tests are the more popular non-nested tests.

The F-test is a variant on the simple F-test given above. Suppose the two models are given by H_1: $Y = X\beta + \varepsilon$ and H_2: $Y = Z\gamma + \nu$ and suppose that neither X nor Z are subsets of each other; take H_1 as the null hypothesis and construct the set of regressors Z* which consists of those variable in Z not included in X. Now run the regression of Y on X and Z* and test the significance of the coefficients attached to Z* via an F-test. Reversing the roles of the models, now take H_2 as the null hypothesis and run Y on Z and

X^*, where X^* is that set of regressors in X not common to Z, and test the significance of the coefficients on X^* via an F-test. If H_1 is the correct model then the contribution of Z^* to the explanation of Y over and above that of X will be due to sampling variation only; similarly if H_2 is the correct model then the contribution of X^* to the explanation of Y over and above that of Z will be due to sampling variation only. Thus if the F-test on the coefficients on Z^* is not significant, while that on X^* is significant, H_2 is rejected in favour of H_1 and *vice versa*. If both F-tests are significant then neither model is individually adequate and both are rejected in their current form, while if both F-tests are insignificant neither model could, on this evidence, be rejected in favour of the other. The F-test must, of course, be carried out within the usual framework which stresses the importance of diagnostic tests.

The J-test (Davidson and MacKinnon, 1981) is run as follows: with H_1 as the null hypothesis first run Y on Z and construct the predicted values of Y under H_2, namely $\hat{Y}(H_2) = Z\hat{\gamma}$. Now run the auxiliary regression of Y on both X and $\hat{Y}(H_2)$; if H_1 is true $\hat{Y}(H_2)$ will offer no significant contribution to the explanation of Y or, equivalently, if $\hat{Y}(H_2)$ does make a significant contribution to the explanation of Y, then H_1 cannot be the 'true' model. Hence the test proceeds via a t-test of the coefficient on $\hat{Y}(H_2)$, and if this leads to the rejection of the null hypothesis that this parameter is zero, then H_1 is rejected. One can now reverse the roles of H_1 and H_2 by running Y on X to yield $\hat{Y}(H_1) = X\hat{\beta}$ and run Y on both Z and $\hat{Y}(H_1)$. If the t-test on the coefficient on $\hat{Y}(H_1)$ is such as to reject the hypothesis that the parameter is zero, then H_2 is rejected. In this test it is, of course, possible to reject both models, to not reject both models, or to reject one while not rejecting the other. Again, the J-test (like the F-test) must be seen as operative within a framework which stresses the importance of diagnostic tests of model adequacy. It should be noted that even though the additional variable in the auxiliary regressions, $\hat{Y}(H_i)$, is a random variable, the ratio of its coefficient to its standard error is asymptotically a t-variate under the appropriate hypothesis.

The Cox test (1961) is a variant of the Neyman–Pearson likelihood ratio test. Denoting the log-likelihood function of $(\beta, \sigma_1^2|Y, H_1)$ by $\ell n L_1(\theta_1)$ and that of $(\gamma, \sigma_2^2|Y, H_2)$ by $\ell n L_2(\theta_2)$, the Cox test is based on the statistic:

$$c_{12} = \ell n L_1(\hat{\theta}_1) - \ell n L_2(\hat{\theta}_2) - E_1[\ell n L_1(\hat{\theta}_1) - \ell n L_2(\hat{\theta}_2)]$$

where $\hat{\theta}_1$ is the maximum likelihood estimate of (β, σ_1^2) and $\hat{\theta}_2$ is the maximum likelihood estimate of (γ, σ_2^2). In computing c_{12} the expectation is carried out under the truth of H_1.

Denoting the maximum likelihood estimator of σ_i^2 by $\hat{\sigma}_i^2$, then $\ell n L_1(\hat{\theta}_1) =$ constant $- (T/2)\ell n\, \hat{\sigma}_1^2$ and $\ell n L_2(\hat{\theta}_2) =$ constant $- (T/2)\ell n\, \hat{\sigma}_2^2$. Hence

$$c_{12} = (T/2)\{\ell n(\hat{\sigma}_2^2/\hat{\sigma}_1^2) - E_1[\ell n(\hat{\sigma}_2^2/\hat{\sigma}_1^2)]\}.$$

To proceed, the expectation under H_1 is replaced by its asymptotic expectation. H_1 is assumed to be true, and so the sum of squared residual from the model H_2 is given by:

$$\hat{\nu}'\hat{\nu} = E(Y'M_zY)$$

where $M_z = I - Z(Z'Z)^{-1}Z$. But under H_i, $Y = X\beta + \varepsilon$ and so:

$$\hat{\nu}'\hat{\nu} = \varepsilon'M_z\varepsilon + \beta'X'M_zX\beta.$$

But $\hat{\sigma}_2^2 = \hat{\nu}'\hat{\nu}/T$ and hence:

$$AE_1(\hat{\sigma}_2^2) = \sigma_1^2 + (1/T)\beta'X'M_zX\beta$$

where AE_1 denotes asymptotic expectation under H_1. Hence:

$$AE_1[\ell n(\hat{\sigma}_2^2/\hat{\sigma}_1^2)] = \ell n[(\sigma_1^2 + T^{-1}\beta'X'M_zX\beta)/\sigma_1^2]$$

which is estimated by $\ell n[(\hat{\sigma}_1^2 + T^{-1}\hat{\beta}'X'M_zX\hat{\beta})/\hat{\sigma}_1^2]$; the inserting this into the expression for c_{12}:

$$\begin{aligned} c_{12} &= (T/2)\{\ell n(\hat{\sigma}_2^2/\hat{\sigma}_1^2) - \ell n[(\hat{\sigma}_1^2 + T^{-1}\hat{\beta}'X'M_zX\hat{\beta})/\hat{\sigma}_1^2]\} \\ &= (T/2)\{\ell n[\hat{\sigma}_2^2/(\hat{\sigma}_1^2 + T^{-1}\hat{\beta}'X'M_zX\hat{\beta})] = (T/2)\ell n[\hat{\sigma}_2^2/\hat{\sigma}_{21}^2] \end{aligned}$$

where $\hat{\sigma}_{21}^2 = \hat{\sigma}_1^2 + T^{-1}\hat{\beta}'X'M_zX\hat{\beta}$.

If H_1 is true then this expression for c_{12} may be shown, asymptotically, to have a zero-mean normal distribution and a variance denoted by $V(c_{12})$; the asymptotic variance may be estimated (see Pesaran, 1974, for details) and denoted by $\hat{V}_{12}$, and then the test statistic used is $c_{12}/\sqrt{\hat{V}_{12}}$ which is asymptotically distributed as a standard normal variate.

If the computed test statistic is significantly negative, then $\hat{\sigma}_2^2$ is significantly smaller than $\hat{\sigma}_{21}^2$ and so H_1 is rejected in favour of H_2. A significant positive value of the test statistic is evidence against H_1, but suggests a model which differs from H_1 in a direction opposite to that of H_2.

Several comments are necessary. First, the small sample distribution of c_{12} is not known, and the statistic has a justification based on asymptotic theory. However, Monte Carlo results indicate that the normality of c_{12} is a good approximation even in samples as small as 20 (see Pesaran, 1974). Second, the statistic is valid only when $X'M_z \neq 0$, which means that if the models are nested or if the competing explanatory variables are orthogonal to each other then the statistic in not valid and tests based upon the classical F-test are applicable. Third, the test is not applicable when there are more than two competing models, and there is no ready generalization to the case of $M > 2$ models. Finally, in using the Cox test the roles of H_1 and H_2 should be reversed and c_{21} should be examined; however, the test is not symmetric in the hypotheses and great care should be exercised if the conclusions from an analysis of c_{21} are in conflict with those from c_{12}.

The simplest possible outcomes, having reversed the roles of the hypotheses, are that H_1 is rejected in favour of H_2 (c_{12} is significantly negative while c_{21} is not significantly different from zero), H_2 is rejected in favour of H_1 (c_{21} is significantly negative while c_{12} is not significantly different from zero), neither H_1 nor H_2 are rejected in favour of the other (both c_{12} and c_{21} are insignificantly different from zero), or both hypotheses are rejected (both test statistics are significantly positive). Of the other possibilities, suppose c_{12} is significantly negative, suggesting a rejection of H_1 in favour of H_2, but c_{21} is significantly positive, suggesting that H_2 is to be rejected, but in favour of some other model opposite to H_2 in a direction different from that of H_1; both models must be rejected in this situation.

The non-nested tests described here are attempts to offer practical means by which to reject one model in favour of an alternative; neither theoretical nor Monte Carlo results are sufficient to draw a clear conclusion as to which test to use in any specific situation. Moreover, several important questions remain: what is the appropriate size of a non-nested test? what are the finite sampling properties of the J-test and Cox statistics? how does one deal with the asymmetry of the models, whereby the choice of reference hypothesis (the model chosen as the null hypothesis) can appear to determine the conclusion? Further work on these, and other questions, is necessary before non-nested tests will be able to play a more significant role in applied work. Increasingly common, however, is the use of encompassing tests, described in the entry of that title.

Empirical evidence suggests that the J-test performs better than the F-test in rejecting the false model, but that the J-test also tends to reject the true model too often. Also, both models should be assessed by reference to their associated diagnostic tests (see **Diagnostic tests**) as these are good indicators of false models.

Further reading

See Davidson and McKinnon (1981), Cox (1961 and 1962), Pesaran (1974), Pesaran and Deaton (1978), Mizon and Richard (1986) and Pesaran and Hall (1989). The symposia by White (1982) and (1983) draw together much recent research on non-nested model selection, and see also MacKinnon (1983) and Godfrey (1984).

Normality tests

Tests of normality are a part of the econometrician's set of diagnostic tests. There are many non-parametric tests of a random variable's distribution, but the most popular test in regression analysis is the Jarque–Bera test. In small samples the normality of the ordinary least squares estimator $\hat{\beta}$ is assured if the errors are normally distributed; in large samples recourse may be made to asymptotic theory to demonstrate this result, under a wider class of assumptions about the error (see **Large sample theory** and **Ordinary least squares in large samples**). However, a test of the normality of the error, via a test of the fitted residuals, can provide evidence not only of a possible non-normal distribution, but also of the presence of outliers (see **Outliers**).

The Jarque–Bera test treats the normal distribution as a special case of a more general family of distributions; the correspondence of the observed residuals, $\hat{e}$, to the general family is examined and those restrictions which yield normality as a particular case are tested. The implied test statistic depends upon the moments of the actual $\hat{e}$ observations. The rth moment of a random variable u_i is denoted by μ_r and is given by $E(u_i^r)$; a normal distribution is uniquely defined by its first moment (its mean) and by its second moment (which together define the variance). The Jarque–Bera test examines the residual distribution via its third and fourth moments; under the null hypothesis of normality they are related and it may be shown that for normally distributed variables for which $\mu_1 = 0$:

$$\text{if } \theta_1 = \mu_3^2/\mu_2^3 \qquad \text{and } \theta_2 = \mu_4/\mu_2^2, \qquad \text{then } \sqrt{\theta_1} = \theta_2 - 3.$$

This test statistic effectively examines the shape of the distribution of the observed residuals and determines whether this is consistent, or not, with a zero mean normal density function. Thus, within a regression model having T observations, if $\hat{e}_i$ is the ith ordinary least squares residual, $s^2 = \hat{e}'\hat{e}/T$ is a consistent estimator of σ^2 and θ_1 and θ_2 may be estimated by:

$$\hat{\theta}_1 = T^{-1}\Sigma_{i=1}^{T}(\hat{e}_i/s)^3 \quad \text{and } \hat{\theta}_2 = T^{-1}\Sigma_{i=1}^{T}(\hat{e}_i^2/s^2)^2;$$

then under the hypothesis of normality, the test statistic is:

$$T\{\hat{\theta}_1/6 + (\hat{\theta}_2 - 3)^2/24\}$$

and this is asymptotically distributed as χ_2^2. A large value of the statistic indicates divergence of $\sqrt{\theta_1}$ from $\theta_2 - 3$, and rejection of the null hypothesis of normality takes place in the right-hand tail of the χ_2^2 distribution.

If the Jarque–Bera test statistic is 'significant' this is commonly due to there being a larger proportion of large residuals than is expected under normality and such a result is, then, often interpreted as suggesting the presence of outliers in the data set, as opposed to indicating a non-normal distribution of the errors. Even if the residuals do not exhibit normality in a finite sample, it is shown in **Central limit theorems** that, under appropriate regularity conditions concerning the true error, the standard distributional statements retain asymptotic validity; hence, if the finite sample is sufficiently large to invoke a central limit theorem it is possible to tolerate some departures from normality and retain asymptotic interpretations of the standard test statistics. Notwithstanding this remark, a significant test should be investigated, for it may arise due to outliers or heteroscedasticity, for example.

Further reading

See Jarque and Bera (1980).

Ordinary least squares

Consider the general linear model $Y = X\beta + \varepsilon$, where Y is an n×1 vector of observations on the regressand, X is an n×k matrix of n observations on k regressors (n > k), β is a k×1 vector of the unknown parameters and ε is the n×1 vector of disturbance terms. This model posits that the variable Y is determined linearly by the k variables in X; the parameters β_i (i = 1, 2, . . k) are unknown constants and the error term represents the difference between the observed value of Y and that given by the theoretical model ($X\beta$). The term ε is referred to as the 'error', the 'true error' or the 'true discrepancy' and ε is inherently unknowable since the 'true' parameter vector, β, is unknowable (see **General linear model**); in analysing this model ε is treated as if it were a random variable with a zero mean. Hence the expectation of Y is given by $X\beta$ and $E(Y) = X\beta$ is referred to as the 'true line of regression'. Estimation of this model involves utilizing observed data (Y, X) to calculate an estimate of the vector β. If β is estimated by the value b then Xb represents the estimated value of Y (or the 'fitted' value of Y) and the errors are then estimated by the vector Y – Xb; this vector is referred to as the 'residual' or 'fitted residual' and the process of estimation seeks to minimize the residual.

The method of ordinary least squares is one, very common, approach to the estimation problem. To analyse the mechanics of ordinary least squares it is assumed that the X matrix is non-stochastic and of full rank, $\rho(X) = k$, that is, all the regressors are linearly independent of each other, and that the error term has a zero mean: $E(\varepsilon) = 0$.

From the regression model, $Y = X\beta + \varepsilon$, taking expectations yields $E(Y) = X\beta$, where E(Y) is an n-dimensional vector. This represents n equations in k unknowns, and the k unknowns (the β_i) can be eliminated. Let $E(Y) = \tilde{Y} = X\beta$. Then, pre-multiplying by X':

$$X'\tilde{Y} = X'X\beta.$$

Given that X is of full rank, X'X is a non-singular k×k matrix, and so:

$$(X'X)^{-1}X'\tilde{Y} = \beta.$$

Substituting this expression for β into $\tilde{Y} = X\beta$: $\tilde{Y} = X(X'X)^{-1}X'\tilde{Y}$, hence:

$$(I - X(X'X)^{-1}X')\tilde{Y} = 0 \qquad \text{or} \quad M\tilde{Y} = 0$$

where $M = (I - X(X'X)^{-1}X')$. M is a very important matrix, and it may be shown to be square, symmetric, idempotent, singular and of order n and rank n – k. The symmetry of M is obvious, and idempotency may be demonstrated by verifying that MM = M. For any idempotent matrix its rank is equal to its trace; in this case, using the property of trace that Tr(AB)= Tr(BA) where both A and B exist, $Tr(X(X'X)^{-1}X') = Tr(X'X(X'X)^{-1}) = Tr(I_k) = k$. Hence $Tr(M) = Tr(I_n) - k = n - k$.

The n equations $M\tilde{Y} = 0$ thus represent only n − k independent linear equations in the n variables $(\tilde{Y}_i)$; in n-dimensional space, therefore, $M\tilde{Y} = 0$ represents a k-dimensional hyper-plane. That is, in general, points in the k-dimensional parameter space, $(\beta_1, \beta_2, .. , \beta_k)$, are mapped into n-dimensional space by the n×k matrix X and form a k-dimensional hyper-plane; this hyper-plane is the range of X. If X is not of full rank then X maps points from k-dimensional space into n-dimensional space and there forms a hyper-plane which is of dimension less than k; in general, if X is of rank r then the hyper-plane is of dimension r.

The observation vector, Y, is n-dimensional and is represented by a point in n-dimensional space. From the regression model the expectation of Y, $\tilde{Y}$, must lie on the k-dimensional plane, and the first task may be seen as estimating $\tilde{Y}$. Denote by $\hat{Y}$ the estimate of $\tilde{Y}$; an obvious estimate of $\hat{Y}$ is that point on the plane 'nearest' to Y; this is taken to be the orthogonal projection of Y onto the plane. Measuring distance in Euclidean fashion the distance between the sample point Y and any point $\tilde{Y}$ on the plane is:

$$\sqrt{\Sigma_{i=1}^{n}(Y_i - \tilde{Y}_i)^2}.$$

The estimate of $\tilde{Y}$ is thus given as the solution to:

$$\text{Min } \sqrt{\Sigma_{i=1}^{n}(Y_i - \tilde{Y}_i)^2};$$

with respect to $\tilde{Y}$ subject to $M\tilde{Y} = 0$; i.e. by minimizing $\Sigma_{i=1}^{n}(Y_i - \tilde{Y}_i)^2$ with respect to $\tilde{Y}$ subject to $M\tilde{Y} = 0$. This may be written is matrix notation as:

$$\text{Min } (Y - \tilde{Y})'(Y - \tilde{Y}) \quad \text{subject to } M\tilde{Y} = 0.$$

This is a standard problem in constrained optimization; introducing the n×1 vector of Lagrange multipliers, λ, the Lagrangian is:

$$L = (Y - \tilde{Y})'(Y - \tilde{Y}) - 2\lambda'M\tilde{Y}$$

i.e.
$$L = Y'Y - Y'\tilde{Y} - \tilde{Y}'Y + \tilde{Y}'\tilde{Y} - 2\lambda'M\tilde{Y};$$

Each term in L is a scalar quantity (a 1×1 matrix) and so $Y'\tilde{Y} = \tilde{Y}'Y$; hence:

$$L = Y'Y - 2Y'\tilde{Y} + \tilde{Y}'\tilde{Y} - 2\lambda'M\tilde{Y}.$$

Therefore:

$$\frac{\partial L}{\partial \tilde{Y}} = -2Y + 2\tilde{Y} - 2M\lambda \quad \text{and} \quad \frac{\partial L}{\partial \lambda} = -2M\tilde{Y}.$$

Setting to zero (and using $\hat{Y}$ and $\hat{\lambda}$ to denote the solutions):

$$\hat{Y} = Y + M\hat{\lambda} \qquad \text{and} \quad M\hat{Y} = 0.$$

Pre-multiplying the first equations by M yields:

$$M\hat{Y} = MY + M\hat{\lambda},$$

since M is idempotent, and using the second equations yields:

$$0 = MY + M\hat{\lambda};$$

i.e. $M\hat{\lambda} = -MY$; hence $\hat{Y} = Y - MY$; i.e. $\hat{Y} = X(X'X)^{-1}X'Y$, and since $\hat{Y} = X\hat{\beta}$, where $\hat{\beta}$ is the estimator of β:

$$\hat{\beta} = (X'X)^{-1}X'Y.$$

To check that the $\hat{Y}$ obtained minimizes the distance demands that the second-order condition is satisfied; this requires that the matrix of second-order derivatives of the objective function is a positive definite matrix subject to the constraint; in this case $\partial^2 L/\partial\tilde{Y}'\partial\tilde{Y} = 2I$ and this is positive definite subject to any constraint.

As an example, consider the simple case of three observations and two parameters:

$$\tilde{Y}_1 = \beta_1 + \beta_2 X_1; \quad \tilde{Y}_2 = \beta_1 + \beta_2 X_2 \quad \tilde{Y}_3 = \beta_1 + \beta_2 X_3;$$

which solve to yield: $\tilde{Y}_1(X_2 - X_3) + \tilde{Y}_2(X_3 - X_1) + \tilde{Y}_3(X_1 - X_2) = 0$. This is the form of $M\tilde{Y} = 0$ in this example, and in general this is a plane in $(\tilde{Y}_1, \tilde{Y}_2, \tilde{Y}_3)$ space. The process of estimating $\hat{Y}$ and $\hat{\beta}$ in this simple case is illustrated in the figure below.

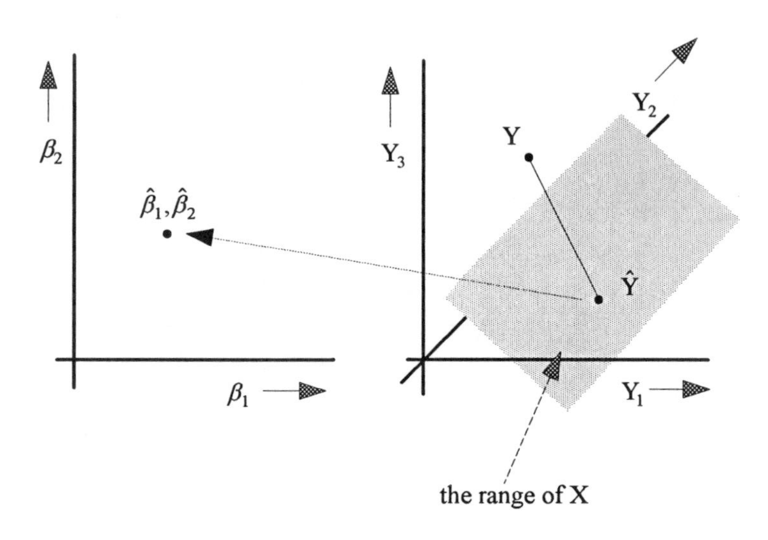

Thus ordinary least squares estimation seeks that point on the plane of expected Y values nearest to the observed Y vector; this point is $\hat{Y}$ and it may then be mapped back into parameter space to yield the OLS estimate $\hat{\beta}$.

If X is of full rank then $\hat{\beta}$ is unique. If X is not of full rank then the hyperplane given by $M\tilde{Y} = 0$ is of dimension less than k and when mapped back into β space the resultant $\hat{\beta}$ is not unique; in this case there is no unique solution to the problem of estimating β by ordinary least squares.

Before proceeding to examine the properties of $\hat{\beta}$ it is profitable to offer a different approach to ordinary least squares estimation.

Suppose β is estimated by some vector b; in that case the relationship is estimated as $Y^* = Xb$, and Y^* then denotes the predicted values of the regressand. The observed discrepancies between the actual observations of the regressand and the predicted values are given by the vector of fitted residuals $Y - Y^*$, whose typical element is $Y_i - \sum_{j=1}^{k} X_{ij} b_j$. A 'good' estimate b is one for which these discrepancies are, in some sense, small, and the method of ordinary least squares seeks that value of b for which the sum of squared discrepancies is a minimum. In the case of the simple model:

$$Y_i = \alpha + \beta X_i + \varepsilon_i;$$

this process may be illustrated as in the figure below. The line $E(Y_i) = \alpha + \beta X_i$ is the 'true line of regression' and the fitted line, $Y_i = \hat{\alpha} + \hat{\beta} X_i$, minimizes the sum of squared residuals.

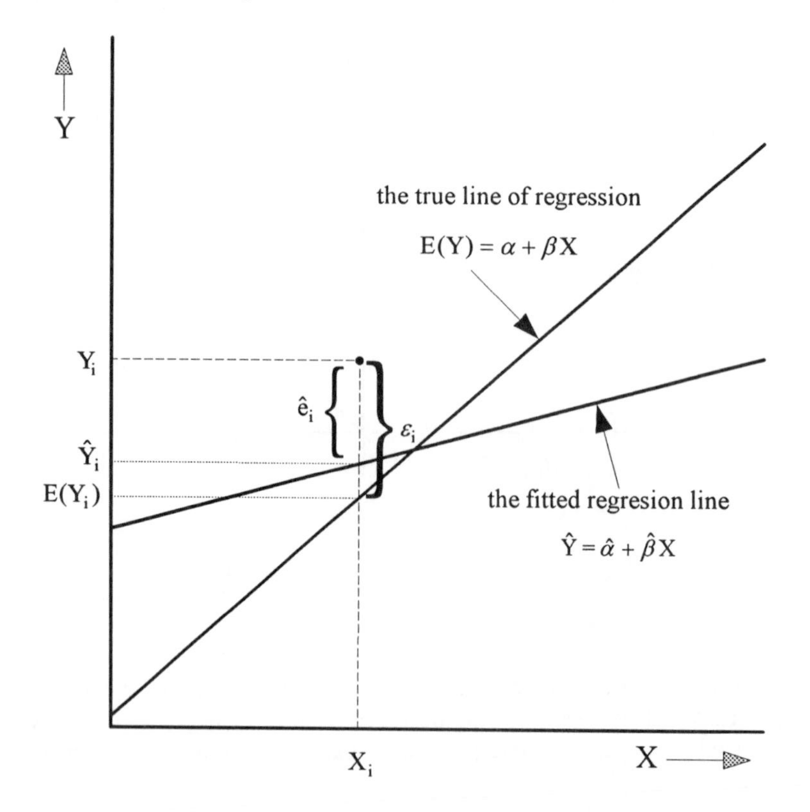

The residuals are the vertical distances between the observed points and the fitted line, whereas the vertical distances between observed points and the (unknowable) true line of regression are the true errors. The parameters of the fitted line are chosen to minimize the sum of squared residuals, and this is a relatively straightforward application of the differential calculus In the simple case this may be accomplished easily, but the general case requires the use of the rules of differentiating matrix expressions. The sum of squares may be written as:

$$\sum_{i=1}^{n}\left[Y_i - \Sigma_{j=1}^{k} X_{ij} b_j\right]^2 = (Y - Y^*)'(Y - Y^*) = (Y - Xb)'(Y - Xb)$$

and so the OLS problem may be written as follows:

Find that b such that $(Y - Xb)'(Y - Xb)$ is a minimum.

$(Y - Xb)'(Y - Xb)$ may be expanded as $Y'Y - Y'Xb - b'X'Y + b'X'Xb$; since each term is a scalar quantity (a 1×1 matrix) it follows that $b'X'Y$ is equal to its transpose given by $Y'Xb$; thus the sum of squares may be written as $Y'Y - 2Y'Xb + b'X'Xb$. Differentiating this with respect to b:

$$\frac{\partial(Y'Y - 2Y'Xb - b'X'Xb)}{\partial b} = -2X'Y + 2X'Xb$$

Setting to zero and denoting the solution vector by $\hat{\beta}$ yields:

$$X'X\hat{\beta} = X'Y.$$

X'X is a square, symmetric matrix of order k; denoting the typical element of this matrix by v_{ij} the expression $X'X\hat{\beta} = X'Y$ may be written as:

$$\sum_{j=1}^{k} v_{1j}\hat{\beta}_j = \sum_{i=1}^{n} X_{i1}Y_i$$

$$\sum_{j=1}^{k} v_{2j}\hat{\beta}_j = \sum_{i=1}^{n} X_{i2}Y_i$$

$$\vdots \quad = \quad \vdots$$

$$\vdots \quad = \quad \vdots$$

$$\sum_{j=1}^{k} v_{kj}\hat{\beta}_j = \sum_{i=1}^{n} X_{ik}Y_i$$

There are k equations here in k unknowns, and these equation are usually referred to as the 'normal equations'; they may be solved on the assumption that the equations are linearly independent. This assumption is valid given the assumption that the k regressors (the columns of the X matrix) are linearly independent (equivalent to the assumption that X is of full rank).

Although the equations could be solved using the techniques of scalar algebra, it is far easier to use matrix notation. The assumption of linear independence of the k columns of X ensures that $\rho(X) = k$ and, since $\rho(X'X) = \rho(X)$, $\rho(X'X) = k$; X'X is a square k×k matrix of full rank and so X'X is non-singular: $(X'X)^{-1}$ exists. Hence:

$$X'X\hat{\beta} = X'Y \quad \Rightarrow \quad \hat{\beta} = (X'X)^{-1}X'Y$$

The second-order condition is that the matrix of second-order derivatives of the objective function is a positive definite matrix; in this case:

$$\frac{\partial^2(Y'Y - 2Y'Xb - b'X'Xb)}{\partial b' \partial b} = 2X'X$$

which is independent of the parameters and is always a positive definite matrix, given that $\rho(X) = k$. Therefore, this approach to the method of ordinary least squares yields the solution as before:

$$\hat{\beta} = (X'X)^{-1}X'Y.$$

The properties of the ordinary least squares estimator

$\hat{\beta} = (X'X)^{-1}X'Y$ is a very important expression; the properties of this estimator may now be examined. Substituting $X\beta + \varepsilon$ for Y:

$$\hat{\beta} = (X'X)^{-1}X'(X\beta + \varepsilon);$$

i.e.

$$\hat{\beta} = \beta + (X'X)^{-1}X'\varepsilon;$$

that is, the estimator $\hat{\beta}$ is given by its true value, β, plus a linear combination of the error terms. From any one sample of data (Y, X) it is, then, an easy task to compute the estimate $\hat{\beta}$ However, since neither β nor ε are knowable no particular estimate $\hat{\beta}$ may be broken down into its constituent parts. The importance of the decomposition lies in its use as a means of examining the properties of $\hat{\beta}$. If ε is treated as a random variable, then for given observations on the regressors the actual observations of the regressand, Y, may be treated as the outcome of drawing a sample; Y is seen as a single realization of a random experiment, and so Y is treated as a single drawing from a multivariate distribution. The expected value of Y is $X\beta$ but from any one sample the observed Y will, in all probability, not coincide with its expected value. This is equivalent to the remark that the elements of ε, although each is a drawing from a zero mean distribution, are most unlikely all to be exactly zero for any particular sample. Hence any one estimate, $\hat{\beta}$, is, with probability 1, not equal to the parameter β. The expression $\hat{\beta} = (X'X)^{-1}X'Y$ provides a rule which may be applied to any sample of observations and which may, therefore, be used to compute an estimate, but without knowledge of β there is no way by which one could say how close that particular estimate is to β. The formula for $\hat{\beta}$ is the estimator, which is to be contrasted with an estimate which is the actual value of $\hat{\beta}$ given one sample of data. Since one would wish to judge an estimate by reference to the true, but unknowable, value of β, the route adopted is to judge an estimate by reference to the properties of the rule which generates the estimate. If the rule, the estimator, has desirable properties then any one estimate from this rule is also viewed favourably. Taking expectations:

$$E(\hat{\beta}) = E[\beta + (X'X)^{-1}X'\varepsilon];$$

since β is a vector of fixed parameters its expectation is itself; the expectation of the linear combination of error terms may be expanded:

$$E[(X'X)^{-1}X'\varepsilon)] = (X'X)^{-1}X'E(\varepsilon) \quad \text{since X is a non-stochastic matrix;}$$

$$= 0 \quad \text{since } E(\varepsilon) = 0.$$

Thus, $E(\hat{\beta}) = \beta$, that is, $\hat{\beta}$ is an unbiased estimator. The unbiased property means that, on average, the estimates are 'right'. This is, perhaps, best understood in the context of repeated sampling: if all possible samples of Y were taken and if, for each sample, the estimate $\hat{\beta}$ were constructed according to the formula, then the arithmetic average of those $\hat{\beta}$ values is the true value β. This may be expressed as follows: let $\hat{\beta}_{(p)}$ denote the value of $\hat{\beta}$ (the estimate) obtained from the p$^{\underline{th}}$ sample, and then:

$$\lim_{m \to \infty} (1/m) \sum_{p=1}^{m} \hat{\beta}_{(p)} = \beta.$$

Alternatively one can imagine the sampling distributions of the elements of $\hat{\beta}$ (the $\hat{\beta}_j$ where $\hat{\beta}_j$ is the estimator of β_j); $E(\hat{\beta}) = \beta$ implies that the mean of the distribution of each $\hat{\beta}_j$ is β_j. Each distribution has a variance, and to determine the spread of the distributions around their mean values, it is necessary to compute the variance of $\hat{\beta}$. Knowing that $\hat{\beta}$ is an unbiased estimator does not necessarily mean that $\hat{\beta}$ is a 'good' estimator.

If the distribution of the conceivable estimates around β, their average value, is widely spread then any one estimate of β is likely to be distant from the expected value; however, if the conceivable estimates are tightly distributed around the true β then any one estimate is more likely to be close to the true value. This argument leads one to prefer, of two unbiased estimators, that with the smaller spread, the smaller variance. It may be shown that, given the assumptions of OLS, $\hat{\beta}$ is the minimum variance estimator of all linear unbiased estimators. This result is demonstrated by the Gauss–Markov theorem. Hence, of all linear unbiased estimators, none has smaller variance than $\hat{\beta}$; since $\hat{\beta}$ is a k-dimensional vector, the variance of $\hat{\beta}$ is a k$\times$k matrix having the variances of the elements of $\hat{\beta}$ along its diagonal, and covariances off the diagonal. Denoting this matrix by $V(\hat{\beta})$, it is given by

$$V(\hat{\beta}) = E[\hat{\beta} - E(\hat{\beta})][\hat{\beta} - E(\hat{\beta})]'$$

and since $E(\hat{\beta}) = \beta$, $V(\hat{\beta}) = E[\hat{\beta} - \beta][\hat{\beta} - \beta]'$. Further, given the formula for $\hat{\beta}$, $\hat{\beta} - \beta = (X'X)^{-1}X'\varepsilon$ and so:

$$V(\hat{\beta}) = E[(X'X)^{-1}X'\varepsilon\varepsilon'X(X'X)^{-1}]$$

Since X is a non-stochastic matrix, the expectation operator only affects the stochastic term, ε:

$$V(\hat{\beta}) = (X'X)^{-1}X'E(\varepsilon\varepsilon')X(X'X)^{-1};$$

but $E(\varepsilon\varepsilon')$ is simply the variance matrix of ε. The usual assumptions of ordinary least squares are:

1. ε is a zero mean random variable;
2. $\rho(X) = k$; that is, there is no exact linear relationship amongst the k regressors;
3. the regressors are non-stochastic.
4. ε has elements which are mutually independent and homoscedastic;
5. $\varepsilon \sim MVN(0, \sigma^2 I)$;

The first and second assumptions were used in the 'mechanical' derivation of $\hat{\beta}$ above, and together with the third assumption it was shown that $\hat{\beta}$ is an unbiased estimator. Using the fourth assumption $V(\hat{\beta})$ may be examined. This assumption provides two pieces of information. The mutual independence of the elements of ε ensures that $E(\varepsilon_i \varepsilon_j) = 0$ for all $i \neq j$, and homoscedasticity implies $V(\varepsilon_i) = E(\varepsilon_i^2) = \sigma^2$ for all i and so $V(\varepsilon) = \sigma^2 I$.

Hence: $V(\hat{\beta}) = (X'X)^{-1}X'(\sigma^{22}I)X(X'X)^{-1} = \sigma^2(X'X)^{-1}X'X(X'X)^{-1}$

i.e.
$$V(\hat{\beta}) = \sigma^2(X'X)^{-1}.$$

Hence $V(\hat{\beta}_j) = \sigma^2 v_{jj}$ where v_{jj} is the jth diagonal term of $(X'X)^{-1}$. Denoting by $\hat{\beta}_{j(p)}$ the estimate of $\hat{\beta}_j$ obtained from the pth sample and following the interpretation of unbiasedness by reference to the sampling properties of $\hat{\beta}$, $V(\hat{\beta}_j) = \sigma^2 v_{jj}$ may be expressed as:

$$\lim_{m\to\infty} (1/m)\sum_{p=1}^{m}(\hat{\beta}_{j(p)} - \beta_j)^2 = \sigma^2 v_{jj}.$$

Thus the estimator $\hat{\beta}$ is unbiased and has a variance–covariance matrix given by $\sigma^2(X'X)^{-1}$; now using the last assumption regarding the distribution of ε, the distribution of $\hat{\beta}$ may be derived: given $\varepsilon \sim N(0, \sigma^2 I)$, for any r×n matrix B which is of full rank ($r \leq n$), $B\varepsilon \sim N(0, \sigma^2 BB')$; setting $B = (X'X)^{-1}X'$, $(X'X)^{-1}X'\varepsilon \sim N(0, \sigma^2(X'X)^{-1})$ and so:

$$\hat{\beta} - \beta \sim N(0, \sigma^2(X'X)^{-1})$$

However, if to make inference of the parameter β from this distributional statement, an estimator of the nuisance parameter σ^2 is required; the obvious starting point is to take the sum of squared residuals; the vector of fitted residuals is given by:

$$\hat{e} = Y - X\hat{\beta}$$

and, substituting $X\beta + \varepsilon$ for Y and $\beta + (X'X)^{-1}X'\varepsilon$ for $\hat{\beta}$:

$$\hat{e} = (X\beta + \varepsilon) - X(\beta + (X'X)^{-1}X'\varepsilon)$$

i.e. $$\hat{e} = \varepsilon - X(X'X)^{-1}X'\varepsilon = (I - X(X'X)^{-1}X')\varepsilon = M\varepsilon$$

where M is defined as before: $M = I - X(X'X)^{-1}X'$, a square, symmetric and idempotent matrix. The residual sum of squares is thus:

$$\hat{e}'\hat{e} = \varepsilon'M\varepsilon.$$

$\varepsilon'M\varepsilon$ is a quadratic form of a multivariate normal random variable, ε, and M is idempotent with rank $n - k$. Therefore:

$$\hat{e}'\hat{e}/\sigma^2 \sim \chi^2_{n-k} ;$$

it follows, then, that $E(\hat{e}'\hat{e}/\sigma^2) = n - k$ (since the expectation of a χ^2 variate is its degrees of freedom) and so:

$$E(\hat{e}'\hat{e}/(n-k)) = \sigma^2;$$

hence, $s^2 = \hat{e}'\hat{e}/(n-k)$ is an unbiased estimator of σ^2.

It is also to be noted that the residuals and the regressors are independent:

$$X'\hat{e} = X'M\varepsilon \equiv 0 \text{ since } X'M \equiv 0.$$

This result may be interpreted as meaning that the ordinary least squares estimator represents the method of moments: in the population X and ε are independent, hence $X'\varepsilon = 0$ and the estimator solves the k sample analogue moment equations $X'\hat{e} = 0$. These equations are simply the normal equations: $X'X\hat{\beta} = X'Y \Rightarrow X'(Y - X\hat{\beta}) = 0 \Rightarrow X'\hat{e} = 0$.

Also, the variance–covariance of the residuals is not scalar:

$$V(\hat{e}\,\hat{e}') = V(M\varepsilon\,\varepsilon'M') = \sigma^2MM = \sigma^2(I - X(X'X)^{-1}X')$$

and so the residuals exhibit heteroscedasticity and are not mutually independent, even when the true errors are.

The unbiasedness of $\hat{\beta}$ has been derived using only the assumptions of a fixed data matrix and a zero mean error; the derivations of the true and estimated variances of $\hat{\beta}$ and the unbiasedness of s^2 require further assumptions. From these results one may proceed to examine hypotheses regarding β (see **Confidence intervals** and **Confidence regions**, **Linear hypotheses** and **Non-linear hypothesis testing**), but in so doing it is important to have checked that the assumptions are valid; this is examined in **Diagnostic tests**, and related entries. Failure of the assumptions is also examined in other entries including **Autocorrelation**, **Chow test**, **Heteroscedasticity**, **RESET tests**, **Normality tests** and **Varying parameter models**.

Finally, although the method of OLS provides the 'best fitting' regression by minimizing the residual sum of squares, this does not answer any question of 'how good is the fit?'. A common approach to answering this question is to examine the degree of closeness of the fitted values (the $\hat{Y}_i$ values) to the observed values (the Y_i). This is usually examined by computing the so-called R^2 statistic, the coefficient of determination. In the case of a regression with a constant term, this is simply the squared correlation coefficient between the fitted and observed values. See **R²**.

Further reading
All the standard texts provide comprehensive coverage of the method of ordinary least squares and the reader is referred to those texts for further discussion of this topic. For an exposition of the geometry of least squares, and of other estimation techniques, see especially Wonnacott and Wonnacott (1979).

Ordinary least squares in large samples

In the general linear model, $Y = X\beta + \varepsilon$, suppose that the error term is assumed to be independently and identically distributed with zero mean and finite variance (written as $\varepsilon \sim \text{IID}(0, \sigma^2 I)$) and the X matrix is non-stochastic. This model differs from the standard presentation only in that the error term is here not assumed to have any specific form. The OLS estimator of β is given by:

$$\hat{\beta} = \beta + (X'X)^{-1}X'\varepsilon \quad \text{and} \quad V(\hat{\beta}) = \sigma^2(X'X)^{-1}.$$

To demonstrate the (weak) consistency of $\hat{\beta}$ it is sufficient, by Chebyshev's inequality (see **Large sample theory**), to show that $\lim V(\hat{\beta}) \to 0$. This demands some assumptions regarding the behaviour of the regressors as $n \to \infty$. It is most common to assume that:

$$\lim_{n\to\infty} (n^{-1}X'X) = Q,$$

where Q is some non-singular matrix. Since the variance of $\hat{\beta}$ may be written as $V(\hat{\beta}) = \sigma^2 n^{-1}(n^{-1}X'X)^{-1}$, in this case:

$$\lim_{n\to\infty} V(\hat{\beta}) = 0.Q^{-1} = 0.$$

The condition $\lim(n^{-1}X'X) = Q$ is sufficient for consistency but is not necessary. To interpret this condition, note that the typical element of $n^{-1}X'X$ is given by $\sum_{t=1}^{n} X_{ti}X_{tj} / n$ (where X_{ti} is the tth observation of the ith variable). Hence the condition that $\lim(n^{-1}X'X) = Q$ is equivalent to requiring that the second moments of all regressors have a finite limit and form a non-singular matrix. One immediate example in which this condition fails is when the data matrix contains a time trend; however, it may then be shown that the matrix $(X'X)^{-1}$ has a zero limit which is itself sufficient to demonstrate the consistency of $\hat{\beta}$. In other cases when variables have a stochastic trend it may not be possible to demonstrate consistency, and specific cases require specific analysis.

The OLS residuals may be written as:

$$\hat{e} = Y - X\hat{\beta} = X(\beta - \hat{\beta}) + \varepsilon$$

and if $\hat{\beta}$ is consistent then $\text{plim}(\beta - \hat{\beta}) = 0$; hence $\text{plim}(\hat{e} - \varepsilon) = 0$ and so the limiting distribution of the residuals is that of the errors: $\hat{e} \xrightarrow{D} \varepsilon$. By the central limit theorem of Khinchine (a weak law of large numbers), $E(\varepsilon_t^2) = \sigma^2$ implies that $\text{plim}(\varepsilon'\varepsilon/n) = \sigma^2$. Now the OLS estimator of the variance, s^2, is given by $\hat{e}'\hat{e}/(n-k)$ whose limiting behaviour, since $\hat{e} \xrightarrow{D} \varepsilon$, is given by $\varepsilon'\varepsilon/n$; hence $\text{plim}(s^2) = \text{plim}(\varepsilon'\varepsilon/n) = \sigma^2$. Thus s^2 is a consistent estimator of σ^2.

The limiting distribution of $\hat{\beta}$ given that the second moments of X all have finite limits and form a non-singular matrix and that the errors are independently and identically distributed, may be shown by noting that, in this case:

$$n^{-½}X'\varepsilon \xrightarrow{D} \eta \sim MVN(0, \sigma^2 Q).$$

This result is an application of the Lindeberg–Feller central limit theorem (see **Central limit theorems**) whose conditions are satisfied in this case. Given this result:

$$\hat{\beta} = \beta + (X'X)^{-1}X'\varepsilon \Rightarrow \sqrt{n}.(\hat{\beta} - \beta) = (n^{-1}X'X)^{-1}n^{-½}X'\varepsilon$$

but $\lim(n^{-1}X'X) = Q$ and $n^{-½}X'\varepsilon \xrightarrow{D} \eta \sim MVN(0, \sigma^2 Q)$; hence, by Cramer's Theorem:

$$\sqrt{n}.(\hat{\beta} - \beta) \xrightarrow{D} Q^{-1}\eta \sim MVN(0, \sigma^2 Q^{-1}QQ^{-1}) = MVN(0, \sigma^2 Q^{-1}).$$

In a large sample, then, one may write:

$$(\hat{\beta} - \beta) \text{ is approximately distributed as } MVN(0, \sigma^2 n^{-1}Q^{-1})$$

or:

$$\hat{\beta} \text{ is approximately distributed as } MVN(\beta, \sigma^2 n^{-1}Q^{-1}).$$

Since Q^{-1} is defined as the limit of $(n^{-1}X'X)^{-1}$, an approximate finite sample representation of $n^{-1}Q^{-1}$ is simply $(X'X)^{-1}$. Hence, in large samples:

$$\hat{\beta} \text{ is approximately distributed as } MVN(\beta, \sigma^2(X'X)^{-1}).$$

The assumptions required for this approximation to hold are that the sample second moments of X have finite limits and form a non-singular matrix and that the errors are identically and independently distributed with zero mean and finite variance; if any of these conditions fails, the results are not necessarily valid. In particular, if the errors do not have finite first and second moments (i.e. if the mean and variance of the errors are not both finite) the results do not necessarily hold.

As a further relaxation of the familiar OLS assumptions, suppose now that X is a matrix of random regressors. If X and the error term, ε, are strongly independent all the elements of X are independent of all the elements of ε and in this special case the estimator $\hat{\beta}$ retains its unbiasedness:

$$E(\hat{\beta}) = \beta + E[(X'X)^{-1}X'\varepsilon]$$

and since the expectation of the product of independent random variables is the product of expectations:

$$E(\hat{\beta}) = \beta + E[(X'X)^{-1}X']E(\varepsilon)]$$

and so $E(\hat{\beta}) = \beta$ (since $E(\varepsilon) = 0$). Further analysis of this model is then best undertaken using the familiar results all of which are then expressed as conditional on the observed X.

Suppose that X is random but not strongly independent of ε. The consistency of $\hat{\beta}$ may be examined as below:

$$\text{plim}\hat{\beta} = \beta + \text{plim}[(n^{-1}X'X)^{-1}]\text{plim}(n^{-1}X'\varepsilon).$$

If the regressors, in the limit, form a finite non-singular moment matrix, Q, then:

$$\text{plim}(\hat{\beta}) = \beta + Q^{-1}\text{plim}(n^{-1}X'\varepsilon)$$

and the consistency of $\hat{\beta}$ is assured if $\text{plim}(n^{-1}X'\varepsilon) = 0$. The jth element of this vector is given by: $\sum_{t=1}^{n} X_{ti}\varepsilon_t / n$; since ε has a zero mean, this may be interpreted as the covariance between the jth regressor and the error term. If all such terms tend to zero as the sample size gets large, as $n \to \infty$, this is described as a situation in which all regressors are uncorrelated, in the limit, of the error. Hence, if the regressors are, in the limit, uncorrelated with the error term the ordinary least squares estimator is consistent. Attempts to derive the large sample distributional behaviour of $\hat{\beta}$ when X is random are not amenable to general results but may be facilitated if it is assumed that in the case of random X the above result:

$$n^{-\frac{1}{2}}X'\varepsilon \xrightarrow{D} \eta \sim MVN(0, \sigma^2 Q)$$

still holds. If this remains true when X represents a set of regressors, at least some of which are stochastic, and $\text{plim}(n^{-1}X'X) = Q$, then the distributional analysis above holds and:

$$\sqrt{n}.(\hat{\beta} - \beta) \xrightarrow{D} Q^{-1}\eta \sim MVN(0, \sigma^2 Q^{-1})$$

in which case large sample test statistics may be constructed. However, if this result is not valid the particular model must then be analysed as a special case. A most useful, if surprising, result in the regression model is that in the case of stochastic regressors the ratio $(\hat{\beta}_i - \beta_i)/s\sqrt{v_{ii}}$, where $\hat{\beta}_i$ is a slope parameter estimator and s^2v_{ii} is its estimated variance, has the t_{n-k} distribution, whether the regressors are all fixed, all stochastic or some combination, so long as the errors are independently and identically normally distributed.

Further reading
For discussion of the use of the various concepts of convergence see, for example, Greenberg and Webster (1983); for applications of the Lindeberg–Feller central limit theorem in econometrics see, especially, Schmidt (1976) and White (1984).

Outliers

An outlier is an observation that is substantially different from the rest of the observations, and is an observation which has usually been generated by unique factors. A data set may, of course, contain more than one outlier. Since outliers are usually the result of unique factors not incorporated in the model, the estimation of a relationship from data which include outliers will be misleading unless some adjustment is made for their presence. The presence of outliers may be detected by analysing the residuals from the OLS regression, and outliers will appear as observations associated with unusually large residuals. However, the ordinary least squares method minimizes the sum of squared residuals and the method seeks to minimize the number of large residuals in estimating the parameters; hence an outlier in the population will not necessarily be reflected by an outlier in the residuals. Outliers in the data will distort the fitted regression plane to minimize their occurrence, and this is precisely the source of concern: outliers exert an undue influence on the estimation process and need to be identified and, in some way, accounted for in subsequent inference.

A significant diagnostic test statistic which rejects the hypothesis of normally distributed errors (see **Normality test**), can be interpreted as an indication of outliers, since the larger is the proportion of large residuals the less likely is the null hypothesis of normality. A significant Jarque–Bera statistic, followed by a plot of the residuals, may provide the relevant information.

If a data set is found to contain outliers then a common response is to delete those particular observations and re-estimate the equation. There are two specific objections to this proposal: first, the OLS residuals are not homoscedastic and in consequence outliers in the residuals may not necessarily reflect population outliers and, second, the importance of outliers should be measured not by the size of the residuals but rather by their influence on the estimates and on all subsequent tests. The above proposal does not constitute an attempt to assess their importance in this sense. A response to the heteroscedasticity in the fitted residuals is to examine standardized residuals: the OLS residual standardized by its standard error.

In order to identify outliers in the data set used to estimate the regression $Y = X\beta + \varepsilon$ the so-called hat matrix, H, is of particular importance:

$$H = X(X'X)^{-1}X'.$$

HY is equal to the ordinary least squares fitted values and the OLS residuals are given by $\hat{e} = Y - HY = MY$ where M is the idempotent matrix $I - X(X'X)^{-1}X'$. The variance matrix of the residuals is given by $V(\hat{e}) = \sigma^2 M = \sigma^2(I - H)$, and so the standardized residuals are calculated as:

$$\hat{e}_i/[s(1 - h_{ii})^{1/2}],$$

where h_{ii} is the ith diagonal element of H and s^2 is the OLS estimator of σ^2. The hat matrix provides a measure of 'leverage' since the larger is h_{ii} the smaller is the variance of the OLS residual and the larger is the standardized residual. Hence a large value of h_{ii} is an indicator that observation i is a potential outlier.

Another indicator of outliers may be obtained by considering the influence of the ith observations by running the regression of Y on X having deleted that observation. Let $Y_{(\neg i)}$ and $X_{(\neg i)}$ denote the regressand and the matrix of regressors having deleted the ith row of each so that, in the absence of the ith observations, the estimate $\hat{\beta}_{(\neg i)}$ is obtained where:

$$\hat{\beta}_{(\neg i)} = (X'_{(\neg i)}X_{(\neg i)})^{-1}X'_{(\neg i)}Y_{(\neg i)}.$$

The (normalized) difference between $\hat{\beta}$ and $\hat{\beta}_{(\neg i)}$, known as DFBETA, provides a measure of the influence of the ith observations on the estimated coefficients. Further, if the ith row of X is denoted by the $1\times k$ vector x'_i, the omitted observation, Y_i, is then predicted by $x'_i\hat{\beta}_{(\neg i)}$ and a large prediction error is a further indication that Y_i may be an outlier. The normalized prediction error is known as the Studentized residual, and may be denoted by $\tilde{e}_i$. This predicted value may be compared with that from the full regression given by $x'_i\hat{\beta}$, and if the difference is scaled by $h_{ii}s_{(\neg i)}$, where $s^2_{(\neg i)}$ is the estimated regression variance having dropped the ith observations, the measure is known as $DFFITS_i$. It may be shown that:

$$DFFITS_i = [h_{ii}/(1 - h_{ii})]^{1/2}\tilde{e}_i.$$

One simple way to construct the predicted value of Y_i, given by $x'_i\hat{\beta}_{(\neg i)}$, is to use a dummy variable. Consider running the following regression:

$$Y = X\delta + D\gamma + \varepsilon$$

where Y and X incorporate all available T observations, and D is a $T\times 1$ dummy variable; denote the first $T - 1$ observations on the regressand and regressors by $Y_{(T-1)}$ and $X_{(T-1)}$ respectively, and those for the final, T^{th} observation, by Y_T and X'_T respectively. The dummy variable takes the value zero for all observations, except the last for which it takes the value unity. Hence this model may be written as:

$$\begin{bmatrix} Y_{(T-1)} \\ Y_T \end{bmatrix} = \begin{bmatrix} X_{(T-1)} & 0 \\ X'_T & 1 \end{bmatrix} \begin{bmatrix} \delta \\ \gamma \end{bmatrix} + \begin{bmatrix} \varepsilon_{(T-1)} \\ \varepsilon_T \end{bmatrix}$$

If the stacked dependent variable is denoted by Y, the matrix of regressors is denoted by Z, the stacked coefficient vector by θ, and the error term by ε, this regression may be written as $Y = Z\theta + \varepsilon$. By OLS, the normal equations are given by $(Z'Z)\hat{\theta} = Z'Y$, which may be written out in full as:

$$[X'_{(T-1)}X_{(T-1)} + X_T X'_T]\hat{\delta} + X_T\hat{\gamma} = X'_{(T-1)}Y_{(T-1)} + X_T Y_T$$

and
$$X_T'\hat{\delta} + \hat{\gamma} = Y_T.$$

Hence: $\hat{\gamma} = Y_T - X_T'\hat{\delta}$ and $\hat{\delta} = [X'_{(T-1)}X_{(T-1)}]^{-1}X'_{(T-1)}Y_{(T-1)}$.

Thus, $\hat{\delta}$ is given by OLS estimator of the coefficient from the regression of $Y_{(T-1)}$ on $X_{(T-1)}$, that is, using only the first T – 1 observations, having effectively deleted the Tth observation, and so $\hat{\delta} = \hat{\beta}_{(\neg T)}$. Therefore, the coefficient on the dummy is seen as precisely equal to the forecast error, that is $\hat{\gamma}$ equals the observed value of Y for the last period (Y_T) less that predicted from the model using only the first T – 1 observations, $X'_T\hat{\delta}$. Moreover, the reported standard error on the coefficient on the dummy is the standard error of the forecast error, and this then represents a very simple way of computing what is, otherwise, a burdensome calculation. The t-statistic on the dummy coefficient is then equivalent to the Studentized residual and provides a test that the Tth observation is 'consistent' with the original model and is, hence, a test that Y_T is not an outlier. This may be generalized to a set of potential outliers, as is described in **Chow test**. If all T observations are tested by reference to their Studentized residuals, the appropriate size of each individual test is then $(1/T)\alpha/2$.

This approach to testing for outliers has appeal, but in any such analysis an observation deemed worthy on this basis of special treatment should not be so treated merely on the mechanical outcome of any such tests. The identification of an outlier by such tests is a prompt for further research: are there any identifiable special factors which might have generated the observation as an outlier? If there are, then special treatment is justifiable. If the dummy variable approach is used it is to be noted that the Tth residual is given by:

$$\hat{e}_T = Y_T - X'_T\hat{\delta} - \hat{\gamma} \equiv 0$$

and so one form of special treatment is to include a dummy variable so as to force the corresponding residual to zero and effectively ignore the outlier in the estimation of the model. This is, of course, equivalent to dropping the observation on the outlier. In this analysis the demonstration of the use of the dummy variable for the Tth observation is without any loss of generality and the dummy could have been used for the jth observation with exactly the same conclusions. Moreover, any observation-specific dummy, D_j, which is defined by $D_j = 1$ for observation j and is otherwise zero, has the effect of ensuring that in the OLS regression including D_j the jth residual is identically zero, and any number of such dummies may be included (subject to the retention of sufficient degrees of freedom). Observation-specific dummies, then, generate a particularly simple way of accommodating outliers, and t-tests of their parameter estimates provide statistical tests of the extent of the difference between those observations and the relationship which is estimated by ignoring those observations.

In cross-section data the recognition of an outlier may lead the investigator to the identification of some unique factors relating to that specific case, and in time-series data the recognition of an outlier may lead the investigator to identify some special circumstances at that particular point in time. However, if no such special factors are identifiable then dropping the variable would appear to be *ad hoc* and, in consequence, lacking justification and problematic.

If the presence of outliers is deemed to be evidence of non-normal errors, then an alternative estimation technique to OLS may be used, and details of other estimation techniques are described in **Robust estimation**.

Further reading

Belsey *et al.* (1980) provides an excellent discussion of outliers, presents statistics by which to measure the influence of observations, and discusses how to respond to the presence of outliers.

Panel data and variance components models

Panel data are data which relate to a number of specific economic agents over a period of time; in the analysis of such data the variance components model has proved most useful. Suppose data are available for n economic agents (individuals or firms, for example) over T time periods. For ease of exposition it will be assumed that there are T observations per agent, and no missing observations; the case when there are identical numbers of observations per cross-section unit is described as balanced, whereas if there are unequal numbers of observations the model is unbalanced. The dependent variable, Y_{it}, is to be explained by some regressor, X_{it}; Y_{it} is the observation on the variable Y for agent i at time t, and might be a measure, for example, of the output of firm i, while X_{it} is the observed 'explanatory' variable which might be a measure of the labour input utilized by firm i at time t. For exposition only one regressor will be used, but the model generalizes to many explanatory variables with ease. The model which relates the variables is given by:

$$Y_{it} = \alpha_i + \beta_i X_{it} + \varepsilon_{it} \qquad i = 1, 2, \ldots, n \quad t = 1, 2, \ldots, T.$$

This general model proposes that the relationship, as described by the parameters α_i and β_i is unique to each cross-section unit but is constant over time for each such unit. Such a model is further analysed in **Pooling data**.

In the fixed effect variance-components model the slopes are treated as identical over all cross-section units (so that $\beta_i = \beta$, all i) but the intercepts, α_i, are treated as random variables, not fixed constants. This model, via the device of random α_i terms, captures unobservable individual specific explanations; in this sense, the error term ε_{it} may be seen as capturing general ignorance of the process while α_i capture ignorance specific to the behaviour of agent i.

The random variables α_i are each assumed to be zero mean, are mutually independent, homoscedastic and independent of the errors, ε_{it}. The errors are also assumed each to be zero mean, mutually independent and homoscedastic:

$$E(\alpha_i) = 0, \qquad \text{all i}$$

$$\mathrm{Cov}(\alpha_i, \alpha_j) = \sigma_\alpha^2, \qquad \text{if i = j}$$

$$= 0 \qquad \text{otherwise.}$$

$$\mathrm{Cov}(\alpha_i, \varepsilon_{it}) = 0, \qquad \text{for all i, j and t.}$$

$$E(\varepsilon_{it}) = 0, \qquad \text{all i and t.}$$

$$\mathrm{Cov}(\varepsilon_{it}, \varepsilon_{js}) = \sigma_\varepsilon^2 \qquad \text{if i = j and t = s.}$$

$$= 0 \qquad \text{otherwise}$$

Since the α_i are random, this model may then be written as:

$$Y_{it} = \beta_i X_{it} + \nu_{it} \qquad i = 1, 2, \ldots, n$$
$$t = 1, 2, \ldots, T$$

where ν_{it} is the composite error given by $\alpha_i + \varepsilon_{it}$; ν_{it} has a zero mean, is homoscedastic, and for composite errors relating to different cross-section units there is a zero covariance, but for composite errors relating to the same cross-section unit at different points in time the covariance is not zero:

$$E(\nu_{it}) = 0, \quad \text{all i and t.}$$

$$\begin{aligned} Cov(\nu_{it}, \nu_{js}) &= Cov[(\alpha_i + \varepsilon_{it}), (\alpha_j + \varepsilon_{js})] \\ &= \sigma_\alpha^2 + \sigma_\varepsilon^2 \qquad \text{if i = j and t = s;} \\ &= \sigma_\alpha^2 \qquad \text{if i = j and t} \neq \text{s;} \\ &= 0 \qquad \text{if i} \neq \text{j, all t and s.} \end{aligned}$$

This correlation amongst the ν_{it} means that ordinary least squares will result in inefficient estimators, and a generalized least squares approach is required. Define the following sums of squares:

$$T_{yy} = \sum_{i=1}^{n}\sum_{t=1}^{T}(Y_{it} - \overline{Y})^2$$

where $\overline{Y}$ is the overall sample mean of Y_{it}. Then:

$$T_{yy} = \sum_{i=1}^{n}\sum_{t=1}^{T}\left[(Y_{it} - \overline{Y}_i) + (\overline{Y}_i - \overline{Y})\right]^2$$

where $\overline{Y}_i$ is the sample mean of Y_{it} for agent i. Hence:

$$T_{yy} = \sum_{i=1}^{n}\sum_{t=1}^{T}(Y_{it} - \overline{Y}_i)^2 + \sum_{i=1}^{n}\sum_{t=1}^{T}(\overline{Y}_i - \overline{Y})^2 + 2\sum_{i=1}^{n}\sum_{t=1}^{T}(Y_{it} - \overline{Y}_i)(\overline{Y}_i - \overline{Y}).$$

The cross-product term is zero, since it may be written as $\Sigma_{i=1}^{n}(\overline{Y}_i - \overline{Y})\Sigma_{t=1}^{T}(Y_{it} - \overline{Y}_i)$ and $\Sigma_{t=1}^{T}(Y_{it} - \overline{Y}_i) = 0$ by definition. Hence:

$$T_{yy} = \sum_{i=1}^{n}\sum_{t=1}^{T}(Y_{it} - \overline{Y}_i)^2 + \sum_{i=1}^{n}\sum_{t=1}^{T}(\overline{Y}_i - \overline{Y})^2.$$

Now $\Sigma_{t=1}^{T}(Y_{it} - \overline{Y}_i)^2$ is the total variation of Y within the class of the $i^{\underline{th}}$ agent, and so the first term is the total variation within all n classes; the second term measures variation between classes, as measured by the differences between the class means and the overall mean. Denoting the two terms by W_{yy} and B_{yy}:

$$T_{yy} = W_{yy} + B_{yy}.$$

Similarly,

$$T_{xx} = W_{xx} + B_{xx} \quad \text{and} \quad T_{xy} = W_{xy} + B_{xy}.$$

If OLS were applied to all n×T observations, imposing a common slope and intercept for all cases, the resulting estimator is:

$$\hat{\beta} = T_{xy}/T_{xx} = (W_{xy} + B_{xy})/(W_{xx} + B_{xx}).$$

Applying generalized least squares, the estimator may be shown to be:

$$\hat{\beta}_{GLS} = (W_{xy} + \theta B_{xy})/(W_{xx} + \theta B_{xx})$$

where $\theta = \sigma_{\varepsilon}^2/(T\sigma_{\alpha}^2 + \sigma_{\varepsilon}^2)$; and if the regression were run by OLS imposing a common slope for all cases but allowing different intercepts for each case, the resulting slope estimator would be:

$$\tilde{\beta} = W_{xy}/W_{xx}.$$

This last estimator is known as the least-squares-with-dummy-variable (LSDV) estimator (since it may be computed by running the regression of Y on X using all the available data and including a set of n dummy variables, D_j, where $D_j = 1$ if observation j relates to agent j and is zero otherwise).

The OLS and LSDV estimators are special cases of the variance-components GLS estimator, with $\theta = 1$ and $\theta = 0$ respectively. One argument against the LSDV estimator is that it is expensive in terms of degrees of freedom, but this objection is valid only in small samples and when T is large, $\theta \to 0$ and the GLS estimator $\to$ the LSDV estimator. When the GLS estimator is used it is to be noted that θ is not known and must be estimated; this may be accomplished in several ways but empirical evidence suggests that the method of estimating θ has little bearing on the final estimates of β. One common route is to estimate the model by LSDV (which imposes a fixed β but allows α_i to be case-specific) and from the n estimates $\tilde{\alpha}_i$ compute the estimate of σ_{α}^2 as the sample variance of the estimates; σ_{ε}^2 is estimated by the estimated residual variance of this regression. Both estimators are biased and inconsistent, but the feasible GLS estimator which results from the implied estimate of θ outperforms, by the mean square error criterion, estimators from other techniques.

The variance-component model has the advantage over the LSDV model in that in the latter the fixed, but different, effects (α_i) must each be estimated, whereas the variance-component model seeks only to estimate the mean and variance of the α_i distribution. It also has the advantage of consistency of treatment: just as ε_{it} represents general ignorance, and is modelled as a random variable, so α_i represents case-specific ignorance and is modelled as a random variable. However, if one were interested in only one cross-section then it would be proper to treat the intercept as fixed, but in pooling the data the more interesting questions concern the population from which the data are drawn, in which case it is better to model the intercepts as random effects.

Another argument for using the random effects model occurs when there are time-invariant regressors. Suppose the cross-section units are individuals, and the model seeks to analyse individuals' earnings, using as one explanatory variable their educational background:

$$Y_{it} = \alpha_i + \beta_i X_{it} + \gamma_i Z_i + \varepsilon_{it} \qquad i = 1, 2, \ldots, n$$

$$t = 1, 2, \ldots, T.$$

In this model, were α_i fixed it would be impossible to estimate γ_i: since Z_i is time invariant the separate case-specific constant term and the effect of Z_i cannot be distinguished. The random effects model allows estimation γ by avoiding the multicollinearity between a fixed α_i and Z_i through the device of α_i as a random variable.

The variance components model may be extended to accommodate dynamics, and this is done in one of two ways: the error term may be allowed to be autocorrelated (known as error dynamics), or lagged dependent variables may be included as regressors (known as equation dynamics). Finally, the model may be extended to allow the unobservable case-specific random effects to be correlated with the regressors which may be estimated by instrumental variables.

The variance component model has, for example, found application in studies of firms' output/input relationship over time (where the random effect may be due to differing, unobservable, managerial inputs) and in studies of individuals' earnings over time (where the random effect may be due to innate, unobservable, differences or to non-measurable background differences). It has advantages over the imposition of common, fixed intercepts and slopes since it is a more general model; and as suggested above, it has advantages over the imposition of fixed, common slope and fixed, but case-specific, intercepts. It is, however, a quite different model from the varying parameter models in which the slopes (the β_i) are treated as random variables; in the variance-component model the case-specific effects are random (due to ignorance of unobservable effects), and the objective is to construct an efficient estimator of the common response coefficient, β. In random coefficient models (see **Random coefficient model** and **Varying parameter models**) the objective is to estimate the distribution from which the (assumed) β_i terms are drawn.

Further reading

See, especially, Balestra and Nerlove (1966), Maddala (1971), Maddala and Mount (1973) and Wallace and Hussain (1969).

Partial correlation

In the general linear model including a constant term the coefficient of determination, R^2, measures the proportion of variation in Y explained by the regressors. If the model is described by the equation:

$$Y_i = \alpha + \beta_1 X_{i1} + \beta_2 X_{i2} + \ldots + \beta_k X_{ik} + \varepsilon_i$$

then are k + 1 regressors (a constant term and k other explanatory variables) and R^2 may be described as the square of the correlation between the observed Y values and the fitted Y values, that is as $R^2 = [\mathrm{Cor}(Y_i, \hat{Y}_i)]^2$. To denote the fact that R^2 measures the variation explained by all k regressors, this may be written as $R^2_{Y\bullet 12\ldots k}$. In order to determine the incremental contribution to the explained variation of Y by X_j, having already included in the regression all other regressors, X_i where $i \neq j$, it is necessary to define the partial correlation coefficient and its square, the partial coefficient of determination.

The partial coefficients of determination of the first order are denoted by $r^2_{Yi.i\neq j}$, $i = 1, 2, \ldots k$; $r^2_{Yi.i\neq j}$ measures the proportion of the variation in Y explained by X_i having already accounted for that variation in Y explained by the other regressors, X_j, $j \neq i$. There are k such partial coefficients of determination. To illustrate the partial correlation, consider the simple regression of Y on two regressors only:

$$Y_i = \alpha + \beta_1 X_{i1} + \beta_2 X_{i2} + \varepsilon_i .$$

Then the residual sum of squares from this regression may be written as RSS $= (1 - R^2) \sum_{i=1}^{n} y_i^2$ where $\sum_{i=1}^{n} y_i^2$ is the sum of squared deviations of the dependent variable about its sample mean. If X_2 were deleted from the regression, the residual sum of squares from the restricted regression of Y on X_1 alone is equal to $RSS_1 = (1 - r^2_{Y1})\sum_{i=1}^{n} y_i^2$, where r^2_{Y1} is the squared correlation between Y and X_1. The partial coefficient of determination, $r^2_{Y2.1}$ is defined as the proportion of the unexplained variation of Y remaining after accounting for the influence of X_1 which may then be explained by X_2:

$$\begin{aligned} r^2_{Y2.1} &= (RSS_1 - RSS)/RSS_1 = 1 - (RSS/RSS_1) \\ &= 1 - (1 - R^2)/(1 - r^2_{Y1}) \end{aligned}$$

hence:

$$(1 - R^2) = (1 - r^2_{Y1})(1 - r^2_{Y2.1}).$$

With three explanatory variables this becomes:

$$(1 - R^2) = (1 - r^2_{Y1})(1 - r^2_{Y2.1})(1 - r^2_{Y3.12}).$$

In the general linear regression $Y = X\beta + \varepsilon$, assumed to include a constant term, the partial coefficients of determination $r^2_{Yi.i\neq j}$ measure the incremental contribution of X_i to the explanation of variation in Y, having taken into account the contribution of the other k − 1 regressors, X_j, $j \neq i$. They are 'purged' correlation coefficients, having purged both Y and X_i of the influence of the other regressors. $r^2_{Yi.i\neq j}$ may be computed with relative ease. Denote the residual vector and the residual sum of squares which result from regressing Y on the constant and the regressors X_j, $j \neq i$, by $\hat{e}(i)$ and RSS(i) respectively; denote by $\hat{u}$ the residuals obtained by regressing X_i on the constant and the other regressors X_j, $j \neq i$. Then $\hat{e}(i)$ is the variation left in Y having taken account of the other regressors, and $\hat{u}$ is the variation left in X_i having taken account of the other regressors. The definition of $r^2_{Yi.i\neq j}$ means that it is proportion of RSS(i) which is explained by $\hat{u}$. This may be computed as the coefficient of determination from the auxiliary regression of $\hat{e}(i)$ on $\hat{u}$. Now the Frisch–Waugh theorem indicates that the coefficient on $\hat{u}$ in this regression is identical to the coefficient on X_i from the multiple regression of Y on the constant and all the original regressors (including X_i). Further, the estimated variance of the coefficient in this auxiliary regression is identical to that from the full regression of Y on all the original regressors. Hence the t-statistic reported from the auxiliary regression of $\hat{e}(i)$ on $\hat{u}$ is identical to that of the coefficient on X_i from the full regression.

In a simple regression of a dependent variable on one regressor the square of the t-statistic is identical to the F-statistic which tests the significance of the R^2, and is related to the coefficient of determination by the expression:

$$t^2 = (n - 1)R^2/(1 - R^2);$$

this may be rearranged to yield:

$$R^2 = t^2/[t^2 + (n - 1)].$$

The expression n − 1 is simply the degrees of freedom in such a simple regression; in the particular case here, the dependent variable is $\hat{e}(i)$ which has only n − (k − 1) degrees of freedom to begin with (where there are a total of k regressors in the original regression, including the constant term) and so the R^2 statistic from the regression of $\hat{e}(i)$ on $\hat{u}$ is given by the expression:

$$\begin{aligned} R^2 &= \hat{t}_i^2/[\hat{t}_i^2 + (n - (k - 1) - 1)] \\ &= \hat{t}_i^2/(\hat{t}_i^2 + n - k). \end{aligned}$$

But this R^2 statistic is identical to the required partial correlation coefficient, and so:

$$r^2_{Yi.i\neq j} = \hat{t}_i^2/(\hat{t}_i^2 + n - k)$$

where $\hat{t}_i$ is the t-ratio on the parameter in the regression of $\hat{e}(i)$ on $\hat{u}$ which is, by the Frisch–Waugh theorem, identical to the t-ratio attached to X_i in the multiple regression of Y on all k regressors. Hence, to compute the partial coefficient of determination, or the squared partial correlation coefficient, the simple expression to use is to run the multiple regression including all k regressors and compute $\hat{t}_i$, the t-statistic on X_i; then use the simple expression:

$$r^2_{Yi.i\neq j} = \hat{t}_i^2/(\hat{t}_i^2 + n - k).$$

Partial correlation coefficients may be used to detect the presence of multicollinearity: if the overall R^2 from a regression is large, but the individual partial correlations are low then this means that although the regressors, taken together, account for a large part of the variation in Y, the partial contributions of the regressors taken individually is low. One way to explain this phenomenon is that there is common variation in the regressors which is reflected in the high overall R^2 but which, since it is of course ignored in computing the partial contributions, accounts for the relatively small partial correlations.

Further reading
The basis of this analysis is that of Frisch and Waugh (1933).

Pooling data

Suppose that data on m units are available and that there are T_i observations on the mth unit; the observations per unit may be observations over time, but need not be – the m units could be cross-section units (m firms, for example) and each comprise observations over time, or the m units could represent m sub-classes of a large cross-section, where the units have been constructed by reference to some criterion (a large cross-section of households might be divided into m classes by reference to income, or region, for example). This data provides a pool of N available observations (where $N = \sum_{i=1}^{m} T_i$). Suppose the economic model takes the form of a set of m equations, of which the ith may be written as:

$$Y_i = X_i\beta + \varepsilon_i$$

where Y_i is a $T_i \times 1$ vector of observations on the ith equation's regressand, X_i is a $T_i \times k$ matrix of observations on k regressors and ε_i is the $T_i \times 1$ vector of the ith equation's disturbances. This statement of the model assumes that the response vector, β, is identical within each unit, and is identical across all units. This is, of course, a testable assumption, and before the data are pooled to estimate a common response vector it is necessary to test the hypothesis of commonality. If the more general model is written as:

$$Y_i = X_i\beta_i + \varepsilon_i \quad i = 1, 2, \ldots, m$$

then a direct way to test the hypothesis $\beta_i = \beta$ for all i is to run the m equations separately to obtain the m residual sums of squares, RSS_i, and then run one single equation of Y on X using all N observations (and thereby constraining the response vector to be constant). The sum of squared residuals from the latter constrained equation is the restricted residual sum of squares (RRSS) which may be compared with the unrestricted residual sum of squares obtained as URSS = $\sum_{i=1}^{m} RSS_i$. A test of commonality is then a simple F-test: under H_o: $\beta_i = \beta$ for all i

$$\frac{[RRSS - URSS]/m}{URSS/(N-k)} \sim F_{m,N-k}.$$

This test of commonality is based on the assumption that the error term per equation is homoscedastic and non-autocorrelated and that all the errors have a common variance. This is very restrictive.

If commonality of the response vectors is to be tested then the m equations may be analysed more efficiently by the application of Zellner's seemingly unrelated regression technique which can accommodate cross-equation heteroscedasticity, cross-equation covariances and also autocorrelation within each equation. The unconstrained parameters of the most general model may be estimated efficiently by feasible generalized least squares, and the model may then be re-estimated subject to a set of simple linear constraints which impose commonality of either the entire response vector (or just the slope components of that vector to allow each equation to have a different constant term). If those restrictions are data acceptable then pooling is appropriate.

Suppose that the commonality of the entire response vector is acceptable; then the full set of m equations may be written as:

$$\begin{bmatrix} Y_1 \\ Y_2 \\ \vdots \\ \vdots \\ Y_m \end{bmatrix} = \begin{bmatrix} X_1 & 0 & \cdots & \cdots & 0 \\ 0 & X_2 & & & \vdots \\ \vdots & & \ddots & & \vdots \\ \vdots & & & \ddots & \vdots \\ 0 & \cdots & \cdots & \cdots & X_m \end{bmatrix} \beta + \begin{bmatrix} \varepsilon_1 \\ \varepsilon_2 \\ \vdots \\ \vdots \\ \varepsilon_m \end{bmatrix}$$

which may be compactly written as:

$$Y = X\beta + \varepsilon.$$

If has been assumed, for purposes of exposition only, that each equation has exactly the same number of regressors; suppose also that there are identical numbers of observations for each equation, T_i = T for all i. Both these assumptions may easily be relaxed.

The variance–covariance matrix of ε is given by:

$$\Sigma = V(\varepsilon) = E\begin{bmatrix} \varepsilon_1\varepsilon_1' & \varepsilon_1\varepsilon_2' & \dots & \dots & \varepsilon_1\varepsilon_m' \\ \varepsilon_2\varepsilon_1' & \varepsilon_2\varepsilon_2' & & & \varepsilon_2\varepsilon_m' \\ \vdots & & \ddots & & \vdots \\ \vdots & & & \ddots & \vdots \\ \varepsilon_m\varepsilon_1' & \dots & \dots & \dots & \varepsilon_m\varepsilon_m' \end{bmatrix}$$

Each 'element' of this matrix, $E(\varepsilon_i\varepsilon_j')$, is itself a matrix; $E(\varepsilon_i\varepsilon_j')$ is a T×T matrix which, if i = j is the variance–covariance matrix of the ith equation's error term and if $i \neq j$ is the covariance matrix relating errors attached to different equations (which, if the observations per unit are over time represents the contemporaneous and lagged covariances between errors relating to different units). Suppose that each equation has a homoscedastic and non-autocorrelated error term and suppose further that the error terms relating to different equations are wholly uncorrelated; then:

$$E(\varepsilon_i\varepsilon_j') = \sigma_i^2 I \qquad \text{if } i = j \text{ and is otherwise zero.}$$

This model is then described as the groupwise heteroscedastic model. Defining Σ_c as $\text{diag}\{\sigma_1^2 \dots \sigma_m^2\}$, then $\Sigma = \Sigma_c \otimes I$ where $\otimes$ is the Kronecker product and the model of all m equations may be estimated by GLS so that:

$$\hat{\beta} = (X'\Sigma^{-1}X)^{-1}X'\Sigma^{-1}Y = (X'(\Sigma_c^{-1} \otimes I)X)^{-1}X'(\Sigma_c^{-1} \otimes I)Y$$

(since $(\Sigma_c \otimes I)^{-1} = \Sigma_c^{-1} \otimes I$).

This generalized least squares estimation cannot, typically, be performed, since the matrix Σ_c is not known. The feasible GLS estimator is constructed by using an estimator of Σ_c formed by applying OLS to the m equations separately, and then using the residuals from these regressions to construct the estimates of σ_i^2. If the residuals from the ith equation are denoted by $\hat{e}_i$, then a consistent estimator of σ_i^2 is given by $s_i^2 = \hat{e}_i'\hat{e}_i/T$.

If σ_i^2 is constant across all cross-section units the groupwise heteroscedasticity disappears and the model may then be estimated by applying OLS to the pooled set of equations. It is of interest, then, to test the hypothesis that $\sigma_i^2 = \sigma^2$ for all i.

In order to test for cross-sectional (groupwise) heteroscedasticity the unrestricted estimates, s_i^2, may be compared with the restricted variance estimator assuming $\sigma_i^2 = \sigma^2$ for all i. The restricted estimator of σ^2 is obtained by running the pooled model $Y = X\beta + \varepsilon$ and computing the error variance from this regression. From the analysis of seemingly unrelated equations, the lack of cross-equation correlation means that the estimates of the ith equation's parameters, $\hat{\beta}_i$, are identical to those obtained from running the m equation separately, and so the pooled model yields an estimator of the common error variance given by $s^2 = (1/m)\sum_{i=1}^{m} s_i^2$ from which the Lagrange multiplier test may be constructed:

$$LM = (T/2)\sum_{i=1}^{m}[(s_i^2/s^2) - 1]^2$$

which, under the null hypothesis $\sigma_i^2 = \sigma^2$, has a χ_m^2 distribution, and since, under the null hypothesis s_i^2/s^2 is approximately unity, rejection of the null hypothesis takes place in the right-hand tail. This hypothesis could also be examined by a likelihood ratio test, or a Wald test (and the latter may be modified to allow for non-normality of the errors).

If this hypothesis is rejected then the efficient estimator of β is obtained from the pooled data by applying feasible generalized least squares to take account if the groupwise heteroscedasticity. This model may also be extended to accommodate autocorrelation within each cross-section over time, and also to non-zero covariances across the equations' error terms. The latter is dealt with easily (in principle) by positing that Σ_c is a full matrix with typical element σ_{ij}, so that Σ_c may be estimated by running the m equations individually and then constructing the estimate of the σ_{ij} by $\hat{e}_i'\hat{e}_j/T$. The hypothesis that Σ_c is a diagonal matrix may be tested by the Lagrange multiplier statistic given in **Seemingly unrelated regression equations**.

If the T observations are over time, then autocorrelation, of small orders, may also be accommodated by first estimating each individual cross-section equation and effecting the appropriate transformation on each of those equations to generate a non-autocorrelated error. If, for example, each cross-section equation is characterized by first order autocorrelation then each of those equations should be transformed by the Prais–Winsten transformation appropriate to it (described in **Autocorrelation – estimation methods**) and then the set of transformed equations satisfies the assumption of no autocorrelation and the possibility of groupwise heteroscedasticity and cross-equation correlation may be dealt with as above. If the time-series is short, autocorrelation may be dealt with by imposing a common autocorrelation parameter on all the equations.

The pooling of data provides a larger data set from which to estimate the common response rate, β. Pooling is a commonly used technique which, by using all the available data, provides consistent and asymptotically efficient estimates of the common parameters. If the parameters are not common across cross-sections then Zellner's seemingly unrelated regression equations approach is appropriate.

Further reading

This model is a relatively straightforward way to deal with panel, or longitudinal, data; for applications see, for example, Grunfeld and Griliches (1960) and Boot and de Witt (1960). Other methods for analysing such data are discussed in **Panel data and variance components models, Varying parameter models** and **Seemingly unrelated regression equations**.

Power function

In testing a null hypothesis against an alternative, a test Γ defines a rejection region R so that if the computed test statistic T lies in R then H_o is rejected. The power function of Γ, denoted by π, defines the probability of rejecting the null hypothesis whatever the true state of the world:

$$\pi = \Pr\{T \in R\}.$$

In hypothesis testing it is common for the null hypothesis to be stated as a simple hypothesis, in which case the test statistic, T, has a well-defined distribution when the null hypothesis is true. Hypothesis testing then proceeds by setting the size of the test (the significance level, denoted by α) which defines R (see **Hypothesis testing**). To take a simple example, if the null and alternative hypotheses are H_o: $\lambda = 0$ and H_1: $\lambda \neq 0$ the power function indicates, for all values of λ, the probability that H_o is rejected. For this two-sided test, $\pi(\lambda)$ when plotted against λ has the typical shape:

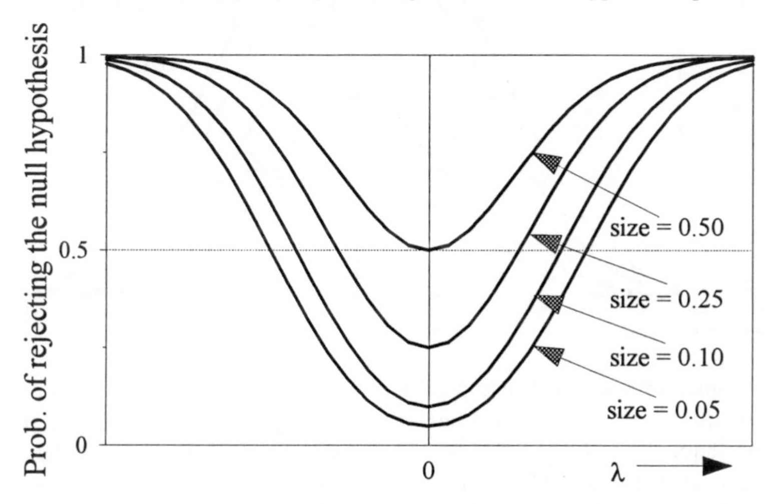

Four different functions are drawn; each corresponds to a different rejection region, R. The smaller is R the lower is the probability of rejecting H_0, whatever the true value of λ. The size of the test is formally defined by:

$$\text{size of the test} = \text{Sup}\ \pi(\lambda | H_o \text{ is true});$$

and in this simple example:

$$\text{size of the test} = \pi(\lambda = 0).$$

The literature typically eschews the label 'size of the test' for the more familiar expression 'Type I error', denoted by α, which is defined by:

$$\alpha = \Pr\{H_o \text{ is rejected} | H_o \text{ is true}\}.$$

α is the probability of making a Type I error, but one is also interested in the probability of making a Type II error, namely that of not rejecting H_o when it is false. In this example, when H_o is false λ takes some non-zero value, and so the probability of not-rejecting H_o when it is false depends critically on 'how false' H_o actually is. Given the definition of the power function:

$$\Pr\{H_o \text{ is not rejected}|\lambda\} = \Pr\{T \notin R|\lambda\} = 1 - \pi(\lambda).$$

This probability, known as the operating characteristic of the test, may also be plotted against λ, and four such curves, which correspond exactly with the power curves, are shown below.

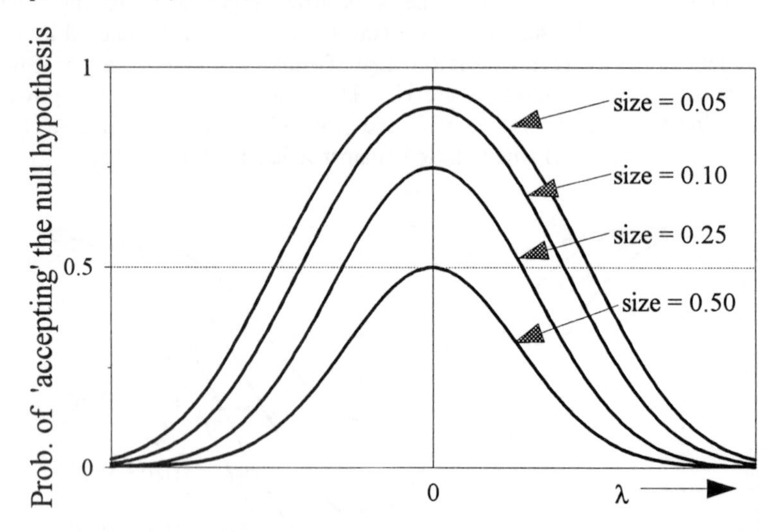

To illustrate the construction of a power function, consider the familiar regression model, $Y = X\beta + \varepsilon$, and a test of H_o $\beta_i = 0$. Let the estimator of β_i be denoted by $\hat{\beta}_i$, and the estimated variance of $\hat{\beta}_i$ be denoted by v_i^2. Then, under the usual assumptions of the model, the variable $t = \hat{\beta}_i/v_i \sim t_{n-k}$ under the truth of the hypothesis that $\beta_i = 0$. The test, Γ, is defined thus:

> If $|t| \geq t^*_{n-k}$ then H_o is rejected; t^*_{n-k} is chosen to be such that $\Pr\{|t| \geq t^*_{n-k} | H_o \text{ is true}\} = \alpha$, where α is chosen, prior to the test, as some small number, typically 0.05.

To examine the power of this test, note that:

$$t = \hat{\beta}_i/v_i = [\hat{\beta}_i/\sigma_i]/[v_i/\sigma_i]$$

where σ_i is the true sampling variance of $\hat{\beta}_i$. The numerator of the right-hand side of the expression is distributed as a normal variate with mean β_i/σ_i and unit variance; the square of the denominator is distributed as an augmented χ^2 variate with n – k degrees of freedom. Thus:

$$t = \hat{\beta}_i / v_i \sim t_{n-k}(\lambda)$$

where λ is the non-centrality parameter, given by β_i/σ_i; when the null hypothesis is true λ is zero, and then $t \sim t_{n-k}$, that is as a central t-variate. When the null hypothesis is false, t is distributed as a non-central t-variate with non-centrality parameter λ. For large degrees of freedom the distribution of t approximates well to the standard normal under the truth of the null hypothesis, and to a non-central, unit variance, normal distribution under the alternative. It is then possible to use standard normal tables to examine the probability of failing to reject the null hypothesis when it is false, for given values of λ.

The procedure of testing, following Neyman–Pearson, consists of fixing the Type I error of the test at some small number (typically one of 0.10, 0.05 or 0.01) and choosing the most powerful of the available tests. Considering the power and operating curves which correspond to a 5% Type I error (the lowest of the power curves and the highest of the operating curves), it can be seen that the probability of not rejecting the null when it is false has a supremum of 95%; this occurs when the null hypothesis is 'only just false', that is when λ is arbitrarily close to zero. As the falsity of the null hypothesis becomes more marked, as λ diverges from zero, the probability of making the error of not rejecting H_0 diminishes to zero.

It is worth noting that as the sample size increases, the standard error of $\hat{\beta}_i$, σ_i, decreases necessarily (since $\hat{\beta}_i$ is a consistent estimator) and so, for a given value of β_i, for a given falsity of H_o, λ is an increasing function of the sample size; thus as the sample size increases the fixed α value guarantees that the probability of 'accepting' the (false) null falls monotonically to zero; effectively, then, the benefits of more information (that is, a larger sample) translate only in the dimension of a smaller Type II error (the power approaches 1 as the sample size increases). This observation has led to the proposal that the size of the test (the α value) should itself be a function of the sample size in order that the benefits of more information which accrue from the larger sample be shared between the probabilities of the two sorts of error.

In this simple example it is possible to examine the power function analytically. Not all tests have power functions which are amenable to analysis, and in such cases the functions may be approximated by the device of constructing repeated samples of data via Monte Carlo methods.

Further reading

The concept of the power of a test is useful in determining the appropriate size of a test, since there is a trade-off between size and power; it is also useful in examining the properties of a test (described in **Hypothesis testing**) and is a necessary element in discussing the properties of pre-test estimators (see **Pre-test estimators**).

Pre-test estimators

In the estimation of economic relationships, and the ultimate testing of such relationships, economic theory is usually silent on some important questions of model specification. Economic theory will identify some candidate explanatory variables in a regression equation, but the full set of regressors will not be known with certainty (neither prior to nor after an empirical analysis); equally, the functional form will not (typically) be specified by theory, nor, in a model using time-series data, will the dynamic processes be specified *a priori*. In the absence of *a priori* information the available data are often used both in the determination of the model's specification and in the estimation and testing of the relationship. *A priori* information (from economic theory or from previous empirical studies, for example) may be incorporated in estimation, and such information will result in more efficient estimators, whether or not that information is correct. However, if the information is incorrect then the gain in efficiency is obtained only at the cost of biased estimators. Some information used in a model's specification does not arise as *a priori* information, but is derived from the data set used subsequently for estimation purposes

In order to avoid the use of incorrect information it is common for investigators first to test the validity of the information and to incorporate it in the estimation process only if its validity is not denied. In this way the choice of the estimator is determined, in part, by the outcome of a previous test. In general terms, if a particular estimator is adopted by reference to the outcome of a previous test then that estimator is described as a pre-test estimator. For example, suppose the validity of some restrictions is tested and the unrestricted estimator is used if those restrictions are not accepted and the restricted estimator is used if the restriction are not rejected. In this case the final estimator is defined by reference to the outcome of the test of the restrictions and is a classic example of a pre-test estimator. One of the commonest cases arises in the regression of a variable, Y, on regressors which may be partitioned into two sets of variables X and Z (where X and Z are data matrices containing k_1 and k_2 variables respectively):

$$Y = X\beta + Z\gamma + \varepsilon.$$

The investigator is uncertain about the role of the k_2 variables in Z and proceeds to test the hypothesis $\gamma = 0$ by an F-test; if this hypothesis is rejected the unrestricted estimators, $\hat{\beta}$ and $\hat{\gamma}$, become the basis for further analysis and if it is not rejected then the restricted estimator, $\tilde{\beta}$ (having constrained γ, and hence $\hat{\gamma}$, to zero), becomes the basis for further analysis. There are two case to consider:

1. The variables in Z are irrelevant. In this case the F-test will reject the (true) null hypothesis $\gamma = 0$ on $100\alpha\%$ of all occasions, where α is the

chosen size of the F-test. Thus, on such occasions, Z will be incorrectly retained in the regression and the unrestricted estimators of β and γ will be inefficient, in general, but no bias will be generated. In the rare case when Z and X are orthogonal in the sample the unrestricted estimators would not be inefficient (indeed, there would then be a spurious superficial gain in efficiency as the effect of including the irrelevant variables of Z is to reduce the estimated regression variance). With probability $(1 - \alpha)$ the F-test correctly indicates that γ is zero and the restricted estimator then has the desirable unbiased and efficient characteristics. Overall, however, the pre-test estimator in this case does not have the desirable properties of unbiasedness and efficiency since efficiency is denied on the $100\alpha\%$ of occasions when $\gamma = 0$ is rejected.

2. Some of the variables in Z are relevant. In this case the parameter γ is non-zero, and the F-test will correctly reject the false null hypothesis $\gamma = 0$ with probability $\pi(\gamma)$, where π is the power of the test which is, of course, a function of the unknown parameter. As γ approaches zero, $\pi(\gamma)$ approaches α, and as γ diverges from zero $\pi(\gamma)$ increases monotonically (and is unity in the limit). Hence, with probability given by $\pi(\gamma)$ the unrestricted estimator will be correctly employed, but on $100[1 - \pi(\gamma)]\%$ of all occasions a Type II error will be committed, the null hypothesis will not be rejected and the restricted estimator will be incorrectly adopted. The restricted estimator from the regression of Y on X alone will be biased (except in the rare case when X and Z are orthogonal in the sample), and the variance estimators from the restricted regression will always be biased. Overall, as in case 1 above, the pre-test estimator does not exhibit the desirable properties of unbiasedness and efficiency since the estimator is biased when the incorrect model is adopted.

The failure of the pre-test estimator always to exhibit desirable properties is known as pre-test bias. The important and immediate implication is that the traditional method of hypothesis testing relies upon the estimator having those desirable properties and, in the case of a pre-test estimator, the investigator faces an uncertain situation: is the pre-test estimator based on a correctly specified model or not? This uncertainty cannot be removed and complicates hypothesis testing.

Pre-test bias is often ignored by applied workers, on the grounds that in the absence of a pre-test the restrictions which would have been tested are either incorporated or not by assumption. It is better, it is argued, to replace such an assumption by the outcome of a statistical test and accept pre-test bias as the cost of this procedure. This amounts to presuming that the pre-test yields the correct outcome more often that does an untested assumption. A formal approach may be utilized which examines the mean square error properties of the pre-test estimator.

Consider the relatively simple case of running the regression of Y on k regressors, denoted by X, subject to r exact linear restrictions $R\beta - r = 0$. Let the restricted least squares estimator be denoted by $\tilde{\beta}$, and the unrestricted estimator be denoted by $\hat{\beta}$. The pre-test estimator, β^*_λ is then $\tilde{\beta}$ if the F-test of the restrictions fails to reject the restrictions, and $\hat{\beta}$ if the F-test rejects the restrictions (see **Conditional omitted variable estimator**). If the variance of the regression error is σ^2, and $\delta = R\beta - r$, the 'falsity' of the restrictions may be measured by the scalar quantity λ where $\lambda = \delta'\delta/2\sigma^2$; λ is known as the hypothesis error. When the null hypothesis is true, $\lambda = 0$ and is otherwise positive. The mean square error of the vector β^* may be measured by the sum of the mean squared errors of the individual components of β^*, and this is the measure of the risk of the estimator. The unrestricted estimator is always unbiased, and has constant variance, whatever the value of δ; since mean square error is the sum of the squared bias and the variance, $\hat{\beta}$ has constant risk for all values of δ. The restricted estimator, $\tilde{\beta}$, is always more efficient than $\hat{\beta}$, whatever the status of the restrictions, but is only unbiased when the restrictions are true (when $\delta = \lambda = 0$); when the restriction are false $\tilde{\beta}$ is biased, and the bias increases with the 'falsity' of the restrictions. Hence the risk of $\tilde{\beta}$ is less than of $\hat{\beta}$ when $\lambda = 0$, but increases monotonically with λ. The pre-test estimator, β^*, is defined by:

$$\beta^* = \begin{cases} \hat{\beta} & \text{if } F \geq F_{r,n-k;1-\alpha} \\ \tilde{\beta} & \text{if } F < F_{r,n-k;1-\alpha} \end{cases}$$

where F is the computed test statistic for the restrictions, and $F_{r,n-k;1-\alpha}$ is the critical value from the F distribution with r and n−k degrees of freedom defined by $\Pr\{F \geq F_{r,n-k;1-\alpha} | F \sim F_{r,n-k}\} = \alpha$.

When $\lambda = 0$, the restrictions are true and so β^* is unbiased (because both $\hat{\beta}$ and $\tilde{\beta}$ are each unbiased when $\lambda = 0$); the null hypothesis, being true, will be rejected with probability α, the size of the test, and so with probability α β^* will equal $\hat{\beta}$ and will equal $\tilde{\beta}$ with probability $1 - \alpha$. Being a combination of the restricted and unrestricted estimators, both of which are here unbiased, its variance lies between the variances of its components. The variance of β^* is a weighted average of the variances of its components, and the weights clearly depend upon the probability of rejecting the (true) null hypothesis at the pre-test stage. The greater the probability of rejecting the null hypothesis when it is true, the greater is the size of the F-test, the greater is the probability of employing the unrestricted, less efficient, estimator. The larger is α, then, the greater is the risk of β^* when $\lambda = 0$.

When the restrictions are false, $\lambda \neq 0$ and then $\tilde{\beta}$ is biased; the F-test will (correctly) reject the null hypothesis with a probability which may be written as $\pi(\lambda)$ and (incorrectly) fail to reject it with probability $1 - \pi(\lambda)$; $\pi(\lambda)$ depends critically upon the size of test, α. The greater is α the greater is

$\pi(\lambda)$ for all values of λ; hence the larger is α the greater is $\pi(\lambda)$ and the smaller is the probability of the F-test incorrectly failing to reject the null hypothesis. β^* will thus be equated with the restricted estimator with probability $1 - \pi(\lambda)$ and will, then, be biased. The greater is the 'falsity' of the restrictions the more will this bias contribute to the risk, and for some values of λ the bias will be so great that the risk of β^* exceeds that of the unrestricted estimator; however, for some small values of λ, the bias will be so small as to ensure that the risk of the pre-test estimator is less than that of the $\hat{\beta}$. Since $\pi(\lambda) \to 1$ as $\lambda \to \infty$ for all values of α, the greater is λ, the more likely is the F-test to reject the (false) restrictions. The risk of the pre-test estimator may be sketched against λ as below:

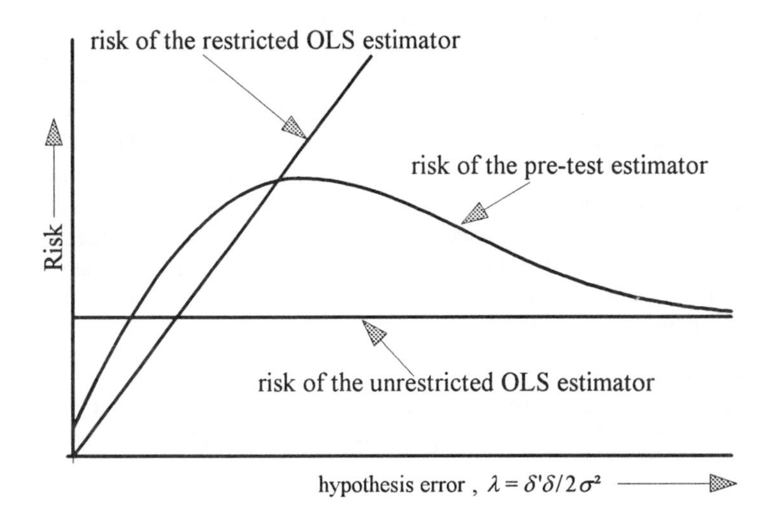

No one estimator dominates the others – no one estimator has least risk for all values of λ; in applied work, since the value of δ, and hence that of λ, is unknown, the choice amongst the estimators is not unambiguous. This is an uncomfortable position.

An estimator which is chosen by reference to the outcome of an earlier test is a pre-test estimator; the classic examples concern those occasions in which the model's specification is developed in response to the outcome of a pre-test (such as excluding a set of regressors if the associated F-statistic is insignificant); however, pre-testing also occurs when the outcome of a test does not lead to a change in the model. For example, if a regression is run and diagnostic tests are then employed the regression will be interpreted in standard fashion if the equation passes all the diagnostic tests. Since the inference of the model's parameters is then conditional upon no Type II errors having been committed at the diagnostic stage, the outcome has the characteristics of a pre-test: if the diagnostic tests lead to no change in the model's specification (since it appears to be adequate) then the later inferences are only strictly valid if a Type II error has not been committed.

Whenever the results of a pre-test inform the model's specification the sampling properties of the resulting estimators are not known. Confidence in the final model (and therefore in inferences made from its estimation) is, of course, enhanced when that model has been subjected to, and has passed, a battery of specification tests of its adequacy, but all subsequent inference is subject to *caveats* which arise from pre-testing.

Pre-testing abounds and is not always acknowledged; pre-testing should lead to lower levels of confidence in the chosen model than the nominal levels used in the formal tests, since pre-testing introduces a source of uncertainty which is not formally captured by those later tests. Pre-testing includes tests of assumptions (as in diagnostic tests) and tests of restrictions on parameters and it is far better to use assumptions and restrictions which are supported by the data, than to ignore or impose them without test (for then the investigator would have no evidence at all upon which to defend the chosen model). The outcome of pre-test processes should, however, be evaluated in the light of economic theory and not be applied in mechanical fashion. Ultimately, pre-testing should have the effect of tempering over-confident conclusions via recognition (albeit informal) of the uncertainty introduced by the pre-test.

Further reading

Pre-test estimators are examined in great detail in Judge and Bock (1978 and 1983) and also in Feldstein (1973). See also Wallace and Ashar (1972) and Wallace (1977).

Principal components

Principal components analysis (PCA) is a statistical device by which a set of k correlated variables is transformed into a set of k uncorrelated variables; the uncorrelated variables are called the principal components, and each principal component is a linear combination of the original variables. The technique originates in analyses when the variables arise 'on an equal footing' but has also been used in regression analysis when there is one 'dependent variable' and a set of 'independent variables'. Specifically, in the regression context PCA has been suggested as a response to multicollinear data.

One objective of principal components analysis is to examine whether a small number of components accounts for most of the variation in the original data; if this is the case then the analysis may be reduced to a set of variables smaller than the original k and the dimensionality of the problem may be correspondingly reduced. If the original variables are denoted by X_1, X_2, . . ., X_k and some of the variables are highly correlated then at least one variable has a similar information content to that of a linear combination of other variables and, in this sense, some of the variables could be discarded with little loss of information. The principal components, denoted P_j, j = 1, 2, . . , k, are constructed in a descending order of importance, so that P_1 has the maximum possible variation, P_2 has the maximum possible variation subject to the condition that it is uncorrelated with P_1 and so on. In this way if the original data are highly correlated it is likely that the first few principal components will account for so much of the original variation that a small number of the $\{P_i\}$ can be effectively used in subsequent analysis, rather than the full set of components. Of course, if the $\{X_i\}$ variables are (almost) uncorrelated then the number of required principal components will be very close to k (and the components will be very like the original variables, but ordered by variance) and no reduction in the dimensionality of the problem will be achieved. PCA is a mathematical device which makes no assumptions about the generation process underlying the original data.

Denoting the tth observation (t = 1, 2, . . ., n) of the ith original variable (i = 1, 2, . . , k) by X_{ti}, and the tth observation of the jth principal component by P_{tj} (t = 1, 2, . . , n; j = 1, 2, . . . , k) one can construct the P_j vectors as linear combinations of the original data:

$$P_{tj} = \Sigma_{i=1}^{n} X_{ti} \alpha_{ij}$$

where the α_{ij} are constants. Denoting by α_j the k×1 vector $[\alpha_{1j} \ \alpha_{2j} \ . . . \ \alpha_{kj}]'$, this combination may be written compactly as:

$$P_j = X\alpha_j$$

and hence in obvious notation as: $P = X\alpha$. These equations contain arbitrary scale factors and the normalization condition $\alpha_j' \alpha_j = \Sigma_{i=1}^{n} \alpha_{ij}^2 = 1$ for all j = 1, . . , k is imposed.

P_1 is the first principal component, P_2 is the second principal component and so on; the variation in P_j is measured by the sum of squares $P_j'P_j$, and so the construction of the principal components may be written as a constrained optimization problem:

$$\text{Max } P_1'P_1 = \alpha_1'X'X\alpha_1 \qquad \text{subject to } \alpha_1'\alpha_1 = 1.$$

Defining a Lagrange multiplier by λ_1, the Lagrangian is:

$$\alpha_1'X'X\alpha_1 - \lambda_1(\alpha_1'\alpha_1 - 1)$$

which yields the first order conditions: $(X'X - \lambda_1 I)\alpha_1 = 0$.

Hence λ_1 is an eigenvalue of X'X and α_1 is the corresponding eigenvector (see **Matrix algebra**). In order to maximize the variation of P_1, λ_1 is chosen as the largest eigenvalue of X'X, λ_2 is then chosen as the next largest eigenvalue, and so on. In the absence of perfect collinearity amongst the $\{X_i\}$ variables, X'X is a positive definite matrix which ensures that all the eigenvalues are strictly positive. Defining the orthogonal matrix of normalized eigenvectors, α, by $[\alpha_1 \ldots \alpha_k]$, the principal components are then defined by $P = X\alpha$.

The variation in the ith original variable is given by $X_i'X_i$ and so the total variation in the set of original variables is $\sum_{i=1}^{n} X_i'X_i = Tr\{X'X\}$. However, since α is orthogonal, $\alpha\alpha' = I$, and the total variation may be written as $Tr\{X'X\alpha\alpha'\}$; using the rules of trace, $Tr\{X'X\alpha\alpha'\} = Tr\{\alpha'X'X\alpha\} = Tr\{P'P\}$. Hence the total variation of the original data is exactly that of the principal components. Moreover, $P'P = \Lambda = diag\{\lambda_1 \ldots \lambda_k\}$, and so the ratio $\lambda_i/(\sum_{j=1}^{k}\lambda_j)$ represents the proportion of the total variation accounted for by the jth principal component. If some of the eigenvalues are small the corresponding principal component accounts for a small proportion of the total variation and it may, then, be possible to discard those components associated with small eigenvalues.

This discussion requires that one can attach meaning to 'the total variation of the original data' and that one can interpret a quantity such as $\sum_{i=1}^{n} X_i'X_i$; if the original data are measured in different units it is difficult to interpret such a quantity and it is therefore common, prior to a principal components analysis, to transform the original data into standardized units such that the X'X matrix in transformed variables is the sample correlation matrix. The advantage of this prior transformation is that the correlation matrix is invariant to the units of the original data; of course, the eigenvalues, eigenvectors and principal components which are derived from the transformed data will, in general, be different from those derived from the raw data.

PCA has several objectives; it may be used to 'get a feel' for the data, it may suggest the presence of underlying linear relationships within the data and it may facilitate reducing the dimensionality of the data set. Use of PCA as a route to understanding the correlation structure within the data is only one way to gain an appreciation of any correlation structures and may not be the best way; one of the prime objections to PCA is that the resulting components, the linear combinations of the original variables, are not amenable to interpretation (or, worse, are easily misinterpreted). As a means of reducing the dimensionality of the problem, however, PCA has found application in regression analysis when the regressors are collinear.

Principal components may be seen as simply a data transformation; take the standard regression model: $Y = X\beta + \varepsilon$ and, as above, let $\Lambda = diag(\lambda_1 \ldots \lambda_k\}$ be the matrix of eigenvalues of X'X and let α be the corresponding orthogonal matrix of eigenvectors. Then one may write $X\beta$ as $X\alpha\alpha'\beta = P\theta$ where $P = X\alpha$ and $\theta = \alpha'\beta$; thus the models:

$$Y = X\beta + \varepsilon \quad \text{and} \quad Y = P\theta + \varepsilon$$

are equivalent. The second form of the model is known as the principal components regression. If X is of full rank then, by ordinary least squares, $\hat{\theta} = (P'P)^{-1}P'Y = (\alpha'X'X\alpha)^{-1}\alpha'X'Y = \alpha'(X'X)^{-1}\alpha\alpha'X'Y = \alpha'\hat{\beta}$ (since $\alpha\alpha' = I$ and where $\hat{\beta}$ is the OLS estimator of β). If X were not of full rank this does not hold; in the case of 'near perfect collinearity' some eigenvalues of X'X will be very small and it may then be deemed appropriate to utilize only the first, say, r (r < k) principal components rather than the full set of k components. Suppose that the last k − r eigenvalues are deemed to be so small that the proportion of the total variation accounted for by the corresponding principal components is itself so small as may be discarded without significant loss of information. In this way the dimensionality of the problem may be reduced. Let α_r denote the matrix of the first r eigenvectors and so $P_r = X\alpha_r$ is the matrix of the first r principal components. Then consider:

$$Y = P_r\theta_r + v \quad \text{so that} \quad \hat{\theta}_r = (P_r'P_r)^{-1}P_r'Y$$

It may be shown that

$$\hat{\theta}_r = P_r'\hat{\beta}.$$

The advantage of principal components in this example is that the r components retain most of the information contained in the variation of the original variables but are a set of mutually uncorrelated variables which facilitate the efficient (although biased) estimation of θ_r. $\hat{\theta}_r$ is a vector of r linear combinations of the ordinary least squares estimates, and there is nothing to guarantee that those linear combinations have any economic meaning; it is not, typically, obvious how one might interpret any one of the r regressors of P_r nor is there, in the absence of a statistical model which describes the generation of the original regressors, an obvious rule by which to declare some eigenvalues so small as to be discarded in subsequent analysis. Moreover, this has not provided an estimation method for the original k parameters, β; the principal components model, having discarded some components, generates the r-dimensional estimator $\hat{\theta}_r$. However:

$$\hat{Y} = P_r\hat{\theta}_r = X\alpha_r\hat{\theta}_r = X\alpha_r\alpha_r'\hat{\beta} = X\hat{\beta}_p$$

where $\hat{\beta}_p = \alpha_r\alpha_r'\hat{\beta}$ and is described as the principal components estimator. It is to be noted that $\alpha_r\alpha_r'$ is not an identity matrix when X is of full rank. Clearly, since $\hat{\beta}$ is unbiased, $\hat{\beta}_p$ is then biased, but is more efficient. Notwithstanding the efficiency gain, the estimator is biased, and if the principal components defy interpretation then so does the principal components estimator defy interpretation.

This approach to reducing the dimensionality of a regression which is characterized by multicollinearity has been suggested, though it appears to be of very limited practical use. Not only is it difficult, if not impossible, to give a meaning to a principal component, but the fact that the first component is that linear combination of regressors with greatest variance says nothing of its relationship to the dependent variable, Y. The technique may be seen to be of use in the rare cases when a small number of components accounts for almost all the variation of the regressors and when those components may be given economic meaning.

Further reading
Chatfield and Collins (1986) is a most useful source of material on principal components analysis, and also on other multivariate techniques. Fomby *et al.* (1978) discuss the principal components estimator as a special case of a restricted ordinary least squares estimator.

Prior information

Prior information (otherwise known as extraneous or *a priori* information) is to be contrasted with sample information; it is information known (with or without certainty) prior to the current sample of observations having been drawn from the material world. The typical sources of such information are economic theory, previous empirical studies or the presently available data set. Within the sampling theory approach to estimation and inference, only the information contained in the sample to hand is utilized; in many cases additional information is available and the issue is how to utilize it. Within econometric investigations, prior information may be used in one of two distinct ways: it may be incorporated into the estimation method in order to increase the efficiency of the estimators or the prior information may be treated as a composite hypothesis (exact or stochastic) which is tested by the sample information.

If used in the former way within an otherwise correctly specified model, prior information always increases the efficiency of estimators, whether or not the information is materially correct (though if it is materially false then bias will result). Both the Bayesian and the classical approach provide formal methods by which to incorporate prior information, the former through the use of Bayes Theorem and the latter through the techniques of restricted estimation and mixed estimation.

Prior information may be known with certainty or it may be stochastic. If it is known with certainty, then such information constitutes a set of exact restrictions (which may be equalities or inequalities, linear or non-linear) upon the parameters of the model in question. If the information takes the form of exact equality restrictions on the parameters then it may be incorporated formally into the estimation technique through the application of restricted least squares, for example. If the restrictions are non-linear, their incorporation is analytically more difficult and, typically, numerical non-linear routines must be used; also, when the information takes the form of linear or non-linear inequality restrictions, numerical solutions are typically required.

If the information is not known with certainty, but takes the form of a linear stochastic restriction on the slope parameters of a model, then it may be incorporated through the technique of mixed estimation, which is a relatively simple application of the generalized (Aitken) least squares method. Alternatively, the information may take the form of a prior density function on the model's parameters, in which case Bayes estimation is appropriate.

Not surprisingly, the properties of estimators which utilize both sample and non-sample information have properties which are, in part, dependent both upon the correctness of the theoretical model with which the non-sample information is combined, and upon the correctness of the non-sample information itself. The real issue is not whether or not to use such information, but how to use it. Several cases are of interest.

If the prior information is in the form of exact linear equality constraints on the slope parameters then, within the general linear model $Y = X\beta + \varepsilon$, the information is $R\beta = r$, and is known with certainty; there is no sampling variability in this information from one sample to another, and $R\beta = r$ comprises exact constraints on the sampling and estimation process. This may be formally incorporated in the estimation process by using restricted least squares which seeks to minimize the residual sum of squares subject to the restriction. Denoting the unrestricted OLS estimator of β by $\hat{\beta}$ and the restricted estimator by $\tilde{\beta}$, $\tilde{\beta}$ differs from $\hat{\beta}$ by a linear function of the difference vector $R\hat{\beta} - r$, i.e. the difference between $\hat{\beta}$ and $\tilde{\beta}$ is a simple function of the discrepancy between the sample information and the prior information. If the prior information is correct, then $\tilde{\beta}$ is the best linear unbiased estimator of β which also satisfies the non-sample information. However, if the information is incorrect, i.e. $R\beta - r = \delta$ and δ is non-zero, then $\tilde{\beta}$ is biased but is more efficient than $\hat{\beta}$, the unrestricted estimator. This leads to the familiar problem of choosing between two estimators, one of which is unbiased but which has a larger sampling variability than an alternative biased estimator. However, choosing that rule which is 'right on average' has little operational appeal once it acknowledged that economists act within a largely non-experimental field of enquiry in which the repeated experiment is not typically possible and, hence, one in which the concept of 'right on average' can be difficult to justify. What is required is a measure which allows a trade-off between bias and efficiency and the mean squared error criterion is one common approach (see **Restricted least squares**, **Pre-test estimators** and **Stein estimators**).

If the prior information is in the form of stochastic linear equality constraints on the slope parameters such as $R\beta = r - \eta$ where η is stochastic with a zero mean and known variance–covariance matrix. The information may arise from previous empirical studies which provide unbiased estimators of some components (or linear combinations) of the β vector (with their associated variances and covariances), or the information may arise in the form of inequalities which stipulate upper and lower bounds on particular coefficients (in which case the variance of would attach only low probability to $R\beta$ lying outside those bounds. Stochastic information of this form may be combined with the model $Y = X\beta + \varepsilon$ and estimated by generalized least squares. This case is described further in **Mixed estimation**.

If the prior information is in the form of linear inequality constraints on the slope parameters, then $R\beta \geq r$; there are many instances in which non-sample information dictates that some coefficients are, for example, non-negative, or lie within certain well-defined bounds. This case could be handled by treating the inequalities as a stochastic restriction which attaches very low probability to $R\beta < r$, but may also be reduced to a programming problem using the Kuhn–Tucker conditions (the classical Lagrangian techniques are not applicable). The numerical solution will require the use of an appropriate algorithm since analytic solutions do not exist to such problems, but the technology is readily available to solve inequality-constrained optimization problems. The resulting estimator, denoted by $\tilde{\beta}$, however, has sampling properties which are not easily examined.

The sampling properties may, however, be characterized by the following: $\tilde{\beta}$ is a combination of an unbiased estimator (resulting when the constraint is true) and a biased estimator (resulting when the constraint is untrue but has been imposed); as a result $\tilde{\beta}$ is biased. The variance of $\tilde{\beta}$ is, of course, less than that of the unconstrained estimator (the use of non-sample information, whether true or false, results in improved precision); however, the mean square error of $\tilde{\beta}$, relative to that of the unconstrained estimator, cannot be determined.

A common estimator in the presence of an inequality constraint such as $R\beta - r \geq 0$ is to estimate β from the unconstrained regression of Y on X to yield $\hat{\beta}$, and then use the pre-test estimator:

$$\beta^* = \hat{\beta} \qquad \text{if } R\hat{\beta} - r \geq 0$$

and

$$\beta^* = \tilde{\beta} \qquad \text{otherwise,}$$

where $\tilde{\beta}$ is the inequality constrained estimator. This can become complicated for the case of several parameters, but is easily applied to the simple case when one parameter is constrained to be non-negative, in which case the inequality constrained estimator is either the unconstrained estimate if it is non-negative or zero if the unconstrained estimate is negative.

Finally, the prior information may take the form of a prior density function on the parameters. An informative prior distribution is one which encapsulates information on the parameter in the form of its expected value and the precision of that prior belief. The resulting estimator will be a weighted average of the unconstrained estimate (the sample information) and the prior mean, where the weights are in inverse proportion to the precision associated with the information. If the sample precision is greater than that of the prior (the sampling variance of the estimators is small relative to their prior variances) then the sample information will be given greater weight, and *vice versa*. In consequence, if the belief held prior to the data analysis is strong, so that the prior distribution has a relatively small variance (reflecting a high degree of precision), the prior will tend to dominate the sample evidence. This is further discussed in **Bayesian theory** and **Bayesian estimation**.

The issue regarding prior information is not whether, but how, to use it; however, if the information is incorporated into the estimation process, without checking its validity with that particular data set, then the resulting estimates can be misleading. Clearly, if the prior information were to be rejected by the data it would be unwise to incorporate it into the estimation process (although the information may still be correct); on the other hand, if it is not rejected it may still be false but is almost certainly then to be incorporated. In all cases a pre-test estimator results, and this results in the usual difficulties of evaluating the sampling properties of such estimators. Finally, extraneous information may not always be relevant; for example, information from cross-section studies may not be readily incorporated into time-series analyses since the former is not necessarily an appropriate reflection of the adjustment processes inherent within time-series data.

Further reading

Stein (1956) and James and Stein (1961) discuss the use of nonlinear estimators in the presence of exact restrictions (see also **Stein estimators**). See Judge and Yancy (1981) on the use of inequality constraints and estimation in their presence.

Probability

There are many interpretations of the word probability; different interpretations derive from the axiomatic, frequentist and subjective approaches. Whatever approach is adopted, probabilities obey certain rules; what differs, from one approach to another, is the interpretation put upon probability. Probability, whatever is meant by that term, is the foundation of statistics; however, those foundations are controversial. The main controversy concerns the distinction between the so-called Bayesian methods and the sampling theory methods, but there are also subdivisions within each category which are of importance. At one level the distinction is that between objective and subjective concepts of probability.

From an axiomatic viewpoint, probability is a set function satisfying three axioms; the interpretation of the (non-controversial) axioms is dependent upon the particular understanding of probability held. If U is a universal, or reference set; a function P which assigns to every subset U a real number is a probability measure on U provided that three conditions are met:

1. for every subset A of U, $P(A) \geq 0$;
2. $P(U) = 1$;
3. if A and B are any two disjoint subsets of U, and their union is denoted by C, then $P(C) = P(A) + P(B)$.

These three axioms form no bone of contention, but objectivists and subjectivists hold quite distinct views about the interpretation of P.

Objective probability

The views of objectivists are best explained by reference to the idea of a repeated experiment (see **Random variables**); indeed, many of the ideas, as originally formulated, have their basis in games of chance and gambling. Consider the simple experiment of rolling a fair die, and confine attention to the six possible outcomes. To an objectivist the 'probability' of any one outcome is 1/6, and the reasoning is as follows:

> Since each outcome is equally likely, the probability of any one outcome is simply the ratio of the number of times that that outcome can occur to the total number of possible outcomes.

This statement has been adopted as a definition, and it has become known as the classical definition of probability. There is, however, a serious objection to this definition: if by 'equally likely' is meant 'equally probable' then there would appear to be a presupposition of a definition of probability in defining probability.

No doubt behind this simple conception is a frequentist interpretation. If the number of trials is denoted by n and the number of occurrences of the event A is denoted by m, then the frequentist view suggests that the probability of A, P(A), is given by the ratio m/n. Of course, as the number of trials increases, the ratio of m to n will change, and in order to avoid the undesirable result of the probability measure depending upon the number of trials, the frequency definition of probability is:

$$P(A) = \lim_{n \to \infty} (m/n).$$

Thus probability is defined as the limit of a relative frequency; this definition requires the limit to exist, and of course the limit (even if it exists) cannot be empirically determined. Clearly, this version of probability relies upon the concept of a repeated trial in which the conditions of the trial are held essentially constant across trials (i.e. the trials must constitute a random experiment).

However, examples abound, in everyday language, of 'probability-type' statements regarding events which are essentially or necessarily non-repeatable: the 'chance' of a particular horse winning a particular race, the 'chance' of Labour winning the next election, etc. Neither the classical approach nor the frequentist approach can provide non-trivial answers to such questions: the named events will either occur or they will not and there is no possibility of repeating the trial. A frequency may only be identified within the context of a well-defined class of experiments, and no such class exists in the examples given above: frequencies are identified with respect to classes of events, not a particular event. It may be said that a 'fair die' will exhibit a probability of 1/6 of showing a six, but what does this say about the outcome of any one *individual* roll of the die?

Regarding the probability of an individual event (whether or not as part of a repeated experimental framework), three distinct responses are possible:

1. probabilities are only defined for stochastic events which have not occurred; probability then does not apply to historical 'facts';
2. probabilities do not apply to individual events, but only to classes of events;
3. probabilities are defined for individual events, past and future, under specific conditions.

The first view requires the timing of the event to be known and thus, adopting this position, 'probability' is defined with reference to a specific information set held at time t, Ω_t, and events to which probability is attached are dated at time t + s, where s is strictly positive. The second view effectively denies the application of probability to individual events. The final view asserts that meaningful probability statements can only be made about some individual events; the circumstance under which this is possible requires that there are no recognizable subsets within the class. A recognizable subset exists when its frequency of occurrence is known to be different from that of the class as a whole. Most classical inferential procedures seem to adopt either the first or the second interpretation. Of the many possible reasons for this position, one of the more important is that the third view makes demands upon the investigator's personal information set: information regarding the presence (or otherwise) of recognizable subsets is required and this makes demands on a personal definition of probability. Thus, in order to make any meaningful statements about the 'probability' of a single event, both objective and frequentist probability have limited applicability: within those approaches it is only meaningful to speak of the probability of a class of events.

This denial of probability statements with respect to single events is particularly restrictive. For example, in a simple experiment of tossing a fair coin the 'probability' of a head, prior to the toss, is said to be a half; the traditional argument which substantiates this view is based upon either a (possibly circular) concept of what constitutes a 'fair coin' or relates to the class of events in which the long-run frequency of a head is asserted to be a half. However, a single toss results in either a head or a tail, and what, then, is to be understood by the probability attached to the outcome of a single toss? Moreover, suppose one were told that a fair coin had been tossed, but the outcome were not divulged; what is to be understood by the question: 'what is the probability that the coin, having been tossed, is a head?' (the issue here is that the event is now historic and is knowable yet unknown).

Social scientists often wish to make probability-type statements regarding single events which have occurred, and often wish to quantify ignorance regarding events which are essentially non-stochastic (such as the quantification of our ignorance regarding the size of a theoretical parameter which is deemed to be fixed). Moreover, the social scientist (amongst others) often deals with non-experimental data in a non-standardized and non-standardizable environment

Subjective probability

The view that probability is not a physical but a personal concept suggests that probability is a 'degree of confidence' which an individual associates with an uncertain event; clearly this probability measure will vary from one individual to another, with regard both to what events are 'uncertain' and to the degree of confidence held. This conceptualization of probability, therefore, places great weight upon the individual's personal information set: when an individual lacks perfect knowledge regarding an event, that event will be identified as uncertain, whereas to an individual who holds perfect knowledge that same event will be deemed certain. Similarly, for events deemed by any two individuals to be uncertain, the 'degree of confidence' will be determined by the information available to each and the method used to process that information. Thus, even if individuals hold identical, but imperfect, information sets regarding an event, they may process that information differently and thus hold different degrees of belief; equally, they may hold different information sets, use different methods of processing the information, and actually hold the same degree of belief.

To take an example from statistics, and one encountered frequently in economics, consider the construction and interpretation of a classical confidence interval: the $(1 - \alpha)\%$ confidence interval for some parameter θ is described, prior to data analysis, as the interval (A, B), where A and B are both functions of the data. From a particular sample this is computed to be (a, b) where a and b are the estimates of A and B and are non-random numbers. This is interpreted as follows: were the formula for A and B to be applied to each and every possible sample drawn randomly from the population, then $(1 - \alpha)\%$ of all intervals so constructed would contain the true parameter while $\alpha\%$ would not. However, the one sample to hand yields the interval (a, b) where a and b are each numbers not formulae (that is, a and b are estimates not estimators). Neither a nor b is a random number and, equally, θ is not random; the particular interval (a, b) either contains the unknown parameter or it does not. What probability interpretation may then be made? In the absence of any recognizable subsets, the response might be that the relevant probability is $(1 - \alpha)\%$, but this probability statement is now being made *ex post*, not *ex ante*; *ex ante* objective probability might be applied to such an individual event, but *ex post* there are no random variables to which objective probability might be attached. One answer, therefore, would appear to be that no objective probability statement applies after constructing a particular interval but one can, nevertheless, make intelligent statements using other forms of probability. This is examined further in **Confidence intervals** and **Confidence regions**. An important question regarding subjective probability which must be posed is this: in what sense are subjective probabilities (personal degrees of belief) interpretable as probabilities and how, if at all, are degrees of belief measurable? (See **Coherence principle**.)

One may take the view that all events (whether historical or otherwise) may have a 'degree of belief' attached to them. Such a view is a consequence of asserting, as an axiom, that given a body of knowledge (what has been referred to above as an information set) and given two uncertain events X and Y, then either X is deemed more likely than Y, or vice versa, or X and Y are deemed equally likely. This does not require any specific (cardinal) measurement of 'likelihood', but merely the ordering of the 'likelihood' of the events. From this ranking, it is then reasonable to ask under what conditions this leads to a probability measure, P, such that $P(X) > P(Y)$ if and only if X is deemed more likely than Y. Of the conditions necessary, the first is that the ranking order is transitive: if X_1 is more likely than X_2, and X_2 is more likely than X_3, . . and X_{n-1} is more likely than X_n, then X_1 is more likely than X_n.

Objective probability statements arise from a world in which material measurement of uncertainty is possible. However, this typically denies the attachment of probability to events which are not deemed random, denies the attachment of probability to events which have occurred and denies the attachment of probability to single events. Subjective probability may be seen to originate in a ranking of events by reference to an individual's assessment of their likelihood. If that subjective view is then translated into a numerical measure which obeys the axioms of a 'probability measure' those degrees of belief are transformed into real numbers, lying in the closed interval [0, 1]. Essentially, then, subjective degrees of belief, however stated, merely reflect a ranking whereas objective probability purports to have a material counterpart in an experimental framework. The use of subjective probability allows single events, in a non-repeatable environment, to be described according to their 'chance' of occurrence.

Importantly, the use of probability as a measure of a degree of belief allows any individual to hold a personal view of the probability of any event, and this, therefore, allows the use of probability language with respect to any event about which that individual is less than perfectly informed. If the individual's information set regarding some event, X, is not complete the individual does not know, with certainty, the outcome of event X. When viewed in this context the concepts and the calculus of probability may be utilized in the analysis of any event for which the individual has less than perfect information; specifically, this approach allows 'ignorance' to be modelled using the concept of a random variable. This provides, in part, a rationalization of the use of stochastic models of non-repeatable phenomena, and hence rationalizes the use of stochastic models using data drawn from a non-experimental world: an analysis of any phenomenon may proceed by using a less than perfect information set which specifies a stochastic model of the phenomenon in which the error term is deemed to behave as if it were a random variable and which may then be analysed using the probability calculus.

Further reading

For an introduction to the notion of probability, see, for example, Meyer (1971) and Mood, Graybill and Boes (1974); Leamer (1978) provides an excellent overview of alternative concepts of probability in the context of econometric investigation. See also Barnett (1973), Keynes (1921), Ramsey (1926), deFinetti (1937), Savage (1954) and Jeffreys (1967). See also **Bayesian theory**, **Coherence principle**, **Distribution theory**, **Error term**, and **Random variables**.

Proxy variables

A particular example of the errors in variables issue (see **Errors in variables**) is that of proxy variables, and occurs when the econometrician would like to include in the analysis a variable which is not observable and observations on a proxy variable are available. Amongst the commonest examples are models which seek to utilize variables such as an individual's characteristics as indicated by theoretical concepts, for example educational experience, intelligence, etc. In the specific example of educational experience, one might construct a dummy variable of years of schooling as a proxy. The question arises: is it better, in some sense, to use a proxy variable or omit the variable from analysis altogether? If a regression equation is specified so that:

$$Y_i = \alpha + \beta X_i + \varepsilon_i$$

and X_i is not observable, but there is a variable Z_i such that:

$$Z_i = X_i + \eta_i$$

then this may be seen as a classic errors in variables problem, in which the true regressor is a 'latent', inherently unobservable, variable. There may be no measurement error at all in the variable Z, but even an exactly known Z is but a proxy for the latent variable X.

If the regression model is specified in terms of many regressors, one of which is unobservable, and interest focuses on the parameters attached to the observable regressors, one might ask whether it is better to omit the unobservable variable's proxy altogether. Using ordinary least squares to estimate the 'complete' model with the proxy will lead to inconsistent estimators (see the argument in **Errors in variables**) and using ordinary least squares to estimate the reduced model without the proxy will lead to biased and inconsistent estimators due to the omission (see **Specification analysis**).

It may be shown that, even if the proxy is a very poor proxy (its measurement error has a high variance), the degree of inconsistency of the ordinary least squares estimator from the mis-specified model is worse than that from the full model including the proxy. However, there are no unambiguous results regarding the precision of the estimators, and so the balance of evidence would suggest that it is better to include proxy variables, however poor they are.

This result depends upon the treatment of the proxy variable as a case of errors in variables and not all proxies fall into this category. In a multiple regression model with one latent variable, X, it is possible that an available proxy, Z, is merely some variable which depends on X and the other regressors of the model; in this case it is not necessarily true that omitting the proxy leads to smaller asymptotic bias in the estimators of the other parameters. Further, if the unobservable latent variable is proxied by a dummy variable when the former is known in terms of ranges (for example, an individual's extent and type of education is used as a dummy variable to proxy their educational experience) the result which leads to the inclusion of the proxy does not necessarily hold. Moreover, the question of including the proxy cannot be answered unambiguously if the other regressors are measured with error. Definitive results in case of the proxy variables are not available unless the issue is treated as a particular example of errors-in-variables, and even then the results are asymptotic, and ambiguous with regard to precision.

Further reading

McCallum (1972) and Wickens (1972) consider the asymptotic bias issue relating to the inclusion of proxy variables, and Aigner (1974) analyses the problem incorporating the precision of the estimators. For extensions of Aigner's results, see Kinal and Lahiri (1983).

R^2

In the standard linear regression model $Y = X\beta + \varepsilon$ with a constant term the goodness of fit statistic, R^2, is defined as the squared correlation between the observed values of Y and the fitted values, $\hat{Y}$; R^2 is also known as the coefficient of multiple determination and the positive root, R, is also known as the multiple correlation coefficient. To examine this statistic, note that by including a constant term the average fitted residual is necessarily zero. This follows from noting that the regression normal equations may be written as:

$$X'\hat{e} = 0$$

where $\hat{e}$ is the vector of regression residuals; with a constant term the first row of X' is given by ι' (a row vector, every element of which is unity) and so the first normal equation is $\iota'\hat{e} = 0$ which implies that the sum of the residuals is zero, and hence that the average regression residual is zero. (The average residual will also be zero if a constant is implicitly, rather then explicitly, included.) Given that the average residual is zero, this implies that the average predicted value of Y, $(1/n)\iota'\hat{Y}$, is identical to the sample average of Y. This follows because:

$$Y = \hat{Y} + \hat{e} \Rightarrow (1/n)\iota'Y = (1/n)\iota'\hat{Y} + (1/n)\iota'\hat{e} \Rightarrow \overline{Y} = \overline{\hat{Y}}.$$

Defining the deviations of the fitted values from their sample average (which is identical to the sample average of the observations on Y) by $\hat{y}$, then: $y = \hat{y} + \hat{e}$ and this implies that $y'y = \hat{y}'\hat{y} + \hat{e}'\hat{e} + 2\hat{y}'\hat{e}$. Denoting by A the matrix $I - (\iota\iota')/n$, the effect of multiplying any vector by A is to transform the variable to a zero mean: $\hat{y} = A\hat{Y}$, $y = AY$ and $A\hat{e} = \hat{e}$ (since $\hat{e}$ has a zero mean). $\hat{y}'\hat{e}$ may then be written as $= \hat{Y}'A\hat{e} = \hat{Y}'\hat{e}$; but since the ordinary least squares estimator $\hat{\beta} = (X'X)^{-1}X'Y$, $\hat{Y} = X(X'X)^{-1}X'Y$ and so $\hat{y}'\hat{e} = Y'X(X'X)^{-1}X'\hat{e} \equiv 0$ since $X'\hat{e} \equiv 0$ by the normal equations. Thus, when the regression includes a constant term the total variation of the dependent variable may be decomposed to yield $y'y = \hat{y}'\hat{y} + \hat{e}'\hat{e}$; i.e. the total variation of Y about its sample mean is the sum of the variation of the fitted values around their sample mean plus the variation of the fitted residuals. This is usually written as:

$$TSS = ESS + RSS$$

where ESS is the explained sum of squares and RSS is the residual sum of squares. This decomposition is not valid without a constant term, for without a constant term there is a difference between the average fitted and average observed values (due to the non-zero average of the residuals). Hence, with a constant term, the correlation between Y and $\hat{Y}$ may be written as:

$$\frac{\sum_{i=1}^{n} y_i \hat{y}_i}{\sqrt{\sum_{i=1}^{n} y_i^2 \sum_{i=1}^{n} \hat{y}_i^2}}$$

The numerator may be expressed in vector notation as $y'\hat{y}$, and since $y = \hat{y} + \hat{e}$, $y'\hat{y} = \hat{y}'\hat{y} + \hat{e}'\hat{y} = \hat{y}'\hat{y}$ (because $\hat{e}'\hat{y} \equiv 0$ in this case). The numerator, then, is equal to the explained sum of squares, ESS. The denominator is the square root of the product of the total and explained sum of squares, and so the R^2 may be written as:

$$R^2 = \frac{ESS}{TSS}$$

which, since ESS = TSS – RSS, may be written as:

$$R^2 = 1 - \frac{RSS}{TSS}.$$

R^2 is then 1 minus the ratio of the unexplained variation to the total variation, which is equal to the ratio of the explained variation to the total variation.

Ordinary least squares, by minimizing the residual sum of squares, clearly maximizes the R^2 statistic and, since $0 \leq R^2 \leq 1$, a large R^2 is evidence of a well-fitting regression equation. A value of 0 indicates no degree of fit whatsoever, which implies that the inclusion of the regressors over and above the constant term offers no explanation of Y. Without a constant term, and when the variables are in uncentred form, this formula no longer represents the correlation between the fitted and observed values of Y, but in some applications (notably the construction of Lagrange multiplier tests) the uncentred R^2 is employed, defined as the ratio of the total sum of squares of the fitted values to the total sum of squares of the regressand (that is, using the raw data rather than, as above, using data standardized by the sample mean): since $\hat{Y} = X(X'X)^{-1}X'Y$ the sum of squared fitted values is $\hat{Y}'\hat{Y} = Y'X(X'X)^{-1}X'Y$, and the uncentred R^2 is the ratio:

$$\frac{Y'X(X'X)^{-1}X'Y}{Y'Y}.$$

The uncentred R^2 will always be positive, but may exceed unity, and does not, then, represent a sample correlation coefficient.

Models having the same dependent variable may be compared by their R^2, but larger models will almost certainly have higher R^2 (additional regressors will lead to an fall in the residual sum of squares and the R^2 statistic will rise, except in the rare case when the estimated coefficients on the additional regressors are identically zero). To overcome this deficiency of R^2 the $\overline{R}^2$ corrects for the degrees of freedom and, for the model $Y = X\beta + \varepsilon$ using n observations and where β is a k-dimensional vector, $\overline{R}^2$ is defined by:

$$\overline{R}^2 = 1 - \frac{RSS/(n-k)}{TSS/(n-1)}.$$

The effect of adding more regressors is to cause the residual sum of squares to fall, and the $\overline{R}^2$ statistic will only increase if the reduction in RSS more than offsets the loss of degrees of freedom.

Further reading
See **Constant term**, **Ordinary least squares**, **Partial correlation** and **Selection of regressors**.

Random coefficient model

A special case of the varying parameter model is the pure random coefficient model. In the simplest case it is assumed that $Y_i = \alpha + \beta_i X_i + \varepsilon_i$ and the response rate β_i is determined according to $\beta_i = \beta + \eta_i$ where η_i is a random term; thus the response rate is, on average, β, but there is random variation about this value. The pure random coefficient model may be used to allow non-systematic variation in the parameter vector, and may also be used to test for the constancy of the vector; it may also be used to analyse the pooling of cross-section and time-series data. In the simplest case, suppose:

$$Y_i = \alpha + \beta_i X_i + \varepsilon_i$$

and

$$\beta_i = \beta + \eta_i.$$

Substitution yields:

$$Y_i = \alpha + \beta X_i + \nu_i$$

where $\nu_i = \varepsilon_i + X_i \eta_i$. This regression equation has a heteroscedastic error: $V(\nu_i) = \sigma_\varepsilon^2 + X_i^2 \sigma_\eta^2 = \sigma_\varepsilon^2 (1 + \lambda X_i^2)$ where $\lambda = \sigma_\eta^2 / \sigma_\varepsilon^2$ which is, of course, not known. However, given that the implied heteroscedasticity is of a very simple form estimation may proceed by maximum likelihood, assuming that ε and η are both normally and independently distributed. The log-likelihood is given by:

$$\text{constant} - (n/2)\ell n\, \sigma_\varepsilon^2 - (1/2\sigma_\varepsilon^2)\sum_{i=1}^{n} \frac{(Y_i - \alpha - \beta X_i)^2}{(1+\lambda X_i^2)}$$

$$-(1/2)\sum_{i=1}^{n} \ell n(1+\lambda X_i^2).$$

For a given λ the weights $w_i = (1 + \lambda X_i^2)^{½}$ may be computed and the weighted least squares regression of Y_i/w_i on $(1/w_i)$, and (X_i/w_i) may then be run; denoting the residual sum of squares from the weighted regression by RSS(λ), the concentrated log-likelihood is given by:

$$\text{constant} - (n/2)\ell n\text{RSS}(\lambda) - (1/2)\sum_{i=1}^{n}\ell n(1+\lambda X_i^2)$$

and this may then be maximized with respect to the unknown parameter, λ. If $\tilde{\lambda}$ maximizes the log-likelihood the estimators of α and β may be derived from the weighted least squares regression using the weights given by $\tilde{w}_i = (1+\tilde{\lambda}X_i^2)^{1/2}$; the resulting estimators of α and β are then maximum likelihood estimators. This is usually referred to as the Hildreth and Houck model. Since random coefficients give rise to such a particular form of heteroscedasticity it is possible, then, to interpret observed heteroscedasticity of this form as an indication of random coefficients.

The random coefficient model may also be used to analyse pooled cross-section and time-series data; suppose there are n cross-section units and T observations on each unit:

$$Y_{it} = \alpha_i + \beta_i X_{it} + \varepsilon_{it}; \qquad i = 1, 2, \ldots, n; \quad t = 1, 2, \ldots T$$

and

$$\alpha_i = \alpha + u_i, \qquad \beta_i = \beta + \eta_i.$$

The variation of the intercept and response rate is thus by reference to the cross-section units but for each such unit are constant over time. It is assumed that the errors ε_{it} are all independent with zero mean and the variance of ε_{it} is given by σ_i^2 for all t so that over time the variation in each cross-section unit is homoscedastic but variation in the variance across cross-section units is allowed. The errors u_i and η_i are assumed to be zero mean, non-autocorrelated and homoscedastic term and the errors ε_{it}, u_i and η_i are assumed independent. Substitution yields:

$$Y_{it} = \alpha + \beta X_{it} + \varepsilon_{it} + u_i + \eta_i X_{it}.$$

Denoting the composite error, $\varepsilon_{it} + u_i + \eta_i X_{it}$, by ν_{it}, and assuming the X_{it} are non-stochastic:

$$\begin{aligned}
\text{Cov}(\nu_{it}, \nu_{js}) &= \text{Cov}(\varepsilon_{it} + u_i + \eta_i X_{it}, \varepsilon_{js} + u_i + \eta_j X_{js}) \\
&= \sigma_i^2 + \sigma_u^2 + X_{it}^2\sigma_\eta^2 && \text{if } i = j \text{ and } t = s; \\
&= \sigma_u^2 + \sigma_\eta^2 X_{it}X_{is} && \text{if } i = j \text{ and } t \neq s; \\
&= 0 && \text{if } i \neq j, \text{ for all t and s.}
\end{aligned}$$

Application of ordinary least squares (OLS) to the pooled data will, therefore, yield an inefficient estimator, and application of OLS to each of the n cross-sections will indicate heteroscedastic errors, but if this is recognized in the separate estimation of each of the n equations the commonality of the source of the heteroscedasticity would be ignored, leading again to a loss of efficiency. To accommodate the restrictive group-wise heteroscedasticity a generalized least squares approach is required using the pooled data, but application of GLS demands knowledge of the n + 2 variances, σ_i^2 (i = 1, . . , n), and σ_u^2 and σ_η^2. Feasible generalized least squares may be applied, however, by first estimating the original equation separately for each cross section unit, using OLS. This yields individual estimators $\hat{\alpha}_i$ and $\hat{\beta}_i$ with their associated estimated variance–covariance matrix, $\hat{V}_i$, and corresponding residuals $\hat{e}_i$ (i = 1, 2, . , n) from which consistent estimators of the variances may be obtained; s_i^2, s_u^2 and s_η^2 are consistent estimators of σ_i^2 (for all i), σ_u^2 and σ_η^2 respectively where:

$$s_i^2 = \hat{e}_i'\hat{e}_i/T \quad i = 1, 2, \ldots, n;$$

and

$$s_\eta^2 = (1/n)\Sigma_{i=1}^n(\hat{\beta}_i - \hat{\beta})^2$$

$$s_u^2 = (1/n)\Sigma_{i=1}^n(\hat{\alpha}_i - \hat{\alpha})^2.$$

Although these estimators are biased, they are consistent and guarantee that the estimated variance matrix of ν is positive definite as required. The estimated variance of ν may then be constructed and feasible generalized least squares may be applied to obtain (asymptotically) efficient estimators of α and β. Let $\hat{\alpha}$ and $\hat{\beta}$ denote the estimators obtained; they are unbiased estimators of the means of the distributions from which the α_i and β_i are drawn; to predict an individual α_i and β_i, a linear combination of the feasible GLS and OLS *seriatim* estimators will be unbiased, and it may be shown that the best linear predictor is given by:

$$A_i\begin{bmatrix}\hat{\alpha}\\ \hat{\beta}\end{bmatrix} + (I - A_i)\begin{bmatrix}\hat{\alpha}_i\\ \hat{\beta}_i\end{bmatrix}.$$

A_i is a function of the precision of the random coefficients and the estimated coefficients; denoting the variance–covariance of the random coefficients, $[\alpha_i \ \beta_i]'$, by V, and recalling that the estimated variance–covariance of $[\hat{\alpha}_i \ \hat{\beta}_i]'$ is denoted by $\hat{V}_i$, A_i is defined by $[V^{-1} + \hat{V}_i^{-1}]^{-1} V^{-1}$. Clearly, if the coefficients are not random, V is a null matrix and the best predictor is the ordinary least squares estimators. A test of the random coefficient model may be constructed by testing the variability of the ordinary least squares from estimating the equations separately, but this may be shown to be formally equivalent to the standard F-test of the joint hypothesis $\alpha_i = \alpha$ and $\beta_i = \beta$ for all i. This equivalence leads to an observational equivalence between the random coefficient model and one in which the parameters are different for each cross-section unit, but not random.

Random coefficient models offer an approach by which to take into account non-systematic changes in the response parameters and are particularly useful in pooling cross-section and time-series data when the responses are assumed to vary randomly over the cross-section units. Since the fixed parameter model is a special case of the random coefficient model, the model also offers a way to examine the assumption of fixed parameters. However, if the model has the appearance of random coefficients, this is also compatible with the hypothesis that the response rates are fixed for each cross-section unit, but different across those units. Whether heterogeneity is attributed to fixed, but different, effects, or to a random coefficient model, is largely a matter of interpretation and choice.

Further reading
For further analysis and examples of random coefficient models see, for example, Hildreth and Houck (1968), Swamy (1970, 1971 and 1974) and Hsiao (1975). See also **Kalman filter models**, **Time-varying parameter models** and **Varying parameter models**.

Random variables

A random number is a theoretical, mathematical construct which is defined within the framework of a random experiment. A random experiment, R, has the following characteristics:

1. The experiment is capable of being repeated indefinitely under essentially the same conditions; each repeat of the experiment is called a **trial**.
2. Although it is not possible to state what a *particular* outcome will be from any one trial, it is possible to provide a complete description of the set of *all possible* outcomes of the experiment.
3. When the experiment is repeated a large number of times, a pattern or regularity appears. It is this regularity which makes it possible to construct a precise mathematical model with which to analyse the experiment.

With each experiment, R, there is a sample space, S, which is the set of all possible outcomes of R. A function f, assigning to every element s of S a real number f(s), is a random variable. Defined in this way a 'random variable' is a conceptual construct, not a material construct (one may *conceive* of an experiment which is repeatable under essentially the same conditions but not demonstrate in the material world that any experiment fits this description under infinitely repeated trials). An essential characteristic of a random variable is that its realized value from any one trial is not known *a priori*; however, as the number of trials increases any one particular outcome demonstrates some relationship to other outcomes.

A random variable may be discrete or continuous; a discrete random variable can take on only a limited, though possibly infinite, number of values whereas a continuous random variable can take all values within a given range (and the range may or may not be finite). An example of a discrete random variable that may take an infinite number of values is a variable whose value is any non-negative integer. An example of a discrete variable which may take only a finite number of values is the outcome of rolling a die. As examples of continuous random variables one could consider a variable which may take any value on the real line (an infinite number of possibilities within an infinite range) or one which may take all values within the [0, 1] interval (an infinite number of possibilities within a finite range).

To develop this, if the trial involves enquiring of individuals whether or not they own a personal computer, then the sample space, S, is {Yes, No}; assigning the value zero to 'no' and one to 'yes' (that is, f(No) = 0 and f(Yes) = 1) the random variable is discrete – taking either the value zero or one. On the other hand, consider spinning a pointer and measuring its displacement in radians from its start position: the sample space is then $[0, 2\pi)$ and if the displacement is denoted by s, and f(s) = s, then s is a continuous random variable within the interval $[0, 2\pi)$. It is possible to repeat the trials and it is reasonable to suppose that there is agreement that the conditions remain essentially the same across all trials; however, one of the difficulties in recognizing a random experiment in practice is in knowing when the experiment in question has been repeated under essentially the same conditions. What are these 'conditions', and when may it be assumed that there has been no material change from one trial to another? At a trivial level, for the sample space to consist of more than one element, at least one condition of the experiment must be different, from one trial to another.

Indeed, if one adopts the position of a determinist (one who believes that *all* outcomes may be wholly explained as the result of a set of causes, whether or not that set is known) then to generate a sample space of more than one member requires that in the repeated trials of the experiment at least one of the salient (determining) conditions varies as the trials are repeated. On the other hand, a non-determinist (one who believes that not all events may be wholly explained as the result of a set of known causes, and who, therefore, believes that some events have an inherently unpredictable, stochastic, random, component) would argue that there exist some experiments whose outcomes are not wholly determined by material conditions, and that those outcomes are simply a **stochastic** event.

To take the deterministic position, the outcome of an experiment, say the familiar die-rolling experiment, is, in principle, actually determined if the initial conditions, the environment of the experiment, and the way in which the entirety of its determining causes combine to yield the outcome, are fully known. If all salient variables are denoted by a vector X then the process may be denoted by the relation g so that g(X) takes on the integer values 1 to 6 inclusive. However, were knowledge of X or g incomplete, the outcome of any one trial could not be foretold with certainty; ignorance of the 'true' determinants (X) or of the 'true' process (g) has, as its consequence, the unpredictability of any specific outcome. In the material world, perfect knowledge is an unattainable position and to model that of which we are ignorant as a random variable is a useful and most productive device.

To the non-determinist, neither X nor g exists such that g(X) is knowable and describes the outcomes completely; it is possible that there is some set of determinants, X, and some relation, g, but g(X) does not describe the process completely. Thus, the non-determinist might describe the process by $g(X) + \eta$ where η is a random variable: this view encapsulates the perspective that *even if* both X and g were, in principle, perfectly knowable then knowledge of the outcome would still be incomplete, and the representation of that 'incompleteness' is the random variable η.

Scientific determinism (the view that the physical world is governed by a set of deterministic equations) was seriously challenged by the physicist Heisenberg, who, notwithstanding Einstein's objections encapsulated in his famous remark that 'God does not play dice', demonstrated in his 'Uncertainty Principle' that it is impossible to know, with absolute accuracy, both the present position and the present velocity of a particle. Thus, while one might maintain the *conceptual* model in which the universe follows deterministic laws, it is not possible to know those deterministic laws with certainty. This leads to the use of stochastic models in which the uncertainty is modelled by a stochastic term.

Following this line of reasoning, investigations of phenomena utilize the concept of a model. A model is, necessarily, an abstraction of reality and this means that enquiry into the set of determining variables, X, and the relation, g, does not seek to discover the 'true' X nor the 'true' g; neither will be known fully (indeed, in practice neither could be known fully nor measured exactly as a consequence of Heisenberg's principle). A model utilizes a reduced set of determinants, say x where $x \subset X$, and utilizes a relation, say g^* where $g^* \neq g$; the (deliberate) omissions and approximations may then be seen as having been relegated into a composite contribution (denoted by ν) which need not necessarily be further decomposed. All unobservable, and some observable, features of the process are ignored and the model focuses upon 'salient' observable variables. One goal of a model is to ensure that the composite, non-modelled contribution is not predictable (for if it were it would be profitable to enquire further of this component and include such predictability explicitly in the model). When this has been achieved the omissions and approximations may be treated *as if* they comprised a random variable (since a particular realized value of a random variable is not predictable with certainty). Suppose the outcome of an experiment is denoted by Y; then:

$$Y = g(X) + \lambda \eta$$

where $\lambda = 0$ for a deterministic perspective, and $\lambda = 1$ for a non-deterministic perspective. Further:

$$Y = g^*(x) + \nu + \lambda \eta;$$

that is, Y = g*(x) + a non-predictable variable. The latter form constitutes the typical model used in analysis, namely:

$$Y = g^*(x) + \varepsilon,$$

where ε is treated as a random variable, and may always be treated as a random variable whether $\lambda = 0$ or not. The concept of a random variable may, therefore, be used profitably to encapsulate a form of 'ignorance': in modelling any process the objective is to identify salient features of that process and relegate the remainder to a non-predictable term. The mathematical construct of a random variable has proved to be an eminently suitable mathematical model by which to analyse models in all areas of enquiry, from the 'hard' sciences to the social sciences.

A continuous random variable is characterized by its probability density function (pdf): if Z is a continuous random variable defined on a range R, then f(Z) is the probability density function of Z if f(Z) takes strictly non-negative values and:

$$\int_R f(Z)dZ = 1 \qquad \text{and} \qquad \int_a^b f(Z)dZ = \Pr\{a<Z<b\}.$$

It is to be noted as an immediate consequence of the second integral that the probability of a continuous random variable taking on any given specific value, say a, is zero:

$$\Pr\{Z = a\} = \lim_{b \to a} \int_a^b f(Z)dZ = 0.$$

The mean, or expected value, and the variance of Z are defined as:

$$E(Z) = \int_R Zf(Z)dZ = \mu \qquad \text{and} \qquad V(Z) = \int_R (Z-\mu)^2 f(Z)dZ = \sigma^2.$$

The mean is a measure of central tendency, and the variance is a measure of the spread of the distribution about the mean (for some distributions the variance may not be finite). If $f(Z - \mu) = f(-Z + \mu)$ the distribution is described as symmetric about its mean, and for non-symmetric distributions (otherwise known as skewed distributions) the variance may not be an appropriate measure of spread, since it is a measure of variation about the mean. The positive square root of the variance, σ, is the standard deviation of the variable. Two other common measures of central tendency are the median and the mode. The median is defined as that value m such that:

$$\int_{-\infty}^{m} f(Z)dZ = 0.5$$

and the mode is that value of Z for which f(Z) is maximized. The median divides the distribution into two, so that values of Z below m occur with probability one half, and is commonly used as the central tendency of skewed distributions such as earnings. The mode is not uniquely defined, and a distribution may, for example, be bi-modal. Other measures of variation are available, and include quartiles and deciles, where the ith quartile (i = 1, 2, and 3) is defined as that value Z_i such that Pr $\{Z_{i-1} < Z < Z_i\} = 0.25$ from which the inter-quartile range may be computed as $Z_3 - Z_1$ within which the central 50% of values of Z lie.

The distribution function of Z, F(z), is the cumulative probability function:

$$F(z) = \int_{-\infty}^{z} f(Z)dZ = \Pr\{Z \leq z\}$$

that is, F(z) is the probability that Z takes on values up to and including z. Clearly, by the fundamental relationship of calculus, f(z) = dF(z)/dz. F(m) = 0.5 thus defines the median, $F(Z_i) = i/4$ defines the ith quartile and $F(Z_j) = j/10$ defines the jth decile.

If Z and Y are two random variables with a joint density function given by f(Z, Y) then f(Z, Y) ≥ 0 for all Z and Y, and:

$$\iint f(Z,Y)dZdY = 1$$

and $$\int_c^d \int_a^b f(Z,Y)dZdY = \Pr\{a < Z < b,\ c < Y < d\}.$$

From the joint density function, the marginal density function of one variable is obtained by integrating out the other over its range:

$$f(Z) = \int_{-\infty}^{\infty} f(Z,\ Y)dY$$

and the conditional probability density function is given by:

$$f(Z|Y) = f(Z,\ Y)/f(Y) \quad \text{and} \quad f(Y|Z) = f(Z,\ Y)/f(Z).$$

Z and Y are statistically independent if their conditional and marginal probability density distributions are identical; hence Z and Y are independent if:

$$f(Z) = f(Z|Y)$$

which implies that f(Z, Y) = f(Z).f(Y).The same conclusion follows from consideration of f(Y) = f(Y|Z). Thus, two random variables are independent if and only if their joint pdf is given by the product of their individual pdfs.

The covariance between Z and Y is defined by:

$$\sigma_{ZY} = \iint [(Z - E(Z))(Y - E(Y))]f(Z,\ Y)dZdY.$$

σ_{ZY} is a measure of the linear association between the variables. If the variables are independently distributed then their covariance is zero, but the converse is not necessarily true; that is, zero covariance does not imply independence in general. However, in the special case when the variables are normally distributed, zero covariance and independence are equivalent. From the covariance, which is not dimensionless, the dimensionless correlation coefficient is defined as:

$$r_{ZY} = \sigma_{ZY}/\sigma_Z\sigma_Y$$

that is as the covariance divided by the product of standard deviations, and may be shown to be such that $|r_{ZY}| \leq 1$. If $r_{ZY} = 1$ then Z and Y are perfectly related, linearly, and if $r_{ZY} = 0$ there is no linear association at all between the variables. It should be stressed that correlation is only a measure of linear association, and not association in general.

The concept and manipulations of the joint density function over two variables are readily generalized to a joint density function over many variables.

For a discrete random variable, the equivalent of the probability density function is the probability function; if Z is a discrete random variable which takes only specific values, say $Z_1, Z_2, \ldots, Z_n$, where n need not be finite the probability function is $\Pr\{Z = Z_i\} = p_i \geq 0$, all i, and $\sum_{i=1}^{n} p_i = 1$. In constructing the expectation and variance, summations then replace integrals. The joint probability function of many discrete random variables may also be defined, and in all subsequent manipulations summations replace integrals.

In econometrics, the commonest random variable used is the normal variate, which is defined over the entire real line and whose probability density function is defined given two parameters, the mean (μ) and variance (σ^2). The probability density function is given by:

$$f(Z) = (2\pi\sigma^2)^{-\frac{1}{2}} \exp\{-\tfrac{1}{2}[(Z - \mu)/\sigma]^2\}.$$

From this distribution, other particular distributions in common use may be derived, including the chi-squared (χ^2), t- and F-distributions. See **Distribution theory**).

Further reading

Material on random variables is available in almost all econometrics texts; the literature of mathematical statistics also provides an excellent source; see, for example, Mood, Graybill and Boes (1974).

Recursive residuals

Suppose $Y = X\beta + \varepsilon$, $\varepsilon \sim MVN(0, \sigma^2 I)$, T observations available, and the parameter vector β contains k parameters. Recursive residuals are obtained by estimating the equation using a subset of the T observations, say the first t observations only, and from the estimated value of β, denoted by $\hat{\beta}_{(t)}$ the next period's value of Y may be predicted as $\hat{Y}_{t+1}$ and the prediction error, given by $Y_{t+1} - \hat{Y}_{t+1}$, may be constructed. This may be repeated for t = k, k+1, . . , T−1 and the resulting prediction error contain useful information regarding the specification of the model. The set of T−k prediction errors forms the basis from which the recursive residuals are constructed.

Consider constructing the ordinary least squares estimate of β from the first k observations, and then expanding the estimation sample by one so as to estimate β from the first k+1 observations, and carry on in this fashion so as to have estimated β a total of T–k+1 times. These T–k+1 regressions are known as ordinary least squares recursions, and from these the recursive residuals may be constructed. Let $X_{(t)}$ denote the t×k matrix of the first t observations on the regressors, so that $X_{(t)} = [x_1\ x_2 \ldots x_t]'$ where x_i' denotes the 1×k vector of observations on all k variables at time i. Let $Y_{(t)}$ denote the t×1 vector of the first t observations on the regressand, $[Y_1\ Y_2 \ldots Y_t]'$, and let $\hat{\beta}_{(t)}$ denote the k×1 estimate of β using the first t observations; then:

$$\hat{\beta}_{(t)} = [X_{(t)}'X_{(t)}]^{-1}X_{(t)}'Y_{(t)} \qquad \text{for } t = k, k+1, \ldots, T;$$

it may be shown that $\hat{\beta}_{(t+1)}$ is updated from $\hat{\beta}_{(t)}$ by:

$$\hat{\beta}_{(t+1)} = \hat{\beta}_{(t)} + [X_{(t)}'X_{(t)}]^{-1}x_{t+1}(Y_{t+1} - x_{t+1}'\hat{\beta}_{(t)})/\theta_{t+1} \quad \text{for } t = k+1, \ldots, T;$$

where
$$\theta_{t+1} = 1 + x_{t+1}'\,X_{(t)}'X_{(t)}]^{-1}x_{t+1}$$

and:
$$[X_{(t)}'X_{(t)}]^{-1} = [X_{(t-1)}'X_{(t-1)}]^{-1}[I - x_t x_t'[X_{(t-1)}'X_{(t-1)}]^{-1}/\theta_t].$$

Using the expression for $\hat{\beta}_{(t)}$ for t = k yields $\hat{\beta}_{(k)} = X_{(k)}^{-1}Y_{(k)}$ and then, from the updating formulae all subsequent estimates may be obtained; only the inverse of $X_{(k)}$ is required, as all subsequent inversions may be derived from the updating formula. This yields the recursive estimates $\{\hat{\beta}_{(t)}\}$, and T–k prediction errors are generated:

$$\tilde{\varepsilon}_t = Y_t - x_t'\hat{\beta}_{(t-1)} \qquad t = k+1, \ldots, T.$$

By definition, $\tilde{\varepsilon}_t$ is the one-step-ahead prediction error of Y_t given $\hat{\beta}_{(t-1)}$ which has been estimated using all observation up to, and including, t–1. The expectation of $\tilde{\varepsilon}_t$ is clearly zero, and since Y_t and $\hat{\beta}_{(t-1)}$ are independent, the variance of $\tilde{\varepsilon}_t$ is $\sigma^2 + x_t'V(\hat{\beta}_{(t-1)})x_t$ which is easily shown to equal $\sigma^2\theta_t$; moreover, it may be shown that the prediction errors are uncorrelated with each other. This may be understood by noting that $\tilde{\varepsilon}_t$ is constructed given $\hat{\beta}_{(t-1)}$ and so the only new stochastic information used to form the one-step-ahead prediction error is contained in Y_t; $\hat{\beta}_{(t-1)}$ already incorporates the information arising from previous values of Y_s, s = k+1, . . , t–1 and assuming that the model is free of autocorrelation it follows that the one-step-ahead predictions are mutually independent. They are not, however, homoscedastic since $V(\tilde{\varepsilon}_t) = \sigma^2\theta_t$.

Let $\hat{v}_t = \tilde{\varepsilon}_t/\sqrt{\theta_i}$; then the random variables $\hat{v}_t$ are uncorrelated, have zero mean and constant variance. Also, because the $\hat{v}_t$ are linear in the observations, if the original disturbances are normally distributed, then the $\hat{v}_t$ variables are also normal and hence independent (since uncorrelated normal variables are independent); $\hat{v}_t$ are the recursive residuals. They clearly have very different properties from the ordinary least squares residuals: the former are independent and homoscedastic while the latter are not.

The recursive residuals can also be used in the updating formula for the ordinary least squares residual sum of squares. Having estimated the model using the first t observations only, the vector of OLS residuals, denoted by $\hat{e}_{(t)}$, is given $Y_{(t)} - X_{(t)}\hat{\beta}_{(t)}$; this may be written as: x_t'

$$\hat{e}_{(t)} = \begin{bmatrix} Y_{(t-1)} \\ Y_t \end{bmatrix} - \begin{bmatrix} X_{(t-1)} \\ x_t' \end{bmatrix} \left[\hat{\beta}_{(t-1)} + [X_{(t-1)}'X_{(t-1)}]^{-1} x_t (Y_t - x_t'\hat{\beta}_{(t-1)})/\theta_t \right].$$

Multiplying out yields:

$$\hat{e}_{(t)} = \begin{bmatrix} \hat{e}_{(t-1)} - X_{(t-1)}[X_{(t-1)}'X_{(t-1)}]^{-1} x_t \tilde{\varepsilon}_t/\theta_t \\ \tilde{\varepsilon}_t - (\theta_t - 1)\tilde{\varepsilon}_t/\theta_t \end{bmatrix}$$

but, by definition, $\tilde{\varepsilon}_t = \hat{v}_t\sqrt{\theta_i}$, and so:

$$\hat{e}_{(t)} = \begin{bmatrix} \hat{e}_{(t-1)} - X_{(t-1)}[X_{(t-1)}'X_{(t-1)}]^{-1} x_t \hat{v}_t/\sqrt{\theta_t} \\ \hat{v}_t/\sqrt{\theta_t} \end{bmatrix}.$$

Therefore, denoting the residual sum of squares using only the first t observations by $RSS_{(t)}$:

$$RSS_{(t)} = \hat{e}_{(t)}'\hat{e}_{(t)} = \hat{e}_{(t-1)}'\hat{e}_{(t-1)} + (\hat{v}_t^2/\theta_t)x_t'[X_{(t-1)}'X_{(t-1)})]^{-1}x_t + (\hat{v}_t^2/\theta_t)$$

i.e.
$$RSS_{(t)} = \hat{e}_{(t-1)}'\hat{e}_{(t-1)} + (\hat{v}_t^2/\theta_t)(\theta_t - 1) + (\hat{v}_t^2/\theta_t).$$

(All cross-product terms involving $\hat{e}_{(t-1)}'X_{(t-1)}$ are zero as the OLS residuals and regressors from the recursions are orthogonal.)

Hence:
$$RSS_{(t)} = RSS_{(t-1)} + \hat{v}_t^2.$$

Thus the recursive residuals play a crucial role in the updating of the residual sum of squares.

The recursive residuals may be used to great effect in analysis of mis-specification. Suppose that the relationship between Y and X is actually non-linear, but a linear form is used. As an example suppose there is one regressor only and the relationship between Y and X is quadratic, with all coefficients positive; then, having ordered the observation by the size of X, the one-step-ahead prediction will be an underestimate on average and the recursive residuals will tend to be positive (and are all positive in expectation). Simply plotting the recursive residuals can yield important information about the specification of the model, and this may be formalized by plotting the cumulative sum (CUSUM) and the cumulative sum of squares (CUSUMSQ) of the recursive residuals. The CUSUM of the recursive residuals is given by:

$$W_t = s^{-1} \sum_{j=k+1}^{t} \hat{v}_j$$

where $s^2 = \hat{e}'\hat{e}/(T-k)$, i.e. s^2 is the OLS estimator of the regression variance using all T observations.

If the model is mis-specified there may be a tendency for a disproportionate number of recursive residuals to have the same sign, and this will manifest itself in W_t moving away from zero. W_t may be plotted against t and values of W_t which are significantly different from zero are indications of mis-specification (including, for example, non-linearities in the functional from and the presence of a structural break which has not been modelled). How large a value of W_t provides such an indication may be determined by reference to critical values given by:

$$\pm a(T-k)^{-\frac{1}{2}}\{(T-k)+2(t-k)\}$$

where a is chosen according to the significance level of the test; a = 0.850 for 10% and 0.948 for 5% for example. Plotting W_t and this pair of lines then provides a test of mis-specification.

The CUSUMSQ is based upon the quantities WW_t defined by:

$$WW_t = \frac{\sum_{j=k+1}^{t} \hat{v}_j^2}{\sum_{j=k+1}^{T} \hat{v}_j^2}.$$

When the model is properly specified WW_t has a known Beta distribution and a plot of WW_t may be used as a test of mis-specification. Large values of WW_t indicate mis-specification, and values lying outside the lines given by:

$$\pm c_o + (t-k)/(T-k)$$

are indications of mis-specification. The constant c_o is determined by the significance level. Plotting WW_t and this pair of lines then provides a test of mis-specification.

The plots of W_t and WW_t are useful supplements to other tests of mis-specification, and in conjunction with other tests based upon OLS residuals can be of great help in, for example, detecting functional form mis-specification or detecting the point at which a (hitherto unsuspected) structural break occurs. The tests are based upon the assumption that the errors in the original regression are normally and independently distributed with constant variance.

Other applications of the recursive regressions include plotting the values of the recursive estimates, $\hat{\beta}_{(t)}$ for t = k, . . . T. Clearly, if the underlying parameter is constant, then after some initial variation of $\hat{\beta}_{(t)}$ it is expected that the $\hat{\beta}_{(t)}$ will converge to a stable (and narrow) band. Moreover, one may use the residual sum of squares at each recursion to generate a recursive Chow test of stability via the test of predictive failure (see **Chow test**). Using the first t observations, the Chow statistic of one-step-ahead predictive failure having estimated the model using the regression over the first t − 1 observations is given by:

$$[RSS_{(t)} - RSS_{(t-1)}]/[RSS_{(t)}/(t-k)] \sim F_{1,t-k}.$$

This may be calculated for all t = k+1, . . . , T; given the updating formula for the residual sum of squares the numerator is simply $\hat{v}_t^2$, the square of the tth recursive residual. Since each test statistic has, under the null hypothesis, a different F distribution (the degrees of freedom in the denominator increase by one at each stage) it is common to use the 'scaled recursive Chow test':

$$C_t = \frac{(t-k)\hat{v}_t^2}{RSS_{(t)}F_{1,t-k;\alpha}}$$

where $F_{1,t-k;\alpha}$ is the α% right-hand critical value from the $F_{1,t-k}$ distribution. These test statistics may then be plotted; any value greater than unity implies that the null hypothesis of structural stability between periods t and t−1 is to be rejected at a significance level of α.

Further reading

The use of recursive residuals as a test of stability was introduced by Brown *et al.* (1975); CUSUMSQ tables may be found in Harvey (1990). See also Harvey and Collier (1977). For an application, see, for example, Galpin and Hawkins (1984).

Recursive systems

A recursive system is a particular form of a simultaneous system. A general simultaneous system in G endogenous variables and K exogenous (and predetermined) variables may be written as:

$$BY_t + \Gamma_t = \varepsilon_t \qquad t = 1, 2, \ldots, T$$

where there are T observations, B is a square G×G matrix and Γ is a G×K matrix; these two matrices contain the structural parameters of the system. Suppose, as a special case, that the error term in equation i is independent of that in equation j (for all i ≠ j), and that the error term in equation i is homoscedastic and not autocorrelated. If ε_{it} denoted the elements of the error term attached to equation i, then $\varepsilon_t = [\varepsilon_{1t}\ \varepsilon_{2t}\ \ldots\ \varepsilon_{Gt}]'$ and:

$$V(\varepsilon_{it}) = \sigma_i^2 I \qquad i = 1, 2, \ldots, G \text{ and all } t = 1, 2, \ldots, T;$$

$$Cov(\varepsilon_{it}, \varepsilon_{is}) = 0 \qquad \text{for } t \neq s \text{ and all } i;$$

$$Cov(\varepsilon_{it}, \varepsilon_{js}) = 0 \qquad \text{for all } t \neq s \text{ and for all } i \neq j.$$

In this case the variance matrix of ε is diagonal, and may be written as $\Sigma_c \otimes I$, where $\Sigma_c = diag(\sigma_1^2 \ldots\ldots \sigma_G^2)$. Hence any admissible transformation of the structure must maintain this covariance structure (see **Identification**), and specifically any admissible transformation must maintain the lack of covariance across the structural equations.

If, in addition to the restrictions on the error structure, the matrix B is lower triangular, so that equation 1 contains only the first of the endogenous variables (and any number of the exogenous variables), equation 2 contains only the first two endogenous variables (and any number of the exogenous variables), and so on, so that equation i contains only the endogenous variable $Y_1, Y_2, \ldots, Y_i$, the system is described as fully recursive. Suppose that B has been normalized so that its diagonal elements are all unity:

$$\begin{aligned}
Y_{1t} + \sum_{j=1}^{K} \gamma_{1j} X_{jt} &= \varepsilon_{1t} \\
\beta_{21} Y_{1t} + Y_{2t} + \sum_{j=1}^{K} \gamma_{2j} X_{jt} &= \varepsilon_{2t} \\
\beta_{31} Y_{1t} + \beta_{32} Y_{2t} + Y_{3t} + \sum_{j=1}^{K} \gamma_{3j} X_{jt} &= \varepsilon_{3t} \\
\cdots\cdots\cdots\cdots\cdots\cdots &= \cdots \\
\cdots\cdots\cdots\cdots\cdots\cdots &= \cdots \\
\beta_{G1} Y_{1t} + \beta_{G2} Y_{2t} + \cdots\cdots + Y_{Gt} + \sum_{j=1}^{K} \gamma_{Gj} X_{jt} &= \varepsilon_{Gt}
\end{aligned}$$

The matrix B is a lower triangular matrix and, in principle at least, the matrix Γ is full, so that the only exclusion restrictions embodied in the above are that equation i excludes all endogenous variables Y_{jt} for $j > i$. Each equation contains all the exogenous variables of the system, which means that the necessary order condition for identification, that the equation in question exclude at least as many exogenous variables as there are endogenous variables on the right-hand side, fails for all equations except the first.

By the order condition the first equation is identified since it includes only one endogenous variable and may, then, be treated as a single equation and estimated by ordinary least squares. However, in this system the second equation may be written as a regression of Y_2 on Y_1 and all the exogenous variables, and since Y_1 is stochastically dependent on ε_1 only which is, by definition, stochastically independent of ε_2, the second equation may also be estimated by ordinary least squares to yield consistent estimators of the structural parameters. The usual simultaneous bias does not arise in a recursive system. If the exogenous variables are all truly exogenous and contain no pre-determined variables (such as lagged values of the endogenous variables), then ordinary least squares applied in turn to each of the G equations will yield unbiased estimators of the structural parameters; if lagged endogenous variables are included amongst the variables of X then OLS will yield biased but consistent estimators.

The second equation is identified by virtue of the restrictions placed on the covariance structure of the errors in the structural form. The question of identification concerns the observational equivalence of linear combinations of structural equations, and the sort of restrictions which are usually examined in identification are exclusion restrictions on variables, and restrictions on other linear combinations of parameters. In a recursive system there are no exclusion restrictions on any exogenous or predetermined variables, and hence it would seem that the traditional order condition for identification fails for all equations but the first. In this particular system, however, there are covariance restrictions, and these provide a sufficient set of identification conditions. Consider the first and second equations:

$$Y_{1t} + \sum_{j=1}^{K} \gamma_{1j} X_{jt} = \varepsilon_{1t}$$

$$\beta_{21} Y_{1t} + Y_{2t} + \sum_{j=1}^{K} \gamma_{2j} X_{jt} = \varepsilon_{1t}$$

A linear combination of these two equations yields:

$$(1+\lambda\beta_{21})Y_{1t} + \lambda Y_{2t} + \sum_{j=1}^{K} (\gamma_{1j} + \lambda\gamma_{2j}) X_{jt} = \varepsilon_{1t} + \lambda\varepsilon_{2t}$$

and this looks like the second equation – it includes Y_1, Y_2 and all K exogenous and predetermined variables. It may be described as a bogus second structural equation; however, the restrictions on the covariances of the errors in the structure require that the errors in the first and second equations have a zero covariance; the error of the bogus second equation is given by $\varepsilon_{1t} + \lambda\,\varepsilon_{2t}$ and the error of the true first equation is given by ε_{1t}; hence the covariance between these two errors is given by σ_1^2, the variance of ε_1, which is not zero. Hence the bogus second equation is distinguishable from the true second equation by the zero covariance restriction. This argument may be applied to the equations in turn, and ordinary least squares applied individually to each equation yields consistent estimators of all the structural parameters, all of which are identified, notwithstanding the fact that the order condition for identification is denied for all but the first equation.

There is a clear causal chain in this system: Y_1 is determined only by the exogenous variables and a stochastic term, Y_2 is determined by Y_1, the exogenous variables and a stochastic term, and so on, so that Y_i is determined by all endogenous variables Y_1 to Y_{i-1}, all the exogenous variables and a stochastic term. Y_i is, therefore, related to all stochastic terms ε_i where $j \leq i$, but is independent of all error terms ε_i where $j > i$. This produces a uni-directional causal chain, known as a Wold causal chain, and the system is not one of simultaneous determination, but is hierarchical so that Y_1 feeds into Y_2 which feeds into Y_3 and so on but there is no feedback.

Given that the nature of the dependences amongst the available data are dictated, in part, by the frequency of observations, a recursive system demands that the current value of Y_i is determined by current values of all Y_j, $j < i$ and there is no feedback; clearly, the greater is the frequency of observations the more persuasive is the argument of no feedback, but the less frequent are the data, the longer is the unit of time measurement, the less acceptable does such a proposition become. Institutional realities may deny feedback and allow only one-way causal chains if the frequency of the data is high. If, for example, daily data are available on some variables, it may be quite reasonable to impose a hierarchical causal chain, but if the data are monthly the strict hierarchy may be subsumed within the data and will appear, then, as simultaneous determination of the variables via feedback with all the commensurate identification and estimation issues which affect simultaneous models.

This general result, that ordinary least squares applied individually to each equation of a recursive system yields consistent estimators of the structural parameters, is derivable from the analysis described further in **Full information maximum likelihood**.

Further reading

See Wold (1954) for a discussion of recursive systems and causality, and see also Strotz (1960), who views simultaneity as the limiting case of a recursive system as agents' response times shorten and the data frequency lengthens.

RESET tests

The general linear model $Y = X\beta + \varepsilon$ is assumed to be linear in the regressors, and if the assumption of linearity is false then any estimation of the model restricted by this assumption will lead to false inferences. The simplest test of the assumption of a linear functional form is that due to Ramsey (1969, 1970). It is to be noted that economic theory rarely (if ever) indicates a specific functional form of the relationship, and the assumption of linearity is an acknowledged approximation. In the absence of an obvious alternative hypothesis to that of linearity, the **R**egression **E**quation **S**pecification **E**rror **T**est (RESET) can be used.

This is computed as follows: from the ordinary least squares regression of $Y = X\beta + \varepsilon$, compute $\hat{Y}$, the vector of OLS predicted values of the dependent variable. Now form the auxiliary regression of Y on X and the additional regressors given by powers of the predicted Y values, $\hat{Y}^i$ for $i = 2, 3, \ldots p$. This regression may be written as: $Y = X\beta + Z\gamma + \varepsilon$ where Z has $p - 1$ columns comprising the squares, cubes and higher powers of the $\hat{Y}$ values, up to the pth power. A simple F-test of the hypothesis that $\gamma = 0$ is then a test of the linearity hypothesis. It should be noted that Z contains only the squares and higher powers of $\hat{Y}$; Z does not include $\hat{Y}$ itself for then Z and X would be perfectly collinear.

The rationale for the test is as follows: if Y is related to the variables X linearly, then the regression of Y on X and the additional variables in Z (which captures the squares and higher powers of X via the powers of the $\hat{Y}$ values) will, in fact, be a regression which includes a set of irrelevant variables, namely those in Z; thus, under the hypothesis of linearity, the additional variables are redundant. Linearity is therefore rejected if the computed F-statistic lies in the right-hand tail of the relevant F-distribution. A common form of this test includes only the squared values of the fitted dependent variable, and the Ramsey test is then computed as a simple t-test on the one additional variable ($\hat{Y}^2$); if higher powers are also included the simplest way to conduct the test, unless the test statistic happens to be a standard output of the regression package, is to run the regression of Y on X and Z, and then examine the reduction in the sum of squared residuals by virtue of having included the variables in Z. Denoting the original sum of squared residuals by RRSS (since that regression restricts γ to be zero) and that from the auxiliary regression by URSS (since it allows $\gamma \neq 0$), under the hypothesis of linearity $\gamma = 0$ and the test is conducted by:

$$\frac{[\text{RRSS} - \text{URSS}]/(p-1)}{\text{URSS}/(T-k)} \sim F_{p-1,T-k}$$

where there are T observations available and β is k-dimensional. A value of this statistic which is so large as to exceed the chosen critical value leads to a rejection of the hypothesis of linearity. Even though $\hat{Y}$ is stochastic, the F-test proposed is exact when the error term is MVN(0, σ^2I) and X is either non-stochastic or otherwise independent of ε.

Other forms of linearity tests are available through use of the Box and Cox transformation which has received extensive attention within econometrics as both a test of linearity and as a technique for estimating the functional form. (See **Box and Cox transformations**.)

If the RESET test rejects the hypothesis of linearity it should be noted that no precise alternative functional form has been utilized as an alternative hypothesis (nor, indeed, has *any* precise alternative hypothesis been stated), and so the investigator is merely alerted to the presence of a problem but is not necessarily alerted to the direction in which a better specification lies. Moreover, a significant RESET statistic is not necessarily an indicator of a mis-specified functional form; for example, if there is a structural break in the relationship this too can give rise to a significant RESET F-statistic. Hence, the response to a significant test statistic requires further investigation of the issue. Also, since the test is an F-test of a restriction, it requires that in other respects the model is well-specified, and in particular that the auxiliary regression successfully passes the other diagnostic tests.

Further reading
See Ramsey (1969 and 1970) and also Godfrey (1988).

Restricted least squares

The regression model $Y = X\beta + \varepsilon$ may be estimated subject to restrictions on its parameters. The purpose of performing a restricted estimation may, for example, be to test a restriction suggested by economic theory or to test a restriction implied by the data. Imposing a restriction will improve the efficiency of estimation – utilizing restrictions in the estimation process means that additional information is incorporated in the estimators, fewer parameters are estimated, and that information, whether correct or not, will lead to an improvement in efficiency. However, if the information is incorrect the resulting estimators will be more efficient, but biased. Such constraints, or restrictions, may take the simple form of hypothesized exclusion of certain regressors (as in the test of a regressor's significance or in the search for a more parsimonious model) or they may take the form of linear restrictions on the parameters (such as the imposition of constant returns to scale in a production function) or they may take the form of non-linear restrictions on the parameters (such as in a test for common factors). It is important, clearly, to test that any restrictions which are imposed are not rejected by the data, for otherwise any gain in efficiency is (almost) necessarily at the expense of biased estimators. In many common cases it is possible to test the restrictions by running the regression of Y on X subject to the constraints; in cases where the restricted regression cannot be easily estimated an alternative testing route is required, and for details see **Wald test**.

Constraints commonly arise from theoretical considerations and many hypotheses may be examined within the context of a restricted regression; if those hypotheses are not rejected they may then be incorporated in the estimation process and an efficiency gain results. Hypotheses of exclusion (no-effect hypotheses) such as $\beta_i = 0$ are easily examined as restricted least squares: the regression of Y on the regressors of X having dropped the $i^{\underline{th}}$ variable provides the restricted estimation. In this example it is clear that the unrestricted regression of Y on all the regressors provides sufficient information with which to test the hypothesis $\beta_i = 0$, since the simple t-test on the coefficient is an appropriate test. The relationship between the unrestricted and restricted regressions is, however, most illuminating regarding the truth of the hypothesis. In general, consider the regression of Y on X subject to m linear restrictions ($m < k$, the number of parameters in β).

$$Y = X\beta + \varepsilon \qquad \text{subject to } R\beta = r$$

where R is an m×k matrix of known constants and is of full rank. $R\beta = r$ represents m linear equations in the k elements of β, and for each of the m restrictions to contain independent information it is necessary that $\rho(R) = m$. This ensures that none of the restrictions is redundant. r is a k×1 vector of known constants. To estimate β subject to the constraint is a simple exercise in constrained optimization: find that estimate which minimizes the residual sum of squared residuals and which satisfies the m restrictions. The Lagrangian is given by $(Y - Xb)'(Y - Xb) - 2\lambda'(Rb - r)$, where λ is an m×1 vector of multipliers. Differentiating this first with respect to the k-parameter vector b, and then with respect to the m-parameter vector λ, setting both expressions to zero and denoting the solutions by $\tilde{\beta}$ and $\tilde{\lambda}$:

$$-2X'Y + 2X'X\tilde{\beta} - 2R'\tilde{\lambda} = 0 \quad \text{and} \quad -2(R\tilde{\beta} - r) = 0.$$

From the first expression:

$$\tilde{\beta} = (X'X)^{-1}X'Y + (X'X)^{-1}R'\tilde{\lambda}.$$

Denoting the familiar term $(X'X)^{-1}X'Y$ by $\hat{\beta}$, the unconstrained ordinary least squares estimator:

$$\tilde{\beta} = \hat{\beta} + (X'X)^{-1}R'\tilde{\lambda}.$$

The constrained estimator thus comprises the unconstrained estimator plus a linear combination of the multipliers; it is immediately apparent that the two estimators coincide if and only if all the multipliers are zero (in which case the constraint does not bind – it is satisfied in the data without imposition). To solve this equation for $\tilde{\beta}$ an expression for the multipliers is required. Pre-multiplying the first order condition by $R(X'X)^{-1}$:

$$R(X'X)^{-1}X'Y - R\tilde{\beta} + R(X'X)^{-1}R'\tilde{\lambda} = 0$$

i.e.

$$R(\tilde{\beta} - \hat{\beta}) = R(X'X)^{-1}R'\tilde{\lambda}.$$

Now the matrix $R(X'X)^{-1}R'$ is of order m×m and, given that R and X are each of full rank, this matrix is also of full rank and is therefore non-singular. This equation may, then, be used to solve for the Lagrange multipliers:

$$\tilde{\lambda} = [R(X'X)^{-1}R']^{-1}R(\tilde{\beta} - \hat{\beta}).$$

It is to be noted that the multipliers depend, linearly, on the difference between the unconstrained and the constrained estimators $(\tilde{\beta} - \hat{\beta})$. This expression may then be substituted into the expression for $\tilde{\beta}$ to yield:

$$\tilde{\beta} = \hat{\beta} + (X'X)^{-1}R'[R(X'X)^{-1}R']^{-1}R(\tilde{\beta} - \hat{\beta}).$$

However, $R\tilde{\beta} = r$; hence the constrained estimator may be written as:

$$\tilde{\beta} = \hat{\beta} - (X'X)^{-1}R'[R(X'X)^{-1}R']^{-1}(R\hat{\beta} - r).$$

Suppose $R\hat{\beta} - r = \delta$; then:

$$\tilde{\beta} = \hat{\beta} - (X'X)^{-1}R'[R(X'X)^{-1}R']^{-1}\delta$$

and, taking expectations, given that the unconstrained model is properly specified and the regressors are non-stochastic:

$$E(\tilde{\beta}) = \beta - (X'X)^{-1}R'[R(X'X)^{-1}R']^{-1}E(\delta).$$

The constrained estimator is, then, unbiased only if $E(\delta) = 0$ and is otherwise biased. Turning to the variances:

$$V(\hat{\beta}) = \sigma^2(X'X)^{-1}$$

and $$V(\tilde{\beta}) = \sigma^2(X'X)^{-1} - \sigma^2(X'X)^{-1}R'[R(X'X)^{-1}R']^{-1}R(X'X)^{-1}.$$

Hence $V(\hat{\beta}) - V(\tilde{\beta}) = \sigma^2(X'X)^{-1}R'[R(X'X)^{-1}R']^{-1}R(X'X)^{-1}$ which is a positive definite matrix and so the elements of $\hat{\beta}$ each have a larger variance than the corresponding elements of $\tilde{\beta}$ and thus the constrained estimator is more efficient whether or not the constraints are true. To test the restrictions, define the constrained residuals as $\tilde{e} = Y - X\tilde{\beta}$:

$$\tilde{e} = Y - X\hat{\beta} + X(\hat{\beta} - \tilde{\beta})$$

i.e. $$\tilde{e} = \hat{e} + X(\hat{\beta} - \tilde{\beta}).$$

Defining the restricted residual sum of squares by RRSS:

$$RRSS = \tilde{e}'\tilde{e} = [\hat{e}' + (\hat{\beta} - \tilde{\beta})'X'][\hat{e} + X(\hat{\beta} - \tilde{\beta})];$$

this may be simplified since the unrestricted OLS residuals, $\hat{e}$, and the data matrix, X, are orthogonal; that is, $\hat{e}'X = 0$; thus:

$$RRSS = \hat{e}'\hat{e} + (\hat{\beta} - \tilde{\beta})'X'X(\hat{\beta} - \tilde{\beta}).$$

Denoting the unrestricted residual sum of squares, $\hat{e}'\hat{e}$, by URSS:

$$RRSS = URSS + (\hat{\beta} - \tilde{\beta})'X'X(\hat{\beta} - \tilde{\beta})$$

i.e. $$RRSS - URSS = (\hat{\beta} - \tilde{\beta})'X'X(\hat{\beta} - \tilde{\beta}).$$

From this it is immediately obvious that since X'X is a positive definite matrix, the restricted residual sum of squares exceeds the unrestricted sum of squares except in the case of $\hat{\beta} = \tilde{\beta}$, i.e. except when the restrictions are exactly satisfied by the data. The difference between the two residual sums of squares may, then, be used as a test of the restrictions. From the previous analysis:

$$\hat{\beta} - \tilde{\beta} = (X'X)^{-1}R'[R(X'X)^{-1}R']^{-1}(R\hat{\beta} - r);$$

but $\hat{\beta} = \beta + (X'X)^{-1}X'\varepsilon$ and, under the null hypothesis, $R\beta = r$; hence, under the null hypothesis $R\hat{\beta} = r + R(X'X)^{-1}X'\varepsilon$ and so:

$$X(\hat{\beta} - \tilde{\beta}) = X(X'X)^{-1}R'[R(X'X)^{-1}R']^{-1}R(X'X)^{-1}X'\varepsilon.$$

Denote the matrix $R(X'X)^{-1}R'$ by A and $X(X'X)^{-1}R'$ by B then:

$$X(\hat{\beta} - \tilde{\beta}) = BA^{-1}B'\varepsilon$$

and so:

$$\begin{aligned} RRSS - URSS &= \varepsilon'BA^{-1}B'BA^{-1}B'\varepsilon \\ &= \varepsilon'BA^{-1}B'\varepsilon \end{aligned}$$

since $B'B = A$. This is a quadratic form in ε and since $BA^{-1}B'$ is a square m× m matrix of full rank:

$$(RRSS - URSS)/\sigma^2 \sim \chi^2_m$$

under the null hypothesis.

Moreover, $URSS = \varepsilon'(I - X(X'X)^{-1}X')\varepsilon = \varepsilon'M\varepsilon$ where M is the idempotent matrix $I - X(X'X)^{-1}X'$; hence:

$$URSS/\sigma^2 \sim \chi^2_{n-k} \quad \text{always.}$$

Using the result from **Distribution theory** that two quadratic forms z'Pz and z'Qz are independent if Q'P = 0, it may be noted that in this case:

$$MBA^{-1}B' \equiv 0 \text{ since } MX \equiv 0.$$

Hence under H_o: $R\beta = r$, $(RRSS - URSS)/\sigma^2 \sim \chi^2_m$; $URSS/\sigma^2 \sim \chi^2_{n-k}$ always and the two distributions are independent. Therefore, under H_o:

$$\frac{[RRSS - URSS]/m}{URSS/(n-k)} \sim F_{m,n-k}.$$

This is a particularly useful result; to test a set of linear restrictions two regressions are run: one unconstrained (to yield URSS) and the other constrained by the hypothesis (to yield RRSS). Except in the very rare case when the hypothesis is exactly satisfied in the data, the restricted sum of squares exceeds the unrestricted. If the hypothesis is true, though not exactly satisfied in the data, any difference between RRSS and URSS will be the result of sampling variation only; however, if the hypothesis is false, then imposing it will effect a very large RRSS relative to URSS. The F-test, expressed in terms of residual sums of squares, can easily be translated into a difference of R^2: denote by R^2_r and R^2_u the goodness of fit statistics from the restricted and unrestricted regressions respectively; then it is easy to show that:

$$\frac{(R^2_u - R^2_r)/m}{(1-R^2_u)/(n-k)} \sim F_{m,n-k}$$

and this form of the test of restrictions has great intuitive appeal: if the restrictions are true then the impact of imposing the restrictions on the regression will result in only a slight reduction of the goodness of fit statistic, whereas if the restrictions are false the impact will be large. Hence if R_r^2 is insignificantly different from R_u^2 the restrictions may be accepted.

The technique of restricted least squares is not, of course, confined to linear restrictions on the parameters, and may easily be extended, in principle, to non-linear restrictions. In using restricted estimation as a means of testing non-linear restrictions it is possible to proceed by using one of two asymptotically equivalent non-linear tests: the likelihood ratio test and the Lagrange multiplier test. These are described in **Likelihood ratio tests**, **Lagrange multiplier tests** and **Non-linear hypothesis testing**; in some cases it is awkward to construct the restricted estimator when the restriction is non-linear, and then the appropriate test which utilizes only the unrestricted estimator is the popular Wald test (see **Wald test**).

If the restrictions are not rejected by the data then the result of estimating the model subject to those restrictions leads to a gain in efficiency, and there is no evidence to suggest that the estimators lose their unbiasedness.

Further reading

Restricted least squares is covered in all econometrics texts, and the reader is referred to the standard texts for further discussion, but also to the related entries here on **Hypothesis testing**, **Linear Hypotheses** and **Non-linear hypothesis testing**.

Ridge regression

Ridge regression is one proposed 'solution' to the 'problem' of multicollinearity. It is a mechanical device, relying on statistical theory, and has no obvious basis in economic theory. In the familiar regression model the ordinary least squares estimator is given by:

$$\hat{\beta} = (X'X)^{-1}X'Y \quad \text{and} \quad V(\hat{\beta}) = \sigma^2(X'X)^{-1}.$$

In the presence of multicollinearity the estimators are imprecise, and this is manifested in large diagonal elements of $(X'X)^{-1}$. Ridge regression reduces this imprecision mechanically by choosing a constant, $c > 0$, and defining a new estimator of β by:

$$\hat{\beta}_R = (X'X + cI)^{-1}X'Y.$$

This is, in general, a biased estimator but is more efficient than $\hat{\beta}$:

$$E(\hat{\beta}_R) = (X'X + cI)^{-1}X'X\beta \quad \text{and} \quad V(\hat{\beta}_R) = \sigma^2(X'X + cI)^{-1}X'X(X'X + cI)^{-1}.$$

The bias is zero only if $c = 0$ or $\beta = 0$; however, there is always an efficiency gain since $V(\hat{\beta}) - V(\hat{\beta}_R)$ is a positive definite matrix for $c > 0$. To develop this analysis, let Q be the matrix of orthogonal eigenvectors of X'X (and so

$QQ' = I$) and let the eigenvalues of X'X be $(\lambda_1, \ldots, \lambda_k)$ (for details of these constructs see **Matrix algebra**). Then $Q'X'XQ = \Lambda = \text{diag}\{\lambda_1, \ldots, \lambda_k\}$; also $Y = XQ\theta + \varepsilon$ is the principal components model (see **Principal components**) and $\theta = Q'\beta$ is the parameter vector associated with that model. Since Q is the orthogonal matrix of eigenvectors of X'X, it is also the orthogonal matrix of eigenvectors of $(X'X)^{-1}$, of $(X'X + cI)^{-1}$ and of $(X'X + cI)^{-2}$. Specifically: Q is an orthogonal matrix, therefore:

$$Q'Q = QQ' = I \Rightarrow Q' = Q^{-1};$$

also $$Q'X'XQ = \Lambda \quad \text{and} \quad Q'(X'X)^{-1}Q = \Lambda^{-1}$$

and $$Q'(X'X + cI)^{-1}Q = (\Lambda + cI)^{-1}$$

and $$Q'(X'X + cI)^{-2}Q = (\Lambda + cI)^{-2}$$

The mean square error matrix of $\hat{\beta}_R$ is given by:

$$MSE(\hat{\beta}_R) = E[(\hat{\beta}_R - \beta)'(\hat{\beta}_R - \beta)] = V(\hat{\beta}_R) + [E(\hat{\beta}_R) - \beta]'[E(\hat{\beta}_R) - \beta]$$

and the scalar measure of mean square error is the trace of $MSE(\hat{\beta}_R)$, often called the mean squared error, or the average loss or risk. The mean squared error is given by the trace of $V(\hat{\beta}_R)$ (the sum of the variances of the elements of the estimator) plus the sum of the squared biases. Now:

$$\begin{aligned} Tr\{V(\hat{\beta}_R)\} &= Tr\{\sigma^2(X'X + cI)^{-1}X'X(X'X + cI)^{-1}\} \\ &= \sigma^2 Tr\{(X'X + cI)^{-2}X'X\} \end{aligned}$$

but $Q'(X'X + cI)^{-2}Q = (\Lambda + cI)^{-2} \Rightarrow (X'X + cI)^{-2} = Q'^{-1}(\Lambda + cI)^{-2}Q^{-1} = Q(\Lambda + cI)^{-2}Q'$; hence:

$$\begin{aligned} TrV(\hat{\beta}_R) &= \sigma^2 Tr\{Q(\Lambda + cI)^{-2}Q'Q\Lambda Q'\} = \sigma^2 Tr\{(\Lambda + cI)^{-2}Q'Q\Lambda Q'Q\} \\ &= \sigma^2 Tr\{(\Lambda + cI)^{-2}\Lambda\} = \sigma^2 \textstyle\sum_{i=1}^{k} \lambda_i/(\lambda_i + c)^2, \end{aligned}$$

and as c increases the sum of the ridge estimators' variances decreases. The bias of $\hat{\beta}_R$ equals $(X'X + cI)^{-1}X'X\beta - \beta = [(X'X + cI)^{-1}X'X - I]\beta$, and by the rules of inverses:

$$(X'X + cI)^{-1} = (X'X)^{-1} - (X'X)^{-1}[(X'X)^{-1} + c^{-1}I]^{-1}(X'X)^{-1}$$

hence $(X'X + cI)^{-1}X'X = I - (I + c^{-1}(X'X)^{-1})^{-1} = I - c(cI + (X'X)^{-1})^{-1}$.

Thus the bias is given by: $-c(cI + (X'X)^{-1})^{-1}\beta$ and the bias element of the mean square error is then:

$$\begin{aligned} Tr\{c^2\beta'(cI + (X'X)^{-1})^{-2}\beta\} &= c^2 Tr\{\beta'Q(\Lambda + cI)^{-2}Q'\beta\} \\ &= c^2 Tr\{\theta'(\Lambda + cI)^{-2}\theta\} \\ &= c^2 \textstyle\sum_{i=1}^{k} [\theta_i/(\lambda_i + c)]^2 \end{aligned}$$

and as c increases the sum of squared biases increases. Hence the mean square error comprises two components, one of which is decreasing in c and the other increasing in c. For some values of c the mean square error of $\hat{\beta}_R$ is less than that of the OLS estimator, $\hat{\beta}$; indeed, in the range $0 \leq c \leq \sigma^2/\max(\theta)$, where $\max(\theta)$ is the maximum element of $\theta = Q'\beta$, it may be shown that the ridge estimator has a smaller mean square error than the OLS estimator. It is worth noting that the ridge estimator may be written as:

$$\begin{aligned}\hat{\beta}_R &= (X'X + cI)^{-1}X'Y \\ &= (X'X + cI)^{-1}X'X(X'X)^{-1}X'Y \\ &= (I + c(X'X)^{-1})^{-1}\hat{\beta}\end{aligned}$$

and as $c \to \infty$, $\hat{\beta}_R'\hat{\beta}_R \to 0$; that is, the effect of increasing c is to 'shrink' the estimator towards zero and c is known, therefore, as the shrinkage factor.

One problem with using ridge regression is that the upper bound on c, $\sigma^2/\max(Q'\beta)$, depends on the unknown parameters and if c is estimated then the properties derived above, on the basis that c is not stochastic, can no longer be guaranteed. Specifically, if c is estimated then the mean square error of the ridge estimator is not necessarily less than that of the OLS estimator and resulting tests based on t- and F-distributions are not valid (and may, therefore, be misleading). Nevertheless, this has not prevented investigators using ridge regression. Some researchers have investigated the use of stochastic shrinkage factors and the resulting 'generalized ridge regression'.

Notwithstanding such developments, ridge regression is somewhat mechanical in nature and produces results which are not immediately amenable to economic interpretation; it is a method driven by statistical considerations and has not proved particularly successful in applied econometrics work. It is difficult, if not impossible, to offer an economic interpretation of the shrinkage factor and this does not, then, offer an appealing 'solution' to multicollinearity.

Further reading

See Hoerl and Kennard (1970), Smith and Campbell (1980), Judge *et al.* (1985) and Schmidt (1976).

Robust estimation

If the model $Y = X\beta + \varepsilon$ with $\varepsilon \sim MVN(0, \sigma^2 I)$ and a non-stochastic data matrix is estimated by ordinary least squares to yield the estimator $\hat{\beta}$, then this is the best linear unbiased estimator if all the assumptions of the model are met; however, if any one of the assumptions fails, then OLS estimators do not have such optimal properties. Robust estimation concerns the construction of alternative estimators which are less sensitive to violations of the assumptions than is the OLS estimator. A robust estimator is not the best if the assumptions are all met.

Robust estimators could, in principle, be constructed for any violation of the assumptions of the general linear model, but the focus of robust estimation concerns violations of the assumed distribution of the error term. If the errors are normally distributed the OLS estimator is not only the best linear unbiased estimator (BLUE) but it is the best unbiased estimator. If the errors are distributed other than normally there is, usually, a more efficient non-linear unbiased estimator available. Of particular concern is the case when the errors have fat tails; fat tails give rise to a greater number of large errors than is expected under the assumption of normality, and one route to examining the nature of the error distribution is to look for large residuals. An observation associated with a large error is an outlier (see **Outliers** and **Normality tests**), but since OLS seeks to minimize the sum of squared errors a large true error will not necessarily translate into a large fitted residual. In this sense the fitted regression using all the observations will not yield the necessary information, as the presence of a large error will cause the OLS regression line to be so constructed as to minimize its influence. It is this very fact that results in the suboptimality of OLS: outliers will have an undue influence on the estimated parameters. Methods for identifying such observations are described in **Outliers**.

If particular observations which appear as outliers can be 'explained' in some way by reference to economic theory or to some particular events which led to 'unusual' outcomes, then treating those observations as special by the use of dummy variables, or simply discarding them, is an acceptable and proper route. However, if outliers remain after such a procedure, then attention should be directed to the possible presence and implications of a fat-tailed error distribution.

One immediate possibility is to employ maximum likelihood estimation, but using a density function other than the normal. For example, if the true errors are assumed to be distributed according to the Laplace distribution:

$$f(\varepsilon_i) = (1/2\sigma)\exp\{-|\varepsilon_i|/2\sigma\}$$

then the maximum likelihood estimator of β is that which minimizes the sum of absolute residuals; this is the MAD (minimum absolute deviation) estimator and is also known both as the LAR (least absolute residual) estimator and as the LAE (least absolute error) estimator; in small samples it is far less sensitive to outlying observations than is the OLS estimator.

Many of the more common forms of robust estimators may be written as the solution to:

$$\text{Min}_\beta S(\beta) = \textstyle\sum_{i=1}^{n} h(\hat{e}_i)$$

where h is some function, and $\hat{e}_i$ is the ith fitted residual.

The estimator which results from this is known as the M-estimator, where M stands for maximum-likelihood-type-estimator. OLS is a special case, where $h(z) = z^2$, and MAD is also a special case, where $h(z) = |z|$. Other forms of h which have been suggested include $h(z) = |z|^p$ where $1 < p < 2$ (this yields the so-called L_p estimator); p is chosen according to the fatness of tails: the fatter the tails the closer should p be to unity. Another form of h is $h(z) = z^2$ if $|z| < c$, and $c|z|$ otherwise. A variant on this is:

$h(z)$	$= z^2$	if $\|z\| < c$ and otherwise:
	$= g(\|z\|)\|z\|$	where $g(\|z\|) < \|z\|$ and is chosen as a decreasing function
	$= 0$	for all z such that $g(\|z\|) < 0$.

This estimator effectively discards all observations which would have been associated with residuals so large that $g(|z|) < 0$. This is a form of 'bounded influence regression'; ordinary least squares does not provide any bounds on the influence of any one observation, but using h as defined above provides a particular weighting scheme which ensures that the influence of any one observation is strictly limited. A particular form of bounded regression which has been proposed is to weight observations according to their Studentized residuals or their DFFITS measure (see **Outliers** for discussion of these measures). A particularly simple example of bounded regression using DFFITS is to choose the parameters to minimize the weighted sum of squares $\sum_{i=1}^{n} w_i \hat{e}_i^2$ where $w_i = 1$ if $|DFFITS| \leq 1$ and $w_i = 0$ otherwise.

A variant on the above method is to fit the OLS regression and then discard the observations associated with the most extreme residuals; if the observations associated with residuals lying in the extremes of the residual distribution are discarded and the regression then rerun, the result is the 'trimmed' least squares estimator. If the observations associated with residuals lying in the $100(\alpha/2)\%$ and $100(1 - \alpha/2)\%$ quantiles are discarded then about $100\alpha\%$ of the observations are effectively discarded.

Given the somewhat arbitrary *ad hoc* nature of the robust estimators which depend upon the choice of the weighting function these approaches have had limited application in econometrics.

Further reading

An extensive survey of robust estimators may be found in Amemiya (1985). See also Huber (1981), Koenker and Bassett (1982) and Welsch (1980).

Sampling theory

An estimator is a rule by which a sample of data is used to construct an estimate of an unknown parameter; the rule, a formula, is the estimator, while the particular value obtained from the application of that formula to a given sample yields the estimate. If the sample is viewed as a random drawing from a population then the estimator is a random variable and the estimate is a single realization of that random variable; an estimate is not, in this approach, a random variable but is a number determined by the sample at hand. In order to judge how good any particular estimate is it is not possible to compare the estimate directly with the underlying parameter, since the latter is unknown. An estimate is judged by reference to the properties of the rule, the estimator, which generates the estimate.

Several criteria are applied to an estimator, and the method by which an estimator is judged consists of conceptualizing the whole spectrum of estimates which would be produced if the estimator rule were applied to repeated random samples drawn from the population. It is to be stressed that this need only be a conceptualization of random sampling – it is not necessary that it be actually performed (nor, indeed, is it necessary that repeated sampling could be performed); what is important is that the experiment of repeated sampling is considered conceptually, and the properties of the estimator in repeated samples are then derived.

Suppose the parameter is denoted by θ, and the estimator by $\hat{\theta}$; suppose a repeated random sampling experiment is conceptualized in which samples of a fixed size are taken at random from the population; let the estimate from the ith sample be denoted by $\hat{\theta}_{(i)}$. The properties of an estimator which are deemed important include:

1. unbiasedness; this requires that $E(\hat{\theta}) = \theta$, and this implies that $E(\hat{\theta}) = \text{Lim}_{m\to\infty}(1/m)\sum_{i=1}^{m}\hat{\theta}_{(i)} = \theta$; that is, the average of $\hat{\theta}$ tends to the true value as the number of samples increases without bound;
2. efficiency; this requires that the distribution of all the possible estimates is tightly clustered and for an unbiased estimator this ensures that the estimates are clustered around θ. Efficiency is a measure of the variance of $\hat{\theta}$ values. In comparing two unbiased estimators it is clear that the one with the smaller variance is preferred. A single estimate may be conceived as a random drawing from the 'population' of the values which the estimator generates via (conceptualized) repeated sampling, and the smaller is the variance of $\hat{\theta}$ the more likely it is that any one estimate drawn at random will be close to the mean. The smaller is the variance of the estimator the more efficient it is; equivalently, the estimator is more precise the smaller is its variance. The variance of $\hat{\theta}$ may be defined by $V(\hat{\theta}) = \text{Lim}_{m\to\infty}(1/m)\sum_{i=1}^{m}(\hat{\theta}_{(i)} - E(\hat{\theta}))^2$, i.e. the variance is the limit of the average squared deviation of the estimates from their mean;

3. in comparing two estimators, both may be biased and they may have different variances; if the more biased is the less efficient the choice is clear, but otherwise it is not an obvious choice. By considering the properties of the estimators in repeated samples, the Mean Square Error (MSE) criterion is often used; $\text{MSE}(\hat{\theta}) = \text{E}(\hat{\theta} - \theta)^2 = \text{V}(\hat{\theta}) + \text{B}^2$, where B is the bias in $\hat{\theta}$, defined as $\text{E}(\hat{\theta}) - \theta$;
4. for some estimators it is not possible to derive exact finite sample results, in which case concepts such as consistency are required: the estimator $\hat{\theta}$ is consistent if $\text{plim}(\hat{\theta}) = \theta$. (See **Large sample theory**.)

An estimator which has desirable properties by reference to its sampling properties is more likely to produce a good estimate than an estimator which has undesirable features; however, since the choice of an estimator rule is made by reference to its sampling properties, and economists usually operate with non-experimental data, this does not guarantee that the estimate will be 'good'; a biased and inefficient estimator might, from a given sample, produce a better estimate than an estimator which is unbiased and more efficient but the fact that this is unlikely leads to the judgement in favour of the unbiased and efficient estimator. In the absence of repeated sampling in the material world, the sampling properties of estimators are derived theoretically or, when this is not possible, by constructing hypothetical samples from a known population and computing the corresponding estimates. This device is described in **Monte Carlo methods** and is a most useful approach. Sampling theory is at the heart of classical econometric procedures, and is the basis of the common method of statistical inference.

Also, unless the population is known or asserted to follow a specific distribution the actual sampling distribution of $\hat{\theta}$ will not be known. To make inferences of θ from the sample estimate and to perform hypothesis tests it is necessary to use a specific distribution of $\hat{\theta}$; in large samples and under certain regularity conditions the results of central limit theorems may be used to approximate the distribution of $\hat{\theta}$ by the normal. For the conditions under which this is legitimate see **Central limit theorems**.

Further reading

Sampling theory is discussed in all econometric texts. For the application of sampling theory to economic data, which is typically non-experimental, see, especially, Haavelmo (1944); see also Leamer (1978) for a further discussion of sampling and Bayesian theory as applied to the non-experimental data of economics. See **Error term**, **Central limit theorems** and **Large sample theory**.

Seasonality

Many time-series exhibit a regular pattern; it is common to break time-series into three components: trend, seasonal variation and a random component. Seasonal variation is seen as comprising intrayear movement in an economic series, which is, relatively speaking, largely predictable, and is commonly assumed to be due to exogenous, typically non-economic, uncontrollable forces. For this reason such variation is often removed from a time-series prior to any economic analysis and once a series has been purged of such variation the result is a 'seasonally adjusted, or deseasonalized, series'; the original series is often described as the 'raw series'. Many official statistics are available in both 'raw' and 'deseasonalized' form.

Before discussing actual methods of deseasonalizing a time-series it is useful to identify some simple desirable properties of any deseasonalization method. If the raw and the deseasonalized data are denoted by X and X^a respectively, the following are desirable properties:

1. the method is 'sum preserving': $X_t^a + Y_t^a = (X_t + Y_t)^a$. This implies, for example, that the sum of the seasonally adjusted components of nominal GNP equals seasonally adjusted nominal GNP, and that the sum of seasonally adjusted employment and seasonally adjusted unemployment equals the seasonally adjusted labour force;
2. the method is 'product preserving': $X_t^a Y_t^a = (X_t Y_t)^a$. This implies, for example, that for any good the product of seasonally adjusted quantity and seasonally adjusted price equals seasonally adjusted value.

It may be shown, disappointingly, that any method which is both sum and product preserving is trivial, for it implies that $X_t^a = 0$ or $X_t^a = X_t$. One cannot, therefore, require both these properties for a given method of deseasonalization.

3. orthogonality: $\mathrm{Cor}(X_t^a(X_t - X_t^a)) = 0$. This implies that there is zero correlation between the deseasonalized series and the difference between the raw and deseasonalized series. The series $X_t - X_t^a$ represents the seasonal component, and if this is correlated with the adjusted series, X_t^a, then the deseasonalization procedure would be deemed deficient since it has left some seasonal variation in X_t^a;
4. idempotency: $(X_t^a)^a = X_t^a$. This, like the orthogonality property, implies that the deseasonalization operator removes all seasonal variation, for it requires that applying the deseasonalization operator to a deseasonalized series leaves the already deseasonalized series unchanged;
5. symmetry:

$$\frac{\partial X_t^a}{\partial X_s} = \frac{\partial X_s^a}{\partial X_t}.$$

This property requires that the effect of a change in the raw variable at time s on the deseasonalized variable at time t is symmetric and is, therefore, equal to the influence of the raw variable at time t on the adjusted variable at time s.

These properties form a set of minimal consistency requirements for a deseasonalization method; however, no method can be both sum and product preserving. If product preserving is discarded and attention is concentrated on sum preserving methods, it may be shown that (i) the properties of orthogonality, idempotency and symmetry are not independent for a method which is sum preserving, and (ii) a sum preserving method which has two of those three properties necessarily satisfies the third.

If a series is thought of as consisting of three elements, a seasonal component (S), a trend component (T) and a residual (R), these may be combined in additive or multiplicative form:

$$X = S + T + R \quad \text{or} \quad X = S \times T \times R.$$

The multiplicative form may be linearized by taking logarithms. Deseasonalization is concerned with estimating the S component, and forming the new, adjusted, series X – S (in the additive form) or X/S (in the multiplicative form). Deseasonalization methods address a series in isolation from other series and the objective is to remove, rather than explain, the seasonal component. The deseasonalized and detrended series from the two models are given by X – S – T and X/(S.T) respectively; the 'residual' is thus designed to reflect the underlying, adjusted, series.

There are two main approaches to seasonal adjustment: moving average methods and regression methods. The typical method used by official agencies is a moving average method (which does not satisfy the above properties); regression methods do satisfy the consistency properties (excluding product preserving) and regression methods have greater appeal on these grounds.

Moving average methods take the general form:

$$X_t^a = \sum_{s=0}^{p} w_s X_{t-s}$$

where the w_s are chosen weights; hence the deseasonalized series is simply a weighted average of p + 1 consecutive terms of X_t (the present value and p lagged terms), and by taking an average any seasonalities in the data will (at least partly) be removed as a 'seasonal high' in the period will be averaged with a 'seasonal low', given that p is properly chosen. Moving average methods typically consist of three stages:

- having chosen p (say p = 4 for quarterly data) an initial estimate of the seasonal component (S) is made by the constructing the moving average and an initial deseasonalized series is constructed;

- this series will contain the trend component, and at stage two the trend is estimated and removed;
- this series may still contain some seasonalities, and these are then removed by applying the moving average once again.

This method is incorporated into many software packages and has certain advantages. Notably, since the adjustment of X_t is based on the most recent p + 1 observations, it allows the seasonal component to vary over the entire length of the series. It does not suffer, then, from having imposed a constant form of seasonal variation on the data. For example, with quarterly data the seasonal component in any given quarter may be estimated from analysis of data extending over one calendar year and the adjustment applied to quarter i observations may then differ from one year to another. An immediate disadvantage of this method is that the adjustments applied to the most extreme data points are less reliable than the adjustment applied to other data points, and in consequence there are, typically, frequent revisions to the most recently adjusted data. This method may, of course, be applied to the data in natural units (additive seasonality) or in logarithms (multiplicative seasonality).

In the regression method it is assumed that the seasonal component is constant over the entire series, and that the trend component may be captured by a deterministic term; for example, in the case of quarterly data and an additive model, a regression involving three dummy variables and a trend is run:

$$X_t = \alpha + \sum_{i=1}^{3} \beta_i D_{ti} + \gamma t + \varepsilon_t$$

where $D_{ti} = 1$ if the observation t is in quarter i and is zero otherwise; for a multiplicative model, the regressand would be $\ell n(X_t)$.

This model may be extended to accommodate more complex forms of trend by, for example, incorporating terms in t^2 and higher powers (i.e. by using a higher polynomial in t), and more complex forms of the seasonal pattern may be accommodated. The ordinary least squares residuals are then the deseasonalized and detrended series; this method is appealing as the adjusted series satisfies the consistency checks of sum preserving, orthogonality, idempotency and symmetry. It is also very easy to implement. The disadvantage of the approach lies in its assumptions: the trend is assumed to be deterministic, and the seasonal pattern is also deterministic, so that the seasonality embodied in a quarter i observation is always given by a constant.

In estimating relationships between variables which are subject to systematic seasonal variation, investigators face a simple choice: to use the raw (unadjusted) data and seek to accommodate the seasonality in the estimated relationship or to use deseasonalized (adjusted) data. The option of using raw data and ignoring the seasonality is not a recommended option, as it may give rise to a form of 'spurious regression': two variables which are unrelated but which are both subject to seasonal variation may appear to be related. It is important to distinguish between the appearance of a relationship which is due only to a common seasonal component and that which is due to an economic relationship between the underlying (adjusted) variables.

One of the problems of using adjusted data is that the method of adjustment is not under the control of the investigator. This has several implications. In the estimation of the relationship between two variables, Y and X, if adjusted data are used this may then distort the apparent economic relationship, especially if the series have been adjusted by different methods. Official deseasonalization procedures use a moving average method which may be the source of autocorrelation in the residuals of the regression of adjusted Y on adjusted X. Also, since deseasonalization utilizes a univariate approach, the possibility that seasonal variation in Y is due to seasonal variation in X will be obscured by the use of adjusted data: in this case, deseasonalization will have removed variation in the variables which should, more properly, be used in estimating the economic relationship. In the light of this it is recommended that unadjusted data are used, with proper recognition of the seasonal variation embodied in the subsequent analysis; this allows the investigator to identify the most appropriate form of seasonal model.

It is to be noted that if a variable Y and potential explanatory variables X_1, . . , X_k were to be deseasonalized by regressing each on seasonal dummies and the residuals used as the adjusted series, then the estimates obtained of the relationship between Y and X_1, . . , X_k from the adjusted data would be identical to those obtained from using the raw data in a regression augmented by seasonal dummies. This is an application of the Frisch–Waugh theorem (see **Frisch–Waugh theorem**).

In the analysis of the stationarity of a variable which is subject to seasonal variation, the typical procedure is as follows. If Y_t is measured s times per year the seasonal differences $Y_t - Y_{t-s} = \Delta_s Y_t$ are constructed, and Y is said to be seasonally integrated of order (d, D) if by applying D s-differences and then taking d first differences a stationary series results (s = 4 for quarterly data and s = 12 for monthly data, for example). The series $\Delta_s Y_t$ will also be detrended if Y_t is subject to a linear trend. If Y_t is subject to additive seasonal components it is not uncommon that $\Delta_s Y_t$ is stationary. If $\Delta_s Y_t$ is non-stationary it is unusual to take a second seasonal difference, and stationarity is typically sought by taking first differences of the s-differences. If the seasonality is multiplicative then seasonal differences may be constructed from the logarithm of Y_t: $\Delta_s \ell n Y_t = \ell n Y_t - \ell n Y_{t-s}$. Methods for testing the degree of integration of a series subject to seasonal variation are more complex than those for a non-seasonal variable, but are all based on extension of the Dickey–Fuller test (see **Integration** and **Unit root tests**).

Further reading

Lovell (1963) discusses the simple consistency requirements of a deseasonalization method; see Wallis (1974) on the potential distortions which arise from using adjusted data. See also Dickey, Hasza and Fuller (1984) and Osborn *et al.* (1988) on seasonal integration.

Seemingly unrelated regression equations

The generalized least squares estimation technique may be appropriate when the economic model in question defines a set of equations which are related via the error structure. A common example is a set of m equations which define demand equations for a set of m goods. If an economic model defines m equations, the ith of which may be written as:

$$Y_i = X_i\beta_i + \varepsilon_i$$

where Y_i is an n×1 vector of observations on the ith equation's regressor, X_i is an n×k matrix of observations on k regressors and ε_i is n×1 vector of the ith equation's disturbances then the full set of equations may be written as:

$$\begin{bmatrix} Y_1 \\ Y_2 \\ \vdots \\ \vdots \\ Y_m \end{bmatrix} = \begin{bmatrix} X_1 & 0 & \dots & \dots & 0 \\ 0 & X_2 & & & \vdots \\ \vdots & & \ddots & & \vdots \\ \vdots & & & \ddots & \vdots \\ 0 & \dots & \dots & \dots & X_m \end{bmatrix} \begin{bmatrix} \beta_1 \\ \beta_2 \\ \vdots \\ \vdots \\ \beta_m \end{bmatrix} + \begin{bmatrix} \varepsilon_1 \\ \varepsilon_2 \\ \vdots \\ \vdots \\ \varepsilon_m \end{bmatrix}$$

which may be compactly written as:

$$Y = X\beta + \varepsilon.$$

It has been assumed, for purposes of exposition only, that each equation has exactly the same number of regressors and that there are identical numbers of observations for each equation. The variance–covariance matrix of ε is given by:

$$\Sigma = V(\varepsilon) = E\begin{bmatrix} \varepsilon_1\varepsilon_1' & \varepsilon_1\varepsilon_2' & \dots & \dots & \varepsilon_1\varepsilon_m' \\ \varepsilon_2\varepsilon_1' & \varepsilon_2\varepsilon_2' & & & \varepsilon_2\varepsilon_m' \\ \vdots & & \ddots & & \vdots \\ \vdots & & & \ddots & \vdots \\ \varepsilon_m\varepsilon_1' & \dots & \dots & \dots & \varepsilon_m\varepsilon_m' \end{bmatrix}$$

Each 'element' of this matrix, $E(\varepsilon_i \varepsilon_j')$, is itself a matrix; $E(\varepsilon_i \varepsilon_j')$ is an n×n matrix which, if i = j is the variance–covariance matrix of the ith equation's error term and if $i \neq j$ is a covariance matrix of the contemporaneous and lagged covariances between errors relating to different equations. Suppose that each equation has a homoscedastic and non-autocorrelated error term and suppose further that the error terms relating to different equations are contemporaneously correlated but non-contemporaneously uncorrelated; then:

$$E(\varepsilon_i \varepsilon_j') = \sigma_{ij} I$$

so that:

$$\Sigma = \{\sigma_{ij} I\} = \begin{bmatrix} \sigma_{11} I & \sigma_{12} I & \cdots & \cdots & \sigma_{1m} I \\ \sigma_{21} I & \sigma_{22} I & & & \vdots \\ \vdots & & \ddots & & \vdots \\ \vdots & & & \ddots & \vdots \\ \sigma_{m1} I & \cdots & \cdots & \cdots & \sigma_{mm} I \end{bmatrix}$$

$$= \begin{bmatrix} \sigma_{11} & \sigma_{12} & \cdots & \cdots & \sigma_{1m} \\ \sigma_{21} & \sigma_{22} & & & \vdots \\ \vdots & & \ddots & & \vdots \\ \vdots & & & \ddots & \vdots \\ \sigma_{m1} & \cdots & \cdots & \cdots & \sigma_{mm} \end{bmatrix} \otimes I$$

i.e. $\Sigma = \Sigma_c \otimes I$, and $\Sigma_c = \{\sigma_{ij}\}$ and $\otimes$ is the Kronecker product (see **Matrix algebra** for operations involving $\otimes$).

The model of all m equations may then be estimated by generalized least squares (GLS) so that:

$$\hat{\beta} = (X'\Sigma^{-1}X)^{-1}X'\Sigma^{-1}Y = (X'(\Sigma_c^{-1} \otimes I)X)^{-1}X'(\Sigma_c^{-1} \otimes I)Y$$

(since $(\Sigma_c \otimes I)^{-1} = \Sigma_c^{-1} \otimes I$).

This GLS estimator cannot, typically, be computed, since the matrix Σ_c is not known. The feasible GLS estimator is constructed by using an estimator of Σ_c formed by applying ordinary least squares to the m equations separately, and then using the residuals from these regressions. If $\hat{e}_j$ represents the residuals from the jth equation, then the typical element of Σ_c is estimated consistently by $s_{ij} = \hat{e}_i' \hat{e}_j / n$.

Two special cases are of great interest and importance. If Σ_c is a diagonal matrix, then the m equations are not related via cross-equation covariances of the errors. Let $\Sigma_c = \text{diag}\{\sigma_{11} \ldots \sigma_{mm}\}$. In that case:

$$\Sigma_c^{-1} = \text{diag}\{1/\sigma_{11} \ldots 1/\sigma_{mm}\}$$

and so $X'(\Sigma_c^{-1}\otimes I)X$ is a block diagonal matrix given by $\text{diag}\{(1/\sigma_{11})X_1'X_1 \ldots (1/\sigma_{mm})X_m'X_m\}$; hence:

$$(X'(\Sigma_c^{-1}\otimes I)X)^{-1} = \text{diag}\{\sigma_{11}(X_1'X_1)^{-1} \ldots \sigma_{mm}(X_m'X_m)^{-1}\}$$

also $X'(\Sigma_c^{-1}\otimes I)Y$ is a blocked vector, whose typical element is the matrix $1/\sigma_{ii}X_i'Y_i$. Hence $\hat{\beta}$ is also a blocked vector, whose typical element is given by:

$$\hat{\beta}_i = \sigma_{ii}(X_i'X_i)^{-1}(1/\sigma_{ii})X_i'Y_i = (X_i'X_i)^{-1}X_i'Y_i \qquad i = 1, 2, \ldots, m$$

but this is simply the OLS estimator from the regression of Y_i on the regressors X_i, and so the GLS estimator is identical to the OLS estimator. Not surprisingly, when the cross-equation covariances are zero the GLS estimator offers no gains.

More surprising is the result that if the m individual equations have *identical* regressors, then the GLS estimator is identical to the application of OLS on each equation separately. This follows from using the rules applying to Kronecker products:

$$X = \text{diag}\{X_1 \ldots X_m\} = I\otimes X^* \qquad \text{if } X_i = X^*, \text{ for all i.}$$

Hence:

$$\begin{aligned} X'(\Sigma_c^{-1}\otimes I)X &= (I\otimes X^{*\prime})(\Sigma_c^{-1}\otimes I)(I\otimes X^*) \\ &= (\Sigma_c^{-1}\otimes X^{*\prime})(I\otimes X^*) = \Sigma_c^{-1}\otimes X^{*\prime}X^* \end{aligned}$$

and:

$$X'(\Sigma_c^{-1}\otimes I)Y = (I\otimes X^{*\prime})(\Sigma_c^{-1}\otimes I)Y = (\Sigma_c^{-1}\otimes X^{*\prime})Y$$

But $$\hat{\beta} = (X'(\Sigma_c^{-1}\otimes I)X)^{-1}X'(\Sigma_c^{-1}\otimes I)Y$$

and so $$\begin{aligned} \hat{\beta} &= (\Sigma_c^{-1}\otimes X^{*\prime}X^*)^{-1}(\Sigma_c^{-1}\otimes X^{*\prime})Y \\ &= (\Sigma_c^{-1}\otimes(X^{*\prime}X^*)^{-1}))\Sigma_c^{-1}\otimes X^{*\prime})Y \end{aligned}$$

hence $$\hat{\beta} = (I\otimes X^{*\prime}X^*)^{-1}X^*)Y$$

and so $\hat{\beta}$ is a blocked vector, with typical element given by $(X^{*\prime}X^*)^{-1}X^*Y_i$ which is, of course, simply the result of regressing Y_i on X^*. Hence, when the regressors in all m equations are identical, ordinary least squares applied to each equation *seriatim* yields the best linear estimator of β and GLS offers no gain. This is an important result and has application in, for example, the estimation of vector autoregressions.

Systems of equations related only via the cross-equation covariance of the error terms are known as 'seemingly unrelated regression equations' (SURE), after the title of the paper in which they were first analysed by Zellner (1962). The gain in efficiency from using the GLS estimator increases with the correlation between equations' errors, and decreases with the correlation between equations' regressors. Having estimated the system of equations satisfactorily, and obtained the m k-dimensional estimates $\hat{\beta}_i$, i = 1, 2, . . , m, tests of restrictions on the model's parameters, both within equations (that is, tests on an individual k-dimensional vector $\hat{\beta}_i$) and tests across equations (tests involving several of the $\hat{\beta}_i$ vectors) may be carried out in the usual fashion using t- and F-statistics. A necessary condition for a satisfactory estimation of the system of equations is acceptable diagnostic tests.

It is critically important whether or not Σ_c is diagonal, and a likelihood ratio test is available:

$$\text{LR} = n\left[\left(\Sigma_{i=1}^{m} \ell n s_{ii}\right) - \ell n|\hat{\Sigma}_c|\right]$$

where s_{ii} is the estimated variance of the ith equation's variance, $\hat{e}_i'\hat{e}_i/n$ and $\hat{\Sigma}_c$ is the maximum likelihood estimator of Σ_c; the statistic is distributed as a χ^2 variate with ½m(m−1) degrees of freedom. The rationale for this test is that if Σ_c is diagonal then its determinant is given by the product of its diagonal terms, and so under the null hypothesis $\left(\Sigma_{i=1}^{m} \ell n s_{ii}\right) - \ell n|\hat{\Sigma}_c|$ is close to unity and if the null hypothesis is false this quantity will exceed unity.

An alternative which does not require the maximum likelihood estimate of Σ_c is the Lagrange multiplier test based only on the OLS residuals:

$$\text{LM} = n\Sigma_{i=2}^{m}\Sigma_{j=1}^{i-1} r_{ij}^2$$

where r_{ij} is the estimated correlation between ε_i and ε_j, computed as the sample correlation between the OLS residuals having estimated the m equations *seriatim*: $r_{ij} = s_{ij}/(s_{ii}s_{jj})^{½}$. This statistic is also distributed as a χ^2 variate with ½m(m−1) degrees of freedom. Under the null hypothesis r_{ij} differs from zero when $i \neq j$ only by virtue of sampling variation, and so rejection takes place in the right-hand tail of the χ^2 distribution.

The model of SURE may be extended to cover cases when the individual equations' errors are autocorrelated; estimation then involves applying a Prais–Winsten transformation (see **Autocorrelation**) to each equation so as to transform the individual equations' errors to a non-autocorrelated form, and then estimating by feasible generalized least squares, as described above.

Further reading

The original paper introducing SURE is that by Zellner (1962); see also Revankar (1974) and Conniffe (1982) for further results and a Monte Carlo examination of the FGLS estimator.

Selection of regressors

In selecting the regressors to be included in a regression equation investigators do not know *a priori* which variables should be included and which excluded; indeed, choosing the set of regressors is an important function of empirical analysis. Economic theory identifies a list of potential regressors and, in the absence of more detailed information, the final choice of the set of regressors may be seen as a statistical decision, based upon the empirical performance.

In the 1960s a popular method by which to select the regressors was stepwise regression; this method was incorporated in many software packages, but is not at all popular today. Stepwise regression involves the choice of a set of k_1 regressors from a list of k potential regressors, where $k_1 < k$. A forward stepwise regression begins by regressing Y on that regressor with which Y is most highly correlated, and then adds as a second regressor that variable with the highest partial correlation coefficient, and so on until the contribution of an additional regressor is insignificant. A backward stepwise regression begins with the regression of Y on all k regressors and successively eliminates regressors which have t-statistics less than some pre-specified value (often unity). There is, of course, no guarantee that a forward and backward stepwise regression with the same data will culminate in the same model, and this very mechanical route to model choice is not in common use today.

In choosing the regressors it is attractive to consider the goodness of fit of the regression; but the R^2 statistic cannot fall as regressors are added and it takes no account of the parsimony of the model. If different models (all of which include a constant term) are to be compared, and they are indexed by j, so that model j includes k_j regressors, the adjusted R^2 statistic, $\overline{R}^2$, may be considered since this incorporates a penalty for the use of additional degrees of freedom as regressors are added:

$$\overline{R}^2 = 1 - \frac{RSS_j/(n-k_j)}{TSS/(n-1)}$$

where RSS_j is the residual sum of squares from regressing Y on k_j regressors, TSS is the total sum of squares of Y and there are n observations. Since $R^2 = 1 - RSS_j/TSS$, this may be written as:

$$\overline{R}^2 = 1 - [(n-1)/(n-k_j)](1-R^2).$$

As regressors are added the R^2 statistic cannot fall, but the $\overline{R}^2$ may fall due to the reduction in degrees of freedom. It may be shown that if the parameter attached to the additional regressor, divided by its standard error, is (absolutely) greater than unity then the $\overline{R}^2$ will rise but will otherwise fall. It is to be noted that, for a given set of observations on the dependent variable, as the number of regressors is changed $\overline{R}^2$ varies inversely with $RSS_j/(n-k_j)$; but this is simply the estimated regression variance, s_j^2. Hence choosing the regressors by maximizing the $\overline{R}^2$ is equivalent to choosing that regression with the smallest estimated variance. The rationale for this approach is that $E(s_j^2) = \sigma^2$ if the k_j regressors specify the correct model, and otherwise $E(s_j^2) \geq \sigma^2$. Unfortunately, if the number of regressors is too large, but all relevant regressors are included, so that some irrelevant variables are also included, $E(s_j^2) = \sigma^2$ and the regression variance remains unbiased, and is likely to indicate too large a model. The adjusted R^2 criterion does not penalize the loss of degrees of freedom sufficiently.

One route by which to address this issue is to consider the predictive performance of alternative models; this involves running alternative regression models over the available observations and then using the estimates to predict future observations of Y. To proceed requires particular assumptions about the behaviour of the regressors in the future, and if it is assumed that the regressors behave in the future as they did in the sample period, the mean squared error may be shown to be approximately equal to:

$$2k_j\sigma^2/n + RSS_j/n$$

where RSS_j is the residual sum of squares from model j. Since σ^2 is not known it may be estimated by either $RSS/(n-k)$, the estimated regression variance using all k regressors, or by $RSS_j/(n-k_j)$, the estimated regression variance using only k_j regressors. If the former estimate is used the resulting measure is known as Mallows' C_p criterion, and if the latter is used the resulting measure is known as Amemiya's PC criterion:

C_p uses the measure $2k_js^2 + RSS_j$

PC uses the measure $2k_jRSS_j/(n - k_j) + RSS_j = RSS_j(n + k_j)/(n - k_j)$.

The PC criterion assumes that the model with k_j regressors yields an appropriate measure of σ^2, whereas the C_p criterion uses an estimate which is unbiased, so long as the k candidate regressors do not exclude any salient variables. On this ground the C_p is to be preferred. Using either of these criteria the model with the least mean squared error is deemed the preferred model.

If the regressors are assumed to follow a multivariate normal distribution then the mean squared error of prediction may be derived as Hocking's S_p criterion:

$$S_p = RSS_j/(n - k_j)(n - k_j - 1).$$

Choosing a model by reference to any of these measures condenses to a choice by reference to the residual sum of squares. The adjusted R^2 criterion seeks to discover the 'true' model, and is based on the fact that the estimated regression variance is biased upwards in a model mis-specified through exclusion. The other criteria value parsimony more highly, and are concerned with comparisons of competing models; they will accept the more parsimonious model if this generates an improved mean square error of the prediction, even if this model has omitted a salient variable. Of course, if a model is chosen by reference to any such criteria then estimates of the chosen model are pre-test estimators and their exact sampling properties are not well defined; inference should proceed with caution.

Other criteria for model choice are available, notably the so-called 'information criteria'; these seek to combine measures of the precision of a model's estimates with parsimony. The Akaike Information Criterion (AIC) suggests that the regressors should be chosen by reference to the likelihood function:

$$\text{AIC} = -(2/n)\ell n L + 2k_j/n$$

where the model whose likelihood function appears in the AIC has k_j parameters, and the model should be chosen so as to minimize this expression. Since the variance of the regression is not known, and is required to compute the likelihood, it must be estimated, and the AIC criterion becomes either the Mallows' or the Amemiya criterion, depending on the estimation method for σ^2.

Yet other criteria are available, including the reformulated AIC and the Bayesian posterior odds ratio.

The criteria are each associated with a particular loss function, and have the appearance of being somewhat *ad hoc* approaches to model selection. Choosing regressors by reference to statistical criteria seems an uncritical approach for economists to adopt, and relegates considerations of economic theory to identifying the original list from which the regressors are to be chosen. Model selection, and the selection of regressors, is best seen as an exercise which involves the interaction of data-based inferences and economic theory, and the use of the criteria listed above is a rather more mechanical approach. It should also be noted that any subsequent inference from the chosen model is liable to suffer from the fact of pre-testing.

Further reading

The adjusted R^2 criterion is due to Theil (1961); for the other criteria listed, see Mallows (1973), Amemiya (1980), Hocking (1976) and Akaike (1973). See Draper and Smith (1980) on stepwise regression.

Specification analysis

The standard presentation of the regression model and the inferential methods applied to it are predicated on the assumption that the regression model is well-specified. This has been encapsulated by Leamer (1978) who described the Axiom of Correct Specification:

1. the set of explanatory variables thought to influence the dependent variable (linearly) must be:
   (a) unique
   (b) complete

   (c) small in number
   (d) observable;
2. all other influences may be captured by a random error whose probability density function has few parameters;
3. all unknown parameters are constant.

Leamer then argued that were this axiom true one would observe only one equation per phenomenon; since this is not the case he argued that the axiom must be false and that investigators actually indulge in specification searches in order to discover the correct specification (see, for example, **Specification searches**, **Data generating processes** and **General to specific modelling**).

One of the most common potential sources of a failure of the axiom is mis-specification due to an incomplete regressor set; this occurs when the regression equation is mis-specified through the erroneous omission of at least one salient variable. The 'true' model is:

$$Y = X\beta + Z\gamma + \varepsilon$$

but the estimated model is: $\quad Y = X\beta + \eta.$

X and Z are each sets of non-stochastic regressors, comprising k_1 and k_2 regressors respectively; the error term ε, associated with the properly specified model, is assumed to have the usual properties of a zero mean, no autocorrelation and homoscedasticity. The error term η will not have such properties, and the fact that η is not a well-behaved error term implies that the ordinary least squares estimator of β from the mis-specified equation does not have the properties of a best linear unbiased estimator. The OLS estimator of β is derived from the regression of Y on X alone, omitting Z; this yields:

$$\hat{\beta} = (X'X)^{-1}X'Y = (X'X)^{-1}X'(X\beta + Z\gamma + \varepsilon)$$

$$= \beta + (X'X)^{-1}X'(Z\gamma + \varepsilon).$$

Taking expectations:

$$E(\hat{\beta}) = \beta + (X'X)^{-1}X'Z\gamma$$

and so $\hat{\beta}$ is unbiased only if either $\gamma = 0$ or $X'Z = 0$. The former condition is equivalent to the proposition that the regressors of Z together comprise irrelevant variables; if the variables of Z are not irrelevant, $\gamma \neq 0$, and $\hat{\beta}$ is unbiased only if $X'Z = 0$. This condition requires that the included regressors, X, are orthogonal to the excluded regressors, Z. This is a very rare occurrence in economic data sets, and so the conclusion is that if a salient variable is omitted from the regression then the resulting estimators of parameters on the included regressors are biased. The bias depends on two factors; since $E(\hat{\beta}) - \beta = (X'X)^{-1}X'Z\gamma$ the bias depends on $(X'X)^{-1}X'Z$

and on γ. Now $(X'X)^{-1}X'Z$ represents the regression coefficients which would result were Z regressed on X: hence the more marked is the linear relationship in the data between the included and the excluded regressors, the more marked will be the bias. This is closely associated with issues of multicollinearity (see **Multicollinearity** and **Venn diagrams**). Also, the greater is γ the greater will the bias be; this is almost self-evident: the more important is the set of omitted regressors, the larger is γ and the more serious are the consequences of exclusion as measured by the induced bias. The bias in $\hat{\beta}$ induced by the exclusion of relevant variables may, of course, result in the elements of $\hat{\beta}$ having signs (or sizes) which are in conflict with *a priori* beliefs.

By omitting salient regressors some of their influence will, to the extent that there is collinearity between the included and excluded regressors, be taken up by the included variables; this is manifested in the bias in $\hat{\beta}$. However, not all the influence of the excluded regressors can be reflected in $\hat{\beta}$ (except in the case of perfect multicollinearity between X and Z, in which case the 'true' model could not be estimated). That part of the influence of Z not taken up by X will be reflected in the residuals, and the regression residuals from the mis-specified equation will have a greater variance; defining the OLS residuals from the mis-specified model by $\hat{e} = Y - X\hat{\beta}$, and the idempotent matrix M by $I - X(X'X)^{-1}X$:

$$\hat{e} = M_x Y = M_x(X\beta + Z\gamma + \varepsilon)$$

hence:

$$\hat{e} = M_x(Z\gamma + \varepsilon)$$

and so:

$$\hat{e}'\hat{e} = (Z\gamma + \varepsilon)'M_x(Z\gamma + \varepsilon).$$

Since the model defined between Y, X and Z is assumed to be the 'true' model the error term ε is assumed to be distributed with a zero mean, have a constant variance of σ^2 and is not autocorrelated; assuming also that the regressors are all non-stochastic and that there are k_1 regressors in X, taking expectations:

$$E(\hat{e}'\hat{e}) = E(\varepsilon'M_x\varepsilon) + E(\gamma'Z'M_xZ\gamma) = (n - k_1)\sigma^2 + \gamma'Z'M_xZ\gamma.$$

In the mis-specified model the regression variance will be estimated as s^2 where $s^2 = \hat{e}'\hat{e}/(n - k_1)$; however it is apparent that:

$$E(s^2) = \sigma^2 + \gamma'Z'M_xZ\gamma/(n - k_1) \neq \sigma^2$$

and so s^2 is clearly biased, and the bias is given by $\gamma'Z'M_xZ\gamma/(n - k_1)$ which is, necessarily, not negative. Indeed, the bias is only zero if $\gamma = 0$, and even if the excluded and included regressors are orthogonal, so that $X'Z = 0$, the bias in s^2 remains, and is then equal to $\gamma'Z'Z\gamma/(n - k_1)$. It is, of course, possible that the estimated precision of $\hat{\beta}$ is greater than that of the estimator of β from the properly specified model (see **Multicollinearity**), but this is of little comfort: not only is $\hat{\beta}$ biased but so is the reported variance of $\hat{\beta}$, and this invalidates hypothesis testing and the construction of confidence intervals and regions. In a regression model which is mis-specified by having excluded salient regressors the standard inferential techniques are invalid.

On the other hand, suppose that the model is mis-specified by the erroneous inclusion of regressors: the 'true' model is:

$$Y = X\beta + \varepsilon$$

but the estimated model is:

$$Y = X\beta + Z\gamma + \eta.$$

By the above analysis, the estimator $\hat{\beta}$ from the regression of Y on both X and Z will be unbiased, since in this case the 'true' value of γ is zero. By the same token, the reported estimator of the error variances will also be unbiased. The problem in such a regression is that additional degrees of freedom have been consumed in estimating γ, and that there will be some consequential loss of precision in the estimator of $\hat{\beta}$.

Tests of inclusion are amongst the most straightforward hypothesis tests in econometrics, and involve the use of F-tests applied to linear hypotheses (see **Linear hypotheses**).

Since some of the influence of an omitted regressor will be felt via the fitted residuals, it is possible that having incorrectly omitted the regressors Z, the systematic effect of those regressors (over and above that accommodated by the included regressors) will manifest itself in the residuals and be identified by standard diagnostic tests (residual autocorrelation and heteroscedasticity may, for example, be apparent). In using the diagnostic tests in this way they are actually performing the role of tests of mis-specification, rather than tests of specification. This subtle distinction arises from describing a test which has well-defined null and alternative hypotheses as a test of specification, and one which has a composite alternative capable of many interpretations as a test of mis-specification. A simple F-test to examine whether or not the variables in Z should be included is a specification test: the null hypothesis is one of exclusion, while the alternative hypothesis is one of inclusion, and the model's specification is well-determined under both hypotheses. However, if a diagnostic test is run, whether it be concerned with autocorrelation, heteroscedasticity, linearity of functional form, constancy of parameters, etc., the alternative hypothesis does not define a unique direction in which to respecify the equation. The failure of a diagnostic test is a general indicator that the model is mis-specified, but does not offer any clear guidance as to the appropriate response and the investigator is faced with a range of possible respecifications (which must then be examined in the light of economic theory and the resulting estimation of the suggested models).

Further reading

All econometric texts discuss the issue of specification and tests of specification, and the reader is referred to such texts and the references therein, but see especially Leamer (1978). Tests of specification may be seen to include tests of non-nested hypotheses (see **Non-nested hypotheses**); also, one common test of specification is to compare the linear versus the log-linear model – see **Linear and log-linear models**.

Specification searches

The standard presentation of the inferential tools used in regression models assumes that the specification of the model is known *a priori* and that the reported estimation is the first and only regression which has been run on the available data; in practice, however, some form of exploration is almost always carried out. The model which an investigator finally reports is usually the outcome of a process in which a number of equations have been estimated sequentially, each equation being some modification of its immediate predecessors. The modifications include both the addition and deletion of regressors, changes to the functional form, alternative estimation techniques, etc., and the specification of the final equation is the result of data-based inferences. Modifications are made in the light of an equation's performance, especially with reference to its associated diagnostic test statistics, the significance of particular parameters and its goodness of fit. To the extent that any such data-based inferences may be in error, this process suffers from the charge of being subject to pre-test bias (see **Pre-test estimators**) and standard textbook inference is, strictly, not valid when applied to the final equation. This is a form of datamining (see **Datamining**), and is seen by purists as a non-legitimate activity. However, to avoid data-based specification and pre-test bias demands that the model's specification is given *a priori* and that diagnostic tests are not even carried out. This is not a tenable position. It is important to recognize that in practice a model's specification is based on the data set used in the final estimation of the equation, for it means that the confidence implied by the uncritical use of standard inferential techniques is not warranted, and that the investigator must temper the conclusions with appropriate, if less than precise, *caveats*.

Leamer (1978) provided a taxonomy of six forms of specification search: hypothesis testing, interpretative, simplification, proxy variable, data selection and post-data model construction.

A *hypothesis testing search* concerns the unconstrained estimation of a model which may then be re-specified if a constraint which reflects an economic hypothesis is found to hold across the parameters. As an example, in analysing a production function, if the hypothesis of constant returns to scale is not rejected, then the production function may be respecified and re-estimated with fewer parameters and a consequent gain in efficiency.

An *interpretative search* is designed to facilitate the reporting of complex multidimensional evidence and may be seen as related to a hypothesis testing search in that both seek to incorporate prior beliefs into the estimation process. Suppose that some parameters of an equation are imprecisely estimated (they have large standard errors) and some of those estimates may even have the 'wrong' sign with respect to the prior belief; if there is some constraint across such parameters which is not rejected by the data and which aids the interpretation of the equation then this constitutes model specification via an interpretative search. As an example, an estimated demand equation may be more easily interpreted when homogeneity of order zero is imposed than when estimated freely. This differs from a hypothesis testing search in that the former search is not motivated by interpretative difficulties with the original model, whereas an interpretative search is specifically constructed to aid interpretation.

A *simplification search* is one which seeks to produce a more parsimonious equation, having first estimated some more general equation. Simplification searches are familiar to all empirical workers, and is a characteristic of the general to specific approach: variables are deleted from an equation on the basis of an F-test. (See **General to specific modelling**.)

A *proxy variable search* is designed to choose the 'best' of the available, alternative, measures of some variable to act for the theoretical variable; it is recognized that theoretical models use theoretical variables, that in the material world only proxies exist, and that investigators often have a choice of data to represent any one variable. Some theoretical variables have several material world proxies (consider, for example, income, money, interest rates, etc.) and some theoretical variables have no obvious measured counterpart; a proxy variable search chooses that proxy which is best suited to the investigator's purpose, and may be chosen on some simple grounds such as an improvement in the R^2 statistic, or more precisely estimated parameters.

A *data selection search* is one which chooses the data set by reference to the results which are generated; the data set might, then, be chosen so that the results accord with the investigator's prior. In this sense, like the outcome of a proxy search, the implied precision of the estimates will be overstated by the final equation since the data set has been used to perform two functions: it is first used to inform the investigator's choice of data and is then used as the basis for inference, as if other data sets had not been considered.

Finally, a post-data model construction search involves the search for hypotheses which explain estimated models. This is commonly referred to as 'Sherlock Holmes inference'. The criticism of such a search is that if the hypothesis which is tested by a model has in fact also been suggested by that same model, then there has been some 'double counting' of the evidence. This form of search is also at variance with a falsificationist approach to hypothesis testing, for falsification demands that the investigator should state, prior to a test being carried out, what observations would be deemed sufficient to falsify that hypothesis; if the hypothesis to be tested is not even identified before the data analysis begins this clearly introduces biases into the testing procedure.

In all specification searches the important issue is the extent to which others can interpret the finally chosen model properly; to be able to interpret an estimated model it is important to know something of the process by which that model was produced. Knowing how the estimated model was arrived at (that is, knowing the search procedure and the criteria used at each stage to modify the equation) allows a better appreciation of the confidence which might properly be attached to it; the extent of pre-test bias, and the consequent tempering of inferential conclusions, are important considerations. Most importantly, if a finally reported equation has been specified by reference to the investigator's own prior beliefs, then this is important information to any subsequent user of that model. One of the most substantial messages from the taxonomy of specification searches is that the search process should, itself, form part of the reporting in order that the final model might be better understood and used as the basis for inference of the phenomenon under consideration.

Further reading

The book by Leamer (1978) sets out the taxonomy of specification searches. See also Darnell and Evans (1990). For details of one very popular form of specification search, see **General to specific modelling;** see also **Pre-test estimators**, **Specification analysis** and **Selection of regressors**.

Spline functions

Consider the simple model regression model in which a dependent variable, Y, is determined by one a single regressor, X:

$$Y_t = \alpha + \beta X_t + \varepsilon_t \qquad t = 1, 2, \ldots, T.$$

Suppose it is suggested that the parameters are not constant, but that for observations such that $X_t \leq c$ the parameters are α_1 and β_1 and for observations such that $X_t \geq c$ the parameters are α_2 and β_2;

i.e. $$Y_t = \alpha_1 + \beta_1 X_t + \varepsilon_t \qquad \text{for } X_t \leq c$$

and $$Y_t = \alpha_2 + \beta_2 X_t + \varepsilon_t \qquad \text{for } X_t \geq c.$$

A simple dummy variable approach appears to be a candidate estimation technique (equivalent here to running two separate regressions, one for observations where $X_t \leq c$, and another for the remainder). However, such an approach is likely to yield not only two distinct regression lines but two lines which indicate different values of $E(Y_t|X_t = c)$. As written, however, the model contains the implicit restriction that when $X_t = c$ the expected value of Y is given by both $\alpha_1 + \beta_1 c$ and $\alpha_2 + \beta_2 c$, which must, then, be equal. The simple application of dummy variables would cause the fitted line to be discontinuous: at $X = c$ the line would jump from a value of $\alpha_1 + \beta_1 c$ to a value of $\alpha_2 + \beta_2 c$. Forcing the line to be continuous at the point of change is an application of spline functions.

As an example of such a phenomenon in which continuity might be imposed, consider an individual's income over time; it might be expected that at all times the individual's income is rising with time, but that at various points in a lifetime the rate of increase changes. Specifically, as the individual gains qualifications and promotion the rate of increase is likely to shift upwards, and in the later years of working life the rate may shift to a lower value; the time profile might, then, have the appearance of a sequence of linear segments which are continuous at the points of change. Such a profile is described as piecewise linear continuous (and its first derivatives are continuous almost everywhere, the exceptions being at the points of change where the left- and right-hand derivatives both exist but are unequal). The points of change are referred to as knots. Another example in which knots arise concerns the effects of income tax rates which exhibit constant marginal rates within certain income bands, but the marginal rate shifts at the knots. Spline functions may also be used to examine structural change when the investigator believes that the function shifts with a continuity at the knot.

In the simple application of dummy variables the continuity restriction is not imposed, but it is a straightforward matter to introduce this constraint. Suppose, for the sake of exposition, a model in one regressor and one knot is considered; the model with the constraint may be written as:

$$Y_t = \alpha_1 + \beta_1 X_t + \varepsilon_t \qquad \text{for } X_t \le c$$

and

$$Y_t = \alpha_2 + \beta_2 X_t + \varepsilon_t \qquad \text{for } X_t \ge c.$$

and

$$\alpha_1 + \beta_1 c = \alpha_2 + \beta_2 c.$$

Defining the dummy variable $D_t = 0$ if $X_t \le c$ and $D_t = 1$ if $X_t > c$:

$$Y_t = \alpha_1 + (\alpha_2 - \alpha_1)D_t + \beta_1 X_t + (\beta_2 - \beta_1)(D_t X_t) + \varepsilon_t$$

but using the constraint, $(\alpha_2 - \alpha_1) = -c(\beta_2 - \beta_1)$:

$$Y_t = \alpha_1 - c(\beta_2 - \beta_1)D_t + \beta_1 X_t + (\beta_2 - \beta_1)(D_t X_t) + \varepsilon_t$$

i.e.

$$Y_t = \alpha_1 + \beta_1 X_t + (\beta_2 - \beta_1)D_t(X_t - c) + \varepsilon_t .$$

Running this regression of Y_t on a constant, X_t, and the interactive term $Z_t = D_t(X_t - c)$ yields a simple linear spline regression. Given that this is well specified it allows the hypothesis of the existence of a knot to be tested: a test of the hypothesis $\beta_1 = \beta_2$ is a test of no shift in the response of Y to X at the knot, and this may be performed easily by a simple t-test of the coefficient on the constructed variable, Z_t. Of course, if this hypothesis is not rejected then the model with constant parameters (both the intercept and the slope) is the accepted model.

The simple model with one knot may be thought of as a model with two 'regimes'; in general, a process could be modelled with p knots and p+1 'regimes'. The same principle as in the simple example then applies.

$$Y_t = \alpha_i + \beta_i X_t + \varepsilon_t \qquad \text{for } c_{i-1} \leq X_t < c_i,\ i = 1, 2, \ldots, p+1,$$

and c_o may be set at $-\infty$, and c_{p+1} may be set at ∞.

If dummy variables are defined, so that $D_{it} = 1$ if $c_{i-1} \leq X_t < c_i$, $i = 2, \ldots, p+1$, and is otherwise zero, then the model may be written as:

$$Y_t = \alpha_1 + \Sigma_{i=2}^{p}(\alpha_i - \alpha_1)D_{it} + \beta_1 X_t + \Sigma_{i=2}^{p}(\beta_i - \beta_1)D_{it}X_t + \varepsilon_t.$$

At the jth knot, when $X_t = c_j$, $j = 1, 2, \ldots, p$, $E(Y|X{=}c_j)$ may be defined in terms of the parameters α_j and β_j or in terms of α_{j+1} and β_{j+1}; for the function to be piecewise continuous it is necessary that:

$$\alpha_j + \beta_j c_j = \alpha_{j+1} + \beta_{j+1} c_j \qquad j = 1, 2, \ldots, p$$

which implies that: $\alpha_2 - \alpha_1 = -(\beta_2 - \beta_1)c_1$, $\alpha_3 - \alpha_2 = -(\beta_3 - \beta_2)c_2$, and so on up to $\alpha_{p+1} - \alpha_p = \beta_{p+1} - \beta_p$.

Incorporating these constraints, using dummy variables, allows one regression to be run over the whole data set and, as an immediate by-product, means that the hypothesized changes at the knots may be tested by simple t-tests; the joint hypothesis of constant parameters is also directly testable as an F-test in this regression.

As noted above, the linear spline function has discontinuities in the first derivative at each knot; if this is considered inappropriate it may be overcome by modelling the relationship between Y and X as a non-linear function, and imposing continuity in the first derivatives. As a simple example, suppose Y is a quadratic function of X, and there is one hypothesized knot at X = c:

$$Y_t = \alpha_1 + \beta_1 X_t + \gamma_1 X_t^2 + \varepsilon_t \qquad \text{for } X_t \leq c$$

and

$$Y_t = \alpha_2 + \beta_2 X_t + \gamma_2 X_t^2 + \varepsilon_t \qquad \text{for } X_t \geq c.$$

Imposing piecewise continuity implies that:

$$\alpha_1 + \beta_1 c + \gamma_1 c^2 = \alpha_2 + \beta_2 c + \gamma_2 c^2$$

and imposing continuity of the first derivative implies that:

$$\beta_1 + 2\gamma_1 c = \beta_2 + 2\gamma_2 c.$$

Discontinuity in the second derivative is represented by the inequality $\gamma_1 \neq \gamma_2$. The polynomial spline function with the constraint that some, but not all, of its derivatives are continuous, may be extended to higher orders with relative ease. Estimation of the model is accomplished by restricted least squares having imposed a set of linear constraints across its parameters.

The general polynomial spline function may be extended to cases of bilinear splines involving two explanatory variables, with spline constraints defined for the main effect of each variable and interaction effects at a set of knots. The use of polynomial splines when the number of knots is relatively small, and their precise position is known, is a flexible way to model change in a relationship; if, however, the existence of the knots were posited, but their position not known, the model becomes very much more complicated. Estimating the position of the knots is not an easy problem. Moreover, fitting knots according to the data becomes an exercise in curve-fitting as opposed to the testing of theory of the fitting of theoretical relationships. All knots should either be posited *a priori* according to theoretical considerations or be identified by data analysis and then justified by reference to theoretical considerations which utilize information peculiar to those specific data points. For other tests of change, the Chow test of stability is described in **Chow test** and in **Diagnostic tests**, and for a device by which to identify points of change see **Recursive residuals**.

Further reading
The text by Poirier (1976) is an excellent source of the theory and application of spline functions in economics.

Spurious regressions

In a paper of 1926, Yule noted that in analysing time-series data, it is possible to observe spurious correlations; a spurious correlation is an observed sample correlation between two series which, though appearing to be statistically significant, is a reflection of a common trend rather than a reflection of any underlying association. In the context of regressions using time-series data it is possible to regress a variable Y on another variable X, obtain a very high R^2 statistic, very large computed t-values, and a very low Durbin–Watson statistic. This combination of statistics is a classic symptom of a spurious regression: one which has some superficial appearance of being a good fit, with estimates that appear statistically significant. If the Durbin–Watson statistic were to be ignored (or the model were re-estimated using some adjustment for autocorrelation such as Cochrane-Orcutt) then the investigator might feel able to report the equation and seek to interpret it in standard fashion.

Of particular interest in economics are variables which are subject to a trend; the simplest form of a trend is a deterministic linear trend, and a variable which evolves according to such a trend grows by some fixed amount (α%) every time period:

$$X_t = X_0 + \alpha t \qquad \text{all } t \geq 0;$$

hence:

$$\Delta X_t = X_t - X_{t-1} = \alpha$$

where X_t is the natural logarithm of the variable in question.

Such a simple model is inadequate for many purposes, for it imposes a linear trend on X_t, and the obvious extension is to model a variable as increasing by some fixed amount per time period on average, but at any given time the change in the trend is unpredictable. If a stationary error term is added to the deterministic growth equation in first differences, the variable contains what is called a stochastic trend:

$$\Delta X_t = X - X_{t-1} = \alpha + \varepsilon_t .$$

If the error term, ε_t, is merely stationary, X_t is integrated of order one, denoted by I(1); however, if ε_t is not only stationary, but also white-noise, X_t is called a random walk with drift. Clearly, then, a random walk with drift is a special case of an integrated variable. In general a variable which is integrated of order q, denoted by I(q), is one which must be differenced q times before stationarity is achieved (see **Integration** and **Stationarity**).

Empirical analysis has shown that many macroeconomic variables may be modelled as if they were integrated processes of order one, and the techniques associated with integration and cointegration have been developed to address the implications of integrated variables for standard regression results (see **Cointegration**).

The immediate implication of a non-stationary variable is that its probability distribution is not invariant to time and so any model which attempts to model such a variable as if it were stationary will lead to improper inferences.

In a most important paper, Granger and Newbold (1974) argued that investigators, having paid insufficient attention to the warnings implicit in very low Durbin–Watson statistics in regressions involving time-series data, had been led, wrongly, to conclude that their regression results constituted evidence of significant relationships. Specifically, they argued that many macroeconomic time series are non-stationary and integrated of order one, denoted by I(1), and a regression involving a dependent variable which is I(1) and a regressor which is also I(1) invalidates the assumptions of the regression model and generates t- and F-statistics which do not have their assumed distributions; further, a spurious regression will generate a very high R^2 and a low Durbin–Watson statistic. The standard assumption of the regression model is that the variables are stationary; however, if X_t is an I(1) variable then it is non-stationary, has an exploding variance and, if used as a regressor, invalidates the traditional interpretations of the regression results. An I(1) variable which evolves according to $\Delta X_t = \varepsilon_t$ exhibits no trend in the mean, but since X_t may be written as $\sum_{s=0}^{\infty} \varepsilon_{t-s}$, the variance of X_t is not bounded and X_t is described as trended in the variance. If the process generating X_t is given by:

$$X_t = \mu + X_{t-1} + \varepsilon_t, \quad \mu \neq 0$$

where ε_t is stationary, then X_t has a trend both in the mean (since $\mu \neq 0$), and in the variance.

The usual assumptions of regression analysis are that:

1. the error term is a zero mean, homoscedastic, non-autocorrelated random variable which is uncorrelated with the regressors; and
2. the regressors are either deterministic or are stationary random variables.

It may then be shown that the ordinary least squares estimators have their desirable properties. However, when some of the regressors are integrated processes, assumption 2 clearly fails (since then some regressors are stochastic and are not stationary), and it is of great interest and importance to understand the implications.

The first point to note is that, in the regression of Y on X, if Y and X are both integrated, but of different orders, then the error term cannot be stationary. If $Y \sim I(p)$ and $X \sim I(q)$ but $p > q$, say, then the difference $Y - \beta X$ will be integrated since an I(p) variable dominates an I(q) variable in linear combination to produce an integrated variable. A necessary, though not sufficient, condition that the error term is stationary is that the regressand and regressor are, if integrated, integrated of the same order. Such an equation is described as balanced.

To demonstrate one implication of using *independent* I(1) variables in a regression, consider the model:

$$Y_t = \alpha + \beta X_t + \varepsilon_t$$

where both Y and X are independent I(1) variables. It may be shown, through Monte Carlo studies, that even though the variables are independent the simple linear regression will, with high probability, generate the appearance of a significant regression – even though the true β is zero its computed t-statistic will exceed conventionally used critical values, and the R^2 will be high. The probability of this outcome is even more pronounced if the I(1) variables are drifting in their means as well as their variances. In such a regression the assumptions of the OLS model are violated since the regressor is not stationary and in consequence the t-statistic does not have a t-distribution, and the R^2 is similarly misleading. The signal that such a regression result may be spurious and due to trends in the series is a low

Durbin–Watson statistic; indeed the DW statistic in such a regression tends to zero in probability. If the regression were to be re-run with differenced data (a regression of ΔY_t on ΔX_t) then this amounts to a regression of one stationary random variable on an independent stationary random variable, and all appearance of a relationship will disappear. The important message from such a demonstration is that it is important to know when a regression is spurious and when it is not.

In a simple regression of one variable, Y, on a variable, X, by taking first differences and using those series in a regression of ΔY_t on ΔX_t, the spurious regression problem is avoided, and the resulting statistics have their assumed distributions, at least asymptotically; if first differencing is not necessary, and the regression in levels is not spurious, then the resulting error term in the differenced equation is a moving average process given by $\varepsilon_t - \varepsilon_{t-1}$, and OLS then yields unbiased but inefficient estimators; they are, however, consistent. The consequences of differencing the data unnecessarily are far less serious than those of not differencing the data when it is necessary.

If the regressors are not stationary but integrated and either:

1. the parameters of interest are attached to zero mean stationary regressors; or
2. some of the parameters of interest are attached to integrated regressors but the regression equation can be re-written (re-parameterized) so that all parameters of interest are coefficients on zero mean stationary variables,

then, given that the error term is a zero mean, homoscedastic, non-autocorrelated random variable which is uncorrelated with the regressors, the OLS estimators are consistent, and the usual t- and F-statistics for the coefficients of interest have t- and F-distributions in large samples. A parameter of interest is a coefficient which is the focus of a meaningful economic hypothesis. The device of re-parameterizing the equation involves writing it in terms of stationary differences of integrated variables, and is notable in the error correction mechanism (see **Error correction models** and **Johansen method**).

In some cases when the regression equation involves integrated regressors it will be impossible to re-parameterize it in order that one or other of the above conditions holds. In such a case suppose that the dependent variable is integrated and is cointegrated with at least one integrated regressor. Two I(1) variables are said to be cointegrated if there exists a linear combination of the variables which is stationary; thus two integrated variables, say Y_t and X_t, are cointegrated if there is some combination, such as $Y_t - \beta X_t$, which is stationary. Hence if Y_t and X_t are individually integrated of order 1 and also cointegrated, then the cointegrating relationship between them may be written as:

$$Y_t = \alpha + \beta X_t + \varepsilon_t$$

where ε_t is a stationary, zero mean, random variable. If two variables are cointegrated then there is a non-spurious relationship between them: in the long run they are related linearly (see **Cointegration**). The critical characteristic of a cointegrating relationship is that the error term is stationary, and if the dependent variable is cointegrated with the regressors so that the error term is stationary (though not necessarily non-autocorrelated) the ordinary least squares estimators of the parameters attached to the integrated regressors will be consistent, though they will not have normal distributions, even asymptotically.

Finally, suppose that the dependent variable and at least one regressor are integrated, but not cointegrated; in that case the regression necessarily involves an error term which is itself integrated and hence not stationary. It follows that, since the OLS assumption of a stationary error is violated, the estimators are inconsistent.

The intuitive explanations of these propositions are as follows. Suppose one were to regress a stationary dependent variable on a stationary regressor which is uncorrelated with a stationary and non-autocorrelated error; OLS yields a consistent estimator since, in large samples, the mean squared residual is minimized at (or near) the true parameter values. At values of the coefficients other than the true values, the mean squared residual is larger, but finite.

Now consider a regression involving an integrated dependent variable which is cointegrated with at least one regressor; the residuals will themselves be non-stationary for all parameter values other than the true parameters. Since a non-stationary process has a variance which tends to infinity as the sample size gets large, for all parameters other than the true parameters the mean squared residual from the regression will tend to infinity; in large samples the only finite mean squared residual is achieved at the true parameter values and this suggests (paradoxically) that estimation in this case will be extremely precise. For any value of the coefficients other than the true parameter values the mean squared residual increases without limit, and this curious feature of the behaviour of the squared residuals suggests that the standard asymptotic theory may need modification.

Consider now the case of a regression of a dependent variable on two regressors; the dependent variable is integrated of order 1, and is cointegrated with one regressor (which itself is integrated of order 1), the other regressor is stationary and the error term is uncorrelated with either regressor and is stationary. Since the stochastic trend dominates the integrated variable, the two regressors will have a zero correlation in large samples and so, for the large sample case, the regressors can be treated as orthogonal. The coefficient on the integrated regressor will be consistent and precisely estimated, by the argument above, and because the regressors can be treated as independent of each other, this is true even if the regression is mis-specified by the omission of the stationary regressor. Since the regressors are independent, the properties of the estimator of the coefficient on the stationary regressor are not affected by the presence of the integrated regressor (though, of course, if the integrated regressor were omitted the error would then not be stationary and OLS estimation would be inconsistent). The argument which leads to the conclusion that the parameter of an I(1) regressor which is cointegrated with the I(1) dependent variable is known as the super-consistency result; this is used in the estimation of cointegrated relationships.

In seeking to establish the nature of trends in data, to test for integration and cointegration, see **Integration**, **Cointegration**, **Stationarity** and **Unit root tests**.

Further reading

The paper by Granger and Newbold (1974) presents important results regarding stochastic trends and spurious regressions; Yule (1926) is a precursor of much of this literature. An excellent survey is to be found in Stock and Watson (1988).

Standardized random variables

If y is a single random variable with a mean, μ, and finite variance, σ^2, and λ and θ are both fixed numbers then $z = \lambda + \theta y$ is a random variable with a mean of $\lambda + \theta\mu$ and a variance of $\theta^2\sigma^2$. This result is of particular importance: if $\lambda = -\mu/\sigma$ and $\theta = 1/\sigma$, then z is equal to $(y - \mu)/\sigma$ which has a zero mean and unit variance and the transformed variable is then described as having been standardized. If the random variable y is defined uniquely by its mean and variance then any probability statement regarding y may be written in terms of the standardized variable, and this implies that if probability tables are available for the standard form of the variable then probability statements may be constructed for y, for any μ and σ^2. This is one purpose of standardizing random variables, namely to enable probability statements to be made; a second purpose is to enable other distributions to be constructed.

To illustrate the first purpose, suppose, for the random variable y and a given probability p, it is required to find two numbers a and b such that:

$$\Pr\{a < y < b\} = p.$$

But

$$a < y < b \Rightarrow (a - \mu)/\sigma < (y - \mu)/\sigma < (b - \mu)/\sigma,$$

and so

$$\Pr\{a < y < b\} = p \Rightarrow \Pr\{(a - \mu)/\sigma < z < (b - \mu)/\sigma\} = p.$$

If tables exist of the standardized distribution $z = (y - \mu)/\sigma$, then those tables can be used to construct probability statements about y whatever the values of μ and σ^2. Suppose y has a probability density function which may be written as $f(y;\ \mu,\ \sigma)$; this distribution is parameterized by μ and σ; however, the density function of the standardized variable $(y - \mu)/\sigma$ is given when those parameters are set to zero and unity respectively: $f(y;\ 0,\ 1)$. If this standard form is tabulated any probability statement on y may be constructed as below. If, from tables, the numbers l and u satisfy the probability statement:

$$\Pr\{l < z < u\} = p$$

then:
$$\Pr\{l < (y - \mu)/\sigma < u\} = p$$

i.e.
$$l = (a - \mu)/\sigma \quad \Rightarrow \quad a = \mu + \sigma l$$

and
$$u = (b - \mu)/\sigma \quad \Rightarrow \quad b = \mu + \sigma u$$

$$\Rightarrow \qquad \Pr\{\mu + \sigma l < y < \mu + \sigma u\} = p$$

and so from knowledge of the mean and variance of y any probability statement on y may be constructed from the probability distribution of the standardized form.

To generalize the technique of standardization, consider the random vector y where y is a vector of n random variables with a mean of μ and a variance–covariance matrix of Ω; the mean of y, μ, is an $n \times 1$ vector and Ω is a square, $n \times n$, symmetric, positive definite matrix. $\Omega = E[(y - \mu)(y - \mu)']$, the diagonal elements of Ω are the variances of the individual elements of y and the off-diagonal elements are the covariances between the different elements of y. A standardized vector of random variables is defined as having a zero mean, all elements have a variance of unity, and all covariances are zero; hence it is required that the variance matrix is the identity: all the diagonal terms of unity and all off-diagonal terms are zero. This generalizes the standardizing of a single variable and what is required, therefore, is a transformation of y so that the new variable has a zero mean and an identity varaince matrix.

Consider the general linear transformation $A + By$ where A is some $n \times 1$ vector of constants and B is some $n \times n$ matrix of constants. The new variable $A + By$ has n elements, each of which is a linear combination of elements of y, and has a mean vector given by $A + B\mu$; hence the random variable given by $B(y - \mu)$ has a zero mean and its variance matrix may be derived as:

$$V[B(y - \mu)] = E[B(y - \mu)][B(y - \mu)]'$$
$$= E[B(y - \mu)(y - \mu)'B'] = B\Omega B'.$$

The vector of random variables $B(y - \mu)$ has a zero mean and a variance matrix of $B\Omega B'$; to standardize y what is required is that matrix B such that this variance matrix is the identity. Since the variance matrix of y, Ω, is a square symmetric n×n matrix there exists a matrix Q such that:

$$QQ' = \Omega.$$

Pre-multiplying this equation by Q^{-1} and post-multiplying by $(Q')^{-1}$ yields:

$$Q^{-1}QQ'Q'^{-1} = Q^{-1}\Omega Q'^{-1} \qquad \text{i.e.} \qquad I = Q^{-1}\Omega' Q'^{-1}.$$

Hence, requiring that $B\Omega B'$ is the identity matrix requires that B is equal to Q^{-1} for then the random variable $Q^{-1}(y - \mu)$ has a zero mean and a variance–covariance matrix given by $Q^{-1}\Omega Q'^{-1}$ which is, by the above result, an identity matrix.

Thus, to standardize a general random vector y, subtract the mean and then transform that zero mean variable by Q^{-1}; the matrix Q, defined by $QQ' = \Omega$, plays the same role in matrix algebra as does the concept of the 'square root' in scalar algebra. The original variable y has a variance–covariance matrix of Ω and, in general, Ω is not a scalar matrix. In general, then, the elements of y are neither independent of each other nor homoscedastic. However, the random vector $Q^{-1}(y - \mu)$ has a variance–covariance matrix which is the identity and therefore this transformed variable has elements each of which has a unit variance and have zero covariances (which, in the case of normality also implies mutual independence).

Further reading
See **Distribution theory**; this analysis is used in all statistical work and further details may be found in any statistical or econometrics text.

Stationarity

The property of stationarity is an important aspect of a time series. An infinite sequence $\{y(t); t = 0, \pm 1, \pm 2 \ldots\}$ of random variables is said to be strictly stationary if the joint probability function of any finite subset such as $y(t_1), y(t_1+1), \ldots y(t_1+n)$ is identical to that of $y(t_1+t), y(t_1+1+t), \ldots y(t_1+n+t)$ for all (integer) values of t_1, n and t. The implication of stationarity is that the process which generates the random variables is, in this precise sense, invariant with respect to time. Stationary time-series form the basis of many models in the natural sciences, and are also common within economics. An immediate and important implication of a stationary time-series is that it has a time independent mean and is homoscedastic, i.e. y(t) has a constant mean and variance for all t. This follows from the definition, setting $n = 0$: $y(t_1)$ then has the same distribution function as $y(t_1+t)$ for all t_1 and t and this implies, particularly, that the mean and variance of $y(t_1)$ are identical to those of $y(t_1+t)$ for all t_1 and t; hence y(t) has a constant mean and is homoscedastic. Stationarity does not imply that the series is white-noise; for example, a series which is autoregressive of order one, denoted AR(1), is clearly not white-noise, but it is stationary so long as the autocorrelation parameter is (absolutely) less than unity.

Stationarity is an important concept within econometrics, for the standard regression model makes assumptions regarding the stationarity of the error term and also regarding the stationarity of the variables in the regression. In particular, the standard linear regression assumes that the errors are drawn independently from a white-noise process and that the independent variables in the regression are either 'fixed in repeated sampling' or, if random, are stationary and independent of the error term. A particular case of non-stationary variables which arises within economics is a trended variable, and when variables are trended it has long been recognized (since Yule, 1926) that by regressing one trended variable on another trended variable a 'spurious regression' is likely to result (see **Spurious regressions**). It is often argued that while stationary series are common in the natural sciences, such series are far less common in the social sciences due to the continuous evolution of social phenomena.

Strict stationarity demands not only that the mean and variance of the series are independent of time, but also that all other higher moments are independent of time; this is a very strong requirement, and a weaker requirement is that the series has a mean which is time independent and that its autocorrelation function depends only on the lag (see **Autocorrelation function**). A series is weakly stationary if $E(y_t) = \mu$ for all t, $V(y_t) = \sigma^2$ for all t and the covariance between y_t and y_{t+s}, $\tau_{t,s,}$ is a function of s only, for all t. This form of stationarity is also known as wide-sense, covariance or second-order stationarity. If the distribution is multivariate normal, then weak stationarity implies strong stationarity since a normal distribution is described completely by its first and second moments.

Non-stationary time-series are frequently subject to detrending procedures before any subsequent analysis; two common methods exist, namely regressing the time series as a simple linear (or higher order) function of time and then using the residuals as the detrended series and alternatively using first (or higher) differences of the time series. The first method assumes that the series, Y_t, is generated according to the equation:

$$Y_t = \alpha + \beta t + \varepsilon_t$$

where ε_t is white noise.

The regression of Y_t on a constant and time results in residuals which have an arithmetic mean of zero and are orthogonal to t. The first difference of Y_t, ΔY_t, is given by $\beta + \Delta\varepsilon_t$ and so $\Delta^2 Y_t = \Delta^2\varepsilon_t$ which is a mean zero stationary series given that ε_t is stationary. If, however, Y_t is generated according to the random walk with drift:

$$Y_t = Y_{t-1} + \beta + v_t$$

where v_t is white noise, then:

$$Y_t = Y_o + \beta t + \sum_{j=1}^{t} v_j .$$

Since v_t is assumed to be white noise, the variance of this error term is given by $t\sigma_v^2$ which is time-dependent and so this equation demonstrates that Y_t, when generated by a random walk with drift, has a linear time trend and a non-stationary error. If Y_t is generated by a random walk without drift (a pure random walk) then $\beta = 0$. The first model, that of a deterministic time trend and a white-noise error is described as a trend-stationary process (TSP), whereas the second model, which describes a random walk with or without drift, is a difference-stationary process (DSP).

All three models (TSP, DSP without trend and DSP with tend) generate a trended, non-stationary series and to distinguish between the models they may be nested as:

$$\Delta Y_t = Y_t - Y_{t-1} = \gamma_o + \gamma_1 t + (\lambda - 1)Y_{t-1} + \eta_t .$$

If η_t is stationary and $\lambda - 1 = 0 = \gamma_1 = 0$ and $\gamma_o \neq 0$ then the model is one of a random walk with drift; if η_t is stationary and $\lambda - 1 = 0 = \gamma_1$ and $\gamma_o = 0$ then the model is a pure random walk; and if η_t is stationary but $\lambda - 1 < 0$ the model denies a difference stationary model and indicates a trend stationary (or some other) model. The importance of distinguishing between the models is that if the process is trend stationary then detrending by a regression of the series on time is appropriate, whereas it is inappropriate for a difference stationary series, even though the regression on time is likely to appear to be significant (a form of spurious regression). The practical issue to be addressed is that if the nested regression is run and the process is difference stationary, then this involves regression of a stationary series (ΔY_t) on a non-stationary process (Y_{t-1}) and the usual F-statistics one might use do not have the assumed distribution. Details of the appropriate tests are given in **Unit root tests**.

Further reading
Box and Jenkins (1984) provide a thorough study of stationarity, with numerous examples. Nelson and Kang (1981 and 1984) discuss differentiating between TSP and DSP processes, and see also the related entries here on **ARMA and ARIMA models**, **Integration** and **Cointegration**.

Stein estimators

A pre-test estimator commonly results when, in the regression of a dependent variable, Y, on a set of k_1 regressors, X, the investigator is uncertain whether or not to include the additional k_2 regressors Z and runs the unrestricted regression:

$$Y = X\beta + Z\gamma + \varepsilon$$

where X and Z are both matrices of regressors, containing k_1 and k_2 variables respectively.

The hypothesis $\gamma = 0$ is examined by an F-test; if this hypothesis is rejected the unrestricted estimators, $\hat{\beta}$ and $\hat{\gamma}$, become the basis for further analysis and if it is not rejected then the restricted, conditional omitted variable estimator, $\tilde{\beta}$ (having constrained γ, and hence $\hat{\gamma}$, to zero), becomes the basis for further analysis. The pre-test estimator of β is, therefore, either $\hat{\beta}$ (if $\gamma = 0$ is rejected) or $\tilde{\beta}$ (if $\gamma = 0$ is not rejected). As is shown in **Pre-test estimators**, the consequence is that, overall, the pre-test estimator is biased and inefficient. The undesirable properties arise, in part, from the dichotomous nature of the pre-test estimator – it jumps from the unrestricted to the restricted estimator according to the outcome of the F-test. The Stein estimator is simply a weighted average of the unrestricted and the restricted estimators, with weights which are a function of the computed F-statistic used to test $\gamma = 0$. One way to write the Stein estimator is:

$$\begin{aligned} \beta^* &= \hat{\beta} && \text{if } F < F_{crit} \\ &= \hat{\beta} + (1 - K/F)(\tilde{\beta} - \hat{\beta}) && \text{if } F \geq F_{crit} \end{aligned}$$

where F_{crit} is the chosen critical value from the relevant F distribution, and K is a positive constant which depends on the particular data under consideration. Clearly, the larger is the computed the F-statistic the close is β^* to $\tilde{\beta}$: as $F \to \infty$, $\beta^* \to \tilde{\beta}$, and the effect of Stein estimators is sometimes referred to as 'shrinking' the estimator towards the restricted ordinary least squares estimator.

Since the weight $(1 - K/F)$ is a non-linear function of the observations, the resulting estimator, β^*, is also non-linear. This estimator, in terms of risk as measured by the mean square error, has the remarkable property that its risk is always less than that of $\hat{\beta}$, the unrestricted ordinary least squares estimator; of course, when the restrictions are very false, the unrestricted estimator has lower risk than the traditional dichotomous pre-test estimator, and so the Stein estimator necessarily has lower risk than the usual dichotomous pre-test estimator when γ is very different from zero.

This means that, as measured by the risk, the Stein estimator combines the sample information and the constraints in a way superior to that of the usual pre-test estimator; the disadvantages are that Stein estimators are non-linear, biased, have unknown small sample properties, their variances are difficult to estimate and the improvement over other, more traditional, estimators, can only be easily analysed in particular cases when special orthogonality conditions on the regressor matrix hold, conditions which fail in the presence of collinear regressors. In consequence the Stein estimators cannot readily be used for hypothesis testing, nor for the construction of confidence intervals.

Nevertheless, Stein estimators do provide superior point estimates of parameters, and if this is the overriding criterion for choosing an estimator, then the Stein estimator may provide an appropriate point estimation method in the presence of testable restrictions on doubtful variables. However, given the disadvantages listed above, especially the fact that hypothesis testing cannot be carried out with a Stein estimator, this method has not been widely applied in the econometrics literature.

Further reading
See Stein (1956); see also Judge and Bock (1978) who discuss pre-test estimators and Stein estimators, and Efron and Morris (1973, 1975 and 1977) for a presentation of Stein estimation.

Syllogistic reasoning

A syllogism is a form of deductive reasoning which consists of two statements from which a conclusion is drawn; it therefore highlights the logical structure of an argument in which the relationship between the premiss(es) and the conclusion is emphasized. Syllogisms are used, implicitly, in all hypothesis tests. Consider the following:

1. All firms seek to maximize their profits.
2. Retailers are firms.
3. Therefore retailers seek to maximize their profits.

This may be stated in general terms as:

1. All objects in the class A have the property B.
2. Object C belongs to the class A.
3. Therefore object C has the property B.

The statements 1 and 2 are called the premisses of the syllogism, statement 1 is the major premiss and statement 2 is the minor premiss. Statement 3 is the conclusion which follows logically (is deduced) given the logical truth of the premisses (different forms of truth are recognized below). Such a syllogism, because its premisses are assertions, is called a categorical syllogism. In contrast, a syllogism whose major premiss takes the form of 'If . . then . .' is called a hypothetical syllogism:

1. If A is true then B is true.
2. A is true.
3. Therefore B is true.

The major premiss in such a syllogism is a conditional statement; the 'If . .' component is called the antecedent and the 'then . . ' component is known as the consequent. It is to be noted that the antecedent may contain many clauses, and the hypothetical syllogism may be written in a the general form:

1. If $A_1, A_2, \ldots, A_n$ are true then B is true.
2. $A_1, A_2, \ldots, A_n$ are true.
3. Therefore B is true.

This form of the syllogism plays a very important role in science, and therefore in economics; the antecedent clauses are known as the assumptions (or tentative hypotheses), and the consequent is known as the prediction. The major premiss is often referred to as the universal law, and the minor premiss is the statement of relevant initial conditions.

In order to answer the question 'when is a syllogism true?', it is necessary to distinguish between logical truth and material truth. A statement is said to be logically true if it is accepted as true purely for the purpose of argument; this contrasts with material truth (or factual truth) which is the quality of being true in the real world. It is to be noted, then, that given the logical truth of the major and minor premisses, the conclusion of a 'true' syllogism is logically true; indeed, the logical truth of the conclusion is merely a consequence of the nature of the reasoning which leads to it – the logical truth of the conclusion is independent of the material truth of the premisses. The premisses may be materially true or materially false and the conclusion logically true; however, a logically true conclusion is necessarily materially true if its premisses are materially true.

Syllogistic reasoning is at the heart of economic theorizing, and plays a critical role in the testing of economic theories; indeed, all attempts to 'verify' or 'falsify' theories utilize syllogisms. (See **Deductive fallacies**, **Falsification**, **Induction**, **Hypothetico-deductive method** and **Verification and confirmation**.

Further reading

Stewart (1979) provides an excellent source of further material on syllogisms, their use and misuse. See also Blaug (1992).

t- and F-tests

In the general linear model $Y = X\beta + \varepsilon$ it is common to perform tests on the elements of the parameter vector β; such tests may be single hypotheses which concern only one element of the β vector, or joint hypotheses which concern two or more elements. To perform a test of a simple null hypothesis against a composite alternative:

$$H_o: \beta_i = \beta_i^o$$

$$H_1: \beta_i \neq \beta_i^o$$

is straightforward. Given the standard assumptions of the model the ordinary least squares estimator, $\hat{\beta}$, is distributed as a multivariate normal with mean β and variance–covariance matrix given by $\sigma^2(X'X)^{-1}$; denoting the $(i, j)^{th}$ element of $(X'X)^{-1}$ by v_{ij}, the distribution of the ith element of β, $\hat{\beta}_i$, is given by:

$$\hat{\beta}_i \sim N(\beta_i, \sigma^2 v_{ii}).$$

Standardizing:

$$\frac{\hat{\beta}_i - \beta_i}{\sigma\sqrt{v_{ii}}} \sim N(0, 1).$$

Also, σ^2 is estimated by s^2 where, denoting the ordinary least squares residuals by $\hat{e}$, $s^2 = \hat{e}'\hat{e}/(n - k)$. s^2 is an unbiased estimator of σ^2, and:

$$(n - k)s^2/\sigma^2 \sim \chi^2_{n-k}.$$

The distributions of $\hat{\beta}_i$ and s^2 are independent, from which the familiar t-distribution may be derived:

$$(\hat{\beta}_i - \beta_i)/s\sqrt{v_{ii}} \sim t_{n-k}.$$

Under H_o: $\beta_i = \beta_i^o$, and so:

$$(\hat{\beta}_i - \beta_i^o)/s\sqrt{v_{ii}} \sim t_{n-k}.$$

Given an estimate, $\hat{\beta}_i$, the test statistic is $\hat{t}_i$ $(= (\hat{\beta}_i - \beta_i^o)/s\sqrt{v_{ii}})$ and the decision rule is: if $|\hat{t}_i| > t^*$, where t^* is the α% critical value, $t_{n-1;\alpha/2}$, then H_o is rejected in favour of H_1 using a significance level of α. Similarly, were one testing:

$$H_o: \beta_j = \beta_j^o$$

$$H_1: \beta_j \neq \beta_j^o$$

then if the observed $\hat{t}_j$ $(= (\hat{\beta}_j - \beta_j^o)/s\sqrt{v_{jj}})$, exceeds (absolutely) t^*, then H_o is rejected at a significance level of α%.

In testing the *joint* hypothesis:

$$H_o: \beta_i = \beta_i^o \text{ and } \beta_j = \beta_j^o$$

$$H_1: \text{at least one equality fails}$$

then, from consideration of the distribution of the vector $[\hat{\beta}_i \; \hat{\beta}_j]'$, the F distribution may be constructed as:

$$\frac{(\hat{\beta}_i - \beta_i)^2 v_{jj} - 2(\hat{\beta}_i - \beta_i)(\hat{\beta}_j - \beta_j)v_{ij} - (\hat{\beta}_j - \beta_j)^2 v_{ii}}{2s^2(v_{ii}v_{jj} - v_{ij}^2)} \sim F_{2,n-k}$$

which may be simplified markedly, and is equivalent to:

$$\left[\frac{(\hat{\beta}_i - \beta_i)^2}{s^2 v_{ii}} - \frac{2(\hat{\beta}_i - \beta_i)(\hat{\beta}_j - \beta_j)r_{ij}}{\sqrt{s^2 v_{ii} s^2 v_{jj}}} + \frac{(\hat{\beta}_j - \beta_j)^2}{s^2 v_{jj}}\right]\left[\frac{1}{2(1-r_{ij}^2)}\right] \sim F_{2,n-k}$$

where r_{ij} is given by $v_{ij}/\sqrt{(v_{ii}v_{jj})}$, the correlation coefficient between the estimators $\hat{\beta}_i$ and $\hat{\beta}_j$. (See **Confidence regions** and **Linear hypotheses**.) Under the joint null hypothesis, replacing β_i and β_j by β_i^o and β_j^o respectively:

$$F = \left[\frac{(\hat{\beta}_i - \beta_i^o)^2}{s^2 v_{ii}} - \frac{2(\hat{\beta}_i - \beta_i^o)(\hat{\beta}_j - \beta_j^o)}{\sqrt{s^2 v_{ii} s^2 v_{jj}}} + \frac{(\hat{\beta}_j - \beta_j^o)^2}{s^2 v_{jj}}\right]\left[\frac{1}{2(1-r_{ij}^2)}\right] \sim F_{2,n-k}.$$

Using the sample statistics the joint null hypothesis is rejected, using a significance level of α, if $F > F_{2,n-k;\alpha}$, where $F_{2,n-k;\alpha}$ is the α% critical value from the right-hand tail of the $F_{2,n-k}$ distribution. This hypothesis could, equivalently, be tested by constructing the $(1 - \alpha)$% confidence regions for (β_i, β_j), given by the ellipse defined by:

$$\left[\frac{(\hat{\beta}_i - \beta_i)^2}{s^2 v_{ii}} - \frac{2(\hat{\beta}_i - \beta_i)(\hat{\beta}_j - \beta_j)r_{ij}}{\sqrt{s^2 v_{ii} s^2 v_{jj}}} + \frac{(\hat{\beta}_j - \beta_j)^2}{s^2 v_{jj}}\right]\left[\frac{1}{2(1-r_{ij}^2)}\right] < F_{2,n-k;\alpha}$$

and reject the null hypothesis if the hypothesized point (β_i^o, β_j^o) lies outside the ellipse. The ellipse, when $r_{ij} = 0.2$ is drawn below in Figure 1, and that for $r_{ij} = 0.9$ is drawn in Figure 2. Both figures also indicate the $(1 - \alpha)$% confidence regions for the individual parameters. The sides of the rectangle which encloses the confidence region are, in general, $s\sqrt{(2v_{ii}F^*)}$, in the β_i direction, and $s\sqrt{(2v_{jj}F^*)}$ in the β_j direction, where F^* is the critical value, $F_{2,n-k;\alpha}$. The inner rectangle which defines the two individual confidence intervals has sides of length $2s\sqrt{(v_{ii}t^*)}$ and $2s\sqrt{(v_{jj}t^*)}$ respectively, where t^* is the α% critical value, $t_{n-1;\alpha/2}$. It is to be noted that the larger the correlation between the estimators $\hat{\beta}_i$ and $\hat{\beta}_j$ (equally, the larger the collinearity between X_i and X_j) the more narrow is the confidence region and the more tilted is its major axis); also, the vertices of the inner rectangle lie strictly outside the

Figure 1

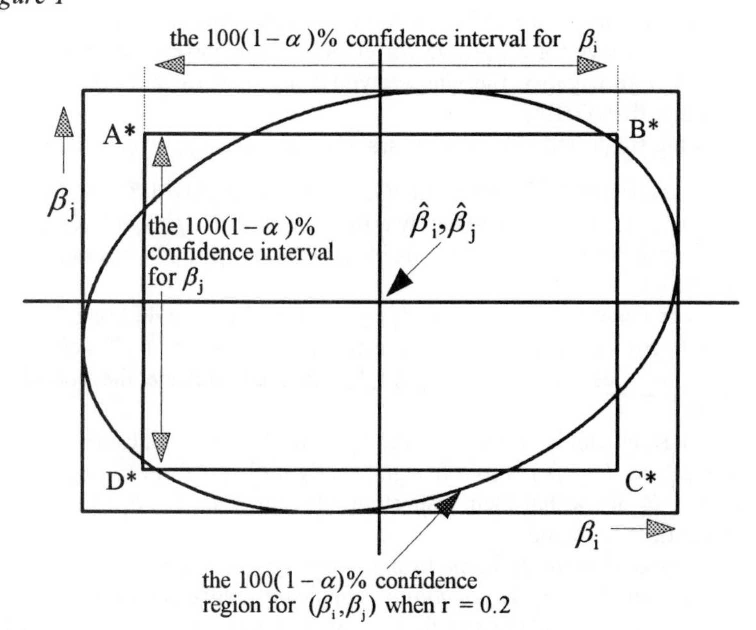

Figure 2

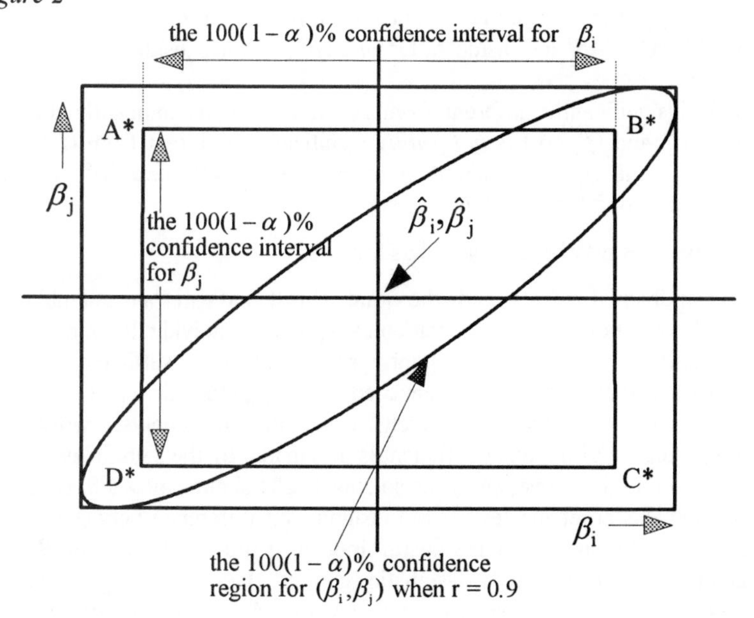

region when r_{ij} is small (0.2) but lie inside the rectangle when r is large (0.9); this is a critical difference and is explored in interpretation 4 below. The two diagrams are drawn for a positive correlation; if the correlation between the regressors were negative the ellipses would be tilted towards the diagonal A*C* rather than D*B*.

In testing single and joint hypotheses, one can envisage several situations:

1. β_i is significantly different from β_i^o, β_j is significantly different from β_j^o and (β_i, β_j) is *jointly* significantly different from (β_i^o, β_j^o): β_i^o lies outside the interval A*B* *and* β_j^o lies outside A*D* *and* (β_i^o, β_j^o) lies outside the confidence region;
2. β_i is significantly different from β_i^o, β_j is insignificantly different from β_j^o and (β_i, β_j) is *jointly* significantly different from (β_i^o, β_j^o): β_i^o lies outside A*B*, β_j^o lies inside A*D*, *but* (β_i^o, β_j^o) lies outside the confidence region;
3. β_i is insignificantly different from β_i^o and β_j is insignificantly different from β_j^o but (β_i, β_j) is *jointly* significantly different from (β_i^o, β_j^o): both β_i^o and β_j^o lie within their respective intervals *but* (β_i^o, β_j^o) lies outside the confidence region;
4. β_i is insignificantly different from β_i^o and β_j is insignificantly different from β_j^o but (β_i, β_j) is *not jointly* significantly different from (β_i^o, β_j^o): both β_i^o and β_j^o lie outside their respective intervals *but* (β_i^o, β_j^o) lies outside the confidence region;
5. β_i is significantly different from β_i^o, β_j is insignificantly different from β_j^o and (β_i, β_j) is *not jointly* significantly different from (β_i^o, β_j^o): β_i^o lies outside A*B*, β_j^o lies inside A*D* *and* (β_i^o, β_j^o) lies inside the confidence region;
6. β_i is insignificantly different from β_i^o and β_j is insignificantly different from β_j^o and (β_i, β_j) is *not jointly* significantly different from (β_i^o, β_j^o): both β_i^o and β_j^o lie within their respective intervals *and* (β_i^o, β_j^o) lies inside the confidence region;

These six cases may be interpreted as follows:

1. The individual t-tests and the joint F-test indicate an unambiguous conclusion: not only are the variables X_i and X_j individually important in explaining Y, but they are jointly significant; it is sufficient, but not necessary, that both t-statistics exceed $\sqrt{(F_{2,n-k;\alpha})}$ for this result.
2. This case can occur relatively frequently in applied work; the insignificance of the one coefficient is dominated by the significance of the other within the F-test, and β_i is so statistically significantly different from β_i^o that this compensates for the insignificant difference between β_j and β_j^o to yield a significant F-statistic. Indeed, if the significance of β_i is so great as to result in a t-statistic greater than $\sqrt{(F_{2,n-k;\alpha})}$, this will necessarily result in a significant F-statistic when tested *jointly* with β_j,

however insignificant β_j is. If $|\hat{t}_i| > \sqrt{F_{2,n-k;\alpha}}$ then β_i^o lies outside the outer rectangle and, therefore, so must (β_i^o, β_j^o) lie outside the rectangle.

3. This case is, perhaps, that seen as the main consequence of multicollinearity – the superficially paradoxical possibility that the individual t-tests indicate insignificance of both regressors yet the F-test results in a significant statistic. In the special case when both β_i^o and β_j^o are equal to zero, this situation is one in which the F-test indicates that the regressors make a significant *joint* contribution to the explanation of Y, but the individual t-tests indicate that neither is individually significant. This case is examined in more detail in **Multicollinearity**. The greater the degree of collinearity between the regressors the narrower is the ellipse and the less area it covers; hence the greater is the collinearity between the regressors that the greater is the extent of parameter space outside the confidence region and the more conceivable is this particular case.
4. This case also presents a superficial paradox: the individual t-tests indicate significance yet the joint test denies this; this can only occur if the vertices of the inner rectangle lie within the confidence region and can only occur, therefore, if the collinearity between the regressors is large. The explanation is as follows: suppose that $r_{ij} > 0$; if H_o: $\beta_i = \beta_i^o$ is true and H_o: $\beta_j = \beta_j^o$ is also true, then if the observed $\hat{\beta}_i$ happens to be an underestimate ($\hat{\beta}_i < \beta_i^o$) it is most likely that $\hat{\beta}_j$ is also an underestimate; it is most likely then that the pair (β_i^o, β_j^o) lies to the north-east of $(\hat{\beta}_i, \hat{\beta}_j)$. Moreover, since both null hypotheses are individually rejected, (β_i^o, β_j^o) lies outside the square A*B*C*D*, and to the north-east of B*. The F-test takes into account the correlation between the estimators and the fact that both t-tests lead individually to a rejection of their respective null hypotheses is not, of itself, sufficient to ensure that the joint hypothesis is also rejected; in this case neither individual null hypothesis is sufficiently strongly rejected and the pair (β_i^o, β_j^o) lies outside A*B*C*D* but within the confidence region. For this case to occur it is necessary (though not sufficient) that each t-statistic exceeds $t_{n-1;\alpha/2}$ (absolutely) but is less than $\sqrt{(2F_{2,n-k;\alpha})}$. This is not a common case in applied work and can only arise when the relationships between the dependent variable and the individual regressors is weak yet statistically significant, and there is collinearity between the regressors so that when the regressors are examined together the relationship is so weak as to be statistically insignificant.
5. This case is not dissimilar from case 2, but here the significance of the one coefficient is insufficient to compensate for the insignificance of the other. Both t-statistics are less than $\sqrt{(2F_{2,n-k;\alpha})}$ and *one and only one* (in this case $\hat{t}_j$) is less than $t_{n-1;\alpha/2}$ (absolutely).
6. This case is not dissimilar from case 1, in that the three tests indicate an unambiguous conclusion – not only do the regressors not make a jointly

significant contribution to the explanation of Y, but neither is individually significant.

Further reading
The relationships between single and joint hypothesis tests are discussed in Geary and Leser (1968).

Three-stage least squares

Three-stage least squares is a method designed to estimate the structural parameters of a system of simultaneous equations; it combines an instrumental variable approach (to yield consistent estimators) with the seemingly unrelated regression equation approach (so as to use the information from the full system of equations to gain efficiency). It is, therefore, a full system method, and all the equations are estimated at the same time. It differs from limited information methods (such as two-stage least squares and limited information maximum likelihood, for example) and utilizes all the available information contained in the system of equations to estimate the parameters. Limited information methods estimate one equation's parameters only using information on that one equation, and do not utilize any information from the other equations; by using more information three-stage least squares is expected, typically, to yield more efficient estimators. Suppose a simultaneous system of G equations is written as:

$$\begin{bmatrix} Y_1 \\ Y_2 \\ \vdots \\ \vdots \\ Y_G \end{bmatrix} = \begin{bmatrix} Z_1 & 0 & \cdots & \cdots & 0 \\ 0 & Z_2 & & & \vdots \\ \vdots & & \ddots & & \vdots \\ \vdots & & & \ddots & \vdots \\ 0 & \cdots & \cdots & \cdots & Z_G \end{bmatrix} \begin{bmatrix} \delta_1 \\ \delta_2 \\ \vdots \\ \vdots \\ \delta_G \end{bmatrix} + \begin{bmatrix} \varepsilon_1 \\ \varepsilon_2 \\ \vdots \\ \vdots \\ \varepsilon_G \end{bmatrix}$$

where Y_i is the endogenous variable in the ith equation whose coefficient has been normalized to unity, and Z_i represents the other variables in the ith structural equation, both endogenous and exogenous; the vectors δ_i thus contain all the structural parameters of the ith equation. This may be written compactly as:

$$Y = Z\delta + \varepsilon$$

where $E(\varepsilon) = 0$ and $V(\varepsilon) = \Sigma$ where:

$$\Sigma = \{\sigma_{ij}I\} = \begin{bmatrix} \sigma_{11}I & \sigma_{12}I & \dots & \dots & \sigma_{1G}I \\ \sigma_{21}I & \sigma_{22}I & & & \vdots \\ \vdots & & \ddots & & \vdots \\ \vdots & & & \ddots & \vdots \\ \sigma_{G1}I & \dots & \dots & \dots & \sigma_{GG}I \end{bmatrix}$$

i.e. $$\Sigma = \Sigma_c \otimes I$$

where $\otimes$ is the Kronecker product, and $\Sigma_c = \{\sigma_{ij}\}$. If ordinary least squares were applied to this stacked set of equations the estimator of δ would, in general, be inconsistent, since the regressors Z_i are generally not independent of the error term; moreover, even if OLS were to yield a consistent estimator, the analysis of seemingly unrelated equations (see **Seemingly unrelated regression equations**) demonstrates that OLS would be inefficient (in general) since it ignores the information contained in the covariances between the equations' error terms. Both issues may be addressed simultaneously, the first by an instrumental variable (IV) approach and the second by a generalized least squares approach. If a set of instruments, W, is available, a consistent, if inefficient, estimator would be given by:

$$\hat{\delta} = (W'Z)^{-1}W'Y;$$

By analogy with the seemingly unrelated regression estimator, the alternative estimator given by:

$$\tilde{\delta} = [W'(\Sigma_c \otimes I)^{-1}Z]^{-1}W'(\Sigma_c \otimes I)^{-1}Y$$

will be more efficient.

The issues to be resolved in order to use this estimator concern the nature of the instruments, and the estimation of the cross-equation variance matrix. From the analysis of two-stage least squares, an obvious candidate for the instruments is to use the variables given by:

$$W = \begin{bmatrix} X(X'X)^{-1}X'Z_1 & 0 & \dots & \dots & 0 \\ 0 & X(X'X)^{-1}X'Z_2 & & & \vdots \\ \vdots & & \ddots & & \vdots \\ \vdots & & & \ddots & \vdots \\ 0 & \dots & \dots & \dots & X(X'X)^{-1}X'Z_G \end{bmatrix}$$

where X represents the matrix of all the exogenous variables of the system. This blocked diagonal matrix has, as its typical element, $X(X'X)^{-1}X'Z_i$, and this is simply the matrix of predicted value of Z_i obtained from the regression of Z_i on all the exogenous variables. Hence, the suggested instruments may be written as $W = \hat{Z} = \text{diag}\{\hat{Z}_1 \ldots . \hat{Z}_G\}$, and then the IV estimator $\hat{\delta} = (\hat{Z}'Z)^{-1}\hat{Z}'Y$ is simply the two-stage least squares estimator, applied separately to each equation (this requires, of course, that all the equations are identified by the rank condition – see **Identification**). This may be shown to be a consistent estimator since the variables of W are valid instruments for estimation of the system equation by equation. However, this estimator is expected to be inefficient, and its efficiency may be improved by taking into account the covariances between the errors of different structural equations. It may be shown that the three-stage least squares estimator defined by:

$$\tilde{\delta} = [\hat{Z}'(\Sigma_c^{-1}\otimes I)Z]^{-1}\hat{Z}'(\Sigma_c^{-1}\otimes I)Y$$

is consistent and, amongst the instrumental variable estimators which only use sample information (and require that all the equations are identified by the rank condition), it is asymptotically efficient. To show consistency it is necessary to demonstrate that the instruments are valid for the purpose of system estimation. In this case the requirements are that:

$$\text{plim}(T^{-1}\hat{Z}'(\Sigma_c^{-1}\otimes I)\varepsilon) = 0$$

and

$$\text{plim}(T^{-1}\hat{Z}'(\Sigma_c^{-1}\otimes I)Z) \neq 0$$

and is a non-singular matrix. The first condition is met by an argument which follows that used in establishing that two-stage least squares is a consistent technique (see **Two-stage least squares**), and identification of every equation by the rank condition is sufficient to satisfy the second condition.

Clearly, if the equations' errors are unrelated (and so have zero covariances), then the matrix Σ_c is diagonal and, following the analysis of seemingly unrelated equations, three-stage least squares is then equivalent to estimation equation by equation, and is identical to two-stage least squares in this case. To estimate Σ_c it is suggested that each equation is first estimated individually by two-stage least squares; from the ith structural equation this yields the $T\times 1$ vector of residuals:

$$\hat{e}_i = Y_i - Z_i\hat{\delta}_i$$

where $\hat{\delta}_i$ is the two-stage least squares estimator of the ith equation's structural parameters. The covariance between ε_i and ε_j may then be estimated by:

$$s_{ij} = \hat{e}_i'\hat{e}_j/T,$$

and this yields the estimator $\hat{\Sigma}_c$. The three-stage least squares estimator is thus constructed as:

$$\tilde{\delta} = [\hat{Z}'(\hat{\Sigma}_c^{-1}\otimes I)Z]^{-1}\hat{Z}'(\hat{\Sigma}_c^{-1}\otimes)Y.$$

In using the information in the full system this estimator is designed to be a more efficient estimator than its limited information counterparts. However, the efficiency gain is zero if the equations are unrelated by their covariance structure, and is slight if the covariances are small. Moreover, it may be shown that if every equation is identified by the rank condition and is just identified by the order condition, then three- and two-stage least squares estimates are identical. Finally, if there is extraneous information on the structure of the covariance matrix then incorporating it via a method such as full information maximum likelihood will be yet more efficient. It should also be noted that the three-stage least squares estimates are not invariant to the choice of normalization; the original system of equations was written having placed one of the endogenous variables on the left-hand side of the equation, effectively by normalizing its structural parameter in that equation to unity. In some structural equations there may be a natural candidate variable whose parameter is set to unity, but the normalization is essentially arbitrary since a structural equation's parameters can only be known up to a multiplicative factor. Three-stage least squares estimates are not invariant to the choice of normalization, and if the original equations were written differently, with a different choice of normalized endogenous variable, the estimates from a finite sample would also be different. This is not surprising, given that two-stage least squares estimates are not invariant to the normalization.

Further reading
The three-stage least squares estimator was introduced by Zellner and Theil (1962). Schmidt (1976) provides formal proofs of the properties of this estimator, and discusses its efficiency relative to two-stage least squares. Mikhail (1975) provides some Monte Carlo evidence on the efficiency of the estimator.

Time-varying parameter models

Extensions of the general linear regression model to the case of non-constant parameters may take several forms (for simple models of the varying parameter model, see **Varying parameter models** and **Random coefficient model**, and for more complex forms, see **Kalman filter models**). One form of varying parameter model allows the parameters to 'drift'. The Cooley–Prescott model models the parameters as a random walk, so that the parameter variation derives from two sources: one transitory and the other permanent. To illustrate the model, suppose there are T observations and that only the intercept term is allowed to drift:

$$Y_t = \alpha_t + \beta X_t + \varepsilon_t \quad \text{and} \quad \alpha_t = \alpha_{t-1} + \eta_t.$$

This model is also known as the adaptive regression model; it may be rationalized in terms of allowing for slow structural change or (perhaps equivalently) in terms of omitted variables, where the omitted variables are believed to be drifting. Straightforward application of maximum likelihood is not possible since the intercept term is generated by a non-stationary process. Choosing one value of α, say $\alpha_{T+1} = \alpha$, as the reference value, the model may be written as:

$$Y_1 = \alpha + \beta X_1 + \varepsilon_1 - \sum_{t=1}^{T} \eta_t$$

$$Y_2 = \alpha + \beta X_2 + \varepsilon_2 - \sum_{t=2}^{T} \eta_t$$

$$\cdots\cdots\cdots\cdots\cdots\cdots\cdots$$

$$\cdots\cdots\cdots\cdots\cdots\cdots\cdots$$

$$Y_T = \alpha + \beta X_T + \varepsilon_T - \eta_T.$$

The composite error term is now both heteroscedastic and autocorrelated, and assuming the errors ε_t and η_t are both independently and identically distributed, but have different variances, the variance matrix of the composite error may be written in terms of σ_ε^2 and λ, where $\lambda = \sigma_\eta^2 / \sigma_\varepsilon^2$, and all the parameters (α, β, σ_ε^2 and λ) may be estimated by maximum likelihood. This approach may be extended to the general varying parameter model in which:

$$Y_t = x_t' \beta_t.$$

This model takes Y_t to be determined by the k variables of the row vector x_t' (and is written deliberately omitting an error term) and the time-varying response rate β_t where $\beta_t = \beta_t^p + u_t$ and $\beta_t^p = \beta_{t-1}^p + \nu_t$, so that $\beta_t = \beta_{t-1}^p + \nu_t + u_t$. β_t^p is the permanent component of β_t; the first element of x_t' is assumed to be a constant term. This presentation of the model allows more detail to be explored. It is assumed that the errors u and ν are each zero mean independent homoscedastic random variables with variance–covariance matrices given by:

$$V(u_t) = (1-\gamma)\sigma^2 \Sigma_u \text{ and } V(\nu_t) = \gamma \sigma^2 \Sigma_\nu.$$

Σ_u and Σ_ν are assumed to be known (up to a scale factor) and have been normalized so that the element corresponding to the intercept term is unity; the transitory component of the constant term thus becomes the additive error in the regression equation. Substitution yields:

$$Y_t = x_t' \beta_t^p + x_t' u_t$$

and as in the simpler adaptive regression model, the model's parameters (σ^2, γ and the permanent components of β_t) cannot be estimated by maximum likelihood; however, by choosing one point in time as the focus of interest, say time T+1, repeated substitution using the equation for β_t yields:

$$Y_t = x_t'\beta_{T+1}^{p} + \varepsilon_t$$

where $\varepsilon_t = x_t'u_t - x_t' \sum_{j=t+1}^{T+1} \nu_j$.

This model now comprises T observations of the dependent variable which are determined by the k regressors and a response rate given by the vector β_{T+1}^{p} (assumed, for estimation purposes, to be fixed) and the error term is both heteroscedastic and autocorrelated. However, assuming that the covariance matrices of u and ν are known, this model has parameters σ^2, β_{T+1}^{p} and γ; the latter parameter is a measure of the relative importance of the permanent and transitory components of the time-varying response. The likelihood of this model may be concentrated to be a function only of γ, and the maximum likelihood estimates of all the parameters may be obtained by first estimating γ within the range $0 \leq \gamma \leq 1$. While estimation and subsequent interpretation of this general model are possible, the information requirements are considerable, since both covariance matrices Σ_u and Σ_ν must be specified; a further difficulty arises because the response parameters are allowed to follow a random walk. If the time-varying parameters are interpreted as representing structural drift, the parameters do not converge and if there are genuine 'drifts' this may well be a most appropriate way to model the phenomenon, but an alternative approach which allows convergence of the parameters to some 'population' mean value might be more appropriate.

Rosenberg developed the random walk model to allow convergence, and this model may be written as:

$$Y_t = x_t'\beta_t + \varepsilon_t \qquad \text{and } \beta_t = (I - \theta)\beta + \theta\beta_{t-1} + \eta_t$$

where β is the population mean vector and θ is a diagonal matrix whose i^{th} element, θ_{ii}, is such that $0 \leq \theta_{ii} \leq 1$. The behaviour of β_t may also be written as:

$$\beta_{it} = \beta_{i,t-1} + (1 - \theta_{ii})(\beta_i - \beta_{i,t-1}) + \eta_t$$

so that θ_{ii} represents that proportion of the difference between β_i and $\beta_{i,t-1}$ which survives to period t. Using the lag operator, the expression for β_t may be written as:

$$(1 - \theta L)\beta_t = (I - \theta)\beta + \eta_t$$

and so:

$$\beta_t = \frac{(I-\theta)\beta}{(1-\theta L)} + \frac{\eta_t}{(1-\theta L)}$$

hence:

$$Y_t = x_t'\left[\frac{(I-\theta)\beta}{(1-\theta L)} + \frac{\eta_t}{(1-\theta L)}\right] + \varepsilon_t$$

and multiplying by $(1 - \theta L)$:

$$(1 - \theta L)Y_t = x_t'(1 - \theta)\beta + x_t'\eta_t + \varepsilon_t - \theta\varepsilon_{t-1}$$

which may be estimated by running the regression

$$Y_t = x_t'(1 - \theta)\beta + \theta Y_{t-1} + v_t$$

where $v_t = x_t'\eta_t + \varepsilon_t - \theta\varepsilon_{t-1}$. This error term is heteroscedastic, due to the term $x_t'\eta_t$, and autocorrelated, due to the moving average component; furthermore, the error is correlated with the lagged dependent variable. Notwithstanding those complications, this model may be estimated and details may be found in Rosenberg (1973).

A natural extension of this model is to allow the current parameter vector, β_t, to be related to the previous vector in some general known (or posited) way such as:

$$\beta_t = \Gamma\beta_{t-1} + \eta_t$$

where Γ is a known k×k matrix, and η_t is a white-noise random term. This model is described further in **Kalman filter models**.

Further reading

Cooley and Prescott (1973a and 1973b) discuss the random walk, adaptive regression, model and Rosenberg (1973) extends this to the model in which the parameters are convergent.

Truncated variables

In some data sets the dependent variable is constrained to lie within a particular range; this can arise as a consequence of the sampling process, so that some cases within the population are deliberately excluded from the sample (for example, a sample of individuals who are chosen by reference to their low, below median, incomes, excludes all individuals with incomes above the population median). Truncated variables arise when the sampling process concentrates on a restricted set of a population. In general a truncated variable, Y, is observed if $Y > c$, where c is some constant, and it follows that the sampling distribution of $Y|Y > c$ is not that of Y, since the probability density function (pdf) of Y will integrate to less than unity over the range $Y > c$. In order to construct the pdf of the truncated variable it is necessary, then, to reallocate the probability of $Y < c$ over the range $Y > c$:

$$f(Y|Y > c) = f(Y)/\Pr(Y > c) = f(Y)/[1 - F(c)]$$

where f is the pdf of Y and F is the cumulative probability function.

Suppose that Y is normally distributed with mean μ and variance σ^2; denote the probability density function by ϕ and the cumulative probability function by Φ. Then the mean and variance of the truncated variable are given by:

$$E(Y|Y > c) = \mu + \sigma\lambda(\alpha) \quad \text{and} \quad V(Y|Y > c) = \sigma^2(1 - \delta(\alpha))$$

where:

$$\alpha = (c - \mu)/\sigma,\ \lambda(\alpha) = \phi(\alpha)/[1 - \Phi(\alpha)],\ \text{and}\ \delta(\alpha) = \lambda(\alpha)(\lambda(\alpha) - \alpha).$$

The function $\lambda(\alpha)$ is known as the hazard function (and also as the inverse Mills ratio); as the truncation point increases so $\Phi(\alpha)$ increases and a greater proportion of the population (in the left-hand tail) is discarded and so the mean rises accordingly. An important result is that $0 < \delta(\alpha) < 1$ for all α. If the truncation cuts off values in the right-hand tail of the distribution of Y, so that $Y < c$, then $\lambda(\alpha)$ is defined by $-\phi(\alpha)/\Phi(\alpha)$, and the definitions of α and δ are unchanged. If the non-truncated model is given by:

$$Y_i = x_i'\beta + \varepsilon_i \qquad \text{and}\ \varepsilon \sim N(0, \sigma^2 I)$$

then the conditional mean of Y_i is given by:

$$E(Y_i|Y_i > c) = x_i'\beta + \sigma\phi(\{c - x_i'\beta\}/\sigma)/[1 - \Phi(c - x_i'\beta)/\sigma)].$$

The marginal effects of changes in x_i are given, in the non-truncated model, by $\partial E(Y_i)/\partial x_i = \beta_i$, but in the truncated model the marginal effect of is given by $\partial E(Y_i|Y_i > c)/\partial x_i = \beta_i(1 - \delta(\alpha_i))$ where $\alpha_i = (c - x_i'\beta)/\sigma$, and since $0 < \delta(\alpha) < 1$ it is clear that the marginal effect in the truncated model is unambiguously less than that in the full population. Whether or not this is of importance depends on the focus of the investigation: if the entire population is of interest then this result must be acknowledged, but if the sub-population, defined by $Y_i > c$, is the focus of interest then the marginal effects from the truncated model are relevant.

From the statement of the conditional mean of $Y_i|Y_i > c$ it is clear that this is not equal to $x_i'\beta$ by virtue of the additional term arising from the truncation; the additional term is non-linear both in the explanatory variables and in the parameters. As a result of this additional non-linear term, if the linear regression of Y determined by x_i' were estimated by ordinary least squares using the truncated data this would omit the non-linear term and in consequence will result in biased and inconsistent estimators of the population parameter β. If the full population is the focus of interest then the model may be estimated consistently by maximum likelihood using only the truncated data by writing the density function of the truncated Y_i as:

$$f(Y_i) = \sigma^{-1}\phi((Y_i - x_i'\beta)/\sigma)/[1 - \Phi((Y_i - x_i'\beta)/\sigma)].$$

The log-likelihood function is then:

$$\ell n L = -(n/2)\ell n(2\pi\sigma^2) - (1/2\sigma^2)\Sigma_{i=1}^{n}(Y_i - x_i'\beta)^2$$

$$- \Sigma_{i=1}^{n} \ell n\left[1 - \Phi\left(\frac{Y_i - x_i'\beta}{\sigma}\right)\right]$$

and this may be maximized using non-linear optimization routines. This model is applicable when the data are truncated and the entire population is of interest. It is quite different conceptually from the censored data model in which the sampling process is not exclusive, but systematically sets some values of dependent variable to zero (see **Censored data**).

Further reading
Details of truncated distributions may be found in Johnson and Kotz (1970); for further details of this model, see, for example, Hausman and Wise (1977) and Greene (1983).

Two-stage least squares

Two-stage least squares (TSLS) is a limited information estimation technique applied to over-identified equations of a simultaneous system and yields consistent estimators of the structural parameters. Suppose that the first structural equation of a simultaneous system of G equations is given by:

$$Y_{1t} = \sum_{q=2}^{g_1} \beta_{1q} Y_{qt} + \sum_{r=1}^{k_1} \gamma_{1r} X_{rt} + \varepsilon_{1t}$$

where Y_{it} represents the endogenous variables of the system, and Y_{it}, $i = 1, 2, \ldots, g_1$ are included in the first equation; X_{rt} represents the exogenous and pre-determined variables of the system and for $r = 1, 2, \ldots, k_1$ represents those which are included in the first equation. The equation has been normalized so that variable Y_1 has been given a unit coefficient. This equation may be written as:

$$Y_1 = Z\beta_1 + X_1\gamma_1 + \varepsilon_1.$$

Z represents the endogenous variables placed on the right-hand side of this equation and is of order $T\times(g_1 - 1)$; X_1 represents all the included exogenous and pre-determined variables and is of order $T\times k_1$. Since the regressors include endogenous variables, the application of ordinary least squares to this structural equation will, in general, result in biased and inconsistent estimators of the parameters (but see **Recursive systems**). This may easily be seen as the equation in question is one of the G structural equations, described by the equations:

$$BY_t + \Gamma X_t = \varepsilon_t, \qquad t = 1, 2, \ldots, T$$

where B and Γ are the matrices of structural coefficients, of order G×G and G×K respectively; Y_t is a G×1 vector of observations on all the endogenous variables at time t and X_t is a K×1 vector of observations on all the exogenous (and pre-determined) variables at time t. The reduced form may be derived as:

$$Y_t = -B^{-1}\Gamma X_t + B^{-1}\varepsilon_t, \qquad t = 1, 2, \ldots, T.$$

i.e. $$Y_t = \Pi X_t + v_t.$$

The estimation of any one of the structural equations will involve an equation in which one endogenous variable is regressed on other endogenous variables and some of the exogenous and pre-determined variables. Since, as demonstrated by the reduced form, all the endogenous variables are, in general, correlated with the error, ε, the regression of Y_1 on Z and X_1 violates one of the assumptions of OLS, namely that the regressors, if they are stochastic, are independent of the error. Hence the OLS estimators of β_1 and γ_1 are biased and inconsistent.

The first equation excludes $K - k_1$ exogenous variables and the order condition for identification requires that $K - k_1 \geq g_1 - 1$. Suppose this is satisfied and that the rank condition for this equation is also satisfied. The first stage of the two-stage least squares estimation technique proceeds by running the reduced-form regressions of each of the right-hand-side endogenous variables on all the exogenous and pre-determined variables:

$$Y_{it} = \sum_{j=1}^{K} \pi_{ij} X_{tj} + v_t \qquad i = 2, 3, \ldots, g_1.$$

These $g_1 - 1$ regressions yield consistent estimators of the reduced-form parameters and consistent estimators of the predicted values of Y_{it}, denoted by the vectors $\hat{Y}_i$ $i = 2, 3, \ldots, g_1$. The application of ordinary least squares to these reduced form equations, one by one, yields consistent and efficient estimators of the reduced-form parameters, notwithstanding the fact that the equations are related via correlations amongst the errors attaching to them. Even if the covariance between v_{it} and v_{jt} is non-zero, that is the equations are related by the errors, there is no gain in efficiency by acknowledging the non-zero covariances. This uses a result of seemingly unrelated regression equations (see **Seemingly unrelated regression equations**) which shows that if, as here, the equations have identical regressors then the application of OLS *seriatim* yields efficient estimators.

If all G reduced-form equations were estimated in this way then the estimators $\hat{\pi}_{ij}$ are linear, consistent and efficient (and indeed best if the X matrix contains only exogenous and no pre-determined variables). If it is then possible to solve for the structural form coefficients, given this estimate of Π, the resulting structural parameter estimates are known as indirect least squares estimates. To construct the structural parameters from reduced-form parameters requires a non-linear transformation of the estimates $\hat{\pi}_{ij}$, and so the structural parameters will be consistent, but not unbiased. The technique of ILS is equivalent to two-stage least squares for exactly identified equations, but yields multiple solutions of structural parameters in over-identified equations (see **Indirect least squares**). TSLS provides a method of combining such multiple solutions in an optimal way to generate consistent estimators, and since ILS and TSLS are equivalent for exactly identified equations, and TSLS provides consistent estimators in cases of over-identification, ILS is not commonly used, whereas TSLS is one of the most popular techniques.

From the regressions of the reduced form a series of OLS fitted values are obtained: $[\hat{Y}_2 \ \hat{Y}_3 \ . \ . \ . \ \hat{Y}_{g_1}]$. Denote this $T \times (g_1 - 1)$ matrix by $\hat{Z}$. By the mechanics of OLS:

$$Z = \hat{Z} + \hat{v} \quad \text{and} \quad \hat{v} = M_x Z \quad \text{and} \quad \hat{Z} = X(X'X)^{-1}X'Z$$

where M_x is the idempotent matrix $I - X(X'X)^{-1}X'$. The endogenous variables, Z, are equal to their fitted values plus the fitted residuals. Substituting in the first structural form equation produces the equation:

$$Y_1 = (\hat{Z} + \hat{v})\beta_1 + X_1\gamma_1 + \varepsilon_1$$

i.e.

$$Y_1 = \hat{Z}\beta_1 + X_1\gamma_1 + \eta_1$$

where $\eta_1 = \varepsilon_1 + \hat{v}\beta_1$ and $\hat{v} = [\hat{v}_2 \ \hat{v}_3 \ . \ . \ \hat{v}_{g_1}]$.

By construction, $\hat{Z} = X(X'X)^{-1}X'Z = X\hat{\pi}_1'$ where $\hat{\pi}_1'$ represents the $K \times (g_1 - 1)$ estimated reduced form coefficients attaching to the $g_1 - 1$ endogenous variables, $Y_2, . . Y_{g_1}$. As a direct consequence of OLS estimation of the reduced form equations, the residuals $\hat{v}$ may be written as $M_x Z$. Hence:

$$\text{plim}[T^{-1}\hat{Z}'\eta_1] = \text{plim}[T^{-1}\hat{\pi}_1'X'(\varepsilon_1 + \hat{v}\beta_1)]$$

$$= \text{plim}(\hat{\pi}_1')\text{plim}[T^{-1}X'\varepsilon_1] + \text{plim}[\hat{\pi}_1'T^{-1}X'\hat{v}\beta_1]$$

but the reduced form estimator $\hat{\pi}_1'$ is consistent and the exogenous variables, X, and the error, ε_1, are definitionally uncorrelated in the limit; therefore, the first term is zero. Also, since $\hat{v} = M_x Z$, $X'\hat{v} = X'M_x Z$ which is identically zero (since X and M_x are orthogonal) and so the second term is also zero. Hence:

$$\text{plim}[T^{-1}\hat{Z}'\eta_1] = 0.$$

The effect of replacing Z by $\hat{Z}$ in the structural equation has been to purge Z of its dependence on the error term (in the limit). The application of OLS to this equation will, therefore, yield consistent estimators. Thus the second stage of two-stage least squares consists of regressing, by OLS, Y_1 on the predicted values $[\hat{Y}_2 \ \hat{Y}_3 \ . \ . \ . \ \hat{Y}_{g_1}]$ (obtained from the first stage) and the exogenous and pre-determined variables $X_1, \ . \ . \ . \ X_{k_1}$. The resulting estimators are consistent. It is worth noting that this equation may be written as:

$$Y_1 = X\hat{\pi}_1'\beta_1 + X_1\gamma_1 + \eta_1$$

and estimation of this equation demands that the matrix of regressors, given by $[X\hat{\pi}_1' \ X_1]$, be of full rank, which requires that $\rho[X\hat{\pi}_1' \ X_1] = g_1 - 1 + k_1$. The information in the $g_1 - 1$ regressors $X\hat{\pi}_1'$ must, then, be distinct from that in the k_1 regressors X_1; however, X may be written as the partitioned matrix $X = [X_1 \ X_2]$ where X_2 represents the $K - K_1$ ($= K_2$) exogenous variables excluded from the first structural equation. If $\hat{\pi}_1'$ is partitioned conformably so that:

$$\hat{\pi}_1' = \begin{bmatrix} \hat{\pi}_{11}' \\ \hat{\pi}_{12}' \end{bmatrix},$$

then $X\hat{\pi}_1' = X_1\hat{\pi}_{11}' + X_2\hat{\pi}_{12}'$; the information in $X_1\hat{\pi}_{11}'$ is not independent of that in X_1, since $X_1\hat{\pi}_{11}'$ is simply a linear combination of the variables X_1; hence $X\hat{\pi}_1'$ contains $g_1 - 1$ pieces of independent information if and only if $X_2\hat{\pi}_{12}'$ contains $g_1 - 1$ independent columns. Since X_2 is of order $T \times K_2$ and $\hat{\pi}_{12}'$ is of order $K_2 \times (g_1 - 1)$, $\rho(X_2) \geq \min(T, K_2) = K_2$ and $\rho(\hat{\pi}_{12}) \geq \min(K_2, g_1 - 1)$ and so $\rho(X_2\hat{\pi}_{12}') \geq \min(\rho(X_2), \rho(\hat{\pi}_{12}')) = \min(K_2, g_1 - 1)$. For $\rho(X_2\hat{\pi}_{12}') = g_1 - 1$ it is necessary (though not sufficient) that $g_1 - 1 \leq K_2$, which is a statement of the order condition for identification, namely that the number of excluded exogenous and pre-determined variables from the equation must be at least as great as the number of included endogenous variables on the right-hand side. If this condition fails then the second stage of the TSLS technique involves a regression with perfect multicollinearity and cannot be estimated. It is, of course, possible that the order condition is satisfied, but the rank condition is not; in such a case TSLS will produce estimates, but they will be inconsistent.

The second stage is a regression of the form:

$$Y_1 = \begin{bmatrix} \hat{Z} & X_1 \end{bmatrix} \begin{bmatrix} \beta_1 \\ \gamma_1 \end{bmatrix} + \eta_1$$

which denoting $[\hat{Z} \ X_1]$ by $\hat{W}$ and the coefficient vector by θ, may be written as:

$$Y_1 = \hat{W}\theta + \eta_1$$

from which: $\hat{\theta}_{TSLS} = (\hat{W}'\hat{W})^{-1}\hat{W}'Y_1.$

The reported estimated variance–covariance of $\hat{\theta}_{TSLS}$ is given by $s^2(\hat{W}'\hat{W})^{-1}$ where s^2 is derived from the sum of squared residuals from this regression. This is an inappropriate estimator, as s^2 is an estimate of the variance in η_1, rather than ε_1. To illustrate how to derive an appropriate variance estimator, it is helpful to show that TSLS is a form of IV estimation. Denoting $[Z\ X_1]$ by W, the first equation of the structural system may be written as:

$$Y_1 = W\theta + \varepsilon_1.$$

Consider using $\hat{W}$ as instruments for W. That $\text{plim}(T^{-1}\hat{W}'\varepsilon_1) = 0$ has already been shown and so these instruments satisfy the first condition of instrumental variables. The second condition is that $\text{plim}(T^{-1}\hat{W}'W) = Q$, some non-singular matrix. Since $\hat{Z}$ is correlated with Z, this is also satisfied. Indeed, $\hat{Z}$ has been constructed from the regression of Z on X, is a linear combination of the exogenous variables and the method of ordinary least squares ensures that the correlation between $\hat{Z}$ and Z is maximized; hence there is no other linear combination of exogenous variables more highly correlated with Z. These instruments are therefore efficient. By the IV method, $\hat{\theta}_{IV} = (\hat{W}'W)^{-1}\hat{W}'Y_1$. To compare the TSLS and IV estimators, the respective solutions may be written out in full as:

$$\begin{bmatrix} \hat{Z}'Z & \hat{Z}'X_1 \\ X_1'Z & X_1'X_1 \end{bmatrix} \hat{\theta}_{IV} = \begin{bmatrix} \hat{Z}'Y_1 \\ X_1'Y_1 \end{bmatrix}$$

and:

$$\begin{bmatrix} \hat{Z}'\hat{Z} & \hat{Z}'X_1 \\ X_1'\hat{Z} & X_1'X_1 \end{bmatrix} \hat{\theta}_{TSLS} = \begin{bmatrix} \hat{Z}'Y_1 \\ X_1'Y_1 \end{bmatrix}$$

The matrices on the left-hand side of these equations have identical second columns, and the right hand side vectors are identical, and so the estimators are equivalent if and only if $\hat{Z}'Z = \hat{Z}'\hat{Z}$ and $X_1'Z = X_1'\hat{Z}$. Given the derivation of $\hat{Z}$:

$$Z = \hat{Z} + \hat{v},$$

and by the mechanics of OLS:

$$\hat{Z} = X(X'X)^{-1}X'Z \quad \text{and} \quad \hat{v} = M_xZ$$

hence $\quad X'\hat{v} \equiv 0, \ \text{and}\ \hat{Z}'\hat{v} \equiv 0;\ \text{since}\ X'M_x \equiv 0$

hence $\quad \hat{Z}'Z = \hat{Z}'\hat{Z} + \hat{Z}'\hat{v} = \hat{Z}'\hat{Z};$

and $$X'Z = X'(\hat{Z} + \hat{v}) = X'\hat{Z} \quad \text{since } X'\hat{v} \equiv 0;$$

hence $$X_1'Z = X_1'\hat{Z}.$$

Thus TSLS estimators are equivalent to, and may be interpreted as, IV estimators using $\hat{Z}$ as the instruments for the right-hand side endogenous variables. The estimated variance–covariance matrix is thus given by:

$$\hat{\sigma}^2(\hat{W}'W)^{-1}\hat{W}'\hat{W}(\hat{W}'W)^{-1}$$

and since $\hat{W}'W \equiv \hat{W}'\hat{W}$, this is equal to:

$$\hat{\sigma}^2(\hat{W}'\hat{W})^{-1}$$

where $\hat{\sigma}^2 = \tilde{e}'\tilde{e}/(T - g_1 + 1 - k_1)$ and $\tilde{e}$ is the vector of IV residuals (whether one uses $T - g_1 + 1 - k_1$ or T as the denominator is not important since the results have only asymptotic validity). The estimator of the variance –covariance reported by the application of OLS in the second stage of the TSLS process is: $s^2(\hat{W}'\hat{W})^{-1}$, where $s^2 = \hat{e}'\hat{e}/(T - g_1 - 1 - k_1)$ and $\hat{e}$ is the vector of TSLS residuals.

Since $\tilde{e} = Y_1 - W\hat{\theta}_{IV}$, and $\hat{e} = Y_1 - \hat{W}\hat{\theta}_{TSLS}$, even though $\hat{\theta}_{IV} \equiv \hat{\theta}_{TSLS}$, the two variance estimators differ, and that reported by the OLS procedure in the second stage of TSLS is incorrect. To derive the correct estimated variance–covariance matrix from the reported TSLS matrix, the latter must be multiplied by $\hat{\sigma}^2/s^2$, which is identical to $\tilde{e}'\tilde{e}/\hat{e}'\hat{e}$. If the software used recognizes the estimation as the TSLS method, as opposed to carrying out the estimation in two separate stages of OLS, this correction may be made automatically but should otherwise be made manually.

One further aspect of TSLS which is deserving of attention is the question of normalization; normalization refers to the rule by which the coefficient of one of the endogenous variables in a structural equation is set to unity. It is common to set the coefficient of Y_i in the ith structural equation to unity (equivalent to setting all the diagonal elements of B to unity), i.e. the ith structural equation is usually normalized with respect to the ith endogenous variable. This act of normalization determines which endogenous variable is placed as the 'regressand' and which are set as 'regressors' when estimation proceeds via TSLS, and ideally the estimation would not be sensitive to the normalization, but unfortunately it is. This arises because in an important sense normalization flies in the face of the spirit of a simultaneous system. In a system of equations the endogenous variables are jointly determined, and so there is no immediately meaningful sense in which, in any given structural equation, one could label one endogenous variable as the dependent variable and the remaining endogenous variables as 'explanatory' variables (and hence as regressors). By using this limited information approach, in which the focus of attention is just one equation rather than the system as a whole, the normalization choice has an impact on the estimates of over-identified equations. The choice of which structural coefficient is set to unity does not, however, have any implications if the equation is exactly identified.

Further reading

The TSLS method is a special case of the so-called k-class estimators; see Theil (1971) or Schmidt (1976). For a survey of Monte Carlo results on the performance of TSLS see, for example, Challen and Hagger (1983). On normalization see, for example, Fisher (1976).

Unit root tests

Unit root tests are designed to test the order of integration of a variable. If the variable x_t is integrated of order d then $\Delta^d x_t$ is stationary, while $\Delta^q x_t$ is non-stationary for all $0 \leq q < d$. If x_t is integrated of order 1 without drift, then:

$$x_t = x_{t-1} + \varepsilon_t$$

where ε_t is stationary; this equation is clearly a special case of the relationship $x_t = (1 + \theta)x_{t-1} + \varepsilon_t$ when $\theta = 0$ and the coefficient on lagged x is then unity. Test of integration are, for obvious reasons, known as unit root tests. An easily computed statistic is the Integrated Durbin–Watson (IDW) statistic defined by:

$$\text{IDW} = \frac{\sum_{t=2}^{T}(x_t - x_{t-1})^2}{\sum_{t=2}^{T}(x_t - \bar{x})^2}.$$

If $x_t \sim I(1)$ (with or without drift) then the numerator is equal to $\sum_{t=2}^{T}\varepsilon_t^2$, but the denominator is not bounded and so one would expect, if $x_t \sim I(1)$, the IDW statistic to be small. The IDW provides a very quick impression of the behaviour of the variable, and if the computed statistic is low, say less than 0.5, further, and more formal, investigation is required. If x_t is white-noise, then $x_t = \varepsilon_t$ and ε_t is not autocorrelated with a constant variance denoted by σ^2; in that case the numerator of the IDW statistic is approximately $2T\sigma^2$ and the denominator is approximately $T\sigma^2$. Hence if the computed IDW statistic is close to 2 stationarity may be safely inferred. For a more formal approach to testing, an immediately attractive approach is to run the regression of x_t on itself lagged once and test that the coefficient is unity. This approach is flawed as the ordinary least squares estimator from this regression is biased and, even when the error term is white-noise, when x_t is integrated the resulting t-statistic does not have the familiar t-distribution, even in large samples. The breakdown of the t-test arises as this test is constructed assuming that the variables in the regression equation are stationary. A simple, and appropriate, test is the Dickey–Fuller (1979) test which is based on a regression of Δx_t on x_{t-1}. Suppose:

$$\Delta x_t = \theta x_{t-1} + \varepsilon_t; \qquad \text{then:} \quad x_t = (1 + \theta)x_{t-1} + \varepsilon_t.$$

If $\theta = 0$ and ε_t is stationary then $x_t \sim I(1)$ and if $-2 < \theta < 0$ x_t is a stationary AR process. (If $\theta > 0$ or $\theta \leq -2$ then x_t is a non-stationary AR process.) The Dickey–Fuller (DF) test is a test of H_0: $\theta = 0$ against H_1: $\theta < 0$ (that is, the null hypothesis is that $x_t \sim I(1)$ and the alternative is that $x_t \sim I(0)$). The test statistic is constructed from the regression of Δx_t on x_{t-1} and is a test of the significance of the θ. The t-statistic is the natural candidate test statistic but, under the null hypothesis $x_t \sim I(1)$, the regression represents the regression of a stationary variable (Δx_t) on a non-stationary variable, and so the resulting t-statistic is not distributed as a t-variate under H_o. In fact the t-statistic obtained from this equation is negatively skewed and the appropriate critical values are not amenable to analytic construction. Unique critical values for the DF statistic do not exist, but tables exist giving upper and lower critical values which depend only on T, the number of observations; given the skewness of the distribution, all critical values are negative and are smaller (that is, more negative) than their t-variate counterparts; for example, with 100 observations the upper and lower 1% critical values are of the order –2.70 and –2.39 so that if the observed statistic is less than –2.70 the null hypothesis is rejected. The inconclusive range applies to all observed statistics between –2.70 and –2.39, and if the observed statistic is negative, but greater than –2.39, the null is not rejected.

Suppose the observed t-statistic is 'significant' and the null hypothesis is then rejected; the conclusion is that the series is stationary. However, if the null is not rejected the valid conclusion is that x_t is not stationary (not that x_t is integrated of order 1). If the null is not rejected then x_t may be integrated of any order, and so the next step is to test the null hypothesis that $x_t \sim I(2)$ against the alternative that $x_t \sim I(1)$. If $x_t \sim I(1)$ then $z_t = \Delta x_t \sim I(0)$, but if $x_t \sim I(d)$ where $d > 1$ then Δx_t is not stationary; hence the DF test is repeated replacing x by $z = \Delta x_t$:

$$\Delta z_t = \theta z_{t-1} + \varepsilon_t; \qquad \text{i.e.} \qquad \Delta^2 x_t = \theta \Delta x_{t-1} + \varepsilon_t.$$

If, in this equation, the null hypothesis $\theta = 0$ is rejected against the alternative that $\theta < 0$ then one may conclude that z is stationary, and hence that $x_t \sim I(1)$. Again, if the null hypothesis cannot be rejected the test should be repeated using the regression of $\Delta^3 x_t$ on $\Delta^2 x_{t-1}$. Most integrated economic series are of order 1 or 2, and repeated non-rejection of the null hypothesis as higher and higher orders of integration are examined may occur because the series is not integrated or because the test is insufficiently sensitive to identify the order of integration. In the iterated process to discover the order of integration over-differencing is possible; if the series is over-differenced a positive DF statistic is likely to result, accompanied by a very large goodness-of-fit statistic.

The above example is one in which the variable is tested as an integrated series without drift. The test can easily be applied to a series which incorporates drift so that then the regression becomes:

$$\Delta x_t = \mu + \theta x_{t-1} + \varepsilon_t.$$

To test $\theta = 0$ the reported t-statistic is used, and the critical values are non-conventional Dickey–Fuller critical values, this time those for the Dickey–Fuller test with drift.

The tabulated critical DF values are simulated from experiments which utilize a white-noise error (i.e. a homoscedastic, non-autocorrelated, wholly unpredictable error term), and if, in the regression of Δx_t on x_{t-1} the residuals exhibit autocorrelation then the test becomes inefficient. To capture possible autocorrelation in ε_t Dickey and Fuller suggest the simple method of using lagged values of Δx as additional regressors to approximate the process, so that the test equation becomes:

$$\Delta x_t = \theta x_{t-1} + \sum_{i=1}^{k} \theta_i \Delta x_{t-i} + \varepsilon_t.$$

Given that k has been chosen as the minimum number of lags to ensure that ε_t is free of autocorrelation, a test of the unit root of x_t is now a test of the significance of θ, and if x_t is stationary $\theta = 0$. This is the Augmented Dickey–Fuller test (ADF), and while there is no formal way of choosing k, the number of lags, it should be chosen to be just sufficiently large to remove evidence of autocorrelation, but not so large as to use many degrees of freedom. The critical values for the ADF test are identical to those for the more simple DF test.

Further reading

See the important papers by Dickey and Fuller (1979 and 1981), and also the earlier work of Mann and Wald (1943) and Rubin (1950). See also Nelson and Plosser (1982), Evans and Savin (1981 and 1984), Nerlove and Diebold (1990) and Charemza and Deadman (1992). See also **Johansen method**.

Variance inflation factor

In the standard general linear model $Y = X\beta + \varepsilon$, under the usual assumptions that X is not stochastic and $\varepsilon \sim N(0, \sigma^2 I)$, the ith element of the ordinary least squares estimator $\hat{\beta}_i$ has a true variance given by $\sigma^2 v_{ii}$, where v_{ii} is the ith diagonal term of $(X'X)^{-1}$; the true variance of $\hat{\beta}_i$ is determined, in part, by the extent of the interrelationships amongst the regressors (as reflected in the terms of the $(X'X)^{-1}$ matrix). If the regressors were orthogonal then the entire information in the variation if the ith regressor is used to determine the variance of $\hat{\beta}_i$, but if X_i and the other regressors are correlated then only that variation in X_i which is uniquely associated with Y is used to determine $\hat{\beta}_i$, and any collinear variation is not allocated uniquely to any regressor. The reduced information is reflected in a lower level of precision in the estimator $\hat{\beta}_i$. Since the inclusion of additional regressors reduces the precision of $\hat{\beta}_i$ when the regressors are not orthogonal it may be useful to compare the actual variance of $\hat{\beta}_i$ with that which would obtain were the regressors orthogonal, and the ratio of the actual variance in $\hat{\beta}_i$ to that which would obtain in the absence of any intercorrelations amongst the regressors is referred to as the variance inflation factor (VIF). The larger is the VIF the lower is the precision of $\hat{\beta}_i$.

To examine the VIF it is necessary to analyse $(X'X)^{-1}$ whose typical term is v_{ij}. Let X be partitioned as $[X_1|Z]$ where X_1 is the column vector of observations on the first regressor and Z is the $n\times(k-1)$ matrix of observations on the regressors X_2 to X_k. Then:

$$(X'X) = \begin{bmatrix} X_1'X_1 & X_1'Z \\ Z'X_1 & Z'Z \end{bmatrix}$$

and using the rules of inverting a partitioned matrix, denote $(X'X)^{-1}$ by:

$$(X'X)^{-1} = \left[\begin{array}{c|c} A_{11} & A_{12} \\ \hline A_{21} & A_{22} \end{array}\right]$$

then: $$A_{11} = (X_1'X_1 - X_1'Z(Z'Z)^{-1}Z'X_1)^{-1}$$

and: $$A_{21} = -(Z'Z)^{-1}Z'X_1A_{11}$$

Hence: $$A_{11} = [X_1'(I - Z(Z'Z)^{-1}Z')X_1]^{-1} = [X_1'M_ZX_1]^{-1}$$

where $M_Z = (I - Z(Z'Z)^{-1}Z')$. But $X_1'M_ZX_1$ is simply the sum of squared residuals obtained from regressing, by ordinary least squares, X_1 on Z; hence v_{11} $(= A_{11})$ is given by the reciprocal of the sum of squared residuals from the auxiliary regression of X_1 on all the other regressors. Denoting these residuals by RSS_1, $v_{11} = 1/RSS_1$. Also, examining the expression for A_{21}, it is clear that the term $(Z'Z)^{-1}Z'X_1$ is the vector of ordinary least squares coefficients from that auxiliary regression of X_1 on Z. Denote by $\hat{b}_{1j}$ the OLS estimate of the coefficient on X_j in this auxiliary regression, then the remaining elements in the first column of $(X'X)^{-1}$ are given by $\hat{b}_{1j}/RSS_1$, j = 2, . . . , k. This may be generalized so that:

$$v_{ii} = 1/RSS_i$$

$$v_{ij} = -\hat{b}_{ij} v_{ii}$$

where RSS_i is the residual sum of squares from the auxiliary regression of the regressor X_i on all the other regressors $[X_1, \ldots X_{i-1}, X_{i+1}, \ldots, X_k]$ and $\hat{b}_{ij}$ is the OLS estimate of the coefficient on X_j in this regression. Hence:

$$V(\hat{\beta}_i) = \sigma^2/RSS_i.$$

However, were the regressors orthogonal, then RSS_i, which is the residual sum of squares from the auxiliary regression of the regressor X_i on all the other regressors, would be given by:

$$RSS_i = \Sigma_{t=1}^{T} x_{it}^2$$

but the R^2 from the auxiliary regression of X_i on the other regressors may be written as

$$R_i^2 = 1 - RSS_i/\Sigma_{t=1}^{T} x_{it}^2$$

and so:

$$RSS_i = (1 - R_i^2)\Sigma_{t=1}^{T} x_{it}^2 .$$

Hence:

$$V(\hat{\beta}_i) = \sigma^2/[(1 - R_i^2)\Sigma_{t=1}^{T} x_{it}^2]$$

which, in the special case of orthogonality, since then $R_i^2 \equiv 0$, is given by:

$$V(\hat{\beta}_i) = \sigma^2/\Sigma_{t=1}^{T} x_{it}^2 .$$

Hence:

$$VIF = 1/(1 - R_i^2)$$

Thus the VIF ratio is equal to $1/(1 - R_i^2)$, which is necessarily greater than or equal to unity, and the actual variance of $\hat{\beta}_i$ is $1/(1 - R_i^2)$ times greater than that which would obtain were the ith regressor orthogonal to the other regressors. The greater is the extent of multicollinearity between the ith regressor and the others the greater is R_i^2, the greater is $V(\hat{\beta}_i)$, the lower is the precision of $\hat{\beta}_i$ and the greater is the VIF. Equivalently, the more is X_i collinear with any one or more of the other regressors the greater is the variance of $\hat{\beta}_i$. This demonstrates the well-known consequence of multicollinearity, namely that it implies imprecise estimators, and the VIF is one simple measure of the extent and consequences of multicollinearity.

Further reading

The variance inflation factor is further discussed in **Confidence regions** and **Multicollinearity**.

Varying parameter models

The standard analysis of economic phenomena assumes that the relationship being studied is stable within the sample of estimation; in the simple linear model $Y = X\beta + \varepsilon$ this assumption includes the presumption that the β vector is constant. The parameter vector represents the effect of changes in explanatory variables upon the dependent variable, and it is often appropriate to allow those effects to vary. The so-called switching regime model proposes that within the sample there are (at least) two distinct regimes so that, within regime 1 $Y = X\beta_1 + \varepsilon_1$ and within regime 2 $Y = X\beta_2 + \varepsilon_2$. If the point of the switch of the parameter vector from β_1 to β_2 is known *a priori* this is easily analysed (under various assumptions about the errors) by techniques such as dummy variables (see **Dummy variables**), and if the switch is not discontinuous models using spline functions may be appropriate (see **Spline functions**); tests of the difference between β_1 and β_2 are straightforward (see **Chow tests**) and if the point of the switch is not known then this may be explored by, for example, the use of recursive residuals (see **Recursive residuals**).

In cross-section analysis it may, for example, be appropriate to allow parameter variability across the units of analysis and in time-series studies it may be appropriate to allow parameters to vary over time. Several approaches to varying parameters exist (see **Kalman filter models**, **Random coefficient model** and **Time-varying parameter models**), and one of the simplest approaches is to identify some measurable variable which itself determines the changes in the parameter in question.

Let $Y_i = \alpha + \beta_i X_i + \varepsilon_i$ and let $\beta_i = \delta + \xi Z_i$; only one regressor is used for the purposes of exposition. In this example the response of Y to X is allowed to vary across observations, and the response parameter, β_i, is modelled by the second deterministic equation which identifies the variable Z as the only determinant of the response rate. The parameters of the auxiliary relationship which defines the parameter, δ and ξ, are known as hyper-parameters. Substitution leads to:

$$Y_i = \alpha + \delta X_i + \xi Z_i X_i + \varepsilon_i.$$

The variable Z enters the determination of Y via the multiplicative term $Z_i X_i$, and the error term in this equation is identical to that of the original equation. This equation may be estimated by ordinary least squares, given that the variables X and Z are non-stochastic (or otherwise independent of the error term) and that ε_i has all the characteristics of a white-noise variable. This model may be used when Z_i is a policy variable which affects behaviour via the parameters, and it is to be noted that when modelled as a determinant of the response rate the policy variable Z_i does not enter the equation additively, but multiplicatively via $Z_i X_i$. Alternatively the determination of the response rate may be seen as a stochastic relationship: $\beta_i = \delta + \xi Z_i + \eta_i$. Substitution leads to:

$$Y_i = \alpha + \delta X_i + \xi Z_i X_i + \eta_i X_i + \varepsilon_i.$$

The variable Z enters the determination of Y again via the multiplicative term $Z_i X_i$. If the variables X and Z are non-stochastic the composite error term is independent of the regressors, and assuming that the individual random errors, ε_i and η_i, are both white-noise terms, then the composite term has a zero mean, is not autocorrelated but is seen to have a variance given by $X_i^2 \sigma_\eta^2 + \sigma_\varepsilon^2$ which is heteroscedastic. This variance may be written as σ_ε^2 $(1 + \lambda X_i^2)$ where λ is the ratio $\sigma_\eta^2 / \sigma_\varepsilon^2$. If λ were known this equation could be estimated by weighted least squares (see **Heteroscedasticity – estimation methods**), but in practice such knowledge is rarely (if ever) available. Estimation may proceed by maximum likelihood, assuming that ε and η are both normally distributed. The log-likelihood is given by:

$$\text{constant} - (n/2)\ell n\, \sigma_\varepsilon^2 - (1/2\sigma_\varepsilon^2)\sum_{i=1}^{n} \frac{(Y_i - \alpha - \delta X_i - \zeta Z_i X_i)^2}{(1+\lambda X_i^2)}$$

$$- (1/2)\sum_{i=1}^{n} \ell n(1+\lambda X_i^2).$$

For a given λ the weights $w_i = (1 + \lambda X_i^2)^{½}$ may be computed and the weighted least squares regression of Y_i / w_i on $(1/w_i)$, (X_i / w_i) and $(Z_i X_i / w_i)$ may then be run; denoting the residual sum of squares from the weighted regression by RSS(λ), the concentrated log-likelihood is given by:

$$\text{constant} - (n/2)\ell n \text{RSS}(\lambda) - (1/2)\sum_{i=1}^{n} \ell n(1+\lambda X_i^2)$$

and this may then be maximized with respect to the unknown parameter, λ. If $\tilde{\lambda}$ maximizes the log-likelihood the estimators of α, δ and ξ may be derived from the weighted least squares regression using the weights given by $\tilde{w}_i = (1 + \tilde{\lambda} X_i^2)^{½}$; the resulting estimators of α, δ and ξ are then maximum likelihood estimators. This model may be extended to the case of several regressors. If, as a special case, $\xi = 0$ so that $\beta_i = \delta + \eta_i$, this becomes the Hildreth and Houck model described in **Random coefficient model**.

Varying coefficient models of this kind offer an approach by which to take into account systematic changes in parameters in response (typically) to changes in policy variables and to model pure random coefficients (an approach most useful in pooling cross-section and time-series data). If the parameters are allowed to drift over time (with and without convergence) the models described in **Kalman filter models** and **Time-varying parameter models** are appropriate. Since the fixed parameter model is always a special case of the varying coefficient model, the above models also offer a way to test the common assumption of fixed parameters. In terms of modelling parameter variation as a reflection of policy changes, the models also provide an approach to accommodate criticisms of fixed parameters such as the Lucas Critique. If economic agents take account of the general policy environment into their decision-making, and there are shifts in policy, then a random coefficient model is an attractive device by which to examine such possibilities, and is more attractive than simply adding a policy variable to the list of an equation's regressors.

Further reading
Hildreth and Houck (1968), Swamy (1970, 1971 and 1974) and Hsiao (1975) are examples of random coefficient models; for the Lucas Critique, see Lucas (1976). See also **Time-varying parameter models** and **Random coefficient model**.

Vector autoregressions

The traditional approach to modelling a simultaneous equation system considers a complete set of G independent structural equations defined on G endogenous variables and a set of exogenous and pre-determined variables; each equation of the structural form includes both endogenous and exogenous (and pre-determined) variables and there are identifying restrictions (typically of the form of exclusion restrictions) which enable the structural parameters to be identified and, hence, estimated (see **Identification**). It has been argued that the identification requirements, expressed as exclusion restrictions, are incredible; this argument may have its source in a complete general equilibrium analysis in which all variables affect all others which implies that no structural parameters are zero. The exclusion of some variables from the ith structural equation is a standard textbook requirement for identification, and as a counter to the argument of incredibility, exclusion may be seen as merely setting some coefficients which are 'sufficiently close' to zero as if they were zero. In this sense exclusion restrictions are equivalent to the usual approach to the specification of a single equation model in which variables whose influence is thought to be 'small' (a testable proposition) are excluded, and analysis concentrates on those other variables whose influence is thought to be 'salient'.

In the familiar representation of a simultaneous system, each endogenous variable at time t, Y_{it} ($i = 1, \ldots, G$; $t = 1, \ldots T$), is determined by other endogenous variables and a set of exogenous and pre-determined variables, and an error term; this structure may be written as:

$$BY_t + \Gamma X_t = \varepsilon_t$$

which may be 'solved' to yield the reduced form:

$$Y_t = \Pi X_t + v_t$$

where $\Pi = -B^{-1}\Gamma$ and $v_t = B^{-1}\varepsilon_t$. If Z_t is defined as the vector of all the current variables of the system, both endogenous and exogenous, then this could be written as:

$$Z_t = \sum_{i=1}^{m} A_i Z_{t-i} + \varepsilon_t$$

where the maximum lag length in X is m. This is a **V**ector **A**uto**R**egression (VAR) model, and each variable in Z_t is determined by the lagged values of all the variables in the system, $Z_{t-1}, Z_{t-2}, \ldots, Z_{t-m}$, and an error term. The advocates of vector autoregressive modelling argue that such this general equation is an appropriate way to model a simultaneous system: all the original variables are treated as endogenous, each is determined only by lagged values of the full set of variables and the lag length m is to be determined empirically. If Z_t contains a total of g variables, then the m matrices A_j are each of order g×g, and economic theory is not called upon to set any elements of any of these matrices to zero; m is to be determined. In the simplest case the error ε_t is non-autocorrelated, but this assumption may be relaxed. The g equations may be estimated as is described below, but further manipulations are of use in the VAR approach.

The set of g equations may be written in the lag operator, L, and then solved:

$$\phi(L)Z_t = \varepsilon_t \quad \text{where } \phi(L) = I - A_1L - A_2L^2 - \ldots - A_mL^m$$

hence:

$$Z_t = [\phi(L)]^{-1}\varepsilon_t = \sum_{j=0}^{\infty} \Psi_j \varepsilon_{t-j}.$$

This 'solution' has effectively eliminated all the lagged variables, and each of the g variables is now expressed as an (infinite) sum of the current and all lagged values of the error, i.e. each Z_t is in the form of an infinite moving average.

Since the variables of Z have been assumed to be stationary, the error term is also assumed to be stationary. Let the variance–covariance of ε_t be Ω; it is important to note that, by virtue of the stationarity of ε, Ω is not time-dated, i.e. $V(\varepsilon_t) = \Omega$ for all t. The diagonal elements of Ω are the variances of the errors from the g equations, and its off-diagonal elements are the contemporaneous covariances between those errors. Since Ω is a symmetric, positive definite matrix there exists a non-singular lower triangular matrix, P, such that:

$$P\Omega P' = I.$$

Define the random variable η_t by $P\varepsilon_t$; this new random variable represents, in the terminology of VAR, a set of g orthogonalized innovations: $E(\eta_t) = 0$, $V(\eta_t) = PV(\varepsilon_t)P' = I$ and, since P is a lower-triangular matrix, η_{1t} depends only on ε_{1t}, η_{2t} depends on ε_{1t} and ε_{2t}, and so on. The elements of η_t are mutually independent and are describe as 'orthogonalized innovations'. Z_t may then be written as:

$$Z_t = \sum_{j=0}^{\infty} \Psi_j P^{-1} P\varepsilon_{t-j} \quad \text{and so:}$$

$$Z_t = \sum_{j=0}^{\infty} \Psi_j P^{-1} \eta_{t-j}$$

$$Z_t = \sum_{j=0}^{\infty} H_j \eta_{t-j}.$$

This expression states that each element of Z_t is a linear combination of η_t, the 'orthogonalized innovations'. Equally, this transformation could be applied to the original representation:

$$Z_t = \sum_{i=1}^{m} A_i Z_{t-i} + \varepsilon_t$$

and so:

$$PZ_t = \sum_{i=1}^{m} A_i PZ_{t-i} + P\varepsilon_t$$

i.e.

$$PZ_t = P\sum_{i=1}^{m} A_i Z_{t-i} + \eta_t$$

and so the variables of PZ_t are orthogonal. Because P is a lower triangular matrix:

$$\eta_t = \begin{bmatrix} \eta_{1t} \\ \eta_{2t} \\ \vdots \\ \vdots \\ \vdots \\ \eta_{gt} \end{bmatrix} = \begin{bmatrix} p_{11} & 0 & \cdots & \cdots & \cdots & 0 \\ p_{21} & p_{22} & 0 & & & \vdots \\ p_{31} & p_{32} & p_{33} & 0 & & \vdots \\ \vdots & & & \ddots & & \vdots \\ \vdots & & & & \ddots & \vdots \\ p_{g1} & p_{g2} & \cdots & \cdots & \cdots & p_{gg} \end{bmatrix} \begin{bmatrix} \varepsilon_{1t} \\ \varepsilon_{2t} \\ \vdots \\ \vdots \\ \vdots \\ \varepsilon_{gt} \end{bmatrix}$$

Thus:

$$\eta_{1t} = p_{11}\varepsilon_{1t}$$

$$\eta_{2t} = p_{21}\varepsilon_{1t} + p_{22}\varepsilon_{2t}$$

$$\cdot \quad \cdot \quad \cdot \quad \cdot$$

$$\cdot \quad \cdot \quad \cdot \quad \cdot \quad \cdot$$

$$\eta_{gt} = p_{g1}\varepsilon_{1t} + p_{g2}\varepsilon_{2t} + \ldots\ldots\ldots + p_{gg}\varepsilon_{gt}$$

and, since $V(\eta_t) = I$, $Cov(\eta_{it}, \eta_{jt}) = 0$ for all $i \neq j$. Also, since the ε_{it} are assumed to be non-autocorrelated, $Cov(\eta_{it}, \eta_{js}) = 0$ for all $t \neq s$ and all i and

j. An immediate implication of this is that an 'innovation' is uncorrelated with all other present and previous 'orthogonal innovations' and this is intended to facilitate simulation and policy analysis, as is described below. To perform a VAR analysis, the steps are as follows.

First choose as large a dimension of Z as is possible given the available data (that is, choose the g variables of Z to be as large a set of variables as can be accommodated given the data availability) and then transform the g variables so that each is stationary and has a zero mean; this transformation is necessary as the statistical theory requires that the variables are stationary, and many economic time-series, when viewed as univariate time-series, are integrated. This step typically involves taking first or higher order differences of each variable (see **Integration** and **Stationarity**).

It is then necessary to choose as large a value of the lag length, m, as is possible given the available data, and fit the VAR; having chosen m this involves running g equations, each of which has identical regressors. The g equations are of the form:

$$Z_{it} = \sum_{j=1}^{m}(A_j)_{i1}Z_{1,t-j} + \sum_{j=1}^{m}(A_j)_{i2}Z_{2,t-j} + \ldots + \sum_{j=1}^{m}(A_j)_{ig}Z_{g,t-j} + \varepsilon_{it},\ i = 1, \ldots, g$$

where Z_{it} is the tth observation on the ith variable of Z, and $(A_j)_{ik}$ is the $(i, k)^{th}$ element of the matrix A_j. In the absence of autocorrelation amongst the errors this is a special case of 'seemingly unrelated regression equations' (see the entry of that title) as each of the g regressions has exactly the same regressors, namely the m lagged values of all the g variables of Z. Hence ordinary least squares may be used *seriatim* to estimate each equation's parameters and the resulting estimators are efficient. The required variance–covariance matrix of ε may then be estimated from the average sums of squares and cross-products of the residuals from the g regressions.

There are, however, many parameters to estimate: each equation involves mg parameters and there are g equations to estimate implying a total of mg^2 parameters plus the means of each Z_i which have been removed in transforming the variables to zero-mean variables. Nevertheless, each equation involves only mg parameters, and given sufficient degrees of freedom, this is not an issue in principle. The lag length, m, may be chosen by first 'overfitting' the equations and then reducing the lag length as a result of a sequence of tests of exclusions, or by imposing some restricting structure on the lags (although this latter proposal would seem to be incompatible with the original view that there are no exclusion restrictions on the structural form).

Finally, the equations are transformed by the construction of orthogonalized innovations; this step of the process has been the subject of much criticism. The model, when transformed into orthogonal innovations, takes the form:

$$PZ_t = P\sum_{i=1}^{m} A_i Z_{t-i} + \eta_t$$

and the variables of PZ_t are orthogonal to each other. The algebra is not contentious, but the intention is to be able to examine the effect of an innovation in one variable of PZ_t while leaving the other variables unchanged. To attempt to do so poses two awkward questions: firstly, if the effect of an innovation in one variable is to be examined this requires that the innovations be treated as exogenous variables (rather than as the random errors of the above formulation), and secondly, for an innovation to have an effect on just one variable of the system (since it is uncorrelated with all other current innovations) does not have an easy interpretation in a simultaneous system. Moreover, the innovations, η_t, are orthogonal and it is proposed that they may be varied independently, but the device of creating the orthogonal innovations is not unique, since the variables in Z may be entered in any order. Furthermore, the interpretation of an orthogonal innovation is, in this context, the impact of a policy change and the ordering of the equations is critically important in determining these innovations. One approach used in a VAR analysis is to establish a causal ordering of the variables and use the information from such an analysis, but any such causal chain is arbitrary. As such, interpretation of the orthogonal innovations is not unambiguous and has been the source of much criticism. While the mathematics of orthogonal innovations is well understood, their interpretation is illusive.

Since the VAR equations are seemingly unconstrained by any theoretical considerations, and no equation of the VAR need bear any obvious resemblance to an equation implied by theory, this approach has been labelled as 'atheoretical'. Since the role of economic theory has been wholly minimized, inference of economic *behaviour* based on a VAR may be grossly misleading. Although theory appears to have no role in the construction of a VAR, its role is, however, implicit: the choice of the dimension and specific elements of Z represents the investigator's prior beliefs (held, possibly, as a consequence of theoretical considerations) and that choice is a determinant in the finally chosen lag length. For example, if the dimension of Z is small, a larger number of lags may be required to proxy omitted variables. Atheoretical modelling may well have a role if the objective is to construct forecasting models; however, their use in examining the impact of policy changes, via orthogonal innovations, is most contentious, and their use as a vehicle for the testing of theory would appear to be extremely limited. Importantly, it is not an easy matter to communicate the outcome of a VAR exercise, and this fact further diminishes their usefulness.

Further reading

See Sims (1980 and 1982), and on the use of zero restrictions as identifying conditions, see Liu (1960) and Fisher (1961). See Cooley and LeRoy (1985) for an important critique, and also Pagan (1987) and Charemza and Deadman (1992) for surveys and overviews of the approach.

Venn diagrams

Many results of regression analysis may be illustrated by the use of Venn diagrams. Venn diagrams can be used to illustrate some, but not all, arguments; in some senses they are deficient as a tool of presentation because, while they can show an association between variables, they cannot show the sign of that association. Nevertheless, although association as demonstrated by a Venn diagram is signless, the Venn diagram remains a most useful pedagogic device.

Consider the simple bivariate ordinary least squares regression of Y on a constant and a single variable X, using the standard model $Y_i = \alpha + \beta X_i + \varepsilon_i$; this is illustrated by Figure 1.

Figure 1

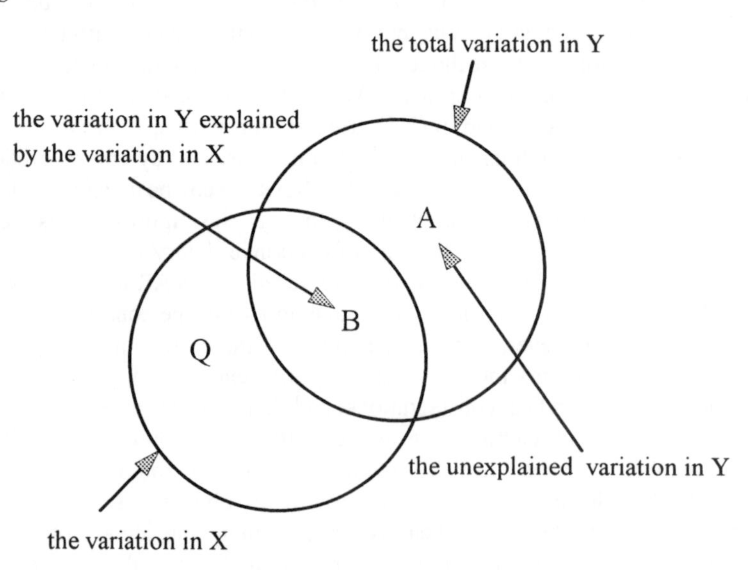

The two sets represent the sample variation in Y and X as labelled. In order to compare the two sets the entire figure is to be understood as drawn in the units of the variation in Y; hence the set labelled 'the variation in X' is a measure of that variation but is more properly described as the variation in βX since βX and Y are measured in the same units. For simplicity of language, in what follows the term 'variation in X' is used throughout to describe this set.

The intersection of the variation in Y and that of X, area B measured in the units of the variation of Y, represents that variation of Y 'explained' by X and the remaining variation in Y, area A, represents the 'unexplained' variation of Y (the sum of squared residuals from the regression of Y on X). Since the units of this diagram are those of variation in Y, there is no obvious interpretation of that variation in X complementary to area B, area Q. This is important, for one might be led to interpret Q as the sum of squared residuals from regressing X on Y (the unexplained variation in X in a regression of X on Y). This is improper since the units of the diagram are those of the variation in the regressand, Y, whereas the residuals involving a regression of X on Y are in the units of X squared.

Area B represents the association between Y and X as measured by the regression of Y on X and is that information which is used to compute $\hat{\beta}$; area A, representing the unexplained variation in Y, is that information used to compute s^2 (the estimator of the variance of the error term, σ^2). Since the estimated variance of $\hat{\beta}$ is, in part, determined by s^2, the smaller is area A (the larger is area B) the smaller is the estimated variance of the ordinary least squares estimator. Formally, of course, area A measures $\sum_{i=1}^{n}\hat{e}_i^2$ (where $\hat{e}_i$ is the ith OLS residual), which is equal to $(1 - R^2)\sum_{i=1}^{n}y_i^2$ (where R^2 is the goodness of fit statistic and $y_i = Y_i - \overline{Y}$); B is a measure of $\hat{\beta}^2\sum_{i=1}^{n}x_i^2$ which is equal to $R^2\sum_{i=1}^{n}y_i^2$ (where $\hat{\beta}$ is the ordinary least squares estimator of β and $x_i = X_i - \overline{X}$).

One can infer, immediately, from this simple representation that the OLS residuals (which form the unexplained variation in Y) are orthogonal to the regressor; this follows from noting that areas A and B have a null intersection, and so a regression of the residuals (area A) on X will result in a zero regression coefficient.

The R^2 statistic may be written as the ratio of the explained to the total variation of Y, and so is measured by the ratio B/(A+B). Clearly, the R^2 statistic is non-negative and cannot exceed unity.

If the model were to include a second regressor, Z, then the expanded model $Y_i = \alpha + \beta X_i + \gamma Z_i + \varepsilon_i$ may be analysed using Figure 2.

Some of the sample variation in Z is coincident with that of Y only (area C) and some is coincident with both X and Y (area D). The sample variation in Z which is coincident with that of X is a measure of the degree of sample collinearity between the regressors, and the area D is an indicator of the degree of multicollinearity. The larger is D relative to B or C, the greater is the degree of multicollinearity between the regressors.

Whereas in the simple regression of Y on X it was the entire intersection of the variation in X and Y which determined the estimated coefficient on X, the introduction of the second regressor has the effect of reducing the

Figure 2

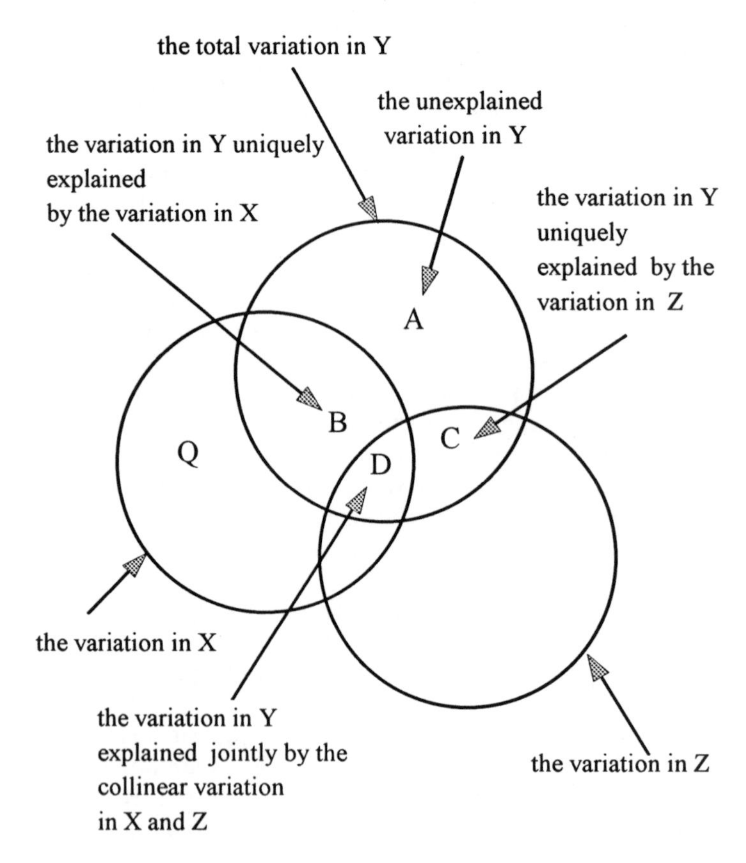

information in X which is used to determine $\hat{\beta}$ (and its precision). The reduction in the information in X used to compute $\hat{\beta}$ is reflected by the extent of the multicollinearity, namely area D. In the case of this multiple regression only that variation in X which is uniquely associated with the variation in Y, labelled as area B, is used to estimate β. Similarly, only that information in Z which is uniquely associated with Y is used to estimate γ. The collinear variation in X and Z which is associated with variation in Y is effectively discarded in the OLS estimation of the coefficients, but it is not discarded in estimating the variance of ε and hence it is not discarded in estimating the variance of the regression coefficients. The introduction of the second regressor has reduced the unexplained variation in Y, and has therefore reduced the estimated variance of ε. Thus area D is utilized in estimating the variances of the coefficients, but not in estimating the coefficients *per se*. Further, areas B, C and D are used to predict Y (that is to 'explain' the variation in Y). The estimated variance of regression coefficients depends on two factors: one is the estimated variance of the regression, and the other is the variation in the regressors uniquely associated with the regressand. The introduction of regressors reduces the estimated regression variance, which improves the precision of the estimators, but when the regressors are not orthogonal it also reduces the amount of information in the individual regressors uniquely associated with the dependent variable, which reduces the precision of the estimators (this effect is further described in **Variance inflation factor**). It is not possible to say *a priori* how the estimated variance of the coefficients will change as regressors are introduced.

To see that the information in area D is discarded in the OLS estimation of the coefficients, consider the following. The regression coefficients measure the partial influence of each regressor on the regressand, that is, having controlled in some sense for the other regressors. Suppose X were regressed on Z, as an auxiliary regression, and the residuals were computed from this regression; the information contained in these residuals is denoted by the sum of areas B and Q and this represents that information in X which is orthogonal to (independent of) Z; if Y is now regressed on these residuals the information used to estimated the regression coefficient is determined by the area B, which is intersection of the information in these residuals (X 'residualized' of Z) and Y. Since exactly the same information is used to estimate β in this method as that used in the regression of Y on X and Z together, exactly the same estimate $\hat{\beta}$ is obtained by both methods. Since regression coefficients are interpreted as measures of the influence of each regressor on the regressand while controlling for the influence of any other regressors, it is not expected that the information which is common to X and Z will be used in the determination of either regression estimate and this diagram demonstrates that this is, indeed, the case.

Taking this analysis one step further, note that if β were estimated by using only that information in X orthogonal to Z this effectively uses area B to estimate β and area A + D + C to estimate the variance of the error. This is clearly an overestimate of the regression variance, and the source of this persistent bias is due to this regression using no information in Z to predict Y, and hence using no information in Z to determine the explained component of Y. If the model is, indeed, correctly specified by the inclusion of Z then accounting for the influence of Z by using only the regressor X residualized of Z will certainly lead to an overestimate of the variance of the error. However, if Y were also residualized of Z (by regressing Y on Z to obtain residuals represented by the area A + B) and Y residualized of Z were to be regressed on X residualized of Z, the information used to estimate the regression coefficient is given by the intersection of A + B and B + Q, that is area B, and the unexplained variation is given by area A. Hence the $\hat{\beta}$ obtained by this route is exactly the same $\hat{\beta}$ obtained by either of the previous two routes, but it is important to note that in this case the estimate of the variance is determined by area A, which produces an unbiased estimator of σ^2.

This illustrates the general proposition that, in the multiple regression of Y on X and Z, where X and Z may be sets of (not perfectly collinear) variables, the ordinary least squares estimates of the coefficients attached to X and their variances are identical to those obtained by using ordinary least squares in the regression of Y 'purged' of Z on X 'purged' of Z (where 'purging' is achieved by using the residuals of Y on Z and X on Z respectively, see **Frisch–Waugh theorem**).

The familiar test of null restrictions (as in hypotheses such as H_o: $\beta = 0$ and H_o: $\gamma = 0$) may be constructed by considering the significance of the increase in the residual sum of squares due to the imposition of the implied restriction. Consider testing the null hypothesis $\beta = 0$; this is carried out by running the unrestricted regression of Y on X and Z and comparing the residual sum of squares with that from the regression of Y on Z alone. In the diagram this amounts to comparing the unrestricted sum of squares, area A, with the restricted sum of squares, area A + B. The F-test, then, is a formal route by which to answer the question: is area B significant? Similarly, the F-test of H_o: $\gamma = 0$ formalizes the answer to the question: is area C significant?

If the regression is properly specified as $Y_i = \alpha + \beta X_i + \gamma Z_i + \varepsilon_i$ but the investigator omits Z and actually runs $Y_i = \alpha + \beta X_i + \varepsilon_i$, this diagram can be used to illustrate the consequences: β is now estimated by reference to both areas B and D and so the $\hat{\beta}$ obtained will be biased due to the incorrect use of D as a measure of the influence of X. The extent and direction of this mis-specification bias will depend, therefore, on the extent of the multicollinearity between X and Z (area D) and also on the degree of the relationship between Y and Z (area C). Further, because the variance of the error term is now estimated using the area A + C, this will also be biased (unambiguously upwards) by an extent determined by the degree of the relationship between Y and Z (for further details see **Specification analysis**).

The Venn diagram may be used to illustrate the consequence of multicollinearity, namely that the precision of individual estimators falls. This is shown in Figure 3.

The larger is the degree of multicollinearity the larger is area D and the smaller are areas B and C. If area D is large relative to B and C it is quite possible for the individual hypotheses $\beta = 0$ and $\gamma = 0$ not to be rejected while the joint hypothesis $\beta = 0 = \gamma$ is rejected, i.e. neither areas B nor C are sufficiently large to be statistically significant, but area B + C + D is statistically significant. This diagram may also be used to illustrate the partial correlation coefficients. The partial correlation coefficient between Y and X

Figure 3

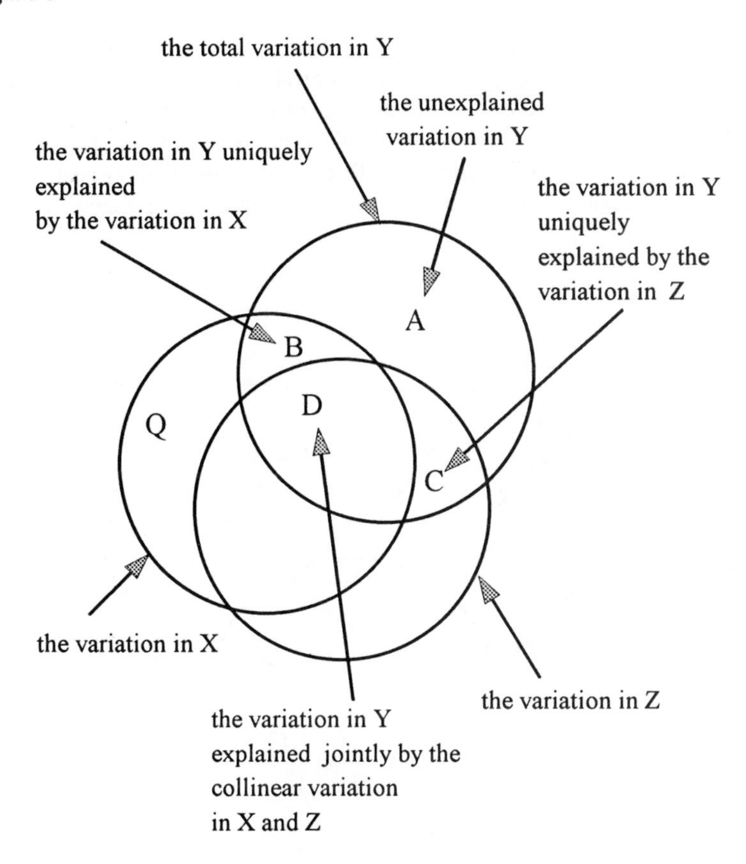

is the proportion of the unexplained variation in Y having accounted for all other regressors which may be accounted for by X (see **Partial correlation**). If, in the general linear model (with a constant) Z represents all other regressors except X, then the unexplained variation in Y after taking account of Z is given by A + B, of which X then accounts for area B; hence the partial correlation between y and X is given by the ratio B/(A + B). In the particular case of $Y_i = \alpha + \beta X_i + \gamma Z_i + \varepsilon_i$ the partial correlation coefficients of Y with respect to X and Z are given by B/(A+B) and C/(A+C). Clearly, then, if the two partial coefficients are small relative to the multiple correlation coefficient, R^2 = (B+C+D)/(A+B+C+D), this may be seen as evidence of multicollinearity. This diagram may also be used to illustrate the formula which links the correlations:

$$(1 - R^2) = (1 - r^2_{YX})\,(1 - r^2_{YZ.X})$$

r^2_{YX} is the simple square of the correlation between Y and X and is (B+D)/(A+B+C+D), $r^2_{YZ.X}$ is the partial correlation between Y and Z, given by C/(A+C) and R^2 is the squared multiple correlation coefficient.

The case of a high degree of multicollinearity is shown in Figure 3; in the limit, when the multicollinearity is perfect, areas B and C disappear, and the regression is unable to distinguish the separate influences of X and Z.

Figure 4

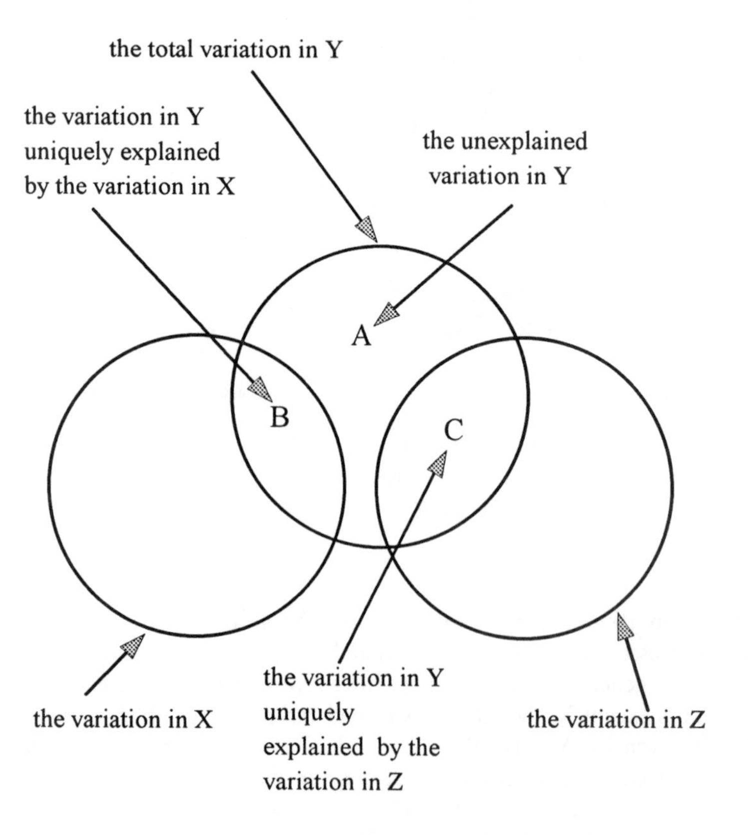

If X and Z are perfectly non-collinear in the sample, that is they are orthogonal regressors, then area D disappears and the sample variations of X and Z have a null intersect as in Figure 4. In this case the estimated coefficients on X and Z in the multiple regression of Y on both X and Z are each invariant to the inclusion of the other variable, and exactly the same information is used in estimating $\hat{\beta}$ ($\hat{\gamma}$) from this multiple regression as that used in the simple regression of Y on X alone (Y on Z alone); the important consequence of including both variables is to ensure an unbiased estimator of the regression variance and so improve the efficiency of the estimators by reducing the unexplained variation in Y. Hence, when the regressors are orthogonal to each other, the consequence of erroneous omission is inefficient but unbiased estimators of the coefficients, and biased estimators of the variances.

If Z were erroneously included in the regression, that is the 'true model' is $Y_i = \alpha + \beta X_i + \varepsilon_i$ but the regression $Y_i = \alpha + \beta X_i + \gamma Z_i + \varepsilon_i$ is run, then area C is expected to be insignificant; this is drawn in the diagram as a relatively small area, as in Figure 5.

Figure 5

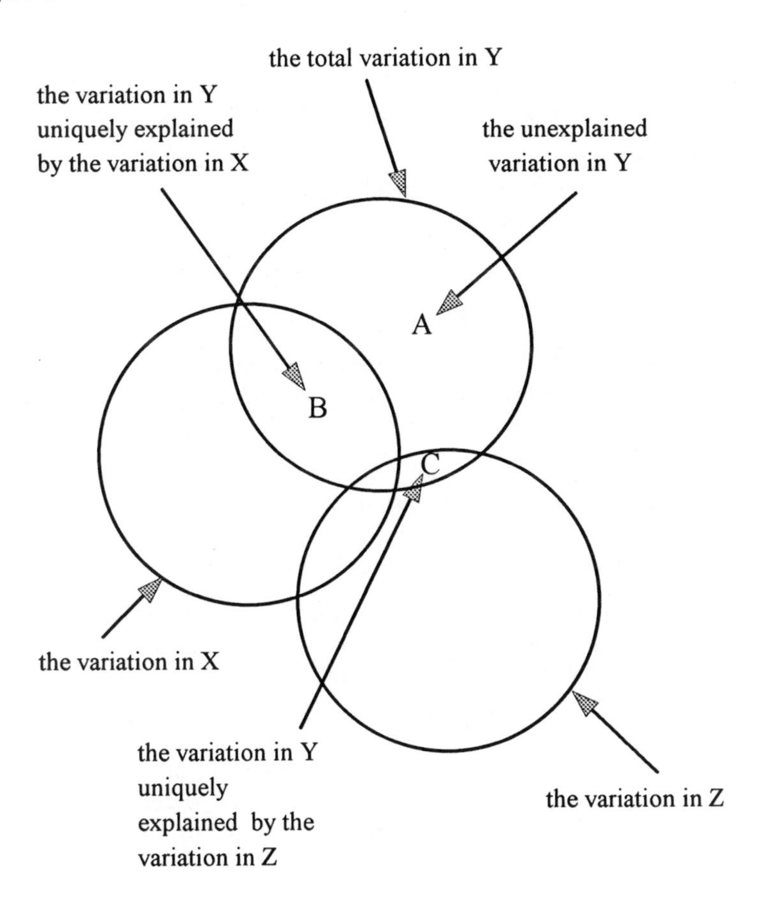

It is likely that area C will be non-null since, even though there is no relationship between Y and Z in the population, it is most unlikely that the sample correlation between Y and Z will be exactly zero. Also, since Z has no relationship with Y in the population, it is likely that the sample relationship between X and Z will be slight, and so area D is drawn as small (and is not marked in the figure). The consequence of including Z erroneously is seen to be a slight reduction in the information used to estimate β, due to the low sample collinearity between X and Z, and also some spurious gain in efficiency as the non-zero sample correlation between Y and Z implies that the unexplained variation in Y is reduced by area C.

Since, in the population, area C is zero, the OLS estimators using areas B and A (for $\hat{\beta}$ and s^2 respectively) will be unbiased. However, it is to be noted that the very presence of area C ensures that the goodness of fit statistic, R^2, will either increase by the inclusion of a variable (whether or not that variable is relevant) or, in the unlikely case of the introduction of a regressor which has an exact zero sample correlation with the regressand, will be unchanged. In the rare case when there is no sample correlation between Y and Z area C is zero and it is to be noted that in this case neither $\hat{\beta}$ nor R^2 are changed by the introduction of Z, and in this case $\hat{\gamma}$ is identically zero.

Further reading

The Venn diagram was introduced by Cohen and Cohen (1975) and has been extended by Kennedy (1981b and 1989).

Verification and confirmation

Verification is the attempt to demonstrate, by empirical testing, that a theory is materially true. By a simple reference to the syllogism required for such an attempt verification is seen to have no demonstrative validity since it involves the fallacy of affirming the consequent:

1. If H and $A_1, A_2, \ldots, A_n$ are all true then the prediction, P, is true;
2. P is true;
3. therefore H and $A_1, A_2, \ldots, A_n$ are all true.

In this form, the minor premiss is an affirmation of the consequent (not the antecedent), and while the conclusion may be true, it is not necessarily true. The rules of formal logic only allow a weak conclusion, which reads:

3, therefore each of H and $A_1, A_2, \ldots$ and A_n is not-necessarily-not-true.

However, there is information content in an empirical test which fails to refute a hypothesis; moreover, repeated attempts to refute a hypothesis which all result in non-refutation may be thought to contain even more information. One has to be careful with such a position, for a theory may be insufficiently well defined to allow falsification or it may be that there are only very few conceivable states of the world which would contradict the hypothesis. However, if a well-defined theory withstands all attempts to falsify it then one may say that it is well corroborated; equivalently one may say that, in consequence of the confidence with which the theory is now held, the degree of confirmation is high.

In statistical testing of theories it is important to formalize what constitutes a confirming instance; specifically, one would wish to control, to some extent, the probability of failing to reject a hypothesis when it is false. If the main hypothesis of interest is stated as the alternative hypothesis of the statistical test this probability is then the Type I error of the test, and control is exercised by setting a small Type I error. This approach may be called 'academic conservatism': there is a reluctance to confirm main hypotheses on the basis of other than strong evidence. If the hypothesis of interest is actually stated as the null hypothesis then the error to be controlled in order not to confirm the theory if the evidence is slight is the Type II error and, technically speaking, this is generally more difficult. One approach is to use a larger Type I error, for this automatically reduces the Type II error (for a fixed sample size).

A most important area of confirmation arises when it is recognized that the statistics used in testing hypotheses have their assumed probability distributions only when the auxiliary hypotheses (for example, those regarding the non-systematic nature of the error term in a regression) are true; thus it is necessary to have 'confirmed' those hypotheses before the main hypothesis of interest may be examined. This illustrates that falsificationism may only proceed once the auxiliary hypotheses, whether they are stated explicitly or implicitly, have been 'confirmed', and so practical falsificationism can only proceed within an accepted methodological norm of confirmation. That is, 'practical falsification' requires not only a methodological norm which sets the acceptable levels of error in a test of a main hypothesis, but also sets the methodological norms of 'confirmation' of the necessary auxiliary hypotheses and of the main hypothesis itself.

This identifies that in statistical testing there is a sequence of steps to the process: before proceeding to test a main hypothesis the necessary conditions for the validity of the statistic must have been confirmed. This highlights the pre-testing nature of all tests, namely that a given statistic only has its assumed distribution when all necessary conditions are either assumed to be true (a dangerous and potentially misleading position to adopt) or have been confirmed by a previous test. To the extent that any test may result in a decision which is at variance with the material world (a Type I or II error) all subsequent tests take their validity on the assumption that no error has occurred at a pre-testing stage.

Further reading

On verification and confirmation in economics, see especially Popper (1968), Stewart (1979) and Blaug (1992). On the non-demonstrative nature of verification, see **Deductive fallacies**, on tests of confirmation of an equation's specification see, for example, **Diagnostic tests** and on pre-testing, see **Pre-test estimators**.

Wald test

The Wald test may be used to construct tests of linear hypotheses in situations for which no exact finite sample results are available, but is used more particularly to test non-linear hypotheses. Suppose a model is parameterized by some set of parameters denoted by β, and the model is estimated freely, that is without any constraints, by maximum likelihood to yield an unconstrained ML estimator $\tilde{\beta}$. In order to examine some general hypothesis of the form $f(\beta) = 0$ the Wald test examines the value of $f(\tilde{\beta})$ and compares the computed value with its hypothesized value, namely zero. This is a direct test of the hypothesis $f(\beta) = 0$ and is in the classical mould of testing. Clearly, if the null hypothesis is true, then $f(\tilde{\beta})$ will be close to zero. The Wald test is a traditional test in that it measures the closeness of $f(\tilde{\beta})$ to zero by reference to the estimated covariance of $f(\tilde{\beta})$. The hypothesis $f(\beta) = 0$ may represent a set of joint hypotheses, that is $f(\beta) = 0$ may, in general, be a set of m equations. It may be shown that:

$$V(f(\tilde{\beta})) = \left[\frac{\partial f(\tilde{\beta})}{\partial \tilde{\beta}}\right]' V(\tilde{\beta}) \left[\frac{\partial f(\tilde{\beta})}{\partial \tilde{\beta}}\right]$$

where $[\partial f(\tilde{\beta})/\partial \tilde{\beta}']$ is the m×k matrix whose (i, j)th term is the derivative of ith equation of $f(\beta)$ with respect to β_j, evaluated at the maximum likelihood estimator of β; let this matrix of derivatives be denoted by $D(\tilde{\beta})'$. To evaluate $V(\tilde{\beta})$ the information matrix may be used; the information matrix, I, is formally defined as:

$$I(\beta) = E\left[\frac{-\partial^2 \ell n L(\beta)}{\partial \beta \partial \beta'}\right].$$

$I(\beta)$ is a measure of the curvature of the log-likelihood function. Under a set of general regularity conditions, the inverse of the information matrix, evaluated at $\tilde{\beta}$, provides the variance–covariance matrix for $\tilde{\beta}$ (see **Maximum likelihood** and **Method of scoring**), and so the Wald statistic takes the form:

$$W = f(\tilde{\beta})'[D(\tilde{\beta})'[I(\tilde{\beta})]^{-1}D(\tilde{\beta})]^{-1}f(\tilde{\beta}).$$

It is to be noted that the Wald test utilizes the curvature of the log-likelihood function evaluated at the unconstrained maximum likelihood value of the parameter, namely $I(\tilde{\beta})$. It may be shown that, under very general conditions, the large sample distribution of the W statistic is χ^2_m where m is the number of constraints defined by the restrictions $f(\beta) = 0$. Expanding $f(\tilde{\beta})$ around β:

$$f(\tilde{\beta}) \cong f(\beta) + D(\tilde{\beta})'(\tilde{\beta} - \beta)$$

and so under H_o: $f(\beta) = 0$:

$$f(\tilde{\beta}) \cong D(\tilde{\beta})'(\tilde{\beta} - \beta)$$

Now $$\sqrt{n}.(\tilde{\beta} - \beta) \xrightarrow{D} Q^{-1}\eta \sim N(0, Q^{-1})$$

where $Q = \lim(n^{-1}I(\beta))$ (see **Method of scoring**). Hence:

$$\sqrt{n}.D(\tilde{\beta})'(\tilde{\beta} - \beta) \xrightarrow{D} D(\tilde{\beta})'Q^{-1}\eta \sim N(0, D(\tilde{\beta})'Q^{-1}D(\tilde{\beta}))$$

$$\Rightarrow \quad \sqrt{n}.f(\tilde{\beta}) \xrightarrow{D} D(\tilde{\beta})'Q^{-1}\eta \sim N(0, D(\tilde{\beta})'Q^{-1}D(\tilde{\beta}))$$

i.e. $$nf(\tilde{\beta})'[D(\tilde{\beta})'Q^{-1}D(\tilde{\beta})]^{-1}f(\tilde{\beta}) \xrightarrow{D} \chi^2_m$$

and thus $$f(\tilde{\beta})'[D(\tilde{\beta})'(nQ)^{-1}D(\tilde{\beta})]^{-1}f(\tilde{\beta}) \xrightarrow{D} \chi^2_m$$

and replacing nQ by $I(\tilde{\beta})$ results in:

$$f(\tilde{\beta})'[D(\tilde{\beta})'[I(\tilde{\beta})]^{-1}D(\tilde{\beta})]^{-1}f(\tilde{\beta}) \xrightarrow{D} \chi^2_m$$

and the left-hand side expression is the Wald statistic, W.

A large value of W leads to rejection of the null hypothesis, as this would constitute evidence that the difference between $f(\tilde{\beta})$ and zero is too large to be explained by sampling variation.

In testing linear restrictions in the general linear model $Y = X\beta + \varepsilon$, the Wald test has a very simple form. If $f(\beta) = R\beta - r$ then the null hypothesis takes the form $f(\beta) = R\beta - r = 0$, where R is some m×k matrix of constants, denoted by r_{ij}, and r is a known m-dimensional vector; the (i, j)th term of $D(\tilde{\beta})'$ is then r_{ij} and so $D(\tilde{\beta})' = R$. Hence:

$$W = (R\tilde{\beta} - r)'[R\tilde{V}(\tilde{\beta})R']^{-1}(R\tilde{\beta} - r) \sim \chi^2_m \quad \text{(asymptotically)}$$

where $\tilde{V}(\tilde{\beta})$ is the estimated variance–covariance matrix of $\tilde{\beta}$. This is the large-sample χ^2 test of linear restrictions and may be compared with the familiar F-test which arises in the regression context and which is derived from the exact expression:

$$F = (R\tilde{\beta} - r)'[R\,\hat{V}(\tilde{\beta})R']^{-1}(R\tilde{\beta} - r)/m \sim F_{m,n-k}.$$

where $\hat{V}(\tilde{\beta}) = s^2(X'X)^{-1}$ and s^2 is the ordinary least squares estimated variance of the regression. As $n \to \infty$, $F_{m,n-k} \xrightarrow{D} C^2_m$ (the augmented chi-squared distribution); hence:

$$F \to (R\tilde{\beta} - r)'[R\hat{V}(\tilde{\beta})R']^{-1}(R\tilde{\beta} - r)/m \xrightarrow{D} C^2_m = \chi^2_m/m$$

i.e. $$(R\tilde{\beta} - r)'[R\hat{V}(\tilde{\beta})R']^{-1}(R\tilde{\beta} - r) \xrightarrow{D} \chi^2_m$$

which demonstrates the above special case. The computed test statistic is given by:

$$(R\tilde{\beta} - r)'[R(X'X)^{-1}R']^{-1}(R\tilde{\beta} - r)/s^2.$$

The Wald test is commonly used in econometrics; it has intuitive appeal and has the very great advantage of requiring the model only to be estimated freely. It is used particularly for large-sample tests of linear constraints when no small-sample exact results are available, and especially for testing non-linear hypotheses. Since it requires only that the model be estimated freely, there are computational gains from this aspect of the test.

Further reading
The derivation and use of the Wald test is examined in comprehensive detail in Godfrey (1988). See also **Non-linear hypothesis testing**, where it is compared with the alternative large sample tests of hypotheses, the Lagrange multiplier and the likelihood ratio tests.

White-noise

White-noise is the label given to a particular form of random variable; the random variable ε_t is a white-noise term if it is wholly unsystematic and therefore wholly unpredictable. A white-noise random variable is formally defined as one which is independently and identically distributed (IID) with a zero mean. By definition, therefore, if ε_t is white-noise if it has constant variance, and it is usually written as $\varepsilon_t \sim \text{IID}(0, \sigma^2)$; ε_t and ε_s have a zero covariance, for all $t \neq s$; hence the autocorrelation function for a white-noise random variable is zero for all non-zero lags (see **Autocorrelation function**). A white-noise process is clearly a particular form of a stationary process (see **Stationarity**).

A white-noise process is the assumed form of the error in the standard regression model, for this reflects the fact that the error exhibits no systematic components. Failure of the assumption of white-noise errors is a major focus of econometric investigations, and failures may be due to any specification errors; for this reason it is common to employ diagnostic tests of the fitted residuals (which are the estimated analogues of the true errors) to test the assumption of white-noise. Such tests include all tests of the errors' autocorrelation structure and all tests of heteroscedasticity; importantly, a white-noise error is a stationary random error, and so tests of the stationarity of the residuals are critically important.

Further reading
See **Error term**, **Autocorrelation tests**, **Heteroscedasticity tests** and also **Stationarity** and **Unit root tests**.

White's test

In making inference from the model $Y = X\beta + \varepsilon$ when it is assumed that the error terms are heteroscedastic, but that the specification is otherwise acceptable, the ordinary least squares estimator of β is known to be linear and unbiased but inefficient. Importantly, the standard OLS formula for the true variance of $\hat{\beta}$ is no longer appropriate, and the standard OLS formula for the estimated variance of ε, s^2, provides a biased estimator in this case and so the estimated variance of $\hat{\beta}$ is, in the case of heteroscedasticity, like that of autocorrelation, biased.

Specifically, if $Y = X\beta + \varepsilon$ and $V(\varepsilon) = \sigma^2\Omega$ where $\Omega = \text{diag}\{\lambda_1, \lambda_2, \ldots, \lambda_n\}$, then:

$$\hat{\beta} = \beta + (X'X)^{-1}X'\varepsilon$$

and $$E(\hat{\beta}) = \beta; \qquad V(\hat{\beta}) = \sigma^2(X'X)^{-1}X'\Omega X(X'X)^{-1}$$

$$s^2 = \hat{e}'\hat{e}/(n-k) \quad \text{where } \hat{e} = Y - X\hat{\beta} = M\varepsilon, \quad M = I - X(X'X)^{-1}X';$$

hence: $$E[(n-k)s^2] = E(\varepsilon' M\varepsilon) = \sigma^2 \textstyle\sum_{i=1}^{n} \lambda_i m_{ii}$$

where m_{ii} is the ith diagonal term of M. In general, $\sum_{i=1}^{n} \lambda_i m_{ii} \neq n - k$ and so s^2 provides a biased estimator of σ^2; the direction of the bias cannot, in general, be ascertained. Of course, if the λ_i weights are known then generalized least squares (in the special case of weighted least squares) can be applied; if the λ_i weights are not known but can be estimated consistently then feasible generalized least squares can be applied. In the case when the weights are not known and cannot be estimated, the problem remains that although the OLS estimator $\hat{\beta}$ is unbiased, its standard errors, as reported by the OLS method, are biased and so the application of the usual inferential techniques (such as t- and F-tests) are no longer valid. To proceed with inference in such circumstance, White (1980) provided a method by which to generate estimators of the variance of $\hat{\beta}$ which are consistent under heteroscedasticity and may, therefore, be used to construct asymptotically test statistics. Moreover, the White heteroscedastic-consistent variance estimators provide the basis for a most general test for heteroscedasticity (see **Heteroscedasticity tests**).

If $Y = X\beta + \varepsilon$, and the error term is heteroscedastic, and the model can neither be re-specified into a model with a white-noise error term nor can the form of the heteroscedasticity be modelled by a small number of estimable parameters, then the White procedure allows inference from the OLS estimators by the following device. The true variance of $\hat{\beta}$ is given by:

$$V(\hat{\beta}) = \sigma^2(X'X)^{-1}X'\Omega X(X'X)^{-1}$$

and Ω is not known. Now $V(\varepsilon_i) = E(\varepsilon_i^2) = \sigma^2\lambda_i$, ε_i is not observable and the weights, λ_i are not known; however, the OLS residuals, $\hat{e}$, provide a proxy for the unobservable and unknowable errors, ε. Given $\hat{e}_i$ as the proxy for ε_i, $\hat{e}_i$ may be viewed as a sample of size 1 from the distribution of the ith residual and so $\hat{e}_i^2$ may be viewed as an estimator of σ_i^2, the true variance of ε_i. Although $\hat{e}_i^2$ is not a consistent estimator of $V(\varepsilon_i)$, it is possible, under very general conditions, to generate a consistent estimator of $\sigma^2 X'\Omega X$. Let $\hat{\Phi} = \text{diag}\{\hat{e}_1^2, \ldots\ldots, \hat{e}_n^2\}$; then $X'\hat{\Phi}X$ may be written as:

$$X'\hat{\Phi}X = \sum_{i=1}^{n} \hat{e}_i^2 x_i x_i'$$

where x_i' is the $1 \times k$ i^{th} row of X, the ith observations on all k regressors. This provides a consistent estimator of $\sigma^2 X'\Omega X$ and $(X'X)^{-1}X'\hat{\Phi}X(X'X)^{-1}$ provides a consistent estimator of $\sigma^2(X'X)^{-1}X'\Omega X(X'X)^{-1}$ as:

$$\hat{V}(\hat{\beta}) = (X'X)^{-1}[\sum_{i=1}^{n} \hat{e}_i^2 x_i x_i'](X'X)^{-1}$$

from which large-sample consistent tests of β may be constructed.

By this method, then, a heteroscedastic-consistent estimator of the variance of the ordinary least squares estimator may be constructed in the absence of any specific assumptions regarding the form of the heteroscedasticity. By using no explicit assumption of the form of that heteroscedasticity, this method has very general applicability, but is inferior to an approach which enables a specific form of the heteroscedasticity to be employed.

Were an adequate specific form of heteroscedasticity available, it would be possible to estimate the weights λ_i consistently, in which case it would be optimal to employ a feasible generalized least squares estimator which is (at least asymptotically) more efficient than the ordinary least squares estimator. In this present case, however, it has been assumed that the λ_i cannot be estimated consistently, but it has been shown that it is possible to generate a consistent estimator of the variance of the (inefficient) ordinary least squares estimator. Hence the White procedure uses the linear unbiased but inefficient ordinary least squares estimator, $\hat{\beta}$, and then proceeds to estimate its variance consistently. No alternative linear unbiased more efficient estimator is available.

The greatest use of White's heteroscedastic-consistent variance estimator is in those situations when no re-specification can eliminate the heteroscedasticity in the original model and when that heteroscedasticity cannot be modelled satisfactorily by imposing some specific structure. The White method simply provides consistent estimators of the variances of the linear unbiased but inefficient OLS estimators of the regression coefficients and thereby enables inference to be made via the usual techniques of t- and F- tests which, in this case, are asymptotically valid. The White estimator of the variance matrix also provides a very general, though not powerful, test of heteroscedasticity.

Further reading

White (1980) provides details of the test and of the heteroscedastic-consistent variance estimators; see Ali and Giacotto (1984) for a survey of tests for heteroscedasticity, which compares their power.

REFERENCES

Afifi, T. and R. Elashoff (1966), 'Missing Observations in Multivariate Statistics', *Journal of the American Statistical Association*, 61, 595–604.

Afifi, T. and R. Elashoff (1967), 'Missing Observations in Multivariate Statistics', *Journal of the American Statistical Association*, 62, 10–29.

Aigner, D. (1974), 'MSE Dominance of Least Squares with Errors of Observation', *Journal of Econometrics*, 2, 365–372.

Aitken, A. (1935), 'On Least Squares and Linear Combinations of Observations', *Proceedings of the Royal Statistical Society*, 55, 42–48.

Akaike, H. (1973), 'Information Theory and an Extension of the Maximum Likelihood Principle', in B. Petrov and F. Csake (eds), *2nd International Symposium on Information Theory*, Budapest, Akademiai Kiado.

Ali, M. and C. Giaccotto (1984), 'A Study of Several New and Existing Tests for Heteroscedasticity in the General Linear Model', *Journal of Econometrics*, 26, 355–374.

Almon, S. (1965), 'The Distributed Lag Between Capital Appropriations and Expenditures', *Econometrica*, 33, 178–196.

Amemiya, T. (1973), 'Regression Analysis when the Dependent Variable is Truncated Normal', *Econometrica*, 41, 997–1016.

Amemiya, T. (1980), 'Selection of Regressors', *International Economic Review*, 21, 331–354.

Amemiya, T. (1981), 'Qualitative Response Models: a Survey', *Journal of Economic Literature*, 19, 481–536.

Amemiya, T. (1984), 'Tobit Models: a Survey', *Journal of Econometrics*, 24, 3–63.

Amemiya, T. (1985), *Advanced Econometrics*. Cambridge, Mass.: Harvard University Press.

Anderson, T. and H. Rubin (1949), 'Estimation of the Parameters of a Single Equation in a Complete System of Stochastic Equations', *Annals of Mathematical Statistics*, 20, 46–63.

Anderson, T. and H. Rubin (1950), 'The Asymptotic Properties of Estimators of the Parameters of a Single Equation in a Complete System of Stochastic Equations', *Annals of Mathematical Statistics*, 21, 570–582.

Arrow, K. J. (1960), 'Decision Theory and the Choice of a Level of Significance for the t–test', in I. Olkin *et al.* (eds), *Contributions to*

Probability and Statistics: Essays in Honour of Harold Hotelling, Stanford, Cal.: Stanford University Press.

Balestra, P. and M. Nerlove (1966), 'Pooling Cross Section and Time Series Data in the Estimation of a Dynamic Model: the Demand for Natural Gas', *Econometrica*, 34, 585–612.

Banerjee, A., J. Dolado, D. F. Hendry and G. Smith, (1986), 'Exploring Equilibrium Relationships in Econometrics Through Static Models: Some Monte Carlo Evidence', *Oxford Bulletin of Economics and Statistics*, 48, 253–277.

Barnett, V. (1973), *Comparative Statistical Inference*. New York: John Wiley.

Bartlett, M. S. (1946), 'On the Theoretical Specification of Sampling Properties of Autocorrelated Time Series', *Journal of the Royal Statistical Society*, Series B, 8, 27–41.

Bartlett, M. S. (1949), 'Fitting a Straight Line when Both Variables are Subject to Error', *Biometrics*, 5, 207–212.

Belsley, D., E. Kuh and R. Welsch (1980), *Regression Diagnostics: Identifying Influential Data and Sources of Collinearity*. New York: John Wiley.

Berndt, E. B., R. Hall and J. Hausman (1974), 'Estimation and Inference in Nonlinear Structural Models', *Annals of Economic and Social Measurement*, 3/4, 653–665.

Berndt, E. and N. E. Savin (1977), 'Conflict among Criteria for Testing Hypotheses in the Multivariate Regression Model', *Econometrica*, 45, 1263–1278.

Blaug, M. (1992), *The Methodology of Economics; or, How Economists Explain*, 2nd edn, Cambridge: Cambridge University Press.

Blundell, R. (ed.) (1987), 'Specification Testing in Limited and Discrete Dependent Variable Models', *Journal of Econometrics*, 34, 1/2.

Bollerslev, T. (1986), 'Generalized Autoregressive Conditional Heteroscedasticity', *Journal of Econometrics*, 31, 307–327.

Boot. J. and G. deWitt (1960), 'Investment Demand: an Empirical Contribution to the Aggregation Problem', *International Economic Review*, 1, 3–30.

Box, G. E. P. and D. Cox (1964), 'An Analysis of Transformations', *Journal of the Royal Statistical Society*, Series B, 211–264.

Box, G. E. P. and G. Jenkins (1984), *Time Series Analysis: Forecasting and Control*, 2nd edn. San Francisco: Holden-Day.

Box, G. E. P. and D. Pierce, (1970), 'Distribution of Residual Autocorrelations in Autoregressive Moving Average Time Series Models', *Journal of the American Statistical Association*, 65, 1509–1526.

Box, G. E. P. and G. C. Tiao (1973), *Bayesian Inference in Statistical Analysis*. Reading, Mass.: Addison-Wesley.

Breusch, T. (1978), 'Testing for Autocorrelation in Dynamic Linear Models', *Australian Economic Papers*, 17, 334–355.

Breusch, T. and L. G. Godfrey (1986), 'Data Transformation Tests', *Economic Journal*, 96 (Supplement), 47–58.

Breusch, T. and A. Pagan (1979), 'A Simple Test for Heteroscedasticity and Random Coefficient Variation', *Econometrica*, 47, 1287–1294.

Breusch, T. and A. Pagan (1980), 'The LM Test and its Applications to Model Specification in Econometrics', *Review of Economics Studies*, 47, 239–254.

Brown, R., J. Durbin, and J. Evans (1975), 'Techniques for Testing the Constancy of Regression Relationships over Time', *Journal of the Royal Statistical Society*, Series B, 37, 149–172.

Buse, A. (1982), 'The Likelihood Ratio, Wald, and Lagrange Multiplier Tests: an Expository Note', *American Statistician*, 36, 152–157.

Caudill, S. (1988), 'An Advantage of the Linear Probability Model over Probit or Logit', *Oxford Bulletin of Economics and Statistics*, 50, 425–427.

Challen, D. W. and A. J. Hagger (1983), *Macroeconomic Systems: Construction, Validation and Applications*. New York: St Martin's Press.

Chalmers, A. F. (1976), *What is This Thing Called Science?* Milton Keynes, Bucks.: Open University Press.

Charemza, W. W. and D. D. Deadman (1992), *New Directions in Econometric Practice*. Aldershot, Hants.: Edward Elgar.

Chatfield, C. (1975), *The Analysis of Time Series: Theory and Practice*. London: Chapman & Hall.

Chatfield, C. and A. J. Collins (1986), *Introduction to Multivariate Analysis*. London: Chapman & Hall.

Chatterjee, S. and B. Price (1977), *Regression Analysis by Example*. New York: John Wiley.

Chong, Y. T. and D. F. Hendry (1986), 'Econometric Evaluation of Linear Macro-econometric Models', *Review of Economic Studies*, 53, 671–690.

Chow, G. (1960), 'Tests of Equality Between Sets of Coefficients in Two Linear Regressions', *Econometrica*, 28, 591–605.

Chow, G. (1968), 'Two Methods of Computing Full Information Maximum Likelihood Estimates in Simultaneous Stochastic Equations', *International Economic Review*, 24, 100–112.

Chow, G. (1983), *Econometrics*. Tokyo: McGraw–Hill.

Christ, C. F. (1966), *Econometric Models*. New York: John Wiley.

Chung, K. L. (1974), *A Course in Probability Theory*, 2nd edn. New York: Academic Press.

Cohen J. and P. Cohen (1975), *Applied Multiple Regression/Correlation Analysis for the Behavioural Sciences*. Hillside, N.J.: Laurance Erlbaum Associates.

Conniffe, D. (1982b), 'A Note on Seemingly Unrelated Regressions', *Econometrica*, 50, 229–233.

Cooley, T. and S. LeRoy (1985), 'Atheoretical Macroeconomics: a Critique', *Journal of Monetary Economics*, 16, 283–308.

Cooley, T. and E. Prescott (1973a) 'An Adaptive Regression Model', *International Economic Review*, 14, 364–371.

Cooley, T. and E. Prescott (1973b) 'Varying Parameter Regression: a Theory and Some Applications', *Annals of Economic and Social Measurement*, 2/4, 463–473.

Cox, D. (1961), 'Tests of Separate Families of Hypotheses', in *Proceedings of the 4th Berkeley Symposium on Mathematical Statistics and Probability*, Vol. 1, Berkeley, Cal.: University of California Press.

Cox, D. (1962), 'Further Results on Tests of Separate Families of Hypotheses', *Journal of the Royal Statistical Society*, Series B, 24, 406–424.

Cragg, J. (1982), 'Estimation and Testing in Time Series Regression Models with Heteroscedastic Disturbances', *Journal of Econometrics*, 20, 135–157.

Cuthbertson, K, S. G. Hall and M. P. Taylor (1992), *Applied Econometric Techniques*. Hemel Hempstead, Herts.: Harvester Wheatsheaf.

Darnell, A. C. and J. L. Evans (1990), *The Limits of Econometrics*. Aldershot, Hants.: Edward Elgar.

Davidson, J., D. F. Hendry, F. Srba and S. Yeo (1978), 'Econometric Modelling of the Aggregate Time-Series Relationship between Consumers' Expenditure and Income in the United Kingdom', *Economic Journal*, 88, 661–692.

Davidson, R. and J. MacKinnon (1981), 'Several Tests for Model Specification in the Presence of Alternative Hypotheses', *Econometrica*, 49, 781–793.

Davidson, R. and J. MacKinnon (1983), 'Small Sample Properties of Alternatives Forms of the Lagrange Multiplier Test', *Economics Letters*, 12, 269–275.

Davidson, R. and J. MacKinnon (1984), 'Convenient Specification Tests for Logit and Probit Models', *Journal of Econometrics*, 25, 241–262.

Davidson, R. and J. MacKinnon (1985), 'Testing Linear and Loglinear Regressions Against Box–Cox Alternatives', *Canadian Journal of Economics*, 18, 499–517.

Davidson, R. and J. MacKinnon (1993), *Estimation and Inference in Econometrics*, New York: Oxford University Press.

de Finetti, B. (1937), 'Foresight: Its Logical Laws, Its Subjective Sources', in H. E. Kyburg and H. G. Smokler (eds) (1964), *Studies in Subjective Probability*, New York: John Wiley.

De Long, J. B. and K. Lang (1992), 'Are All Economic Hypotheses False?', *Journal of Political Economy*, 100, 1257–1272.

Denton, F. T. (1985), 'Data Mining as an Industry', *Review of Economics and Statistics*, 67, 124–127.

Denton, F. T. (1988), 'The Significance of Significance: Rhetorical Aspects of Statistical Hypothesis Testing in Economics', in A. Klamer, D. N. McCloskey and R. M. Solow (eds) (1988), *The Consequences of Economic Rhetoric*, Cambridge: Cambridge University Press.

Dhrymes, P. (1971), *Distributed Lags: Problems of Estimation and Formulation*. San Francisco: Holden-Day.

Dickey, D. and W. Fuller (1979), 'Distribution of the Estimators for Autoregressive Time Series with a Unit Root', *Journal of the American Statistical Association*, 74, 427–431.

Dickey, D. and W. Fuller (1981), 'Likelihood Ratio Tests for Autoregressive Time Series with a Unit Root', *Econometrica*, 49, 1057–1072.

Dickey, D., D. P. Hasza, and W. Fuller (1984), 'Testing for Unit Roots in Seasonal Time Series', *Journal of the American Statistical Association*, 79, 355–367.

Draper, N. and H. Smith, (1980) *Applied Regression Analysis*. New York: John Wiley.

Duncan, G. (ed.) (1986), 'Continuous/Discrete Econometric Models with Unspecified Error Distribution', *Journal of Econometrics*, 32, 1.

Durbin, J. (1954), 'Errors in Variables', *Review of the International Statistical Institute*, 22, 23–32.

Durbin, J. (1960), 'Estimation of Parameters in Time-Series Regression Models', *Journal of the Royal Statistical Society*, Series B, 22, 139–153.

Durbin, J. (1970), 'Testing for Serial Correlation in Least Square Regression When Some of the Regressors are Lagged Dependent Variables', *Econometrica*, 38, 410–421.

Durbin, J. and G. Watson (1950), 'Testing for Serial Correlation in Least Squares Regression – I', *Biometrika*, 37, 409–428.

Durbin, J. and G. Watson (1951), 'Testing for Serial Correlation in Least Squares Regression – II', *Biometrika*, 38, 159–178.

Durbin, J. and G. Watson (1971), 'Testing for Serial Correlation in Least Squares Regression – III', *Biometrika*, 58, 1–42.

Eatwell, J., M. Milgate and P. Newman (eds) (1990a), *The New Palgrave Dictionary: Econometrics*. London: Macmillan.

Eatwell, J., M. Milgate and P. Newman (eds) (1990b), *The New Palgrave Dictionary: Time Series and Statistics*. London: Macmillan.

Edwards, A. W. F. (1972), *Likelihood*. Cambridge: Cambridge University Press.

Efron, B. and C. Morris (1973) 'Stein's Estimation Rule and its Competitors', *Journal of the American Statistical Association*, 68, 117–130.

Efron, B. and C. Morris (1975), 'Data Analysis Using Stein's Estimator and its Generalisations', *Journal of the American Statistical Association*, 70, 311–319.

Efron, B. and C. Morris (1977), 'Stein's Paradox in Statistics', *Scientific American*, 236, 119–127.

Engle, R. (1982), 'Autoregressive Conditional Heteroscedasticity with Estimates of the Variance of United Kingdom Inflations', *Econometrica*, 50, 987–1008.

Engle, R. (1983), 'Estimates of the Variance of U.S. Inflation Based on the ARCH Model', *Journal of Money, Credit, and Banking*, 15, 286–301.

Engle, R. (1984), 'Wald, Likelihood Ratio, and Lagrange Multiplier Tests in Econometrics', in Z. Griliches and M. Intriligator (eds., *Handbook of Econometrics*, Vol. 2, Amsterdam: North-Holland.

Engle, R. and C. Granger, (1987), 'Co-integration and Error Correction: Representation, Estimation and Testing', *Econometrica*, 35, 251–276.

Engle, R. and D. Kraft (1983), 'Multiperiod Forecast Error Vacancies of Inflation Estimated from ARCH Models', in A. Zellner (ed.), *Applied Times Series Analysis of Economic Data*, Washington, D.C.: Bureau of the Census.

Engle, R. and M. Rothschild (1992), 'ARCH Models in Finance', *Journal of Econometrics*, 52, 1/2.

Engle, R., D. F. Hendry and J.-F. Richard (1983), 'Exogeneity', *Econometrica*, 51, 277–304.

Evans, G. and N. Savin (1981), 'Testing for Unit Roots: I', *Econometrica*, 49, 753–779.

Evans, G. and N. Savin (1984), 'Testing for Unit Roots: II', *Econometrica*, 52, 1241–1269.

Fair, R. (1984), *Specification and Analysis of Macroeconomic Models*. Cambridge, Mass.: Harvard University Press.

Farebrother, R. (1980), 'The Durbin–Watson Test for Serial Correlation When There is No Intercept in the Regression', *Econometrica*, 48, 1553–1563.

Farrar, D. and R. Glauber (1967), 'Multicollinearity in Regression Analysis: the Problem Revisited', *Review of Economics and Statistics*, 49, 92–107.

Feldstein, M. (1973), 'Multicollinearity and the MSE of Alternative Estimators', *Econometrica*, 41, 337–346.

Fisher, F. M. (1961), *The Identification Problem in Econometrics*. New York: R. E. Krieger.

Fisher, F. (1970), 'Tests of Equality Between Sets of Coefficients in Two Linear Regressions: an Expository Note', *Econometrica*, 28, 361–366.

Fisher, W. (1976), 'Normalisation in Point Estimation', *Journal of Econometrics*, 4, 246–252.

Fletcher, R. (1980), *Practical Methods of Optimization*. New York: John Wiley.

Fomby, T., C. Hill and S. Johnson (1978), 'An Optimal Property of Principal Components in the Context of Restricted Least Squares', *Journal of the American Statistical Association*, 73, 191–193.

Fomby, T., C. Hill and S. Johnson (1984), *Advanced Econometric Methods*. Needham, Mass.: Springer-Verlag.

Frisch, R. and F. Waugh (1933), 'Partial Time Regressions as Compared with Individual Trends', *Econometrica*, 1, 387–401.

Galpin, J. and D. Hawkins (1984), 'The Use of Recursive Residuals in Checking Model Fit in Linear Regression', *American Statistician*, 38, 94–105.

Garber, S. and S. Klepper (1980), 'Extending the Classical Normal Errors in Variables Model', *Econometrica*, 48, 1541–1546.

Geary R. and C. Leser (1968), 'Significance Tests in Multiple Regression', *American Statistician*, 22, 20–1.

Geweke, J. (1982), 'Causality, Exogeneity and Inference', in W. Hildenbrand (ed.), *Advances in Econometrics*, Cambridge: Cambridge University Press.

Geweke, J. (1984), 'Inference and Causality in Econometric Time Series Models', in Z. Griliches, and M. Intriligator (eds), *Handbook of Econometrics*, Vol. 2. Amsterdam: North-Holland.

Gilbert, C. L. (1986), 'Professor Hendry's Econometric Methodology', *Oxford Bulletin of Economics and Statistics*, 48, 283–307.

Glesjer, H. (1969), 'A New Test for Heteroscedasticity', *Journal of the American Statistical Association*, 64, 316–323.

Godfrey, L. (1978a) 'Testing for Multiplicative Heteroscedasticity', *Journal of Econometrics*, 8, 227–236.

Godfrey, L. (1978b) 'Testing against General Autoregressive and Moving Average Error Models when the Regressors Include Lagged Dependent Variables', *Econometrica*, 46, 1293–1302.

Godfrey, L. (1979) 'Testing the adequacy of a time series model', *Biometrika*, 66, 67-72.

Godfrey, L. (1984), 'On the Use of Misspecification Checks and Tests of Non-nested Hypotheses in Empirical Economics', *Supplement to Economic Journal Conference Papers*, 95, 69–81.

Godfrey, L. (1988), *Misspecification Tests in Econometrics*. Cambridge: Cambridge University Press.

Godfrey, L. and D. Poskitt (1975), 'Testing the Restrictions of the Almon Lag Technique', *Journal of the American Statistical Association*, 70, 105–108.

Goldfeld, S. and R. Quandt (1965), 'Some Tests for Homoscedasticity', *Journal of the American Statistical Association*, 60, 539–547.

Goldfeld, S. and R. Quandt (1971), *Nonlinear Methods in Econometrics*. Amsterdam: North-Holland.

Goldfeld, S., R. Quandt and H. Trotter (1966), 'Maximization by Quadratic Hill Climbing', *Econometrica*, 541–551.

Granger, C. (1969), 'Investigating Causal Relations by Econometric Models and Cross-spectral Methods', *Econometrica*, 37, 424–438.

Granger, C. (1980), *Forecasting in Business and Economics*. New York: Academic Press.

Granger, C. (ed.) (1990), *Modelling Economic Series*. Oxford: Clarendon Press.

Granger, C. and P. Newbold (1974), 'Spurious Regressions in Econometrics', *Journal of Econometrics*, 2, 111–120.

Granger, C. and P. Newbold (1977), *Forecasting Economic Time Series*. New York: Academic Press.

Greenberg, E. and C. Webster (1983), *Advanced Econometrics: A Bridge to the Literature*. New York: John Wiley.

Greene, W. (1983), 'Estimation of Limited Dependent Variable Models by Ordinary Least Squares and the Method of Moments', *Journal of Econometrics*, 21, 195–212.

Greene, W. (1993), *Econometric Analysis*, 2nd edn. New York: Macmillan.

Greene, W. and T. Seaks (1991), 'The Restricted Least Squares Estimator: a Pedagogical Note', *Review of Economics and Statistics*, 73, 563–567.

Griliches, Z. (1967), 'Distributed Lags: a Survey', *Econometrica*, 35, 16–49.

Griliches, Z. (1986), 'Economic Data Issues', in Z. Griliches and M. Intriligator (eds), *Handbook of Econometrics*, Vol. 3. Amsterdam: North-Holland.

Griliches, Z. and P. Rao (1969), 'Small Sample Properties of Several Two Stage Regression Methods in the Context of Autocorrelated Errors', *Journal of the American Statistical Association*, 64, 253–272.

Grunfeld, Y. and Z. Griliches (1960), 'Is Aggregation Necessarily Bad?', *Review of Economics and Statistics*, 42, 1–13.

Haavelmo, T. (1944), 'The Probability Approach in Econometrics', Supplement to *Econometrica*, 12, 1–118.

Halvorsen, R. and R. Palmquist (1980), 'The Interpretation of Dummy Variables in Semilogarithmic Equations', *American Economic Review*, 70, 474–475.

Hansen, L. (1982), 'Large Sample Properties of Generalized Method of Moments Estimators', *Econometrica*, 50, 1029–1054.

Harvey, A. (1981), *Time Series Models*. Deddington, Oxford: Philip Allan.

Harvey, A. (1990), *The Econometric Analysis of Time Series*, 2nd edn. Cambridge, Mass.: MIT Press.

Harvey, A. and G. Collier (1977), 'Testing for Functional Misspecification in Regression Analysis', *Journal of Econometrics*, 6, 103–119.

Harvey, A. and G. D. A. Phillips (1973), 'A Comparison of the Power of Some Test for Heteroscedasticity in the General Linear Model', *Journal of Econometrics*, 2, 307–316.

Hatanaka, M. (1974), 'An Efficient Two Step Estimator for the Dynamic Adjustment Model with Autoregressive Errors', *Journal of Econometrics*, 2, 199–220.

Hausman, D. M. (1992), *The Inexact and Separate Science of Economics*. Cambridge: Cambridge University Press.

Hausman, J. (1975), 'An Instrumental Variable Approach to Full-information Estimators for Linear and Certain Nonlinear Models', *Econometrica*, 43, 727–738.

Hausman, J. (1978), 'Specification Tests in Econometrics', *Econometrica*, 46, 1251–1271.

Hausman, J. (1983), 'Specification and Estimation of Simultaneous Equations Models', in Z. Griliches and M. Intriligator (eds), *Handbook of Econometrics*, Amsterdam: North-Holland.

Hausman, J. and D. Wise (1977), 'Social Experimentation, Truncated Distributions, and Efficient Estimation', *Econometrica*, 45, 919–938.

Heckman, J. and T. MaCurdy (1985), 'A Simultaneous Equations Linear Probability Model', *Canadian Journal of Economics*, 18, 28–37.

Hendry, D. (1980), 'Econometrics: Alchemy or Science?', *Economica*, 47, 387–406.

Hendry, D. F. (1984), 'Monte Carlo Experimentation in Econometrics', in M. Intriligator (ed.), *Handbook of Econometrics*, Vol. II, Amsterdam: North-Holland.

Hendry, D. F. and G. E. Mizon (1978), 'Serial Correlation as a Convenient Simplification, Not a Nuisance', *Economic Journal*, 88, 549–563.

Hendry, D. and J.-F. Richard (1982), 'On the Formulation of Empirical Models in Dynamic Econometrics', *Journal of Econometrics*, 20, 193–220.

Hendry, D. and J-F. Richard (1983), 'The Econometric Analysis of Economic Time Series', *International Statistical Review*, 51, 3–33.

Hendry, D., A. Pagan and J. Sargan (1984), 'Dynamic Specification', in Z. Griliches and M. Intriligator (eds), *Handbook of Econometrics*, Vol. 2, Amsterdam: North-Holland.

Hildreth, C. and C. Houck (1968), 'Some Estimators for a Linear Model with Random Coefficients', *Journal of the American Statistical Association*, 63, 584–595.

Hocking, R. R. (1976), 'The Analysis and Selection of Variables in Multiple Regression', *Biometrics*, 32, 1–49.

Hoerl, A. and R. Kennard (1970), 'Ridge Regression: Biased Estimation for Nonorthogonal Problems', *Technometrics*, 12, 69–82.

Holden, K., D. A. Peel and J. L. Thompson (1990), *Economic Forecasting: An Introduction*. Cambridge: Cambridge University Press.

Hsiao, C. (1975), 'Some Estimation Methods for a Random Coefficient Model', *Econometrica*, 43, 6, 305–325.

Hsiao, C. (1983), 'Identification', in Z. Griliches and M. Intriligator (eds), *Handbook of Econometrics*, Amsterdam: North-Holland.

Hsu, Y. S. *et al.* (1986), 'Monte Carlo Studies on the Effectiveness of the Bootstrap Method on 2SLS Estimates', *Economics Letters*, 20, 233–239.

Huber, P. J. (1981), *Robust Statistics*. New York: John Wiley.

Hume, D. (1955), *An Inquiry Concerning Human Understanding*, originally printed 1748. Indianapolis: Bobbs-Merrill.

James, W. and C. Stein (1961), 'Estimation with Quadratic Loss', in J. Neyman (ed.), *Proceedings of the 4th Berkeley Symposium on Mathematical Statistics and Probability*, Vol. 1, Berkeley, Cal.: University of California Press, 361–379.

Jarque, C. and A. Bera (1980), 'Efficient Tests for Normality, Heteroscedasticity, and Serial Independence of Regression Residuals', *Economics Letters*, 6, 255–259.

Jeffreys, H. (1967), *Theory of Probability*, 3rd edn. London: Oxford University Press.

Jeffreys, H. (1973), *Scientific Inference*, 3rd edn. Cambridge: Cambridge University Press.

Johansen, S. (1988), 'Statistical Analysis of Cointegration Vectors', *Journal of Economic Dynamics and Control*, 12, 231–254.

Johansen, S. and K. Juselius (1990), 'Maximum Likelihood Estimation and Inference on Cointegration – with Applications to the Demand for Money', *Oxford Bulletin of Economics and Statistics*, 52, 169–210.

Johnson, N. and S. Kotz (1970), *Distributions in Statistics – Continuous Univariate Distributions*, Vol. 2. New York: John Wiley.

Johnston, J. (1984), *Econometric Methods* 3rd edn. New York: McGraw-Hill.

Jorgenson, D. (1966), 'Rational Distributed Lag Functions', *Econometrica*, 34, 135–149.

Judge, G. and M. Bock (1978), *The Statistical Implications of Pre–tests and Stein Rule Estimators in Econometrics*. Amsterdam: North-Holland.

Judge, G. and M. Bock (1983), 'Biased Estimation', in Z. Griliches and M. Intriligator (eds), *Handbook of Econometrics*, Vol. 1, Amsterdam: North-Holland.

Judge, G. and T. Yancey (1981), 'Sampling Properties of an Inequality Restricted Estimator', *Economics Letters*, 4, 327–333.

Judge, G., C. Hill, W. Griffiths, T. Lee and H. Lutkepol (1982), *An Introduction to the Theory and Practice of Econometrics*. New York: John Wiley (2nd edn, 1988).

Judge, G., C. Hill, W. Griffiths and T. Lee (1985), *The Theory and Practice of Econometrics*. New York: John Wiley.

Kalman, R. (1960), 'A New Approach to Linear Filtering and Prediction Problems', *Journal of Basic Engineering*, Transactions ASME, Series D, 82, 35–45.

Karni, E. and B. K. Shapiro (1980), 'Tales of Horror from Ivory Towers', *Journal of Political Economy*, 88, 210–212.

Kelejian, H. (1969), 'Missing Observations in Multivariate Regression – Efficiency of a First Order Method', *Journal of the American Statistical Association*, 64, 1609–1616.

Kennedy, P. (1981a) 'Estimation with Correctly Interpreted Dummy Variables in Semilogarithmic Equations', *American Economic Review*, 71, 802.

Kennedy, P. (1981b) 'The "Ballentine": a Graphical Aid for Econometrics', *Australian Economic Papers*, 20, 414–416.

Kennedy, P. (1989), 'Non–nested Hypothesis Tests: a Diagrammatic Exposition' *Australian Economic Papers*, 28, 160–165.

Kennedy, P. (1990), 'An Exercise in Computing the Variance of the Forecast Error', *International Journal of Forecasting*, 6, 275–6.

Kennedy, P. (1992), *A Guide to Econometrics*, 3rd edn. Oxford: Basil Blackwell.

Keynes, J. N. (1921), *A Treatise on Probability*. New York: Harper & Row.

Kinal, T. and K. Lahiri (1983), 'Specification Error Analysis with Stochastic Regressors', *Econometrica*, 51, 1209–1219.

Klepper, S. and E. Leamer (1983), 'Consistent Sets of Estimates for Regressions with Errors in All Variables', *Econometrica*, 52, 163–184.

Koenkar, R., and G. Bassett (1982), 'Robust Tests for Heteroscedasticity Based on Regression Quantiles', *Econometrica*, 50, 43–61.

Kosobud, R. (1963), 'A Note on a Problem Caused by the Assignment of Missing Data in Sample Surveys', *Econometrica*, 31, 562–563.

Koyck, L. (1954), *Distributed Lags and Investment Analysis*. Amsterdam: North-Holland.

Leamer, E. (1973), 'Multicollinearity: a Bayesian Interpretation', *Review of Economics and Statistics*, 55, 371–380.

Leamer, E. (1978), *Specification Searches: Ad Hoc Inferences with Nonexperimental Data*. New York: John Wiley.

Leamer, E. (1983), 'Let's Take the Con Out of Econometrics', *American Economic Review*, 73, 31–43.

Leamer, E. (1985), 'Vector Autoregressions for Causal Inference', in K. Brunner and A. H. Meltzer (eds), *Understanding Monetary Regimes*, Supplement to *Journal of Monetary Economics*, Amsterdam: North-Holland.

Leamer, E. (1986), 'A Bayesian Analysis of the Determinants of Inflation', in D. A. Belsey and E. Kuh (eds), *Model Reliability*, Cambridge, Mass.: MIT Press.

Leamer, E. and H. Leonard (1983), 'Reporting the Fragility of Regression Estimates', *Review of Economics and Statistics*, 64, 306–317.

Lehmann, E. L. (1959), *Testing Statistical Hypotheses*. New York: John Wiley.

Levi, M. (1973), 'Errors in the Variable in the Presence of Correctly Measured Variables', *Econometrica*, 41, 985–986.

Liu, T. (1960), 'Underidentification, Structural Estimation, and Forecasting', *Econometrica*, 28, 855–856.

Ljung, G. and G. Box (1979), 'On a Measure of Lack of Fit in Time Series Models', *Biometrika*, 66, 265–270.

Lovell, M. C. (1963), 'Seasonal Adjustment of Economic Time Series', *Journal of the American Statistical Association*, 58, 993–1010.

Lovell, M. C. (1983), 'Data Mining', *Review of Economics and Statistics*, 65, 1–12.

Lucas, R. E. (1976), 'Econometric Policy Evaluation – a Critique', in K. Brunner and A. H. Meltzer (eds.), *The Philips Curve and Labour Markets*, vol. 1, 19–46, Carnegie–Rochester Conferences on Public Policy, supplement to *Journal of Monetary Economics*, Amsterdam: North-Holland.

McAleer, M., C. R. McKenzie and A. D. Hall (1988), 'Testing Separate Time Series Models', *Journal of Time Series Analysis*, 9. 169–189.

McCallum, B. (1972), 'Relative Asymptotic Bias from Errors of Omission and Measurement', *Econometrica*, 40, 757–758.

McCloskey, D. N. (1985), 'The Loss Function Has Been Mislaid: the Rhetoric of Significance Tests', *American Economic Review, Papers and Proceedings*, 75, 201–205.

MacKinnon, J. G. (1983), 'Model Specification Tests against Non–nested Alternatives', *Econometric Reviews*, 2, 85–110.

MacKinnon, J. G. (1992), 'Model Specification Tests and Artificial Regressions', *Journal of Economic Literature*, 30, 102–146.

Maddala, G. (1971), 'The Use of Variance Components Models in Pooling Cross Section and Time Series Data', *Econometrica*, 39, 341–358.

Maddala, G. (1977), *Econometrics*. New York: McGraw-Hill.

Maddala, G. (1983), *Limited Dependent and Qualitative Variables in Econometrics*. New York: Cambridge University Press.

Maddala, G. (1992), *Introduction to Econometrics*, 2nd edn. New York: Macmillan.

Maddala, G. and T. Mount (1973), 'A Comparative Study of Alternative Estimators for Variance Component Models', *Journal of the American Statistical Association*, 68, 324–328.

Magnus, J. (1978), 'Maximum Likelihood Estimation of the Generalized Regression Model with Unknown Parameters in the Disturbance Covariance Matrix', *Journal of Econometrics*, 18, 83–114.

Mallows, C. L. (1973), 'Some Comments on C_p', *Technometrics*, 15, 661–676.

Mann, H. and A. Wald (1943), 'On the Statistical Treatment of Linear Stochastic Difference Equations', *Econometrica*, 11, 173–220.

Meyer, P. L. (1971), *Introductory Probability and Statistical Applications*. Reading, Mass.: Addison-Wesley.

Mikhail, W. M. (1975), 'A Comparative Monte Carlo Study of the Properties of Econometric Estimators', *Journal of the American Statistical Association*, 70, 94–104.

Mills, T. (1990), *Time Series Techniques for Economists*. New York: Cambridge University Press.

Mizon, G. E. (1977), 'Model Selection Procedures', in M. J. Artis and A. R. Nobay (eds), *Studies in Modern Economic Analysis*, Oxford: Basil Blackwell.

Mizon, G. E. and J.-P. Richard (1986), 'The Encompassing Principle and its Application to Non–nested Hypotheses', *Econometrica*, 54, 657–678.

Mood, A., F. Graybill and D. Boes (1974), *Introduction to the Theory of Statistics*. New York: McGraw-Hill.

Morgan, M. S. (1990), *The History of Econometric Ideas*. Cambridge: Cambridge University Press.

Morrison, D. E. and Henkel, R. E. (1970), *The Significance Test Controversy – A Reader*. Chicago: Aldine.

Nelson, C. and H. Kang (1981), 'Spurious Periodicity in Inappropriately Detrended Time Series', *Econometrica*, 49, 741–751.

Nelson, C. and H. Kang (1984), 'Pitfalls in the Use of Time as an Explanatory Variable in Regression', *Journal of Business and Economic Statistics*, 2, 73–82.

Nelson, C. and C. Plosser (1982), 'Trends and Random Walks in Macroeconomic Time Series: Some Evidence and Implications', *Journal of Monetary Economics*, 10, 139–162.

Nerlove, M. (1972), 'Lags in Economic Behavior', *Econometrica*, 40, 221–251.

Nerlove, M. and F. Diebold (1990), 'Unit Roots in Economic Time Series: a Selective Survey', in T. Bewley (ed.), *Advances in Econometrics*, Vol. 8, New York: JAI Press.

Newey, W. (1984), 'A Method of Moments Interpretation of Sequential Estimators', *Economics Letters*, 14, 201–206.

Newey, W. (1985a), 'Maximum Likelihood Specification Testing and Conditional Moment Tests', *Econometrica*, 53, 1047–1070.

Newey, W. (1985b), 'Generalized Method of Moments Specification Testing', *Journal of Econometrics*, 29, 229–256.

Neyman, J. and E. S. Pearson (1933), 'On the Problem of the Most Efficient Tests of Statistical Hypotheses', *Transactions of the Royal Statistical Society*, Series A, 231, 289–337.

Ohtani, K. and M. Kobiyashi (1986), 'A Bounds Tests for Equality Between Sets of Coefficients in Two Linear Regression Models', *Econometric Theory*, 2, 230–231.

Osborn, D. R., A. P. L. Chui, J. P. Smith and C. R. Birchenhall (1988), 'Seasonality and the Order of Integration for Consumption', *Oxford Bulletin of Economics and Statistics*, 50, 361–377.

Pagan, A. (1987), 'Three Econometric Methodologies: a Critical Appraisal', *Journal of Economic Surveys*, 1, 3–24.

Pagan, A. and F. Vella (1989), 'Diagnostic Tests for Models Based on Individual Data: a Survey', *Journal of Applied Econometrics*, 4, Supplement, S29–S59.

Pagan, A. and M. Wickens (1989), 'A Survey of Some Recent Econometric Methods', *Economic Journal*, 99, 962–1025.

Pesaran, M. H. (1974), 'On the General Problem of Model Specification', *Review of Economics and Statistics*, 41, 153–171.

Pesaran, M. H. and A. Deaton (1978), 'Testing Non–nested Nonlinear Regression Models', *Econometrica*, 46, 677–694.

Pesaran, M. H. and A. Hall (1989), 'A Test of Non–nested Linear Regression Models Subject to Linear Restrictions', *Economics Letters*, 27, 341–348.

Peters, S. C. and D. A. Freedman (1984), 'Some Notes on the Bootstrap in Regression Problems', *Journal of Business and Economic Statistics*, 2, 406–409.

Phillips, A. W. (1954), 'Stabilisation Policy in a Closed Economy', *Economic Journal*, 64, 290–323.

Plosser, C. I., G. W. Schwert and H. White (1982), 'Differencing as a Test of Specification', *International Economic Review*, 23, 535–552.

Poirier, D. (1976), *The Econometrics of Structural Change*. Amsterdam: North-Holland.

Poirier, D. (1988), 'Frequentist and Subjectivist Perspectives on the Problems of Model Building in Economics' (with discussion), *Journal of Economic Perspectives*, 2, 121–144.

Poirier, D. (1991), 'Bayesian Empirical Studies in Economics and Finance', *Journal of Econometrics*, 49.

Popper, K. (1968), *The Logic of Scientific Discovery*, 2nd edn. London: Hutchinson (1st edn, 1965).

Quandt, R. (1983), 'Computational Problems and Methods', in Z. Griliches and M. Intriligator (eds), *Handbook of Econometrics*. Amsterdam: North-Holland.

Ramsey, F. P. (1926), 'Truth and Probability', in H. E. Kyburg and H. G. Smokler (eds) (1964), *Studies in Subjective Probability*, New York: John Wiley.

Ramsey, J. (1969), 'Tests for Specification Errors in Classical Linear Least Squares Regression Analysis', *Journal of the Royal Statistical Society*, Series B, 31, 350–371.

Ramsey, J. (1970), 'Models, Specification Error and Inference: a Discussion of Some Problems in Econometric Methodology', *Bulletin of the Oxford Institute of Economics and Statistics*, 32, 301–318.

Ramsey, J. (1974), 'Classical Model Selection Through Specification Error Tests', in P. Zarembka (ed.), *Frontiers in Econometrics*, New York: Academic Press.

Rao, C. R. (1973), *Linear Statistical Inference and Its Applications*, 2nd edn. New York: John Wiley.

Revankar, N. (1974), 'Some Finite Sample Results in the Context of Two Seemingly Unrelated Regression Equations', *Journal of the American Statistical Association*, 69, 187–190.

Ringwald, K. (1980), *A Critique of Models in Linear Aggregation Structures*. Boston, Mass.: Oelgeschlager, Gunn & Hain.

Rosenberg, B. (1973), 'The Analysis of a Cross-Section of Time Series by Stochastically Convergent Parameter Regression', *Annals of Economic and Social Measurement*, 2/4, 399–450.

Rubin, H. (1950), 'Consistency of Maximum Likelihood Estimators in the Explosive Case', in T. Koopmans (ed.), *Statistical Inference in Dynamic Economic Models*, New York: John Wiley.

Salkever, D. (1976), 'The Use of Dummy Variables to Compute Predictions, Prediction Errors, and Confidence Intervals', *Journal of Econometrics*, 4, 393–397.

Sargan, J. D. (1964), 'Wages and Prices in the United Kingdom: a Study in Econometric Methodology', in P. E. Hart, G. Mills and J. K. Whittaker (eds), *Econometric Analysis for National Economic Planning*, London: Butterworths.

Savage, L. J. (1954), *The Foundations of Statistics*. New York: John Wiley.

Schmidt, P. (1974), 'Choosing among Alternative Linear Regression Models', *Atlantic Economic Journal*, 2, 7–13.

Schmidt, P. (1976), *Econometrics*. New York: Marcel Dekker.

Simon, H. A. (1953), 'Causal Ordering and Identifiability', in W. C. Hood and T. J. Koopmans (eds), *Studies in Econometric Method*, Cowles Commission Monograph No. 14, New York: John Wiley.

Simon, H. A. (1970), 'The Concept of Causality in Economics', *Kyklos*, 23, 226–252.

Sims, C. A. (1972), 'Money, Income, and Causality', *American Economic Review*, 62, 540–552.

Sims, C. A. (1977), 'Exogeneity and Causal Ordering in Macroeconomic Models', in C. A. Sims (ed.), *New Methods in Business Cycle Research*, Minneapolis: Federal Reserve Bank of Minneapolis.

Sims, C. A. (1980), 'Macroeconomics and Reality', *Econometrica*, 48, 1–48.

Sims, C. A. (1982), 'Policy Analysis with Econometric Models', *Brookings Papers on Economic Activity*, 1, 107–152.

Smith, G. and F. Campbell, (1980), 'A Critique of Some Ridge Regression Models', *Journal of the American Statistical Association*, 75, 74–103.

Spanos, A. (1986), *Statistical Foundations of Econometric Modelling*. Cambridge: Cambridge University Press.

Spanos, A. (1988), 'Towards a Unifying Methodological Framework for Econometric Modelling', *Economic Notes*, 1, 1–28.

Spitzer, J. (1982), 'A Primer on Box–Cox Estimation', *Review of Economics and Statistics*, 64, 307–313.

Stein, C. (1956), 'Inadmissibility of the Usual Estimator for the Mean of a Multivariate Distribution', *Proceedings of the Third Berkeley Symposium*, Vol. I, Berkeley, Cal.: University of California Press.

Stewart, I. (1979), *Reasoning and Method in Economics: An Introduction to Economic Methodology*. London: McGraw-Hill.

Stock, J. H. (1987), 'Asymptotic Properties of Least Squares Estimators of Cointegrating Vectors', *Econometrica*, 55, 1035–1056.

Stock, J. H. and M. W. Watson (1988), 'Variable Trends in Economic Time Series', *Journal of Economic Perspectives*, 2, 147–174.

Strotz, R. (1960), 'Independence as a Specification Error', *Econometrica*, 28, 428–442.

Suits, D. (1984), 'Dummy Variables, Mechanics vs. Interpretation', *Review of Economics and Statistics*, 66, 177–180.

Swamy, P. (1970), 'Efficient Inference in a Random Coefficient Regression Model', *Econometrica*, 38, 311–323.

Swamy, P. (1971), *Statistical Inference in Random Coefficient Regression Models*. New York: Springer-Verlag.

Swamy, P. (1974), 'Linear Models with Random Coefficients', in P. Zarembka (ed.), *Frontiers in Econometrics*, New York: Academic Press.

Taylor, W. E. (1977), 'Small Sample Properties of a Class of Two Stage Aitken Estimators', *Econometrica*, 45, 497–508.

Theil, H. (1961), *Economic Forecasts and Policy*. Amsterdam: North-Holland.

Theil, H. (1963), 'On The Use of Incomplete Prior Information in Regression Analysis', *Journal of the American Statistical Association*, 58, 401–414.

Theil, H. (1971), *Principles of Econometrics*. New York: John Wiley.

Theil, H. and A. Goldberger (1961), 'On Pure and Mixed Estimation in Economics', *International Economic Review*, 2, 65–78.

Tobin, J. (1958), 'Estimation of Relationships for Limited Dependent Variables', *Econometrica*, 26, 24–36.

Trivedi, P. and A. Pagan (1979), 'Polynomial Distributed Lags: a Unified Treatment', *Economics Studies Quarterly*, 30, 37–49.

Wald, A. (1940), 'The Fitting of Straight Lines if Both Variables are Subject to Error', *Annals of Mathematical Statistics*, 11, 284–300.

Wallace, T. (1977), 'Pretest Estimation in Regression: a Survey', *American Journal of Agricultural Economics*, 59, 431–443.

Wallace, T. and V. Ashar (1972), 'Sequential Methods in Model Construction', *Review of Economics and Statistics*, 54, 172–178.

Wallace, T. and A. Hussain (1969), 'The Use of Error Components in Combining Cross Section with Time Series Data', *Econometrica*, 37, 55–72.

Wallis, K. (1972), 'Testing for Fourth Order Autocorrelation in Quarterly Regression Equations', *Econometrica*, 40, 617–636.

Wallis, K. (1974), 'Seasonal Adjustment and Relations between Variables', *Journal of the American Statistical Association*, 69, 18–31.

Welsch, R. E. (1980), 'Regression Sensitivity Analysis and Bounded Influence Estimation', in J. Kmenta and J. Ramsey (eds), *Evaluation of Econometric Models*, New York: Academic Press.

White, H. (1980), 'A Heteroscedasticity-Consistent Covariance Matrix Estimator and a Direct Test for Heteroscedasticity', *Econometrica*, 48, 817–838.

White, H. (ed.) (1982), 'Model Specification', *Journal of Econometrics*, 20, 1.

White, H. (ed.) (1983), 'Non–nested Models', *Journal of Econometrics*, 21, 1.

White, H. (1984), *Asymptotic Theory for Econometricians*. New York: Academic Press.

Wickens, M. (1972), 'A Note on the Use of Proxy Variables', *Econometrica*, 40, 759–760.

Winckler, R. L. and S. Makridakis (1983), 'The Combination of Forecasts', *Journal of the Royal Statistical Society*, Series A, 146, 150–157.

Wold, H. (1954), 'Causality and Economics', *Econometrica*, 22, 162–177.

Wonnacott, R. J. and T. H. Wonnacott (1979), *Econometrics*, 2nd edn. New York: John Wiley.

Wu, D. (1973), 'Alternative Tests of Independence between Stochastic Regressors and Disturbances', *Econometrica*, 41, 733–750.

Yule, G. U. (1926), 'Why Do We Sometimes Get Nonsense Correlations Between Time Series?', *Journal of the Royal Statistical Society*, 89, 1–64.

Zarembka, P. (1968), 'Functional Form in the Demand for Money', *Journal of the American Statistical Association*, 63, 502–511.

Zarembka, P. (1974), 'Transformations of Variables in Econometrics', in P. Zarembka (ed.), *Frontiers in Econometrics*, New York: Academic Press.

Zellner, A. (1962), 'An Efficient Method of Estimating Seemingly Unrelated Regressions and Tests of Aggregation Bias', *Journal of the American Statistical Association*, 57, 500–509.

Zellner, A. (1971), *Introduction to Bayesian Inference in Econometrics*. New York: John Wiley.

Zellner, A. (1985), 'Bayesian Econometrics', *Econometrica*, 53, 253–269.

Zellner, A. and H. Theil (1962), 'Three Stage Least Squares: Simultaneous Estimation of Simultaneous Equations', *Econometrica*, 30, 63–68.

Ziemer, R. F. (1984), 'Reporting Econometric Results: Believe It or Not?', *Land Economics*, 60, 122–127.